LATIN
AMERICAN
WRITERS

LATIN AMERICAN WRITERS

Carlos A. Solé

EDITOR IN CHIEF

Maria Isabel Abreu

ASSOCIATE EDITOR

VOLUME I

CHARLES SCRIBNER'S SONS
MACMILLAN LIBRARY REFERENCE USA

NEW YORK

Charles Scribner's Sons

1633 Broadway
New York, NY 10019-6785

Library of Congress Catalog Card Number: 88–35481

PRINTED IN THE UNITED STATES OF AMERICA

printing number
10

Library of Congress Cataloging-in-Publication Data

Latin American writers / Carlos A. Solé, editor in chief,
Maria Isabel Abreu, associate editor.
p.   cm.
Includes bibliographies and index.
ISBN 0-684-18463-X (Set)
ISBN 0-684-18597-0 (Volume I)
ISBN 0-684-18598-9 (Volume II)
ISBN 0-684-18599-7 (Volume III)
1. Latin American literature—History and criticism.   2. Authors,
Latin American—Biography.   I. Solé, Carlos A.   II. Abreu, Maria
Isabel.
PQ7081.A1L37   1989
860'.9'98—dc19
[B]   88-35481
                                              CIP

The paper in this book meets the guidelines for permanence and
durability of the Committee on Production Guidelines for Book Longevity
of the Council on Library Resources.

EDITORIAL STAFF

CONTENTS

VOLUME III

PREFACE

It was the year 1492 when the Bishop of Avila, Fray Hernando de Talavera, accompanied the famous humanist Elio Antonio de Nebrija to present his *Arte de la lengua castellana*, the first grammar of Spanish as well as the first of a Romance language, to Isabel de Castilla. When the queen inquired about its usefulness, Bishop Talavera, a friend of Christopher Columbus, responded without hesitation that it would serve to introduce the language to the many peoples and "naciones de peregrinas lenguas" (nations of strange languages) that her Highness was to bring under her crown and "que necesitarían recibir las leyes que el vencedor pone al vencido" (who would need to receive the laws that the conqueror imposes on the conquered). Only months later, on 12 October 1492, Columbus would land on Hispaniola; eight years later, in 1500, during the reign of Manuel I of Portugal, Pedro Álvares Cabral would discover Brazil. In 1536, Fernão de Oliveira would write the first grammar of Portuguese.

Nearly five hundred years have passed since Spain and Portugal brought their languages to the New World, using them to propagate the Christian faith, impose their laws, and spread a rich and ancient cultural tradition, introducing an entirely different system of values and, in short, a new way of thinking and seeing the world. Thus, two very different cultures collided and, later incorporating other European and African influences, over several centuries molded themselves into what would become known as the Ibero-American world. The term Latin America—broader in meaning, since it includes not only the countries conquered by the Iberian powers but all the nations of the Western Hemisphere south of the Rio Grande—is used here to refer exclusively to the Spanish- and Portuguese-speaking countries of the New World. The term Spanish America, which includes only those countries conquered by Spain, will be used to refer only to New World literature in the Spanish language, including that of Puerto Rico.

Latin American literature was born at the moment of discovery; from the beginning, the inhabitants of the new continent felt the need to bear witness to the unfolding human, political, and social drama that formed the foundation for five centuries of Latin American life. The monarchs of Spain and Portugal never imagined that their languages would be the means of such aesthetic expression; Latin American literature has traveled a long and difficult road, and its enormous variety and richness have secured its place among the world's most important literatures. *Latin American Writers* is dedicated to the celebration of the fifth centennial of the discovery of the New World.

In the last four decades, this literature has increasingly captured North American attention, largely because of the recognition of its productivity, especially in prose fiction and poetry, but also because of the public's curiosity about Latin America itself. This interest is reflected in the increasing number of translations of Latin American writing, not only into English, but also into many other languages. The English translations, oftentimes appearing simultaneously with the publication of the original version, are immediately reviewed in popular magazines like *Time* and *Newsweek*. Other publications like the *New York Times* Book Review and the literary sections of magazines like *The Nation, The New Republic, The New Yorker,* and *Saturday Review* have been giving more and more attention to the works of Latin American writers. Since the 1920's, *Books Abroad* has been an important American forum for the discussion of Latin American literature; now titled *World Literature Today,* this publication has had special issues dedicated to Carlos Fuentes, Julio Cortázar, Jorge Luis Borges, Gabriel García Márquez, and Mario Vargas Llosa, as well as an issue devoted entirely to Brazilian literature. Fuentes and García Márquez also have the honor of receiving *World Literature Today's* prestigious Neudstaat International Award.

Scholarly publications have also helped disseminate current Latin American writing among the Anglo-Saxon literary public. *Tri-Quarterly* dedicated an issue to Borges; in 1971 *Studies in Short Fiction* dedicated a special issue (8/1) to the Latin American short story; *The Literary Review: An International Journal of Contemporary Writing* dedicated its Winter 1978 issue to Brazil; *Novel,* published by Brown University, has added an important dimension; and above all *Review,* published by the Center for Inter-American Relations in New York, is perhaps the best source of literary criticism in English on Latin American literature. Today the Latin American writer also has greater contact with U.S. universities and cultural institutions. Enormous academic interest in Latin American literature has attracted the writers themselves to teach courses at North American universities, give lectures, and participate in symposia and round-table discussions. Latin American literature continues to influence the writers of other cultures, and at the same time, the North American writer has become more interested in reviewing and analyzing the work of Latin American writers, as in the cases of John Updike on Guillermo Cabrera Infante, Anthony West on Alejo Carpentier, and John Barth on Borges, among others. In fact, this "literature of the future," as it was called by the French critic Roger Caillois shortly after World War II, has steadily attracted not only the attention of the North American public but also the world at large. In fact, four Latin American writers have been honored with the Nobel Prize: two Chileans, Gabriela Mistral (1945) and Pablo Neruda (1971), the Guatemalan Miguel Ángel Asturias (1967), and the Colombian Gabriel García Márquez (1982). Other Latin American writers have been nominated for the Nobel award, and many have been recognized by other important international prizes, most notably the Mexican Octavio Paz, who in 1963 won the International Poetry Prize in Belgium.

Latin American Writers is a comprehensive effort to acquaint the English-speaking world, and other countries where Spanish and Portuguese are not the mother tongue, with the rich and varied literature of Spanish America and Brazil. Since Latin American literature traces its origins to Europe and has been influenced by modern Western literatures throughout its development, in a certain sense *Latin American Writers* is complemented by other titles in the Scribner writers series: *European Writers, British Writers,* and even *American Writers. Latin American Writers* was conceived as a reference work for specialists and nonspecialists alike: it is intended for a readership that includes high school and university students, teachers and professors, scholars, critics, editors, and commentators, as well as the general public. The essays that appear in these three volumes are designed to introduce the reader to the life, work, and literary contribution of 176 writers representative of Latin American letters, 149 Spanish-American and 27 Brazilian.

Our primary goal in this selection of Latin American authors has been to offer a panoramic view of Latin American literary history, beginning with its origins during the colonial period and continuing to the present. Thus, the authors are presented in chronological order according to their date of birth. At the same time, we have worked to represent the various literary genres—chronicle, poetry, theater, prose fiction, and essay—throughout several periods. Because of historical and cultural circumstances, literary production varies from country to country; nonetheless, we have included representatives of every Spanish-American country and of Brazil, although in some cases it has been possible to include only one or two writers for a particular country. Another criterion for our selection of authors takes into account the evaluation that literary critics have made of these writers. Because of the restrictions imposed by this work's length, it has been impossible to include many writers whose work, nevertheless, should not be underestimated.

In considering literature, the Latin American does not necessarily think in terms of nationality. Many of these writers have lived and written outside of their countries of origin. For instance, in 1842 the Venezuelan classicist Andrés Bello, a prominent figure in Chile's public and intellectual life, and the Argentine romanticist Domingo Faustino Sarmiento, also in exile in Chile, engaged in a fascinating public discussion on the cultural and literary future of the new republics; the Cuban José María Heredia arrived in Mexico at the age of sixteen and spent a considerable part of his life occupying official posts there; the Nicaraguan Rubén Darío published his book *Azul* while living in Chile and later launched the modernist movement in Argentina; the Chilean Vicente Huidobro began his aesthetic program of creationism in Argentina; the Mexican Alfonso Reyes had close ties to Brazil; and two of the best women poets of Latin America—Gabriela Mistral of Chile and Cecília Meireles of Brazil—were close friends.

It is true that, especially since independence, regional literary trends have developed in various Latin American countries, among them the indigenist literature of Mexico, Guatemala, Brazil, and the Andean countries, the gaucho literature of Argentina and Uruguay, the novel of the Mexican Revolution, the abolitionist novel of Cuba, and the current of Afro-Caribbean poetry. Although it is perfectly legitimate to speak of a Peruvian, Argentine, Mexican, or Cuban literature, in the end it is of no importance that Clorinda Matto de Turner was Peruvian, José Hernández Argentine, Martín Luis Guzmán Mexican, Cirilo Villaverde and Nicolás Guillén Cuban, or that Luis Palés Matos was Puerto Rican. Since Spanish-Americans share a common language and cultural heritage, they see these writers as belonging to a single body of literature, superseding political and geographical boundaries. This is clearly the case with the most recent group of writers, which includes among others Borges, García Márquez, Octavio Paz, Vargas Llosa, José Donoso, and Carpentier. Even with Brazilian writers, who write in Portuguese rather than Spanish, a spiritual bond exists—the result of commonly shared problems and aspirations—that unites them with the other writers of their continent, creating a sort of literary Pan-Americanism encompassing the essence of Latin America.

PREFACE

Since the 1950's a new and promising generation of writers has emerged, especially in prose fiction and theater. Although we have not been able to include all of them, we hope that a positive reception of these first volumes of *Latin American Writers* will necessitate the publication of supplementary volumes, doing justice to the literary creation of this exciting generation of writers, whose work continues to evolve. For now, the quality of critical attention they have attracted, and the number of translations made of their works, have played an important role in the final selection of this group of contemporary voices.

The essays presented here vary in length from approximately 2,500 to 10,000 words, according to the extent of each writer's work. We have tried to maintain a format, tone, and style that is as uniform as possible, while still allowing the contributor to present his or her own unique appraisal of each subject's work. The essays begin with a brief biographical description of each writer, relating him or her to the sociohistorical and literary influences that have motivated that subject's work. The majority of the text is dedicated to presenting each writer's production, evaluating it in its totality, and indicating its contribution to Latin American literature as a whole. Each essay ends with a selected bibliography of the writer's works, appearing in chronological order and grouped by genre. Individual works, collections or anthologies, important modern editions, and notable translations into English are given in alphabetical order. With the goal of guiding the interested reader in continued research of the subject, the bibliography concludes with a section of biographical publications and selected critical books and articles.

An array of distinguished contributors, including university professors, recognized scholars and critics, historians, intellectuals, and writers have prepared the essays that appear in *Latin American Writers*. They come not only from North America but also Latin and European intellectual and academic circles. In many cases, the contributor is internationally recognized as the best critic of the author discussed. (A complete list of contributors and their professional affiliations appears after the Index in Volume III.) Their task has been one of introduction and exposition; their principal concern has been to explain as completely as possible the literary contribution of the subject—not to acclaim or censure, nor to establish judgment of merit in comparison with other writers. In those cases where essays were translated into English from the Spanish or Portuguese, this is noted at the conclusion of the text.

Throughout *Latin American Writers* we have adopted a certain style when referring to titles of works. On first mention of a Spanish or Portuguese title, an English translation follows in parentheses with the date of publication of the original-language title. Dates of translations are given in the bibliography. The important distinction is that if the English title that appears in parentheses is set in *italic* type, then this represents a published English translation of the original. The published English title will be used on subsequent reference in the essay. If, however, the title in parentheses is set in roman type, the reader should note that that title is merely a literal translation of the original title. In the latter case, subsequent reference is to the published title in the original language. The reader should also note that occasionally a contributor has chosen to give a literal translation of the original title even though a published translation may exist, with the understanding that the existing translations are either unavailable, out of print, or not adequate renditions of the original.

Regarding translations of a subject's work in an extract: if no published translation is cited following an extract, the reader may assume that the translation in question is the work of the author of the essay or, as noted above, the translator of the essay. If the contributor or the translator of the essay has translated only *some* of the quoted work of the subject, then in the first instance of such a translation a footnote indicates that translations of the subject's writing were the work of the contributor (or translator) unless otherwise noted. English translations of titles of Spanish or Brazilian journals and newspapers are provided parenthetically in some cases where the titles are not obvious cognates, or when the title in its original language bears some special significance or would simply be of interest to those who do not read Spanish or Portuguese.

In order to provide the reader with a panoramic view of the political and sociocultural milieu of the lives of these writers a chronological table offers a historical, cultural, and literary backdrop to the essays. In the following pages, we will attempt to broaden this historical and literary outlook by presenting a brief outline of Latin America's literary journey.

Nevertheless, we wish to make clear that we did not design *Latin American Writers* as a literary encyclopedia or as a comprehensive series of essays that includes every Latin American writer of historical or literary importance. The character of these volumes is rather that of a critical anthology of representative Latin American writers and thus possesses the virtues and limitations of such a collection. On the one hand, it does not offer the schematic organization of an encyclopedia nor the integrated perspective of a literary history. But, on the other hand, we believe that the present work is neither limited by the impersonality of the one nor the rigidity of the other. We trust that these essays will arouse the reader's enthusiasm for Latin American literature and stimulate interest in the writers included here, and at the same time provide the student of this literature with the basic materials for further study.

Finally, we wish to thank all of our contributors for their excellent cooperation and patience. We also wish to express our appreciation to our colleagues Enrique Anderson Imbert, Afrânio Coutinho, Wilson Martins, Klaus Müller-Bergh, and George Schade for their many valuable suggestions, to the translators of some of these essays for their difficult labor, and to Carlos A. Solé III for his meticulous care in the preparation of the Chronological Table. We must acknowledge Marshall De Bruhl for his enthusiastic reception of the project in its initial stages, Helen McInnis for her support, and especially we express our profound gratitude to Jonathan Aretakis, who with Scribner's excellent editorial team brought this work to publication.

—C.A.S.
—M.I.A.

LATIN AMERICAN LITERATURE

Spanish-American Literature

On the basis of external history it could be said that Spanish-American literature has developed roughly in three stages: the colonial era, the nineteenth century, and the contemporary period. Within each period, however, there are distinct phases that correspond to the influence of various external, literary and ideological tendencies and movements, primarily European. These influences provoke various reactions at different times, in different countries.

The colonial period of Spanish-American literature, lasting somewhat more than three centuries, extended from the time of discovery, in 1492, to the triumph of the struggles for independence in 1825, and consisted of three literary moments. The sixteenth century, the century of discovery, exploration, and conquest, was marked by the further cultivation of medieval genres—the chronicle and theater—within a framework of Italian Renaissance structures, and influenced by Erasmus' advanced humanistic thinking. The seventeenth century, the century of colonization, brought with it the baroque, which in Spanish America occurred gradually and remained longer than in the Iberian peninsula. In this period, it was poetry that achieved the greatest artistic maturity. The eighteenth century, the "French" century, announced the beginning of the disintegration of the colonial structure. It brought the ideas of the Enlightenment, followed by rococo and neoclassicism, which remained dominant until 1825, when the separatist movement reached its peak. Poetry and especially prose were the best-cultivated genres, particularly toward the end of this period.

Literature first appeared in Latin America when the first discoverers and conquerors—men of action rather than letters—recorded their own experiences. The New World's first writers, inspired by a great interest in historical studies in Europe and Spain, have left us abundant testimony as to the scenery, the characters, the events and the very meaning of discovery and conquest. They did this using literary forms of medieval origin: the diary, the narrative letter, and the memoir. Above all, these early writers of the New World employed the chronicle, which blends reality and fantasy, history and fiction, prose and poetry.

In a very broad sense it might be said that Columbus himself was the New World's first writer, but many others also began writing chronicles to acquaint the Old World with American life in all its detail. This, however, was not always their only motivation. Bernal Díaz del Castillo (ca. 1496–1584), with his *Historia verdadera de la conquista de la Nueva España* (*The True History of the Conquest of New Spain*, 1632), sought not only to leave an account of the events that he witnessed, but also to recognize the Spanish soldier by exalting his participation in the conquest, allowing him to share in the glory of captains and commanders. On the other hand, Fray

Bartolomé de las Casas (1474–1566) dedicated his works to a passionate defense of the rights of the indigenous inhabitants of the New World.

The most important chronicles were written throughout the sixteenth century, narrating discoveries and explorations, conquests and colonizations. Today it is estimated that there were more than one hundred chroniclers, but many of their accounts have never been published. Many of these writers were Spaniards, among them Bernal Díaz and Gonzalo Fernández de Oviedo y Valdés (1478–1557); many were born in the New World, as was the Peruvian Garcilaso de la Vega, known as El Inca (1539–1616); many were clergymen, including Las Casas and Father Joseph de Acosta (1540–1600). While many wrote out of a sense of the urgency of the moment, others wrote official chronicles commissioned by the crown, like Oviedo, whose *Historia general y natural de las Indias,* first published between 1851 and 1855, is the first general work on the New World. Many of these chronicles were written by people who had participated in the events they described, as was the case of Bernal Díaz, a soldier under Hernán Cortés in the Conquest of Mexico. Others, though, made use of witnesses' testimony and other sources, as was the case with Oviedo, who had been authorized by the crown to ask the conquistadores for reports concerning their experiences. In his *Comentarios reales* (Royal Commentaries of the Incas, 1609–1617), El Inca Garcilaso de la Vega proudly exalts the past ways and customs of his people and then describes the conquest of Peru, using as sources his own experiences and the memories of older Indians.

The chronicles combine elements of history, narration, essay, and even fiction, resulting in a literary genre unique in theme and technique. Although they lack the artistic or intellectual maturity of Renaissance literature, and often have fictitious anecdotal elements, the chronicles constitute the most interesting historical prose written in Spanish during the sixteenth century. They are written with spontaneous vitality, great human emotion, and a little imagination and invention. In the chronicles we find the origins of the Spanish-American novel and the seeds of Spanish America's consciousness. This is their historical, literary, and linguistic value.

America was not conquered only by soldiers and adventurers. Along with them came clergymen, men of letters, poets, dramatists and even philosophers, who carried with them new aesthetic doctrines and tendencies that stimulated literary activity in the New World and allowed it to thrive. They brought with them the printing press, and they circulated books that were being read in Spain at the time. Universities were soon founded and important cultural centers established. Many illustrious Spaniards visited the New World; among them, Eugenio de Salazar y Alarcón, Gutiérrez de Cetina, and Juan de la Cueva were perhaps the three most influential Spanish authors during this period of literary formation. There were others who came and never returned to Spain. Two of these men of letters who remained in America produced work that sealed the first century of colonial literature: in theater, Fernán González de Eslava (1534–1601?), born in Seville; and in epic poetry, Don Alonso de Ercilla y Zúñiga (1553–1594), born in Madrid. Although neither was born in Spanish America, both were completely absorbed by this new reality and felt it their own. Therefore, their work is considered a part of Spanish-American literature.

The task of educating the Indians as Christians fell to the missionaries. In addition to learning Indian languages and writing grammars and vocabularies of them, these men of faith made use of dramatic compositions that the Indians themselves performed in churches and convents. In this manner theater made its first appearance in Spanish America. This was religious theater, dominated by the forms of Spanish medieval drama (the allegorical play, the dialogue, and the *villancico*, a type of carol), combined with elements of the Indians' own dramatic practices: ritual ceremonies, chants, dances, mimicry, and pantomime. Unfortunately, little is known of this short-lived *teatro misionero* (missionary theater) which the chroniclers identify as a highly original form.

Toward the end of the sixteenth century, the colonial cities were becoming important cultural centers and their expansion produced new tastes and changes in habits, demanding a theater of simple entertainment and diversion; hence the appearance of popular and profane theater. Because of his simple style, humor, and grace, his interest in the secular, and the popular elements he incorporated into his religious drama, González de Eslava is today considered the best playwright of sixteenth-century Mexico and America, and a precursor of the *teatro criollo* ("creole" theater) that flourished a century later with Sor Juana Inés de la Cruz (1651–1695). In fact, this early interest of Spanish-American writers in depicting their social milieu and regional setting developed into a trend known as *criollismo* ("creolism"), one of the most important elements of this literature, particularly in prose fiction and theater, although manifested at times in poetry and to a lesser degree in the essay.

All forms of epic poetry, highly esteemed in Europe during the sixteenth century, were intensely cultivated during Spain's Golden Age: the heroic and historical, the novelesque and fantastic, the sacred. The heroism, the violence and intrigue, and the variety of events in the conquest of America were ideal material and of sufficient aesthetic value to promote a flourishing of this genre in Spanish America's nascent literature. In fact, the period's best epic poets in Spanish had been born in the New World: the Chileans Alonso de Ercilla y Zúñiga and Pedro de Oña (1570–1643?), the Mexican Bernardo de Balbuena (1561?–1627), and the Peruvian Diego de Hojeda (1571–1615). The latter, although not included in our essays, bears mention here as a writer of religious epic, complementing our presentation of the various forms taken by the genre in Spanish America.

The first Spanish-American literary work to achieve real artistic maturity was an epic poem, Ercilla's *La Araucana* (*The Araucaniad*), published in three parts in 1569, 1578, and 1589. It is the first epic written about the New World and about the birth of an American nation. Ercilla was not only its author, but also an actor in the events narrated, and his extraordinarily realistic descriptions, perceptive character development, and skillful and surprising use of metaphor, along with the ease and elegance of his verse and the complexity of the poem, won him the praise of Lope de Vega and Voltaire. Now translated into all modern languages, *The Araucaniad* is considered by many to be the best epic poem ever written in Spanish.

As the sixteenth century ended and the seventeenth century began, the decline of an optimistic Renaissance mentality—which, among other things, idealized human potential and the world's future—resulted in a spiritual disequilibrium that soon became evident in all artistic efforts, from architecture to literature. Disillusioned and listless in the realization that human life is, in the end, ephemeral and fleeting, artists turned away from the Renaissance and from classical standards of balance, harmony, judgment, order, and reason, and sought to hide their anguish behind dynamic, contorted structures, overdressed with profuse ornamentation.

The arrival of the baroque in Spain coincided with the beginning of the nation's political and military decline, but in spite of the spiritual discontent produced by this decay the baroque was an artistic and intellectual movement of great creativity, expressive of the ideals and the consciousness of the moment. In fact, Spain's literary Golden Age achieved its greatest splendor precisely when the baroque style reached its apogee, during the first decades of the seventeenth century.

The baroque's philosophy and artistic techniques fit well with the new American reality of the seventeenth century. Peninsular institutions had been consolidated, and society was organized on a feudal and aristocratic basis, resulting in a rigid social stratification. Ready to break with this tradition, the affluent elite of *peninsulares* (those born on the Iberian peninsula), and the rising bourgeoisie of *criollos* (the children of *peninsulares*, who were born in America), developed new tastes and favored the importation of the new style. With the patronage of viceroys, the Church, and the universities, a new period of intense artistic and intellectual activity began, spiritually based on Catholicism and dogmatic scholasticism. The great centers of political power, located near rich mines of precious metals—principally Mexico City and Lima, followed by Quito and Bogotá—were also the great cultural centers.

The baroque came slowly to Spanish-American literature, as the colonial intellectual community could receive only few of the latest trends in European thought. Quevedo, Lope de Vega, Calderón, and above all Góngora, were among the most influential Spanish writers. The Mexican poet Bernardo de Balbuena best represents this transitional period of Renaissance to baroque. Although at this point Balbuena still employed forms and themes of the Renaissance—notably the epic and hendecasyllabic verse—he decorated his language richly and used baroque images in his poetry. His poem *Grandeza mexicana* (1604), in which he magnificently describes Mexico at the end of the sixteenth century, is actually baroque in its form and essence. In fact, the literary genre that attained greatest artistic maturity in Spanish America's baroque period is poetry, although it has neither the profundity nor the complexity of Spain's Golden Age poetry. Nevertheless, Spanish-American baroque has its own mark of distinction: many of its themes are American, with abundant references to indigenous cultures and mythologies; its language is sprinkled with native words, phrases, and expressions; its motifs and ornamentation are of folk and *criollista* origin.

The most important and prolific writer of the Spanish-American baroque is, without doubt, Sor Juana Inés de la Cruz, "the Tenth Muse," whose work incorporated every literary current of her time. Her style is baroque, like Calderón and Góngora's, yet her attitude is rationalistic, her conceptions of nature mystical, her expression popular. Her poetry is the most valuable aspect of her literary production: in the opinion of many critics, her *El sueño* (*The Dream*, 1962), a complex philosophical poem already expressing some ideas of the Enlightenment, is the most important work of colonial Spanish-American literature. In addition, her famous *Carta athenagórica* (1690) is considered one of the first manifestations of feminist literature in Latin America. Sor Juana was also an excellent dramatist. Apart from Juan Ruíz de Alarcón (1580?–1639), whose insuperable dramatic work belongs more to the Golden Age of Spain—where he spent the last twenty-six years of his life—the central figure of Spanish-American theater was Sor Juana, who combined reality, fiction, and a sense of humor in her drama.

The other important figure in Spanish-American baroque poetry is the Peruvian

Juan del Valle y Caviedes (1645?–1697?), who wrote satirical poetry after the style of Quevedo, without achieving the latter's poetic aestheticism. Nevertheless, Valle y Caviedes is the first Peruvian writer to paint faithfully the customs and conditions of life in seventeenth-century Lima society, as Ricardo Palma would do in prose two centuries later with his *Tradiciones peruanas*.

We complete our view of Spanish-American baroque literature with Carlos de Sigüenza y Góngora (1645–1700), a historian, mathematician, astronomer, geographer, and philosopher, who was also a poet and essayist. Although it may be argued that Sigüenza y Góngora belongs more to the history of ideas and culture than to literary history, his essays show him to be one of the precursors of the Enlightenment. His essays in *Libra astronómica y filosófica* (1690) are considered important in the history of Mexican ideas. But Sigüenza y Góngora also was important to baroque prose, as evidenced by the style of his *Infortunios de Alonso Ramírez* (*The Misadventures of Alonso Ramírez*, 1690), a book of adventures combining history and imagination, and influenced by picaresque fiction. According to many critics, this book is the Spanish-American colonial work that most closely approaches what is now called the novel.

The last century of colonial life opened as the first Bourbon monarch, the Frenchman Philip V, ascended the Spanish throne in 1700. In Europe, this was the French century, the century of enlightenment and reason, a period when the Encyclopedists established the ideological bases of the modern world, of neoclassicism. The transition from the baroque to neoclassicism was signaled by the flourishing of rococo, characterized by *preciosité* and refinement in the most minute detail, in all artistic production patronized by the nobility and the wealthy bourgeoisie. By around 1750, this frivolity would be rejected in favor of the renewed sobriety of neoclassicism. Neoclassicism, enlightenment, reason, and revolutionary encyclopedism were simultaneous tendencies in European thought and philosophy, reflected in literature throughout this period. The Age of Reason inhibited great works of pure creativity and literary aestheticism: prose turned to philosophy, history, the sciences, mathematics, criticism, and linguistics; poetry focused more on form than on profoundly sentimental content; and neoclassicism stimulated the translation of the Greek and Latin classics. Even the drama of Molière and Jean Racine was essentially rationalistic. The best works of the time were essays, treatises, and criticism.

In Spain all that was French became fashionable. Although in the rest of Europe the Enlightenment was already well under way at the beginning of the century, the rationalistic and classicist spirit did not take root in Spain until relatively late, in the 1730's, and dominated during the reign of Charles III (1759–1788).

The currents of the Enlightenment and neoclassicism arrived in Spanish America much later. Although at mid-century Spanish America still cultivated the baroque, already out of style in Spain, it was inevitable that the new European currents would influence the ideas and customs of the affluent *criollos*, who in spite of having attained impressive economic and cultural status enjoyed neither the political power nor the social prestige of the *peninsulares*. Spain's increasing political decadence, and, more importantly, the ideas of the French Encyclopedists, realized by the French and North American revolutions, roused the consciousness of the *criollos*. This awakening of the colonies provoked a crisis in their scholastic, political, economic, and cultural thinking. These changes were expressed in neoclassicism and culminated in the breaking of imperial power and the dawn of romanticism. It was in literature that neoclassicism best thrived in Spanish America. Although all genres were cultivated, it was primarily through the political and social essay and lyric poetry that Spanish-American writers celebrated their intellectual, cultural, literary, and artistic emancipation.

The writer who best represents and expresses the essence of the entire period was Andrés Bello (1781–1865) of Venezuela. Bello was a true Encyclopedist and humanist: his thinking was European and his outlook cosmopolitan, but like his countryman Simón Bolívar his heart and soul were profoundly Spanish American. Through his valuable work as an educator, his numerous essays, and his poetry, Bello reaffirmed with words what Bolívar accomplished with arms. Not surprisingly, he has often been described as the patriarch of Spanish-American letters. Like Channing in his essay "On National Literature" (1823), and Emerson in his speech "The American Scholar" (1837), Bello proclaimed the intellectual and cultural independence of the colonies in his "Alocución a la poesía" ("Allocution to Poetry," 1823). Three years later, in another classic of Spanish-American poetry, "La agricultura de la zona tórrida" ("Agriculture in the Torrid Zone," 1826), Bello lauds nature's beauty and commends the fertility of the American soil. His style is elegantly neoclassical, with certain elements of romanticism.

The Cuban José María Heredia (1803–1839), neoclassical lyric poet par excellence, was one of the first Spanish-American poets to be recognized in Europe. The story of one of the two poems that earned him such fame is well known. He wrote the ode "Niágara" in 1824, after visiting Niagara Falls, a copy of François René de Chateaubriand's *Atalá* in hand. Although Heredia also wrote patriotic and philosophical poetry, his lyric poetry describing natural settings in America won him unequaled fame. The melancholy, nostalgic, personal tone of his poetry marks the transition from neoclassicism to romanticism.

The end of the long colonial period coincides with an event of vast importance to Spanish-American letters: the novel appeared, in 1816, with the publication of *El Periquillo Sarniento (The Itching Parrot)*, written by the Mexican José Joaquín Fernández de Lizardi (1776–1827). The mother country had given the world one of the great novelists of all time—Miguel de Cervantes, creator of the modern novel—but three centuries of colonial literature had produced only chronicles, epics, lyric poetry, drama, and essays; no novelist had emerged. We can mention only a few of the diverse reasons that have been offered in explanation of the curiously belated appearance of the novel in Spanish-American literature. Among them are the censorship and restrictions that prohibited the importation and printing of novels in the New World; the insufficient circulation of Spanish masterpieces, which could reach only a few readers; the decadence of the novel itself in Spain; and the very attitude of Spanish America's writers, who were more concerned with describing and publishing the new and fascinating reality of their world than with creating their own fictional realm. Although there were elements of fiction in their writing, what these writers were actually seeing seemed more unreal to them than any fantasy.

The Spanish-born Peruvian Alonso Carrió de la Vandera (ca. 1715–1783) had already made an initial attempt at the genre when, around 1773, he wrote *El lazarillo de ciegos caminantes desde Buenos-Ayres, hasta Lima (El Lazarillo: A Guide for Inexperienced Travelers Between Buenos Aires and Lima)*, clandestinely published in Lima around 1775. A lively account of a traveler's experiences, it was narrated with Quevedian irony in the first person and followed the model of the picaresque novel. But when the novel finally appeared it was almost by accident, more as the result of Lizardi's intellectual commitment to effect sweeping social change than of any deliberately creative aesthetic or artistic process. A true liberal, inspired by the ideals of the Enlightenment, Lizardi was critical of the abuses, vices, and virtues of Mexico's civil and religious authorities. He decided to abandon journalism and defend his ideas with a new type of literature. *The Itching Parrot,* published in three volumes (the last one posthumously, due to censorship), was an extremely original account of Mexico's social environment. Lizardi's work is profoundly realistic, even naturalistic, in some descriptions. Although picaresque in style, it had certain preromantic traits, and a moralistic tone, since it was conceived more to propagate the author's modern ideas than to demonstrate his aesthetic principles. Years later Lizardi would demonstrate his gifts as a narrator in his masterwork *Don Catrín de la Fachenda* (written in 1818 but published posthumously, in 1832). This work was also picaresque and moralistic, but its structure was more coherent and its narrative irony highly refined; it was, simply, more of a novel. Both works had enormous influence in the development of Spanish-American narrative, *Don Catrín* for its literary value, and the *Itching Parrot* for its importance in literary history.

The second period of Spanish-American literary history opens with independence from Spain—presaged by the victories of Junín, Argentina, and Ayacucho, Peru, in 1824—and with the inception of the romantic movement, propagated by Andrés Bello, José María Heredia, and Esteban Echeverría (1805–1851). This period extends roughly through the second decade of the twentieth century. In 1916 the death of Rubén Darío (1867–1916) marked the end of *modernismo.* That same year the Chilean Vicente Huidobro (1893–1948), published *El espejo del agua,* in which his poem "Arte poética" proclaimed the new aesthetic of creationism in Buenos Aires. This vanguard movement broke away from the traditional rhythms of verse and the "artificiality" of the modernist movement and defended "absolute" poetic creation, inventing fresh images as it surged naturally and spontaneously from the music of the poet's soul.

The social and political situation, emerging liberal and socialist doctrines, new currents of scientific and philosophical thought, and the artistic and literary trends arriving from Europe all make this period one of extreme historical and literary complexity. In Europe, the break with the ancien régime, based on the precepts of the Enlightenment, was not easy; all nineteenth-century European political history revolved around the struggles between liberalism and despotism. The transition was even more difficult for the newborn Spanish-American republics. The ideology of independence required modern systems of government for which these countries were not prepared. The Enlightenment approach to government and Anglo-Saxon political maturity, which had made possible the American revolution, did not correspond with Spanish America's socioeconomic structure. For three centuries all political power had been in the hands of the *peninsulares;* hence the "founding fathers" of the new nations, the *criollos,* had no experience in self-government. The great task of organizing the republics was made still more difficult by America's vast territories, racial mixtures, and uneven demographic and geographic profiles.

It is hardly surprising, then, that these were years of anarchy and confusion. Despots and *caudillos* emerged and forged dictatorships: two of the harshest, among many, were

Argentina's Juan Manuel de Rosas (1829–1852), and Ecuador's Gabriel García Moreno (1860–1875); other strongmen tempered their strength with a national mission, among them Argentina's Domingo Faustino Sarmiento (1868–1874) and Mexico's Porfirio Díaz (1876–1911). The imperative need for radical social change produced fierce internal struggles, such as the War of the Reform (1855–1860) in Mexico, led by Benito Juárez. Territorial and economic ambitions sparked international conflict: the Cisplatine War (1825–1828) between Brazil and Argentina, for the possession of Uruguay; the War of the Triple Alliance (1865–1870) of Argentina, Brazil, and Uruguay against Paraguay; and the War of the Pacific (1879–1883) between Peru and Chile for the nitrate-producing provinces, among others. Political instability also facilitated foreign intervention: in 1848, Mexico lost a war with, and a great part of its territory to, the United States; Spain attempted to reconquer Peru (1862–1866); the French made Maximilian von Hapsburg the emperor of Mexico (1863–1867); Spain, losing the war with the United States in 1898, was forced to give up Cuba and Puerto Rico; and in 1903 the United States created the new nation of Panama, finally dissolving Bolívar's dream of Great Colombia. These were traumatic decades in which Spanish America strove to reconcile its Spanish heritage with its new identity as a continental region of politically and culturally free and independent nations, confronting grave organizational problems—many of them shared but others very different—yet spiritually united by similar ways of thinking, similar causes, similar goals.

The new literary movements and trends coming from Europe—romanticism, realism, naturalism, Parnassianism, symbolism, decadence—acquired unique characteristics as they developed within different countries and spread across Spanish America during the nineteenth century. Beginning in the 1850's—the second generation of the romantic movement—the transition to realism became most apparent in narrative prose, essay and theater, first taking the form of *costumbrismo*, or sketches of manners, and later, toward the turn of the century, naturalistic realism. At the same time, from the 1880's onward, poetry and prose were also influenced by the French Parnassians and symbolists, resulting in the modernist movement. Thus, between 1880 and 1910, modernism, naturalism, and realism coincided.

It could be said that the first century of independence also represented the securing of literary expression in Spanish America. All genres flourished and there was intense literary production. The novel was cultivated as never before, and great technical strides were made. European models were adapted to the continent's reality. The strong desire for national identity, supported by the romantic movement, produced both the popular *criollista* literature (whose roots are found in the baroque and cultivated during the neoclassical period) and the national literature of the *gaucho*, the legendary cowboy-hero of Argentina; customs and traditions were valued, as *costumbrismo* flourished; and a new genre, the *tradiciones*, was invented. The essay, a genre still highly favored by the best Spanish-American writers, became the indispensible medium for comprehension of the social, political, and ideological unfolding of Spanish America. As the century closed, the modernist movement, one of Spanish America's greatest contributions to world literature, took poetry and prose to new heights of aestheticism. Throughout the period, in spite of a regional and national focus, the aesthetic of Spanish-American writers operated on a continental, even universal, level.

The birth of the American republics coincided with the peak of European romanticism, which proclaimed the complete freedom of the individual, rebellion against all forms of oppression and injustice, nationalism in all aspects, and the glorification of indigenous values and the cult of nature. Romanticism was a reaction against the cold dictates of the Enlightenment and the ordered, traditional style of the neoclassical period. The romantics searched for truth, not through reason and neoclassical order, but through subjectivity and unrestrained sentiment; confronting the disappointment of life's reality, they fell into nostalgia, a kind of anguish for the "paradise lost," oftentimes sinking into pessimism.

The desire to reaffirm total independence from Spain brought Spanish-American nations to view non-Spanish Europe as the model to imitate, particularly in the arts. Nowhere was this sentiment so strong as in the River Plate countries of Uruguay and, especially, Argentina. It is not surprising then that the first waves of romanticism came directly from France, where the movement was consecrated, and to a lesser extent, from England. In other countries, on the other hand—Mexico, Cuba, Colombia—Spanish roots remained culturally influential and were a source of pride. Toward the second half of the century, Argentina and Uruguay also turned to the Spanish romantics as spiritual leaders.

Nor is it surprising that the first romantic work published in Spanish, the poem *Elvira; o, La novia del Plata* (1832), was written by an Argentine, Esteban Echeverría. We have already mentioned Bello, and especially Heredia, as the poets of transition from neoclassicism to romanticism, but Echeverría brought fervent passion to his defense of this new orientation in its spiritual, aesthetic, and—as romanticism and liberalism go hand in hand—political ramifications. To promote the movement, Echeverría founded in Buenos Aires the famous Asociación de Mayo, an important group of young Argentine intellectuals and idealists dedicated to advancing the romantic agenda. In no other country of Spanish America was there any group of writers so decidedly romantic. The Argentines went so far as to speak of a "national language." Two outstanding works in Spanish-American letters distinguish Echeverría as the father of romanticism: the poem "La cautiva" (1837), the first to praise the beauty of the Argentine pampa as an American landscape, and above all his short story *El matadero* (*The Slaughter House*, 1871), a classic in its genre and of enormous influence in the development of Argentina's narrative prose.

The sociopolitical scene in nineteenth-century Spanish America explains why romanticism was so well received there, lasting nearly a century, longer than in any European country. Spanish-American romanticism in the latter half of the nineteenth century distinguished itself from that of European romanticism by becoming a movement of political and social ideals with liberal, progressive, and democratic values. In fact, many romantic writers were also public figures, driven by nationalistic conscience to struggle against tyranny and oppression with actions as well as words. In Spanish America romantic literature was not mere artistic expression, but a device used for education and socialization. Eager to express what was genuinely American and to reaffirm national values, the Spanish-American writer exalted America's beauty and unique character. The Indian's status was raised from "noble savage" to romantic hero, the black slave became the object of compassion, and the *gaucho* was glorified and immortalized. Native characters and their lore, as well as the customs of different social classes, were valued, and regional variations in language were incorporated into literary works. Spanish-American romanticism focused on the people, developing the popular literature of *criollismo*, making sketches of manners important, and creating the *tradiciones*, all the while preparing the way for the realistic novel.

Romanticism began in Spanish America with lyric and epic poetry, but perhaps the best literary production was in prose; the essay was most important, and the novel took on a definitive form. Theater was also cultivated. This was a period of great literary activity and many of these writers excelled in more than one genre. Argentina produced not only Echeverría but also José Mármol (1817–1871), a lyric poet whose *Cantos del peregrino* (1847) was inspired by Lord Byron's *Childe Harold's Pilgrimage*. Primarily a protest writer, Mármol was called "the poetic executioner of Rosas" by Spanish critic Menéndez y Pelayo. Cuba, which had continued under Spanish domination during the romantic period and had given us one of the movement's outstanding precursors, José María Heredia, likewise produced one of the most important lyric poets of Spanish-American romanticism, Gertrudis Gómez de Avellaneda (1814–1873), who was also claimed by Spain, where she spent a significant part of her literary life. La Peregrina, or La Avellaneda, as she was known, was romantic in her sensitivity and choice of theme, sincerely and passionately treating art, politics, and love as both human and divine. Yet, her style was cautious and her language polished and precise. La Avellaneda, who was also an excellent dramatist, wrote America's first important novel about slavery (*Sab*, 1841).

The Uruguayan Juan Zorrilla de San Martín (1855–1930), was another great romantic poet. His masterwork *Tabaré* (finished and published in 1888), which contains a more lyric, nostalgic, and elegiac than epic tone, describes in metaphysical terms the destiny of the Charrúa Indians, who symbolize nature, in their struggle against the Spaniards during the conquest. But in its pictorial and musical language, Zorrilla de San Martín's poetry already announces the symbolism and linguistic renovation that the modernists would later bring.

Argentina and Ecuador produced two of Spanish America's greatest prose writers, Domingo Faustino Sarmiento (1811–1888) and Juan Montalvo (1832–1889). Both were romantics, possessed with rebellious and idealistic spirits. Personally identifying with the problems of their countries, their literary (and in Sarmiento's case, public) lives were unswervingly dedicated to the battle against America's social and political malaise. With intellectual courage, they combated abominable dictatorships: Sarmiento against Rosas in Argentina, Montalvo against García Moreno in Ecuador. Among their volumes are two of the most outstanding essayistic works in the Spanish language: Sarmiento's *Facundo* (1845), a sociopolitical essay with historical, biographical, *criollista*, and novelistic elements, written to tell the world of the Argentine tyrant's cruelty; and Montalvo's *Catilinarias* (1880–1882), a collection of twelve brilliant essays in the same spirit of protest, a book whose pages modernist poet Rubén Darío described as being filled with "odio santo" (holy hatred). The romantic spirit carried Sarmiento still further in linguistic expression, but also in the realm of action; for six years he was president of Argentina. Contrary to Montalvo, who exercised extreme care in perfecting the form and purity of his language, Sarmiento's style was more spontaneous, his language much less rigorous. He was a passionate defender of linguistic independence: "America's language must . . . be its own." *Facundo* was historically important because it introduced the conflict between "civilization" (the

European culture of the cities) and "barbarism" (the pampa and the desert); its literary value lay in its creation of a romantic myth centered on the figure of the *gaucho* and the idealization of his environment, the Argentine pampa. All of this continued to develop as a part of *gaucho* literature.

In fact, nowhere in Spanish America was the nativist and folkloric tendency more dominant than in the River Plate region. *Gaucho* literature thrived there during the nineteenth and into the twentieth century and produced classic works in several literary periods: during the romantic period *Martín Fierro* (1872) was written by José Hernández (1834–1886); the Uruguayan Florencio Sánchez (1875–1910) produced important realist theater including such plays as *M'ijo el dotor* (1903) and *Barranca abajo* (1905); and the novel *Don Segundo Sombra* (1926) by Ricardo Güiraldes (1886–1927) appeared during the vanguardist movement. This attempt to create a "national" literature was successful in that it was a step toward defining Spanish-American literature's unique personality. The works written within this nativist/criollista current have no equivalent in other literatures.

In *Facundo*, Sarmiento had defined the *gaucho*'s character; three romantic Argentine writers consecrated it, elevating the *gaucho*'s language to its maximum artistry and creating the most genuine exaltation of the *gaucho*'s environment. Hilario Ascasubi (1807–1875), with *Santos Vega, o Los mellizos de la Flor* (published in Paris, 1872), drew a vivid picture of *gaucho* society, narrated with humor and irony; Estanislao del Campo (1834–1880), with *Fausto* (*Faust*, 1886), parodied Goethe's work, placing it within a *gaucho* context, penetrating *gaucho* psychology with his sense of humor and perfecting the language of Ascasubi, whose disciple he considered himself; and, above all, José Hernández' *Martín Fierro* and its sequel, *Vuelta de Martín Fierro* (1879). In Hernández' work, the language of the *gaucho* reached the apex of its aesthetic development. His nostalgic, even tragic, poem idealizes a character who seems to take on real life as he struggles against injustice and the abuses of "civilized" society; it is also realistic in its descriptions of the geographic and social setting of the Argentine pampa. *Martín Fierro* is a work of extreme originality, mixing lyric, epic, novelistic, and folkloric elements.

During the nineteenth century, the novel flourished as an important literary genre, improving considerably over Lizardi's first efforts. The romantic novel was oriented toward politics, abolition, sentiment, history, the idealization of Indians, and popular tradition. Its momentum derived from its social themes, its sense of justice for the oppressed, and its glorification of indigenous and local customs and characteristics. Thus many of these novels at times reflect a sense of historic mission, becoming social documents.

José Mármol's *Amalia* (1851–1855) represents the romantic political and autobiographical novel. Although written without aesthetic concern, it is of historical importance as the first Argentine novel and as the best literary document of Rosa's abominable tyranny. Until 1880 the Caribbean sugar cane plantations were worked by black slaves, and the first abolitionist novels were written in Cuba, many years before Harriet Beecher Stowe published *Uncle Tom's Cabin*. Two Cuban writers produced the best abolitionist novels: Gertrudis Gómez de Avellaneda's *Sab* is full of compassion for the black slave; still more important was *Cecilia Valdés, o La Loma del Angel* (*Cecilia Valdés, or Angel's Hill*, begun in 1839 and finished in 1882) by Cirilo Villaverde (1812–1894), a work that marked the peak of abolitionist literature, combining realistic and folkloric elements to present Cuba's racial problems as a whole. The preeminent romantic novelist was the Colombian Jorge Isaacs (1837–1895), whose *María* (1867), an idealization of love—idyllic, melancholy, sentimental in tone, but written in an elegant and sober style—is one of Spanish America's most widely read novels.

An important element of the romantic novel was the author's description of the social environment, manners and customs, social and political conditions, human nature, and components of the society in which the plot unfolds. This technique, known as *costumbrismo,* which featured sketches of manners, was one of the most salient features of Spanish-American romanticism. It culminated in the creation of a new genre, the *tradiciones,* short narratives mixing the historical and the anecdotal with humor and irony. This genre, created by Ricardo Palma (1833–1919), synthesized all the elements of *costumbrismo.* Palma's *Tradiciones peruanas* (Peruvian Traditions, written between 1872 and 1896) is a fascinating overview of the manners of each social class, from the time of the Incas to the author's own period.

During the last twenty-five years of the nineteenth century and the first decade of the twentieth, Spanish-American society experienced profound changes, the inevitable consequence of Europe's evolution. Industry began to develop, banks were created, the means of communication were expanded with the construction of the railroads, the diffusion of information intensified with the appearance of numerous newspapers and literary magazines, public education received great attention, and the population grew, especially in the urban centers. In some areas, such as the River Plate, masses of European immigrants arrived. All of this brought sudden and rapid material progress, and a new capitalist bourgeoisie, with "democratic" ideas, secured its place in the economy. Nevertheless, there was little improvement in the quality of life for the masses, and the gap between the classes became even more striking. Public and political life became dominated by the old landholding oligarchies who protected their own economic interests, while the materialistic bourgeoisie became the instrument of foreign capital. Education was a privilege reserved for only a few.

The thought and work of the Spanish-American writer were also influenced by the rich variety of ideas in vogue in Europe: the new political ideologies of Marxism and socialism, and the new philosophical schools, including the positivism of Comte, who defended real experience, observed and researched, as the basis of knowledge; the German idealism of Hegel, attempting to rationalize social and individual ideals; the "pessimistic voluntarism" of Schopenhauer; the "creative voluntarism" of Nietzsche; and the existentialism of Kierkegaard. Darwin and Haeckel's hypotheses on the evolution of species led to the theories of natural selection and social determinism. The international exposition of Paris in 1889 emphasized the intense desire for artistic renovation that was stirring in the arts, music, and letters. Symbolists, impressionists, pre-Raphaelists, decadents, neosensualists, and Parnassians all searched for a new aesthetic to relieve the widespread *mal du siècle.*

The romantic ideal no longer fit the social, ideological, and artistic framework, and literature turned in several directions. For one, the writer wished to describe life as it was, painting social reality, events, and characters, including the most sordid, in full color, relying on the observation of real experience, without subjective idealization. At the same time, there was a tendency toward apoliticism and an intense desire to blend the intellectual with the aesthetic.

Thus, the two European literary currents of realism and naturalism entered Spanish America, bringing both novel and drama toward greater artistic refinement. Almost simultaneously, the desire for some artistic renovation and the yearning for an aestheticism that would not diminish an essentially romantic vision culminated in the creation in Spanish America of the movement known as *modernismo*, whose greatest production was in poetry, while also influencing the essay, short story, and novel.

Realism, naturalism, and modernism are not exactly parallel phenomena in Spanish-American literature. Nevertheless, the three movements do coincide to a certain extent in the period between 1880 and 1910. In 1862, *Martín Rivas*, by Chilean Alberto Blest Gana (1830–1920), announced the beginning of realism in the novel. Twenty years later, in 1882, before romanticism had expired, the Cuban José Martí (1853–1895) published his collection of poems *Ismaelillo*, initiating the modernist movement. Between 1881 and 1887, the Argentine Eugenio Cambaceres (1843–1889) published several strongly realistic and naturalistic novels. This coincidence of trends demonstrates why it is sometimes difficult to place a writer of this period precisely within a rigidly defined literary movement. The different movements, and the writers themselves, influenced each other; thus we find writers who began their literary careers in one movement, only later to follow another current. There are writers who treat romantic themes, integrating them with realistic motifs and descriptions. Others tend more to incorporate naturalistic elements, resulting in "romantic realism" and "naturalistic realism." The aesthetic renovation that brought about modernism influenced the style of the twentieth-century novel, while the techniques of narration and description were influenced by realism and naturalism.

Generally speaking, the development of realism and naturalism in Spanish-American narrative followed European patterns—especially the French and the Spanish—but also maintained unique properties. In their zeal to accurately depict reality, customs, and people the writers describe those things they know best. Spanish-American realism was primarily regional and social in character, taking the form of *criollismo*; it neglected to some degree the character analysis which was so important to European realism.

Nor did Spanish-American naturalism adopt the excesses of French naturalism. Although the writers do treat subjects previously considered taboo, they avoid the extremism of Zola's clinical cases and the typically repugnant descriptions of sordid environments and characters, shunning the excessive determinism of the French. The Spanish-American writers who followed the naturalist current chose to observe and present as precisely as possible the environment and the human and social problems that plagued a society in crisis: social injustice, exploitation of workers, political and moral corruption, intellectual and philosophical crises. Naturalist writers denounced these evils and demanded reform. Spanish-American naturalism is generally a mixture of *costumbrismo* and realism with naturalistic elements. Compared to the romantic period, technique in the novel improved considerably as a result of the influences of realism and naturalism. The structure of the novel became more precise and cohesive, the characters better drawn, and the descriptions of environment, customs, and characters better integrated with the plot.

Alberto Blest Gana is considered the first important realistic novelist of Spanish America. His writing marks the transition from romanticism to realism, and his novels *Martín Rivas* and *Durante la reconquista* (1897) are possibly the best realistic works of all nineteenth-century Spanish-American literature. Others followed him, although not all are included here. Eduardo Acevedo Díaz (1851–1921) introduced both realism and naturalism to Uruguay. If his glorification of the *gaucho* and the pampa is romantic, his veracity and precision in observation and narration are decidedly realistic, and his work has had considerable influence on the *gaucho* literature of his country. In Peru, Clorinda Matto de Turner (1852–1909) broke with the romantics' poetic, idealized view of the Indians, presenting them as a living, suffering human and social reality. Her novel *Aves sin nido* (*Birds Without a Nest*, 1889) initiated the modern indigenist novel. The Colombian Tomás Carrasquilla (1858–1940), whose work was forgotten for a time, is perhaps the novelist who found the best combination of *costumbrismo*, realism, and naturalism, introducing a great variety of characters and personalities in his works. Another realistic writer of naturalist inclination is the Argentine Roberto Jorge Payró (1867–1928), who wrote in a picaresque style. The authenticity of his descriptions of the environment and the varied characters he presents, not without sarcasm and cynicism, impart great sociological value to his works. The Argentine Manuel Gálvez (1882–1962) left an impressive novelistic production, in which he offered with deep social concern a picture of his country's life and people, their social mores, their national conscience and psychology. Yet Gálvez' reputation rests in his early works as a realist-naturalist writer.

In the ranks of the naturalists we have also included the Mexican Federico Gamboa (1864–1939), whose themes most closely approach those of Zola, despite his lack of the Frenchman's rigor and the romantic elements of his works. The Puerto Rican Manuel Zeno Gandía (1855–1930) also merits a place in the development of the Spanish-American novel; his medical training expanded his capacity for observation and enabled him to describe in detail the world of poverty, hunger, and vice.

In theater realism served to strengthen technique, theme, and objective. Although local settings and characters make it principally a regional and national theater, the human and social conflicts it portrays are of more universal interest, paving the road for contemporary drama. Payró's drama was realistic; however, the playwright most representative of the period was the Uruguayan Florencio Sánchez. In spite of the regional flavor of his works and the important role of the "noble *gaucho*" in them, his theater is essentially serious and its subjects are universal. Sánchez' work illustrates such difficulties as social breakdown due to rapid social and economic transformation, family problems and intergenerational conflicts, poverty, alcoholism, and other diseases, with an intensity imparted by excellent characterizations and dialogue.

In the West, the transition from the nineteenth to the twentieth century awakened an enormous desire for spiritual renovation, translated into an insatiable appetite for modernity in all art. In literature, French Parnassians and symbolists soon made their influence felt among Spanish-American poets and prose writers, who began to experiment with new forms and themes.

For the first time in Spanish-American literary history, writers saw the purpose of creation as essentially aesthetic and apolitical, without a social message or a moral doctrine, believing now in art for the sake of art. They began to feel the need to function aesthetically on the world plane, integrating their work with the currents of universal culture.

Poetic language and structure were modernized, breaking with neoclassical norms. New metric combinations began to appear; synesthesia and chromatic images predominated; rhythm, musicality, and plasticity occupied the artistic imagination. Costumbrist, *criollista*, regional, and social themes no longer excited interest. Images and settings became more refined: luxury, elegance, sensuality, exoticism, cosmopolitanism, paganism, and fantasy became fashionable.

This renovation in Spanish-American letters, known as *modernismo*, was not only a literary tendency or school; it was rather a spiritual movement which elevated the artistic consciousness of the writer. Literary creation ceased to be considered the product of mere vocation and became the work of professional artists. In this vein, the modernists propagated total aesthetic freedom to create, conserve, and integrate literary and artistic elements. At the same time they announced a new ambience of high culture in harmony with the select spirit of artists and intellectuals. When reality failed to reach the lofty heights of their sensibilities, the modernists, like the romantics before them, suffered the same torturous melancholy, anguish, and pessimism. It is true that modernism had its roots in romanticism, recovering the ideals of artistic liberty proclaimed by the latter; but it was also a reaction against certain aesthetic traits that distinguished the romantic movement.

Although linguistic renovations associated with modernism had first been introduced in the prose of Montalvo's essays and Palma's *tradiciones*, two poetic works are considered the starting point of the modernist movement. In 1882, the Cuban José Martí published *Ismaelillo,* a collection of fifteen poems inspired by his son. In 1888, the Nicaraguan Rubén Darío published his landmark book *Azul* in Chile, incorporating various innovations which had already appeared in the poetry and prose of earlier writers.

Martí was an extremely prolific writer whose works consist of more than thirty volumes. He was equally versatile in writing poetry, drama, and short stories, as well as critical and political essays, speeches, letters, and even a novel. Following a stay in Paris, Martí became, in Darío's words, the first "maestro" of modernism by introducing Parnassian and symbolist innovations to his work upon his return to Cuba. Although his refined and elegant style, the melody and rhythm of his language, and the structure of his works earned him recognition as the creator of "artistic prose," Martí was distinguished from other modernists by his active interest in Cuban politics and his intense concern for the future of the American republics. Thus, the aesthetic value of his copious literary production is supported by the sense of ethics, humanitarianism, and Americanism which it conveys.

Martí was accompanied by a group of artistically talented writers who, in spite of being essentially romantic in temperament, were the actual creators of the pictorial, plastic, and musical language of modernism. Several of these writers stand out: the Peruvian Manuel González Prada (1844–1918), a magnificent prose writer, primarily ideological in orientation, but also an excellent poet who created new forms; the Mexican Manuel Gutiérrez Nájera (1859–1895), who wrote short stories and poetry and, in the area of artistic journalism, created the chronicle; the Cuban Julián del Casal (1863–1893), perhaps the Spanish-American poet most influenced by the French Parnassians, despite the subjective, nostalgic, and elegiac tone of his poetry; and the Colombian José Asunción Silva (1865–1896), who also wrote prose, today considered one of the period's best lyric poets, even though much of his greatest work was lost in a shipwreck as he returned home from Europe.

In a matter of three years, between 1893 and 1896, four of these precursors or true initiators of modernism died: del Casal in 1893, Gutiérrez Nájera and Martí in 1895, and Silva in 1896. Rubén Darío then consolidated the movement, bringing it to its culmination and becoming the most representative modernist and one of the great innovators of all Spanish-language poetry. But Darío also represents the transition of Spanish-American literature into the new century. His *Prosas profanas* (1896) signaled the high point of the literary *préciosité* radiating from France. Later, without abandoning linguistic refinement and ingenious metaphor, Darío changed course and in *Cantos de vida y esperanza* (1905) turned his attention to metaphysics and the problems of America. While it is true that apoliticism was one of the characteristics of modernism, it cannot be said that the movement was exclusively aesthetic, as it also developed a new and more penetrating view of American reality. Martí and González Prada, among others, contributed to this acute vision.

The figure of greatest renown, after Darío, was the Uruguayan José Enrique Rodó (1871–1917), the most outstanding modernist essayist. His *Ariel* (1900), addressed to the youth of Latin America, is a landmark in modern Spanish-American thought and in the stylistic development of the essay, bringing lexical enrichment, syntactical flexibility, structural precision, and the fluidity of expression.

The writers of this generation and those who followed Darío, by virtue of the artistic quality and richness of their literary production as well as the variety of themes and genres they employed, raised Spanish-American literature to a level of international prestige never before achieved. While poetry was the preferred genre of the modernists, they also cultivated the essay and the short story; some even wrote novels. Nonetheless, in contrast to realist and naturalist narrative—with which it intertwines—in the modernist short story and novel there is a reaction against folklore and *criollismo*, and social commentary is avoided. Plot development is of less concern, overshadowed by lyrical elements, stylized language, and *préciosité* in form. Further adorned with exotic settings and aristocratic characters, the works almost become prose poems. The value of modernist narrative lies primarily in the artistic effort invested in its creation; its works cannot be seen as literary documents reflecting the epoch's social concerns. It should be noted, nevertheless, that the confluence of various currents—*criollismo*, realism, naturalism—with the modernist movement resulted in many novelists and story writers mixing elements of all the styles in their narrative; or the writers themselves may have begun with one current and crossed over to another. Therefore, many modernist works, while not ignoring the movement's basic formula for aesthetic renovation, are amalgams of several tendencies.

As for the modernist essay, it should be mentioned that these writers go beyond aesthetic preoccupations, adding an ideological and philosophical dimension which was primarily oriented toward idealism, humanism, and liberalism. Although there is a constant concern for the destiny of Spanish America, American society is not the only theme; many universal problems are considered, including liberty, materialism, utilitarianism, spirituality, and human fulfillment.

While modernism came to maturity with Darío and Rodó, there were other important modernists such as the Bolivian Ricardo Jaimes Freyre (1868–1933), the recreator of the Nordic fantasy and mythology (*Castalia bárbara*, 1899) and a great revolutionary of technique and meter (*Leyes de la versificación castellana*, 1912); the Venezuelan Manuel Díaz Rodríguez (1871–1927), perhaps the best modernist novelist (*Sangre patricia*, 1902); Amado Nervo (1870–1919), Mexico's most important modernist poet, whose work is distinguished by its mystical, pantheistic, religious focus and its subjective tone (*Místicas* and *Perlas negras,* 1898); José Juan Tablada (1871–1945), also Mexican, whose poetry exerted great influence over later vanguardist and surrealist writers; the Guatemalan Enrique Gómez Carrillo (1873–1927), recognized as the creator of the modern chronicle on such topics as travel, personalities, and books; the Colombian Guillermo Valencia (1873–1943), Parnassian in his plastic imagery and his painstaking form; the Peruvian José Santos Chocano (1875–1934), known as the "bard of America" because of the nearly epic tone of his poetry and his great interest in the continent's destiny (*Alma América,* 1906); the Argentine Enrique Larreta (1873–1961), author of the modernist novel par excellence, *La gloria de Don Ramiro* (*The Glory of Don Ramiro,* 1908); the Argentine Leopoldo Lugones (1874–1938), a poet and prose writer whose literary work runs the gamut from socialism and romantic nationalism to brash symbolism and cosmopolitan *preciosité,* to *criollismo;* and the Uruguayan Julio Herrera y Reissig (1875–1910), the most symbolist of the modernists. Lugones and Herrera y Reissig are perhaps modernism's two most important poets, after Darío. In their work, as in that of other writers of their inclination—Tablada, Valencia, and Santos Chocano—new forms and images appear, which later are integrated into postmodernism, a prelude to the vanguard.

Modernism was still in its apogee as the twentieth century began, ushering in an epoch that saw the world divided by profound changes and in which all aspects of human life were substantially altered. World War I (1914–1918) destroyed faith in traditional institutions, leaving society spiritually, aesthetically, and ideologically disoriented. The Bolshevik Revolution of 1917, followed by the Stalinist era, produced the world's most categorical ideological schism as it installed an unprecedented system of political and social organization. In 1922, Italy fell to fascism; beginning in 1933, German nazism also negated the traditional values of liberty and human rights, eventually leading to a second armed conflict of even greater magnitude which involved the great powers of East and West. Between 1936 and 1939, Spain was the scene of the world's bloodiest civil war, a struggle which attracted international sympathy and support from both the right and the left of the political spectrum. Science, technology, and industry jolted the twentieth century with their startling vigor; the international markets were dominated by the great economic powers.

The international crises of the century's first decades demanded a violent break with the past and required a total renovation of society. The world's deep divisions and confusion made the fragmentation of art and thought inevitable. As thinkers, artists, and writers sought explanations and solutions to the chaos, Europe became a crucible of opposing artistic doctrines, theories, and orientations which ran parallel and commingled, influencing and modifying each other, gradually molding the thought of the second half of the twentieth century.

In 1907 in *Creative Evolution* Henri Bergson postulated the predominance of intuition over reason in arriving at knowledge, thus rejecting the positivism of the previous century. The ideas of Sigmund Freud and Carl Jung brought new interpretations to psychology, and Albert Einstein revolutionized physics. In 1909, the Italian poet Filippo Tommaso Marinetti's *Manifesto of Futurism* inaugurated the futurist movement, a glorification of the twentieth century's technological dynamism and all its consequences. By World War I, cubism, as an early form of abstract art, had emerged in France. In 1916, another Italian writer, Tristan Tzara, launched dadaism in Zurich, proposing a new nihilistic art based on imitation of the infantile, deliberately incoherent and meaningless. At the same time, the Chilean poet Vicente Huidobro—followed by Pierre Reverdy of France—was proclaiming a vanguard movement he called creationism, which compared the process of artistic creation with that found in nature. "To make a poem as Nature makes a tree," Huidobro prescribed in the prologue to his book *Horizon carré*, written in French and published in Paris in 1917.

But of all the vanguard's movements, surrealism was the most important and the most influential in the development of twentieth-century art and literature. Initiated by André Breton in *Manifesto of Surrealism* (1924), surrealism emerged amid the influence of Tzara's dadaism and Freud's theories of the unconscious, and held as its main tenet that the artist and the writer should express not exterior reality but pure thought and the functioning of the mind, excluding all formal logic and moral concerns. Art must flow from the stream of consciousness, where dreams, fantasies, allusions, and images appear without logical order or calculated effort.

In the first decades of the century, the nations of Spanish America found themselves in circumstances no less complex than the rest of the world. Mexico's revolution of 1910 would last for eleven years, and was the first in Spanish America geared toward agrarian reform, breaking with the semifeudal system inherited from the colonial period and striving for social justice and democratic stabilization. Later, under the government of Lázaro Cárdenas (1934–1940), Mexico again underwent important socioeconomic and political changes. In Mexico in 1924, meanwhile, the Peruvian leader Víctor Raúl Haya de la Torre founded APRA—the Alianza Popular Revolucionaria Americana (American Revolutionary Popular Alliance)—a program of social reform for Peru. Such events created important ideological repercussions throughout the continent.

Although some countries appeared to have found stability—Uruguay carried out a program of advanced political and socioeconomic reforms from 1911 to 1927, and Argentina made electoral and educational reforms between 1912 and 1918—for the most part unrest, military dictatorships, internal struggles, and instability continued in Spanish America as the century progressed. Some South American countries further endured external strife, as with Paraguay and Bolivia's unfortunate Chaco War (1932–1935) and other conflicts of lesser magnitude.

North America's easy victory in Cuba in 1898 and the ensuing Platt Amendment of 1901 were still fresh in Spanish-American memory when, in 1903, the United States separated Panama from Colombia in order to acquire the rights of the French company building the interoceanic canal. In the years that followed, the "great colossus of the North" continued to intervene in Caribbean political and economic affairs. Nonetheless, there was some effort to consolidate the inter-American system. In 1933, President Franklin Delano Roosevelt proclaimed the short-lived Good Neighbor policy, and in Montevideo, the American nations celebrated the first Inter-American Conference for the Maintenance of Peace, followed in 1940 by the Havana Economic Conference.

The Latin American panorama, in light of global events and their ideological repercussions—anarchism, socialism, communism, fascism, imperialism, nationalism—meant that Spanish-American writers and thinkers inevitably shared in the spiritual and cultural crisis affecting the world. Like artists elsewhere they searched for new themes and new channels of thought, gradually abandoning old forms of expression and participating in the movements of aesthetic renovation radiating from Europe at the beginning of the twentieth century.

By the first decade of this century modernism had abandoned its initial *preciosité* and had taken on a new tone of metaphysical anguish and patriotic anxiety. This latter mood was expressed by Darío in 1905 in *Cantos de vida y esperanza* and *Los cisnes y otros poemas*, culminating in 1910 with his famous "Canto a la Argentina." A year later, on the other hand, Leopoldo Lugones had published *Lunario sentimental*, in which he satirized human ills using concrete, grotesque, and fantastic images that would have been inconceivable within modernist poetics.

Modernism was dissolving as the process of change and poetic experimentation accelerated. As the movement faded into extinction, writers took up various new paths; diverse tendencies sometimes manifested themselves even within the work of a single author. Some artists did not break completely with modernism but sought a more conservative means of expression, thereby creating products that were distinctly individual. Others who were more radical experimented daringly with the new forms and trends of the vanguard. Postmodernists never congealed into a coherent, classifiable group, except by virtue of their chronological proximity as a new generation of great personalities who had superseded modernism and were producing literature of the highest quality. Postmodernism and the vanguard brought a heightened awareness of the writer's role, the nature of literature, and its contribution to culture as a whole. The postmodernists continued their predecessor's preoccupation with form and aesthetic advancement, including a desire for linguistic and metrical variety and new images, but without the excesses of modernism. Now writers were searching for a more sober form of expression, one of greater simplicity and sincerity; nevertheless, literary renovation and modernity remained as goals. In content, literature became more intellectual and subjective; writers turned to the inner self and to their own immediate surroundings for subject matter. They abandoned the modernist exoticism of princesses, swans, and the Orient for the beauty of the American landscape, indigenous and colonial history, *criollismo*, and social reality. Poetry and the essay yielded brilliant pages. The novel, and to a lesser extent the short story, as well as theater in the tradition of Florencio Sánchez, distinguished the *criollista*/nativist current, which paralleled the vanguard's cerebral poetry. Along with the new themes of subjectivity and spiritual discontent, postmodernism forged new regional literatures, including the novel of the Mexican Revolution, a literature of anti-imperialism and social protest, and the interpretive essay on Spanish-America's destiny.

The development of postmodernist letters was strongly affected by the extraordinary poetic contribution made by a nucleus of women writers. Indeed, the first Nobel Prize ever awarded to a Latin American writer was accepted in 1945 by the Chilean Gabriela Mistral (1889–1957), one of the most intensely lyrical poets of the Spanish language. Mistral never broke absolutely with modernism but she surpassed it, both in the rich metaphors masterfully woven into her sincere verses and children's stories, and in the central theme of her work: love and tenderness as the foundation of universal human harmony. Mistral's love of children and her exaltation of mother-hood made hers some of the most beautiful children's poetry and narrative in Spanish. At the same time, her work was also influential in vanguard poetry.

Another woman, Juana de Ibarbourou (1895–1979) of Uruguay, known as "Juana de América," wrote with joy and spontaneity of love and life, combining nature's pagan sensuality with intimate emotion. Few poets have treated the theme of erotic love with such impressive elegance and aesthetic imagery as another Uruguayan, Delmira Agustini (1886–1914). The Argentine Alfonsina Storni (1892–1938) resembled Agustini without matching her almost obsessive eroticism. Storni, the most feminist of these writers, was one of the first women artists in Spanish America to rebel against the male dominance of her world.

The Mexican Ramón López Velarde (1888–1921) and the Peruvian José María Eguren (1874–1942) were among the postmodernist writers who put the new techniques and images into practice. López Velarde wrote prose as well as poetry, but he became known primarily for the novelty of his poetic language, in which concrete metaphors and highly original adjectivization elevated the ordinary to the level of art. His famous poem "La suave patria" (1921) synthesized the nativist, patriotic, provincial, and nationalist character that he evoked with profound sincerity. Eguren also withdrew from modernism, and although he was forgotten for a time under the shadow of Santos Chocano, today he is recognized for his creation of a symbolic and pictorial poetry with almost superrealistic associations. Both López Velarde and Eguren represent the transition from postmodernism to vanguard.

The same process that diversified lyric poetry's form and deepened its content also affected the postmodernist essay. The period's essayists felt an urgent need to analyze the difficulties afflicting their historical moment and to reaffirm the positive values of Spanish America in order to safeguard its integrity. Rodó, in response to the political and economic threat of imperialist forces, had already glorified the spiritual values of the Hispanic culture. The Venezuelan Rufino Blanco Fombona (1874–1944), also a poet, short story writer, novelist, chronicler, and literary critic, denounced North American imperialist policy in still more eloquent and audacious sociopolitical essays, while the Peruvian José Carlos Mariátegui (1894–1930) devoted himself to the social essay with a radical approach to solving Spanish America's social and political malaise, as for instance in *Siete ensayos de interpretación sobre la realidad peruana* (Seven Interpretative Essays on Peruvian Reality, 1928).

Other essayists were more serene and analytical in their vision of America and in their judgment of the continent's destiny. At the forefront was the Mexican Alfonso Reyes (1889–1959), who abandoned all modernist influence and created a new essayistic prose full of poetic images, original ideas, and accurate observations. His *Visión de Anáhuac* (*Vision of Anáhuac*, 1917), a glorification of American nature as the basis of Spanish-American cultural unity, reflected the literary maturity of these countries as well as the fulfillment of the essay's potential.

Reyes formed the Ateneo de la Juventud (Youth's Forum) in order to combat, among other things, positivism and modernism. Among his collaborators was a fellow Mexican, José Vasconcelos (1882–1959), a brilliant proponent of the role of the *mestizo*—"the fifth race"—and the Indian in the development of Spanish-American culture in opposition to the Anglo-Saxon (*La raza cósmica* [*The Cosmic Race*], 1925; *Indología*, 1926). Another ally was the Dominican Pedro Henríquez Ureña (1884–1946), who laid the foundation of the new Spanish-American literary criticism (*Seis ensayos en busca de nuestra expresión*, 1928, and later *Literary Currents in Hispanic America*, originally published in English, in 1945). Ricardo Rojas (1882–1957) also belonged to this distinguished group of postmodernist thinkers and humanists. His critical works made sage evaluations of the literature and culture of his native Argentina.

Perhaps the world's war-torn and weary state of mind explains the almost simultaneous appearance of the so-called vanguard on both sides of the Atlantic in the early 1920's. As with postmodernism, the new schools of the vanguard were also a reaction against modernism, the very movement within which they had been incubated. While Huidobro defended creationism in Buenos Aires and Paris, in Mexico another group—influenced by Marinetti's futurism—proposed stridentism, a school involving the use of dynamic images and typographical techniques to achieve free expression. In Madrid just after World War I another group of intellectuals and writers, among them Argentina's Jorge Luis Borges (1899–1986), were eager to tighten their bonds to the European vanguard, especially dadaism, and to go beyond what they saw as "carrying aesthetic renovation to its ultimate conclusion," with ultraism. Upon his return to Buenos Aires, Borges became the movement's main spokesman through his journal *Prism* (1921), followed by other vanguard journals such as *Proa* (1924–1925) and *Martín Fierro* (1924–1927). *Contemporáneos* was published in Mexico during the same years, and it consolidated another group of young vanguardists, more influential than the stridentists. Among the new group were José Gorostiza (1901–1979), Jaime Torres Bodet (1902–1974), and Xavier Villaurrutia (1903–1950). In Havana, Jorge Mañach Robato (1898–1961) and Alejo Carpentier (1904–1980) collaborated with others on the *Revista de avance* (1927–1930), forming the group Los Contemplativos.

Vanguardists rejected the traditional principles of beauty—order, harmony, unity, balance—and sought, rather, absolute liberty. The poets were indiscriminate in their choices of words and metaphors, employing grotesque forms, bold comparisons, elliptical and contorted syntax, free verse, internal rhyme, and polymetry. Vanguard poetry, based on intuition, automatism, and the unconscious, was hermetic, abstract, dehumanized; critics have described it as a sort of neobaroque art that bore meaning only after the reader comprehended the metaphors used. Hence, vanguardism was for the minority; its intellectual and elitist poetry expressed personal and metaphysical anguish, skepticism, and defeatism, backed by social, ideological, militant, and nationalist sentiment.

Poetry was the genre in which vanguardism was most successful. In fact, many of the great names in twentieth-century poetry explored one aspect or another of vanguardism before shifting to other movements later. Beyond all doubt, the Spanish-American vanguard's best representative was Vicente Huidobro, who brought creationism to its peak in the fourth canto of his masterpiece *Altazor*, begun in 1919 and published in 1931. Another important vanguardist was César Vallejo (1892–1938) of Peru, whose work extended from the postmodernism of *Los heraldos negros* (1918) through *Trilce* (1922), his best collection of vanguard poetry, to *Poemas humanos* (1939). The profound concern for humanity expressed in the latter work distinguished Vallejo from the rest of the vanguard. Chile's Pablo Neruda (1904–1973), the second Spanish American to receive the Nobel Prize for literature (1971), created some of the most marvelous poetry ever written in the Spanish language. His work also ran the gamut from postmodernism through vanguardism to social and autobiographical poetry. Neruda's work, the crowning glory of modern Spanish-American verse, has been translated into more than twenty-four languages, and his technical and thematic innovations place him among the most influential poets of the twentieth century.

While neither Xavier Villaurrutia nor José Gorostiza was a prolific writer, both deserve a place of honor in twentieth-century Spanish-American poetry for their metaphysical concerns and originality of expression. It is interesting to note that the best works of these two Mexican poets—Villarrutia's *Nostalgia de la muerte* (1938) and Gorostiza's *Muerte sin fin* (*Death Without End,* 1939), perhaps the most important work of transcendental poetry—center around the theme of death in metaphysical terms and existential anguish. Both were also renovators of the theater. Another praise-worthy Mexican was Jaime Torres Bodet, author of one of the most beautiful works of Mexican literature, *Tiempo de Arena* (1955). Torres Bodet, Villaurrutia, Huidobro, and Mañach Robato also represent the best essay writing during the vanguardist movement. In Argentina, Borges, who had been the main defender of ultraist poetics, modified his intuitive position and abandoned the movement, and even seems to have repented of his enthusiasm for the vanguard.

The universalizing nature of vanguardism came to be reflected in an expanding social concern on the part of Spanish-American writers; the resulting literature, in turn, contributed to a heightened social and literary awareness among the Spanish-American people. One of the most important steps in the development of Spanish-American letters was the flourishing of *criollismo.* The interest in *criollismo* reappeared in narrative prose within postmodernism, but developed separately from the vanguard schools—it was poetry rather than narrative that characterized the movement. In fact, during these years, narrative prose reached a level of perfection comparable to that attained by poetry and the essay. The works of the *criollistas* became widely known throughout the continent, attracting an international readership. These novels laid the real foundations for the novel of the second half of the twentieth century. The postmodernist novelists inherited the formal and stylistic guidelines established by the modernists without sharing their disdain for American themes and issues. On the contrary, their interest in the *criollista* came to replace the modernists' use of refined ambience and exotic motifs. Nor did the new novelists try to imitate peninsular models as the realists and costumbrists had earlier; conscious of literary Pan-Americanism, they strove to create a narrative genuinely Spanish-American in form and style—incorporating American motifs, images, symbols, and myths—as well as theme, to describe the land, environment, and people of America. Although *criollismo* also appeared in poetry, essay, and drama, its greatest works were in narrative prose. Thus, alongside the more cultured literature of the vanguard, the *criollismo* born of postmodernism developed a more popular literature that had political, social, and even psychological purposes. So the regional novel emerged: novels of the jungle, of the city, and of the countryside, the indigenist novel and the novel of the Mexican Revolution.

Many writers contributed to the success of the *criollista*/nativist short story and novel. Pedro Prado (1886–1952), also a postmodernist poet and essayist, devoted his novels to human problems and aspirations and to the clash between different cultures, using the characters and settings of his native Chile. Prado's works included *La reina de Rapa Nui* (1914) and *Alsino* (1920), one of Latin America's best novels of fantasy and allegory. Another Chilean, Eduardo Barrios (1884–1963), also wrote of Spanish-American scenes, although he withdrew somewhat from *criollismo.* He contributed several psychological and philosophical novels, among them *El hermano asno* (*Brother*

Ass, 1922), whose profound character analysis and richly lyrical, poetic style make it one of the most accomplished novels of Spanish America. The Venezuelan Rómulo Gallegos (1884–1969) used his country's plains and jungles as the setting of a masterful reelaboration of the conflict between civilization and barbarism—a theme previously treated by Sarmiento and Hernández in the *gaucho* novels of the romantic movement—in his trilogy of *Doña Bárbara* (1929), *Cantaclaro* (1934), and *Canaima* (1935), and in later novels. The work of Colombian José Eustasio Rivera (1888–1928) also bore a social purpose: *La vorágine* (*The Vortex*, 1924) was written in protest of the poor conditions imposed on the rubber plantation workers of the Colombian jungle, but its value as a social document is transcended by its enormous artistic merit and the poetic style in which Rivera described the struggle between society and nature. In Puerto Rico, Enrique A. Laguerre (1906–) used the sugar cane plantations as the setting in which, again, people were pitted against the natural environment.

In Argentina, the theme of the *gaucho* yielded its best novels after the turn of the century. Benito Lynch (1880–1951), who depicted the *gaucho*'s decadence in *El inglés de los güesos* (1924), was the genre's most realistic writer. Ricardo Güiraldes (1886–1927), on the other hand, departed from the realism of the *criollistas* and integrated the vanguard's currents into the native material of *gaucho* life. His *Don Segundo Sombra* (1926), the best of the *gaucho* novels, immortalized the figure of the *gaucho* as the symbol of Argentine consciousness.

The romantic view of the Indian as a hero had already been redefined by Clorinda Matto de Turner. A precursor of the indigenist novel, as opposed to the Indianist novel of the romantics, she portrayed the Indian not as an object of idealization, but as a real social being. But it was not until after modernism, when there was a resurgence of interest in indigenous cultures and a heightening of social consciousness, that the indigenist novel emerged. It was particularly strong in Mexico, Guatemala, Ecuador, Peru, and Bolivia. Perhaps the best-known novelist within this current was the Peruvian Ciro Alegría (1909–1967), whose *El mundo es ancho y ajeno* (*Broad and Alien is the World*, 1941) garnered him a literary prize in New York. Other noteworthy indigenists were Jorge Icaza (1906–1978) of Ecuador, who wrote short stories and novels—among them *Huasipungo* (*The Villagers*, 1934), a powerful and controversial social protest novel in which the radical ideas of the author often cloud his aesthetic intent—and the Guatemalan Miguel Ángel Asturias (1899–1974).

By far the best postmodernist short story writer was the Uruguayan Horacio Quiroga (1878–1937), who began his career as a modernist. Strongly influenced by the terror and inexorable fatalism of Edgar Allan Poe and Rudyard Kipling, Quiroga perfected the technique of storytelling and left an extensive collection of fascinating tales with *criollista* themes and motifs. The vein of *criollismo* in theme and poetic expression also demands mention of Salvador Salazar Arrué, known as Salarrué (1899–1975), the Salvadoran whose collection *Cuentos de barro* (1933) has earned him a place among Spanish-American short story writers of this period.

The Mexican revolution of 1910 produced profound, radical changes in the political, social, and economic life of the country, creating at the same time a new art that was national in nature and eminently popular. Within the complex events that surrounded them—military campaigns, violence, struggles for power, betrayals, rivalries among leaders, charismatic personalities, varied ideologies, and political disappointments—Mexican writers found a wealth of material and themes that they wove into their extensive narrative production. These were not "historical" novels in the technical sense. Because most of these writers had been active participants in the national drama, their works were infused with realistic and autobiographical elements; yet their portrayals of historical events were also colored by fantasy and imagination. Technically, these novels often had no central plot, but rather consisted of a series of episodes or sketches that formed a whole but also had independent aesthetic and narrative value. The true protagonist in such novels was the Mexican *pueblo,* fighting for its identity, its freedom, and its aspirations. The epic-tragic tone of these novels, distinguished by their sense of deep social purpose and their nationalist orientation, also surfaced in the painting of Diego Rivera, José Clemente Orozco, and David Alfaro Siqueiros.

Although the revolution of 1910 yielded a complex proliferation of novels, four great masters stand out among the many notable writers of this regional literature. Mariano Azuela (1873–1952), the novelist *par excellence* of the Mexican Revolution, originated the genre in 1915 with *Los de abajo* (*The Underdogs*), in which he describes the evils that led to the Revolution; Martín Luis Guzmán (1887–1976) wrote several famous novels offering a broad view of the Revolution's leaders; José Rubén Romero (1890–1952) depicted Mexican reality in the picaresque *La vida inútil de Pito Pérez* (*The Futile Life of Pito Pérez,* 1938); and José Vasconcelos, in addition to his essays, wrote a series of autobiographical accounts including the impassioned *Ulises criollo* (*A Mexican Ulysses,* 1935).

The vanguard's *criollista*/nativist current spawned a second popular trend, Afro-Caribbean poetry. This school centered on the soul, psychology, emotions, beliefs, suffering, and environment of Caribbean blacks, an important component of the racial mix in many Spanish-American societies. This was a poetry of rhythmic verse and sensorial tone, saturated with a plasticity and musicality that arose from the use of lively images and metaphors, onomatopoeia, and what Alfonso Reyes called "jitanjáfora," or play on the sounds of a word or expression. Afro-Caribbean poetry evokes black folklore: its language, customs and emotions, rites and ceremonies, music and dance. Within the re-creation of this folk culture, the poets embedded a message of vigorous protest against the injustice, oppression, and discrimination suffered by blacks.

Afro-Caribbean poetry was best represented by three poets, the Puerto Rican Luis Palés Matos (1898–1959) and the Cubans Nicolás Guillén (1902–) and Emilio Ballagas (1908–1954). Palés Matos, who had begun writing as a postmodernist but whose poetry later tended toward the cultured tones of vanguardism, was the first to create a series of poems centered on the theme of the Afro-Caribbean experience. The best of these poems were brought together in his collection *Tuntún de pasa y grifería* (1937). Yet his poetry was primarily objective, descriptive, and lyrical; folklore and social concern were of secondary importance.

Nicolás Guillén was unique among Spanish-American poets in his understanding and portrayal of the heart and soul of the Afro-Caribbean. As a conscious artistic mission, Guillén utilized the black ancestral legacy and masterfully combined aesthetic and social concerns (*Motivos del son,* 1930; *Sóngoro cosongo,* 1931), winning the praise of the great Spanish writer and thinker of the Generation of 1898, Miguel de Unamuno. Guillén's intense interest in universal human problems, and particularly his profound concern for social justice, culminated in a classic example of engagé literature, *El son entero,* published in 1947.

While the black experience was Guillén's inspiration, Emilio Ballagas' cultivation of black poetry was more of a poetic maneuver toward a trend which was in vogue. While Ballagas was recognized as one of the most important poets of the Spanish-American vanguard, he also merged successfully with the Afro-Caribbean current in 1934 with his *Cuaderno de poesía negra*. Ballagas distinguished himself from Palés Matos and Guillén by using vanguardist forms of expression and treating the Afro-Caribbean theme with surrealist techniques. He created a poetry of great intensity and anguish, a poetry which expressed deep human and social concerns and eventually even became religious in tone.

The vanguard began to dissolve in the mid-1930's, first evolving into postvanguardism and then yielding entirely to new currents. Existentialist literature, an offshoot of the philosophy of Jean-Paul Sartre, expressed the contemporary individual's temporal and spatial metaphysical anguish. Another emerging trend was absurdist literature, a cynical vehicle of vehement protest against all cultural and social order, characterized by satire, irony, and mockery.

The horrendous toll of one million left dead by the Spanish civil war, the brutality and violence of World War II (1939–1945), which opened the frightful path to the nuclear age, and the Cold War's menacing chess match of the superpowers were events for which the world was not spiritually prepared. Spanish America was hit by a new wave of military dictatorships. There, as in the rest of the world, an alarming population increase exacerbated the social unrest and economic inequalities which still choke the Third World. In 1959, the hemisphere's first Communist regime was established in Cuba. Meanwhile, "revolutions" and struggles against the old structures were breaking out in various countries. In politics, new voices were raised against oppression and injustice, while Marxism, socialism, materialism, and democracy continued to be debated. Uncertainty, fear, anxiety, desperation, insecurity, and spiritual unease multiplied in a world dominated by the advanced science and technology of the great economic powers. On one hand, humanity now seemed capable of overcoming all physical obstacles and achieving an incomparable level of material well-being, albeit one stained by great social injustice; on the other hand, it was faced with the most acute moral, spiritual, philosophical, and ideological crisis of the twentieth century.

Within this climate of global instability, Spanish-American writers began to feel more than ever the need to merge the expression of their problematic national and personal realities with European influences and trends as harmoniously and completely as possible. Some writers continued, with modifications, the aesthetic tendencies of the vanguard; others were seduced by Sartre and the existentialists. In general, the works of the writers who followed the vanguard manifested a reaction against regionalism, although some local elements persisted. Intellect prevailed over emotion and sentiment, and all genres reflected the period's anguish and solitude. These writers also devoted their works to penetrating human psychology and spiritual isolation; they were interested in people oppressed by hunger and poverty, and in documenting the political and social problems besieging not only Spanish America but the whole world. Poets, playwrights, essayists, and especially narrators sought a harmonious link between American and universal art.

Among the poets who marked the transition from the vanguard to postvanguardism are two Argentines. Ricardo E. Molinari (1898–) began writing as an ultraist (*El imaginero*, 1927), but the publication of *Delta* (1932) announced his poetic evolution toward contemporary themes. Leopoldo Marechal (1900–1970) followed a similar path from ultraism to the themes of human and divine love (*Laberinto de amor*, 1936; *Sonetos a Sophia y otros poemas*, 1940); he was also an important playwright and is considered a pioneer of the contemporary novel (*Adán Buenosayres*, 1948). The Chilean Nicanor Parra (1914–) was a true postvanguardist. His complex poetic work ran from traditional ballads to the sarcastic denunciation of a world which he perceived as absurd and grotesque (*Poemas y antipoemas [Poems and Antipoems]*, 1954). The Cuban José Lezama Lima (1910–1976) was another important poet of this period; he also wrote essays and a single novel, *Paradiso* (1966). This novel, highly acclaimed by the critics for its intellectual content and poetic beauty, became one of the most important narrative works of the boom. Although his poetic development was gradual, the Mexican Octavio Paz (1914–) is undoubtedly, after Neruda, Spanish America's most famous poet (*La estación violenta*, 1958). Paz is also known for the brilliant essays that synthesize and blend his philosophical and ideological views with the aesthetic ideas of the contemporary world. The themes he addresses, including human destiny, nature, time, nothingness, silence, love, and solitude, and his work's ontological, ideological, and even social bent, along with his lyricism and style, make Paz a genuinely universal writer. One of his best-known images reveals the optimism toward human destiny that underlies his work: "la lira que consagra y canta al hombre, y así le da un puesto en el cosmos; la flecha, que lo hace ir más allá de sí mismo y realizarse en el acto" (the lyre which consecrates and sings to man, giving him a place in the cosmos; the arrow, which makes him go beyond himself and become himself in the act," *El arco y la lira [The Bow and the Lyre]*, 1956).

The contributions of Paz aside, the contemporary essay developed through the works of other writers who imparted a more nationalistic and American dimension to their pages. Their new evaluation and interpretation of Spanish-American culture secured their place in the history of the genre: these important essayists include the Colombian Germán Arciniegas (1900–), the Honduran Rafael Heliodoro Valle (1891–1959), and the Venezuelans Mariano Picón Salas (1901–1965) and Arturo Uslar Pietri (1906–), who is also notable as a short-story writer.

Drama also began to make great strides in the 1940's. Of course, the work of earlier playwrights contributed significantly to this development. The realism of Florencio Sánchez laid the foundation of modern Spanish-American drama. The doctrines of realism were carried forward by the Argentine Samuel Eichelbaum (1894–1967), although his work took a more psychological and philosophical perspective. Here, external reality was only the backdrop before which the playwright constructed universal analyses of human behavior. Beginning in the 1930's, experimental drama groups were established in many universities and cities. The demand for the production of plays by national and international authors also stimulated the creation of modern scenographic techniques. While Spanish-American theater retained a national flavor throughout its development, it also cultivated a universal dimension evidenced by its greater sobriety, depth, precision, and balance. The exploration of human consciousness, modern psychological and social conflicts, and philosophical questions, all treated by this new theater, further highlight its universal aspect. The Mexicans Rodolfo Usigli (1905–1979) and Emilio Carballido (1925–), the Puerto Rican René Marqués (1919–1979), the Chileans Jorge Díaz (1930–), Egon Wolff

(1926–), and Luis Alberto Heiremans (1928–1964), the Cuban José Triana (1933–), and the Argentines Osvaldo Dragún (1929–) and Griselda Gambaro (1928–) are among the writers who have contributed most to the current peak in dramatic art.

No genre has dealt better with the new approach to man's existential problem than narrative prose. The contemporary novel and short story are geared toward the exploration and reconsideration of the origin and interpretation of human nature, as well as the unconscious motivations that control behavior. Around 1935, Spanish-American narrators began successfully to incorporate the latest trends of the great European and North American masters of prose fiction: neorealism, neonaturalism, psychologism, existentialism, transcendentalism, superrealism, and neosymbolism, among others. They also began to employ aesthetic and stylistic innovations: counterpoint and different narrative and temporal levels, free association of ideas, incongruities and absurdities corresponding to the stream of consciousness, interior monologue, transference of contemporary characters and circumstances to narrate past events, labyrinthine narrations, symbolic and allegorical elements, mythification of history and of terrestrial forces, techniques of magical realism, collective protagonists, and cinematographic techniques, including flashbacks, close-ups, and multiple viewpoints.

The result was that the new Spanish-American narrative, far removed from the traditional techniques of realism and regionalism, experienced a boom in the 1960's and flourished throughout the following years. While elements of *criollismo* remain, regionalism has been abandoned; the plot unfolds more often in urban centers than in the countryside. Narrative prose became more intellectual, metaphysical, intuitive, and transcendental; its most important element is the stream of consciousness in search of identity in a confusing, conflict-ridden world. In sum, the writers of the boom soon won international prestige for their success in creating an art that was truly universal.

An observer cannot generally classify present-day Spanish-American narrators on the basis of the various trends, currents, and literary techniques developed since the mid-1930's. To greater or lesser degrees, these writers share in all these trends, combining them in various ways so that the entirety of any given writer's work cannot be categorized within a single literary school. Nor will each writer be described here; only a few important milestones will be pointed out.

The reaction against *criollismo* began in Chile as María Luisa Bombal (1910–1980) published two novels, *La última niebla* (*The Final Mist*, 1934) and *La amortajada* (*The Shrouded Woman*, 1938), which were to have great impact on Spanish-American narrative. While never losing sight of reality, Bombal used superrealistic techniques and a very poetic style in both novels to explore the unconscious drives motivating the behavior of her characters, whom she presents in a subjective world of dream, fantasy, and mystery.

The Argentine Eduardo Mallea (1903–1982) was also prominent within the development of the psychological novel. However, his work (consisting of essays as well as narrative prose), was distinctly philosophical and existential in character, addressing such themes as the meaning of life in a world of crisis, the problem of Argentine identity, and the failure of human communication. The Uruguayan Juan Carlos Onetti (1909–) brought the Spanish-American psychological novel to a higher level of maturity with a series of excellent novels and short stories that presented the problem of urban society's moral and spiritual disintegration. The Mexican Agustín Yáñez (1904–1980) was one of the Spanish-American writers who best assimilated contemporary literary currents and techniques. In *Al filo del agua* (*The Edge of the Storm*, 1947), a true artistic achievement and one of the novels in which national and universal concerns are most harmoniously blended, he explored the collective unconscious of a Mexican town in the period just before the Revolution. Man's inability to rid himself of his own psychological complexes was treated by the Argentine Ernesto Sábato (1911–), bringing the psychological novel to its culmination (*El túnel*, 1948, and *Sobre héroes y tumbas* [*On Heroes and Tombs*], 1961).

In 1935, soon after Bombal had published her novel *La última niebla*, Jorge Luis Borges (who, in essays, had earlier posed the problem of creating a *criollismo* that might supersede regionalism) published his first collection of fantastic short stories, *Historia universal de la infamia* (*A Universal History of Infamy*), which was followed by two more important collections, *Ficciones* (1944) and *El Aleph* (1949). Although some of his Spanish-American predecessors had also been interested in fantastic literature, Borges is considered the great master of this field because of the skill with which he harmonized complex structure and artistic form with philosophical and metaphysical content. In his writing, the line which separates the real world from the unreal is almost imperceptible; nearly everything imaginable fits within this reality. Thus Borges created an abstract literature whose themes were eminently intellectual: time and space, infinity and the circularity of time, freedom, destiny, the relationship between life and literature, the problem of identity, death, magic, courage, and humanity imprisoned within the labyrinth of a meaningless universe. The influence of Borges has been such that it is almost impossible to comprehend contemporary Spanish-American narrative without knowing his work. Other writers who contributed to the development of fantastic literature were the Mexican Juan José Arreola (1918–), and the Argentines Enrique Anderson Imbert (1910–), Adolfo Bioy Casares (1914–), and, above all, Julio Cortázar (1914–1984), one of the most complex and prolific writers of the boom.

The German critic Franz Roh first used the term *magical realism* to describe the contemporary pictorial art which began with postexpressionism in the 1920's. The term became popular with some critics and its meaning was broadened to include literature. However, in the plastic arts, magical realism is opposed to expressionism; in literature, the two currents are not in opposition. The magical-realist writer attempts to unravel the mystery of reality, using metaphor, symbol, allegory, and myth to create strange settings in which the characters and the objects that surround them appear to obey immanent forces. While always recognizable, these worlds of magic, dreams, and mystery verge on the fantastic.

There are elements of magical realism in many works of contemporary prose fiction, but in reality the term has a narrower application than that given it by journalistic criticism. The Cuban Alejo Carpentier was perhaps the writer who best captured "lo mágico americano" ("the marvelous American reality"), using his brilliant language, surrealistic techniques, and highly ideological content to probe contemporary psychological, social, and philosophical problems. In a series of narrative works which immediately won him international fame (especially in France), Carpentier sought out the roots of American society (*El reino de este mundo* [*The Kingdom of This World*], 1949). He also took on such themes as the conflict between time and the individual

(*Guerra del tiempo* [*The War of Time*], 1958) and the opposition of the eternity of objects against the brevity of human life, civilization against primitivism (in his masterpiece *Los pasos perdidos*, 1953), and European against American culture (*El siglo de las luces*, 1962; published in English as *Explosion in the Cathedral*).

Juan Rulfo (1918–1986) was very Mexican and at the same time very universal. His narrative, including one of the most complex novels ever written, *Pedro Páramo* (1955), recreated the world of the Mexican peasant, masterfully creating strange settings of magic and fantasy. The Venezuelan Arturo Uslar Pietri, author of some historical novels and a number of important essays, also wrote short stories that serve as excellent examples of American magical realism, particularly "La lluvia," "El venado," "El gallo," and "La voz."

The Guatemalan Miguel Ángel Asturias oriented his narrative toward both the mythological and the social aspects of American reality. It was in the first of these that Asturias best displayed his artistic gifts, leaving some works of lasting importance to contemporary narrative. His *Leyendas de Guatemala* (1930), inspired by the stories of the ancient Popol Vuh, best reflected his interest in "the magical American reality." *Hombres de maíz* (*Men of Maize*, 1949) was a recreation of the magical world of the Mayan Indians of Guatemala as they struggled to reaffirm their identity. *El señor presidente* (*The President*, 1946), his masterpiece, won Asturias the Nobel Prize in 1967. This superrealistic novel described the ambiance of fear and impotence produced by an iron-fist dictatorship. Its universal value resides in the fact that the situation portrayed transcends national boundaries and in the work's tone of social and political protest, which was the axis of Asturias' writing and an orientation that he developed further in his later works.

Although the reaction against *criollismo* grew after the 1940's, there were still some writers who continued to address native issues; yet even they abandoned *criollista* techniques and incorporated contemporary narrative innovations. Within this group two writers stood out for their revitalization of the indigenist novel. José María Arguedas (1911–1969) of Peru recreated the world of the Incas with masterful artistry, using the psychology of an adolescent (*Los ríos profundos* [*Deep Rivers*], 1958), while Mexico's Rosario Castellanos (1925–1974) used a young girl character to present the painful world of the Mexican Indian (*Balún Canán*, 1957; published in English as *The Nine Guardians*). Some writers were oriented toward protest; others combined *criollo* elements with magical-Americanism; still others, fierce existentialists, distanced themselves from tradition and folklore and sought a "transcendental *criollismo*." Such was the case with the Chilean Manuel Rojas (1896–1973), author of short stories and of one very important novel, *Hijo de ladrón* (*Born Guilty*, 1951).

The various literary currents and fashions, the narrative innovations and experiments, and the topics and issues that occupied the attention of the Spanish-American writer beginning in the period 1935–1940 prepared the way for the great boom in narrative prose in the 1960's and after. While the neorealist and existentialist currents continued, many new works took on a tone of protest and social criticism, a more testimonial character, and a commitment to humanity; an absurdist narrative developed as well. But the writers of the boom never forgot their essential mission: to create a work of art. For the first time in the history of Spanish-American letters, prose fiction surpassed the other genres in quality, although several of these authors also wrote essays, poetry, and drama.

Since the end of the 1950's, then, there has been a surge of important works by prominent authors from Spanish-American countries. Some have already been mentioned—Borges, Sábato, Cortázar, Carpentier, Rulfo, Asturias. The majority of these writers are still living: they include the Argentines Marco Denevi (1922–), Manuel Puig (1932–), and Luisa Valenzuela (1938–), the Uruguayan Mario Benedetti (1920–), the Paraguayan Augusto Roa Bastos (1917–), the Chilean José Donoso (1924–), the Peruvian Mario Vargas Llosa (1936–), the Cubans Guillermo Cabrera Infante (1929–) and Severo Sarduy (1936–), the Mexican Carlos Fuentes (1928–), and the Colombian Gabriel García Márquez (1928–), Spanish America's most recent Nobel Prize winner (1982).

The work of these writers—without even addressing the postboom, which would demand a separate volume—continues to occupy the attention of literary critics. It is too early to determine what, in the final analysis, will be their influence on the future of Spanish-American literature. Yet there is no doubt that while these writers have established Spanish-America's literary Pan-Americanism, they have also brought Spanish-American literature to the universal plane, linking the essence of America to the problems and questions of contemporary humanity.

Carlos A. Solé
University of Texas at Austin

Brazilian Literature

In many ways Brazilian literature developed along the same lines as Spanish-American literature, especially during the colonial period. It began with narrations and letters of explorers and missionaries, who described the land and its inhabitants. The first written account of the land is a famous letter to the king of Portugal by Pero Vaz de Caminha, a voyage companion of Pedro Álvares Cabral, who discovered Brazil and claimed it for Portugal. Many other letters as well as books and chronicles followed, and the subjects included the conquest of the land, the exploration of its riches, and domination and indoctrination of Indians.

As in Spanish America, the Jesuits played an important role, representing a moralizing and educational force. Among the second group of Jesuits arriving in Brazil was Father José de Anchieta (1534–1579), the most notable schoolmaster and literary figure of the Society of Jesus during the first two centuries. He wrote a grammar and began work on a dictionary of Tupy (the language common to most Indians of Brazil), translated the catechism, and wrote dramas for theater performances, both in Portuguese and Tupy. Anchieta was also the first poet of Brazil, writing in Latin, Portuguese, Spanish, and Tupy.

Of the European writers who journeyed to Brazil during the sixteenth century and wrote about the land, one should mention, among others, Pero de Magalhães Gandavo, a notable humanist and friend of Luiz Vaz de Camões (1524–1579?) the greatest poet of the Portuguese language. Gandavo lived in Brazil for some time, and on his return to Portugal he published two important books on the fertility and abundance of the land of Brazil.

In the seventeenth century the first writers born in Brazil appeared as a part of the burgeoning sugar plantation civilization of the Northeast. This century revealed the awakening of a nativist feeling both in Brazilian literature and in the struggle of its people against foreign invaders. Works on Brazil at this point frequently reveal evidence of love and pride for the author's native land, as well as a firm belief in its future.

Since the early seventeenth century the baroque had been introduced to Brazil. Influenced by Spanish poets—Luis de Góngora, Francisco Quevedo, and Baltasar Gracián—Portuguese and Brazilian literature were then characterized by metaphors, hyperbole, plays on words, double meanings, antitheses, and paradoxes. A leading figure at this time was Father Antônio Vieira (1608–1697), best known for his sermons, important religiously but also concerned with sociopolitical issues. His rich, elaborate prose is essentially baroque. However, the most striking literary figure of Brazilian baroque and, according to some, of colonial Brazil is Gregório de Mattos (1636–1695). Born in Bahia, he studied in Portugal and later returned to Brazil. His satiric vein brought him into disfavor both in Portugal and Brazil. He would attack everyone in his verses, including powerful clergy and government authorities. Because of this, he earned the nickname of "Hellmouth" and was greatly persecuted. Gregório de Mattos' production can be divided into lyric, religious, and satirical verse. His most lasting contribution to Brazilian literature may be found in the satirical aspect of his work, which first revealed in verse the evils of colonial Brazilian society.

More notable than the works in literature were the baroque achievements in music and the plastic arts, although they arrived later, in the eighteenth century. Production in architecture and sculpture was outstanding, especially in Minas Gerais, where gold and diamonds had been discovered: cities were built overnight, and art flourished. The great Brazilian sculptor Antônio Francisco Lisboa, the "Aleijadinho" (Little Cripple), with his artificial hands created masterpieces still admired today by Brazilians and foreigners in the old cities of Minas Gerais.

In the eighteenth century nativism became more entrenched than in the previous century and caused bloody conflicts between Brazilians and Portuguese. Nativism was reflected in literature's increasing focus on the natural and political history of the country, and it often took the form of exaggerated patriotism, as in Sebastião da Rocha Pita's *História da América Portuguesa* (1730): "In no other region are the skies more serene, nor does the dawn come more fair; in no other hemisphere does the sun have rays more golden, nor are its nocturnal reflections more brilliant; . . . In short, Brazil is the earthly Paradise regained . . ." (quoted in Manuel Bandeira, *A Brief History of Brazilian Literature*, Ralph Edward Demmick, trans., 1964, pp. 42–43).

Literary academies sprang up (the Academy of the Forgotten, the Academy of the Happy, the Academy of the Reborn, the Academy of the Select, among others—all short-lived), as writers, anxious to study things Brazilian, sought the encouragement brought by working in a group. The spirit of such study, and the writing it produced, was rather in the vein of optimistic hyperbole than of historical objectivity. José Veríssimo, author of an important history of Brazilian literature, wrote of these academies that "despite the official nature of their origin, and the fact that they were, after all, an imitation, they evidenced perhaps a certain feeling of rivalry with the mother country, and therefore constitute a first, though slight, symptom of the local spirit of independence" (*ibid.*, pp. 41–42). Many sonnets were written, although few were of any significance. The importance of the literature of this period, however, was in the fact that it expressed a mature and widespread sense of pride for a nation in formation.

The important dramatist Antônio José da Silva (1705–1739), known as "O Juden" (the Jew), was born in Rio de Janeiro during this era. At the age of seven he accompanied his parents, who were following the orders of the Holy Office, to Portugal, and there is a question as to whether Silva, who studied and spent his entire adult life in Portugal, should be considered a Portuguese or Brazilian author. (Silva was denounced by the Inquisition and burned at the stake in Lisbon when he was thirty-four.) A tragic figure, Silva was a social rebel like Gregório de Mattos and was influenced by the father of Portuguese theater, Gil Vicente (1465–1536?), who inspired him to revive a primitive and vigorous kind of comedy.

In the second half of the eighteenth century, as Minas Gerais was experiencing a period of great prosperity, a corresponding flowering of culture occurred. Besides sculptors, architects, and musicians, there appeared a group of poets known as the Arcadia Mineira (Minas Arcadia), or school of Minas. Arcadianism first appeared in Italy in 1690, but it soon spread throughout Europe, including Portugal. Its followers in Brazil took for their models Latin and Greek authors and the French classicists of the seventeenth century.

Although some of the Brazilian Arcadians retained in their work the European landscape, with its pastoral and mythological images, the more sophisticated writers abandoned these European devices, replacing them with Brazilian themes, expressed in precise and concrete terms.

The poets of the school of Minas were involved in a revolution in 1789 in Minas Gerais, called the *Inconfidência* (Disloyalty), which sought to free the province from Portuguese rule. When the revolt failed, its leader was beheaded and all the participants were severely punished, either imprisoned or expelled to Africa.

Among the poets of the Minas school, Cláudio Manuel da Costa (1729–1789) was the most renowned for his use of language and meter. His sonnets, which avoided the artificial devices of other poets of his school, are considered among the best of the period. Thomas Antônio Gonzaga (1744–1810) was another important poet of this era.* His work *Marília de Dirceu,* a collection of poems relating a poet's love and dreams, cruelly interrupted by his trial and sentence, became immensely popular and has undergone many editions since the time of its original publication.

One of the most intriguing documents in the history of Brazilian literature is the famous *Cartas Chilenas,* whose authorship, long disputed, is now ascribed to Gonzaga. It is a long satirical verse composition that constitutes a violent denouncement of the government of the Minas Gerais province. In order to disguise the locale Gonzaga moves the action from Vila Rica, Brazil, to Santiago, Chile.

In the nineteenth century, heroism and a determined desire for freedom had become the essence of Brazilian life. The revolt of Minas Gerais had failed but unrest was intense, and it would not take long for independence to come.

A fortuitous event prevented the goal of independence from taking a violent turn.

---

*Unfortunately, limitations of space have prevented us from including an essay on Gongaza, as well as other notable Brazilian literary figures discussed in this section of the introduction. Readers are encouraged to seek out the general reference sources that appear in the bibliographies of essays on both colonial and modern writers who are included in *Latin American Writers.*

In order to avoid the Napoleonic Wars in Europe, the Portuguese court came to Brazil and established itself in Rio de Janeiro in 1808. Prince John, the regent of the Portuguese throne, took measures which brought significant improvements for Brazil, especially for Rio, which became the capital of the United Kingdom of Portugal, Brazil, and Algarves. In 1821, John, who was by then King John VI, returned to Portugal, leaving his son Pedro as regent of Brazil.

There were many reasons for Brazilian dissatisfaction with Portugal, and therefore Brazilian leaders convinced Pedro to establish the country's independence. As the head of the movement, he declared Brazilian independence on 7 September 1822, and became the first emperor of Brazil. It was a short, turbulent reign. In 1831 the king abdicated in favor of his five-year-old son, also named Pedro. After a tempestuous period of regency, Pedro II was crowned emperor of Brazil in 1841, when he was only fifteen years old. Pedro II ruled Brazil with wisdom and kindness for almost half a century. Monarchy brought stability to Brazil. Unlike Spanish America, which had so many conflicts and split into fourteen countries while trying to attain its freedom, the empire allowed Brazil to enjoy relative peace for many years and to preserve its territorial integrity.

Literature followed its course alongside these political movements. During the difficult period of John VI, Pedro I, and the regency, literary accomplishments were mainly in journalism and oratory, ephemeral but efficacious activities in a time of crisis. In 1836, the romantic movement became manifest with the publication of *Suspiros Poéticos e Saudades* by Domingos José Gonçalves de Magalhães (1811–1882). Romanticism represented perfectly the Brazilian ideals of freedom, patriotism, and nativism that were so fervent at that time. These sentiments were well expressed in the main issues of the romantic revolution in Brazil: literature should reject artifice, the European landscape, and mythology in favor of Brazilian scenery and the Christian religion; it should abandon classical rules and replace them with free individual imagination.

The evolution of romantic poetry in Brazil can be divided into three main phases. In the first phase we find religious inspiration, the beauty of Brazilian nature, and themes based on the life of native Indians. The greatest representative of the poetry in this phase is Antônio Gonçalves Dias (1823–1864), one of the most remarkable poets that Brazil has ever produced. His work dealt mainly with Indianism and Brazilian landscape. He wrote exultant, pantheistic hymns to the beauties of tropical nature. With his imagination and sensibility, he succeeded better than any other in breathing life into the Indian theme. Gonçalves Dias' Indianism is deeply rooted and sincere, although his attitude toward the aborigene is an idealistic one. In addition, he had a greater sense of sobriety and harmony than most romantics, which created balance in his poetry.

The second phase of romanticism in Brazil occurred once the empire of Pedro II was well established. Up to this time, or until about the middle of the nineteenth century—that is, during the colonial epoch and then to an even greater degree during the struggle for national liberation—there had been a constant striving to be Brazilian. However, after independence and the coming of romanticism, with its emphasis on the individual, writers began to look for more aesthetic and individual motivations in literature. The Brazilian works of this period reflected, more than Brazilian life, the literary trends then current in Europe. Lord Byron, Alfred de Musset, Charles

Baudelaire, and their contemporaries in Europe influenced this Brazilian generation. Religious sentiment, patriotism, and Indianism were replaced by disillusion and a despairing, cynical tone. The poets of this period were called "the bohemians" because they were usually addicted to alcohol or drugs and spent their lives in the dissipation of the taverns. Their poetry reveals tedium and obsession with death. Indeed almost all of these poets died young, most between the ages of twenty and thirty; some succumbed to the dissipations of the taverns, while others died of tuberculosis. One of the famous pieces of this school is "Noite na Taverna" ("Night in the Tavern," 1853), by Manuel Antônio Alvares de Azevedo (1831–1852), who died at the age of twenty-one and was the leading poet of this period.

Sociopolitical questions inspired the third phase of romantic poetry, as new ideas were disseminated in the country during the last decades of the empire. The main points debated were the abolition of slavery and the establishment of the republic. In addition, literature of this period reveals the influence of Victor Hugo and Edgar Quinet. This opulent poetry was the product of the so-called Condor School. Stylistically the work was characterized by bombast, audacious metaphors, and the abuse of antithesis. The greatest poet of this school is Antônio de Castro Alves (1847–1871), who, for the first time in Brazil, wrote poetry that became a reflection of the sentiment of the common man. Castro Alves led a tragic life, and died at the age of twenty-four of tuberculosis. Although he died young, Castro Alves left several volumes of splendid poetry. A substantial part of his work was devoted to the abolition of slavery. In his poem "Vozes d'África" he reveals his indignation toward slavery and reproaches even God for this crime of man. Another powerful poem is "O Navio Negreiro," in which the poet pictures all the horrors of the African slave ship, the seething mass of human bodies, the cries and sufferings of the slaves. The scenes in the poem are reminiscent of Dante's *Inferno*.

Romantic prose produced Brazil's first important novel, A *Moreninha* (1844), by Joaquim Manuel de Macedo (1820–1882). A *Moreninha* achieved enormous success and is still read today. It is a highly romantic story, overly sentimental and written without great concern for style, but it remains of interest to modern readers as an artifact that reflects the middle-class customs of its time.

The truly outstanding figure among romantic prose writers is José de Alencar (1829–1877). Two of his most successful productions were Indianist novels: O *Guarani* (1857) and *Iracema* (*The Honey-Lip*, 1865). Both deal with love between Indian and white, a theme encouraging racial assimilation. However, the author did not delve deeply into this issue but used it solely for dramatic and emotional effect. Like Gonçalves' Dias, Alencar's treatment of Indians was "idealistic" in that they possessed European morals and courtesies.

Indianism represents only one feature of José de Alencar's literary focus; his work reflects Brazilian themes and imagery in several other ways. He depicted rural and urban life and studied the psychology of the Brazilian woman. Alencar furthermore introduced stylistic values into Brazilian prose fiction: for instance his depiction of Brazil's natural landscape is rendered in a manner that evokes its mystery as no Brazilian writer had done before. Alencar's artistic production was truly superb. He modernized Brazilian language and literature, and began a nationalistic movement in favor of Brazilian forms.

Besides the novel and poetry other genres developed during the romantic period, including essays, history, journalism, and the theater. Brazilian theater, which had its roots in the Jesuit catechism, first appeared during the colonial period, but it reemerged with vigor at the onset of the nineteenth century. Drama by Gonçalves de Magalhães and Gonçalves Dias, and drama and comedy by José de Alencar and others were performed with great success. The comedy of manners became especially popular, with a large repertory and an eager audience.

In the early 1870's, when the romantic movement already showed signs of ebbing, Brazilian literature experienced its greatest moment, in the person of Joaquim Maria Machado de Assis (1839–1908). Widely considered the eminent prose writer in the Portuguese language, Machado de Assis cannot be included in any school; he was a contemporary of the second generation of romantics, from whom he received some influence in his formative years, but during the succeeding generations of romantics, naturalists, and symbolists Machado de Assis developed a highly unique and charismatic style as a literary figure. Machado de Assis' supremacy in Brazilian literature existed not only during his own lifetime, but has continued to grow since his death. No Brazilian writer before or since has equalled Machado, whose superior talent makes him the classic Brazilian writer par excellence.

Machado de Assis was chiefly concerned with the spirit of man. For Machado man is a lost being with no redemption, no Christian heaven, only a voluptuous nothingness. His image of man is well expressed by Bras Cubas, a character in his *Memórias Póstumas de Bras Cubas* (*Epitaph of a Small Winner*, 1881), who declares: "I have no offspring; I have transmitted to no human being the legacy of our wretchedness." This storyteller, who is so despairing of humankind, has given us human portraits of selfishness, jealousy, vanity, and cruelty, and he does it with complete aloofness if not with a stern, sarcastic humor. A writer with this view of life and man must have a refuge, and for Machado it was found in beauty. Machado's heaven is the aesthetic form, and this is reflected in his superb literary style. Machado's work includes poetry, essays, and criticism, but his true masterpieces are his novels and short stories.

In the late-nineteenth century, during Machado's life, important changes occurred in the literary, social, and political life of Brazil. With its scientific spirit, the new generation of writers rejected the lyricism and subjectivism of the romantics. Their battle cries were "Realism," "New ideas," "Science," and "Social poetry." This generation was strongly influenced by Émile Zola and José Maria Eça de Queiroz.

Romanticism was succeeded by realism-naturalism in the novel and by Parnassianism in poetry. Naturalism included conceptions such as Darwinist, Spenserian, and positivist ideas, the latter having had great repercussions in Brazil. The new schools were all based on the same philosophy, which strongly favored the republic and was opposed to slavery, the clergy, and the aristocracy. Naturalism was the next school to succeed the last generation of romantics, who had likewise been socially oriented. Naturalism emphasized reforms, care for the less privileged, the study of man in his habitat, and the need to maintain a sense of commitment for the organization of a better society. The naturalists believed that humanity and society could improve and that literature should be an instrument of reform. Indeed, literature at this time contributed to drastic reforms in Brazil. Slavery was abolished in 1888, and the monarchy was overthrown in 1889 by a military coup.

The greatest representative of naturalism is Aluísio Azevedo (1857–1913) who began his literary life as a romantic but soon evolved into a naturalist of immense talent, as revealed in *O Cortiço* (*A Brazilian Tenement*, 1890) and his other masterpieces. Azevedo was skilled in molding characters and in depicting scenes. Strongly influenced by Zola, he expressed a complete determinism, disdainful of man, from whom he believed nothing very good could be expected. The author was attracted to the subject of social problems, as for example the place of the *mestizo* in the social scheme, the contrast between urban life in *sobrados* (the multistory homes of the wealthy) and tenement dwellings, the existence in boarding houses, and so on. He gives an excellent impressionistic picture of customs in Brazil during the empire of Pedro II; Azevedo emphasized the ugly side of life, and succeeded in producing important works of art.

In 1878 the "battle of Parnassus" began in the newspaper *Diário do Rio de Janeiro*, in which columnists claimed their antiromantic position and new ideas. This poetic revolution took its name from the group that in 1865 had formed around a magazine in Paris called *Le Parnasse contemporain* (The Contemporaneous Parnassus). Olavo Bilac (1865–1918) in his *Poesias* (1888) marked the victory of Parnassianism in Brazil, and even today, Bilac is still read, enjoyed, and admired in Brazil.

As Parnassianism developed in reaction to romanticism, symbolism, which roughly corresponds to modernism in Spanish-American literature, appeared as a counterreaction. For symbolists, the Parnassian outlook was too objective, too controlled in its emotion, and too dominated by the ideas of form. The symbolists rejected precision, embraced an idea of form that was more musical than visual, and cultivated an atmosphere of dreams. Mysticism and Catholic sentiments were strong in Brazilian symbolism. The finest symbolist in Brazil is João da Cruz e Sousa (1861–1898), a black poet from the southern state of Santa Catarina. He found strong opposition because of his race, his rebellion against the rigid rules of grammar imposed by Parnassians, and the novelty of the poetic school that he introduced. However, the value of his poetry—rich in noble and sincere emotion—succeeded in creating a group of enthusiastic disciples. Admiration and respect for the poetry of Cruz e Souza continues to grow to this day.

The Brazilian republic did not fulfill the hopes and ideals of those who had fought for it. Revolts and messianic movements broke out at the turn of the century: one such messianic movement was superbly portrayed by Euclides da Cunha (1866–1909) in his *Os Sertões* (*Rebellion in the Backlands*, 1902). The movement was headed by a religious fanatic, Antônio "The Counselor." With his followers, he founded the rude stronghold of Canudos in the interior of the *sertão* (backlands). The members of the movement were opposed to the republic without understanding what a republic was; they believed only in the empire of a religious or warrior leader. A trained army of a thousand men was sent by the government to confront this handful of backwoodsmen, who defended themselves heroically but were finally defeated. Most of these people (including women, old people, and children) were barbarously killed. The book depicts the myths, legends, and fanaticism in the *sertão*, where men depend constantly upon nature; this feeling of dependency makes them delve into the supernatural. The book also portrays the crimes of the administration, and the disgrace of intolerable politics. Euclides da Cunha is the author of other works, but *Os Sertões* is by far his masterpiece, and is a high point in Brazilian literature.

Another fiction writer of great stature at the turn of the century was Afonso

Henriques de Lima Barreto (1881–1922). His work takes as its basic theme injustice in the world and, more specifically, injustice in Brazilian society, where he saw mediocrity respected and enthroned. He portrays the drama of people existing at humble levels of society, whom he considered to be truly authentic human beings, the real heroes. Many of them were mulattoes, like himself, and this was in line with his subtheme, racial prejudice. The tone of his writing is one of revolt and aggression against the establishment and its low moral standards. He frequently uses irony, satire, and allegory as literary devices. Lima Barreto's work has been considered symbolist, realist, and more often premodernist.

The political and economic upheaval that marked the end of the nineteenth century gradually affected national attitudes and helped to open the way for great events in the twentieth century. The beginning of the century, however, was not marked by many political changes, and was a period of transition and synchronism in literature. Both naturalism and Parnassianism were stagnant, although authors still wrote according to those models; symbolism had few manifestations; poetry paid more attention to the literary trends in Europe than to Brazilian reality. The atmosphere was one of doubt and hesitation, and a certain uneasiness hinted at the radical reforms that were about to take place.

After World War I, the transformation of the world, the new conception of life, and new ideas coming from Europe resulted in an awakening of Brazilian consciousness. Social and political agitation began, and military uprisings took place. This new spirit called for a reevaluation of Brazil's intelligentsia. Nonconformist young artists and writers sprang into action, manifesting their discontent in a revolution in the arts. This movement took the name of modernism, a school that corresponded in ways to the avant-gardism of Spanish-American literature. Although modernism had already been introduced by writers of the two previous decades, the movement was officially inaugurated at the Semana de Arte Moderna (Modern Art Week), a riotous meeting in São Paulo in February 1922. The basic modernist tenets were then stated: Brazilian art should look to native themes for inspiration; the language used in literature should be Portuguese, as spoken in Brazil, to replace the artificial dialect coming from Portugal and until then the only one acceptable in literature; and the new artistic trends that were dominating Europe should be welcome in Brazil.

Modernism constituted a rupture, a revolt against academicism and tradition. It had a warlike spirit that in the beginning was more destructive than constructive. A great number of books, periodicals, manifestos, and journals appeared. One of the publications is a volume of poems by Mário de Andrade (1893–1945) entitled *Paulicéia Desvairada* (*Hallucinated City*, 1922). This work became something like the bible of the movement, and Mário de Andrade its "pope." Andrade also wrote *Macunaíma* (1928), another central work of modernism, which has been called a novel, an epic, and a rhapsody. Mário de Andrade is one of the greatest analysts of Brazilian culture and a leading literary figure. His versatile work includes fiction, poetry, theater, plastic art, music, and mathematics. Another outstanding literary leader of this period was Oswald de Andrade, who well represented the revolutionary aspect of modernism with his irreverence, the fragmentary structure of his fiction, and his telegraphic style.

In the beginning modernists formed one group, but later they split into several currents. One group, intensely nationalistic not only in its literary implications but also in its political philosophy, eventually developed into a Brazilian fascist movement known as Integralismo. Another group, led by Mário de Andrade, had leftist tendencies. In fact, the revolutionary spirit was everywhere in Brazil: it was among educators who fought for John Dewey's ideas, and it was in the factories, in politics, and among the military. These rebellious ideas culminated in the revolution of 1930, led by Getúlio Vargas, who overthrew the government. Years of great agitation followed, and on 10 November 1937, Vargas brought the country under a dictatorship that would last until 1945.

In the 1930's literature was distinguished by a high degree of social consciousness. On the whole, all forms of literary production—the novel, poetry, criticism, the essay—came to full development during this era. While the generation of the 1920's had been primarily one of poets (although important fiction had appeared as well), the 1930's saw the ascendance of prose, represented mainly by the novel, the short story, and essays on sociology, ethnology, education, politics, and folklore. The Brazilian theater also expanded during this period.

The Northeast developed its own variety of modernism, at the center of which was sociologist Gilberto Freyre (1900–1987). Novelists were concerned with social injustice, the country's overwhelming poverty, the collapse of old social structures, and with economic and social problems generally. The devastating droughts which plague the Northeast of Brazil were also a frequent theme in that region's fiction. Writers wrote about their native states, but they were usually inspired by universal concepts. Graciliano Ramos (1892–1953), one of the greatest Brazilian novelists of any period, was especially interested in Alagoas, his home state, but his work was based on Marxist philosophy, with strong social protest marking his fiction. His novels *São Bernardo* (1934), *Angústia* (*Anguish,* 1936), and *Vidas Secas* (*Barren Lives,* 1938) and his two autobiographies, among other books, are masterpieces and have been translated into many languages. Graciliano Ramos' mastery of style and technique has earned him a special place in Brazilian literature.

José Lins do Rego (1901–1957), from the state of Paraíba, studied the decadence of the patriarchal family and the organization of the working class; Rachel de Queiroz (1910–), from Ceará, the first woman to be elected to the Brazilian Academy of Letters, stressed the suffering brought by drought and by social injustice; Jorge Amado (1912–), from Bahia, is the most widely read and translated Brazilian writer. He describes the struggle among the rich landowners in the cocoa regions of Brazil, and he defends the poor, the prostitutes, and the drunks who roam the low districts of Bahia. Although most fiction in the 1930's was especially sociological, there were exceptions. One example is seen in the work of Érico Veríssimo (1905–1975). Many of his novels are psychological in intent, although his masterpiece is an epic trilogy of the history of the Rio Grande do Sul, his native state, titled *O Tempo e o Vento* (*Time and the Wind,* 1949–1961). The fiction of Dinah Silveira de Queiroz (1910–1982) includes love, religion, history, mystery, science fiction, and children's literature. One of Brazil's most popular novelists, she was the second woman elected to the Brazilian Academy of Letters.

In poetry, Manuel Bandeira (1886–1968), who participated in Modern Art Week, was the leader of modernists in Rio de Janeiro. His group did not fully accept the tenets of modernism, feeling rather the need to stress tradition and spiritual values. Among the participants of this group, another outstanding figure was Cecília Meireles (1901–1964), one of the most important women poets of the Portuguese language.

The striking literary figure of Minas Gerais, Carlos Drummond de Andrade (1902–1987), is widely considered the greatest Brazilian poet. His poetry evolved in several phases: he first made use of the characteristic ironic style of the 1920's; he subsequently adopted as subjects for his work family recollections, social injustice, philosophical reflections, and a serene contemplation of the world. The preeminent poet of the Northeast was Jorge de Lima (1893–1953), whose work included beautiful verse on blacks, and religious poetry.

After 1945, regionalist, folkloric, and populist modernism changed direction. The postmodernists have been called the Generation of 1945. This new generation was shaped by several events, including the ideological debates over fascism versus democracy and socialism versus communism during the years of World War II and the repressive years of the Vargas regime. From its long preoccupation with strictly national questions, Brazilian intellectual consciousness returned to international issues. Writers became more interested in a universal philosophy and paid more attention to form, neglected in previous years. The influence of foreign writers was also felt at this time.

Several important collections of verse appeared, including *O Engenheiro* (1945) by João Cabral de Melo Neto (1920–) who stands out among many fine poets of this period. Perhaps Melo Neto's greatest contribution as an innovator of poetic language is his change in the lyric. He was fiercely opposed to sentimental poetry, adopting instead a rationally constructed poem. Even though he was at first identified with the Generation of 1945, he later came to be separated from the group because of his surrealism, his socially oriented poetry, and his dry and conceptual style based on the visual arts. Melo Neto was widely imitated by younger poets, including the concretists, who singled him out as their predecessor.

Experimentalism, a vanguard trend including concretism, neoconcretism, praxism, semiotics, and the process poem, began in the 1950's. Concretism was launched in São Paulo by members of the Generation of 1945 who broke with the mainstream of their group and were inspired by modern poets such as Stéphane Mallarmé and Ezra Pound. In 1956 the concretists organized in São Paulo the National Exhibition of Concrete Art, an event similar to the Modern Art Week of 1922. Concrete poetry was defined in its manifesto as "a product of a critical evolution of forms . . . aware of the graphic space as a structural agent" ("Post-Modernism in Poetry," in *Dictionary of Brazilian Literature*, Erwin Stern, ed. New York, 1988).

Some of the leaders of the movement, such as José Ribamar Ferreira Goular, did not support the manifesto and later founded a new movement known as neoconcretism, whose manifest was published in *Jornal do Brasil* on 22 March 1959. This manifesto rejected the exclusively mathematical and graphic qualities of poetry as regarded by the concretists. Neoconcretism was short-lived.

Praxism, another response to concretism, appeared in 1962 after Mário Chamie explained the concept in the preface to his book *Lavra-Lavra*. The praxis poem aesthetically organizes and assembles a located reality according to three conditions: a) the act of composition, b) the area of the composition, and c) the act of consuming the work. The praxis poem had a social aim: a praxis poem served as a field for the defense of the values of the work, and praxis literature was the general field for the defense of human values against the alienation of a society that needs to change in order to conquer itself.

Another phase of concretism was the semiotic poetry movement, also known as *Nova linguagem, nova poesia* (New language, new poetry). This movement, launched in the December 1964 issue of the review *Invenção*, presented poetry destitute of words, using instead "code poems" or collages.

The process poem movement, another outgrowth of concretism, began with a manifesto in the journal *O Sol* in December 1969. The process poem represented a radical position within vanguard poetry, emphasizing visual elements that dominated or minimized verbal ones.

The literary scene was not completely dominated by the vanguard positions that formed around the word-space relationship. The neotraditionalists of the Generation of 1945 continued to publish, sometimes playing with the experimental forms, and various other movements appeared. Excellent poetry was produced throughout this era of experimentation.

During the military dictatorship (1964–1979) a new kind of poetry developed: one representing the marginal elements of society. Individualism flourished. The poets borrowed elements from any school that served their purpose, and they became known as the "mimeograph generation" because they distributed their poems in mimeographed copies.

The most remarkable writer of postmodernist fiction, and one of the greatest writers of any period, is João Guimarães Rosa (1908–1967). The thematic content and physical context of his fiction involves almost exclusively the remote backlands of Minas Gerais, his home state, yet his prose is permeated by a metaphysical awareness that leads to problems of conscience and religious inquiry. His preoccupation with language resulted in linguistic innovation in his work, including the use of vocabulary from modern and ancient languages, the creation of neologisms, and experimentation with the infinite possibilities of syntax. He exploited the potentialities of language and restored its poetic character.

Besides experimentation with language, Brazilian writers have introduced new methods in point of view and narrative form. Some authors have written introspective fiction revealing the influence of the French New Novel, Virginia Woolf, and Spanish-American writers like Gabriel García Márques, Jorge Luis Borges, and Julio Cortázar. Famous for her introspective fiction is Clarice Lispector (1925–1977), whose highly abstract narratives are completely devoted to descriptions of states of mind and emotional reactions. Her intensely psychological work was instrumental in helping to move Brazilian fiction away from modernist regionalism. Lygia Fagundes Telles (1923–) is another great writer of psychological fiction. Her most widely read novel, *As Meninas* (*The Girl in the Photograph*, 1973), published during the military dictatorship, is at once a testimony of that time of repression and the author's view of women who are trying to liberate themselves from the pressures of a traditional society.

The short story in Brazil has assumed a variety of aspects: sometimes it is almost a folkloric document, at other times it tries to portray the urban or bourgeois drama; it often represents unlimited fantasy, or it may be solely devoted to the aesthetics of language. It began with Machado de Assis, the great master of the genre; it achieved success in the accomplishments of Lima Barreto; and it reached true excellence in the writing of Mário de Andrade and other modernists. Recent outstanding examples of the short story include João Guimaráes Rosa's regional collections and Lygia Fagundes

Telles' and Clarice Lispector's psychological stories. Indeed, short fiction has seen a boom in the last decades. The urban short story has been of particular interest. It frequently reflects the extreme destitution and great cruelty inflicted on the common man in the modern city. Good examples are the works of Dalton Trevisan (1925–), whose tone is poignant and whose focus is an obsession with the essential, and João Antônio Ferreira Filho (1937–), who like Trevisan depicts the marginal society of prostitutes, drug dealers, street sellers, and thieves. Everything in such fiction is brief, intense, and synthetic, including the lives of its characters, pressed by necessity between the urgency of hunger and the fear of police or of stronger competitors within this marginal culture.

The theater began to improve in the late 1920's with talented playwrights, popular actors, and the emergence of theatrical groups in several parts of the country. Modernism did not reach to the theater, since theatrical activities were already very much rooted in Brazilian themes with the *revista* (musical revue) and the *chanchada* (satire). A few exceptionally good plays were staged in the 1930's and 1940's; excellent theatrical talent appeared and in the 1950's Brazilian drama underwent a boom. A series of fine social plays were produced, with themes taken from Brazilian folklore. The boom was especially mature in the Northeast, mainly in Pernambuco. Using themes from popular literature, often from *cordel* (literally, "from a string"— that is, literature sold in pamphlet form dangling from a string), and employing medieval theatrical forms such as the *auto* (short play), a popular theater was created that continues to be a force throughout Brazil. The puppet theater, which was founded in the Northeast, has also made an important contribution to the Brazilian theatrical tradition. Ariano Vilar Suassuna (1927–) was and still is the most important dramatist of this movement. Suassuna has achieved one of the finest examples of a truly national literature, combining the form of the medieval European theater (for example, the theater of Gil Vicente) with folkloric tales of the Brazilian Northeast. His most popular play, *Auto da Compadecida* (*The Rogues' Trial*, 1957), mixes Christian traditions with popular religion and has important allegorical, social, and nationalistic overtones. Other great playwrights have appeared and first-rate dramas and comedies have been written and staged all over Brazil. However, during the recent military dictatorship the theater suffered a radical change, and in general the golden age of the 1950's has yet to be matched.

Modern literary criticism began with Sílvio Romero (1851–1914), who introduced a sociological approach to Brazilian literary studies. Although many fine critics followed, until the mid-1950's writers lacked a formal critical philosophy and used an impressionistic approach in their work. Alceu Amoroso Lima (1893–1983), considered the dean of modern Brazilian literary criticism, began writing his criticism in 1919. Until 1930 he wrote an expressionist, aesthetic criticism that was influenced by Henri Bergson and Benedetto Croce. Later his work was marked by Catholic moral values, effected by the author's contact with Jackson de Figueiredo, a Brazilian poet and philosopher, and by his readings of Jacques Maritain and Georges Bernanos. During the years 1930–1965, Alceu Amoroso Lima was recognized as the official critic of Brazilian modernism, but later he expanded his sphere of concentration by including in his writings philosophical, poetical, religious, and pedagogical issues. The origin of liberation theology in Brazil has been attributed to Amoroso Lima.

This is merely a brief overview of Brazil's literary history. We trust that the essays and bibliographies offered in these volumes of *Latin American Writers* will awaken the reader's desire to go on and deepen his knowledge of the rich and extensive Brazilian literature. Brazilian writers have developed splendid prose—novels, short stories, and essays—an impressive theater, poetry of great philosophical depth, and most recently have achieved an objective and competent criticism. Brazilian literature, as that of Spanish America, has become a literature of universal stature.

Maria Isabel Abreu
Georgetown University

CHRONOLOGICAL TABLE

1415 Henry the Navigator, Crown Prince of Portugal, begins general plan for the discoveries

1474–1566 Bartolomé de las Casas (Dominican Republic)

1476–1516 Ferdinand of Aragón and Isabel of Castille rule Spain

1478–1557 Gonzalo Fernández de Oviedo y Valdés (Cuba)

1486 "Ordenações Afonsinas" promulgated to regulate Portugal's colonial territories

ca. 1490–
1559? Álvar Núñez Cabeza de Vaca

1492 Christopher Columbus reaches the New World

Antonio de Nebrija publishes his *Arte de la lengua castellana*, the first Spanish grammar and first grammar of a Romance language

1493–1504 Columbus writes his *Cartas sobre el descubrimiento*

1494 Treaty of Tordesillas divides New World between Portugal and Spain

The earliest Spanish settlement, La Isabela, established on the island La Hispaniola (today the Dominican Republic and Haiti)

1495–1521 Manuel I rules Portugal

1496 Bartolomé Colón founds Santo Domingo, first Spanish city in New World

ca. 1496–
1584 Bernal Díaz del Castillo (Mexico)

1499 Portuguese navigator Vasco da Gama finds route to India

1500 Pedro Álvares Cabral discovers Brazil

1503 Spain legalizes the *encomienda*

Casa de Contratación created in Spain to oversee economic regulation of American empire

1510 Dominican friars arrive in La Hispaniola

1512 "Laws of Burgos" constituted to regulate treatment of Indians

ca. 1512 First slaves arrive in Cuba

1513 Vasco Núñez de Balboa discovers Pacific Ocean

1514 "Ordenações Manuelinas" updates Portugal's legal codes for New World

1516–1556 Charles V rules Spain

1516 Spanish explorer Juan Díaz de Solís arrives at mouth of the River Plate

1517 Martin Luther's "Ninety-five Theses" spark Protestant Reformation

1519–1556 Charles V annointed and serves as Holy Roman Emperor

1519 City of Havana founded

1521 Hernán Cortés completes Spain's conquest of Aztec Empire and founds Mexico City

1524 Supreme Royal Council of the Indies instituted in Spain for governance of administrative, political, judicial, and defense matters in American empire

Pedrarias Dávila founds Panama City

1526 Gonzalo Fernández de Oviedo y Valdés' *De la natural historia de las Indias*

1532 Board of Conscience and Religious Orders created in Portugal

Martim Affonso de Soussa founds San Vicente, first permanent settlement in Brazil

1533 Sebastián de Belalcázar seizes Ecuador; founds city of Quito a year later

1533? Bishop Juan de Zumárraga introduces printing press in Mexico, for production of religious books; in 1535 *Escala espiritual para illegar al cielo*, a Spanish translation of a sixth-century Latin book of devotions, is printed

1533–1594 Don Alonso de Ercilla y Zúñiga (Chile)

1534 João III of Portugal divides Brazil into *capitanías*

1534–1601? Fernán González de Eslava (Mexico)

1535 Viceroyalty of New Spain established; comprises Central America, Mexico, parts of California, the Louisiana territories, Texas, New Mexico, and Florida; capital is Mexico City

Francisco Pizarro completes Spain's conquest of Incan Empire and founds city of Lima

Gonzalo Fernández de Oviedo y Valdés writes *Historia general de las Indias;* first complete edition published in Madrid, 1851–1855

1536 Pedro de Mendoza founds city of Nuestra Señora de los Buenos Aires

Fernão de Oliveira writes first grammar of Portuguese

1537 Domingo Martínez serves as governor of newly founded city of Asunción

Papal bull by Paul III declares Indians capable of receiving the faith of Christ

1538 Gonzalo Jiménez de Quesada conquers Colombia and founds city of Santa Fé de Bogotá

First slaves arrive in Brazil

First university in New World established in Santo Domingo

1539 *Breve . . . doctrina cristiana en lengua mexicana y castellana,* the first traceable work published in New World, printed in Mexico City (first book printed in English colonies will be the *Bay Psalm Book,* in Cambridge, Mass., 1640)

1539–1616 El Inca Garcilaso de la Vega (Peru)

1540–1600 Father Joseph de Acosta (Peru)

1541 Pedro de Valdivia conquers Chile and founds city of Santiago

1542 Spain institutes laws to reform *encomienda* system

1544 Viceroyalty of Peru established; comprises Peru, Bolivia, Ecuador, and Chile; capital is Lima

1545 Spaniards discover silver in Potosí (Bolivia)

1545–1536 Council of Trent meets periodically to define Catholic doctrine and reiterate papal authority

1549 Arrival of Jesuits in New World

First governor general, Tomé de Souza, arrives in Brazil with large expedition and founds Salvador as capital of Brazil; six Jesuits accompany the expedition under leadership of Manuel da Nobrega

1551 University of San Marcos de Lima founded in Lima

University of Mexico founded in Mexico City

1552 Bartolomé de las Casas' *Brevísima relación de la destrucción de las Indias*

1553 More Jesuits arrive in Brazil; the group includes José de Anchieta, the first Brazilian poet

1554 Jesuits found School of São Paulo, around which develops city of the same name

1555 French settle in Brazil

1556–1598 Philip II rules Spain

1561?–1627 Bernardo de Balbuena (Mexico)

1567 Portuguese begin to expel French settlements and found the city of Rio de Janeiro; the French sail northward, capture Recife and Maranhão, and remain in Brazil until 1615.

1569 Don Alonso de Ercilla y Zúñiga's *La Araucana* (part 1) appears in Madrid; parts 2 and 3 appear in 1578 and 1589, respectively

1570 First Inquisition tribunal in America created in Lima; others created later in Mexico City (1591) and Cartagena, Colombia (1610)

1570–1643? Pedro de Oña (Chile)

1571 Battle of Lepanto

1572 Luiz Vaz de Camões publishes his epic poem *Os Lusíadas*

1580 Philip II of Spain seizes Portuguese throne; kingdom of Portugal remains under Spanish domain until 1640

1588 Defeat of Spanish Armada by the British

1590 Father Joseph de Acosta's *Historia natural y moral de las Indias*

1596 Pedro de Oña's *Arauco domado*

1598–1665 Under Philip III (1598–1621) and Philip IV (1621–1665) Spain achieves Golden Age in literature and art; the period embraces Cervantes, Lope de Vega, Tirso de Molina, Calderón, Quevedo, Góngora, and Gracián in literature, and Velázqeuz, Ribera, Zurbarán, and Murillo in painting

ca. 1600–
ca. 1720 Baroque period in art and literature

1603 New legal codes (Código Filipino) established for Portuguese colonies

1604 Bernardo de Balbuena's *Grandeza mexicana*

1607	British settlement established in Jamestown, Va.
1609–1617	El Inca Garcilaso de la Vega's *Los comentarios reales*
1618–1648	Thirty Years' War; Protestants revolt against Catholic oppression throughout Europe (particularly in Germany); war ends with Treaty of Westphalia (1648), and Spain loses practically all political power in Europe
1623	University of La Plata founded in Argentina
1624	Bernardo de Balbuena's El *Bernardo, o Victoria de Roncesvalles*
1630–1654	Dutch control the Northeast of Brazil
1632	Bernal Díaz del Castillo's *Historia verdadera de la conquista de la Nueva España*
1636–1695	Gregório de Mattos (Brazil)
1640	Under John IV the Portuguese monarchy is restored in Portugal; Brazil is organized as a viceroyalty, capital Bahia
1642	Overseas Council created in Portugal by John IV to supervise matters concerning the viceroyalty of Brazil.
1645?– 1697?	Juan del Valle y Caviedes (Peru)
1645–1700	Carlos de Sigüenza y Góngora (Mexico)
1651–1695	Sor Juana Inés de la Cruz (Mexico)
1676	University of San Carlos Borromeo founded in Guatemala City
1681	"Recopilación de Leyes de las Indias" promulgated by Spain for the governance of the New World possessions
1682	French claim Lousiana
1689	Sor Juana Inés de la Cruz' *Inundación castálida*
1690	Sor Juana Inés de la Cruz' *Carta athenagórica*, preceded by "Carta de Sor Philotea" Carlos de Sigüenza y Góngora's *Infortunios de Alonso Ramírez*
1691	Sor Juana Inés de la Cruz' *Respuesta a Sor Philotea de la Cruz*
1692	Sor Juana Inés de la Cruz' *El sueño*
1695	Gold discovered in interior of Brazil
1700–1746	**Philip V, the first Bourbon king, rules Spain** Rococo style flourishes
1702–1713	War of Spanish Succession; concludes with Peace of Ultrecht, whereby England gains the right to trade with Spanish America
1706	First printing press in Brazil (later suspended, reestablished in 1808 with arrival of Portuguese royal family)
1710	"Peddlers war" in Pernambuco, Brazil
ca. 1715– 1783	Alonso Carrió de la Vandera (Peru)
1717	Viceroyalty of New Granada established; comprises Panama, Colombia, and Venezuela; capital is Santa Fé de Bogotá;
1718	Quadruple Alliance (Britain, France, Netherlands, and German Empire) in war against Spain
1729–1789	Cláudio Manuel da Costa (Brazil)
ca. 1750– ca. 1810	Neoclassic period
1750	Treaty of Madrid establishes border between Brazil and Spanish America
1750–1777	Marquês de Pombal reconstructs city of Lisbon and undertakes important political, social, religious, and economic reforms in Portugal and Brazil
1750–1816	Francisco de Miranda, the forerunner of Spanish America's independence
1751–1772	Publication in France of the twenty-eight volume *Encylcopedie*, edited by Denis Diderot and Jean d'Alembert
1755	Lisbon destroyed by an earthquake
1759–1788	**Charles III rules Spain**
1759	Jesuits expelled from Portuguese Empire
1762	Jean-Jacques Rousseau publishes his *Du contrat social*; encourages the rise of antimonarchical republicanism
1763	Capital of viceroyalty of Brazil is moved from Bahia to Rio de Janeiro
1767	Jesuits expelled from Spanish Empire
1768	Cláudio Manuel da Costa's *Obras poéticas*
1775?	Alonso Carrió de la Vandera's *El lazarillo de ciegos caminantes desde Buenos-Ayres, hasta Lima . . .* published clandestinely in Lima
1776	Viceroyalty of the River Plate established; comprises Argentina, Uruguay, Paraguay, part of Bolivia; capital is Buenos Aires
1776–1783	American War of Independence

1776–1827 José Joaquín Fernández de Lizardi (Mexico)

1778 Charles III's Decree of Free Trade ends the Spanish monopoly on trade with the colonies.

1778–1842 Bernardo O'Higgins, hero of Chile's independence

1778–1850 José de San Martín, hero of Argentina's independence

1780 Tupac Amaru II revolt in New Granada

1781 Communero and Socorro tax revolts in New Granada

1781–1865 Andrés Bello (Venezuela)

1783–1830 Simón Bolívar, the "Liberator of America"

1789 French Revolution begins

Adoption of U.S. Constitution

In Minas Gerais, Brazil, Joaquim José da Silva Xavier (1748–1791), known as "Tiradentes," and others attempt to liberate Brazil from Portuguese domination

1794 Declaration of the Rights of Man from constitutional convention in Paris is translated into Spanish and secretly printed by Antonio Nariño (1765–1823) in Bogotá and widely read in the Spanish-American colonies

1798 Bahian Conspiracy in Brazil; *quilombos*, groups of runaway slaves of Orobô ad Andarai, are destroyed in Bahia

1799 Napoleon seizes power in France

1799–1804 Geographers Alexander von Humboldt and Amadeus James Alexander Bonpland travel through Venezuela, Colombia, Ecuador, Peru, Mexico, Cuba, and Brazil

ca. 1800–
ca. 1875 Realism in the novel flourishes with works of Dickens and Thackeray in England; Balzac, Flaubert, the Goncourts in France; Tolstoy, Dostoyevski, Gogol, Turgenev in Russia; Meyer, Keller in Germany; Caballero, Alarcón, Pereda, Valera, and Galdós in Spain; paves the way for *costumbrismo* and *criollismo* in Latin American prose fiction and drama after the second half of the nineteenth century

1803–1839 José María Heredia (Cuba)

1805 Battle of Trafalgar

1805–1851 Esteban Echeverría (Argentina)

1806 British squadron occupies Buenos Aires; expelled in 1807

1807 Napoleon invades Spain and Portugal

1807–1875 Hilario Ascasubi (Argentina)

1808 Napoleon occupies Madrid and places his brother Joseph on Spanish throne

Royal family of Portugal arrives in Brazil

French driven from Portugal

1810 Parliament in Spain created to rule in the name of deposed monarch Ferdinand VII

Father Miguel Hidalgo's Grito de Dolores launches Mexican struggle for independence

1810–1884 Juan Bautista Alberdi (Argentina)

1811 Paraguay and Venezuela declare independence

Father Miguel Hidalgo executed by Spanish officials; Father José Morelos continues fight for Mexico's independence

1811–1888 Domingo Faustino Sarmiento (Argentina)

1812 Spanish parliament asserts new, liberal constitution restricting king's authority

1812–1894 Cirilo Villaverde (Cuba)

1813 Inquisition tribunal abolished in Spain

Congress of Chilpancingo declares Mexican independence

1814 Ferdinand VII returns to Spanish throne and annuls 1812 constitution

Congress of Chilpancingo drafts Mexican constitution, the first in Latin America

1814–1840 Populist *caudillo* José Gaspar Rodríguez de Francia dominates Paraguay

1814–1873 Gertrudis Gómez de Avellaneda (Cuba)

1815 Spanish officials capture and execute Father Morelos in Mexico

1816 Argentina declares independence

José Joaquín Fernández de Lizardi's *El Periquillo Sarniento* (the last of three volumes appeared posthumously due to censorship) marks beginning of novel as literary genre in Spanish-American literature

1817 Brazilians in Pernambuco revolt unsuccessfully for independence; a second revolt in 1824 also fails

1817–1871 José Mármol (Argentina)

1818 José Joaquín Fernández de Lizardi's *Don Catrín de la Fachenda* (published posthumously in 1832)

1820 Portuguese parliament asserts new constitution restricting king's authority
José María Heredia's poem "El teocalli de Cholula" (final version in 1832)

1821 Mexico, Peru, and Central America declare independence after Ferdinand VII endorses 1812 constitution
Bolívar and San Martín meet in Ecuador
After thirteen years in Rio de Janeiro, Portuguese royal family returns to Portugal; Prince Pedro stays in Brazil as regent

1822–1823 Emperor Agustín I rules Mexican Empire

1822 Pedro, under advice of José Bonifacio de Andrada e Silva, declares Brazil's independence and reigns as Emperor Dom Pedro I until 1831

1823 U.S. president James Monroe announces Monroe Doctrine
Chile and the nations of Central America are first in Western Hemisphere to abolish slavery
The first of Andrés Bello's *silvas americanas*, *Alocución a la poesía*, appears in the journal *Biblioteca americana*; proclaims intellectual independence of the colonies

1823–1864 Antônio Gonçalves Dias (Brazil)

1824 Bolívar wins battle of Junín and Antonio José de Sucre wins battle of Ayacucho; final defeat of the Spaniards in South America
Brazil adopts a constitution
José María Heredia's poem "Niágara"

1824–1838 United Provinces of Central America formed

1825 Bolivia declares independence
José María Heredia's poems "Himno del desterrado" and "Vuelta al sur"

1825–1828 Cisplatine War between Argentina and Brazil to possess Uruguay results in stalemate and Uruguayan independence

1826 Congress of Panama called by Simón Bolívar meets in Panama
Andrés Bello's *La agricultura de la zona tórrida* appears in the journal *Repertorio americano*

1827 The newspapers *El Mercurio* (Chile) and *Jornal do Comércio* (Brazil) founded
Victor Hugo's "Manifesto," preface to his *Cromwell*, signals beginning of the romantic period

ca. 1827–
ca. 1880 Romanticism flourishes in Latin American literature influenced by works of European romantics—Chateaubriand, Lamartine, Hugo, Vigny, Musset, and Dumas of France; Sir Walter Scott and Lord Byron of Britain; to a lesser extent Goethe and von Schiller of Germany and Manzoni and Foscolo of Italy—but particularly through the works of Spanish romantics Duque de Rivas, José de Larra, Espronceda, Zorrilla, and, later, Rosalía de Castro; Brazilian literature is also influenced by Portuguese romantics Almeida Garrett, Alexandre Herculano, Camilo Castelo Branco, and Antero de Quental

1829–1852 Populist *caudillo* Juan Manuel de Rosas dominates Argentina

1829–1855 Antonio López de Santa Anna dominates Mexico

1829–1877 José de Alencar (Brazil)

1830 Political union of Gran Colombia dissolves, leaving Colombia, Ecuador, and Venezuela as independent nations

1830–1846 José Antonio Páez dominates Venezuela (comes to power again 1861–1863)

1830–1861 Diego Portales dominates Chile

1830–1920 Alberto Blest Gana (Chile)

1831 Emperor Dom Pedro I forced to abdicate in favor of his five-year-old son; Brazil governed by regency until 1940

1832 Esteban Echeverría's *Elvira; o, La novia del Plata* marks beginning of the romantic period in Spanish-American literature

1832–1889 Juan Montalvo (Ecuador)
1833–1919 Ricardo Palma (Peru)
1834–1880 Estanislao del Campo (Argentina)
1834–1886 José Hernández (Argentina)
1835 Slave revolts in Bahia, Brazil
1835–1845 War of secession in Río Grande do Sul, Brazil
1836 Domingos José Gonçalves de Magalhães publishes *Suspiros Poéticos e Saudades*; marks beginning of romanticism in Brazilian literature
1836–1856 Academia de San Juan de Letrán founded in Mexico
1837 Esteban Echeverría founds Asociación de Mayo, a group of prominent young Argentine romantics

The Uruguayan Marcos Sastre founds Salón Literario in Buenos Aires (closed by Rosas in 1838)

Esteban Echeverría's "La cautiva" in his collection *Rimas*
1837–1895 Jorge Isaacs (Colombia)
1838–1840 French navy blockades Buenos Aires (Buenos Aires blockaded again 1845–1848, by French and British navies)
1839 Civil war erupts among federated provinces of Argentina and Uruguay (Montevideo under siege 1843–1852)

The newspaper *El Comercio* (Lima) founded

Cláudio Manuel da Costa's *Vila Rica*

Cirilo Villaverde begins to write *Cecilia Valdés, o La loma del ángel* (final revised edition appears 1882)
1839–1865 Populist *caudillo* Rafael Carrera rules Guatemala
1839–1908 Joaquim Maria Machado de Assis (Brazil)
1840–1862 Carlos Antonio López dominates Paraguay
1840–1889 Dom Pedro II reigns as emperor in Brazil
1841 Gertrudis Gómez de Avellaneda's *Sab*
1842 The Argentine Sarmiento, exiled in Chile, and the Venezuelan Bello, a prominent figure in Chile's public and intellectual life, debate cultural and literary future of Spanish America in a series of polemic exchanges; exchanges between classicists (rep-

resented by Bello) and romantics (represented by Sarmiento) had tremendous influence on literary, cultural, and intellectual development of nineteenth- and early-twentieth-century Latin America
1843 Andrés Bello reorganizes University of Chile according to French models and becomes its first president; University of Chile becomes first in Latin America to publish annuals, books, journals, magazines, and reviews
1843–1889 Eugenio Cambaceres (Argentina)
1843–1909 Miguel Antonio Caro (Colombia)
1844 Joaquim Manoel de Macedo (1820–1882) publishes *Moreninha,* first Brazilian novel
1844–1918 Manuel González Prada (Peru)
1845 Domingo Faustino Sarmiento's *Civilización i barbarie: La vida de Juan Facundo Quiroga*
1846 Antônio Gonçalves Dias' *Primeiros Cantos*

Juan María Gutiérrez' *América poética;* first anthology of Spanish-American poetry published in New World
1846–1848 Mexican-American War; United States acquires Arizona, California, and New Mexico in Treaty of Guadalupe Hidalgo
1847–1903 Cruzoh rebellion in Yucatán leads to Mayan self-government
1847–1871 Antônio de Castro Alves (Brazil)
1848 Karl Marx and Friedrich Engels publish *Communist Manifesto*

Antônio Gonçalves Dias' *Ultimos Cantos*
1848–1855 Populist *caudillo* Manuel Belzu rules Bolivia
1849 Domingo Faustino Sarmiento's *Viajes*
1850 United States and Britain sign Clayton–Bulwer treaty, which checks expansion of each in Central America

Domingo Faustino Sarmiento's *Recuerdos de provincia*
ca. 1850–
ca. 1900 Symbolism, impressionism, neosensualism, Parnassian movement, decadentism flourish in European art and literature—especially in France with works of Gautier, Baudelaire, Sully

Prudhomme, Leconte de Lisle, Verlaine, Mallarmé, Rimbaud—paving the way for Spanish-American *modernismo*

1851 José Mármol's *Amalia* (second part completed in 1855 after the fall of Juan Manuel de Rosas in Argentina)

1851–1852 Brazil and Uruguay help the opposition in Argentina to overthrow the Rosas dictatorship

1851–1921 Eduardo Acevedo Díaz (Uruguay)

1852–1909 Clorinda Matto de Turner (Peru)

1853–1895 José Martí (Cuba)

1854–1861 Ramón Castilla rules Peru

1855–1860 Benito Juárez' War of the Reform in Mexico promises liberal agenda

1855–1930 Manuel Zeno Gandía (Puerto Rico)

1855–1931 Juan Zorrilla de San Martín (Uruguay)

1855–1857 William Walker's occupation of Nicaragua

1856–1939 Sigmund Freud

1857 José de Alencar's *O Guarani*
Antônio Gonçalves Dias' *Os Timbiras*

1857–1913 Aluísio Azevedo (Brazil)

1858–1940 Tomás Carrasquilla (Colombia)

1859 Charles Darwin's *On the Origin of the Species by Means of Natural Selection*

1859–1895 Manuel Gutiérrez Nájera (Mexico)

1860–1875 Gabriel García Moreno rules Ecuador

1860–1930 Expansion of Buenos Aires after two large European immigration waves (by 1895 almost 52 percent of Buenos Aires population is of foreign origin)

1861–1865 American Civil War; President Abraham Lincoln assassinated (1865); abolition of slavery in United States (1865)

1861–1898 João da Cruz e Sousa (Brazil)

1862 Alberto Blest Gana's *Martín Rivas*; marks beginning of realist movement in Spanish-American prose

1862–1866 Spain attempts to reconquer Peru

1862–1868 Bartolomé Mitre serves as first constitutional president of Argentina

1862–1870 Francisco Solano López governs Paraguay

1863–1867 Maximilian von Hapsburg rules Mexico under French protection

1863–1893 Julián del Casal (Cuba)

1864–1939 Federico Gamboa (Mexico)

1865 José de Alencar's *Iracema*

1865–1870 War of the Triple Alliance; Argentina, Brazil, and Uruguay defeat Paraguay

1865–1896 José Asunción Silva (Colombia)

1866 Estanislao del Campo's *Fausto*

1866–1909 Euclides da Cunha (Brazil)

1867 Jorge Isaacs' *María*
Rufino José Cuervo's *Apuntaciones críticas sobre el lenguaje bogotano*

1867–1872 Benito Juárez ousts Maximilian and dominates Mexico

1867–1916 Rubén Darío (Nicaragua)

1867–1928 Roberto Jorge Payró (Argentina)

1868–1874 Domingo Faustino Sarmiento serves as president of Argentina

1868–1878 Ten Years' War in Cuba against Spain in an attempt to assert the island's independence

1868–1933 Ricardo Jaimes Freyre (Bolivia)

1869 The newspaper *La Prensa* (Buenos Aires) founded

1870 The newspaper *La Nación* (Buenos Aires) founded
Conquest of desert begins in Argentina
Republican party founded in Brazil

ca. 1870 Naturalistic movement in prose fiction (best represented by Émile Zola) develops in France

1870–1888 Antonio Guzmán Blanco rules Venezuela

1870–1919 Amado Nervo (Mexico)

1871 Colombian Academy of Language created, the first in Spanish America modeled on Spain's Royal Academy in Madrid; Mexico and Ecuador follow in 1875; Venezuela in 1883
Juan Bautista Alberdi's *Peregrinación de Luz del Día*
Antônio de Castro Alves' *Espumas Flutuantes*
Esteban Echeverría's *El matadero*

1871–1917 José Enrique Rodó (Uruguay)

1871–1927 Manuel Díaz Rodríguez (Venezuela)

1871–1945 José Juan Tablada (Mexico)

1872 José Hernández' *El gaucho Martín Fierro*
Hilario Ascasubi's *Santos Vega*
Ricardo Palma's first series of his *Tradiciones* (complete four-volume series *Tradiciones peruanas* appeared 1893–1896); marks culmination of *costumbrismo* (literature of manners) in

Spanish America and creates new literary genre known as *tradiciones*

1873–1885 Justo Rufino Barrios dominates Guatemala

1873–1927 Enrique Gómez Carrillo (Guatemala)

1873–1943 Guillermo Valencia (Colombia)

1873–1952 Mariano Azuela (Mexico)

1873–1961 Enrique Larreta (Argentina)

1874 First exhibition of impressionist art opens in Paris

1874–1938 Leopoldo Lugones (Argentina)

1874–1942 José María Eguren (Peru)

1874–1944 Rufino Blanco Fombona (Venezuela)

1874–1952 Macedonio Fernández (Argentina)

1875 Juan Montalvo's *La dictadura perpetua*
José de Alencar's *Senhora*

1875–1908 Juan Ramón Molina (Honduras)

1875–1910 Florencio Sánchez (Uruguay)
Julio Herrera y Reissig (Uruguay)

1875–1934 José Santos Chocano (Peru)

1876 Antônio de Castro Alves' *A Cachoeira de Paulo Afonso*

1876–1911 Porfirio Díaz rules Mexico

1877 Chilean governmental decree permits women to receive professional degrees
The fanatic Antônio Vicente Mendes Maciel (known as Antônio Conselheiro, "The Counselor") and his followers provoke disturbances in Brazil's backlands culminating with the Canudo War (1896–1897), as result of Brazilian government intervention

1878–1937 Horacio Quiroga (Uruguay)

1879–1883 War of the Pacific; Chile tries to conquer the nitrate-producing provinces of Bolivia and Peru; in 1881, the National Library in Lima is destroyed

1880 Juan Montalvo's *Las Catilinarias*

1880–1894 Rafael Núñez rules Colombia

1880–1951 Benito Lynch (Argentina)

1881 Buenos Aires established as a federal district
Machado de Assis' *Memórias Póstumas de Braz Cubas*
Aluízio Azevedo's *O Mulato*

1881–1922 Afonso Henriques de Lima Barreto (Brazil)

1881–1973 Pablo Picasso

1882 José Martí's *Ismaelillo* marks beginning

of modernist movement in Spanish American literature

1882–1957 Ricardo Rojas (Argentina)

1882–1959 José Vasconcelos (Mexico)

1882–1962 Manuel Gálvez (Argentina)

1883 Manuel Gutiérrez Nájera's *Cuentos frágiles*
Antônio de Castro Alves' *Os Escravos*

1884 Eugenio Cambaceres' *Música sentimental*

1884–1946 Pedro Henríquez Ureña (Dominican Republic)

1884–1963 Eduardo Barrios (Chile)

1884–1969 Rómulo Gallegos (Venezuela)

1885 Eugenio Cambaceres' *Sin rumbo*

1886 Eloísa Diaz becomes first woman in Latin America to be awarded a medical degree as she graduates from University of Chile
Slavery abolished in Cuba

1886–1891 José Balmaceda governs Chile

1886–1914 Delmira Agustini (Uruguay)

1886–1927 Ricardo Güiraldes (Argentina)

1886–1952 Pedro Prado (Chile)

1886–1968 Manuel Bandeira (Brazil)

1887–1976 Martín Luis Guzmán (Mexico)

1888 Brazil passes "Golden Law," becomes last nation in Western Hemisphere to abolish slavery (in 1871, children born of Brazilian slaves had been declared free; in 1875, sixty-five-year-old slaves had been emancipated)
Rubén Darío's *Azul*
Juan Zorrilla de San Martín's *Tabaré*
Eduardo Acevedo Díaz' *Ismael*

ca. 1888–
ca. 1910 Realism and naturalism flourish in Spanish-American prose fiction, essay, and drama (in Brazilian literature the movement had begun around 1877)

1888–1921 Ramón López Velarde (Mexico)

1888–1928 José Eustasio Rivera (Colombia)

1889 International exposition in Paris featuring Eiffel Tower and early signs of modern style in art
Deodoro da Fonseca leads overthrow of Dom Pedro II in Brazil; Brazil becomes a republic; coffee planters begin domination of Brazil

Clorinda Matto de Turner's *Aves sin nido*
Manuel Gutiérrez Nájera's *Cuentos color de humo*

1889–1890 First Inter-American Conference meets in Washington, D.C.
1889–1957 Gabriela Mistral (Chile)
1889–1959 Alfonso Reyes (Mexico)
1890 Aluízio Azevedo's *O Cortiço*
1890–1936 Ana Teresa de la Parra Sanojo (Venezuela)
1890–1952 José Rubén Romero (Mexico)
1890–1979 Victoria Ocampo (Argentina)
1891 Chilean civil war
José Martí's *Versos sencillos*
Joaquim Maria Machado de Assis' *Quincas Borba*
1891–1959 Rafael Heliodoro Valle (Honduras)
1892 Matilde Throup becomes first female lawyer in Latin America as she graduates from University of Chile law school
1892–1938 César Vallejo (Peru)
Alfonsina Storni (Argentina)
1892–1953 Graciliano Ramos (Brazil)
1893 Santa Fe revolts in Argentina
João da Cruz e Souza's *Missal* and *Broquéis*
1893–1903 President José Santos Zelaya governs Nicaragua
1893–1945 Mário de Andrade (Brazil)
1893–1948 Vicente Huidobro (Chile)
1893–1953 Jorge de Lima (Brazil)
1893–1983 Alceu Amoroso Lima (Brazil)
1894 Prudente de Morais elected first civilian president of Brazil
Eduardo Acevedo Díaz' *Soledad*
Manuel Zeno Gandía's *La charca*
Manuel González Prada's *Páginas libres*
1894–1930 José Carlos Mariátegui (Peru)
1894–1967 Samuel Eichelbaum (Argentina)
1895–1898 Cuban War for Independence
1895–1911 Eloy Alfaro dominates Ecuador
1895–1964 Ezequiel Martínez Estrada (Argentina)
1895–1979 Juana de Ibarbourou (Uruguay)
1896 Rubén Darío's *Prosas profanas y otros cuentos*
Tomás Carrasquilla's *Frutos de mi tierra*
Federico Gamboa's *Suprema ley*
Manuel Zeno Gandía's *Garduña*
1896–1973 Manuel Rojas (Chile)

1897 Alberto Blest Gana's *Durante la reconquista*
Leopoldo Lugones' *Las montañas del oro*
1898 As a result of Spanish-American War, Cuba gains independence from Spain and United States takes possession of Puerto Rico
1898–1920 Manuel Estrada Cabrera dominates Guatemala
1898–1959 Luis Palés Matos (Puerto Rico)
1898–1961 Jorge Mañach Robato (Cuba)
1898– Ricardo E. Molinari (Argentina)
1899 Ricardo Jaimes Freyre's *Castalia bárbara*
Joaquim Maria Machado de Assis' *Dom Casmurro*
1899–1902 Colombia's War of the Thousand Days
1899–1974 Miguel Ángel Asturias (Guatemala)
1899–1975 Salvador (Salarrué) Salazar Arrué (El Salvador)
1899–1986 Jorge Luis Borges (Argentina)
1900 José Enrique Rodó's *Ariel*
1900–1942 Roberto Arlt (Argentina)
1900–1970 Leopoldo Marechal (Argentina)
1900– Germán Arciniegas (Colombia)
1900 Joaquim Maria Machado de Assis' *Dom Casmurro*
1901 Hay-Pauncefote Treaty; Great Britain acknowledges U.S. supremacy in Central America
1901–1957 José Lins do Rego (Brazil)
1901–1964 Cecília Meireles (Brazil)
1901–1965 Mariano Picón Salas (Venezuela)
1901 Manuel González Prada's *Minúsculas*
1901–1979 José Gorostiza (Mexico)
1902 Manuel Díaz Rodríguez' *Sangre patricia*
Euclides da Cunha's *Os Sertões*
1902–1974 Jaime Torres Bodet (Mexico)
1902–1987 Carlos Drummond de Andrade (Brazil)
1902– Rogelio Sinán (Panama)
Nicolás Guillén (Cuba)
1903 Panama gains independence from Colombia and signs treaty with United States for construction of an interoceanic canal
Federico Gamboa's *Santa*
Florencio Sánchez' *M'ijo el dotor*
Tomás Carrasquilla's *Salve, Regina*
1903–1929 José Batlle dominates Uruguayan politics; economic growth and stability brings the middle class to power

1903–1950 Xavier Villarrutia (Mexico)
1903–1982 Eduardo Mallea (Argentina)
1904 U.S. president Theodore Roosevelt declares Roosevelt Corollary to Monroe Doctrine
Florencio Sánchez' *La gringa*
Roberto Jorge Payró's *Sobre las ruinas*
1904–1907 Julio Herrera y Reissig's *Los éxtasis de la montaña*
1904–1973 Pablo Neruda (Chile)
1904–1980 José Marín Cañas (Costa Rica)
Agustín Yáñez (Mexico)
Alejo Carpentier (Cuba)
1905 Albert Einstein publishes his first theory of relativity
Rubén Darío's *Cantos de vida y esperanza*
Florencio Sánchez' *Barranca abajo*
Leopoldo Lugones' *Los crepúsculos del jardín*
Roberto Jorge Payró's *Marco Severi*
1905–1975 Érico Veríssimo (Brazil)
1905–1979 Rodolfo Usigli (Mexico)
1906 José Santos Chocano's *Alma América*
1906–1909 Second U.S. intervention in Cuba
1906–1978 Jorge Icaza (Ecuador)
1906– Enrique A. Laguerre (Puerto Rico)
Arturo Uslar Pietri (Venezuela)
1907 Pablo Picasso's painting "Les Demoiselles d'Avignon" creates sensation at first cubist exhibition, in Paris
Henri Bergson publishes his *Creative Evolution*
1908 Enrique Larreta's *La gloria de Don Ramiro*
Manuel Díaz Rodríguez' *Camino de perfección*
Manuel González Prada's *Horas de lucha*
1908–1912 Augusto Leguía governs Peru (and again, 1919–1930)
1908–1935 Juan Vicente Gómez dominates Venezuela
1908–1954 Emilio Ballagas (Cuba)
1908–1967 João Guimarães Rosa (Brazil)
1909 José Enrique Rodó's *Motivos de Proteo*
Alberto Blest Gana's *El loco estero*
Leopoldo Lugones' *Lunario sentimental*
Manuel González Prada's *Presbiterianas*
Julio Herrera y Reissig's *La torre de las esfinges*

Afonso Henriques de Lima Barreto's *Recordações do Escrivão Isaías Caminha*
1909–1933 U.S. intervention and occupation of Nicaragua
1909–1967 Ciro Alegría (Peru)
1909– Juan Carlos Onetti (Uruguay)
1910 Ordinary Brazilians for the first time participate in the country's presidential campaign
Roberto Jorge Payro's *Divertidas aventuras del nieto de Juan Moreira*
1910 Leopoldo Lugones' *Odas seculares*
1910–1940 Mexican Revolution
1910–1976 José Lezama Lima (Cuba)
1910–1980 María Luisa Bombal (Chile)
1910– Enrique Anderson Imbert (Argentina)
Rachel de Queiroz (Brazil)
1911 Emiliano Zapata advocates agrarian reform in his Plan de Ayala
Manuel González Prada's *Exóticas*
1911–1927 Uruguay undergoes important modern political, social, and economic changes
1911–1969 José María Arguedas (Peru)
1911–1982 Dinah Silveira de Queiroz (Brazil)
1911– Ernesto Sábato (Argentina)
1912 Black leader Evaristo Estenoz organizes Indian Party of Color to support blacks' rights in Cuba
Leopoldo Lugones' *El libro fiel*
1912– Jorge Amado (Brazil)
1913 Victoriano Huerta overthrows Francisco I. Madero in Mexico
Delmira Agustini's *Los cálices vacíos*
José Martí's *Versos libres*
1914 Panama Canal opens
Manuel Gálvez' *La maestra normal*
1914–1918 World War I between the Central Powers, Germany and Austria-Hungary, and the Entente of France, Russia, and Great Britain; United States enters war on side of Entente in 1917
1914–1924 United States intervenes in Dominican Republic (United States occupies that country 1914–1916)
1914–1984 Julio Cortázar (Argentina)
1914– Octavio Paz (Mexico)
Adolfo Bioy Casares (Argentina)
Nicanor Parra (Chile)

1915 Venustiano Carranza overthrows Victoriano Huerta in Mexico
Mariano Azuela's *Los de abajo*
Afonso Henriques de Lima Barreto's *Triste Fim de Policarpo Quaresma*

1916 Vicente Huidobro's *El espejo del agua*, with his famous poem "Arte poética," marks beginning of "creationism" in Spanish-American literature; the same year in a lecture in Buenos Aires' Ateneo Huidobro proclaims the new literary trend
Manuel Gálvez' *El mal metafísico*

1916–1922 Hipólito Irigoyen governs Argentina as its first middle-class president

1917 Bolshevik Revolution
Promulgation of Mexican Constitution, blueprint for the revolution
Earthquake destroys most of Guatemala City
Carl Jung publishes his work *The Unconscious*
Alfonso Reyes' *Visión de Anahuac*

1917– Augusto Roa Bastos (Paraguay)

1918 César Vallejo's *Los heraldos negros*
José Juan Tablada's *Al sol y bajo la luna*

ca. 1918–
ca. 1932 Ultraism, avant-garde, futurism, dadaism, cubism, surrealism develop in art and literature

1918–1986 Juan Rulfo (Mexico)

1918– Juan José Arreola (Mexico)

1919 President Augusto Leguía in Peru declares Indian community a legal corporation
Semana Trágica in Argentina; laborers clash with police
Manuel Gálvez' *Nacha regules*
Afonso Henriques de Lima Barreto's *Vida e Morte de Gonzaga de Sá*
Ramón López Velarde's *Zozobra*

1919–1979 René Marqués (Puerto Rico)

1920 Women granted the right to vote in United States
Juana de Ibarbourou's *Raíz salvaje*
Amado Nervo's *La amada inmóvil*
Pedro Prado's *Alsino*

1920–1924 Obregón serves as president of Mexico
Arturo Alessandri, representing the middle-class interests, governs Chile

1920– João Cabral de Melo Neto (Brazil)
Mario Benedetti (Uruguay)

1921 Ramón López Velarde's poem "La suave patria"
José Eustasio Rivera's *Tierra de promisión*

1922 Modern Art Week in Brazil inaugurates the avant-garde movement in art and literature known in Brazil as *modernismo* (in Spanish America *modernismo* had been result of the French symbolists, impressionists, Parnassians, decadentism, neosensualism)
Mário de Andrade's *Pauliceia Desvairada*
Eduardo Barrios' *El hermano asno*
Enrique Gómez Carrillo's *El evangelio del amor*
Gabriela Mistral's *Desolación*
César Vallejo's *Trilce*
Manuel Zeno Gandía's *Redentores* and *El negocio*

1922–1924 *Tenentes* revolt in Brazil

1922– Marco Denevi (Argentina)

1923 Pancho Villa assassinated in Mexico
Bertha Lutz founds Brazilian Federation for Feminine Progress
Pablo Neruda's *Crepusculario*
César Vallejo's *Escalas melografiadas*

1923– Lygia Fagundes Telles (Brazil)

1924 "Prestes Column" marches inland in Brazil
U.S. intervention in Honduras
In Mexico, Víctor Raúl Haya de la Torre founds American Revolutionary Popular Alliance, a program of social reforms for Peru that has tremendous repercussions throughout Latin America
André Breton's *Manifesto of Surrealism*
Benito Lynch's *El inglés de los güesos*
Gabriela Mistral's *Ternura*
Pablo Neruda's *Veinte poemas de amor y una canción desesperada*
José Eustasio Rivera's *La vorágine*

1924–1934 Plutarco Elias Calles dominates Mexican politics

1924– José Donoso (Chile)

1925 Alfonsina Storni's *Ocre*
José Vasconcelos' *La raza cósmica*

1925–1974 Rosario Castellanos (Mexico)

1925–1977 Clarice Lispector (Brazil)
1925– Emilio Carballido (Mexico)
1926 José Carlos Mariátegui launches journal *Amauta*

Nicolás Guillén and Fernando Ortíz establish society for Afro-Cuban studies

Roberto Arlt's *El juguete rabioso*

Tomás Carrasquilla's *La Marquesa de Yolombó*

Ricardo Güiraldes' *Don Segundo Sombra*

Enrique Larreta's *Zogoibi*

José Carlos Mariátegui's *Siete ensayos sobre la realidad peruana*

José Vasconcelos' *Indología*

1926– Egon Wolff (Chile)
1927 Leopoldo Lugones' *Poemas solariegos*

Ricardo Molinari's *El imaginero*

1927–1933 Augusto César Sandino leads guerilla struggle in Nicaragua to expel U.S. marines

1927–1935 Alceu Amoroso Lima's *Estudos* (five series)

1927– Ariano Suassuna (Brazil)
1928 Mário de Andrade's *Macunaíma*

Martín Luis Guzmán's *El águila y la serpiente*

Pedro Henríquez Ureña's *Seis ensayos en busca de nuestra expresión*

Jorge Mañach's *Indagación del choteo*

1928–1964 Luis Alberto Heiremans (Chile)
1928– Griselda Gambaro (Argentina)

Gabriel García Márquez (Colombia)

Carlos Fuentes (Mexico)

1929 World financial collapses reduce Latin American exports but encour age import-substitution industrialization

Ecuador is first Latin American nation to allow women right to vote

José Carlos Mariátegui founds Socialist party in Peru

Macedonio Fernández' *Papeles de recién-venido*

Rómulo Gallegos' *Doña Bárbara*

Ana Teresa de la Parra Sonojo's *Memorias de Mamá Blanca*

1929– Osvaldo Dragún (Argentina)

Guillermo Cabrera Infante (Cuba)

1930 Revolution in Brazil deposes government of Old Republic, beginning New Republic

Miguel Ángel Asturias' *Leyendas de Guatemala*

Manuel Bandeira's *Libertinagem*

Nicolás Guillén's *Sóngoro cosongo: Poemas mulatos*

Martín Luis Guzmán's *La sombra del caudillo*

Rachel de Queiroz' *O Quinze*

1930–1945 Getúlio Vargas governs Brazil (and again 1951–1954)

1930–1961 Rafael L. Trujillo dominates Dominican Republic

1930– Jorge Díaz (Chile)
1931 Victoria Ocampo founds literary review *Sur* in Buenos Aires

Vicente Huidobro's *Altazor; o, El viaje en paracaídas*

Arturo Uslar Pietri's *Las lanzas coloradas*

César Vallejo's *Tungsteno* and *Rusia en 1931*

1931–1944 Jorge Ubico governs Guatemala
1931– Jorge Edwards (Chile)
1932 José Lins do Rego's *Menino de Engenho*

Ramón López Velarde's *El son del corazón*

Ricardo E. Molinari's *Delta*

ca. 1932 Post-avant-garde movement in art and literature

1932–1935 Bolivia and Paraguay fight Chaco War
1932–1948 Tiburcio Carias Andino governs Honduras

1932– Manuel Puig (Argentina)
1933 Ezequiel Martínez Estrada's *Radiografía de la pampa*

Pablo Neruda's *Residencia en la tierra (1925–1931)*

1933–1945 U.S. president Franklin Delano Roosevelt announces Good Neighbor policy toward Latin America

1933– José Triana (Cuba)
1934 Platt Amendment to Cuban constitution nullified

Emilio Ballagas' *Cuaderno de poesía negra*

Rómulo Gallegos' *Cantaclaro*

Jorge Icaza's *Huasipungo*

Graciliano Ramos' *São Bernardo*

1934–1940 Mexican Revolution reaches its apogee under President Lázaro Cárdenas

1934–1959 Fulgencio Batista dominates Cuba

1935 Communist-inspired revolt in Brazil fails

Emilio Ballagas' *Antología de poesía negra hispanoamericana*

María Luisa Bombal's *La última niebla*

Jorge Luis Borges' *Historia universal de la infamia*

Rómulo Gallegos' *Canaima*

Pablo Neruda's two volumes of *Residencia en la tierra* (1925–1935)

José Vasconcelos' *Ulises criollo*

ca. 1935 Spanish-American novel begins successfully to incorporate contemporary European and American stylistic techniques, ideological trends, and universal themes (leads to boom in Spanish-American prose fiction of 1960's and after)

1936 Spanish army under Francisco Franco revolts against elected republican government, triggering Spanish civil war (1936–1939)

Manuel Bandeira's *Estrela de Manhã*

Graciliano Ramos' *Angústia*

Arturo Uslar Pietri's *Red*

1936–1979 Somoza dynasty in Nicaragua

1936– Mario Vargas Llosa (Peru)

Severo Sarduy (Cuba)

1937 Bolivia nationalizes foreign oil companies

Getulio Vargas seizes power in Brazil and declares Estado Novo

Luis Palés Mato's *Tuntún de pasa y grifería*

1938 Mexico nationalizes foreign oil companies

Germán Arciniegas' *Los comuneros*

María Luisa Bombal's *La amortajada*

Leopoldo Lugones' *Romances de Río Seco*

Gabriela Mistral's *Tala*

José Rubén Romero's *La vida inútil de Pito Pérez*

Xavier Villaurrutia's *Nostalgia de la muerte*

1938– Luisa Valenzuela (Argentina)

1939 Emilio Ballagas' *Sabor eterno*

José Gorostiza's *Muerte sin fin*

Juan Carlos Onetti's *El pozo*

Dinah Silveira de Queiroz' *Floradas na Serra*

César Vallejo's *Poemas humanos* (1923–1938)

1939–1945 World War II (United States enters war after bombing of Pearl Harbor by Japan in December 1941)

1940 Adolfo Bioy Casares' *La invención de Morel*

Samuel Eichelbaum's *Pájaro de barro*

Ezequiel Martínez Estrada's *La cabeza de Goliat*

Xavier Villaurutia's *Invitación a la muerte*

1941 Inter-American Treaty of Reciprocal Assistance signed in Rio de Janeiro, intended to protect Western Hemisphere from foreign intervention

Ciro Alegría's *El mundo es ancho y ajeno*

Octavio Paz' *Entre la piedra y el sol*

Vicente Huidobro's *Ver y palpar* and *El ciudadano del olvido*

Jaime Torres Bodet's *Nacimiento de Venus y otros relatos*

José María Argueda's *Yawar Fiesta*

1942 Jorge Luis Borges' *El jardín de senderos que se bifurcan*

Samuel Eichelbaum's *Un tal Servando Gómez*

Cecília Meireles' *Vaga Música*

Alfonso Reyes' *Ultima Tule* and *Prolegómenos a la teoría literaria*

1943 Jorge Amado's *Terras do Sem Fim*

José Lins do Rego's *Fogo Morto*

1943– Reinaldo Arenas (Cuba)

1944 Brazilian Expedition Force sent to Italy to cooperate with United States in World War II

Jorge Luis Borges' *Ficciones*

Jorge Mañach's *Historia y estilo*

1944–1954 Guatemalan Revolution

1945 Getúlio Vargas overthrown in Brazil

Gabriela Mistral of Chile wins Nobel Prize in literature, the first Latin American so honored

João Cabral de Melo Neto's *O Engenheiro*

Carlos Drummond de Andrade's *A Rosa do Poro*

Cecília Meireles' *Mar Absoluto e Outros Poemas*

Graciliano Ramos' *Infância*

1946 Miguel Ángel Asturias' *El señor presidente*

Emilio Ballagas' *Mapa de la poesía negra americana*

João Guimarães Rosa's *Sagarana*

Javier Villaurrutia's *Nostalgia de la muerte*

1946–1955 Juan Perón, president of Argentina (and again 1973–1974)

1947 Nicolás Guillén's *El son entero* (. . .)

Jorge de Lima's *Poemas Negros*

Pablo Neruda's *Alturas de Macchu Picchu* and *Tercera residencia (1935–1945)*

Agustín Yáñez' *Al filo del agua*

1948 Organization of American States (OAS) charter signed in Bogotá

Leopoldo Marechal's *Adán Bueno-sayres*

Ernesto Sábato's *El túnel*

1948–1956 Manuel A. Odría rules Peru

1948–1966 "La violencia" in Colombia

1949 Miguel Ángel Asturias' *Hombres de maíz* and *Viento fuerte*

Jorge Luis Borges' *El Aleph*

Alejo Carpentier's *El reino de este mundo*

José Lezama Lima's *La fijeza*

Dinah Silveira de Queiroz' *Margarita La Rocque*

Érico Veríssimo's *O Tempo e o Vento 1: "O Continente"* (2: *"O Retrato,"* appeared in 1951; 3: *"O Arquipélago,"* in 1961; 4: *"O Arquipélago,"* in 1962)

1950 Juan Carlos Onetti's *La vida breve*

Octavio Paz' *El laberinto de la soledad*

1951 Jorge Luis Borges' *La muerte y la brújula*

Julio Cortázar's *Bestiario*

Manuel Rojas' *Hijo de ladrón*

Octavio Paz' *¿Aguila o sol?*

1952 Evita Perón dies of cancer

Alberto Blest Gana's *Durante la reconquista*

René Marqués' *La carreta*

1952–1964 Bolivian Revolution

1953 Alejo Carpentier's *Los pasos perdidos*

Juan Rulfo's *El llano en llamas*

1954 Getúlio Vargas, in his second term as president of Brazil, commits suicide

CIA overthrows President Jacobo Arbenz of Guatemala

Juan José Arreola's *La hora de todos*

Miguel Ángel Asturias' *El papa verde*

Adolfo Bioy Casares' *El sueño de los héroes*

Carlos Drummond de Andrade's *Fazendeiros do Ar e Poesia Até Agora*

Nicanor Parra's *Poemas y antipoemas*

Dinah Silveira de Queiroz' *A Muralha*

1954– Alfredo Stroessner dominates Paraguay

1955 Perón and his cabinet excommunicated from Catholic Church

Marco Denevi's *Rosaura a las diez*

Gabriel García Márquez' *La hojarasca*

Juan Rulfo's *Pedro Páramo*

Jaime Torres Bodet's *Tiempo de arena*

1956 Mario Benedetti's *Poemas de la oficina*

João Cabral de Melo Neto's *Morte e Vida Severina*

João Guimarães Rosa's *Grande Sertão: Veredas* and *Corpo de Baile*

Octavio Paz' *El arco y la lira*

1957 Rosario Castellanos' *Balún Canán*

José Donoso's *Coronación*

René Marqués' *La muerte no entrará en palacio*

Octavio Paz' *Piedra de sol*

Ariano Suassuna's *O Auto da Compadecida*

1958 Jorge Amado's *Gabriela Cravo e Canela*

José María Arguedas' *Los ríos profundos*

Emilio Carballido's *Medusa*

Alejo Carpentier's *Guerra del tiempo*

Carlos Fuentes' *La región más transparente*

Jorge de Lima's *Invenção de Orfeu*

Octavio Paz' *La estación más violenta*

1959 Carlos Fuentes' *Las buenas conciencias*

1959–64 Rómulo Betancourt serves as first legitimately elected president of Venezuela; he completes entire term and is electorally succeeded

1959– Cuban revolution begins with advent of Fidel Castro to power; Agrarian Reform Law nationalizes property

1960 Brasília inaugurated as new capital of Brazil

Miguel Ángel Asturias' *Los ojos de los enterrados*
Jorge Luis Borges' *El hacedor*
Mario Benedetti's *La tregua*
Guillermo Cabrera Infante's *Así en la paz como en la guerra*
Clarice Lispector's *Laços de Família*
Augusto Roa Bastos' *Hijo de hombre*
Salvador (Salarrué) Salazar Arrué's *La espada y otras narraciones*
Agustín Yáñez' *La tierra pródiga*

1961 U.S. president John F. Kennedy announces Alliance for Progress
CIA-backed Bay of Pigs invasion fails in attempt to overthrow Castro; United States breaks diplomatic relations with Cuba
Paraguay is last nation in Latin America to grant women the right to vote
Enrique Anderson Imbert's *El grimorio*
Miguel Ángel Asturias' *El alhajadito*
Marco Denevi's *Ceremonia secreta*
Gabriel García Márquez' *El coronel no tiene quien le escriba*
Clarice Lispector's *A Maçã no Escuro*
Juan Carlos Onetti's *El astillero*
Ernesto Sábato's *Sobre héroes y tumbas*

1962 Cuban missile crisis ends in withdrawal of Soviet missiles in Western Hemisphere
Juan José Arreola's *Confabulario total*
Alejo Carpentier's *El siglo de las luces*
Rosario Castellanos' *Oficio de tinieblas*
Carlos Drummond de Andrade's *Lição de Coisas*
Carlos Fuentes' *La muerte de Artemio Cruz*
Gabriel García Márquez' *Los funerales de la Mamá Grande*
Luis Alberto Heireman's *El abanderado* and *Versos de ciego*

1963 Enrique Anderson Imbert's *Vigilia*
Juan José Arreola's *La feria*
Miguel Ángel Asturias' *Mulata de tal*
Julio Cortázar's *Rayuela*
Mario Vargas Llosa's *La ciudad y los perros*
Egon Wolff's *Los invasores*

1964 Brazilian military deposes President João Goulart and establishes dictatorship

Luis Alberto Heireman's *Puerta de salida*
Juan Carlos Onetti's *Juntacadáveres*

1965 United States invades and occupies Dominican Republic
Enrique Anderson Imbert's *El gato de Cheshire*
Luis Alberto Heireman's *Buenaventura*
José Triana's *La noche de los asesinos*

1966 Argentine military ousts President Arturo Illia and establishes dictatorship
José Donoso's *El lugar sin límites* and *Este domingo*
José Lezama Lima's *Paradiso*
Leopoldo Marechal's *El banquete de Severo Arcángelo*
Mario Vargas Llosa's *La casa verde*

1967 Miguel Ángel Asturias of Guatemala wins Nobel Prize in literature
Ernesto "Che" Guevara dies
Guillermo Cabrera Infante's *Tres tristes tigres*
Macedonio Fernández' *Museo de la novela de la Eterna*
Griselda Gambaro's *El campo*
Gabriel García Márquez' *Cien años de soledad*
Octavio Paz' *Corriente alterna*
Severo Sarduy's *De donde son los cantares*

1968 Peruvian military coup establishes dictatorship under General Juan Velasco Alvarado
Military coup in Panama led by General Omar Torrijos Herrera
Gregório de Mattos' *Obras Completas*
Manuel Puig's *La traición de Rita Hayworth*

1969 Reinaldo Arenas' *El mundo alucinante*
Adolfo Bioy Casares' *Diario de la guerra del cerdo*
Mario Vargas Llosa's *Conversación en La Catedral*

1970 For the first time, the number of urban Latin Americans equals the number of rural Latin Americans
In Argentina leftist guerrillas kidnap and murder former president Aramburo and a decade of unrest follows
José Donoso's *El obsceno pájaro de la noche*

José Lezama Lima's *La cantidad hechizada*

Leopoldo Marechal's *Megafón, o la guerra*

1970–1973 President Salvador Allende undertakes profound reforms in Chile

1971 Pablo Neruda of Chile wins Nobel Prize in literature

Mario Benedetti's *El cumpleaños de Juan Angel*

1972 Earthquake devastates city of Managua

Jorge Díaz' *El lugar donde mueren los mamíferos*

Gabriel García Márquez' *La increible y triste historia de la cándida Eréndira y de su abuela desalmada*

Severo Sarduy's *Cobra*

Luisa Valenzuela's *El gato eficaz*

1973 Chilean military overthrows president Salvador Allende and establishes dictatorship under General Augusto Pinochet

Alejo Carpentier's *Concierto barroco*

Lygia Fagundes Telles' *As Meninas*

Mario Vargas Llosa's *Pantaleón y las visitadoras*

1974 Octavio Paz' *Los hijos del limo: Del romanticismo o la vanguardia*

Augusto Roa Bastos' *Yo el supremo*

1974–1976 Isabel Perón serves as president of Argentina; first woman chief of state in Western Hemisphere

1975 Quechua recognized as official language of Peru along with Spanish

Carlos Fuentes' *Terra nostra*

Gabriel García Márquez' *El otoño del patriarca*

1976 General Videla launches the "Dirty War" against leftist guerrillas in Argentina

First International Women's Year Conference convenes in Mexico City

Manuel Puig's *El beso de la mujer araña*

1977 Luisa Valenzuela's *Como en la guerra*

Mario Vargas Llosa's *La tía Julia y el escribidor*

1978 Panama and United States sign treaty returning Canal Zone to Panamanian control and putting Canal under Panamanian direction by 1999

José Donoso's *Casa de campo*

Severo Sarduy's *Maitreya*

1979 Nicaraguan revolution

Guillermo Cabrera Infante's *La Habana para un infante difunto*

Alejo Carpentier's *El arpa y la sombra*

Griselda Gambaro's *Dios no nos quiere contentos*

1981 Carlos Drummond de Andrade's *Esquecer para Lembrar*

Gabriel García Márquez' *Crónica de una muerte anunciada*

Mario Vargas Llosa's *La guerra del fin del mundo*

1982 Argentina invades Falkland Islands and loses war with Great Britain

Gabriel García Márquez of Colombia wins Nobel Prize in literature

Marco Denevi's *Araminta, o El poder*

José Donoso's *Cuatro para Delfina*

Osvaldo Dragún's *Historias para ser contadas*

1983 President Raúl Alfonsín represents return to civilian government in Argentina

United States intervenes in Grenada

Reinaldo Arenas' *El palacio de las blanquísimas mofetas*

João Cabral de Melo Neto's *Auto do Frade*

Severo Sarduy's *Colibrí*

Luisa Valenzuela's *Cola de lagartija*

1984 Griselda Gambaro's *Lo impenetrable*

Mario Vargas Llosa's *Historia de Mayta*

1985 Tancredo Neves elected president of Brazil, marking return to democracy; he dies before taking office, and Vice-President José Sarney assumes the presidency

Adolfo Bioy Casares' *La aventura de un fotógrafo en La Plata*

Jorge Luis Borges' *Los conjurados*

Carlos Fuentes' *El gringo viejo*

Gabriel García Márquez' *El amor en los tiempos del cólera*

Nicanor Parra's *Hojas de Parra*

1986 José Donoso's *La desesperanza*

Mario Vargas Llosa's *¿Quién mató a Palomino Molero?*

1987 Carlos Fuentes' *Cristóbal nonato*

LATIN
AMERICAN
WRITERS

Bartolomé de las Casas

(1474–1566)

Javier Malagón

There has been a tendency to present Bartolomé de las Casas not only as the sole "defender of the Indians," but also as the pioneer and forerunner of Indians' rights. It should not be forgotten, however, that when Las Casas had just been granted an *encomienda* (an estate of land that included the inhabiting Indians), a Dominican friar, Antón de Montesinos, was preaching in the cathedral of Santo Domingo on 30 November and 7 December 1511 (the first and second Sundays of Advent), before the viceroy, Diego Colón, royal officials of Hispaniola, and "all the learned jurists that there were" in Hispaniola, denouncing the conditions in which the Indians lived and worked. This sermon was not a personal position, but rather represented the opinion of the small Dominican community headed by Pedro de Córdoba, author of *Doctrina cristiana* (Christian Doctrine), in which he affirms the equality of Indian and Spaniard, and therefore the right of the Indian to human treatment.

It is, however, Bartolomé Casaus of Seville, whose last name was Hispanicized and definitively adopted as Casas, who has been called "the defender of the Indians," as if he had been the only one who took this position. But in fact, already before him Montesinos confronted both the crown and those who tried to abuse the native population as well as the immi-

grants (who, without power or material goods, could sell the only thing they had, their ability to work); and the position of "defense" of the native was also adopted by other members of religious orders, by lay clergy, by royal and local officials, and even by private citizens, both Creoles and residents of the peninsula.

Las Casas' birthplace has generally been assumed to be one of the parishes of San Lorenzo, San Vicente, or Magdalena of Seville. Born in August 1474, son of Pedro de las Casas, native of Tarifa (Cadiz), he belonged on his father's side to a lineage of converted Jews. His mother, Isabel de Sosa of Seville, was from an old Christian family. Las Casas' contact with the New World began even before the voyages of Christoper Columbus, since his uncle, Juan de Peñalosa, a *contino* (royal official), was sent to Palos in 1492 to aid the leaders of the expedition in recruiting sailors for the discoverer's ships. Upon Columbus' return, Las Casas witnessed his arrival in Seville, accompanied by an "ostentatious show of Indians, parrots, and *papagallos.*" On Columbus' second voyage, the contact was more direct, since Las Casas' father participated in it in search of riches to head off the bankruptcy of his modest business. Las Casas' father returned five years later, bringing with him a Taino boy whom he gave to his son Bartolomé, who

1

used the boy as a page to accompany him in his wanderings in Seville. Another paternal uncle of Las Casas, Francisco de Peñalosa, also embarked on Columbus' second voyage as *jefe de armas*. Diego de Peñalosa, a scribe in Hispaniola (1494), and Gabriel, an *encomendero* (holder of an *encomienda*) in Higüey (from 1514), were also uncles of Las Casas. Las Casas' first cousin, Juan de Sosa, participated in the conquest of Peru, and years later his sister Catalina went to the Indies with her son Augustín de las Casas.

Las Casas' childhood was spent in the city of his birth, where his primary education took place in the cathedral school. He was a member of the Sevillian militias that fought against the Moorish inhabitants of Granada in 1497, a struggle which Las Casas was to remember later in one of his writings. In 1498 he may have studied the Latin classics under the learned master Antonio de Nebrija. In Seville he also received his humanistic education, and it is likely that he entered the lower religious orders there in order that he might later aspire to the position of *doctrinero* (priest in an Indian parish) in Hispaniola.

He departed for the New World with the expedition of Nicolás de Ovando in 1502. When he arrived in Santo Domingo he participated in the military suppression of a general uprising among the Indians. As a result of his good service, he obtained a sizable number of Indians in Higüey. He also had, next to the Xanique River, a landed estate, and in addition, he had in Vega Real large estates which, by his own account, were worth more than 100,000 *castellanos* each year. In 1506–1507 he went to Rome, where he probably entered the diaconate. From there he returned to Hispaniola. He went to Cuba in 1513, and accompanied Diego Velázquez and Pánfilo de Narváez in military expeditions, obtaining a considerable area of land near the port of Xagua. In Cuba, he led a busy life, profiting from agricultural pursuits, sending Indians from his lands into the mines to extract gold and prepare fields for planting. By this time Las Casas was already a priest; he regarded the Indians as infidels and believed that he had the obligation of introducing them to Christian doctrine.

In Hispaniola, in addition to his activities on his *encomiendas*, Las Casas served as a *doctrinero* (1510–1512), and was ordained a presbyter, perhaps by the bishop of Puerto Rico, Alonso Manso. As an *enco-*

mendero, the Las Casas of those days did not relinquish his rights without a struggle.

With Easter approaching in 1514, Las Casas and another priest were the only clergymen in Cuba. Las Casas decided to go to the village of Sancti Spiritus to preach. As he was studying the sermons he began to ponder the poverty and servitude in which the Indians were living. In agreement with his partner Pedro Rentería, he turned over his estate to Governor Velázquez (June 1514), deciding to dedicate his life to the defense of the native Indians. He then went to Hispaniola, where he visited friar Pedro Córodoba, pioneer of the defense of the Indians. From Hispaniola he returned to Seville and to the royal court, where he made pleas for legal reform and for the punishment of corrupt officials on both sides of the ocean. As a result of his efforts, three Jeronymite friars were sent to Hispaniola to "fix matters," and Las Casas was sent with them as their adviser and as Procurator and Protector of the Indians (1516). After strong disagreements with the friars, Las Casas returned to Spain, where for the next five years he very vigorously promoted his ideas. Finally he obtained a grant of a parcel of land in Venezuela in order to carry out his project of colonization with Spanish peasants. The project failed because many of the seventy colonists recruited by Las Casas deserted when they arrived in Puerto Rico.

After the failure of this enterprise, Las Casas in 1523 went to Hispaniola and decided to enter the Order of Preachers (Dominicans), in the monastery maintained by the order in Santo Domingo. He resided in Hispaniola eight years, mainly in the convent of Puerto Plata, where he dedicated himself to study and to religious life. In 1531 he sent to the Council of the Indies a long letter containing a plan for governing the New World. In that year he went to Mexico, where he experienced a series of conflicts (with the *cabildo* of Mexico City and with some Dominican prelates). While in Mexico, he was ordered to go to Peru. It is not known why he did not go, but he returned to Hispaniola, where in January 1534 he participated in the peaceful subjugation of the Indian strongman Enriquillo. In June of the following year he accompanied Tomás de Berlanga (bishop of Panama) to Berlanga's new post and then Las Casas and three other friars embarked for Peru.

They never reached their destination because of bad sailing conditions, and after almost three months they returned and landed in Nicaragua, where Las Casas would spend more than two years. Later he traveled to Guatemala and established his residence there in 1536. The same year Las Casas and a few other New World Dominicans drew up several petitions to Pope Paul III, who on the basis of these reports promulgated his *Bulla sublimis Deus* (2 June 1537), affirming the rationality of the Indians. Las Casas participated in the meeting of the Chapter of the Order in Mexico (1539), after which he traveled to Spain.

During his years on the peninsula, the emperor on 20 November 1542 promulgated New Laws, which responded in part to the ideas of Las Casas. Las Casas, however, was not satisfied with several points and released a letter suggesting a series of amendments. Prince Philip added certain complementary dispositions that, together with the main body of the Laws, seemed to prove the triumph of Las Casas' ideas, including, according to Giménez Fernández, "the suppression of the Conquest, the liquidation of the *encomienda* system, and the care and good treatment of the Indians." Las Casas was designated bishop of Chiapas and consecrated in the convent of San Pablo de Sevilla on 30 March 1544. He left shortly afterward in the fleet of the viceroy's widow, María de Toledo, destined for Hispaniola, from which he was to travel to Mexico. He arrived at the Royal City of Chiapas at the beginning of 1545. His religious work encountered a great number of difficulties: opposition from the faithful, and disagreements with the clergy (he withdrew confessional privileges from almost all the priests), with royal authorities (he excommunicated the president of the Audience of Guatemala), and even with the bishops of neighboring dioceses. Scarcely a year after arriving at his bishopric, he went to Mexico to participate in a meeting of bishops, where he disagreed with, among others, Viceroy Antonio de Mendoza, who opposed any discussion of the legal status and freedom of the Indians or of the crown's obligations toward them. Las Casas decided to return to Spain to obtain the support of the emperor. He embarked in Veracruz but disembarked in the Azores upon receiving news of official disapproval of his conduct. From there he went to Lisbon

and traveled to Salamanca, arriving in May of 1547. This was to be his last voyage; he remained on the peninsula until his death nineteen years later.

Las Casas' confrontation with the emperor's historian, Juan Ginés de Sepúlveda, occurred because Las Casas managed to prevent the publication of Sepúlveda's work, *Democrates alter*. In this work Sepúlveda reiterated his thesis that Indians were "slaves by nature" and thus the wars against them were justified. Sepúlveda, in turn, managed through the Council of the Indies to order the removal of the manuscript or printed copies of Las Casas' *Confessionario* (Confessional), which Las Casas had distributed in his diocese. These events, together with the general alarm caused by the attacks and counterattacks of supporters and foes of the Indians, led the Royal and Supreme Council of the Indies to convoke a meeting. Participants in this meeting included theologians, jurists, and specialists in canonical law, such as Domingo de Soto, Melchor Cano, Bartolomé Carranza, and also Las Casas and Sepúlveda, who were invited to present their respective opinions about "how to constitute the laws according to which the Catholic faith was to be preached." The sessions lasted from July to September of 1550, at which time Domingo de Soto prepared a summary in Spanish of the arguments of both expositors. At about the middle of the next year, there was a second meeting. Although no formal conclusions were reached, subsequent policies of the council were mostly inspired by Las Casas' theses.

During these last years of his life, Las Casas abandoned the political struggle he knew to be lost, dedicating himself instead to the recruitment of zealous bishops and groups of religious men and missionaries for the work in the Indies. He completed and revised his two major works on the New World, and wrote about a number of highly controversial subjects: the *encomienda* system, preaching, personal liberty, conquest, restitution, and the titles of sovereignty of the kings of Castile. He traveled to Salamanca to attend the Chapter of the Order, and went from there to Seville to recruit missionaries (1552). In Seville he published his famous "Treatises," which he gave to a group of clergymen who were embarking for the Indies. Then he went to Toledo, residing in the convent of Saint Peter the Martyr, and from there to Madrid in order to be near the court. He settled in the capital in 1562. He died in the convent of Our Lady of Atocha on 18 July 1566. In fulfillment of his wishes, his remains, which had been buried in Madrid, were moved years later to the convent of Saint Gregory of Valladolid.

"I have written many pages, more than two thousand in Latin and Romance," said Las Casas in a bilingual letter in 1562, which was probably sent to other members of his order in Chiapas. Las Casas' statement was perhaps too modest. Although much of his work has not been published until modern times, the work published in Las Casas' day would fill the two thousand pages to which he referred.

Las Casas was a prolific writer, as evidenced by his immense series of letters, reports, presentations, opinions, petitions, entreaties, proclamations, tracts, and histories, and especially his abundant correspondence. He corresponded with members of his order, colonizers, authorities on the peninsula and in America, the Council of the Indies, university scholars, and even with the king himself and with the Holy Father. Agustín Yáñez, the Mexican historian, says of the work of Las Casas that "his writings run the gamut from natural and political history, from the theological and judicial treatise, to the pamphlet," and adds that "it seems impossible that voyages and vicissitudes have left time and composure to write so copiously."

During Las Casas' life, a minimal part of his writings was published. As Giménez Fernández, professor at the University of Seville, tells us, "in order to give a summarizing body of doctrine to the missionaries he was sending to Chiapas, to his followers there and to his friends scattered from Chile to Texas," he had "private copies of seven so-called Treatises made in Seville in 1552, where he happened to be at the time." *Avisos y reglas para confesores* (Warnings and Rules for Confessors) contains his pastoral letter of 20 March 1545, in which absolution was denied to "all those who did not set their slaves free and make restitution for that which had been extorted from them," as well as clarifications of this letter made at the Council of the Indies. *Treinta proposiciones muy jurídicas* (Thirty Very Judicial Propositions, written possibly in 1549) was pre-

sented before the Council of the Indies as a response to allegations that Las Casas did not accept the authority of the king over the Indians. *Una disputa o controversia entre . . . Bartholomé de las Casas . . . y el doctor Ginés de Sepúlveda . . .* (Dispute and Controversy Between Bartolomé de las Casas and Dr. Ginés de Sepúlveda) is a summary prepared by Domingo de Soto of the session held in Valladolid in 1550, with the addition of the responses of the second session (1551), which took place in that same city. *De los indios que se han hecho en ellas* [Indias] *esclavos* (About the Indians Who Have Been Made Slaves in Them [the Indies]) was apparently prepared for the meeting of bishops in Mexico (1546), and later was presented to the Council of the Indies, when the council commissioned Las Casas to present in writing his feelings on this subject. *Tratado comprobatorio del Imperio soberano 'y principado universal que los Reyes de Castilla y León tienen sobre las Indias . . .* (The Treatise in Proof of the Sovereign Empire and Universal Principality that the Kings of Castile and León Have over the Indies, early 1553), states that said kings possess

> a most just title to the sovereign or universal or high empire of all the area which we call the Indian Ocean, and they are sovereign princes and supreme and natural lords and emperors over the kings and natural lords of the Indies, by virtue of the authority, concession, and grant that the Holy Apostolic Seat interposed and made for them.

This is compatible with the fact that the kings and natural lords of the Indians "have administration, jurisdiction, rights, and dominion over the subjected peoples . . ." *Principia . . . ad . . . defendendam justitiam Yndorum* (Principles for the Defense of the Justice to Indians, early 1553) is a summary in Latin of another, longer work published outside Spain after Las Casas' death. *Octavo remedio contra los repartimientos de indios* (Eighth Remedy Against the Consignments of Indians) was printed on 17 August 1552 by the printer Juan Cromemberger, of Germanic origin, also in Seville.

Finally, the work that was to become a famous, inflammatory libel against Spain, the *Brevísima relación de la destrucción de Indias* (*The Devastation of the Indies: A Brief Account*, 1552) was translated into

Dutch (1578), French (1579), English (1583), German (1597), and Latin (1598), with the engravings of Theodore de Bry. Despite its exaggerations and falsifications, which even Las Casas' admirers and followers recognize, the pamphlet served as a point of attack for the enemies of the Spanish Empire. The Dutch, for example, used this work to kindle the hatred of rebellious patriots toward the Spanish rule: between 1578 and 1670, there appeared twenty-seven Dutch editions of the booklet. The *Account* was used in a similar way by other countries. In less than one century after its publication, eight editions appeared in Italian, six in French, four in German, two in English, and two in Latin. In Spain the work was not reprinted until 1646, in Catalonia, as a part of the policy of France against Philip IV.

Of the numerous writings of Las Casas, only these treatises were printed before his death. Despite the doubtful value of their theological, historical, sociological, and political content, they served well to propagandize Las Casas' ideas. He availed himself of the respect inspired by his title of bishop, and had the treatises printed without royal license or the permission of his superiors in the order. The Franciscan Toribio de Motolinía, in the Indies, was surprised that the Royal Council would authorize the printing of such books, until he later discovered that they had appeared without any such authorization. Juan Ginés de Sepúlveda also accuses Las Casas of having done this without "license."

As for the rest of his writings, including the three large works—*Apologética historia sumaria* (Summary Apologetical History), *Historia de las Indias* (*History of the Indies*), and *De unico vocationis modo omnium gentium ad veram religionem* (The Only Method of Attracting All People to the True Faith)—they were in some cases known only through copies of the originals that Las Casas bequeathed, with the rest of his work, to the Dominicans of the monastery of Saint Gregory of Valladolid. There was some attempt to publish *De unico vocationis* during Las Casas' lifetime. Las Casas' last known writing asks Pope Pius V "to have said book examined, and, if found worthy, printed. . . ." As for the other works, like the *History of the Indies*, Las Casas prohibited that they be published until at least forty years had passed since his death. Some of the known writings of the "procurator

of Indians" had not yet been printed by the second half of the twentieth century.

The *Apologética historia sumaria cuanto a las cualidades, disposición, ciclo y suelo destas tierras, y condiciones naturales, policías, repúblicas, manera de vivir e costumbres de las gentes destas Indias occidentales y meridionales cuyo imperio soberano pertenece a los Reyes de Castilla* (Summary Apologetical History of the Qualities, Disposition, Description, Sky, and Soil of These Lands, And Natural Conditions, Politics, Republics, Way of Living and Customs of These Western and Southern Indies Whose Sovereign Empire Belongs to the Kings of Castile, first printed in full in 1951) is without doubt one of the first works in which the New World is treated like a spectacle. As La Casas says, he began to write the *Apologética historia*, or, rather, to collect the material for it, when he was living in the monastery in the north of Hispaniola in 1527. Originally, he planned to include it in his general history of the Indies, "but, because the subject requires a large treatise, and because it is very diffuse and slightly less than infinite, since infinite nations are to be described, I therefore am resolved to leave it to be written separately" (*History of the Indies* 1, p. 67).

This work consists of 267 chapters (the proposed brevity was not achieved) and an epilogue. As a good scholastic, Las Casas fills his writings with quotations. In addition to the obligatory quotations from Aristotle, there are citations from 246 authors with a total of 448 works. The cited writers are mainly Greek and Roman classics, with the addition of Christian, Jewish, and Arab medieval writers, including Mohammed. There is no lack of contemporary writers or writers from the historical past, such as Marcus Martial, Marcus Quintilian, and Lucius Columella, Saint Isidore of Seville, Alphonse X the Wise, Juan Luis Vives, Averroës, *el Tostado*, and all those who participated in the discovery, conquest, and conversion of the New World: Columbus, Hernán Cortés, Francisco Pizarro, Álvar Núñez Cabeza de Vaca, Andrés Olmos, Father Pane, Motolinía, and others. He intentionally ignores Gonzalo Fernández de Oviedo y Valdés, author of the first book published about the American continent, *Sumario de la natural historia de las Indias* (Summary of the Natural History of the Indies, Toledo, 1526).

This, apparently, was the work that suggested to Las Casas the idea of writing the history of the settlement of the Spaniards in the Indies. Las Casas attacks Oviedo on several occasions in his *History* and claims that Oviedo "presumed to write a history about things he never saw." Las Casas was forgetting that he, as well as Oviedo, was able to work largely because of reports he received from correspondents in the territories that were being occupied. There was, however, one difference. In order to assist Oviedo in writing his *Sumario*, the crown ordered on 15 October 1532 that he be sent information about "history, land relationships, and other things."

In the *Apologética historia*, Las Casas had a well-defined purpose. This consists not only of demonstrating the rationality of the Indians, but also that they are "by nature very clever, lively, clear of understanding, and quite capable of the same; universally and naturally of good character and favorably disposed to being brought to and imbued with our Christian religion."

The *History of the Indies* is a polemical work that gives Las Casas' version of the discovery and conquest from 1492 to 1520 (it appears that he originally planned to include events up to 1550, but if this part was written, it has been lost). The work consists of three books with a total of 417 chapters. In the *History*, Las Casas attempts to disprove the statements of others, especially of his "enemy," Fernández de Oviedo. Oviedo was, in a way, fair to Las Casas, describing him as a "reverend and lettered person, of sound doctrine and life," while at the same time labeling him as "fanatical, shallow, and desirous of giving orders."

In order to write the *History*, Las Casas probably began to gather material before 1527, the date when, according to him, he began the writing. He recounts events in which he was an actor or a spectator, or events known to him through those who participated in them. He met most of the people connected with the discovery of the New World: he knew Columbus, whom he saw upon his return from his first journey, and also Columbus' sons Diego and Ferdinand; Vicente Yáñez Pinzón; Alonso de Ojeda; Juan Ponce de León; Ferdinand Magellan; Cortés; Bernal Díaz del Castillo; Father Pané; Father Córdoba; Father Montesinos; the Jeronymite monks; and many others. In

the royal court, he knew kings Carlos I and Philip II and their collaborators. He also knew Spanish officials in the Indies, including Nicolás de Ovando, Velázquez, Viceroy Mendoza, and others whom he confronted on more than one occasion in his struggle for the Indian. He had at his disposition a unique wealth of material, a large part of which has been saved for posterity only thanks to him. It is safe to say that he was familiar with everything published about the Indies in his day.

Opinions of his work and his personality are highly contradictory. For example Lewis Hanke, a supporter of Las Casas, judges his work in the following way: "The *History* is badly organized, the narrative weaves in and out to the confusion of the reader, and sometimes makes curious detours or stops entirely to introduce what appears to modern readers irrelevant chapters . . ." such as "two long chapters on the Nile River, its history, the height to which it rose every year . . ." or "a long discussion of the exact location of the earthly paradise. . . . These digressions are like island obstacles around which his history flows sluggishly and with great difficulty" (Lewis Hanke, *Bartolomé de las Casas; Bookman, Scholar, and Propagandist*, Philadelphia, 1952, p. 26). Menéndez Pidal is harsh in his opinion of Las Casas: "[Due to] that deformative elaboration of all data received, criticism cannot utilize any data from the *History of the Indies* without taking account of the morbid prejudice that unpardonably deforms any judgment of events to which that prejudice is applied." Augustín Yañez states, "It must be repeated often: Las Casas was not a historian but an apologist." On the other hand, Pedro Henríquiez Ureña says that "Las Casas takes care with the form of his writings; in addition, he is occasionally eloquent in indignation, picturesque, and even humoristic in his descriptions of types and characters."

The *History* was first published in 1875. The best edition is that of Agustín Millares, printed in Mexico City in 1951, with a preliminary study by Lewis Hanke.

De unico vocationis modo, written in Latin, is perhaps the least polemical of Las Casas' works. As Hanke says in his introduction to the first edition, printed in Mexico City in 1942 under the direction of Agustín Millares, for those who have read the vigorous fulminations and the tremendous epithets of Las Casas in his *Brief Account* or in his *History*, the moderate language and the eloquent exhortations of this treatise will be a pleasant surprise. It might appear that he is making a special effort here to practice what he has preached. He rarely mentions the Indies and develops his argument on an elevated plane on which only universal truths are considered.

It is supposed that this work was written during his years of residence in Guatemala (1536–1537), and that, as in the case of all his works, he made additions to it throughout his life. He mainly refers to how to preach to the Indian, a "rational being," and instill in him the Catholic faith. His doctrine is no longer an ideal, but rather is based on his thirty-five years of residence, though not continuous, in the New World.

Like the rest of the important works of Las Casas, this treatise remained unpublished until modern times, although excellent summaries appeared in the seventeenth century. The bilingual (Latin-Spanish) edition was made in Mexico, based on the Oaxaca manuscript, but, as Millares points out, "it only contains chapters 5, 6, and 7, with 36, 8, and 6 paragraphs, respectively." *Los tesoros del Perú* (The Treasures of Peru, 1565) is one of his last writings that has remained unpublished until recently; it is not an archaeological or moral work but one more for the purpose of continuing the polemic regarding the theme, so loved by Las Casas, of the justification of the conquest. He considers the presence of Spain valid in those places where the Indians gave their voluntary consent, as it was in la Verapaz, where "the Dominican fathers were and specifically Fra Bartolomé, who peacefully solicited from the Indians the plot of land that they gladly granted," as the editor of the work, Ángel Losada, tells us.

To summarize, Las Casas' work was judged favorably and unfavorably in his own time and again beginning with the nineteenth century, when he regained prominence with the publication of the *History*. He is accused, with some reason, of contributing to the creation of the anti-Spanish "black legend" by publishing the *Devastation of the Indies: A Brief Account*. Menéndez Pelayo accuses the work of fanaticism and of having soiled the national honor. Serrano y Sanz expresses similar opinions, and, in modern times, Menéndez Pidal says that "Las Casas remains foreign to the great historical moment in which he lives, the time of great explorations. . . ." In none of his works "is a single word of praise spoken for the superhuman effort, or even of affectionate compassion for the terrible labors of those lovers of danger and success involved in risk-filled adventures, who suffered hunger, privations and exhaustion with death always in sight. . . ." But Las Casas insists time and again that the Indians are being stripped of their rights, that they are in need, and that they are the object of cruelties.

Today, the movement against Las Casas has lost strength, and he is no longer presented as the enemy of Spain and Spaniards; instead, the positive aspects of his work are taken into account. There is no doubt that he influenced the political direction and methods of governance of the Indies. Some of his declarations, like that contained in *De regia potestate*, can be considered precursors, by four centuries, of current policies and conduct:

> no emperor, king or prince . . . can legitimately . . . cede any part of his country, no matter how insignificant, to another lord; nor can he negotiate concerning the right of sovereignty without the free consent of his subjects . . . and if the king in fact does this against their will or by forcing their consent, he sins mortally and has no political validity.

Because of this, UNESCO presented Las Casas, in his role as an evangelical prophet and in his political criticism, as an ideal on the twenty-fifth anniversary of the Declaration of Human Rights (1973). The fifth centenary of Las Casas' birth (1974) has also been an occasion for holding a number of conferences in Spain, France, and the United States, in which his work has been examined.

Translated from the Spanish by Philip Donley

SELECTED BIBLIOGRAPHY

Editions

Treatises

Del único modo de atraer a todos los pueblos a la verdadera religión [De unico vocationis modo omnium gentium ad veram religionem]. Latin text edited and annotated by Agustín Millares Carlo. Spanish translation by Atenógenes Santamaría. Mexico City, 1942. 2nd ed. Mexico City, 1975.

Los tesoros del Perú. Translated and annotated by Ángel Losada. Madrid, 1958. Bilingual edition.

Tratado de Indias y el Dr. Sepúlveda. Edited and with a preliminary study by Manuel Giménez Fernández. Caracas, 1962.

Tratados. With prologues by Lewis Hanke and Manuel Giménez Fernández, transcriptions by Juan Pérez de Tudela, and translations by Agustín Millares Carlo and Rafael Moreno. 2 vols. Mexico City, 1965.

De regia potestate; o Derecho de autodeterminación. Critical bilingual edition by Luciano Pereña, J. M. Pérez-Prendes, Vidal Abril, and Joaquín Azcárraga. Madrid, 1969. New ed. 1984.

Brevísima relación de la destrucción de las Indias. With an introduction and notes by Manuel Ballesteros Gaibrois. Madrid, 1977. Facsimile of the 1552 edition.

Histories

Historia de las Indias. Edited by Agustín Millares Carlo, with a preliminary study by Lewis Hanke. 3 vols. Mexico City, 1951. Reprinted Mexico City, 1965.

Apologética historia sumaria . . . destas Indias. . . . Edited and with a preliminary study by Edmundo O'Gorman. 2 vols. Mexico City, 1967.

Translations

In Defense of the Indians. Translated, edited, and annotated by Stafford Poole. Chicago, 1974. A translation of a circa 1552 Latin manuscript held by the Bibliothèque Nationale in Paris.

The Devastation of the Indies: A Brief Account. Translated by Herma Briffault. With an introduction by Hans M. Enzensberger. New York, 1974.

History of the Indies. Translated and edited by Andrée Collard. New York, 1971. Based on the edition by Agustín Millares.

A Selection of His Writings. Translated and edited by George Sanderlin. New York, 1971.

The Tears of the Indians. Translated by John Phillips. London, 1656. Reprinted New York, 1972.

Biographical and Critical Studies

Biographies

Giménez Fernández, Manuel. *Breve biografía de fray Bartolomé de las Casas*. Seville, 1966.

Helps, Arthur. *The Life of Las Casas: "The Apostle of the Indies."* London, 1868. New ed. 1970. With an introduction by Lewis Hanke.

Knight, Alice Jones. *Las Casas, "The Apostle of the Indies."* New York, 1917.

Mahn-Lot, Marianne. *Bartolomé de las Casas: L'Evangile et la force*. Paris, 1964.

Martínez, Manuel María, O.P. *Fray Bartolomé de las Casas, el gran calumniado*. Madrid, 1955.

Menéndez Pidal, Ramón. *El Padre las Casas: Su doble personalidad*. Madrid, 1963.

Ortiz Vidales, Salvador. *Fray Bartolomé de las Casas*. Mexico City, 1937.

Quintana, Manuel José. "Fray Bartolomé de las Casas." In *Vida de españoles célebres* 3. Madrid, 1833. New ed. Buenos Aires, 1943.

Yáñez, Agustín. *Fray Bartolomé de las Casas: El conquistador conquistado*. Mexico City, 1942.

Critical Studies

Bataillon, Marcel, and André Saint-Lu. *Las Casas et la défense des Indes*. Paris, 1971. Translated into Spanish by Javier Alfaya and Barbara McShane as *El Padre Las Casas y la defensa de los indios*. Barcelona, 1976.

Bayle, Constantino, S.J. *España en las Indias: Nuevos ataques y neuvas defensas*. 2nd ed. Madrid, 1939.

Carbia, Romulo D. *Historia de la leyenda negra hispanoamericana*. Buenos Aires, 1943.

Carro, Venancio, O.P. *La teología y los teólogos-juristas españoles ante la conquista de América*. Madrid, 1944. 2nd ed. Salamanca, 1951.

Friede, Juan. *Bartolomé de las Casas*. Bogotá, 1974.

_____, and Benjamin Keen. *Bartolomé de las Casas in History*. DeKalb, Ill., 1971.

Giménez Fernández, Manuel. *Bartolomé de las Casas*. 2 vols. Seville, 1953–1960. Reprinted Madrid, 1984.

Hanke, Lewis. *The First Social Experiments in America*. Cambridge, Mass., 1935.

_____. *The Spanish Struggle for Justice in the Conquest of America*. Philadelphia, 1949.

_____. *Bartolome de las Casas: An Interpretation of His Life and Writing*. The Hague, 1951.

_____. *Bartolome de las Casas: Historian. An Essay in Spanish Historiography*. Gainesville, Fla., 1952.

Imbrighi, Gastone. *Bartolomeo las Casas: Note per una storia della problematica colombiana*. Rome, 1972.

Losada, Ángel. *Fray Bartolomé de las Casas, a la luz de la moderna crítica histórica*. Madrid, 1970.

Muria, José María. *Bartolomé de las Casas ante la historiografía mexicana*. Mexico City, 1974.

O'Gorman, Edmundo. *Cuatro historiadores de India: Siglo XVI*. Mexico City, 1972.

Ríos y Urruti, Fernando. *Religión y estado en la España del siglo XVI*. Mexico City, 1957.

Wagner, Henry R. *The Life and Writings of Bartolomé de las Casas*. Albuquerque, N. Mex., 1967.

Zavala, Silvio. *La encomienda indiana*. Madrid, 1935.

_____. *New Viewpoints on the Spanish Colonization of America*. Philadelphia, 1943.

Bibliographies

Hanke, Lewis and Manuel Giménez Fernández. *Bartolomé de las Casas: Bibliografía crítica. . . .* Santiago, Chile, 1954.

Hernández Ruizgomez, Almudena, and Carlos González. "Materiales para una bibliografía sobre fray Bartolomé de las Casas." In *El V centenario de Bartolomé de las Casas*. Madrid, 1986.

Gonzalo Fernández de Oviedo y Valdés

(1478–1557)

Luis A. Arocena

The discovery of the New World surprised Europe and aroused its curiosity. News spread rapidly, and men of letters immediately recognized the importance of recording the memorable deeds of the discovery and conquest. The Italian humanist Pietro Martire d'Anghiera, for example, began to chronicle Christopher Columbus' exploits even before they had drawn to an end, and the conquest of the Americas was still unfolding when general histories began to treat these noteworthy events, the odd customs and unfamiliar peoples found there, and the marvels and riches of the lands they inhabited. Gonzalo Fernández de Oviedo y Valdés was among those who realized from the start the importance of this vast and surprising New World, and he began to record it in what was to become his monumental *Historia general y natural de las Indias* (General and Natural History of the Indies, 1851–1855).

Oviedo was thirty-six years old when, in 1514, he arrived for the first time in the new city of Santa María de la Antigua, in Castilla del Oro. He came as a member of the expedition of the infamous Pedrarias Dávila, charged with the duties of general scribe of the armada and king's inspector of the gold foundries. He was to repeat the risky crossing of the Atlantic Ocean eight more times, spending twenty-seven years of his life in the Indies—in Darién, Cuba, Nicaragua, and Santo Domingo—interspersed with fifteen years of residence and work in Spain. With good reason he could boast that he wrote not from hearsay or from the works of others but from his personal acquaintance with those who participated in the discovery and conquest and from his own immediate experience of the physical and moral environment in which they acted.

Already a mature man when he arrived in the Indies, Oviedo brought with him experiences that were to serve him well in his future duties as historian. As a member of the Spanish nobility, he had served in the court of the Catholic kings and had come to know the men responsible for political decision-making and action. Later, the need and desire for new horizons led him to Italy, where he pursued his military and literary interests. In the centers of Renaissance humanism Oviedo learned the Tuscan language, struck up acquaintances with artists and writers, and formed more than one lasting friendship. His humanistic education was almost certainly not as complete as his vanity proclaimed, but at any rate he felt confident of his abilities to reconstruct, to judge, and to write about historic reality. Renaissance thought provided him with the keys to understanding it.

Oviedo's literary interests were not limited to the

11

brilliant new world of the Indies, but it is clear that he was immediately seduced by the amazing landscape and by the drama developing in that inordinate setting. Upon returning to Spain after his second stay in America, he was able to dash off from memory, at the special request of Emperor Charles V, a *Sumario de la natural historia de las Indias* (Summary of the Natural History of the West Indies, published in English as *Natural History of the West Indies*), which he published in 1526. It would be difficult to exaggerate the merits of this brief treatise. In it Oviedo reveals himself to be not only a writer gifted in the description of the copious and multiform nature of the American world but also an alert observer, perspicuous and reliable. He admits his debt to Pliny, the Roman naturalist, but clearly leaves a personal mark on his observations. He may lack systematic exactness, but he delights the appreciative reader by making manifest a world of novelties and wonders, of beauty and horror, of unusual or different forms, of attractions and rejections, of vital impulses and unexpected death. What the *Sumario* may lack in scientific method is more than compensated by the merits of this first vision of nature in the New World as it revealed itself to the joyful immediacy of the author's alert senses.

Oviedo's concern with events in the New World began at an early date. By 1532, when he was appointed official chronicler of the Indies, his diligence as a historian was already established. "Of all those who have passed through here," the *cabildo* (municipal council) of Santo Domingo praised him, "none has seen as much territory as he. He has devoted himself to writing about it and to pondering its secrets and has with good style gathered the relations of many things." Oviedo worked for at least thirty-five years on his *Historia general de las Indias.* This work, divided into three parts and fifty books, covers a period of over fifty years and includes every place in America that had been part of Spain's activities of discovery and conquest through 1549. The author's pride in it extended even to its imposing volume. "My work," he declared happily in part 2 of the *Historia*, "is not a minor one, but among the highest and most copious written by man from Adam forward on such subjects."

Few chroniclers have been as concerned as Oviedo with the material and formal problems encountered in the course of their work; few inform the reader so often of the difficulties that the history of the West Indies presented to the task of historical reconstruction and discourse. Oviedo was bewildered by the infinite physical and cultural variety of the New World. "What mortal mind," he wonders, "could comprehend such diversity of languages, of dress, of customs among the men of these Indies?" The simultaneity of events, which prevented any possibility of the desired linear account, was another aggravating problem. His desire to record everything and not to omit any event from the narration ended by giving the structure of his *Historia general* the character of a compote or a stew, a hodgepodge that Oviedo himself noted with a final, worried resignation.

But beyond discontinuities, digressions, and unconnected and sometimes irritating detail, one finds in this work a receptive consciousness transforming the plurality and diversity of occurrences into objects of historical judgment. A unifying value system—distinguishing just from unjust, laudable from reprehensible, divine from profane, and exhibitions of lust and avarice from acts of heroism—is brought to bear upon the heterogeneity of the observations. Certain ideological presuppositions shape the spirit of the discourse and the nature of the judgments. In Oviedo the characteristics typical of a Spaniard of the sixteenth century are clearly visible: militant religiosity, firm adhesion to the ideals of the nobility and of chivalry, devout allegiance to the institution of the monarchy, and the desire for honor, fame, and fortune. Moreover, he belonged to that group of educated men who in the days of Charles V forged an exalted idea of Spanish life, of Spain as a political entity and of its greatness and imperial destiny. For Oviedo the discovery of a new continent and the imposition of Spanish dominion upon its extensive geography summarized the exaltation of Spain as the consummator of a utopian dream—the Catholicity of the Christian republic. Owing to the influence that these convictions may have had on the historian's judgments, some contemporary critics, somewhat excessive in their condemnation, consider the *Historia general* an example of history in servitude, that is, history written in service to and justification of Spain's imperial interests. But throughout his work

Oviedo will protest again and again his adherence to the truth and the pains he has taken to discover it, as well as his desire to expose it, regardless of whom it would benefit or harm. "I know for certain that I speak the truth in what I write," he notes for the reader, "and I admit that in matters that I did not witness, those who related these events to me could have deceived me." In writing about a particularly difficult situation, he adds: "You will excuse me for talking about these subjects with my usual candor, since my hands are clean and since at this age I am not in need of riches and my soul needs no more sins." Although he may have unintentionally concealed his ideologically conditioned consciousness, Oviedo was determined to narrate a true story.

A fundamental and firmly rooted conviction opens the pages of the *Historia general de las Indias*: the belief in the importance of the events destined to change a hitherto unknown continent into a new world. The journeys of discovery, the conquests, the people and cultures that revealed themselves to the wonder and greed of the conquerors, and a geography excessive both in its bounty and in its challenges constituted in his judgment a reality such as had not been observed in the course of all previous human experience. In the European Renaissance mind, historical occurrences were made intelligible through comparison with the exemplary acts of the Greeks and Romans; according to Oviedo, all of them, even the mythical and legendary, were "jokes and trifles compared with what in these our Indies has been seen and is seen every day in our times." The chronicler was convinced that the magnitude and transcendence of the events in the Indies would permit him to give shape to "a history so elevated and heretofore unseen, so desired and true, so famous and great, and so marvelous and authentic as the one I have in hand."

In the dazzling setting of the New World, the action receives its dramatic character from the conflict of two antagonists: the Spanish conqueror and the conquered Indian. The work of Oviedo has been judged, on the evidence of many texts, as justifying and exalting the Spanish exploits in the Indies. Oviedo did not doubt that the conquest was indeed God's design, that Spain had sufficient claims to legalize the imposition of its political dominion over the Indies and the appropriation of all things, that the subsequent religious and cultural imposition was as justified as the political and economic one, and that the *encomienda* (a grant of land including the inhabiting Indians), as an institution designed to organize and exploit Indian labor, conformed to the needs of the conquest and to the condition of the conquered. In short, Oviedo extols the heroic men of a "nation brimming with virtues" who made possible the incorporation into Christendom of a whole new continent. But this shining portrayal had its dark spots, and the historian-turned-moralist did not fail to recognize and expose them. Some *conquistadores* (conquerors) had committed violent acts and abuses; many had participated in acts of gratuitous cruelty; soldiers and *encomenderos* (holders of an *encomienda*), driven by unlimited greed, had engaged in all kinds of barbarities. Even priests and friars bore heavy sins upon their consciences. "I do not want to give or take away credit from Erasmus nor his colloquies," he notes on one occasion, "but in these Indies things have been seen among such secular priests that it is better to hush them than to stir up anything more on this subject."

Oviedo's attitude toward the Indian, of whose tragedy and collapse he was somewhat more than a mere accredited spectator, has provoked the angriest of criticisms against him. Father Las Casas, in the fervor of his Indian apostolate, called him a malicious servant of the interests of the *conquistador* and the *encomendero*. "Whenever he touches on the Indians in his *Historia*," the Dominican friar accuses, "he never opens his mouth without blaspheming them and annihilating them as much as he possibly can." Las Casas' accusation is at least partially correct. Oviedo feels curiosity, but never sympathy, for the Indian world. With the diligence that earned him the title of the first ethnographer of America, he notes everything in detail—the physical appearance of the Indians, their way of life, their political and social institutions, their languages, religions, and customs—but these observations reveal a certain pleasure in underscoring the darker aspects of the indigenous cultures—their barbarity, primitivism, and cruelty. Oviedo recognizes few virtues in the Indian beyond those suitable to servitude, and in their cultural heritage and values he finds nothing that does not deserve destruction and replacement.

Problems of historical research, composition, and exposition persistently claimed Oviedo's attention. In the *Historia general* he repeatedly discusses the arduous tasks of collecting information in order to uncover the truth. He is no less insistent in noting the difficulties of organizing the collected material and then creating a balanced and meaningful portrayal. In both cases he achieved less than he intended. A history that was in progress even as he attempted to narrate it concealed many events from him, and the immediacy and variety of these events made impossible the kind of orderly composition that Oviedo would have liked to achieve.

Oviedo's writing has virtues and defects. To the modern reader his prose seems heavy, his syntax overinvolved, and the pace of his discourse slow and detailed, with serious lapses into insignificant prattle, digression, or admonition. His tone is familiar; it would appear he is conversing with his readers, winning them over to share privately in his investigations, information, and judgments. "Like a soldier," he states, "I say plainly what I have seen and understood." But there is more to it than what he rhetorically calls "the simplicity of stating the case simply, without flattery or adulation." Sixteenth-century Spanish writing has in the author of *Historia general* a perfect representative of its lexical richness. Oviedo never lacks words to describe the variety of things, to express shades of ideas, to describe a heretofore unimagined physical world to the amazed observer, to penetrate the obscure precincts where human feelings are forged and decisions are made. The author eventually wins over the reader by his savoring of the curious detail, the circumstantial event, the revealing anecdote, the recording of human traits and behavior rescued by him from the turbulent tide of history. Oviedo the chronicler redeems Oviedo the historian.

Las Casas, in an angry attack, labeled Oviedo "a deceiver, hypocrite, inhuman, thief, blasphemer, and liar." These insults are unfair. The man who is revealed through frequent glimpses in the pages of his work is not, certainly, a paragon of virtue. He is vain, greedy, ambitious, prejudiced, and slow to condemn the many inhumanities that he saw or knew were committed in the Indies. But he did not shy away from the dictates of a moral conscience in denounc-

ing the crimes against the Indians, the violence of the *conquistadores* and the abuses of the *encomenderos*, or the excesses of those who in the broad Indian world felt free to give rein to their demonic instincts and passions.

Gonzalo Fernández de Oviedo y Valdés died on 26 June 1557 in the fortress of Santo Domingo, where he had served as commander for more than twenty years. For the old, disenchanted *indiano*, the world of his adventures, dreams, and hopes had long since been reduced to the laborious folios of a chronicle, of a *Historia general* destined to become our most valuable source of knowledge concerning the first fifty years of a truly new world.

Translated from the Spanish by Galen Greaser

SELECTED BIBLIOGRAPHY

First Editions

Libro del muy esforzado e invencible caballero de la fortuna, propriamente llamado don Claribalte que según su verdadera interpretación quiere decir don Félix o bienaventurado. Nuevamente imprimido e venido a ésta lengua castellana: el cual procede por nuevo e galan estilo de hablar. Valencia, 1519.

Respuesta a la epístola moral del almirante. Manuscript in the National Library of Madrid, n.d. (Commentary on a letter of moralizing intention written by Fadrique Enríquez.)

Relación de lo sucedido en la prisión del rey de Francia, desde que fué traido en España, por todo el tiempo que estuvo en ella, hasta que el emperador le dió libertad y volvió en Francia, etc. Manuscript in the National Library of Madrid, n.d.

De la natural historia de las Indias; o, Sumario de la natural historia de las Indias. Toledo, 1526. Reissued Madrid, 1749, 1852.

Libro primero del blasón. Tratado de todas las armas é diferencias dellas, é de los escudos, etc. Manuscript in the National Library of Madrid, n.d. (A treatise on heraldry.)

Catálogo real de Castilla, y de todos los reyes de las Españas e de Nápoles y Sicilia, etc. Manuscript in the National Library of El Escorial, written 1532–1535.

Epílogo real, imperial y pontifical. Manuscript draft of this lost work preserved in the National Library of Madrid, written in 1535.

La historia general de las Indias. Books 1–19. Seville, 1535.

Libro de la camara real del príncipe Don Juan, etc. Madrid, 1870. (Written in 1546.)

Batallas y quincuagenas, escriptas por el Capitán Gonzalo Fernández de Oviedo, etc. Manuscript fragments of this lost work preserved in the National Library of Madrid and in the Real Academia de la Historia, n.d.

Las quincuagenas de los generosos e illustres e no menos famosos reyes, príncipes, duques, marqueses, condes e caballeros e personas notables de España, que escribió el Capitán Gonzalo Fernández de Oviedo y Valdés, etc. Manuscript in the National Library of Madrid. First published edition, edited by Vicente de la Fuente. Madrid, 1880.

Libro de linajes y armas que escribío el Capitán Gonzalo Fernández de Oviedo y Valdés, coronista del emperador Carlos V y de las Indias. Manuscript in the Real Academia de la Historia, n.d.

Historia general y natural de las Indias, islas y tierra firme del mar Océano, etc. Autographic manuscripts in the Real Academia de la Historia. First edition of the complete work, 4 vols. Madrid, 1851–1855.

Modern Editions

Historia general y natural de las Indias, islas y tierra firme del mar Océano, etc., edited by J. Natalicio González. 14 vols. Asunción, 1944–1945.

_____, edited by Juan Pérez de Tudela Bueso. 5 vols. Madrid, 1959.

Libro del muy esforzado caballero Don Claribalte, por Gonzalo Fernández de Oviedo. Facsimile reproduction of first edition. Madrid, 1956.

Las memorias de Gonzalo Fernández de Oviedo, edited by Juan Bautista Avalle-Arce. 2 vols. Chapel Hill, N.C., 1974. (A selection from *Las quincuagenas.*)

De la natural historia de las Indias; o, Sumario de la natural historia de las Indias. Madrid, 1942; Mexico City, 1950.

Biographical and Critical Studies

Álvarez López, Enrique. "Plinio y Fernández de Oviedo." In *Anales de ciencias naturales del Instituto Joseph de*

Acosta 1 and 2. Madrid, 1940. Vol. 1, pp. 40–61; vol. 2, pp. 13–35.

_____. Preliminary study to *De la natural historia de las Indias.* Madrid, 1942.

_____. "La historia natural en Fernández de Oviedo." *Revista de Indias* 17/67–70:541–604 (1957).

Amador de los Ríos, José. "Vida y escritos de Gonzalo Fernández de Oviedo y Valdés." Introduction to *Historia general y natural de las Indias.* Madrid, 1851.

Ballesteros Gaibrois, Manuel. *Vida del madrileño Gonzalo Fernández de Oviedo y Valdés.* Madrid, 1958.

Esteve Barba, Francisco. *Historiografía indiana.* Madrid, 1964. Pp. 59–75.

Gerbi, Antonello. "Gonzalo Fernández de Oviedo." In *La naturaleza de las Indias nuevas. De Cristóbal Colón a Gonzalo Fernández de Oviedo.* Spanish translation by Antonio Alatorre. Mexico City, 1978. Pp. 149–477.

Iglesia, Ramón. *Cronistas e historiadores de la conquista de México.* Mexico City, 1942. Pp. 79–93.

Miranda, José. Introduction to *Sumario de la natural historia de las Indias,* Mexico City, 1950.

O'Gorman, Edmundo. "Gonzalo Fernández de Oviedo y Valdés." In *Cuatro historiadores de Indias.* Mexico City, 1972. Pp. 47–84.

Perez de Tudela Bueso, Juan. "Rasgos del semblante espiritual de Gonzalo Fernández de Oviedo: La hidalguía caballeresca ante el nuevo mundo." *Revista de Indias* 17/69–70:391–444 (1957).

_____. "Vida y escritos de Gonzalo Fernández de Oviedo." Preliminary study to *Historia general y natural de las Indias* 1. Madrid, 1959. Pp. vii–clxxv.

Ramos, Demetrio. "Las ideas de Fernández de Oviedo sobre la técnica de colonización en América." *Cuadernos hispanoamericanos* 32/96:279–289 (1974).

Salas, Alberto M. "Fernández de Oviedo crítico de la conquista y de los conquistadores." *Cuadernos americanos* 74/2:160–170 (1954).

_____. "Fernández de Oviedo." In his *Tres cronistas de Indias: Pedro Mártir de Anglería, Gonzalo Fernández de Oviedo, Fray Bartolomé de las Casas.* Mexico City, 1959, Pp. 63–158.

Bibliography

Turner, Daymond. *Gonzalo Fernández de Oviedo y Valdés: An Annotated Bibliography.* Chapel Hill, N.C., 1967.

Bernal Díaz del Castillo

(ca. 1496–1584)

Luis A. Arocena

Spanish-American historical discourse, rich and varied in form and content, resulted in truly notable works in the sixteenth century. Through these works we witness, amidst exploits and tragedies, noble acts and acts inspired by cruelty, greed, and moral turpitude, and amidst the destruction of old social orders and the difficult efforts of transculturation, the birth of a new historic reality, the formation of a world noted for the novelty of its ethnos and ethos. Few of these many books have attained the testimonial merit of *Historia verdadera de la conquista de la Nueva España* (*The True History of the Conquest of New Spain*), produced by the weary and unsteady hand of Bernal Díaz del Castillo. The fate of this chronicle is significant. Publication of the manuscript was delayed over fifty years, and when it finally appeared in 1632, interest in it was far from overwhelming. Disregarded in its time and almost ignored in the eighteenth century, it began to be appreciated in the following century, when it was also translated into French, English, German, and Hungarian. In our century its multiple editions have enjoyed a popularity that extends far beyond the circle of specialized scholars. Hernán Cortés' old soldier, eager to leave an account of his person and services so that his children and grandchildren could say in truth that "[their] father came to these lands to discover and

win them at his own proper cost, and he spent what fortune he had doing so, and he was in conquest among the first," could hardly have foreseen the long survival and literary prestige of *History*.

Everything that is important about the author's life and personality can be found in and between the lines of this work. His own presence stands out to such an extent that the chronicle becomes, in large measure, an autobiography or, at least, the detailed record of a memory guided by its subjectivity. Born in Medina del Campo around 1496 to a family of scant lineage—he alludes vaguely to his nobility—and scanter financial resources, at the age of eighteen Bernal Díaz went to the Indies with the then common hope of attaining glory and riches. Following a brief and disappointing stay in Darién, he went to Cuba, where he lived for three years in inactivity and poverty. Finally, he managed to enlist in the expedition of Francisco Hernández de Córdoba "to try our fortune"—as he says—"in seeking and discovering new lands." This first experience as a conquistador only garnered him for his share the wounds from three Yucatán Indian arrows, "and one of them was quite serious, in my left, passing straight through the flank."

In 1518 he again enlisted as a soldier in an armada under the command of Juan de Grijalva, bound once more for Yucatán, "because it was rumored that the land was rich and that the buildings were of lime and stone." The eager Bernal Díaz gained little benefit from his second visit and even less, certainly, from the six hundred hatchets the expedition proudly recovered, believing them to be fine gold, only to find out later, to the disappointment of some and the merriment of many, that they were copper. Shortly after returning from this second frustrating mission, he embarked in February 1519 with a new expedition headed again for the tempting coast of Yucatán. The fleet was now under the command of Cortés, and with it, in the service of a great captain, the young man of twenty-three sailed to participate in the conquest of lands, to gain renown, to accumulate gold, and to obtain cities, slaves, and Indians in *encomienda*, compensation for demonstrated merits.

Bernal Diáz' military service did not end with the collapse of the Aztec resistance in Tenochtitlán. He participated in punitive or pacifying expeditions to different regions of the conquered empire, the most important being the expedition that Cortés organized to Honduras. The misery of that expedition's calamitous ending equaled the initial ostentation and promise of the march. In 1540, unhappy with what he considered poor compensation for his merits as a conquistador, Bernal Díaz returned to Spain—he made a second trip in 1550—to procure from the court greater recognition and better benefits. Upon returning to the New World, he abandoned Mexico and established himself as a resident of Santiago de los Caballeros de Guatemala, becoming a *regidor* (councilman) for life of that city's *cabildo* (municipal council). Married to Teresa Becerra, the daughter of a conquistador, whose generous dowry increased his wealth as an *encomendero*, he began to enjoy quiet, carefree days, propitious for the careful recollection of past glory, exploits, and adventurous service. Already in his sixties, Bernal Díaz began writing down his memories, and the result was *The True History of the Conquest of New Spain*.

Bernal Díaz declares, and his statement is confirmed, that he had already begun to write his chronicle when he happened to obtain, among other books, the *Historia de las Indias y Conquista de México* (History of the Indies and Conquest of Mexico, 1552) by Francisco López de Gómara. This work,

produced by Cortés' former private secretary and chaplain, impressed Bernal Díaz greatly and left a lasting influence on his work. He noted in Gómara's book a form of composition in which the account shapes a cohesive and lucid historical portrayal. From then on he did not deviate from Gómara's narrative structure. He contested some circumstantial details, adding information that only he as an eyewitness to the event could know (Gómara was never in Mexico), and documented attitudes, feelings, and judgments expressed by his military companions; but the formal structure of the learned cleric's work was the foundation for his own text. Also, reading Gómara's *Historia* inspired, by way of opposition, the key idea and justification of Bernal Díaz' chronicle. The idea is that Gómara, having allowed his palms to be greased—or so Bernal Díaz maliciously charges—presented the heroic conquest of Mexico as the personal and exclusive triumph of Cortés. Everything happened thanks to his heroic will, his military and political virtues, the superiority of his discernment, his prudent foresight, and his exemplary bravery. This reduction of history to the actions of a single hero greatly irritated Bernal Díaz. He did not deny Cortés' virtues as a military chief and astute politician, but the great captain could not have achieved anything without the vigorous assistance of his company, the captains and soldiers who fulfilled his orders at great sacrifice. So Bernal Díaz unfailingly substitutes Gómara's "Cortés did," "Cortés conquered," "Cortés decided" with "we did," "we conquered," "we decided," and so forth. Reading the texts of Gómara and Gonzalo de Illescas (*Historia pontifical y catholica*, 1569) suggested to him on one occasion this annoyed reflection: "All I can see from these writings and in their chronicles is praise for Cortés, and they silence and conceal our illustrious and famous deeds, by which we enhanced the captain, bringing him the rank of marquis as well as the great wealth and fame and renown that he has." Based on many other statements like this, one critic has stressed the populist nature of Bernal Díaz' chronicle, viewing it as a history in which the individual protagonist is replaced by the collective protagonist. This may be going a bit too far, especially since there is good reason to believe that it would have appealed to the vanity of the old soldierconquerer to substitute more frequently the collective "we" with the singular "I." "Among my companions the strong conquistadores"—he states in one of his final considerations—"for some were very courageous, I was considered as one of the most valiant, and I the most ancient of all, and again I say I, I and I, and repeat that I am the most ancient and have served His Majesty as a very good soldier."

The substantive part of Bernal Díaz' narration does not encompass many years, covering 1517 to 1524, the period of the disastrous expedition to Honduras, the region then called Las Hibueras. However, his remembrances permit him to regress or advance in time beyond these dates and, because he continued to work on his manuscripts to a very advanced age ("I am an old man over eighty-four years old"—he informs us in one of his prologues—"and I have lost my vision and hearing"), the additions and corrections bring his information up to the year 1568.

In the judgment of modern critics the work of Bernal Díaz is a priceless source for the study of the history of the Conquest of Mexico. As important as this is, another aspect contributes to make this chronicle one of the great books of Spanish-American literature, namely, the nature of the historical narrative: the resourcefulness of a writer able to retrieve from the depths of a rich and reliable memory everything that could bear on the animated reconstruction of what had been for him a dramatic life experience. "If I could paint and sculpt their bodies and figures and forms and manners and faces and features"—he says when speaking of his brothers-in-arms—"as I now have them in my mind and sense and memory, . . . I would be able to draw all those I have mentioned as it were to the life, each of them in the manner he entered into battle, and the great spirit they showed." In Bernal Díaz' chronicle, as in no other, the reader gathers a lively and vivid impression of the Spanish conqueror in action. As William H. Prescott has stated in his *History of the Conquest of Mexico* (1843), "he introduces us into the heart of the camp, we huddle round the bivouac with the soldiers, loiter with them on their wearisome marches, listen to their stories, their murmurs of discontent, their plans of conquest, their hopes, their triumphs, their disappointments" (book 5, chapter 7). And, one might add, we see played out the

contradictions of their virtues and defects: compelling religiosity and extreme cruelty, unflinching bravery and inexhaustible greed, the capacity to accept deprivations willingly as well as unbridled carnal appetites, faithfulness to their king and to the law objectifying his will, and a capacity for the greatest infringement of the laws.

Confronting the world of the Spaniard was the world of the conquered, for which Bernal Díaz clearly felt little sympathy. The Indian was, first of all, the enemy who must be conquered and then reduced to servile labor on the encomienda. In addition, he was the practitioner of a bloodthirsty idolatry and other abominable vices and customs. Nevertheless, Bernal Díaz' chronicle suggests that he treated the Indians in his service benevolently, that he objected to the enslavement of prisoners taken in the so-called righteous wars, and that he censured the barbaric custom of branding them with hot irons. Bernal Díaz also expressed surprise and admiration before many aspects of Indian life and culture. The vision of Tenochtitlán reminded him of "the enchantments they tell us of in the story of Amadis." The monumental structures, the exquisite luxury of the palaces, the charm of the perfumed gardens, the prodigies of craftsmanship reflected in the incredible variety and abundance of the markets, appreciatively remembered, inspired a melancholy reflection: "Now all is overthrown and lost, nothing left standing." He admired Moctezuma's dignity and honesty, and the consideration he showed toward him. When he died, Bernal Díaz notes "there was no man among us who knew him and dealt with him who did not mourn him as though he were our father, and it is not to be wondered at, considering how good he was." As for Cuauhtémoc—Guatemuz as Bernal Díaz calls him—he praises his bravery, the steadfastness with which he defended his empire, and the manly way in which he endured his misfortune. That Cortés condemned him to the gallows was a great injustice "and seemed wrong"—he concludes—"to all of us there." Bernal Díaz does not accept Father Las Casas' censure of the cruelties committed by Cortés' conquering army, but he admits that on more than one occasion the violence unleashed on the subjugated Indians went too far.

Numerous passages in Bernal Díaz' chronicle reflect his concern with the subject and the problems related to its exposition. For him the Conquest of Mexico was a feat that could not be compared to any other in the annals of history. Even he, a rank-and-file soldier, could glory in having personally participated "in many more battles and skirmishes than the historians claim for Julius Caesar." He believed this conquest was like all human events, providential. "I say that all our works and victories are by the hand of Our Lord Jesus Christ." Nevertheless, it must not be forgotten, Bernal Díaz insists, that the conquering forces' tenacious will and untiring bravery were the instrument of the service rendered to God and king. Further, their feat must be perpetuated in the memory of men, for this is the mission of history; and when history is true—"we know that truth is a blessed and sacred thing"—the deserving are guaranteed rewards, honor, and fame. His chronicle fulfills this obligation. It is a "True History" because it was written under the dictates of personal experience; as an eyewitness he related events just as they occurred. Bernal Díaz chooses to ignore the subjectivity that may characterize such testimony; and he pays even less attention to the frequent occasions in his discourse in which an ubiquitous and omniscient narrator replaces the immediate observer or the actor himself.

In several passages Bernal Díaz deplores the fact that he lacks the literary aptitude to write in the high style befitting the solemnity of history and greatness of the events under discussion. We have no reason to consider these apologies simply rhetorical; his writing is indeed straightforward, familiar, spontaneous. The reader gets the sense of listening to the conversation of an old soldier sifting through his memories, sometimes accurate and detailed, sometimes repetitive and digressive. His long sentences, enumerative to the point of fatigue, the defects of his constructions, the forms of his syntactical connections, as well as his use of popular expressions, proverbs, trite comparisons, all contribute to a style that imitates oral expression. Yet what may have been rhetorically unacceptable to his erudite contemporaries today contributes to the continuing interest and value of Bernal Díaz' chronicle. No other chronicle in the history of West Indian historiography surpasses it in color, vivacity, drama, or in registering the extremes of human experience.

In *True History* Bernal Díaz was able to sketch adroit portraits of his companions in Cortés' armada.

He does not draw his own, but the frequent glimpses we catch of him in those pages enable us to become familiar with the hopeful young man seeking adventure in the Indies, with the soldier well tested in "bloody and treacherous and difficult battles," and with the old encomendero recalling his exploits among gatherings of friends in his large family home. There is a play of light and shadow in the gradually unfolding personality of Bernal Díaz. He was, without doubt, a soldier of proven bravery (though not a *miles gloriosus*), of a pleasant, loyal, friendly character, humane in the treatment of his Indians and prudent in his public and private affairs. Educated more by life than by books, he had nonetheless enjoyed formative and informative readings. The shadows of this portrait are formed by his extreme vanity, his irksome dissatisfaction with the rewards and benefits he was given, his inclination to gossip and to diminish the prestige of others, and the self-importance that leads him to exalt his own modest accomplishments to heroic levels of action and decision. Someone once ventured to suggest that in his chronicle he praised himself excessively. His response is as informative as it is categorical: "And it should have been written"—he tells him—"in gold letters. Were the birds that flew over our heads while in battle or the clouds to give accounts of us?"

Having become a patriarch to his large family and neighbors in Santiago de los Caballeros de Guatemala, diminished physically but not mentally, Bernal Díaz del Castillo "met his death" on 3 February 1584.

Translated from the Spanish by Galen Greaser

SELECTED BIBLIOGRAPHY

Editions

Historia verdadera de la conquista de la Nueva España. Escrita por el capitán Bernal Díaz del Castillo, uno de sus conquistadores. . . . Madrid, 1632. Printed based on a 1575 manuscript.

Historia verdadera de la conquista de la Nueva España por Bernal Díaz del Castillo uno de sus conquistadores. . . . Edited by Genaro García. 2 vols. Mexico City, 1904. Paleographic edition based on the so-called Guatemala Codex.

Historia verdadera de la conquista de la Nueva España. Edited by Joaquín Ramírez Cabañas. 3 vols. Mexico City, 1939. Modernized edition of the text of the Guatemala Codex.

Historia verdadera de la conquista de la Nueva España. . . . Madrid, 1940. Large-format edition prepared by Ramón Iglesia, Ángel Rosenblat, and Antonio Rodríguez-Moñino, although published without the proper recognition. The variations of the Guatemala Codex and those of a new one, now known as the Algería Codex, were added to the text by Alonso Remón. This edition was interrupted at chapter 146.

Translations

The Bernal Díaz Chronicles: The True Story of the Conquest of Mexico. Translated and edited by Albert E. Idell. New York, 1956.

The Conquest of New Spain. Translated and with an introduction by J[ohn] M[ichael] Cohen. Harmondsworth, England, 1963.

The Memoirs of the Conquistador Bernal Díaz del Castillo. . . . Translated by John Ingram Lockhart. 2 vols. London, 1844.

The True History of the Conquest of Mexico. . . . Translated by Maurice Keatinge. London, 1800. Reprint edited by Arthur D. Howden Smith, New York, 1927.

The True History of the Conquest of New Spain. . . . Translated by Alfred Percival Maudslay. 5 vols. London, 1908–1916. Reprinted Nendeln, Liechtenstein, 1967.

Biographical and Critical Studies

Alvar López, Manuel. *Americanismos en la "Historia" de Bernal Díaz del Castillo.* Madrid, 1970.

Barbón, José A. *Bernal Díaz del Castillo.* Buenos Aires, 1968.

Caillet-Bois, Julio. "Bernal Díaz del Castillo, o de la Verdad en la Historia." *Revista iberoamericana* 25/50:199–228 (1960).

Cardoza y Aragón, Luis. "Notas sobre Bernal Díaz del Castillo." *Anales de la Sociedad de Geografía e Historia de Guatemala* 9:452–461 (1933).

Carreño, Alberto María. *Bernal Díaz del Castillo, descubridor, conquistador y cronista de la Nueva España.* Mexico City, 1946.

Cerwin, Herbert. *Bernal Díaz, Historian of the Conquest.* Norman, Okla., 1963.

García, Genaro. "Noticias bio-bibliográficas." In his edition of the *Historia Verdadera.* . . . 1. Mexico City, 1904. Pp. ix–xciv.

Ghiano, Juan Carlos. "Veracidad y naturalidad de Bernal Díaz del Castillo." In *Revista de literatura argentina e iberoamericana.* Mendoza, Argentina, 1959. Pp. 47–73.

Gilman, Stephen. "Bernal Díaz del Castillo and 'Amadis de Guala'." In *Studia Philologica: Homenaje ofrecido a Dámaso.* Madrid, 1961. Alonso 2. Pp. 99–114.

González Obregón, Luis. *El Capitán Bernal Díaz del Castillo, conquistador y cronista de Nueva España. Noticias biográficas y bibliográficas.* Mexico City, 1894.

Graham, Robert B. Cunninghame. *Bernal Díaz del Castillo; Being Some Account of Him, Taken from His True History.* . . . London, 1915.

Hidalgo, Jacinto. "El ideario de Bernal Díaz." In *Estudios Cortesianos.* Madrid, 1948. Pp. 505–536.

Iglesia, Ramón. "Bernal Díaz del Castillo y el popularismo en la historiografía española"; "Las críticas de Bernal Díaz del Castillo a la Historia de la Conquista de México, de López de Gómara"; "Introducción al estudio de Bernal Díaz del Castillo y de su Verdadera historia." In his *El hombre Colón y otros ensayos.* Mexico City, 1944. Pp. 61–116.

Lapesa, Rafael. "La ruptura de la 'consecutio temporum' en Bernal Díaz del Castillo." *Anuario de letras* 6:73–83 (1968–1969).

Madariaga, Juan José. *Bernal Díaz y Simón Ruiz, de Medina del Campo.* Madrid, 1966.

Sáenz de Santa María, S.J., Carmelo. "Importancia y sentido del manuscrito alegría de la 'Verdadera Historia' de Bernal Díaz del Castillo." *Revista de Indias* 11/43–44:123–141 (1951).

_____. "Bernal Díaz del Castillo. Historia interna de su crónica." *Revista de Indias* 16/66:585–604 (1956).

_____. "¿Fue Remón el interpolador de la crónica de Bernal Díaz del Castillo?" In *Missionalia hispanica* (Madrid) 1956. Pp. 561–567.

_____. *Historia de una Historia. La crónica de Bernal Díaz del Castillo.* Madrid, 1984.

Simpson, Lesley B. "Bernal Díaz del Castillo, encomendero." *The Hispanic American Historical Review* 17:100–106 (1937).

Tamez, J.H. *Tras la huella de Bernal Díaz del Castillo.* Mexico City, 1971.

Wagner, Henry R. "Three Studies on the Same Subject." *The Hispanic American Historical Review* 25:153–211 (1945). "Bernal Díaz del Castillo," pp. 153–190; "The Family of Bernal Díaz del Castillo," pp. 191–198; "Notes on Writings By and About Bernal Díaz del Castillo," pp. 199–211.

Don Alonso de Ercilla y Zúñiga

(1533–1594)

Isaías Lerner

Don Alonso de Ercilla y Zúñiga is the most important author of Spanish epic poetry of the era between about 1550 and 1650. Though he wrote only one great epic poem, *La Araucana* (*The Araucaniad*, 1590), he dedicated more than twenty years of his life to its writing. It is divided into three parts: the first appeared in 1569, the second in 1578, and the third in 1589. This long process of poetic creation was carried out during the most active period of Ercilla's public life, and many aspects of his work and his life are interrelated to such an extent that the poet's biography becomes an important element in the comprehension of the poem's text. In effect, the historical events and the ideological, political, and ethical postures of the period form an intimate part of the poetic discourse of Ercilla; and like all overtly historical works, *La Araucana* ·is, on one level of meaning, both political and apologetic.

Like his contemporary Garcilaso de la Vega, an author often considered the archetypal aristocrat, Ercilla represents—perhaps to an even greater extent—the incarnation of all the necessary values of the courtier; that is, his career spans the parallel pursuits of arms and letters, being that of both a valorous soldier and a sensitive artist conscious of the importance of his creation. This combination of valor and knowledge resulted from Ercilla's belonging to a high social class while developing, through his own initiative, those virtues often considered inseparable from authority.

Don Alonso de Ercilla y Zúñiga was born on 7 August 1533 in Madrid, of Basque origins, a fact he mentions in *La Araucana* (canto 27, stanza 30). Ercilla was little more than a year old when his father died. In 1548 his mother managed to have him enrolled in the service of Prince Philip, the future King Philip II. From that point until his death, Ercilla served his liege unconditionally and, not surprisingly, dedicated the three parts of *La Araucana* to him. This dedication was not merely incidental but provided very special characteristics to the poem, as will be seen below.

Ercilla must have completed his education as a page to Prince Philip—an experience less to be scorned than his modern biographers suppose though doubtless less structured than that of his father or any other youth then pursuing studies in the universities of Europe. In any case, *La Araucana* reflects a literary knowledge ranging from the classics to Erasmus, from Dante to the discussions of the day centering on the justice of wars and the rights of nations, including geography, astronomy, and the art of navigation. His life experiences and awareness of cultural variety gained from numerous voyages instilled in Ercilla a cultivated spirit in the European cultural tradition, oriented toward a modern vision of the history and society of his time.

In 1548, Philip left Spain for Flanders to receive the investiture of royal succession from his father, Emperor Charles V. In his entourage was Ercilla. From Barcelona, with the squadron commanded by Andrea Doria (mentioned in *La Araucana* [24.22]), the procession passed to Genoa and on to other parts of Italy and then to Austria and Germany, finally arriving in Brussels on 1 April 1549. The retinue remained in Flanders almost two years, during which time the prince made further travels. It is known that Ercilla was with Prince Philip at the German Diet that took place in August 1549 in Augsburg— mentioned in *La Araucana* by its ancient name of Augusta in the final moving recapitulation of his services to the sovereign.

In 1554 Ercilla returned to Valladolid in anticipation of Prince Philip's trip to England for his marriage to Mary Tudor. In London, news arrived of the uprising of Francis Hernández Girón in Peru and of the death of Pedro de Valdivia in Chile at the hands of the Araucano Indians. Ercilla, then twenty-one years old, resolved to solicit permission from Prince Philip to travel to Peru. (See the dedication of the first part of *La Araucana*.) Philip, already charged with royal authority over the Indies, named Don Andrés Hurtado de Mendoza as viceroy of Peru, with orders to pacify the land and punish the rebels; he also designated Jerónimo de Alderete as governor of Chile. As part of Alderete's company, Ercilla departed London, having obtained the permission of the prince.

The ship in which Alderete traveled and which carried them to America set sail around October 1555. After severe storms, the party landed at Nombre de Dios in Panama; it embarked again, after crossing the isthmus, en route to Peru, but Alderete, sick with fever, died and was buried on the island of Taboga (13.30) in 1556. Meanwhile, the viceroy Hurtado de Mendoza completed his journey to Peru; Ercilla undoubtedly joined his party before the new viceroy's solemn entrance into Lima in June 1556.

Ercilla embarked on the Chilean expedition under the command of Don García Hurtado de Mendoza, the son of the viceroy. This force represented the most powerful Spanish contingent yet to be dispatched to those areas. Eleven weeks later, they disembarked at the port of Coquimbo or La Serena. With some 150 men, the expedition continued toward the south and after a tempestuous voyage, touched land in front of the hill of Penco, on an island off the coast. At that moment, one might say, Ercilla's American experience entered its "epic period," for this event coincided with the beginning of his literary activity. From that point, when Ercilla declares he took quill to hand (17.34), the public and the poetic sides of his career became inseparable. The New World nourished his vocation as a writer; and, until his death, literature was his vital horizon, for he was both creator and official recorder of events.

Ercilla was present at a good number of battles, which he wrote about in *La Araucana*, including the Battle of Biobío (22.25) and that of Millarapue (25 and 26), perhaps the single most bloody battle of the campaign. He also participated in diverse excursions into the interior of Araucano territory with the purpose, not always achieved, of pacifying the indigenous population. The poem mentions other actions and combat but does not detain itself in their description, nor does it supply many particulars (30. 26, 27). Having supplied the fort of Tucapel, the governor (along with Ercilla) goes on to found the city of Cañete and its fort (30.29), while imposing order in the other cities. But Caupolicán, the Araucano chief, decides to change the course of the war by way of a massive attack on the post of Ongolmo (30. 40), as a way of regaining prestige lost in previous defeats.

Betrayed by the Yanacona Indian Andresillo, the Araucanos suffer a bloody defeat and, subsequently, endure brutal repression at the hands of the victors. This is the last great battle on American soil that Ercilla describes in his poem. Although he took part in the search and capture of the chief Caupolicán, Ercilla did not participate in his trial and execution. He traveled throughout the southern territories to the Straits of Magellan, in the expedition organized by Don García Hurtado de Mendoza, in compliance with the king's orders to the deceased governor Alderete. From Valdivia, this expedition made its way to the south, overcoming enormous difficulties, as described in cantos 35 and 36 of *La Araucana*.

The company returned to La Imperial via less hazardous routes, and there Ercilla had his first period of rest since his arrival in Chile. A duel between him and another young aristocrat, alluded to twice in the poem (36.33 and 37.70), placed Ercilla in danger of *ajusticiamiento* (execution) by order of the governor, with the alternative possibility of a long prison sentence. After participating in new and bloody encounters with the Indians, Ercilla left for Peru at the start of 1559. His stay in Chile had lasted almost two years, filled with great adventures and dangers.

Ercilla decided to return to Spain in early 1561 and arrived in Seville in the middle of 1563. From that moment forward, the events of the life of the author diverged, for the most part, from those of the poem he wrote. The perspective supplied by this spatial and temporal distance, combined with the cultural and social environment of the court, left their marks on the epic text. In the restless life of Ercilla, numerous voyages remained to be made; barely returned to Spain, he traveled with Philip (now King Philip II) to the court of Monzón in Aragon. Then he journeyed to Vienna, where his sister, María Magdalena, was the queen's lady and awaited marriage to Don Fadrique de Portugal, as decreed by King Maximilian of Bohemia and Hungary, Philip's cousin. Shortly after the wedding in Madrid, María Magdalena died (1565). Ercilla inherited the major share of her considerable estate. From his relationship with Rafaela de Esquinas, of which little is known, was born a son, Juan de Ercilla, who died in 1588, in the catastrophic enterprise of the "Invincible Armada" against England. During this period Ercilla also dedicated himself to the polishing and preparation of his manuscript for the printing of the first part of *La Araucana*. In fact, in the dedication to Philip II, he reminds us that he wrote the book while on active military service, and in the prologue to the reader, he states that the little available time during those days of war was occupied entirely

> by this book which, because it is most certain and truthful, was composed during the actual war and at the actual battle sites, often written for lack of paper on pieces of leather, some so small that only six verses could be inscribed on them, so that later it cost me no little work to piece them together. . . .

Certainly the proximity to events at the moment of writing gave greater "historicity" to the tale, but there is reason to believe that this declaration was also a rhetorical device designed to capture the good faith of the reader. In fact, the text was not printed until almost six years after the return of Ercilla to Spain, appearing in Madrid in 1569, in the edition of Pierres Cossin. The poem enjoyed immediate success, and to Ercilla's advantageous social position was added literary fame. In 1570 he married Dona María de Bazán, lady-in-waiting of the third wife of Philip II, Isabel de Valois, and thereby attained the highest level of social respectability.

The second part of *La Araucana* appeared in 1578 and renewed the success achieved by the first. In fact, another edition appeared in Saragossa that same year, and a third in Madrid, once again by the editor Cossin, this time with the privilege of publication in the Indies. The monarch entrusted Ercilla with a diplomatic mission on the occasion of the arrival in Spain of the duke and duchess of Brunswick; he was indirectly involved in the Portugal campaign and perhaps was present during the conquest of the Azores Islands (1582), since he wrote a ballad concerning the naval battle between the French armada, captained by Felipe Strozzi, and the Spanish. Around then he must have begun to exercise his office of *examinador de libros* (censor): he passed at least twenty-one books; there is mention of two others, but it is probable that he examined additional books that were never published. In any case, the first book approved by Ercilla dates from 1580.

To Ercilla's social privileges and economic power were added the influence of his literary judgment and his special status in the literary world, thanks to the contacts that his censorship duties provided and the solid fame of his works. He completed the third part of his poem, which appeared in 1589. Then he turned to correcting the first edition of the three parts combined into a single volume, which appeared in Madrid the following year. By that time his financial situation was very solid. The abundant documentation of the economic activities of Ercilla shows that he was interested in luxury items and artworks and owned jewelry and numerous objects of gold and silver, which he frequently bought and sold. Thanks to his ability in making loans and conducting other credit operations, he was able rapidly to augment his capital in such a way that by the end of his life he could consider himself enormously wealthy. His melancholy complaints at the end of the poem (37. 70–74) ought not to be understood on a literal level but rather as a rhetorical formula that points to the vanity of the things of this world, appropriate at the end of such a long poetic discourse for a protagonist who is finally more concerned with salvation and the imperial polity than with heroic deeds. After concluding the poem, Ercilla continued his literary activities; it is known that he had begun to write a long poem about Philip's campaign in Portugal. Without a doubt, part (or all) of the composed text passed into *La Araucana* in the posthumous edition of Madrid, 1597: the final stanzas of canto 36 imply, and almost all of canto 37 (the last of the poem) deals with, the above-mentioned campaign, an affair having little to do with the central theme of *La Araucana*. The text insinuates the possibility of a continuation (36.43), but the poet's health had diminished greatly, and on 29 November 1594 he died in Madrid, at sixty-one. In 1595 his remains were transported to Ocaña, to the monastery of Carmelite nuns founded by Dona María de Bazán, his widow.

Ercilla's life has been summarized in detail because much of *La Araucana* is intimately related to it. It would not be an exaggeration to consider the poem as a kind of partial autobiography: the narrator is in large part the protagonist, and the aspects of the poem that are not strictly autobiographical are nevertheless indicative of the cultural ideals and ideological systems of the author himself. Needless to say, the narrative elements, precisely because they are narrative, cannot be considered verifiable historical facts; but from a very early date the events of the poem—the warfare and the geographical and cultural references to Chile and its inhabitants—have been taken as authentic.

Ercilla should be considered essentially as the author of a single great work. Two other poetic texts have minor significance. One is a gloss, perhaps his first known work (published by López de Sedano in the *Parnaso español* [Madrid, 1770]), the other a "romance" concerning the naval action in the Azores. There are also two sonnets attributed to him. Ercilla dedicated almost two-thirds of his life to

writing his epic, and it is clear that the changes within the poem, perceptible in each of the three parts, reflect the evolution of Ercilla as a poet and a thinker. The poem belongs to a literary tradition that goes back to Homer and Vergil, and it builds upon their works, even when that tradition searches, as in the Renaissance, for other routes.

In Spain, no doubt due to its hegemonic supremacy in Europe and America, the tendency in literature was toward a genre of a markedly historical character. This tendency was already in evidence with the publication of Jerónimo Sempere's first work, *La Carolea* (1540), which narrates, in part, the martial campaigns of Charles V. *La Araucana* is also a narrative poem that describes events not imagined but historically based. This fundamental characteristic should suffice to differentiate it from the "novelistic" tradition established by Lodovico Ariosto, but Ercilla knew how to use renovating elements from *Orlando Furioso* in his own work. His poem does not have any single hero. His plot does not adhere strictly to the "unity of action"; it mixes diverse types of materials; it accepts interruptions in the narration and mixes in distinctive actions, defining itself as a narration not rigidly regulated, but rather free. It is certain that the influence of Ariosto is most profoundly felt in the composition of *La Araucana*: in formal and structural elements like those already mentioned, in the selection of the metric form *octavas reales* (ottava rima), in the use of *exordios* or introductions of a moral theme in each canto, and in the imitation of episodes or stylistic devices.

But since Ercilla's historical purpose is so radically distinct from Ariosto's, it becomes necessary to recognize other literary debts. Lucan's *Pharsalia*, an epic poem in ten books that narrates the battles between Caesar and Pompey, received renewed attention in the sixteenth century. It was translated by Martin Lasso de Oropesa around 1530 and, without a doubt, was read in Spanish or in the original Latin by Ercilla, who utilized it not only in particular episodes but in his preference for a long narration of a single, extensive military campaign.

In the thirty-seven cantos, Ercilla narrated the conquest of the lands of the Araucanos within what today comprises Chile, from the government of Valdivia to the defeat of the indigenous rebellion by the governor Don García Hurtado de Mendoza. More than ten descriptions of encounters with the Araucanos—diverse narrations and lyric episodes—form the material of the poem. Ercilla begins his epic poem with a descriptive introduction of Chile and of the customs, beliefs, and warlike characteristics of the Araucanos that must have fascinated the readers of his day. This description owes, perhaps, too much to the necessities of the epic; but the warlike nature and indomitable ferocity in defense of independence have remained, nonetheless, attached to the character of the Araucanian nation. Ercilla also echoes a tradition that predates the arrival of the Spaniards and that attributes to the inhabitants of the central plain of Chile the defeat of a powerful army sent by the Incas from Peru: he regards their cultivation of physical force and capacity for resistance as synonymous with warlike valor and the capacity to lead. The *prueba del tronco* (contest of the log) in canto 2 converts Caupolicán into the chief of the rebellion against the Spaniards because he proves himself the strongest and most resistant of the chiefs. The rebellion of the Araucanos against the Spaniards is also attributed by the narrator to the greed and tyranny of Valdivia (3.3–5).

Caupolicán, with the aid of the valient Lautaro, who had been the page of Valdivia, prepares new attacks against the Spanish forces now under the command of Francisco de Villagrán. Other bloody combats are narrated in the two cantos that follow, in which the descriptive technique goes from general overviews of the gory losses and fierce determination of both sides to descriptions of individual combats, which exemplify personal valor and the heroic dimensions of the opponents. An accumulation of epithets, parallelistic syntactic structures, comparisons taken from the Greco-Latin tradition, and abundant Latinisms and cultivated terms give to the narration of battles an expressive quality and a conscious hierarchy of lexical choices that are unparalleled in previous Spanish poetry. The poem employs differentiated rhythms in which purely descriptive pauses, detailing the more general actions, alternate with vertiginous accumulations of series of verbs; hyperbolic valor and physical resistance against impossible extremes mark the epic intention of these encounters. At the same time, heroism is deflated by

the ingredients of cruelty toward the defenseless and of fear, which generates acts of selfishness or cowardice as combatants vainly strive to save themselves from sure death.

The Spaniards abandon positions before the enormous numerical advantage of the Indians, which counteracts the Spaniards' advantages of horses and artillery; the latter flee Andalicán, abandon to the Araucanos the city of Concepción, and prepare to defend La Imperial. But the victories obtained by the Araucanos blind them to reality, as they consider the possibility of invading Spain, ignore the dire predictions of their witch doctor, Puchecalco (8.39–43), and opt to return to the attack against the Spaniards at La Imperial. During a sudden storm ordered by the god Eponamon, there appears a celestial apparition that routs the Araucanian army on the outskirts of the city. After this miracle the Indians undergo two years of exemplary sufferings through natural cataclysms, occurrences drawn from a long literary-historical tradition. Food shortages owing to persistent drought result in acts of cannibalism, but the war continues, with renewed acts of valor and additional Spanish defeats. Celebrations, drunken orgies, and athletic games are part of the not always pacific festivals of the Araucanos, which are richly described in the poem. These passages are more influenced by literary tradition than by true observation of customs.

In a new attack Lautaro, who has been growing in strategic expertise, defeats the Spaniards by means of a ruse; he offers conditions of peace unacceptable to the Spaniards, who then retreat to Concepción. When an Indian offers to take the Spaniards toward Lautaro's new fort by way of a hidden path, Villagrán organizes a surprise attack in which Lautaro is killed; the battle that ensues is very bloody (cantos 14 and 15), and all the Indians in the fort die. To the rhetorical devices already employed with great efficacy, Ercilla now adds the spectacular action of the Genovese Andrea and the Araucanian Rengo; the element of fatality that makes possible the surprise attack, which was foreseen in the presentiments of Guacolda (13.43–46), the beloved of Lautaro; the impression of hopeless struggle on the part of the Araucanos; and the implacable advance of the Spaniards, who, not without strong losses, go about eliminating their enemies. The battle continues to be defined in gruesome realistic details which are convincing in their documentary expression. Besides comparing the fighting to forces of nature, intended to underline the blind power that guides violence, Ercilla heightens the poem's impact by this immediacy in the descriptions of acts of war. Although he intertwines rhetorical formulas taken from Vergil and Lucan with impeccable simplicity, what creates the sensation of authenticity that moves the reader so directly is the gory description of the blows of clubs, the stabs of lances, and the cut of swords. At the same time, the cruelty of the Spaniards in dismembering the bodies of the Araucanos creates in the reader a feeling of sympathy for the vanquished that has given to *La Araucana* a humanitarian prestige that today is associated with pacifist ideals. The narrator specifically expresses his repugnance for certain forms of military cruelty, which in his eyes are totally unnecessary.

The episode of the assault on Lautaro's fortress is interrupted at the beginning, with the appearance of the narrator as an actor (13.29–30); he announces his decision to embark for Peru with the marquis of Cañete. The first part closes with the ship carrying Ercilla to Chile, struggling against a strong storm. Thus the fifteen cantos of the first part of *La Araucana* relate events of which Ercilla has only heard, but his later experiences in similar circumstances enable him to give an "authentic" account.

The fact that the narrator comes upon the scene just after the last battle of the first part, as well as that this battle results in the first defeat of the Araucanos, is in itself symbolic. During his military career, Ercilla knew only the triumphs of the Spaniards and the defeat of the enemy. It was not inappropriate that he should dedicate the three parts to Philip II, who seems to become the interlocutor par excellence. The text frequently directs itself to Philip, and the monarch is the ideal reader of this account of the triumph of his armies. Ercilla decided to be, with full consciousness of purpose, the official *cantor* (poet) of the empire, and to this end he dedicated the greater part of his life, both as actor and as epic voice. Thus, in the second part the angle of focus upon the campaign in Chile had to be widened. The testimonial value, stemming from Ercilla's own participation in the events he narrates, might come from the most distant part of the subjugated lands, but this distance acts as a symbol of the universality of Spanish power. The unity of the enterprise of conquest is further conveyed by the relation of similar events in other latitudes. Thus, in the second part, the episodes that describe the battles of Lepanto (canto 24) and San Quentin (canto 18) universalize and unify the imperial venture; French power (San Quentin), Turkish power (Lepanto), and the Araucanian territories—all appear equally subjugated to the rule of Philip II in this utopian poetic space.

For European eyes, the marginal American *epopeya* (epic) acquires real dimensions only when it is seen as united to events occurring at or near the center of world power. The two battles with European settings are introduced by way of a typical epic literary device—the mythological apparition (absent in the first part) in the case of San Quentin, or the magical devices of the witch doctor Fitón in the case of Lepanto; the poem's vertiginous movement through space and time seems almost to require such devices. At the same time, both episodes are connected, in that a mysterious lady dressed in white prophesies the outcome of Lepanto in the same canto (18.60–63), and provides information concerning the future personal life of the narrator (18.70–72).

The Araucanian revolt is punctuated with amorous episodes that introduce individualized female characters. Tegualda (canto 20) recalls the tragic figure of Argeia (from the *Thebaid* of Statius), who renders lugubrious honors to her husband Polynices, along with Antigone. The story of Glaura and her beloved Cariolán (canto 28) reenacts the Byzantine literary motif of the violently separated lovers who are again united by the workings of chance and the generous act of some triumphant protagonist.

Fitón the magician represents the most direct homage to the Latin epic as a literary source; namely, in the objects that he utilizes in his vials (23.48–54) and in the spells calling to the la caterva infernal (infernal gang, 80–82). When he reappears in cantos 26 and 27, the debt to the literary tradition of Spain is clear in an image taken from Juan de Mena—that of the description of the orb. Seen from its American setting, however, this magical astronomical vision of the world acquires a totality completely unknown to the poet of the fifteenth century. From a central point in Spain (in which it is possible to see the minuscule, ancestral land of the author: Bermeo in Vizcaya), Ercilla writes from the secure position of power—the power of a nation that, more so than any other on earth, extends over large areas of Asia, Africa, Europe, and America; lands both known and unknown, which remain to be explored when God wills it.

In this variety of motives and episodes, the Araucanos progressively lose the bellicose advantages displayed in the first part. Acts of valor are carried out by new heroes who replace Lautaro, but in the assault on the fortress of Penco, Gracolano, who had promised to carry the Araucanian flag, (17.31) is killed. He is replaced by Pinol, who in turn is killed and replaced by Tucapel. The descriptive formula that alternates general overviews of the battles with violent, individual combat is modified by psychological elements; the combatants are no longer distinguished only by the trait of fierce personal bravery in battle, but rather, these acts allow the protagonists to be individualized as multidimensional beings. In defeat the bravery of the Araucanos acquires hyperbolic dimensions, at the same time that Spanish repression disproportionately multiplies the level of cruelty. Canto 22, which describes the attack near the *alto monte andalicano* (high Andalicán mountain), includes the combat of Rengo, isolated in a swamp, alone against several Spaniards, among whom the reader finds Ercilla (22.35), and the brutal punishment of Galvarino (22.46–54). Described with admirable rhetorical skill and respectful admiration, these episodes transmit the dimensions of the valor, desperation, and resistance of the indigenous camp, as well as the noble attitude of the narrator regarding the enemy.

The battle of Millarapúe occupies cantos 25 and 26; in it, the Spanish heroes, who in the first part appeared on the defensive, now find themselves in a position of advantage, a situation that permits an occasional act of unexpected humor and the active participation of the narrator in acts of singular daring (26.15–16). From the numerous prisoners, the Spaniards select twelve nobles to make an example of their punishment; in this number is included Galvarino, whom Ercilla fruitlessly attempts to save. The passage juxtaposes the justice of the Araucanos' cause, as proclaimed by Galvarino in his final oratory, with the

unjust harshness of his sentence, as perceived by the narrator.

The third part is the briefest: eight cantos in the complete version of 1597. In it, the narration wanders even farther afield from its initial purpose, the Spanish campaign in Chile; moreover, the poet warns the reader that another writer will have to tell the story of "otros muchos encuentros de importancia" (many other encounters of importance, 30.26), in addition to the recounting of "otra batalla sangrienta de ambas partes y reñida" (another battle bloody for both sides and bitter, 30.27). At the same time, the military rationale of the epic gives way to psychological considerations in order to explain the end of the Araucanian rebellion: Caupolicán is defeated because a Yanacona Indian, Andresillo, betrays the Araucanian cause. The behavior of the Araucanos evokes the memory of similar behavior in the European heroic tradition and makes possible the inclusion of Ercilla's long defense of Vergil's Dido, queen of Carthage. The intercalation of this episode is justified because it has been preceded by the example of the encounter with Lauca, who represents conjugal fidelity even beyond death. This reference to the Vergilian text, which extends from 32.44 to 33.54 (102 octaves), is a significant link to European cultural tradition.

At the same time, the narration acquires a more personal tone. The assault on the Spanish fort at Ongolmo (cantos 30–33) is transformed by the protagonist Ercilla into an agonizing struggle of conscience in which feelings of mercy and hatred battle for supremacy (31.49–50). Additionally, the conflicting sentiments of pity and justice, as understood by the victors, are examined (32.1–5). In the end, the poet is convinced of the validity of the constituted order, and pronounces it legitimate: "Todo le es justo y licito al que vence" (All is just and licit in conquest, 32.5); nevertheless the work protests the ruin and destruction wrought on Araucanian soil, "en parte justo, y lastimoso en todo" (partly just and wholly pitiful, 32.5) and displays the testimony of the personal conscience that narrates these events.

On the other hand, the journey to the south, in search of the Strait of Magellan, offers the chance to describe the dangers of these expeditions through unknown zones, without sure guides and surrounded by an inhospitable nature. The epic account of the conquest per se is transformed into the adventure of discovery and colonization. Ercilla adds the pride of the victorious soldier to the fearlessness of the discoverer of new lands, in which "otro no ha llegado" (no others have arrived, 36.29).

Finally, it is in this last part of the work that the figure of Caupolicán acquires its tragic grandeur. After the Araucanos have been defeated completely at Ongolmo, the battle becomes general and anonymous: each shot puts an end to the life of another enemy warrior (32.10), and the devastation caused by Spanish firearms is more cruelly depicted (32.11–19). The capture and punishment of Caupolicán (33.56) inspires a meditation on the instability of all things human and on the changes of fortune (34.1–2). The victor over Valdivia, the destroyer of Penco and Purén (34.8), is now a prisoner, despised by his wife, Fresia (33.76–81), naked and barefoot, dragging two heavy chains, with a noose about the neck; he is paraded before the frightened and amazed people. The political aspect of defeat and triumph is displaced by the irrationality of the chief's fate; thus, in a gesture that seems to underline the universal dignity bestowed upon authority, Caupolicán refuses a dishonorable death at the hands of the executioner, reproaches the clearly "unchristian" nature of such a death (34.25), and submits "con poca ayuda" (with little help, 34.27) to the brutal impalement to which he has been condemned. The very longbowmen, "aunque en toda maldad ejercitados" (although trained in all kinds of mischief, 34.29) waver when they aim to finish him off. Ercilla opts for an unadorned account of this execution, free of all rhetorical elements; but he himself, as in relating the execution of Galvarino, feels obliged to dissent from the prisoner's sentence which, had he been present, he would have tried to suspend. The bravery of Caupolicán in the face of death runs parallel to the incredulity of his subjects over the spectacle, but the punishment's value as an example of Spanish retribution will be nil; rather than intimidating the Araucanos, the inhuman act will drive them "llena de nueva rabia y mayor ira" (full of new fury and greater ire, 34.25). But Ercilla no longer uses his own voice in relating the chieftain's gathering organized by Colocolo to plan the resistance (36.43–44).

The return of the narrator to Spain facilitates the introduction of events related to the Portuguese campaign, but without the mediation of magical acts. The last four octaves of canto 36 and all of canto 37 (the finale) constitute a commentary on the justice of war and, particularly, the justice of the war to Portugal. The problem of the rights of nations, which had not even been considered pertinent in the bloody Chilean campaign, appears as an obligatory discussion as soon as European territory is at issue. Ercilla never doubts the validity and legitimacy of imperial possessions in the New World. Though he shows genuine sympathy for the Indian rebels, and disdain for the greed and arrogant cowardice of Valdivia or the barbaric administration of "justice" on the part of Don García Hurtado de Mendoza, he nevertheless harbors no doubts concerning the providential character of the conquest of America. The colonialization and subjugation of the Indians, due to its redeeming character (in the Christian sense) is shown to have been celestially ordained, with no need for justification. The taking of Portugal, on the other hand, must be justified under the tenets of international law.

The New World remains in the shadow of his memory as a soldier, brilliantly summarized. The poem closes in Europe, on a melancholy note of Christian regret. Whoever added the final stanzas to the 1597 edition of Madrid understood the primary purpose of the poem from an existential and ideological perspective at the time of the third part's writing. Directed toward a cultivated and elite public, *La Araucana*, throughout its 2,534 octaves, utilizes a vocabulary and a repertory of rhetorical figures from both epic and classical traditions, in addition to the new literary uses imposed on Spanish letters since the time of Garcilaso, yet without ever disdaining the techniques of earlier authors such as Juan de Mena. The result of these diverse elements is the creation of a poetic language that inclines to clarity of expression and a choice of vocabulary with an illustrious literary tradition that is accessible to the competent reader. For that reason, Ercilla at times prefers exceptional Latinisms, while on other occasions he selects colloquial formulas that aid in generating the impression of immediacy, of an experience personally lived. Despite the great length of the poem, only twenty words of indigenous origin appear in the text, and of these, only three are Araucanian. Of course, the place-names and some of the proper names (albeit deformed) are of native origin, but in his ordinary vocabulary Ercilla prefers to use the Spanish equivalent over the truly indigenous word. Ercilla is not unaware that many indigenous terms have already been incorporated into the language of the Spaniards in America, as he points out in the *Declaracion de algunas dudas* (Clarification of Certain Expressions) at the end of the poem; but in recognition of the readers to whom the poem is directed, he offers a list of those few actually used by the poem "por variar" (to vary) the lexical selection.

Ercilla's work was early recognized as a paradigmatic or exemplary text. From the treatise-writers of the sixteenth century to Miguel Cervantes, and from Lope de Vega to Voltaire; from the translations of the seventeenth century to the editions of today, the work of Ercilla has not been relegated to oblivion. His text has received a varied reception and at times has been considered quite removed from its literary context, but such a strong impact testifies to its plurality of meaning and has justified Ercilla's permanent presence among the canonical texts written in Castilian on both sides of the Atlantic.

Whether read as a historical document or for pleasure by Ercilla's contemporaries and during the seventeenth century; whether consulted as a textual authority for the editors of the *Diccionario de autoridades* in the eighteenth century or by the rhetoricians of the previous century; whether taken as a geography manual or as a nationalistic epic of America in the nineteenth, *La Araucana* continues to be read to our own times, attracting the interest and curiosity of readers and scholars in both Europe and America.

Translated from the Spanish by David H. Nagel

SELECTED BIBLIOGRAPHY

First Editions

La Araucana. Madrid, 1569. First edition of the first part.
Primera y segunda parte de La Araucana. Madrid, 1578. In octavo, probably the first edition of the second part.
Segunda parte de La Araucana. Zaragoza, Spain, 1578. First independent edition of the second part.

Tercera parte de La Araucana. Madrid, 1589. First edition of the third part.
Primera, segunda y tercera partes de La Araucana. Madrid, 1590. First edition of the complete poem. The title pages of the second and third parts are dated 1589.
Primera, segunda y tercera partes. Madrid, 1597. First edition with the enlarged text: twenty-two new stanzas in canto 34, canto 35, and canto 36, except for the last four stanzas.

Modern Editions

La Araucana. In *Poemas épicos* 1, edition of Biblioteca de Autores Españoles, vol. 17. Madrid, 1851.
_____. Edition of the Real Academia Española. 2 vols. Madrid, 1866.
_____. Edited by José Toribio Medina. 5 vols. Santiago, Chile, 1910–1918.
_____. With an introduction by Hugo Montes. Santiago, Chile, 1956.
_____. Edited by Arturo Souto. Mexico City, 1962.
_____. Edited by Marcos A. Morínigo and Isaías Lerner. Madrid, 1979.

Translations

The Araucaniad: A Version in English Poetry of Alonso de Ercilla y Zúñiga's "La Araucana." Translated by Charles M. Lancaster and Paul Th. Manchester. Nashville, Tenn. 1945.
The Historie of "Araucana": Written in verse by Don Alonso de Ercilla: Translated out of the spanishe into Englishe Prose allmost to the Ende of the 16: Canto. This oldest known translation by George Carew (Lambeth Palace Library, Ms. 688) was transcribed and annotated with an introduction by Frank Pierce. The probable date of the manuscript is late sixteenth or early seventeenth century. Manchester (England), 1964.

Biographical and Critical Studies

Alegría, Fernando. "Neruda y *La Araucana.*" In *Estudios de literatura hispanoamericana en honor a José J. Arrom,* edited by Andrew P. Debicki and Enrique Pupo-Walker. Chapel Hill, N.C., 1974. Pp. 193–200.
Aquila, August J. "Ercilla's Concept of the Ideal Soldier." *Hispania* (U.S.) 60:68–75 (1977).
Bocaz, Aura S. "El personaje Tegualda, uno de los narradores de *La Araucana.*" *Boletín de filología* (Montevideo), 27:7–27 (1976).

Fernán González de Eslava

(1534–1601?)

Julie Greer Johnson

Fernán González de Eslava, sixteenth-century Spanish America's most renowned dramatist, arrived in the New World in 1559 at the age of twenty-four. Little is known about him before his departure from his native Spain, but several scholars studying linguistic aspects of his works have conjectured that he was originally from Andalusia or León. Once in Mexico, however, he established himself in the literary community and counted among his friends such notable literary figures as Francisco de Terrazas, Pedro Ledesma, Juan Pérez Ramírez, and Juan de la Cueva. Although González de Eslava wrote both poetry and drama, it is his sixteen short dramatic pieces known as *coloquios* (colloquies) for which he is famous. They were written and performed between 1567 and 1600 and were published in 1610 after the dramatist's death in a collection gathered by the Augustinian priest Fernando Vello de Bustamante. In 1572 González de Eslava entered the clergy. Two years later as a priest he became the center of a dispute between the church and the state that resulted in his brief incarceration. He died just after the turn of the century, presumably in Mexico.

A controversial interlude staged in 1574 brought González de Eslava to the attention of Mexico City residents by creating an uproar among the capital's officials. The Inquisition, established there in 1571,

was primarily in charge of censoring works presented to the public, and its main purposes were to protect the moral well-being of the Indians and to preserve the dignity of the clergy. Looking out after its own interests, it occasionally let a critical comment about colonial administration or a royal official go unnoticed, and this was the case with a satiric piece inserted into one of González de Eslava's programs. During a presentation of the dramatist's *Coloquio III* in 1574, Viceroy Martín Enríquez de Almansa became incensed by a comic character who was made up to look like him and who advocated public resistance to his newly implemented sales tax. He ordered the arrest of González de Eslava, several of his friends, and the actor involved, all of whom spent a few weeks in jail. Although the case was thoroughly investigated, it was never clearly determined who had written the politically sensitive material.

The theater played a very important role in the transfer of Spanish culture to the New World and in the development of colonial society. Shortly after the Spaniards established a colony on the island of Hispaniola, plays were performed to entertain the residents of Santo Domingo. According to the famous historian and humanitarian Father Bartolomé de Las Casas, the earliest ones were put on at the home of María de Toledo, the wife of Diego Columbus, the son of Christopher. Although drama provided an excellent diversion for Spanish colonists, its entertainment value was secondary to its importance as a device to indoctrinate and convert the Indians. Many of the first plays written in America were composed by the earliest friars, and quite a few of these pieces were adaptations of Spanish religious drama translated into native American languages and acted by Indians. Actions conveyed Bible stories and Christian doctrine much more effectively than words alone, and the stage representation of religious themes gave the Indians an opportunity to participate in and experience Christianity. One of the best descriptions of a dramatic work presented in the New World is found in the history of Fray Toribio de Benavente (Motolinía), which chronicles the 1538 performance of *La caída de nuestros primeros padres* (The Fall of Our Original Parents) in Tlaxcala, Mexico. Indians playing the roles of Adam and Eve spoke Nahuatl, the language of the Aztecs, and the Garden of Eden, because of its many indigenous elements, appeared to have been located in the Indies. Although the Roman Catholic church dominated the development of the theater during the postconquest years, a tendency that would persist throughout the colonial period, secular elements were gradually introduced into dramatic works by the end of the sixteenth century. González de Eslava was one of the first dramatists to secularize Spanish theatrical productions presented in the New World, and it is through this reorientation that he makes his greatest contribution to early Spanish-American drama.

González de Eslava's dramatic works are similar to the *teatro prelopista* (theater before Lope de Vega) of Spain. They are more developed than the medieval *autos*, short plays based on brief episodes taken from the Bible, but are far less complex than the *comedias* defined by the Golden Age playwright Lope de Vega. Mexican settings are combined with traditional religious themes in González de Eslava's colloquies, and he often employs some current event to illustrate a moral lesson. In *Coloquio V*, for example, he bases his allegory on the construction of fortifications along the road to the mining town of Zacatecas. A traveler advancing along the route represents man as he makes his way through life; the seven fortresses symbolize the seven sacraments of the Catholic faith; and the attacking Indians stand for the ever-present forces of evil.

González de Eslava also interjects themes of local concern into his drama, such as the social conflict between *criollos* (Spaniards born in the New World) and *peninsulares* (those born in Spain), the presence of racial tension between the Spaniards and natives in the colonies, and the continued practice of pagan ritual among the Indians. His language also reflects this regional content, as his colloquies contain Mexican slang and numerous words from Nahuatl.

The structure of the *coloquios* is rudimentary, and action is presented in chronological order. Each work is divided into *jornadas* (acts) and *loas* (short dedicatory or prefatory pieces), and *entreméses* (interludes) often accompany them. Frequently these various parts of the program are interrelated, as characters in one part reappear in another or an action foreshadowed in one takes place in another. González de Eslava's dramatic works are written both in prose and in poetry, but verse prevails. Numerous types of verse—such as octaves, tercets, ballads, and sonnets—are often combined in a single play.

The characters in González de Eslava's dramas are generally symbolic and represent sacraments, virtues, vices, aspects of theology, or abstract elements of life. Figures representing human beings appear only occasionally, as do angels and saints. Even allegorical personages, however, possess human traits and often resemble popular societal or dramatic types. One of the characters, the *bobo* (buffoon), appears frequently and contributes in large measure to the development of comedy in González de Eslava's works. Slapstick as well as *sayagués*, a form of distorted and amusing speech, enhance the performance of this comic character.

González de Eslava's *Coloquio VII* is an excellent example of his talent and possesses many of the characteristics generally found in his drama. Entitled "De cuando Dios nuestro señor mandó al profeta Jonás que fuese a la ciudad de Ninive a predicar su destrucción" (About When God Our Lord Commanded the Prophet Jonah to Go to the City of Nineveh to Predict Its Destruction), the entire work consists of an interlude and a *loa* dedicated to the viceroy, which precede but are intertwined with the principal dramatic action of the colloquy. When the curtain goes up, Teresa and her husband, Diego Moreno, the main characters, are having a marital squabble over the ban on silk in the Spanish-American colonies. Spain forbade its production in accordance with mercantilistic principles—colonies could not produce the same products as the mother country—thus depriving elite colonists of a highly prized luxury item. Teresa is unconcerned with the political ramifications of this prohibition and considers only its effects on her wardrobe.

Teresa is portrayed as a selfish, vain woman who will stop at nothing to get what she wants, and González de Eslava's portrayal of her may reflect his view of some of Mexico's aristocratic women. She is outraged at the suffering she must endure and begins a verbal attack on Diego, who she contends is too poor to buy silk clothing anyway. Her tirade expresses disdain for the native *huipil* (a cotton garment of Aztec origin) and insults Diego's lineage. Because she claims to be a direct descendant of a conqueror and he is a commoner, she speaks to him condescendingly and calls him a good-for-nothing. When she runs out of criticism, she begins assaulting him physically. In order to stop the violence, Diego finally agrees to take his wife to China so that she can obtain all the silk she wants. The couple boards a galleon bound for the Orient at the conclusion of the interlude, and the account of their voyage is interrupted by the *loa*.

In the *loa*, González de Eslava succinctly summarizes Jonah's flight from Nineveh and foreshadows his being swallowed by the whale. When the action resumes in the final segment of the colloquy, Teresa, Diego, and the prophet are passengers aboard the same ship. During the voyage a storm comes up, and all begin to fear for their lives and to do some genuine soul-searching. Both Jonah and Teresa believe that they are responsible for this manifestation of God's wrath and take action to restore calm seas. Jonah hurls himself into the water to enable the ship to continue its safe passage, and Teresa vows to be a good obedient wife.

González de Eslava's last colloquy, "Del bosque divino" (About the Divine Forest) is considered by some critics to be his best because of its complex structure and varied situations. The program is composed of two acts and an interlude; since the second act is so much longer than the first, however, it is conjectured that the dramatist originally meant to divide the action in several more places. The divine forest in this colloquy is a special enclosure set aside by God in which he provides for the protection of all his creatures. This preserve represents the Roman Catholic church, and it is constantly guarded by the allegorical figures of Memory, Understanding, Goodwill, and the cardinal virtues, as well as by its Guardian Angel and several shepherds. The only way to enter the premises is through one of the seven doors or sacraments. The forces of evil, however, want to hunt in the forest and dispatch spies to find out how to gain entry. Among the villains are Prince Worldliness and Princess Flesh, a crippled devil, and the seven capital sins. They succeed to some extent because the representatives of good are not as vigilant as they should be, but the failure of the evil figures to accept the sacraments ultimately brings about their defeat.

As González de Eslava carefully explains the significance and introduces the guardians of each door, he stops at the one representing the sacrament of marriage and intercalates another *entremés* that illustrates the mutual responsibilities of husbands and wives. As with Teresa and Diego, conjugal strife again provides the context for this illustration, but the partners are not actual people but abstractions endowed with human characteristics. The interlude begins with Espión (Spy) beating his wife Ocasión (Occasion) for infidelity. Ocasión is so upset by her husband's actions that she consults an old native woman known as Doña Murmuración (Lady Slander), a midwife and medicine woman who deals in witchcraft to resolve many of her clients' problems. Idol worship and pagan ceremonies were still concerns of the Catholic clergy even after the conversion of the Indians, and the church especially discouraged the use of sorcery. Doña Murmuración is closely linked to native culture, as she includes Nahuatl expressions in her speech and prays to the demon who inhabits the volcano Popocatepetl. The model for this figure, however, comes from Fernando de Rojas' *Tragicomedia de Calisto y Melibea* (1499). The principal character of this masterpiece, Celestina, is an old bawd who deals in all forms of the occult and generally uses her services to resolve problems of the heart. Doña Murmuración, however, is unable to help Ocasión, and when the young wife later confesses what she has done to Voluntad (Goodwill) and Templanza (Temperance), they chide her for even thinking of consulting such a person. Disillusioned by the use of witchcraft, she is encouraged to seek a solution through Christianity and is advised to pray, to attend mass regularly, and to make pilgrimages to the shrine of the Virgin of Guadalupe, who later became Mexico's patron saint.

Although González de Eslava's purpose in writing his *coloquios* follows the general didactic tendency of his predecessors and contemporaries in early Spanish-American theater, his innovative approach to the dramatic presentation of the Christian tradition distinguishes him from other dramatists. Current events and local customs add freshness and vitality to the familiar situations he dramatizes, and comedy lessens the tedium of the moral lesson he teaches. González de Eslava is also one of the first colonial dramatists to explore the satiric possibilities of theatrical pieces, and his conflict with royal officials over an unidentified skit documents the power of censorship in the colonies. These aspects of his life and work confirm his reputation as the sixteenth century's finest colonial playwright, and his efforts to secularize the theater in the New World mark a turning point in its development.

SELECTED BIBLIOGRAPHY

First Editions

Coloquios espirituales y sacramentales y canciones Diuinas, compuestas por el Diuino poeta Fernán Gonçález de Eslaua Clerigo Presbitero. Compiled by Fernando Vello de Bustamante. Mexico City, 1610.

Works Containing Fragments of Poetry

Flores de varia poesía. An anthology gathered in Mexico in 1577. The manuscript is in the Biblioteca Nacional de Madrid.
Farfán, Agustín. *Tractado breve de medicina.* Mexico City, 1579.

Sánchez de Muñon, Sancho. *Doctrina cristiana.* Mexico City, 1579.
Dávila Padilla, Agustín. *Historia de la fundacion y discurso de la provincia de Santiago de Mexico, de la orden de Predicadores.* Madrid, 1596.

Modern Editions

Individual Works

Coloquio IV. Coloquio VI. In *Autos y coloquios del siglo XVI.* Edited by José Rojas Garcidueñas. Mexico City, 1939.
Coloquio V. Coloquio XIV. In *El teatro de Nueva España en el siglo XVI.* Edited by José Rojas Garcidueñas. Mexico City, 1935.
Coloquio VII. In *Teatro Mexicano: Dos obras en un acta.* Edited by Fernando Wagner. Mexico City, 1946.
"Entremes del ahorcado." In *Anthology of Spanish American Literature.* Edited by Herman E. Hespelt. New York, 1946.

Collected Works

Coloquios espirituales y sacramentales. Edited by José Rojas Garcidueñas. 2 vols. Mexico City, 1958.
Coloquios espirituales y sacramentales y poesías sagradas del Presbítero Fernán González de Eslava. Edited by Joaquín García Icazbalceta. Mexico City, 1877.

Works Containing Fragments of Poetry

Castro Leal, Antonio. "Unos versos desconocidos de Francisco de Terrazas y un falso Privilegio." *Revista de literatura mexicana* 1:2 (1940).
Méndez Plancarte, Alfonso. *Poetas novohispanos (1521–1621).* Mexico City, 1942.

Biographical and Critical Studies

Alonso, Amado. "Biografía de Fernán González de Eslava." *Revista de filología hispánica* 2:213–321 (1940).
Jiménez Rueda, Julio. "La edad de Fernán González de Eslava." *Revista mexicana de estudios históricos* 2:102–106 (1928).
Johnson, Harvey L. "The Staging of González de Eslava's *Coloquios.*" *Hispanic Review* 8:343–346 (1940).
Johnson, Julie Greer. "Three Celestinesque Figures of Colonial Spanish American Literature." *Celestinesca* 5/1:41–46 (1981).

Listerman, R. W. "Sobre el arte dramático de Fernán González de Eslava y Sor Juana Inés de la Cruz a través de sus autos sacramentales." *University of South Florida Language Quarterly* (Tampa) 17/3,4:12–18 (1979).

Pasquariello, Anthony M. "The *Entremés* in Sixteenth-Century Spanish America." *Hispanic American Historical Review* 32:44–58 (1952).

Weber de Kurlat, Frida. *Lo cómico en el teatro de Fernán González de Eslava.* Buenos Aires, 1963.

El Inca Garcilaso de la Vega

(1539–1616)

Enrique Pupo-Walker

Gómez Suárez de Figueroa, the gifted man of letters we have come to know as El Inca Garcilaso de la Vega, was born on 12 April 1539 in the old Andean city of Cuzco, capital of the Incan Empire, and originally named after a paternal uncle. In ways that he could not have anticipated, his name and books came to represent in subsequent years the traumatic process of conquest and cultural blending initiated by Spain in the New World. *La Florida del Ynca* (*The Florida of the Inca*, 1605) is the first major work of American history written by a person born in the New World, a person who was, moreover a prominent *mestizo* (of mixed European and American Indian ancestry). In that lengthy and idealized narrative, he repeatedly described American Indians as people of considerable courage who upheld the highest standards of chivalric behavior, although they were not enlightened as yet by European culture and the Christian faith. Even earlier, in the prologue of his elegant translation of Leon Hebreo's 1535 *Dialoghi di amore* from Italian into Spanish as *La traduzión del Indio de los tres diálogos de amor de León Hebreo* (*The Philosophy of Love*, 1590), he alludes with evident pride to his Indian and European roots. Quite obviously he added Ynca to his name to denote his royal ancestry.

His identification with the Incan culture was evident in his most important works, *The Florida* and *Comentarios reales de los Yncas* (*Royal Commentaries of the Incas*, 1609, 1616–1617), known as the *Commentaries*. In those complex narratives, using his knowledge of philology and on methodological grounds, he attempted a systematic correction of errors and misunderstandings contained in the histories and reports written by Spaniards about the conquest of Peru. Citing primarily the Spaniards' ignorance of the Quechua language spoken by the Incas, which Garcilaso many times describes as his native tongue, he dismantled much of what official chroniclers had written about his homeland. This critique focused mainly on Diego Fernández de Palencia's *Primera y segunda parte de la historia del Perú* (First and Second Part of the History of Peru, 1571). Garcilaso's critical and defiant turn of mind was resented by Spaniards who saw in his works the seeds of a political program that could be used by groups of rebellious Indians and *mestizos* who opposed Spanish colonial rule. Indeed, a political reaction led by Tupac Amarú II, a person of noble Incan heritage, eventually led to a royal decree banning Garcilaso's works in Peru. Since the early days of the nineteenth century, the *Commentaries* have been perceived by many as a bright point of departure for a new political ideology in Spanish America. José de San Martín, a prominent Argentine leader in the wars of independence, sought to stimulate nationalistic sentiment by having the *Commentaries* published again, a move consistent with an ideological program that sought cultural as well as political independence from Spain.

Although one can comprehend the cultural and political considerations that led to such a use of the *Commentaries*, most of the ideological tenets held by Peruvians and other South Americans in the nineteenth century were alien to Garcilaso's thought. Political and administrative separation from Spain is not advocated in his works at any time. In fact, the conception of the Spanish Empire as formulated during the reign of Charles I (1500–1588) is one of the cornerstones of Garcilaso's historical perspective, particularly in all theological matters.

Garcilaso's works have been the object of enthusiastic praise and also a source of controversy. Well-known scholars, such as William Robertson, have doubted the validity of Garcilaso's assertions. In his *History of America* (1777), the Scottish historian initiated a trend of negative appraisals that has been expanded, for various reasons, by John Howland Rowe and Clements R. Markham, among others. The controversial Spanish scholar Marcelino Menéndez y Pelayo, in volume 1 of his *Orígenes de la novela* (Origins of the Novel, 1905), attempted to downgrade Garcilaso's contribution to history by describing the *Commentaries* as a utopian novel that led to idealized visions of American history. Ironically, Menéndez y Pelayo's partial reading of the *Commentaries* did not acknowledge the subtle and complex influence of Thomas More's *Utopia* (1516) on Garcilaso's rhetorical and philological reinterpretation of the pre-Hispanic and colonial history of Peru.

Recent scholarship has provided greater balance in the analysis of Garcilaso's narratives. A more sympathetic and informed reading of his texts is evident in the studies of Raúl Porras Barrenechea, Aurelio Miró Quesadà, Carmelo Sáenz de Santa María, John Grier Varner, and José Durand. But scholarly studies have not dispelled, by any means, the intense controversies that Garcilaso's works continue to generate among historians, anthropologists, and literary scholars.

During his childhood Garcilaso lived under the care of his mother, Isabel Suárez Chimpu Ocllo, concubine of Sebastián Garcilaso de la Vega. She was the granddaughter of the great Inca Túpac Yupanki and more than likely was bestowed to Capitán Sebastián as a very special reward. But after ten years of illegitimate union, he gave up the Palla (Inca princess) to marry Luisa Martel, a fourteen-year-old girl of distinguished Spanish ancestry. Yet Garcilaso remained under his father's care and became the captain's personal secretary.

At the age of twenty, in 1560, Garcilaso left Cuzco to settle among his distinguished paternal relatives in Extremadura, a region in the southwest of Spain. Under the protection of his uncle, Alonso de Vargas, he finally settled in the Andalusian village of Montilla, where, guided by the learned friars and supported by a trust arranged by his father, he began to acquire his considerable erudition. Thirty years later, after experiencing the turmoils of a military life, he was able to indulge his scholarly and religious inclinations when he settled in Cordova, a city in the south of Spain that was the headquarters of the royal chronicler Ambrosio de Morales and a group of learned historians known as the Cordova savants. There he died on 23 April 1616, surrounded by his mistress and illegitimate son, a small staff, and a few friends.

The wealth of autobiographical material in Garcilaso's works cannot always be detected immediately. He often left out of his narratives facts of an embarrassing nature or matters on which personal honor compelled him to remain reticent. He tells us that his father had been a captain in the royal armies of Charles I and that his mother was the Incan princess Isabel Chimpu Ocllo, but he omits that his father actually married a Spanish woman of aristocratic lineage and forced Garcilaso's mother into a marriage of convenience with a Spaniard of humble origins. Though Garcilaso refers frequently to his impressive family history, he does not omit the fact that he was illegitimate and a *mestizo*, and that he had endured an uncertain social status. Garcilaso partially offsets these unpleasant facts by displaying, at every turn, his sophistication and knowledge about the dissimilar cultural legacies that shaped his identity.

Through his knowledge of the Quechua language and his familiarity with Incan culture, Garcilaso was able to give his histories, at first glance, a validity and verisimilitude that Spanish historians could not hope to convey to their readers. By using narratives, confessions, and facts learned from his prominent Incan relatives, he appeared to be not merely the best-informed but the only legitimate chronicler of Incan history. Though this considerable authority gave Garcilaso the means to undertake a major revision of the histories that Spaniards had written about his homeland, he did so mainly by relying on philological commentaries and rhetorical devices that demonstrated clearly his acquaintance with the highest forms of Renaissance culture.

To provide immediacy and also to formalize the narrative process, Garcilaso inserted in the *Commentaries* passages in which he recalls with precision and delight events that occurred when his father was *corregidor* (magistrate) of Cuzco. He recalled ceremonies, visits of viceregal authorities to Cuzco, and the well-attended dinners that his father frequently hosted. If we observe with care the large scope of autobiographical material inserted in this narrative, we will understand that for Garcilaso the *Commentaries* were a reconstruction of vast historical periods but also the means to elucidate his own personal status. In a more general sense, he sought to resolve, as well, the precarious social ambivalence attached to the *mestizo*. Beyond these immediate concerns, he wanted to erase, once and for all, accusations made against his father, by which his rivals had brought into question the captain's loyalty to the Spanish crown.

The works of the Inca Garcilaso were read with considerable admiration by eminent historians and learned men who were at the center of important intellectual circles in southern Spain. Among the humanist and biblical scholars that Garcilaso knew were Gerónimo de Prado, Juan de Pineda, and Pedro Maldonado de Saavedra; perhaps the most influential individual of his acquaintance in Cordova was Bernardo de Aldrete, a humanist whose prestige reached beyond Spanish borders. However, the recognition and friendships that Garcilaso enjoyed could not compensate entirely for the frustrations he suffered in Madrid, where he was unsuccessful in obtaining monies he claimed were due him on account of his parents' positions. He began tedious and difficult

solicitations to the courts and councils of the crown around 1561, but many prerogatives were denied him. He was also unsuccessful in attempting to exonerate the memory of his father. After this sequence of reversals, he sought relative isolation, during which he wrote most of his historical narratives. Garcilaso's greatest satisfaction, in a life of sometimes paradoxical fortune, came to him with the publication of his books; the unprecedented recognition they received led him to direct acquaintance with distinguished historians and scholars, who valued him as the foremost authority on Peruvian history.

Fame and its rewards brought a sense of tranquillity to Garcilaso's last years in Cordova. On 18 September 1612 he bought the rights to burial in one of the chapels in the cathedral there. The chapel was prepared by his son, Diego de Vargas. On 18 April 1616, he dictated his last wishes. Earlier in the year, he had concluded the second part of the *Commentaries*, but the book was published late in 1617, a year after his death.

The Philosophy of Love (1590)

The translation from the Italian of Hebreo's *Philosophy of Love* was Garcilaso's first literary achievement. The task was one of considerable complexity. Varner, in his excellent biography of Garcilaso, notes that he was "drawn to the Neo-Platonic *Dialoghi di Amore* of the renowned humanist, Judah Abarbanal [León Hebreo], a Portuguese Jew whose philosophical explanation of the origin of both divine and profane love as early as 1564, if not earlier, had been expurgated in part by the Inquisition" (p. 276).

Garcilaso's translation was published in Madrid in 1590. In the prologue, he says he was inclined to do the translation because of "the sweetness and delicacy contained in [the work]." He also tells us that enlightened friends such as the Jesuit theologian Gerónimo de Prado and the Augustinian scholar Fernando de Zárate encouraged him to undertake the project. Garcilaso must have been aware that previous scholars who commented on the text had been scolded by authorities because of its supposedly theosophic and cabalistic concepts, which many regarded as dangerous. The Latin version had been forbidden by ecclesiastical authorities in 1564. Though Garcilaso wrote to a friend that the translation was undertaken to pass hours of tedious leisure, he knew that eminent scholars admired the dialogues. Moreover, parodies of the work had appeared in *La Galatea* (1585), by Miguel de Cervantes Saavedra, though it is not known whether Garcilaso was acquainted with that novel. He was attracted to the Neoplatonic conceptions that govern the flow of the dialogue in Hebreo's work, in which secular and divine forms of love are explained in an affected manner.

The Philosophy of Love was written by Hebreo in the first years of the sixteenth century, but the publication was delayed until 1535. The central line of discussion focuses on the contrast between love and desire, and suggests that love is fulfilled through a relationship that is consecrated. On the other hand, we are fully cognizant of desire only when seeking fulfillment. The subtle line of argument differentiates intuition, passion, and love, and the relationship that might exist among those states. These speculations lead to the conclusion that one can love either what one knows or what one desires. In each instance, knowledge is achieved on a particular plane of awareness. Desire, in any case, is more frequently linked to intuition. Abundant examples are provided to substantiate these distinctions; yet ultimately *The Philosophy of Love* is concerned with topics that were looked upon by ecclesiastical authorities with suspicion.

Hebreo's concepts of wisdom, virtue, and the existence of objects and beings did not conform in all instances to notions held by Scholastic philosophers and Christian theology in general. For example, the text examines in great detail the objects of human desire and at times does so from a highly individualistic point of view. There is an insistent and articulate defense of the pleasurable, described in highly sensual terms, provided though it was to show that the love of God exceeds in purity and virtue all other forms of love. Although *The Philosophy of Love* appears to the contemporary reader to be marred by excessive idealization, in Garcilaso's time the subject matter of the book was fascinating to many.

This translation afforded Garcilaso a pleasing entry into the intricacies of humanistic thought and phil-

ological concerns. The elaboration of the text in Castilian also served to sharpen his control of the language in which he would write his major works. With concerns typical of a Renaissance scholar, he was fascinated by the challenges and implications of translation as a task that expands and re-creates precious sources of knowledge. Aided by his intense motivation and his extraordinary linguistic skills, he produced the finest Spanish translation of Hebreo's text.

The Florida of the Inca (1605)

More than sixty years after the unfortunate expedition of Hernando de Soto to Florida, Garcilaso published in Lisbon an exhaustive account of the ill-fated adventures of the Spaniards in the southeastern part of North America. This book put Garcilaso's talents to a very different test. All the information he used was secondhand and pertained to a remote area of the New World that he had never visited. In addition, the information was obtained by oral testimony or from personal documents written by humble soldiers who had participated in the conquest of Peru, including many documents that no one else mentions or uses. As with the translation of *The Philosophy of Love*, it is difficult to understand why Garcilaso chose to labor for so long on the preparation of a book that, at first glance, seems so distant from his main historiographical objectives.

This book, as the *Commentaries* would do later, served to consolidate Garcilaso's problematic identity and his desire to identify with the ancient historical legacy of the Incas. Of all the narratives written on the subject, Garcilaso's is the most complete, extensive, and well written. Ironically, the very elegance and literary refinement of Garcilaso's texts would be used by many to discredit the historical contribution made by *The Florida*. Objections that the work was more a creative effort than a contribution to history were raised by the North American historian George Bancroft, in his well-known *History of the United States* (1834–1874). However, the controversial aspects of *The Florida* have been elucidated, to a considerable extent in recent years, by the studies of Miró Quesada, Durand, and Varner, among others.

Although in the nineteenth and twentieth centuries *The Florida* was looked upon as a document of doubtful historical value, that was not the case in Garcilaso's time. The royal chronicler Antonio de Herrera (1559–1625), among others, used *The Florida* rather extensively in his own accounts. He did not acknowledge his debt to the work of Garcilaso, but the practice of appropriation of facts in historical works was not uncommon.

It is possible that Garcilaso was working on the preliminary stages of *The Florida* as early as 1563. He speaks of it in the prologue to *The Philosophy of Love*, but in 1589 he was still polishing several portions of the manuscript. By 1592, he seems to have concluded his final draft. In a letter to the Licenciado Juan Fernández Franco, dated 31 December 1593, he states, "Thanks to God, I have finished *The Florida*, although I have yet to find a scribe who can produce a clean copy of it."

Regarding his sources, it is fair to say that Garcilaso consulted most of the written sources available in his day, although historians have noted with surprise that prominent accounts, such as the ones written by the Hildalgo of Elvas, Rodrigo Rangel, and Luis Hernández de Biedma were not known to Garcilaso. While he depended heavily on the spectacular accounts given by Alvar Núñez Cabeza de Vaca in his *Naufragios* (Journal, 1542), ultimately his most reliable source was his friend Gonzalo Silvestre, an old conquistador who had been with the disastrous expedition that de Soto led to Florida and who lived in the village of Las Posadas near Montilla. Garcilaso also acknowledged having used the narratives composed by the soldiers Alonso de Carmona and Juan de Coles, both survivors of the expedition. But these unknown manuscripts remind us immediately of similar "finds" of mysterious accounts so frequently dramatized in Renaissance literature by Cervantes and other prominent Spanish and Italian authors.

This body of facts and information is the most obvious disguise used by Garcilaso in *The Florida*. He tells us that he writes the narratives of others, including those who experienced the events, but these sources serve as masks or personas adopted by Garcilaso. In other instances, he comes very close to the prerogatives of the omniscient narrator (book 2, chapter 9), and in still other passages he indicates obliquely that the total organization is really his (book 1, chapter 27).

From the beginning books and chapters of *The Florida*, Garcilaso attempts to follow at close range the sequence of events as they occurred. He indulges in anecdotal digressions but on the whole maintains a global perspective of the events. It is evident that these frequent digressions serve to cover up areas or periods about which Garcilaso knew little; it is clear that he has tried to supplement the sometimes slender body of information he had. Often these supplements take the form of short narratives that emerge as imaginative illustrations of the events described (book 3, chapter 20).

The *Commentaries* (1609; 1616–1617)

After a lifetime of gathering information and endless hours of laboring over his manuscripts, Garcilaso published the first part of the *Commentaries* in 1609, with the aid of the famous presses of Pedro Crasbeeck in Lisbon. The book was dedicated to Catalina of Portugal, duchess of Braganza. As was customary at the time, the title of the book is in itself a brief narrative: *Primera parte de los comentarios reales, que tratan del origin de los Yncas. . . . Escritos por el Inca Garcilasso de la Vega, natural del Cozco, y capitán de su Magestad* (First Part of the Royal Commentaries, which Deal with the Origin of the Incas. . . . Written by the Inca Garcilaso de la Vega, Native of Cuzco and His Majesty's Captain). After Garcilaso's death, the second part was published, in 1616–1617 in Cordova by the presses of Andrés Barrera's widow. For arbitrary reasons and against Garcilaso's wishes, the second volume appeared as the *Historia general del Perú* (General History of Perú). These two volumes established Garcilaso as a leading authority on Peruvian history. Indirectly, because of the expository refinement of both volumes, Garcilaso also achieved a considerable literary reputation.

Though there are fundamental elements that link the two volumes, they are in many ways different books. The first is divided into nine books of similar length, in which Garcilaso describes the geographic setting of the Incan Empire, and its history and cultural heritage, including social and political institutions, dynasties, costumes, religious beliefs, mythology, and the languages used. In describing the central figures of the empire, Garcilaso depicts the Incas as generous benefactors. He also characterizes the flora and fauna found in the region, always contrasting this factual knowledge with European realities.

Though Garcilaso describes in book 2 the full range of pagan beliefs maintained by the Incas, he nevertheless indicates, whenever possible, that the forms of worship practiced by his maternal ancestors were in some ways very close to Christian beliefs. Indeed, Garcilaso followed the Augustinian model, portraying the Incan Empire as in a preparatory stage for the advent of Christianity. Cuzco is seen as another Rome, and the Incan Empire as a major civilizing force that facilitated the assimilation of European culture. In this respect, as in many others, Garcilaso's imaginative effort reaches considerable proportions; through it, we come to appreciate the impressive range of his knowledge of historiography, theology, and philology. Within its vast frame of references, his writing reveals a humanistic education of impressive depth.

In composing the ancient history of Tahuantinsuyu (as the Incan Empire was called), Garcilaso claims, on linguistic and philological grounds, a more accurate knowledge of sources than that of the Spanish historians who preceded him. Indeed, much of the thrust of the *Commentaries* was to "correct" errors present in the narratives of Fernández de Palencia, Francisco López de Gómara, and others. He emphasizes at every turn that their lack of knowledge of the Quechua language led them to serious misunderstandings. (See part 1, book 6, chapter 2; part 2, book 6, chapter 26.) While underlining these and other deficiencies, Garcilaso repeatedly documented his detailed knowledge of Incan traditions and his acquaintance with members of the Incan royal family. The *Commentaries* assume an increasing polemical bent. It was his desire to prove the worth and importance of Incan culture that led Garcilaso to assume extreme positions. In describing Incan traditions as if they were valid equivalents of Roman cultural legacies, he portrays the social structure in Cuzco in a highly idealized manner, and these distorted aspects of the text have

diminished Garcilaso's stature as a historian and primary source.

The second part, the *General History of Peru*, is divided into eight books. Garcilaso seeks to describe the conquest of his homeland, while documenting the history of his family and the privileged status that he enjoyed in Cuzco as a youth. He documents his personal knowledge of the events and personalities that dominated the early stages of the conquest. In the initial chapters of the second part, the reader encounters Francisco Pizarro, who had been named governor of Peru by Charles V and is described in positive terms, as well as Pedro de Alvarado, a nobleman from Extremadura who was mentor of Sebastián Garcilaso de la Vega and a rival and later companion of Francisco Pizarro. One meets also Diego de Almagro, with whom Pizarro had formed a pact for the conquest of Peru. Atahualpa, Inca emperor when the Spanish arrived, and Manco Inca, son of Hayna Cápac and legitimate heir to the throne, are also mentioned, as are many of the leading protagonists and victims of the conquest. Special interest is added to this volume by Garcilaso's narrative of the early struggles for power among the Spanish and Incan leaders. Much emphasis is given to the vicious conflicts that developed between the factions led by Francisco Pizarro and those of de Almagro. On several occasions, Francisco's brother Gonzalo led Spanish soldiers into open warfare against the established royal authorities, but this rebellion was weakened by his execution and that of many of his followers. Nevertheless, other leaders, notably Francisco Hernández Girón, repeatedly rebelled against the royal authorities. This extraordinarily violent early period concludes with the execution of Tupac Amarú, heir to the Incan throne, by the Spanish viceroy Francisco de Toledo. Garcilaso provides a detailed and rather morbid account of these bloody incidents.

The character of events and the perspective afforded by the second part are quite different from those of the first part of the *Commentaries*. Because the first part is concerned primarily with events contemporary to Garcilaso, they are often described with surprising immediacy. On the whole, the second part does not provide much new knowledge about the early stages of the conquest. The chronological organization of the narrative is orderly and well established, even though the events described are confusing and often clouded by Garcilaso's prejudices. He had depended heavily on information supplied by his friend Silvestre, his father, and other persons who were close to his family's household. Beyond these testimonies and the reconstruction of his personal experiences, Garcilaso used many of the textual sources that he had called on for the first part. Nevertheless, it must be said that the second part of the *Commentaries* contains several distinctive features. It represents an elaborate effort on Garcilaso's part to redeem the memory of his beloved father. He sought, furthermore, to place the Incan royal family in a better light and to demonstrate the highly disruptive impact of the conquest. This is particularly evident in books 7 and 8, which pertain to the rebellions of Hernández Girón and the brief tenure of the viceroy Antonio de Mendoza.

In the second part, as in previous works, Garcilaso frames the narrative with a prologue that is of special interest. In it, he abandons any hope of royal recognition and simply dedicates the work to the Virgin Mary, admitting that it is also intended as a tribute to the memory of his father. In the prologue, Garcilaso directly addresses the Indians and *mestizos* of Peru. The prologue is of special interest because it provides further clarification regarding Garcilaso's understanding of the purposes of history. This portion of the text is further evidence of the delicate balance of a narrative that, on the one hand, hails the conquest on religious grounds and, on the other, condemns the brutality of its actions; yet he skillfully places this paradoxical context within the framework of Spain's imperial and evangelical enterprises.

Much of the interest in both parts of the *Commentaries* is found in the multiple ironies that are carefully balanced by the delicate twists and turns of the narrative process. It must also be borne in mind that Garcilaso was in many ways at the mercy of royal censors and subject to inspection by authorities of the Inquisition. It is a tribute to his talents that he was able to deal with so many controversial matters without falling into situations of conflict with authorities who knew that he had no special commission to write such books.

SELECTED BIBLIOGRAPHY

Editions

Individual Works

La traduzión del Indio de los tres diálogos de amor de León Hebreo. Madrid, 1590.
La Florida del Ynca. Lisbon, 1605.
Primera parte de los comentarios reales de los Yncas. Lisbon, 1609.
Historia general del Perú. Cordova, 1616–1617.
Relación de la descendencia de Garcí Pérez de Vargas. Lima, 1596. Facsimile ed. 1951.

Collected Works

Obras completas. Edited by P. Carmelo Sáenz de Santa María. 4 vols. Madrid, 1960, 1963.

Translations

The Florida of the Inca. Translated by John Grier Varner and Jeannette Johnson Varner. Austin, Tex., 1951.
The Philosophy of Love. Translated by F. Friedeberg-Seeley and Jean Barnes. London, 1937.
Royal Commentaries of the Incas and General History of Perú. Translated and with an introduction by Harold V. Livermore. 2 vols. Austin, Tex., 1966.

Biographical and Critical Studies

Arocena, Luis A. *El Inca Garcilaso y el humanismo renacentista.* Buenos Aires, 1949.
Castanien, Donald G. *El Inca Garcilaso de la Vega.* New York, 1969.
Crowley, Francis G. *Garcilaso de la Vega, el Inca, and His Sources in the "Comentarios Reales de los Incas."* The Hague, 1971.
Durand, José. *El Inca Garcilaso, clásico de América.* Mexico City, 1976.
Fitzmaurice-Kelly, Julia. *El Inca Garcilasso de la Vega.* Oxford, 1921.
Miró Quesada S., Aurelio. *El Inca Garcilaso y otros estudios Garcilasistas.* Madrid, 1971.
Pupo-Walker, Enrique. *Historia, creación y profecía en los textos del Inca Garcilaso de la Vega.* Madrid, 1982.
Varner, John Grier. *El Inca: The Life and Times of Garcilaso de la Vega.* Austin, Tex., 1968.

Father Joseph de Acosta

(1540–1600)

Luis A. Arocena

Toward the end of the sixteenth century much had already been written about what was for the European an unsuspected New World. General and regional histories, chronicles of discoveries and conquests, travel accounts, geographical descriptions, and fairly reliable observations about the nature of the Indian and his peculiar cultural world constituted by that time a library as voluminous as it was varied. For Father Joseph de Acosta, however, something was lacking, and his purpose in writing a new natural and moral history of the Indies was to remedy the shortcomings of the earlier works.

Father Acosta was thirty-two when, after a brief and uneventful stay in the Greater and Lesser Antilles, he arrived in Lima, instructed by the Society of Jesus to resolve the problems attendant to its expansion in Peru and to evangelize the Indians. Born in Medina del Campo in 1540, he had received a solid humanistic education among the Jesuits, whose novitiate he had entered while yet a boy, and at the University of Alcalá de Henares, where he completed his theological and philosophical studies with singular distinction. At the age of twenty-six, he took priestly orders and very soon gained prestige as a lecturer in theology and as an eloquent pulpit speaker. His American experience lasted sixteen years, most of which he spent in Peru, whose regions, cities, people, and cultures he came to know well. During his stay in Mexico between 1586 and 1587 his diligence as a researcher enabled him to gather information that was more bookish than direct or personal. Nevertheless, when this naturalist and historian reflected on the methodology of his work, he categorically declared that nothing could replace personal experience and methodical observation in the description of nature and in the consideration of human behavior.

During his active stay in Peru, Father Acosta journeyed throughout the country promoting the formation of Jesuit schools. He served as rector of the Lima school and as provincial of the Society in the broad viceregal jurisdiction, while bolstering his fame as a sacred orator and as an evangelist among the Indians. He learned Aymará in order to make his missionary efforts more effective, and he collaborated in the writing of trilingual catechisms in Aymará, Quéchua, and Spanish. Around 1576, his evangelizing experience motivated him to write a treatise about its problems and methodology: *De promulgatione Evangelii apud barbaros, sive De procuranda indorum salute, libri sex* (The Six Books of the Promulgation of the Gospel Among the Barbarians, or the Procuring of the Salvation of the Indians). While furthering his religious efforts, he still found time to satisfy his yearning for knowledge about the physical reality, knowledge that was for him no less compelling than that of the metaphysical. During his missionary travels, he carefully observed the nature around him, took notes, requested information, and drew on existing knowledge. He organized all his data, and around 1586 compiled it in two books called *De natura Novi Orbis* (On the Nature of the New World).

Father Acosta translated *De natura Novi Orbis* into Spanish and made it part of his *Historia natural y moral de las Indias* (*Natural and Moral History of the Indies*). The *History*, completed in 1588, was judged by Fray Luis de Leon, the poet and ecclesiastical censor who approved the work, as "worthy of the great learning and wisdom of the author and of being read by all that they might praise God, whose works are marvelous." Indeed, this treatise is responsible for the privileged position occupied by Father Acosta in the history of Spanish American historiography.

In the initial words of the Proem in his *History*, Father Acosta advises the reader of a fact so decisive for him that it had come to represent the fundamental justification of his work.

> Many authors have written books and accounts about the New World and the West Indies in which they speak of the new and strange things that have been discovered in those regions and of the actions and events that have befallen the Spaniards who have conquered and populated them. But until now I have seen no author attempt to state the causes and reasons for such novelties and oddities of nature or make any discourse or investigation in this area, nor have I found any book about the actions and history of the ancient Indians themselves, the native inhabitants of the New World.

His purpose was quite clear. It was not a question of attempting a mere description of the physical reality of America or of simply narrating the acts of the men who lived there or came as conquerors. The important matters were the discovery and exposition of the real causes operating at the heart of natural phenomena and in historical events, that is, to justify a causal explanation of what previously had been put forth as an assorted collection of oddities. Whether Father Acosta was able to achieve completely the purpose of his historiographic method is less important than the fact that he recognized its importance and put it into pratice with systematic rigor. His attempt to impose a

methodology on the object of his study bore fruit as an early philosophy of nature and of the history of America on the centennial of her discovery.

A simple inspection of the structure of the *Natural and Moral History of the Indies* suffices to verify the extent to which a selective, ordering intelligence has reduced to unity and system what at first appears to be chaos and confusion. For Father Acosta, reality was divided between the world of nature and the world of man. This was not an original idea. What was original was the author's use of this idea as a rigid criterion for systematization.

> So although the New World is no longer new but old, inasmuch as a great deal has been written and said about it, I still believe this *History* can in some way be considered novel, because it is both history and, in part, philosophy, and deals not only with the works of nature, but also with those of free will, which are the actions and customs of men.

But when it came to actually ordering the two worlds that are the object of his study, Father Acosta shared the vigorous providentialism of the men of his times and religious persuasion. The Creator constantly rules his creation. Nature reveals the fullness of his power; history reveals his thought. "Things which seem to us to be chance occurrences," he declares, "are quite deliberately ordained by God." But beneath the high and inscrutable First Cause lies the level of secondary causes. It is on this secondary level that Father Acosta believed he found at work in nature a certain necessity and rigor, whose economy becomes evident upon careful observation and reflection. These secondary causes also exert their constitutive function in the human realm, but there the operation of freedom gives causation its specific character. In history all acts are indeed occurrences, but they do not occur in a haphazard, discontinuous fashion. Acosta believed it was possible to arrive at reasonable explanations, even within the realm of free will, by taking into account the recurrence of events in time and the constants of human nature.

The four books devoted to the systematic exposition of nature in the New World abound with examples of Father Acosta's keen perception, and the results of his work were noteworthy. In an age that broadened geographical knowledge more than any other before it, he contributed not only the correction of old errors, but also a wealth of new knowledge. The nineteenth-century explorer and naturalist Alexander von Humboldt praised the *Natural and Moral History of the Indies,* saying that matters related to the new continent and the physical history of the earth had never before been considered with such admirable generality.

Given Father Acosta's obligatory monogenism, he was compelled to reflect on the problem of tracing the population of the New World to descent from Adam and Eve and the variety of its fauna to the species saved in Noah's ark. He notes in Book 1, chapter 16, when examining how such extraordinary migrations could occur, that "it is not a matter of what God can do, but rather of what conforms to reason and to the order and style of things human." Having examined and rejected as indefensible the theories proposed up to that time, Father Acosta suggested that the passage of people as well as animals probably occurred over land, at a point where the two worlds, the Old and the New, joined or were in close proximity. "Until now, at least," he concludes in Book 1, chapter 20, "there is no evidence to the contrary, because from the Arctic Pole, which is called the North Pole, the entire earth has not been discovered and explored, and there is no lack of people who say that the earth runs continuously from Florida to the North." This idea about the peopling of America represents a notable foresight on the part of Acosta, as do his ideas about the primitivism that must have characterized its first inhabitants and about the progress achieved through the centuries until Europeans appeared as discoverers. The naturalist also attributed to time and environment the varieties noted in the species of American fauna.

In attending to the customs, beliefs, and social and political organizations of the Indian, Father Acosta anticipated to a degree the methods of cultural history. When dealing with the highest cultures of America, those developed in Mexico and Peru, he did not attempt to prepare an account of actions in a chronological sequence, but rather to trace a broad, demonstrative description of the elements that constituted their particular material and spiritual forms of life. In approaching "the moral history, that is, that of the customs and actions of the Indians," he did so realizing that the inhabitants of the New World offered such a complex variety of economic levels, customs and habits, developments in social relations, religious beliefs and rituals, physical appearance, and psychological temperament, that any generalization becomes risky, if not impossible. Nonetheless, in his *History* as well as in *De procuranda indorum salute,* Father Acosta understood that as a basic principle one thing could be stated as a certainty: The Indian was not by nature the irrational, fierce, savage, cruel, and vicious being described by many writers. Acosta was not unaware that many aspects of Indian life and customs were censurable, but these should not be considered an innate necessity but rather explained as the imposition of social experience. "It is known," he says, "that the way men are raised has more bearing on their nature than heredity." Thus, Acosta could state "that the Indian's incapacity for ingenuity and his fierce customs stem less from heredity or lineage, or from the native air, than from his prolonged training and from a way of life not unlike that of the beasts." Father Acosta added two more assertions in defense of the unjustly accused Indian. First, he observed that the barbarity for which the Indians were criticized was not their exclusive patrimony. Even the greatly admired Greeks and Romans, he notes, were guilty of similar, or worse, defects. Second, he emphasized the excellence of the achievements of the more advanced Indian societies. Dissenting energetically with those who believed that the Indians lacked reason and understanding, Acosta declared in Book 6, chapter 1, with support from the opinions of Juan Polo de Ondegardo, the author of a 1572 treatise on the lineage of the Incas, and the Jesuit Juan de Tovar: "The more inquisitive and wiser men who have penetrated and understood their secrets, their ways and ancient government, hold quite a different opinion, amazed that such order and reason existed among them."

Of the three books that comprise his moral history, Acosta devotes the first and most extensive to recording and commenting on the religious beliefs and practices of the Indians. His interest in this subject is obvious and understandable. He believed that one could hardly work to evangelize them without a knowledge of the nature and depth of indigenous religious experience, particularly because the Indian lived immersed in a supernatural world in and for

49

which his acts and behavior acquired meaning. For every aspect of this religious experience that concerned him, Acosta offers a reasoned explanation. Beyond these circumstantial explanations, however, he finds a fundamental, operant cause at work in the religious world of the Indian: the presence of the Devil in the forging of their idolatry. It was hardly original for Acosta to attribute to "him who is envious of the glory of God" and to the "enemy of humankind" such a tenacious and constant intervention in shaping the religious institutions of the Indian. The novelty of his observations is that, while not justifying them, for Father Acosta the Devil represented an excuse that at least relieved the Indians of some responsibility for their odious and abominable practices.

Father Acosta also examined other problems related to the Indian and his destiny in the face of a painful and sometimes tragic process of political and cultural impositions. He showed himself in all things to be a man of balanced judgment, with manifest sympathy for the world of the conquered. He did not attain the radicalism of Fray Bartolomé de las Casas, but neither is he close to those who considered the Indians suitable only for iniquitous servitude and exploitation. He demanded respect for their human condition even in the field of missionary work. "Let us not make greed and tyranny the teachers of their introduction to the gospel," he exorted. Acosta knew the conquest was carried out in the main "by greedy, rough men, ignorant of the way one should proceed when among infidels who had never committed any offense against Christians," but he did not condemn the conquest as a whole, nor did he question the institutions that consolidated it. For him, the religious aim attached to the violent imposition of Spanish control in the Indies justified and condoned the whole. Acosta was, without a doubt, deeply committed to the full incorporation of the world of the Indian into Christianity. The humanist and the man of science gave way to the missionary. Even when writing his *History*, he was not intent so much on increasing the wealth of knowledge as he was on supplying information instrumental for the work of evangelization. His historiographic pragmatism is, in this sense, quite noteworthy.

Acosta probably possessed a somewhat abrasive personality. He himself confessed that his way of dealing with people was "direct, without affectation or qualms." One who praises him acknowledged the dubious merit of his great ability to dissimulate—*et dissimulare in loco doctus*. He made no few enemies in life, and he was reproached for allowing himself to became secularized and for being ambitious, disloyal, and vain about his intellectual gifts. In the opinion of one modern critic, he was even a plagiarist. Father Acosta took it upon himself to respond punctually to those who criticized him in his own time, and proof of his intellectual dishonesty has not been satisfactorily established. In any case, his name has been linked for all time to a body of work that reveals extraordinary knowledge, keen observations, and thoughtful opinions about the physical and human reality of the New World. In the case of the *Natural and Moral History of the Indies*, his work displays not only the merits of an effective structure, but also a rich, clear, and precise prose in which didactic demands yield at times to an eloquence and lyricism elicited by admiration.

In the course of his rugged wanderings and exhausting tasks, Father Acosta fell ill, as he says, with "afflictions of the heart," as heart disease was called. He died of his "afflictions" in Salamanca in February 1600, at peace with all and with himself, surrounded by books and literary projects, faithful in this regard to a vocation he had felt, no doubt, since his childhood.

Translated from the Spanish by Galen Greaser

SELECTED BIBLIOGRAPHY

Editions

Collected Works

Obras del P. José de Acosta, de la Compañía de Jesús. Estudio preliminar y edición del P. Francisco Mateos de la misma Compañía. Madrid, 1954. Works by Father Acosta that are part of this collection are indicated.

Works in Latin

De natura Novi Orbis, libri duo et De promulgatione Evangelii apud barbaros, sive De procuranda indorum salute, libri sex. Salamanca, 1588. The six books corresponding to *procuranda indorum salute* were translated and published by Father Francisco Mateos. See *Obras*, pp. 387–611.

De Christo Revelato, libri novem. Rome, 1590.

De temporibus novissimis, libri quattuor. Rome, 1590. This treatise and the previous one were reissued and published together in Lyon, 1592.

Concilium provinciale Limense celebratum in civitate Regum. Anno MDLXXXIII sub Gregorio XIII, Sum. Pont. Madrid, 1591.

Josephii Acostæ e Societate Jesu, Conciones in Quadragesima. Quarum in singulas Ferias numerarum et locum Index initio præfixus ostendit. Res vero et insigniores Scripturæ locos retractos duo alii indices continent. Salamanca, 1596.

Conciones de Adventu. Salamanca, 1597.

Conciones ab octava Pasche usque ad Adventum. Salamanca, 1599.

Tractatus aliquot de Theologia et de Sacra Scriptura. 6 vols., unpublished manuscript.

Works in Spanish

Carta Anua de 1576 al P. Everardo Mercuriano, Prepósito General de la Compañía de Jesús. Lima 15 de febrero de 1577. See *Obras*, pp. 260–290.

Carta Anua de la Provincia del Perú del año 1578. Lima 11 de abril de 1579. See *Obras*, pp. 290–302.

Tercero cathecismo y exposición de la doctrina christiana por sermones para que los curas y otros ministros prediquen y enseñen a los indios. Lima, 1585.

Peregrinación del Hermano Bartolomé Lorenzo. Written in 1586, first published in 1666. See *Obras*, pp. 304–320.

Parecer sobre la guerra de la China. Written in Mexico, 15 March 1587. See *Obras*, pp. 331–334.

Respuesta a los fundamentos que justifican la guerra contra la China. Written in Mexico, 23 March 1587. See *Obras*, pp. 334–345.

Historia natural y moral de las Indias, en que se tratan las cosas notables del cielo, y elementos, metales, plantas, y animales dellas: y los ritos, y ceremonias, leyes, y gobierno, y guerras de los Indios [. . .] Impresso en Sevilla en casa de Juan de León. Año de 1590. Translations into Italian (Venice, 1596), French (Paris, 1598), Dutch (Amsterdam, 1598), Latin (Coll. Thedor de Bry, 1602), English (London, 1604), and German (Ursel, 1605).

Diario de la embajada a Roma. Roma 22 de diciembre 1592. See *Obras*, pp. 353–368.

Memorial de apología o descargo dirigido al Papa Clemente VIII. Written in 1593; published in 1889. See *Obras*, pp. 368–386.

De la justicia conmutative y distributiva; reglas de buen gobierno dirigidas al Virrey D. Francisco de Toledo y Elogios de varones ilustres de la Compañia de Jesús en el Perú. These two works are cited as unpublished in bibliographical listings, as are many reports, memorials, letters, commentaries on sacred texts and a voluminous collection of sermons. See some of the previously unpublished material in "Escritos menores," *Obras*, pp. 249–386.

Biographical and Critical Studies

Aguirre, E. "Una hipótesis evolucionista en el siglo XVI. El P. José de Acosta, S. I., y el orígen de las especies americanas. *Arbor* (Madrid) 36/134: 176–187 (1957).

Arrom, Juan José. Prologue to *Peregrinación de Bartolomé Lorenzo*, Lima, 1982.

Beddall, Bárbara G. "El P. José de Acosta y la posición de su Historia Natural y Moral de las Indias en la historia de la ciencia." Introduction to *Historia natural y moral de las Indias*. Facsimile of the 1590 edition. Valencia, 1977. Pp. 11–29.

Esteve Barba, Francisco. "José de Acosta." In *Historiografía Indiana*. Madrid, 1964. Pp. 102–111.

Hornberger, Theodore. *Acosta's "Historia natural y moral de las Indias": A guide to the source and the growth of the American scientific tradition.* The University of Texas Publication, 3926, 8 July 1939. Pp. 139–162.

Lopetegui, León, S.I. *El Padre José de Acosta, S. I. y las misiones.* Madrid, 1942.

Mateos, Francisco, S.I. Introduction to *De procuranda indorum salute. Predicación del Evangelio en las Indias*, by Father Joseph de Acosta. Madrid, 1952.

———. "Personalidad y escritos del P. José de Acosta." Introduction in *Obras del P. José de Acosta, de la Compañía de Jesús.* Pp. vii–xlix. Madrid, 1954.

O'Gorman, Edmundo. Prologue to *Historia natural y moral de las Indias [. . .] compuesto por el P. Joseph de Acosta, religioso de la Compañia de Jesús.* 2nd ed., Mexico City and Buenos Aires, 1962. Pp. xi–xcv.

Pereña, Luciano. "Estudio Preliminar." In *De procuranda indorum salute. Pacificación y colonización.* Bilingual edition. Madrid, 1984. Pp. 3–46.

Pinta Llorente, Miguel de la. *Actividades diplomáticas del P. José de Acosta. En torno a una política y a un sentimiento religioso.* Madrid, 1952.

Rivara de Tuesta, María Luisa. *José de Acosta, un humanista reformista.* Lima, 1970.

Rodríguez Carracido, José. *El P. José de Acosta y su importancia en literatura científica española.* Madrid, 1899.

Bernardo de Balbuena

(1561?–1627)

José Rabasa

Almost nothing is known with certainty about Bernardo de Balbuena's early years. It is commonly accepted that Balbuena was born in Valdepeñas, in the province of Ciudad Real, Spain, sometime between 1561 and 1563. Apparently Balbuena was born out of wedlock to Francisca Sánchez de Velasco while his father was in Spain for business and legal affairs. His father, also named Bernardo, arrived in the New World at a young age and obtained a post in the Audiencia of Nueva Galicia, the present-day state of Jalisco in Mexico. Balbuena may have arrived in Mexico with his father as early as 1564. Once settled in Nueva Galicia, he grew up with relatives who had properties in Guadalajara, Compostela, and San Pedro Lagunillas. Balbuena studied in Guadalajara until about 1580, when he went to Mexico City to continue his education. There is no documentation on the college where he earned the title of *bachiller* (bachelor of theology), nor on the education he received at the Real y Pontifica Universidad de México (Royal and Pontifical University of Mexico). It is not even known whether he ever matriculated as a student. More important to his development as a poet, however, is the fact that by the second half of the sixteenth century, Mexico City was already a lively center of literary activities. In his letter *Al Doctor Don Antonio de Ávila y Cadena Arcediano de la Nueva Galicia* (To Doctor Antonio de Ávila y Cadena, Archdeacon of New Galicia, abbreviated as *Carta al Arcediano*) Balbuena mentions how he won the prize in three literary contests celebrated between 1585 and 1590.

In 1586, the year he won his second literary contest, Balbuena apparently initiated his ecclesiastical career as chaplain in New Galicia. He was promoted to the post of priest in San Pedro Lagunillas in 1592. This new post gave him more freedom and time to pursue his own interests, and the following ten years in Lagunillas were his most productive. During this time he composed the greater part of his long epic poem, *El Bernardo, o Victoria de Roncesvalles* (Bernard, or the Victory of Roncesvalles, 1624), and his pastoral novel, *Siglo de oro en las selvas de Erífile* (Golden Age in the Groves of Eriphyle, 1608).

Balbuena's extensive travels took him to San Miguel de Culiacán, where he met Isabel de Tobar y Guzmán, who was in the process of moving to Mexico City to join a convent. During their meeting, Isabel de Tobar asked Balbuena to write her a description of Mexico City. In response Balbuena wrote a long verse epistle between 1602 and 1603, which was almost immediately published as *Grandeza mexicana* (The Grandeur of Mexico City) in 1604. The first edition, printed by Melchior Orchate, is dedicated to the archbishop of Mexico, thereby conveying Balbuena's intention of gaining a post in the church of Mexico City or Tlaxcala. To gain the recognition of dignitaries in Spain, Balbuena also wrote a song dedicating the epistle to the Count of Lemos, Don Pedro Fernández de Castro, who was the president of the Real Consejo de Indias (Royal Council of the Indies) and a prominent patron of letters. In this latter capacity he was the benefactor of Miguel Cervantes and Lope de Vega. The song to Count Lemos was added to copies of the earlier version of the poem destined for Spain and was printed in 1604 by Diego López Dávalos.

Balbuena traveled to Spain in 1606 and remained there until 1610. While in Spain he published his novel *Siglo de oro en las selvas de Erífile* and earned a doctorate in theology from the University of Sigüenza in 1607. The novel was first published in 1608 with a dedication to Count Lemos. From all appearances the dedications to Count Lemos earned Balbuena the abbacy of Jamaica in 1608. This post represented both advantages and disadvantages for Balbuena. On the one hand, the abbacy was surpassed in dignity only by a bishopric, while on the other hand, the independence and authority of the abbacy of Jamaica also entailed a geographic isolation from cultural centers. Balbuena arrived in Jamaica in 1610 and remained there for the next twelve years. He was named bishop of Puerto Rico in 1619, but he did not assume his new post until 1623, after a short stay in Santo Domingo in 1622. It was during his stay in Puerto Rico that Balbuena published his long poem *Bernardo, o Victoria de Roncesvalles* in 1624. Among the critical events in the last days of Balbuena's life was the loss of his library, resulting from the Dutch invasion of Puerto Rico in which San Juan was ransacked and burned in 1625. Balbuena died on 11 October 1627.

Siglo de oro en las selvas de Erífile is a pastoral novel that alternates between prose and verse. The work consists of twelve eclogues in which tercets constitute the main verse form, but it also includes combinations with songs, *silvas* (a form of metrical poetry), ottava rima, and sonnets, among other forms. Balbuena uses these variations to present such topics as lamenting the absence of the loved one or expressing complaint over being spurned. The poems also dwell on the beauty and physical features of the loved one. Along with these conventional contents of the pastoral, Balbuena includes verses of which the poetics of the pastoral are the main topic.

The prose sections of the eclogues further elaborate the discussion of pastoral poetic conventions. As has often been remarked, Balbuena does not follow such Spanish pastoral prototypes as the *Diana* of Jorge de Montemayor and Gil Polo. Instead Balbuena adopts the original paradigm of the *Diana* (1558–1559?) and of other works in France and England, the *Arcadia* (1502) of the Neapolitan Jacopo Sannazaro. His approximation to the *Arcadia* leads Balbuena to accentuate the bucolic element at the expense of traits that define *Siglo de oro* as a novel. Balbuena's divisions of the text with eclogues constitute a self-conscious relegating of the novelistic format to a mere frame function. The narrative is lyrical and tends toward an erratic movement that resembles the wanderings of shepherds and nymphs, the traces of musical sounds, and the flights of fancy in a dream world.

Thus we find the most significant transformation of the novel in Eclogue Six, where a dream serves as the leading motif for introducing a description of Mexico City: ". . . a quiet dream, sweet comfort of evils, bathed my face with a delightful liquor, taking my restless fantasy after it through frightening places worthy of reverence" (1821 ed., p. 130). This eclogue divides the novel in two as it marks a transition from an emphasis on natural landscape, on the description of the grove as a *locus amoenus* (ideal landscape), to the inclusion of cultural features such as monuments, pyramids, altars, and so on. On the threshold of a cave, which seems like death, a beautiful nymph comes out of a fountain and challenges the shepherd to follow her, leading him through the cave on an underworld journey that concludes on the other side of the world, with a vision of Mexico City from under its lagoon: ". . . seated on top of its delicate waves I saw a proud and populous city, and not without great admiration did I say in my thoughts: this undoubtedly is that great Mexico City, about which the world tells so many miracles" (p. 132).

In the passages following this quotation, Balbuena presents the topics of his long epistle to Isabel de

Tobar; this anticipation suggests that *Grandeza mexicana* was not simply a response to her request but a project he had already entertained. Moreover, the model for the inclusion of a city within a dream is already in Sannazaro's Naples in the *Arcadia*. Sannazaro also has a nymph that leads the shepherd through the underworld, but his description from afar lacks the fantastic element of perceiving the city from underneath a lagoon.

Grandeza mexicana, Balbuena's epistolary poem describing Mexico City, consists of nine chapters in terza rima. Balbuena advances the subject of his chapters in the "Argumento," an octave that opens the poem with an enumeration of the main topics. The first editions of the poem were accompanied by two songs (one dedicated to Count Lemos and the other to the archbishop of Mexico), the *Carta al Arcediano* (which includes the poems that earned him prizes in his youth), and the *Compendio apologético en alabanza de la poesía* (Apologetic Compendium in Praise of Poetry), an important text for understanding Balbuena's poetics.

In the latter work, a treatise on poetry that closes the first printings of *Grandeza mexicana*, Balbuena presents his main poetic tenet: ". . . the ordinary and the common said in a particular and extraordinary mode, and what is more, things extraordinary, new and difficult in an ordinary and simple mode." Both movements, from the ordinary to the extraordinary and vice versa, posit the poetic as a defamiliarization of everyday life. The oppositions and the juxtaposition of dissimilar objects, which provoke the estrangement of the ordinary and the extraordinary, explore the bounds of poetic beauty. Balbuena's poetics of defamiliarization pursues new forms of the imagination and artistic freedom that have earned him recognition as the first American poet. This position can be attributed not so much to his descriptions of American nature, for Balbuena is actually disappointing in this respect, but to his inaugurating what critics have called an American baroque, one akin to the profusion of adornment on the baroque altars of Mexican churches.

Balbuena's poetics of defamiliarization are perhaps nowhere better represented than in his descriptions in *Grandeza mexicana*. In reading the work one must look for juxtapositions of sense impressions that approximate pure images, solely sustained by a poetic sense of language:

> *Aqui entre yerua, flor, sombra y descansos,*
> *Las tembladoras olas entapizan*
> *sombrias cueuas a los vientos mansos.*

Here among grass, flower, shadow, and repose,
The trembling waves tapestry shadowy caves to the
  gentle winds.

(1821 ed.; chapter 6, stanza 11)

Along with the production of pure images, there is an idyllic quality to Balbuena's descriptions of nature in the valley of Mexico. If in the *Siglo de oro* the pastoral merges with a description of the city, the valley of Mexico City bears the quality of a perfect landscape and is compared with the legendary Tempe:

> *Es el valle de Tempe, en cuya vega*
> *Se cree que sin morir nacio el verano. . . .*

It is the valley of Tempe, in whose lowlands
It is believed that summer was born without dying. . . .

(6, 17)

This portrayal of the *parayso mexicano* (Mexican paradise) partakes of a celebratory commonplace for the New World since the time of Columbus. But the Mexico whose grandeur Balbuena praises is that of the *criollo*, the Mexico of the Spaniards born in the New World. It is the city built by conquistadors and their descendants. Neither the deeds of the Spanish Conquest itself nor the achievements of prehispanic Mexico concern him in the *Grandeza*:

> *Dexo tambien el aspero concurso,*
> *Y obscuro origen de naciones fieras*
> *Que la hallaron con barbaro discurso. . . .*

I also leave aside the rough concourse,
And dark origin of fierce nations
That found her with barbarous discourse. . . .

(2, 18)

Moreover, the natives disappear from Balbuena's tableaux, with the exception of the incidental, nonetheless highly revealing, mention of the laboring *Indio feo* (ugly Indian), whose production of gold frames Balbuena's praise of the city at the end of the poem,

> *Entre el menudo-aljofar que a su arena*
> *Y a tu gusto entresaca el Indio feo,*
> *y por tributo del tus flotas llena. . . .*

> In between the small pearl that from its sand
> And to your pleasure the ugly Indian selects,
> And with his tribute fills your fleets. . . .
> (9, 125)

Balbuena's praise of Mexico City is ultimately of Spain's imprint in the New World. Balbuena's haughty reduction of Amerindians to "ugly" laborers in *Grandeza mexicana* has its parallel in a correspondingly arrogant passage in *El Bernardo*, where a Tlaxcalan sorcerer predicts Cortés' conquest of Mexico:

> *Ya de un Cortés caudillo el pecho honroso*
> *Premio a mis ricas esperanzas siento,*
> *Y la gloria del hecho mas famoso*
> *Que caber pudo en cuerdo atrevimiento. . . .*

> Already from Cortés does pride swell in my breast
> The prize of my rich hopes,
> And the glory of the most famous deed
> Ever conceived by sane daring. . . .
> (19, 15)

In spite of the conquest's highly suitable material for an epic poem (it is indeed "the most famous deed ever conceived"), the stanzas dedicated to the praise of Cortés are but part of one of the many incidental digressions in *El Bernardo*. This work takes for its main theme the victory of Bernardo del Carpio over Charlemagne and his paladins, from which the poem derives the subtitle *Victoria de Roncesvalles*. This epic poem, which consists of twenty-four cantos and five thousand stanzas in ottava rima, is generally considered Balbuena's most accomplished piece. Each canto closes with a prose explanation, which Balbuena calls an *alegoria*, of its moral meaning. In addition to these short prose pieces, there is a prologue that explicates the poetics informing the text. Noteworthy are Balbuena's discussions of history and poetry, where he states that "poetry must be the imitation of truth, but not truth itself, writing things, not as they happened, since that would no longer be imitation, but as they could have happened, giving them all the perfection that the imagination of he who feigns can lend them" (Van Horne ed., p. 145).

Because *El Bernardo* is a quasi-historical personage, he is preferable to Cortés for exalting the glories of Spain. The imitation of truth does not pertain to a representation of reality but to a whole realm of fantastic entities that make up the stuff of the *verosimil* (the believable), "the gods and demigods with which the ancients made their poems so admirable and pompous." Balbuena adds the fairies and magicians "that have been invented by Boiardo and those that have followed him." As Frank Pierce has aptly put it, the poetics of *El Bernardo* produce a "baroque fantasy." The fantastic, as has been noted, is already an element that separates the city in *Siglo de oro en las selvas de Erífile* from Sannazaro's Naples in the *Arcadia*. And from all appearances it is this sense of baroque fantasy that differentiates *El Bernardo* from its Renaissance models in Boiardo and Ariosto, as well as from the epic poems of antiquity; as Balbuena self-consciously puts it: "This poem can be called the completion and last line and key that fully closes the artifice and machine of their fables."

Critics generally consider *El Bernardo* to be Balbuena's masterpiece. One might add that the early pursuit of a poetic vision in the simplicity of the *Siglo de oro* achieves its finest realization in the baroque ornamentation of his *El Bernardo*. Today, however, as both the pastoral and the epic have lost their attractiveness, *Grandeza mexicana* remains his most-read text.

SELECTED BIBLIOGRAPHY

First Editions

Grandeza mexicana del Bachiller Bernardo de Balbuena. Mexico City, 1604. Contains *Carta al Arcediano.*

Siglo de oro en las selvas de Erífile. Madrid, 1608.
El Bernardo, o Victoria de Roncesvalles. Madrid, 1624.

Modern Editions

El Bernardo, o Victoria de Roncesvalles. In *Poemas épicos 1,* edited by Cayetano Rosell. (Biblioteca de Autores Españoles 17.) Madrid, 1851.

Grandeza mexicana. Edited by Real Academia de la Lengua. Madrid, 1821.

Grandeza mexicana. Edited and with an introduction by John Van Horne. Urbana, Ill., 1930. Van Horne's is the most authoritative and complete contemporary edition; it includes all the texts from the 1604 editions. The following two economical editions for students are incomplete but more accessible.

Grandeza mexicana. Edited and with a prologue by Francisco Monterde. 2nd ed. Mexico City, 1954. This edition includes fragments from *El siglo de oro* and *El Bernardo.*

La grandeza mexicana and *Compendio apologético en alabanza de la poesía.* Edited and with a preliminary study by Luis Adolfo Domínguez. Mexico City, 1971.

Siglo de oro en las selvas de Erífile. Edited by Real Academia de la Lengua. Madrid, 1821.

Biographical and Critical Studies

Fucilla, Joseph G. "Bernardo de Balbuena's *Siglo de Oro* and Its Sources." *Hispanic Review* 15:101–119 (1947).

Leal, Luis. "El *Siglo de Oro* de Balbuena primera novela americana." *Kentucky Romance Quarterly* 23:327–334 (1976).

Pierce, Frank. "*El Bernardo* of Balbuena: A Baroque Fantasy." *Hispanic Review* 13:1–23 (1945).

———. "L'allégorie poétique au XVIe siècle. Son évolution et son traitement par Bernardo de Balbuena." *Bulletin Hispanique* 51:381–406 (1949) and 52: 191–228 (1950).

Roggiano, Alfredo A. "Bernardo de Balbuena." In *Historia de la literatura hispanoamericana 1: Época colonial.* Edited by Luis Iñigo Madrigal. Madrid, 1982. Pp. 215–224.

Rojas Garcidueñas, José. *Bernardo de Balbuena: La vida y la obra.* Mexico City, 1958.

Van Horne, John. *"El Bernardo" of Bernardo de Balbuena: A Study of the Poem with Particular Attention to its Relations to the Epics of Boiardo and Ariosto and to its Significance in the Spanish Renaissance.* Urbana, Ill., 1927.

———. *Bernardo de Balbuena: Biografía y crítica.* Guadalajara, Mexico, 1940.

Pedro de Oña

(1570–1643?)

Raquel Chang-Rodríguez

During the colonial period, the Araucania, a region occupying most of south-central Chile where the Araucanian Indians had lived for centuries, was the battleground for many armed conflicts between the Spaniards and the native population. The numerous military feats that took place there inspired the first epic poem about the New World, *La araucana (The Araucaniad)*, written by Alonso de Ercilla y Zúñiga; the poem appeared in three parts (1569, 1578, 1589). The impact of this work was such that, shortly after its publication, many writers tried to imitate it, and the *Araucana* cycle came into being. Of all the writers who imitated Ercilla, Pedro de Oña, author of *Arauco domado (Arauco Tamed, 1596)*, was the most talented. Oña was born in 1570 in Infantes de Engol, a city located in the heart of the war-torn region. The place and date of Oña's death remain unknown. His father, the Spanish captain Gregorio de Oña, died in battle against the Indians of southern Chile the year his son was born. Shortly afterward, the poet's mother, Isabel de Acurcio, remarried into a distinguished family.

Little is known about the childhood and adolescence of Pedro de Oña. It has been documented that in June 1590 the author registered in Lima as a student at the College of San Martín, an institution established by the Jesuits and devoted to secular education. Later, Oña also attended San Marcos University; and in 1592, Viceroy García Hurtado de Mendoza awarded him a scholarship to continue studying in Lima at the Royal College of San Felipe and San Marcos. Don García, displeased that Ercilla had ignored him and his family in *The Araucaniad*, commissioned the young Oña to compose a poem praising his deeds in the war with the Araucanians and his accomplishments as viceroy. Oña finished *Arauco Tamed* in 1596, the year he began using the title of *licenciado* (lawyer). No one has yet documented where and when the poet earned this title.

As he had been asked, Oña in his first work, *Arauco Tamed*, praised the conduct and deeds of Don García Hurtado de Mendoza as governor of Chile from 1557 to 1561 and viceroy of Peru from 1589 to 1596. As a consequence of the publication of the poem, the author became entangled in litigation. Five representatives of the city of Quito complained to the Royal Tribunal in Lima that Oña accused the *quiteños* of treason and disloyalty in his narration of the Quito rebellion against royal taxation in 1592–1593. They requested that the complete edition be collected and burned. Because of this and other charges, the first edition of *Arauco Tamed* was confiscated and its further sale prohibited. The only copies saved were the ones that Viceroy Hurtado de

Mendoza took with him on his return to Spain. The documents of this litigation reveal that by 1596, Oña had married and had been appointed *corregidor* (magistrate) in the city of Jaén, now a province of the department of Cajamarca, in Peru. This appointment had been sponsored by Viceroy García Hurtado de Mendoza, perhaps to compensate Oña for his favorable poem.

The documents available to us do not indicate how long Oña was in Jaén. However, six years after the court fight, in 1602, Oña was back in Lima, participating actively in the literary life of that city. In 1605, the second edition of *Arauco Tamed* appeared in Madrid. Since the work was printed without the necessary permit from the Royal Council of the Indies, the author was again involved in litigation. Toward the end of 1609, Oña published *Temblor de Lima, año de 1609* (Earthquake in Lima in the Year 1609), a poem of eighty-three stanzas in *ottava rima* in which two friends, Arcelo and Daricio, converse about an earthquake that destroyed much of Lima in that year. The two men praise the prudent measures taken by Viceroy Juan de Mendoza y Luna to repair the devastation. In 1608, this viceroy had appointed Oña to another post as *corregidor*.

In 1639, *El Ignacio de Cantabria* (Ignatius of Cantabria), Oña's second major work, appeared in Seville. This long poem, which took Oña fifteen years to finish, is written in hendecasyllabic verses and divided into twelve books. The poem narrates the life of Saint Ignatius of Loyola, founder of the Jesuit order, with particular focus on his trip to the Monserrat monastery in Spain, his pilgrimage to Rome, and his return to Spain. At the time of its publication, *El Ignacio de Cantabria* was well received by writers of the stature of Lope de Vega and Calderón de la Barca, even though the views of later critics have differed from these early assessments. Oña's last major work is *El vasauro* (The Golden Goblet), finished in 1635 and dedicated to Luis Gerónimo Fernández de Cabrera y Bobadilla, count of Chinchón and viceroy of Peru from 1629 to 1639. In 1630, he had appointed Oña as *corregidor* in yet another town. The poem, using the traditional versification of eleven syllables grouped in *ottava rima* stanzas, is divided into eleven books. In them, Oña recounts the many accomplishments of Ferdinand and Isabella, the Catholic king and queen of Spain, from 1466 to 1492, the year in which they consolidated their power by reconquering Granada, the last Moorish bastion. But more than anything else, the poet stresses the services rendered to the monarchs by Andrés de Cabrera, an ancestor of the count of Chinchón. As a token of their gratitude, the sovereigns gave Cabrera a *vaso de oro* (golden goblet); hence the name of this work. The poem did not appear in print until 1941. It has been favorably viewed by some contemporary critics.

Arauco Tamed is Oña's masterpiece. The author wrote it in order to praise García Hurtado de Mendoza, whose deeds in the Araucanian wars were not given sufficient recognition by Ercilla because of personal disagreements. The poem has nineteen books, arranged in *ottava rima* stanzas. The text includes 131 notes and a brief vocabulary of Indian words. *Arauco Tamed* revolves around three historical events: an expedition against the Araucanian Indians in southern Chile, an expedition to Quito in order to fight the rebellious population there, and a naval war against the English pirate Richarte Aquines (Richard Hawkins). The three expeditions departed from Lima at different times, and García Hurtado de Mendoza was in charge of all of them, first as governor of Chile and later as viceroy of Peru.

To introduce key historical information about the expedition to southern Chile commanded by the young Don García, Oña first reviews the situation of the Spaniards settled in that region (cantos 1–11). He describes the Indian uprisings, the defeat and subsequent death of conqueror Pedro de Valdivia, and the many quarrels among the men who wanted to replace him. The poet also points out the abuses perpetrated by the Spaniards against the native population and how Don García attempted to correct this situation. Later, Oña narrates several military encounters with the Araucanians in order to show the superiority of the Spaniards. The Indians are defeated—although not for long—by the troops under Don García's command, on the banks of the river Bío-bío (canto 10). This battle concludes the first part of the poem.

In order to describe events in the rebellious city of Quito (cantos 14–16), Oña uses the classic literary device of the dream, through which he takes us to a different historical period. Now viceroy of Peru, Don García is forced to deal with an uprising: the *quiteños* have protested against new royal taxes imposed on the viceroyalty of Peru since the beginning of 1592. Unlike other cities, Quito has refused to pay the new royal taxes, and two thousand men have gathered to fight the troops sent from Lima by Viceroy Hurtado de Mendoza. This segment of *Arauco Tamed* is also dedicated to praising the wise decisions of Don García. Even though he did not accompany his troops, from Lima he kept in touch with the commanders and gave them advice. As a result, the city was retaken on 10 April 1593.

The third part (cantos 18–19) is devoted to a description of the naval expedition against the English pirate Richard Hawkins and his defeat by Beltrán de Castro y de la Cueva, brother-in-law of Don García. Even though the hero is Beltrán de Castro, Oña manages to present Viceroy García as overseeing every detail. The poet takes time to explain how Don García, when learning of Hawkins' approach, gets up from his sickbed and calls his council to discuss matters. As would be expected, *Arauco Tamed* concludes with the defeat of the English pirate and the total triumph of the Spanish navy and army.

With regard to the Spanish characters, the most notable is Don García, the hero of the poem. Oña describes him as a good-looking man, capable of attracting even the goddess Diana. His magnetic personality makes him the ideal leader. Shrewd and intelligent, he is always ready to defend himself and to attack the enemy (canto 1). (Although Oña has pictured García as magnanimous with his foes, historical accounts contradict this view.) Prudence is his most praiseworthy trait. The poet transforms his hero into the perfect Renaissance gentleman, ready for war, love, and letters. Among other important characters on the Spanish side are Don Felipe de Mendoza, Don García's brother, General Pedro de Arana, leader of the Quito expedition, and Don Beltrán de Castro, the viceroy's brother-in-law and commander of the Spanish navy in the Pacific.

Among the seventy-three Araucanians appearing in the poem, the most notable are the chieftains Caupolicán, Tucapel, and Galbarino. The gallant behavior and handsome looks of the first remind us of the protagonists of pastoral novels; the second stands out for the ferocity with which he attacks the Spaniards; Don García punishes the third by having his hands chopped off (canto 12). Galbarino's mutilation, a historical fact, is one of the most dramatic events of *Arauco Tamed*. Giving no sign of pain after his hands are cut off, the Araucanian leader demands to be decapitated. Among the feminine characters, Fresia, Gualeva, and Quidora are memorable. Gualeva is Tucapel's wife; Quidora, whose dreams are utilized to bridge events of different periods, is the wife of Talguén, another Araucanian chief. However, even though she appears only once in the poem (canto 5), Fresia is the most notable of these women. Oña presents Fresia and Caupolicán in a beautiful valley. The poet describes her as white as snow, resembling both mythological nymphs and heroines of pastoral novels. Some critics have noted that Fresia's literary model can be found in the women depicted by the Spanish poet Garcilaso de la Vega.

Historical events have provided the nucleus of *Arauco Tamed*. However, three fictitious episodes are considered the best in the poem: the romance of Caupolicán and Fresia (canto 5), Tucapel and Gualeva's adventures (canto 12), and the events that occur in the shepherd Guemapu's cabin (cantos 12–14).

The idyll of Caupolicán and Fresia takes place in the Elicura Valley, inhabited by nymphs and satyrs, and irrigated by a beautiful river that forms a transparent pool where the two play and make love. Even though it is impossible to specify the sources that inspired Oña to create this ideal place, the influence of bucolic poetry and pastoral novels—from Vergil to Ercilla, Jacopo Sannazaro, Garcilaso, Jorge de Montemayor, and Gaspar Gil Polo—is very evident. The poet combines several elements from these literary traditions to create a passage that stands out because of the exquisite nature of its landscape and the physical beauty of its characters. The romance is interrupted by news announcing Don García's arrival in Araucania. Some critics have seen in this abrupt end a moralizing intention—behind happiness, tragedy always lurks.

The episode of Tucapel and Gualeva, in which women search for their men after battle, is typical of the epic genre. In this case, Gualeva finds Tucapel alive but wounded. She then cures him with Chilean herbs; suddenly, a lioness interrupts the lovers' conversation. This last incident is based on the fable of Pyramus and Thisbe, told by Ovid in his *Metamorphoses*. In this as in many other instances, Oña uses his sources judiciously and ingeniously. The tenderness and determination of Gualeva make her one of the most memorable characters of the poem. In Guemapu's cabin, this shepherd and Tucapel discuss in reasoned fashion the virtues of pastoral and military life. Also in this cabin (as frequently occurs in pastoral novels), two lost lovers, Quidora and Talguén, meet. At the group's request, the woman tells her dream about Don García and the rebellion in Quito. In theme and ambience, the three episodes offer similarities with well-known books from the pastoral and bucolic traditions. Oña, however, is not simply copying old models. He fuses his sources to produce characters and events that are different from the originals.

Oña has been criticized because of the lack of American flora and fauna in the landscape of *Arauco Tamed*. It has already been noted that Oña was strongly influenced by a long and prestigious European tradition which required that, in creating his landscape, the writer follow specific patterns having little to do with physical reality. Oña, faithful to these models and well acquainted with what readers preferred, describes the ideal place and the frightful forest that were so dear to Italian, Spanish, and Portuguese writers. It is to his credit that he does it in such an accomplished manner.

Despite the author's efforts, *Arauco Tamed* fails to reach epic stature. The excessive praise of Viceroy Hurtado de Mendoza and perhaps the haste with which the poem was composed affected Oña's work adversely. However, Pedro de Oña is no simple imitator of Alonso de Ercilla. His works, specifically *Arauco Tamed*, have contributed to our understanding of an important characteristic of colonial Spanish-American literature: the rapid adoption of the literary fashions of Spain and Portugal. Throughout the colonial centuries, this desire to imitate and to be a part of European letters shows the dependent character of colonial writers. At the same time, their excesses helped to undermine and transform the European model, diluting and finally supplanting it with a more original cultural product. The lyric quality of *Arauco Tamed* and Oña's ability to fictionalize reality are important steps in the search for a distinct poetic voice in the New World.

SELECTED BIBLIOGRAPHY

First Editions

Poetry

Primera parte de Arauco domado. Lima, 1596.
Temblor de Lima, año de 1609 . . . y una canción real panegyrica. Lima, 1609.
El Ignacio de Cantabria. Seville, 1639.
El vasauro. Edited and with an introduction by Rodolfo Oroz. Santiago, Chile, 1941.

Uncollected Poetry

"A la florentissima universidad de los reyes . . ." In *Constituciones y ordenanzas de la Universidad de San Marcos.* Lima, 1602. Sonnet.
"Hay entre Delo y Delio competencia . . ." In *Primera parte de la miscelánea austral*, by Diego D'Avalos y Figueroa. Lima, 1602. Sonnet.
"En vano recontáis, don Diego insigne . . ." In *Defensa de damas*, by Diego D'Avalos y Figueroa. Lima, 1603. Sonnet.
"Esta infinita [entre las otras] arte . . ." In *Libro de plata reduzida*, by Juan de Garreguilla. Lima, 1607. Sonnet.
"Hasta agora tuvimos por muy cierto . . ." In *Primera parte del Parnaso antártico de obras amatorias*, by Diego Mexía de Fernangil. Seville, 1608. Sonnet.
"Canción real." In *Relación de las exequias que el excmo. S.D. Juan de Mendoza y Luna Marqués de Montesclaros, Virrey del Perú, hizo en la muerte de la reina nuestra S. Doña Margarita.* Lima, 1612.
"Soneto." *Ibid.*, Lima, 1612. Presented by Oña to Fray Martín de León.
"Canción real río Lima al río Tibre." In *Vida, virtudes y milagros del nuevo apóstol del Perú, el venerable P. F. Solano*, by Diego de Córdoba. Lima, 1630.

Modern Editions

Arauco domado. Valparaiso, 1849.
_____. Edited and with an introduction by Cayetano Rossel. Madrid, 1854.
_____. Edited and with an introduction by José Toribio Medina. Santiago, Chile, 1917.
_____. Facsimile ed. Madrid, 1944.

El temblor de Lima de 1609. Facsimile ed., edited by José Toribio Medina. Santiago, Chile, 1909.

Translation

Arauco Tamed. Translated and with an introduction by Charles Maxwell Lancaster and Paul Thomas Manchester. Albuquerque, N. Mex., 1948.

Biographical and Critical Studies

Alegría, Fernando. "Oña: *El Arauco domado.*" In *La poesía chilena.* Mexico, 1954. Pp. 56–106.

Caillet-Bois, Julio. "Dos notas sobre Pedro de Oña." *Revista de filología hispánica* 4:269–274 (1942).

Dinamarca, Salvador. *Estudio del "Arauco domado" de Pedro de Oña.* New York, 1952.

Iglesias, Augusto. *Pedro de Oña: Ensayo de crítica e historia.* Santiago, Chile, 1971.

Johnson, Julie G. *Women in Colonial Spanish American Literature: Literary Images.* Westport, Conn., 1983. Pp. 41–45.

Labandeira Fernández, Amancio. "En torno a la historicidad de *El vasauro.*" *Memorias del XVII Congreso del Instituto Internacional de Literatura Iberoamericana: El barroco en América* 1. Madrid, 1978. Pp. 149–171.

Lazo, Raimundo. *Historia de la literatura hispanoamericana: El periodo colonial.* Havana, 1968. Pp. 163–178.

Matta Vial, Enrique. *El licenciado Pedro de Oña: Estudio biográfico-crítico.* Santiago, Chile, 1924.

Medina, José Toribio. *Historia de la literatura colonial de Chile* 1. Santiago, Chile, 1878. Pp. 132–238.

Neale Silva, Eduardo. "Oña, Pedro de: *Arauco Tamed,* Translated into English . . ." *Hispania* 31/4:498–506 (1948).

Oroz, Rodolfo. "Reminiscencias virgilianas en Pedro de Oña." *Atenea* 115/348:278–286 (1954).

_____. "Pedro de Oña, poeta gongorista." *Atenea* 143/393:122–140 (1961).

Porras Barrenechea, Raúl. "Nuevos datos sobre la vida del poeta chileno Pedro de Oña." *Mercurio peruano* 33/308:524–557 (1952).

Román-Lagunas, Jorge. "Obras de Pedro de Oña y bibliografía sobre él." *Inter-American Review of Bibliography* 31/3:345–365 (1981).

Sánchez, Luis Alberto. *Escritores representativos de América. Primera serie* 1. Madrid, 1963. Pp. 49–58.

Sequel, Gerardo. *Pedro de Oña: Su vida y la conducta de su poesía.* Santiago, Chile, 1940.

Solar Correa, Eduardo. "El patriarca de la poesíá chilena: Pedro de Oña. 1570–1643?" *Atenea* 6/56:5–13 and 6/57:162–173 (1929). Reprinted in his *Semblanzas literarias de la colonia.* 3rd ed. Buenos Aires, 1969.

Vega, Miguel Ángel. *La obra poética de Pedro de Oña.* Santiago, Chile, 1970.

Gregório de Mattos

(1636–1695)

Fernando da Rocha Peres

In the conservative Brazilian literature of the colonial period, the poet Gregório de Mattos (or Matos) e Guerra stands out as a controversial and singular figure. Sometimes known in his day as "O Boca do Inferno" (Hell's Mouth), he was born on 20 December 1636 in the city of Salvador, in Bahia state.

It was not until the second half of the nineteenth century that the public and the critics became aware of the existence of Mattos' texts. His inclusion in the cast of seventeenth-century Brazilian authors was brought about by the historian Francisco Adolfo Varnhagen, viscount of Porto Seguro, who in Lisbon in 1850 published *Florilégio da Poesia Brasileira* (Anthology of Brazilian Poetry), which contained thirty-nine poems by Mattos, copied from the original manuscripts. Other nineteenth-century anthologies, or *parnasos* (collections of poems), contained poems by Mattos, but the first editor to compile a volume of his work only was Alfredo do Vale Cabral who, in 1882, published a collection of his satires.

Between the years 1923 and 1933, the Brazilian Academy of Letters published the poet's apographal work in six volumes, under the direction of Afrânio Peixoto. In 1968 the writer James Amado published Mattos' apographal works in seven volumes that include erotic and fescennine poems censored by Peixoto and omitted from his edition.

From the beginning, there has been controversy regarding the life and the work of Mattos. Concerning his life, research has been directed toward the exploration of archives, files, and other documents that might add new information to the biographical text written by Manuel Pereira Rabelo in the second half of the eighteenth century. Research by Peixoto, Pedro Calmon, and the present writer (see Fernando da Rocha Peres, *Gregório de Mattos e Guerra: Uma Revisão Biográfica*) has led to the drawing of a new profile of the poet. The current description is rather removed from the pictures painted by Tristão A. Araripe Júnior, who referred to Mattos as a "shabby vagrant," and José Veríssimo, who called him a "swaggerer of genius."

The second area of critical discussion concerns Mattos' text. The poet did not publish in his lifetime, nor did he leave any known original autographed manuscripts. The work attributed to him is contained in several codexes, or manuscript books (made up of apographal documents), in archives and libraries in Portugal and Brazil, many of them located by the present writer. Of these, the oldest specimen appears to be the one belonging to the National Library of Lisbon, under the number 3.576 (*Obras do Douctor Gregório de Mattos e Guerra*), in the reserved section of the collection Fundo Geral.

Because Mattos' apographal works exist in codex (the great majority of these from the eighteenth century), the consensus of scholars is that the poet's text contains alterations by copyists and material added by others who wrote in the style popular during the one and a half centuries when his creations were preserved by transcription. The work of other poets who wrote lyrical, religious, satirical, erotic, or burlesque verses, such as the seventeenth-century writer Tomás Pinto Brandão, suffered a similar fate. Doubts about Mattos' authorship will remain until a team of specialists and scholars can produce a critical edition of his works, conclusively establishing his poetic corpus, or, in the words of Antônio Houaiss, his "irreducible residuum."

The question of possible plagiarism by Mattos is another theme that has attracted scholarly attention, especially in the work of Professor João Carlos Teixeira Gomes. What can be said with certainty is that the poet's apographal text was altered in such a way that it reflects the Iberian poetic tradition—from the troubadours, the "vagrant" poets, the Lusitanian classics (Francisco de Sá de Miranda and Luiz Vaz de Camões) and the Golden Age of Spanish poetry, in the figures of Francisco Gómez de Quevedo and Luis de Góngora y Argote.

The poet belonged to the affluent and influential Mattos family, who emigrated before 1618 to Salvador, the leading city of Portuguese America, and its *Recôncavo*, the region of rich soil on its outskirts. He was the grandson of Pedro Gonçalves de Mattos, who was a sugarcane planter, a contractor in public works projects, and the owner of a crane that was used for the transportation of merchandise back and forth from the lower to the upper city of Salvador. Because Gonçalves de Mattos was a member of the religious order of the Holy Office, the tribunal of the Inquisition in Portugal, he and his extensive family held a place among the "good and honorable men" of seventeenth-century Bahia.

Evidence suggests that the Mattos family came from the northern Portuguese region of Guimarães. Pedro and his son Gregório (the poet's father) both married women with the first name Maria and the surname Da Guerra. The family became powerful and counted among its male offspring two worthy and illustrious individuals: the brothers Eusebio de Mattos (a poet and clergyman) and Gregório de Mattos (poet, jurist, and clergyman).

From 1642 to 1650, Gregório de Mattos attended the distinguished Colégio dos Jesuitas in Bahia. There he began the education that prepared him for higher learning in Portugal, where in 1650 he concluded his preparatory studies to enter the University of Coimbra. After his entrance examination, in 1652 he began his education in canonical law.

In 1661 the young Bahian graduated from the revered university and married Dona Michaela de Andrade, who belonged to a family of magistrates and was the daughter of a chief judge. The following year the canonist submitted to the process of "habilitation (*de genere*) for the reading of bachelor" (comprehensive examination for the bachelor's degree). This was the equivalent of an inquest to determine whether the postulant had both the knowledge and the "qualities"—he could not be a descendant of a Jew, a new Christian, a Moor, a Negro, a mulatto, or a mechanical worker—to qualify for a public post in the judiciary. After passing this review process in 1663, Mattos was appointed a *juiz de fora* (county judge) in the town of Alcácer do Sal, south of Lisbon. Again in Lisbon, on 27 January 1668, in the Paço da Ribeira, a government palace, he served as the procurator, or representative, of the "peoples" of his native Bahia in the Portuguese courts, invested by the Senate's Chamber. At this time "Baia" occupied a prominent seat in the São Francisco Monastery; it was well represented and considered important among the kingdom's cities. In 1671 Mattos was appointed judge of civil law in Lisbon. The next year, he was appointed procurator of Bahia in Lisbon but was removed from this position in 1674. On 20 January of the same year, he received a mandate to represent Bahia again as procurator in the courts of Lisbon.

In the parochial registry files in the national archives of Torre do Tombo in Lisbon, I located the baptismal record of an illegitimate daughter of Mattos by the name of Francisca, born to an unmarried woman named Lourença Francisca. I have been unable to locate any record of children born to Mattos and Dona Michaela, who died on 7 August 1678 and was buried in the Carmo Monastery in Lisbon.

A widower at the age of forty-two, Mattos turned to his career as a magistrate and considered returning to Brazil. In 1679, while still in Lisbon, he was appointed chief judge of the "Ecclesiastical Relation" of Bahia, a position created by Archbishop Dom Gaspar Barata in 1678. The canonist also received the tonsure (the first of the traditional clerical degrees), along with minor orders and the designation to exercise in Bahia the office of chief judge and the function of high treasurer of the see. He returned to Brazil in 1683. The same year, he was removed from these posts by the new archbishop, Dom Frei João da Madre de Deus, for having declined to accept major orders and to wear a cassock.

In Emmanuelis Alvarez Pegas' publication *Commentaria ad ordinationes regni portugalliae* (Lisbon, 1682, vol. 7, pp. 294–296), we find two rulings authored by Mattos, which were issued in 1671 when he was a judge in Portugal. They constitute proof of his prominence as a jurist. His knowledge of law, both canonic and civil, permitted his financial survival in Brazil as an attorney and rural landowner. In 1684 he traveled with friends through the Bahia *Recôncavo* (Cachoeira, S. Francisco do Conde, Cajaíba, and Itaparica) from one sugar mill plantation to another. In the 1680's he remarried. With his second wife, Dona Maria de Póvoas, he had a son named Gonçalo.

Because of some of his writings, in 1685 Mattos was denounced by his enemies to the Holy Office as a heretic and as "an unbound man without Christian manners." Because of lack of substantial evidence, the suit did not result in punishment. In 1691 the poet became a patron and administrator of the Santa Casa de Misericórdia (hospital for indigent persons) of Bahia, thus joining the ranks of the prestigious, or status, group. Historical records show that in 1692 he paid a debt of "trinta mil réis" (thirty thousand reis), a sizable amount, which proves his good financial situation at the time.

Mattos' satirical and erotic poetry was responsible for his gaining the epithet Hell's Mouth. The poet was a cruel and contumacious critic of Bahian society from the time of his return to Brazil in 1683 until 1694, the year before he died. He was a caustic and mordacious denouncer of the social and sexual behavior of Salvador's inhabitants. No one was spared his criticism. He scoffed at and ridiculed, among others, rulers, the military, priests, Jews, Negroes, the native nobility, merchants, and usurers. His virulent writings were used as the basis for his banishment to Angola in 1694 by Governor Dom João de Lencastre. The governor was a friend of Mattos' (who "treasured" certain verses of his that are contained in a codex that has not yet been located), an admirer who, through deporting him, saved the poet from being murdered by a foe.

Mattos stayed in Africa only a short time. His involvement in a military rebellion favored Governor Henrique Jacques de Magalhães, and as a reward, he was allowed to return to Brazil in 1695, but this time to Recife; he was forbidden to return to his native Bahia.

The poet died in Recife on 26 November 1695, and was buried in the Old Chapel of Nossa Senhora da Penha hospice, which in 1870 was totally destroyed, with no vestiges, not even his gravestone. In Salvador, a street was named after the poet in the district of Sé, where the Mattos family had lived in the seventeenth century.

Mattos' life and work (be it his own or amended) fully reflect the antinomies of his baroque time, his disharmony in the world and perplexity before its cultural progress, his heterodox heritage, and his schismatic contestations. His very existence and literary output offer a kind of synthesis of the contrasting forces at work during his lifetime.

Mattos' poetry, especially his satirical and erotic creations, parodied and satirized the seventeenth-century Brazilian capital of Salvador. Certain of his poems, some of the religious ones, for instance, record the thinking of his times as well as his own vision. They reflect a critical approach to the foundations of Christianity. The poem "Ao Divino Sacramento" (To The Divine Sacrament) refutes the sacrament of the Eucharist:

> *Quanto a que o sangue vos beba,*
> *isso não, e perdoai-me:*
> *Como, quem tanto vos ama,*
> *há-de beber-vos o sangue?*
>
> *Beber o sangue do amigo*
> *é sinal de inimizade;*

pois como quereis, que o beba,
para confirmarmos pazes?
(*Obras Completas* 1,
1968, pp. 49–50)

As to the drinking of your blood,
I'll say no; and forgive me.
How could anyone who loves you so,
drink your blood?

To drink a friend's blood
is a sign of enmity;
how, then, would you want me to do it,
in order to confirm our peace?

It is most unlikely, as some scholars argue, that Mattos experienced a mystical crisis on his deathbed. His posture vis-à-vis the Catholic religion and the Church (the wielders of ecclesiastical power) was always one of independence. He ridiculed monks and nuns, detailing their sexual relations among themselves and among the laity. There is a description of the people and customs of Bahia in a long text entitled "The Poet Takes Another Stroll About His World," in which he records the religious climate of that world:

Que hajam muitos ateístas,
que pelos costumes seus
não crêem, no que disse Deus
pelos quatro Evangelistas:
que só vivam Dogmatistas,
cuidando por seu prazer,
que há só nascer, e morrer,
não crendo no inferno, e glória!
Boa história.

Mas que outros (como se vê)
sejam com hipocrisia
só cristãos por cortesia
ou fiéis de meia-fé:
que inda que febre lhe dê,
não tratem da confissão,
cuidando, que escaparão
com a amiga à cabeceira!
Boa asneira.
(*Obras completas* 2,
1968, p. 492)

That there are many atheists,
whose customs show they have no faith
in the teachings of God's four evangelists,
but only that their lives are rooted
in desire for their own pleasure,
who do not believe that there is
either hell or heaven,
but rather only birth and death—
What a story!

That there are still others (as one sees)
who are hypocrites
and Christians in name only,
or men of little faith
who even when they are ill with fever
never think of confessing their sins,
believing that they will escape
with the girlfriends who are at their bedsides—
What folly!

Because of limitations of space, several genres of Mattos' poetry, such as the lyrical, sacred, burlesque, and erotic, could not be covered. We refer the reader to the summary bibliography of the publications by and about the poet.

SELECTED BIBLIOGRAPHY

Editions

Collected Works

Florilégio da Poesia Brasileira. Edited by Francisco Adolfo Varnhagen. 3 vols. Lisbon, 1850. 2nd ed. Rio de Janeiro, 1946. Contains thirty-nine poems by Mattos.

Obras. Edited by Afrânio Peixoto. 6 vols. Rio de Janeiro, 1923–1933.

Obras Completas. Edited by James Amado. 7 vols. Salvador, Brazil, 1968.

Obras Poéticas 1: Satyricos. Edited by Alfredo do Vale Cabral. Rio de Janeiro, 1882.

Os Melhores Poemas de Gregório de Matos. Edited by Darcy Damasceno. São Paulo, 1985.

Parnaso Brasileiro 1. Edited by Mello Moraes Filho. Rio de Janeiro, 1885.

Poemas Escolhidos. Edited and with an introduction and notes by José Miguel Wisnik. São Paulo, 1976.

Biographical and Critical Studies

Amado, James. "Notas à Margem da Editoração do Texto I e II." In *Obras Completas* 1 and 7, by Gregório de Mattos. Salvador, Brazil, 1968.

Araripe Júnior, Tristão A. *Gregório de Mattos.* Rio de Janeiro, 1894.

Ávila, Afonso. *O Lúdico e as Projeções do Mundo Barroco.* São Paulo, 1971.

Barquín, Maria del Carmen. *Gregório de Matos: La época, el hombre, la obra.* Mexico City, 1946.

Calmon, Pedro. *A Vida Espantosa de Gregório de Matos.* Rio de Janeiro, 1983.

Campos, Augusto. *Da América que Existe: Gregório de Mattos.* Rio de Janeiro, 1977.

Castello, José Aderaldo. *A Literatura Brasileira 1: Manifestações Literárias da Era Colonial.* São Paulo, 1962.

Dias, Angela Maria. *O Resgate da Dissonancia: Sátira e Projeto Literário Brasileiro.* Rio de Janeiro, 1981.

Dimas, Antonio. *Gregório de Mattos.* São Paulo, 1981.

Goldberg, Isaac. *Brazilian Literature.* New York, 1922.

Gomes, João Carlos Teixeira. *Gregório de Mattos: O Boca de Brasa. Um Estudo de Plágio e Criação Intertextual.* Petrópolis, Brazil, 1985.

Helena, Lúcia. *Uma Literatura Antropofágica.* Rio de Janeiro, 1982.

Houaiss, Antônio. "A Tradição em Gregório de Mattos." In *Primeiro Simposio de Língua e Literatura Portuguesa.* Rio de Janeiro, 1967. Pp. 27–33.

Martins, Heitor. "Gregório de Matos: Mito e Problemas." In *Do Barroco a Guimarães Rosa.* Belo Horizonte, Brazil, 1983. Pp. 235–245.

Martins, Wilson. *História da Inteligência Brasileira 1.* São Paulo, 1976.

Moisés, Massaud. *História da Literatura Brasileira 1.* São Paulo, 1983.

Paes, José Paulo. *Mistério em Casa.* São Paulo, 1961.

Peres, Fernando da Rocha. "Negros e Mulatos em Gregório de Mattos." *Afro-Ásia* (Bahia, Brazil) 4/5:59–75 (1967).

_____. "Gregório de Mattos e Guerra em Angola." *Afro-Ásia* 6/7:17–40 (1968).

_____. "Documentos para uma Biografia de Gregório de Mattos." *Universitas* 1:134–145 (1968).

_____. *Gregório de Mattos e Guerra: Uma Revisão Biográfica.* Salvador, Brazil, 1983.

_____. "Quem Pediu a Bênção a Grégorio de Matos?" *Revista do Brasil* (Rio de Janeiro) 3:4–11 (1985).

Portella, Eduardo. "Gregório de Mattos: Maneirismo e Barroco." *Revista Tempo Brasileiro* 45/46: 8–19 (1976).

Rabelo, Manuel Pereira. *Vida do Dr. Gregório de Mattos Guerra.* In *Obras Poéticas*, edited by Alfredo do Vale Cabral. Rio de Janeiro, 1882.

_____. *Vida e Morte do Doutor Gregório de Mattos Guerra. Escripta pelo Licenciado Manuel Pereira Rabelo. E Mais Apurada Depois por Outro Engenho.* In *Obras 1: Sacra*, edited by Afrânio Peixote. Rio de Janeiro, 1929.

_____. *Vida do Grande Poeta Americano Gregório de Matos.* In *Obras 6: Última*, edited by Afrânio Peixoto. Rio de Janeiro, 1933.

_____. *Vida do Excelente Poeta Lírico, o Doutor Gregório de Matos Guerra.* In *Obras completas 7*, edited by James Amado. Bahia, Brazil, 1968.

Romero, Silvio. *História da Literatura Brasileira 1.* Rio de Janeiro, 1888.

Salles, Fritz Teixeira de. *Poesia e Protesto em Gregório de Matos.* Belo Horizonte, Brazil, 1975.

Spina, Segismundo. *Gregório de Mattos.* São Paulo, 1946.

Veríssimo, José. *História da Literatura Brasileira.* Rio de Janeiro, 1916.

Carlos de Sigüenza y Góngora

(1645–1700)

Raquel Chang-Rodríguez

The Mexican savant Carlos de Sigüenza y Góngora is one of the most fascinating personalities of the colonial period in Spanish America. This mathematician, cosmographer, poet, and novelist wrote profusely on many topics and in diverse genres. However, many of Sigüenza y Góngora's manuscripts were never published, and we know of them only because they are mentioned by other writers of the period. Sigüenza y Góngora's scientific writings reveal both his ability to use logic to present difficult arguments and his stature as a forerunner of modern scientific inquiry in Spanish America. He was not as successful, though, with his literary endeavors. His poetry lacked originality and luster because he carefully imitated the baroque masters such as Góngora and Quevedo. A short novel, *Infortunios de Alonso Ramírez* (*The Misadventures of Alonso Ramírez*, 1690), in which he followed the Spanish picaresque model, is his most memorable literary work.

Sigüenza y Góngora was born 15 August 1645 into a very distinguished family. At the Spanish court in Madrid, his father, Carlos de Sigüenza, was the tutor of Prince Baltasar Carlos. In 1640 the elder Sigüenza came to Mexico, where he married Dionisia Suárez de Figueroa, an Andalusian woman related to the prominent baroque poet Luis de Góngora y Argote. The

young Carlos was the second child of this marriage, and the first son. In 1660, at fifteen, he entered the Jesuit order, from which he was expelled in 1667 for certain late-night escapades. Sigüenza y Góngora attempted to return to the order several times, and it is believed that he was readmitted just before he died. While Sigüenza y Góngora was a Jesuit, he wrote *Primavera indiana* (Indian Spring, 1668), a poem of uneven quality in which he praises the Virgin of Guadalupe, later proclaimed the patron saint of Mexico.

Although Sigüenza y Góngora went through a period of anguish after being expelled from the Jesuit order, he continued his studies in theology at the Royal University of Mexico. While there, he also became interested in other disciplines, particularly pre-Columbian history and mathematics. Soon Sigüenza y Góngora was recognized as an outstanding mathematician, and when the chair of mathematics and astrology at the Royal University of Mexico became vacant, he entered the competition for the position. Aside from his excellent reputation as a mathematician, his two printed *lunarios* (almanacs) corresponding to 1671 and 1672 were ample proof of his abilities in this field. He won the competition and was formally installed as professor of mathematics and astrology on 20 July 1672. Recent research indicates that Sigüenza y Góngora requested numerous leaves of absence and required substitute teachers for his classes. The young professor was often fined for failing to keep proper records of the number of students attending his classes. It is likely that due to his growing fame, he was frequently called by the colonial administration to render various public services. Perhaps this excessive workload, as well as his distaste for astrology, caused Sigüenza y Góngora to neglect his teaching.

In 1680 Sigüenza y Góngora was appointed Royal Cosmographer of the Kingdom of New Spain (Mexico). In that year his poem *Glorias de Querétaro* (Glories of Querétaro) was published. In it he again praised the Virgin of Guadalupe and described the inaugural ceremonies of a church dedicated to her in the city of Querétaro. In 1680 he also published *Panegírico con que la muy noble e imperial ciudad de México aplaudió . . . al Marqués de la Laguna* (Panegyric with which the Very Noble and Imperial City of Mexico Applauded . . . the Marquis of the Laguna) and *Teatro de virtudes políticas que constituyen a un príncipe* (Theater of the Political Virtues that Make a Prince). The first is a composition of seventeen ottava rima stanzas that an allegorical figure recites when the viceregal Marquis of the Laguna and Count of Paredes enters Mexico City; the second is a prose work that integrates the Indian past and the colonial present of Mexico.

The most important event for the life and writings of Sigüenza y Góngora was the comet first sighted in Mexico 15 November 1680, which he observed from 3 January to 20 January 1681. To help clarify the misunderstandings and superstitions surrounding its appearance, he wrote *Manifiesto filosófico contra los cometas* (Philosophical Manifesto Against Comets, 1681). In this work he contradicted those astrologers who viewed the periodic sightings of comets as a tragic omen. The publication of *Manifiesto* brought about attacks against Sigüenza y Góngora, which he refuted in *El belerofonte matemático* (The Mathematical Bellerophon). This extremely erudite work analyzes the appearance of comets as a natural phenomenon and, at the same time, explains why scientific research is superior to knowledge based on astrology.

In 1681 the Austrian Jesuit Eusebio Francisco Kino came to Mexico on a missionary assignment and was quickly befriended by Sigüenza y Góngora. Kino arrived at the height of the comet controversy and contributed to it his *Exposición astronómica* (Astronomical Exposition, 1681). In it he offered a traditional interpretation of comets and also attacked his new Mexican friend. Sigüenza y Góngora, always ready to indulge in polemics, answered Kino with his best-known scientific treatise, *Libra astronómica y filosófica* (Treatise on Astronomy and Philosophy), published nine years later in 1690. After first answering Kino's personal accusations, Sigüenza y Góngora presents a scientific description of the movements of comets and illustrates them with several diagrams. He goes on to refute Kino's thesis with precise and logical arguments. This treatise is of paramount importance in Spanish-American intellectual history, for it reaffirms the value of scientific observation, defends experimentation, and argues that mathematics is an essential tool for measuring natural phenomena. Influenced by René Descartes, Sigüenza y Góngora was one of those early scientists who eventually abandoned Aristotelian postulates and laid the groundwork for a modern science based on observation and experimentation.

In 1682 and 1683 the literati of New Spain were very busy as the University of Mexico invited them to participate in two poetry contests to celebrate the Feast of the Immaculate Conception. Sigüenza y Góngora presided over these contests as master of ceremonies. He later published *Triunfo parténico* (Parthian Triumph, 1683), which collects the poems submitted as well as the amusing verses that were recited when awards were distributed. It is worth noting that the most celebrated writer of colonial literature, the Mexican nun Sor Juana Inés de la Cruz, took part in these contests using a pseudonym. *Triunfo parténico* is especially important for the information it contains about the literary tastes and the cultural ambience of Mexican society in the second half of the seventeenth century.

In 1682 a very good friend of Sigüenza y Góngora, Francisco Aguiar y Seijas, was appointed archbishop of Mexico and selected the savant as chaplain of the Hospital del Amor de Dios (Hospital of the Love of God). This position provided the author with living quarters to which he transferred his extensive library and many scientific instruments. Sigüenza y Góngora resided in the Hospital del Amor de Dios until his death.

By this time, if not before, Sigüenza y Góngora was well known in European scientific circles. He corresponded with noted scientists, among them Athanasius Kircher, the German archaeologist, mathematician, biologist, and physicist. The visit paid him in 1687 by the Flemish Jesuit Pedro Van Hamme attests to his international reputation. Sigüenza y Góngora was always willing to share his knowledge with his many visitors, and thus exercised tremendous influence during and after his lifetime.

In 1689 Sigüenza y Góngora published a fragmentary edition of *Piedad heroica de Don Fernando Cortés* (Heroical Piety of Don Fernando Cortés), in which he narrates the history of the Hospital de la Inmaculada Concepción, founded by a testamentary deposition of the conqueror of Mexico.

From a literary perspective, the most important work by Sigüenza y Góngora is *The Misadventures of Alonso Ramírez*, a narrative account based on the travails of a shipwrecked Puerto Rican who visited the author in Mexico (1690). Following the "autobiographical" pattern of picaresque novels so popular in seventeenth-century Spain, the protagonist, Ramírez, tells of his adventures. Ramírez explains how, as a child, he traveled from Puerto Rico to Mexico seeking a better way of life. He then relates how he arrived in the Philippines, became a prisoner of English pirates, and was finally shipwrecked on the coast of Mexico. Alonso Ramírez is far from the traditional picaresque protagonist who lives by his wits and seeks social advancement at any cost; he is honest, generous, hard-working, and a devout Catholic. Even though the novel employs the picaresque form, Sigüenza y Góngora adapts it to his own taste and interests and to the demands of his story. Departing from picaresque patterns in order to show his vast knowledge, he includes detailed geographical descriptions of Asia and America. Sigüenza y Góngora is also original in not characterizing the masters whom Alonso serves and in describing nature in a very realistic fashion.

Sigüenza y Góngora incorporates into *The Misadventures of Alonso Ramírez* the traditional social criticism of picaresque narratives, using it to point out the lack of charity and the prevalence of hypocrisy and ambition in Mexican society. These qualities become apparent when the local inhabitants seek to deceive Alonso by stealing his belongings and when, after being entertained by Alonso's tales, they dismiss him before lunch or dinner. Only the Indians show compassion, sharing their meager provisions with Alonso and his shipwrecked friends. When the protagonist stresses the freedom enjoyed by English ships to travel undisturbed in America and Asia, we are being told that Spain is no longer mistress of the seas; after all, the Spanish Armada was defeated in 1588. Because of its sharp characterization of the protagonist and its clever adaptation of the picaresque form, *The Misadventures of Alonso Ramírez* is an important link in the development of narrative prose in Spanish America. This work also shows the diverse talents of Sigüenza y Góngora, a man able to write a complex scientific treatise as well as an interesting novel.

In 1691 the Mexican savant published *Relación de lo sucedido a la Armada de Barlovento* (An Account of What Happened to the Barlovento Fleet) and *Trofeo de la justicia española* (Trophy of Spanish Justice). The former recounts the victory of the Spanish forces against French settlers who occupied the northern coast of Santo Domingo; the latter concentrates on the naval aspects of that campaign. It is important to note that the viceroy of New Spain, Gaspar de Sandoval Cerda Silva y Mendoza, ordered these attacks and later gave Sigüenza y Góngora the necessary information to write both accounts in his capacity as chronicler of New Spain. Examples of early journalism, the two tales glorify the triumph of the Spanish navy and the wise decisions made by the viceroy.

One of the better known works by Sigüenza y Góngora is a long letter to his friend the Spanish admiral Andrés de Pez; it describes the Indian revolt that took place in Mexico on 8 June 1692. This document is known as *Alboroto y motín de los indios de México del 8 de junio de 1692* (Riot and Revolt of the Indians of Mexico City, 8 June 1692). This riot was partly caused by the poor wheat harvest of the previous year and the general indifference of the authorities toward the Indian population. The disturbances began in the main market where corn was sold and spread to the principal square of the capital city. Small commercial establishments were burned, and the fire quickly reached the city hall and the viceregal palace. When Sigüenza y Góngora, an eyewitness, realized that the fire could destroy the city archives, he sought help to save precious documents and paintings.

Alboroto y motín reveals Sigüenza y Góngora's contradictory attitudes toward the Indian population. Indeed, in other works he had studied and admired the pre-Columbian past of Mexico, which for him often surpassed European accomplishments. But in *Alboroto y motín* he characterized the Indians as ungrateful complainers. In subsequent letters to colonial authorities, he recommended that the native population be kept far from the center of the city, confined to its own quarters. Following critic Ramón Iglesia, who views the year 1692 as crucial, it is imperative to examine Sigüenza y Góngora's attitude toward the Indian population and his *mexicanidad* (Mexicanness) from a different perspective. It is necessary to distinguish between his admiration for the accomplishments of pre-Columbian peoples and his perception of the role and status of the Indians in colonial society.

Sigüenza y Góngora's expertise in geography was again acknowledged when in March 1693 the viceroy requested that he sail to explore Pensacola Bay and the mouth of the Mississippi River. Because of French incursions in the Gulf of Mexico that threatened Spanish possessions in Texas, Louisiana, and Florida, the crown had decided to settle this region. To carry out this settlement, it was essential to have accurate information and maps. As a result of his expedition, Sigüenza y Góngora prepared a detailed map and various reports on the region's terrain, vegetation, and fauna. In this period, he also wrote *Mercurio volante* (Flying Mercurio, 1693; published in English as *The Mercurio Volante*), an account of the peaceful reconquest by the Spaniards of the Indians of the region known as New Mexico.

On 24 July 1693 Sigüenza y Góngora, suffering from kidney stones, retired from his professorship at the University of Mexico. Already distressed by the death of close friends and relatives, he suffered another hard blow at the demise of his protector, Archbishop Aguiar y Seijas. A trip to San Juan de Ulúa castle, to give a report on the status of this fortress, was the last on-site inspection for Sigüenza y Góngora. But despite his ailments, he kept on studying, and his reputation continued to grow. In 1698 he received the Italian scientist and traveler Giovanni Francesco Gemelli Carreri (1651–1725), who later used some of Sigüenza y Góngora's writings in his own book *Giro del mondo* (A Voyage Round the World, 1699–1700).

The last years of Sigüenza y Góngora's life were made bitter by a dispute with Andrés de Arriola, who had gone on an expedition to settle Pensacola Bay and returned in haste after sighting French ships. In a letter dated 6 April 1699, this navy officer questioned the maps and reports of the Pensacola Bay area done earlier by Sigüenza y Góngora and demanded that the aging savant return to Pensacola with him. Always ready to argue, Sigüenza y Góngora answered in very strong terms, stating his willingness to return to Pensacola to confirm the accuracy of his maps and reports. He was so sure of himself that he wagered his library, worth more than three thousand pesos, against an equal amount to be deposited by his rival. The only demand he made was that Arriola and he travel in separate ships, for he was afraid that Arriola might drown him or that he might drown his rival. Due in part to Sigüenza y Góngora's ill health and in part to his brilliant refutations of Arriola's arguments, the trip to Pensacola was never made.

On 22 August 1700, Carlos de Sigüenza y Góngora died in Mexico City. In his will, he requested that an autopsy be performed in order to learn the exact location of the kidney stone that had caused him so much pain. He further stipulated that the results of the autopsy be made known, so that physicians might learn to treat patients with the same illness more effectively. It was a befitting decision for a man who believed so firmly in the role of observation and experimentation in scientific inquiry.

SELECTED BIBLIOGRAPHY

First Editions

Fiction

Infortunios de Alonso Ramírez. Mexico City, 1690.

Essays

Teatro de virtudes políticas que constituyen a un príncipe. Mexico City, 1680.

Manifiesto filosófico contra los cometas, despojados del imperio que tenían sobre los tímidos. Mexico City, 1681.

Triunfo parténico que en glorias de María Santísima, inmaculadamente concebida, celebró la Pontificia, Imperial y Regia Academia Mexicana. Mexico City, 1683.

Paraíso occidental, plantado y cultivado . . . en su magnífico Real Convento de Jesús María de México. Mexico City, 1684.

Libra astronómica y filosófica. Mexico City, 1690.

Relación de lo sucedido a la Armada de Barlovento a fines del año pasado y principios de este de 1691. Mexico City, 1691.

Trofeo de la justicia española en el castigo de la alevosía francesa. Mexico City, 1691.

Mercurio volante, con la noticia de la recuperación de las provincias del Nuevo México. Mexico City, 1693.

Poetry

Primavera indiana, poema sacro-histórico, idea de María Santísima de Guadalupe. Copiada de flores. Mexico City, 1668.

Glorias de Querétaro en la nueva congregación eclesiástica de María Santísima de Guadalupe. Mexico City, 1680.

Panegírico con que la muy noble e imperial ciudad de México aplaudió . . . al Marqués de la Laguna. Mexico City, 1680.

Oriental planeta evangélico, epopeya sacro-panegírico al Apóstol grande de las Indias, San Francisco Xavier. Mexico City, 1700.

Modern Editions

Fiction

Infortunios de Alonso Ramírez. Madrid, 1902; Mexico City, 1940; Buenos Aires, 1951; Mexico City, 1960; San Juan, 1967; Critical edition by J. S. Cummins and Alan Soons. London, 1984.

Essays

Alboroto y motín de los indios de México del 8 de junio de 1692. Edited and annotated by Irving A. Leonard. Mexico City, 1932.

Documentos inéditos de don Carlos de Sigüenza y Góngora. Edited by Irving A. Leonard. Mexico City, 1963.

Informe sobre el Castillo de San Juan de Ulúa, 31 de diciembre de 1695. Edited by Irving A. Leonard. *Revista de Historia de América* 45:130–143 (1958).

Libra astronómica y filosófica. Mexico City, 1959.

Manifiesto filosófico contra los cometas, despojados del imperio que tenían sobre los tímidos. Mexico City, 1957.

Mercurio volante, con la noticia de la recuperación de las provincias del Nuevo México. In *Documentos para servir a la historia del Nuevo México, 1538–1778.* Madrid, 1962.

Noticia cronológica de los reyes, emperadores, gobernadores, presidentes y virreyes de ésta nobilísima ciudad de México. Mexico City, 1948.

Obras históricas. Edited and with a prologue by José Rojas Garcidueñas. Mexico City, 1944; 2d ed. 1960.

Paraíso occidental, plantado y cultivado en su magnífico Real Convento de Jesús María de México. Mexico City, 1945.

Piedad heroyca de don Fernando Cortés. Edited and with a study by Jaime Delgado. Madrid, 1960.

Relaciones históricas. Selected and with a prologue and notes by Manuel Romero de Terreros. Mexico City, 1972. Includes *Infortunios, Relación,* and *Alboroto.*

Seis obras. Edited and with notes and chronology by William C. Bryant. With a prologue by Irving A. Leonard. Caracas, 1984. Includes *Infortunios, Trofeo, Alboroto, Mercurio volante, Teatro,* and *Libra.*

Triunfo parténico que en qlorias de María Santísima, inmaculadamente concebida celebró la pontificia, imperial y regia Academia Mexicana. Mexico City, 1945.

Poetry

Glorias de Querétaro en la nueva congregación eclesiástica de María Santísima de Guadalupe. Querétaro, Mexico, 1945.

Poemas de Carlos de Siqüenza y Góngora. Compiled and arranged by Irving A. Leonard. With a preliminary study by Ermilo Abreu Gómez. Madrid, 1931.

Primavera indiana, poema sacro-histórico, idea de María Santísima de Guadalupe. Copiada de flores. Mexico City, 1945.

Prose and poetry

Obras. Edited by Francisco Pérez de Salazar. Mexico City, 1928. Includes *Teatro, Trofeo, Relación, Piedad,* and *Primavera.*

Translations

The Mercurio Volante of Don Carlos de Sigüenza y Góngora: An Account of the First Expedition of Don Diego de

Vargas into New Mexico in 1692. Translated and with an introduction and notes by Irving A. Leonard. Los Angeles, 1932. Reprinted New York, 1967.

The Misadventures of Alonso Ramírez. Translated by Edwin H. Pleasants. Mexico City, 1962.

Spanish Approach to Pensacola, 1689–1693. Translated and with an introduction and notes by Irving A. Leonard. Albuquerque, N.M., 1939. Reprinted New York, 1967.

Biographical and Critical Studies

Abreu Gómez, Ermilo. "Carlos de Sigüenza y Góngora." In *Clásicos, románticos, modernos.* Mexico City, 1934. Pp. 13–55.

———. "La poesía de Sigüenza y Góngora." *Contemporáneos* 26–27:61–90 (1930).

Arrom, José J. "Carlos de Sigüenza y Góngora, relectura criolla de los *Infortunios de Alonso Ramírez.*" *Thesaurus, Boletín del Instituto Caro y Cuervo* 42:1–24 (1987).

Bazarte Cerdán, Willebaldo. "La primera novela mexicana." *Humanismo* 7:3–22 (1958).

Burrus, Ernest J. "Sigüenza y Góngora's Efforts for Readmission into the Jesuit Order." *Hispanic American Historical Review* 33:387–391 (1953).

———. "Clavigero and the Lost Sigüenza y Góngora Manuscripts." *Estudios de Cultura Náhuatl* 1:59–90 (1959).

———. "A Sigüenza y Góngora Contribution to the History of Florida." *The Americas* 19:305–313 (1963).

Carreño, Alberto María. "El archivo municipal de la capital de la Nueva España y su salvador, don Carlos de Sigüenza y Góngora." *Memorias de la Academia Mexicana de la Historia* 8:321–352 (1949).

Castagnino, Raúl H. "Carlos de Sigüenza y Góngora o la picaresca a la inversa." In *Escritores hispanoamericanos desde otros ángulos de simpatía.* Buenos Aires, 1971. Pp. 91–101.

Catalá, Rafael. *Para una lectura americana del barroco mexicano: Sor Juana Inés de la Cruz y Sigüenza y Góngora.* Minneapolis, 1987.

Chang-Rodríguez, Raquel. "La transgresión de la picaresca en los *Infortunios de Alonso Ramírez.*" In *Violencia y subversión en la prosa colonial hispanoamericana.* Madrid, 1982. Pp. 85–108.

Cummins, James S. "The Philippines Glimpsed in the First Latin-American 'Novel'." *Philippines Studies* 26:91–101 (1978).

———. "*Infortunios de Alonso Ramírez:* 'A Just History of Facts'?" *Bulletin of Hispanic Studies* 61:295–303 (1984).

Gallegos Rocafull, José M. *El pensamiento mexicano en los siglos XVI y XVII.* Mexico City, 1951. 2nd ed. 1974.

Gimbernat de González, Ester. "Mapas y textos, para una estrategia del poder." *Modern Language Notes* 95:389–99 (1980).

González, Beatriz. "Narrativa de la estabilización colonial." *Ideologies and Literatures* 2:7–52 (1987).

Iglesia, Ramón. *El hombre Colón y otros ensayos.* Mexico City, 1944. Pp. 119–143.

Johnson, Julie G. "Picaresque Elements in Carlos de Sigüenza y Góngora's *Los infortunios de Alonso Ramírez.*" *Hispania* 64:60–67 (1981).

Lagmanovich, David. "Para una caracterización de *Infortunios de Alonso Ramírez.*" *Sin Nombre* 5:7–14 (1974).

Leonard, Irving A. *Don Carlos de Sigüenza y Góngora: A Mexican Savant of the Seventeenth Century.* Berkeley, Calif., 1929.

———. "Don Andrés de Arriola and the Occupation of Pensacola Bay." In *New Spain and the Anglo-American West.* 1. Los Angeles, 1932. Pp. 81–106.

———. "Sobre la censura del *Triunfo parténico* de Sigüenza y Góngora (1683)." *Nueva revista de filología hispánica* 3:291–293 (1949).

———. *Baroque Times in Old Mexico: Seventeenth-Century Persons, Places, and Practices.* Ann Arbor, Mich., 1959.

———. "Sigüenza y Góngora and the Chaplaincy of the Hospital del Amor de Dios." *Hispanic American Historical Review* 39:580–587 (1959).

———. "A Mexican Savant: Don Carlos de Sigüenza y Góngora." In *Portraits and Essays: Historical and Literary Sketches of Early Spanish America,* edited by William C. Bryant. Newark, Del., 1986. Pp. 79–101.

López Cámara, Francisco. "La conciencia criolla en Sor Juana y Sigüenza." *Historia Mexicana* 6:350–373 (1971).

Maza, Francisco de la. "Sor Juana y don Carlos, explicación de dos sonetos hasta ahora confusos." *Cuadernos americanos* 25:190–204 (1966).

Navarro, Joaquina. "Algunos rasgos de la prosa de Carlos de Sigüenza y Góngora." In *Homenaje a Andrés Iduarte ofrecido por sus amigos y discípulos,* edited by Jaime Alazraki et al. Clear Creek, Ind., 1976. Pp. 243–249.

Paz, Octavio. "Ritos políticos en la Nueva España." *Vuelta* 3:4–10 (1979).

Pérez Blanco, Lucrecio. "Novela ilustrada y desmitificación de América." *Cuadernos Americanos* 244:176–195 (1982).

Quiñonez-Gauggel, María Cristina. "Dos pícaros religiosos: Guzmán de Alfarache y Alonso Ramírez." *Romance Notes* 21:91–96 (1980).

Rojas Garcidueñas, José. *Don Carlos de Sigüenza y Góngora, erudito barroco.* Mexico City, 1945.

Sánchez Lamego, Miguel A. *El primer mapa general de México elaborado por un mexicano.* Mexico City, 1955.

Sibirsky, Saúl. "Carlos de Sigüenza y Góngora (1645–1700); la transición hacia el iluminismo criollo en una figura excepcional." *Revista iberoamericana* 31:195–207 (1965).

Soons, Alan B. "Alonso Ramírez in an Enchanted and Disenchanted World." *Bulletin of Hispanic Studies* 53:201–205 (1976).

Trabulse, Elías. *Ciencia y religión en el siglo XVII.* Mexico City, 1974.

Juan del Valle y Caviedes

(1645?–1697?)

Daniel R. Reedy

Juan del Valle y Caviedes occupies an important place at the side of other major poets in seventeenth-century Latin American literature. In particular, one thinks of Mexico's Sor Juana Inés de la Cruz and her compatriot, Carlos de Sigüenza y Góngora, and of Gregório de Mattos Guerra in Brazil. Whereas Sor Juana Inés de la Cruz and Sigüenza y Góngora are usually identified with the heavily stylized current of the Hispanic baroque period and the strong influence of Spanish poet Luis de Góngora y Argote, the poetry of Caviedes and de Mattos is more closely akin to the baroque satirical mode of Spain's Francisco de Quevedo y Villegas.

Caviedes is certainly the most distinguished representative of the several satirical poets who are associated with Lima, the City of the Kings, during the colonial period. It is principally in the creole temperament and in the rebellious spirit of Caviedes that we find the roots of a nascent national literature in Peru. These characteristics are found basically in his critical vision of viceregal Peruvian society and in his intellectual independence.

For more than two hundred years, few details about Caviedes' life were known. Perhaps his personal obscurity was due to the invectives that he hurled at his contemporaries in viceregal Lima. We know, for example, that his poems circulated in manuscript form, but only three were published during his lifetime (1688, 1689, and 1694). It was not until 1873 that a first edition of a portion of his poetry was published under the title *Diente del Parnaso. Poesías serias y jocosas* (Tooth of Parnassus. Serious and Jocular Poems).

The discovery in 1937 of documents concerning Caviedes' marriage and his testament reveal that he was born in the village of Porcuna in Andalusian Spain, probably between 1645 and 1648. The date of his birth and the reasons for his moving to Peru are unverifiable to date. However, in an autobiographical poem entitled "Carta a la monja de México" (Letter to the Mexican Nun), discovered in 1944, Caviedes reveals that at an early age he traveled from Spain to Peru, where he was reared in a mining area, possibly in the Andean region of Huancavelica where his uncle, Don Tomás Berjón de Caviedes, was governor of the town and of the mining area from 1660 to 1664.

By 1671 Caviedes was living in Lima, where he married that same year. Again from his testament, we know that he had five children and that his wife preceded him in death. One of his poems "En la muerte de la mujer del autor" (On the Death of the Author's Wife) describes his grief when Doña Beatriz died. The testament, dictated in 1683, also mentions that he was gravely ill at the time from "la enfermedad que Dios nuestro Señor ha servido darme" ("the illness that God, our Lord, has seen fit to give me"). It may be supposed, therefore, that his many works satirizing Lima's medical doctors were motivated by the inept treatment he received at their hands when he was gravely ill. There abound in his works caustic satires against physicians, with allusions to the poet's illness, the mistreatment he received, and expressions of gratitude to God that he managed to cure himself despite his doctors' incompetence.

Caviedes' poems written during the 1680's and 1690's reveal his keen awareness of contemporary themes and happenings. He mentions the naming of Dr. Vargas Machuca as physician of the Holy Inquisition in 1680, the appearance of an important comet in 1681, the construction of the Hospital of San Bartolomé in 1684, the building of a wall around Lima during 1684–1687 to protect the city against pirate attacks, the devastating earthquake of 1687, the arrival of Viceroy Melchor Portocarrero Lasso de la Vega, conde de Monclova in 1689, the death of Viceroy Melchor de Novarray Rocafull, duque de la Palata in 1691, and the effects of a measles epidemic in the viceroyalty in 1692–1694.

The last poems that can be dated in this manner concern the construction of a dock at the port of Callao during the governance of Viceroy Monclova (1697). After this date, there is a total silence in his verses about contemporary happenings, and we know that his name does not appear in the 1700 census of Lima's inhabitants.

The corpus of Caviedes' literary works consists of some two hundred seventy poems and three short dramatic pieces. The nucleus of the poems is known by the title *Diente del Parnaso*—a reference to the wit and mordant satire in his works. According to their central purpose, subject matter, and style, his poems may be divided into four basic groups. The first of these is traditionally associated with *Diente del Parnaso* and consists of works in which jocular and burlesque satire is directed against all sectors of Lima society. Another group is composed of religious poems whose themes are philosophical or moral in nature. A third group deals with amorous themes, and the final group is made up of his occasional verse

written on different subjects and happenings during his time.

There predominates in the poetry of Caviedes a lyrical attitude that enlivens his verse whether in his invectives against doctors or in his amorous laments, religious prayers, or elegiac verse. In terms of the versification of his poems, he was not an innovator, since he chose the strophes and traditional meters common to his time: octosyllabic and hendecasyllabic verses in *romances*, sonnets, and other popular forms such as *décimas* and quatrains.

In the group of satirical poems, one immediately notes his harsh criticism of doctors, yet he also throws barbs at lawyers, poets, painters, clerics, mulattoes, Indians, drunks, cuckolds, and prostitutes, among others. While his works reflect the general orientation of Quevedo, we also find satirical echoes from such classical Latin poets as Juvenal and Martial.

The topics that Caviedes elects to satirize in his invectives against physicians are, at some times, realistic and, at others, hyperbolic, ridiculous, distorted, and shocking. In these works humor is the factor that unifies the extremes of his poetic vision. Also, his personal involvement, expressed through the lyric "I," is clearly evident, whether in conversation with a doctor or in a dramatic soliloquy addressed to an adversary. In his verbal war against doctors, Caviedes utilizes irony, sarcasm, antitheses, hyperbole, puns, ingenious metaphors, scatological references, and jocular comparisons. For him, doctors are "executioners in Latin," "killers, graduated in skulls," "doctors of the tomb," and "bloody ministers of Death." All of them are soldiers in the army of Death, and they wage war on the health of innocent victims with syringes, purgatives, poultices, enemas, and prescriptions.

Caviedes' condemnation of doctors is not limited to a generic attack on the profession; he also deals with them personally and by name—doctors who belonged to the highest stations of Lima society: Dr. Bermejo y Roldán, physician to the viceroy and rector of the Royal University of San Marcos; Dr. Vargas Machuca, professor in San Marcos and physician to the tribunal of the Holy Inquisition; and some twenty others whose identities have been verified in the annals of Peruvian medicine.

In his attacks on the illustrious Dr. Vargas Machuca, for example, Caviedes mentions that the doctor had alleged that he was a virgin when he was elected to the chair of medicine in the University of San Marcos:

> Machuca que en todo es vano
> alegó que era doncel,
> porque en todo, este crüel
> es contra el género humano.
> No hace de buen cristiano
> el ser casto y continente,
> sino de ser inclemente
> en el oficio que trata,
> que quien gente desbarata
> no es amigo de hacer gente.
> (Obra completa, edited by
> Daniel Reedy, p. 51)

> Machuca, who is in all things vain,
> alleged that he was a virgin,
> because in this case, as in everything,
> this cruel man is against the human race.
> Being chaste and being continent
> are not born of being a good Christian,
> but from being inclement
> in the job that is being undertaken,
> for he who spends time destroying people
> cannot be interested in engendering them.

His most ferocious attack against this doctor was occasioned by Vargas Machuca's inept treatment of Caviedes' cousin, who died as a result of the "cure."

Other topics border on the ridiculous: the poet writes a jocular criticism of the mulatto physician Pedro de Utrilla, who had removed a kidney stone from a woman; he verbally castigates a lawyer who switched from law to medicine; he remembers a fainting spell that a woman suffered as she climbed a high hill near Lima; and he celebrates the marriage of several doctors in ribald verses.

Another characteristic of these poems is Caviedes' interest in the ugly, distorted, and grotesque—a feature that his works share with other writers and artists of the baroque. For example, he addresses poems to two hunchbacked surgeons and offers another hunchback a "Receta para sanarse de la giba" (Prescription to Cure Himself of His Hump). Calling him an "armadillo of doctors," a "monkey of medicines," and "licentiate turtle," Caviedes speculates that this man's physical deformity must somehow

relate to the circumstances of his conception and that he is the product of "dregs of some ethnic love."

Women are also frequently the brunt of Caviedes' satire. There are, in particular, several noteworthy poems dedicated to promiscuous women. In the romance entitled "A una dama que, yendo a Miraflores, cayó de la mula en que iba" (To a Lady Who, on Her Way to Miraflores, Fell from the Mule She Was Riding), the poet provides a detailed metaphorical description of the parts of her body that were revealed as she tumbled from the mule, head over heels. Other poems such as "A una dama que paró en el Hospital de la Caridad" (To a Lady Who Landed in the Charity Hospital) contain graphic references to the lives of prostitutes, particularly to those afflicted with syphilis:

> En la Caridad se halla
> por su mucha caridad,
> si a ningún amor mendigo
> negó limosna jamás. . . .
>
> Las que de amor se resfrían
> es el remedio eficaz
> sudar un francés que es de
> picardía natural.
> (Obra completa, edited by
> Daniel Reedy, p. 159)

> In the Charity Hospital, Anarda finds herself
> because of all the charity she gave,
> for to no beggar of love
> did she ever deny an alms. . . .
>
> Those who suffer the chills of love
> will find the most efficacious remedy
> in a French sweat, which is
> native to Picardy.

Less shocking, and much more witty, is a poem to a famous old bawd from Cuzco, in which Caviedes recounts the advice she gave to her two mestiza daughters about how to conduct themselves, for the greatest advantage and personal profit, with men of all ages.

The language of these satirical poems is noteworthy for the large number of Americanisms: words of Quechua origin and other indigenous terms that refer to the flora and fauna of South America. Additionally, the poet frequently relies on Latinisms related to medical aphorisms and on invented words that imitate the Latinized speech of doctors.

The religious and philosophical-moral poems are among the least original or interesting of Caviedes' works. Their seriousness and somber tone contrast markedly with the wit and vitality of his satirical poetry. The themes are primarily concerned with the Crucifixion, the Immaculate Conception, the Ascension, the Incarnation, and the adoration of Jesus Christ, of God, and of the Virgin Mary. The most extensive of these poems is a "Romance a Jesucristo crucificado" (Romance to the Crucified Jesus Christ), in which the poet speaks of the divine gifts of Jesus and ponders the circumstances of his sacrifice on the Cross in order to save man.

The philosophical and moral poems deal with death, the negative effects of excessive wealth on Peru's inhabitants, ways to guard against lascivious thoughts, how to be a good judge, and similar exemplary themes. Perhaps the most interesting are those poems in which Caviedes reflects on the significance of earthquakes and other natural disasters that the populace tended to interpret as God's punishment of man's errant nature. Caviedes seems to be remarkably enlightened for his time and attempts to debunk such superstitions.

By way of contrast with the satirical and religious poems, those written on amorous themes are quite different in concept, tone, language, and style. They abound in soliloquies, bucolic scenes, mythological allusions, and idyllic subject matter. The nucleus of this group is formed by some twenty octosyllabic pieces describing bucolic settings in which shepherds lament their misfortunes in love. They are reminiscent of similar situations in the pastoral novels and bucolic poetry of sixteenth-century Spain. Some of these poems are addressed to specific women (Lisi, Filis, Catalina, Marcia) by a lyric narrator who chides them for disdaining the love that has been proffered by heartsick suitors. Also, it is not unusual to find descriptions of idealized women strolling through gardens on beautiful May mornings or poetic portraits of women whose beauty is extolled in classic images and metaphors.

The remainder of Caviedes' poetry deals with diverse topics and events relating to daily life in viceregal Peru. He writes about the death of one viceroy as he was returning to Spain; he describes the triumphal arrival of other viceroys in Lima; in several poems he describes the appearance over Lima of the comet of January 1681; he details the horrors and devastation of the earthquake on 20 October 1687; and he treats such ordinary topics as the construction of the Hospital of San Bartolomé, the erection of a wall around Lima, and the building of a dock at Callao.

The three dramatic works that Caviedes authored were not discovered and published until 1947. They share generally similar structures, thematics, and scenic movements. Each presents a burlesque allegory of Love, personified as a character who is the central figure of the work. Jokes, verbal wordplay, and buffoonish actions abound. In seventeenth-century Lima, small indoor theaters and open-air stages were abundant, and while there is every likelihood that Caviedes' works were staged as interludes between the acts of major plays by other dramatists, there is no firm evidence to prove this supposition.

Caviedes is the prototype of the lay poet of his time in Latin America. His is not the intellectualized, erudite writing of many of his European contemporaries; rather, it represents the Creole vein of popular poetry whose origins were rooted in the foibles and weaknesses of the society of his time, in particular in the excesses of moral, spiritual, and economic decay in the Spanish colonial empire. He is best remembered for his impudent humor and the acerbity of his wit.

SELECTED BIBLIOGRAPHY

First Editions

Poetry

Romance, en que se procura pintar, y no se consigue: La violencia de dos terremotos, con que el Poder de Dios asoló ésta Ciudad de Lima, Emporio de las Indias occidentales, y la más rica del mundo. Lima, 1688.
"Quintillas en el certamen que se dio por la Universidad a la entrada del Conde de la Monclova." In Diego Montero del Aguila, *Oración Panegyrica Qve al primer*

feliz ingresso del Excelentissimo Señor Don Melchior Portocarrero Lasso de la Vega, Conde de la Monclova. Lima, 1689.

"Créditos de Avicena, gran Bermejo." In Francisco Bermejo y Roldán, Discvrso de la enfermedad del sarampion experimentada en la civdad de los Reyes del Perú. Lima, 1694.

"Décima" (Tembló la tierra preñada). Mercurio peruano 1/34:312–313 (28 April 1791).

"A un doctor que trayendo anteojos pronosticó a una Señora preñada que pariría hija, y no parió sino hijo. Décimas." Mercurio peruano 2/47:111 (12 June 1791).

"Conversación que tuvo con la Muerte un Médico estando enfermo de riesgo." Mercurio peruano 5/157:152–155 (5 July 1792).

"Respuesta de la Muerte al Médico con este romance." Mercurio peruano 5/158:156–160 (8 July 1792).

Defensa que hace un pedo al ventoso: por don Juan de Caviedes mercader de Lima. Dedícala a los autores y consortes de cierto manifiesto. Un extranjero, layco, mercader de libros que apenas los conoce por el rótulo para venderlos. Lima, 1814.

Modern Editions

Diente del Parnaso. Guerras físicas, proezas medicinales. Hazañas de la ignorancia. In Documentos literarios del Peru 5, edited by Manuel de Odriozola. "Prólogo muy preciso," by Ricardo Palma. Lima, 1873.

Diente del Parnaso. Edited by Luis Alberto Sánchez and Daniel Ruzo. Lima, 1925.

Flor de academias y diente del Parnaso. Edited by Ricardo Palma. Lima, 1899.

Juan del Valle y Caviedes. Obra completa. Edited by Daniel R. Reedy. Caracas, 1984.

Obras de don Juan del Valle y Caviedes. Edited by Rubén Vargas Ugarte. Lima, 1947.

Critical Studies

Bellini, Giuseppe. "Actualidad de Juan del Valle y Caviedes." Caravelle 7:153–164 (1966).

Bueno Chávez, Raúl. "Algunas formas del lenguaje satírico de Juan del Valle Caviedes." In Literatura de la emancipación hispanoamericana y otros ensayos. Lima, 1972.

Cáceres, María Leticia. El Manuscrito de Ayacucho, fuente documental para el estudio de la obra literaria de don Juan del Valle Caviedes. Lima, 1972. Offprint of Fénix 22 (1972).

_____. Voces y giros del habla colonial peruana registrados en los códices de la obra de D. Juan del Valle y Caviedes, (s. XVII) 1. Arequipa, Peru, 1974.

_____. La personalidad y obra de D. Juan del Valle y Caviedes. Arequipa, Peru, 1975.

Guitarte, Guillermo. "Notas para la historia del yeísmo." In Sprache und Geschichte: Festschrift fur Harri Meier zum 65. Geburstag, edited by E. Coseriu and W.-D. Stempel. Munchen, 1971. Pp. 179–198.

Gutiérrez, Juan María. "Juan Caviedes. Fragmento de unos estudios sobre la literatura poética del Perú." In Escritores coloniales americanos, edited by Gregorio Weinberg. Buenos Aires, 1957. Pp. 257–289.

Johnson, Julie Greer. Women in Colonial Spanish American Literature. Westport, Conn., 1983.

Kolb, Glen L. Juan del Valle y Caviedes: A Study of the Life, Times and Poetry of a Spanish Colonial Satirist. New London, Conn., 1959.

Lohmann Villena, Guillermo. "Dos documentos inéditos sobre don Juan del Valle y Caviedes." Revista histórica 11/3:277–283 (1937).

_____. "Una poesía autobiográfica de Caviedes inédita." Boletín bibliográfico de la Universidad de San Marcos 14:100–102 (1944).

_____. "Un poeta virreinal del Perú: Juan del Valle y Caviedes." Revista de Indias 8/33–34:771–794 (1948).

Reedy, Daniel R. "Poesías inéditas de Juan del Valle Caviedes." Revista iberoamericana 29/3:157–190 (1963).

_____. The Poetic Art of Juan del Valle Caviedes. Chapel Hill, N. C., 1964.

_____. "Signs and Symbols of Doctors in the Diente del Parnaso." Hispania 47/4:705–710 (1964).

_____. "The Writer as Seer: Baroque Views of Natural Phenomena in the New World." South Atlantic Bulletin 43/4:85–93 (1978).

Sánchez, Luis Alberto. Los poetas de la colonia. Lima, 1921.

_____. "Un Villón criollo." Nosotros 10:219–226 (1939).

Unánue, Hipólito. "Rasgos inéditos de los escritores peruanos." Mercurio peruano 1/34:312–313 (1791).

_____. "Rasgo de nuestro anti-galeno Caviedes." Mercurio peruano 2/47:111 (1791).

Xammar, Luis Fabio. "Dos bayles de Juan del Valle Caviedes." Fénix 2:277–285 (1945).

_____. "Veintitrés sonetos inéditos de Juan del Valle Caviedes." Fénix 3:632–641 (1945).

_____. "La poesía de Juan del Valle y Caviedes en el Perú colonial." Revista iberoamericana 12/23:75–91 (1947).

Sor Juana Inés de la Cruz

(1651–1695)

Georgina Sabat-Rivers

Sor Juana Inés de la Cruz stands out as one of the most extraordinary personalities of Spanish America. Nothing really explains the enigmas of this paradoxical seventeenth-century Mexican woman's life better than her own well-known autobiography *Respuesta a Sor Filotea de la Cruz* (Reply to Sister Philotea of the Cross; published in English as *A Woman of Genius*), dated 1 March 1691, and Diego Calleja's essay "Aprobación" (Censor's Approval) for the posthumous third volume of her works (Madrid, 1700). These have been our main sources of information, although there are other documents that help with details.

Juana Ramírez de Asuaje (usually written as Asbaje) was born, according to Calleja, on 12 November 1651, on a small farm called San Miguel de Nepantla run by her mother Isabel Ramírez de Santillana, also born in New Spain. The farm was situated to the southeast of Mexico City, between the two famous volcanoes Popocatépetl and Iztaccíhuatl. Sor Juana's father was a military man from Spain, Pedro Manuel de Asuaje y Vargas Machuca, whose family was probably of Basque origin. The date of her birthday given by Calleja has been contested with the discovery of a baptismal certificate in the parochial archive of Chimalhuacán that says: "In December 2 of 648 [1648], I baptized Inez, daughter of the Church. Her godparents were Miguel Ramírez and Beatriz Ramírez. Friar Presbyter of the Monastery." The godparents were the brother and sister of Juana's mother; thus, this certificate belonging to a "Church's daughter," that is, someone of illegitimate birth, has been interpreted by critics as that of the future poet. But in Amecameca, the city closest to where Sor Juana was born, the book in which the names of children born of Spanish parents were recorded is missing. Besides, Juana did not use the name "Inez," the only one appearing in the document, until her vows upon entering the convent. We can speculate on whether she was given that name when she was born or adopted it as a religious name.

Juana's mother undoubtedly contributed greatly to her children's independence of attitude. Although it was not unusual in the Spanish New World for a colonial woman to have children outside of wedlock, it did require a firm independence of character. And Doña Isabel had not only three daughters by Juana's father but three more children by another captain from Spain. Yet it was only late in her life when Doña Isabel finally declared, in her last will and testament, that she was "an unmarried woman." Hence we may believe that for some time Juana did not know about (or ignored) her illegitimate birth, for in her convent's documents she declared herself to be "the

85

legitimate daughter" of her parents. Her contemporaries could hardly have been ignorant of the truth; envy of her obvious superiority must have motivated gossip. But in poetic references to such matters, she shows herself to have been quite self-assured.

> El no ser de padre honrado,
> fuera defecto, a mi ver,
> si como recibí el ser
> de él, se lo hubiera yo dado.

> To have a dishonorable father
> would be bad, in my opinion,
> if, instead of my depending on him,
> his reputation depended on mine.
> (1:230)*

In her *Respuesta* Sor Juana provides details on her precocity and explains her firm vocation as a scholarly woman and her unusual combination of submission and independence. When she was three years old, Juana learned how to read by practicing deceptions unusual for one so young: she persuaded her sister's teacher to allow her to attend the local primary school by saying that her mother had sent her. Two years later she learned to write and to do embroidery, the last a regular task for women, according to the customs of the time. Her inclination to study was so obsessive that it won out over more childish or "feminine" traits: thus she refused to eat cheese, which she loved, because she had heard it would make one stupid; she cut her hair as a punishment for not learning something within a certain time limit, since she did not want to have hair "on an empty head." Later she heard people talking of a university, in the capital city, where one could do advanced studies; she began to pester her mother, "begging and pleading with her to dress me as a boy and send me to Mexico City, to stay with some relatives who lived there and study at the University" (4:446). Since this was out of the question, Juana had to make do "with reading and more reading, studying and more studying" (4:447), poring through the books in her maternal grandfather's library at the

*All references are to volume and page numbers in *Obras completas,* edited by A. Méndez Plancarte et al. (Mexico, 1951–1957).

nearby Hacienda de Panoayan, in spite of frequent punishment and scolding.

She would have to go on studying by herself all of her life, however arid this might seem to her, deciphering "the books in themselves, their soulless characters, without the living voice of a master to explain them" (4:447). At the age of eight her natural enthusiasm for poetry had already produced a Eucharistic *loa* (prologue to a play), as her biographer Calleja tells us, a work that is not now extant. It must have been at about the same time that Juana finally persuaded her mother to send her to the capital, to live with relatives. She learned Latin in less than twenty lessons; this skill lay the foundation for many of her later readings and writings.

The unusual case of the studious little girl came to the notice of the viceroy, the marquis of Mancera, and his wife. Don Antonio Sebastián de Toledo Molina y Salazar was a man of literary inclinations. His wife Doña Leonor Carreto joined him in inviting Juana to their court, where she soon won everyone's admiration and began to write poetry for the vicereine as "Laura." Juana was not only beautiful but also enjoyable company. When the viceroy realized how brilliantly talented she was, he organized a public oral examination by forty scholarly specialists living in the capital. This was her "graduation," the official recognition of that rare phenomenon in a seventeenth-century Hispanic society, a female intellectual.

At court Juana was continually asked to write poetry celebrating social or political events associated with the viceroy, the city authorities, or the clergy. She used all the lyrical and dramatic genres, drawing upon her knowledge of music, painting, mathematics, logic, theology, and physics. Juana accepted everyone's invitations to display her growing brilliance, although she says, exaggerating, in the *Respuesta:* "I have never written anything of my own will, but obliged by others' petitions" (4:444). In this, she followed a long tradition according to what we find, on the same subject, in Bernardo de Balbuena's *Compendio apologético en alabanza de la poesía* (Compendium in Praise of Poetry):

> No cantes cosas que otro te demande
> sino en ocasión propria, o compelido

de que algún grande príncipe lo mande.
En lo que por nosotros fue eligido
todo se vuelve fácil, y al contrario,
lo que nos mandan, duro y desabrido.

Do not sing verses that another demands of you
Except in due season, or if compelled
By some great prince who commands it.
In matters that we ourselves have chosen
All goes very smoothly, but on the contrary
What is forced on us is hard and rough.

If we also consider her personal appearance—svelte, with classic features and imposing big, dark eyes—we can imagine how much Juana must have been considered the rare attraction of the viceregal palace. In literature, her genius paralleled the decline of letters in distant Spain, continuing and giving new life to the baroque style in poetry, of which she is the best representative on this side of the Atlantic.

Perhaps because life at court did not allow her enough time for study, Juana entered the aristocratic Carmelite convent of Mexico City on 14 August 1667, with the marquis and marquise of Mancera as her sponsors. During her years at court, Juana had matured, and had realized how unusual her personal situation was. Since she could not live alone, she decided that "the most appropriate and respectable thing for me to do" was to enter the convent. She knew the case of her sister, who had married and then was abandoned by her husband, and of the many other women who were subordinated to their fathers, brothers, or husbands, with housekeeping and child-bearing as their only possible occupations.

Perhaps the Carmelite order was too rigorous for Sor Juana. More likely it was the snobbish atmosphere of this particular convent, where Spanish-born ladies predominated, that caused the socially modest young Mexican to leave after only three months. But her intellectual vocation, her desire to lead a life of studious withdrawal from the world, was as strong as ever. Somewhat over a year later, at the age of seventeen, Juana Ramírez entered the convent of Saint Jerome with the religious name of Sor Juana Inés de la Cruz, and remained with the Jeronymites for the rest of her life.

Sor Juana seems to have adapted herself easily to life in the Jeronymite convent, even though some-times she felt that the routine did not allow her enough time for study. Cloistered convents in the New Spain of that period permitted a way of life that was not without a degree of social freedom and entertainment. Thus she was able to continue her dialogues and discussions with men of distinction, who sought the intellectual company of her parlor in the convent. Carlos de Sigüenza y Góngora, a Mexican relative of the Spanish poet Luis de Góngora y Argote, was one of these men. And the viceroy's palace, the cathedral, and the city hall continued to demand her contributions, in verse and prose, to their courtly pageants. After the marquis of Mancera came other viceroys; the most important for Sor Juana was the marquis of la Laguna, whose wife had her own title as countess of Paredes. To her (under the poetic name of Fili, Lisi, or Lísida) and to her husband and her son, Sor Juana dedicated a great number of poems. Later, when she returned to Madrid, the countess of Paredes sponsored the publication of *Inundación castálida* (Muses' Flood, 1689), the first edition of volume 1 of Sor Juana's collected works.

Sor Juana's international fame, and her problems in New Spain, began to grow. Hers was a world in which scholarship and intellectual life were always associated with men only: how then could she be allowed to emphasize in the final words of her philosophical poem *El sueño* (Dream, 1692), also known as *Primero sueño*, that it was as a woman that she had explored a dreamworld of scientific and epistemological problems, a strictly masculine area of speculation? But time and again Sor Juana struggled with prioresses, confessors, bishops, and other envious people to maintain her stubborn fidelity to the ideal of a woman self-consciously defending her own intellectual life. Convinced that the two sexes had equal abilities, she persisted in her ingenious and subtle arguments, justifying her right to compose poetry of all sorts. She became known as "the vindication of her sex," a "feminist" in a world with few feminist traditions. This was her most original aspect: she was perhaps submissive and orthodox in every other respect, but she would do nothing to deny her right, as a human being, to develop her mind. This attitude is what makes her unique in the Hispanic world of her time.

Her life and all of her written works, in many different genres, are implicit and explicit defenses of feminism, of her own and other women's intellectual rights. The examples are innumerable. Well-known are Sor Juana's much-anthologized *redondillas* (quatrains) that begin: "Hombres necios que acusáis" (Stupid men who accuse), following the interesting pastoral tradition of the Renaissance, with its invectives against abuse and the inconsistent way in which men treat women. In her play *Los empeños de una casa* (The Tasks of a House, first performed in 1683) she presents the *gracioso* (comic character) Castaño in a scene in which he dresses as a woman and makes fun of the systematic domination of women, the basis for Hispanic machismo. She attacks the nonsensical dichotomies of Golden Age Spanish literature that separate women into the beautiful-stupid and the ugly-erudite. For Sor Juana the most important task for any human being was to master the will in order to obtain knowledge. In her romance dedicated to the duchess of Aveiro she explains the basis of her battle in defense of women and her own main concern: that intelligence does not depend on gender. She tells the duchess:

> claro honor de las mujeres,
> de los hombres docto ultraje,
> que probáis que no es el sexo
> de la inteligencia parte.

> Honor of womankind,
> Insult to men,
> You prove that sex is not
> An intellectual factor.
>
> (1:101)

Women are paragons, also, of loving fidelity, as seen in figures of classical times and ancient history: Lucretia, Thisbe, Julia, Portia. Cleopatra is justified in her suicide because of her honor, according to Sor Juana's very feminist *villancico* (carol) to Saint Catherine of Alexandria:

> Porque no triunfase Augusto
> de su beldad soberana,
> se mata Cleopatra, y precia
> más que su vida la fama;
> que muerte más prolija
> es ser esclava.

So that Augustus wouldn't triumph
Over her sovereign beauty
Cleopatra kills herself and prizes
Her fame more than her life,
For it is a more prolonged death
To be a slave.

(2:167)

Saint Catherine is a perfect example of a Christian woman, and Sor Juana, because of the many traits they held in common, could easily identify with her:

> Porque es bella la envidian,
> porque es docta la emulan:
> ¡oh qué antiguo en el mundo
> es regular los méritos por culpas!
> . . . .
> De una mujer se convencen
> todos los sabios de Egipto,
> para prueba de que el sexo
> no es esencia en lo entendido.
> ¡Víctor, víctor!
> . . . .
> Estudia, arguye y enseña,
> y es de la Iglesia servicio,
> que no la quiere ignorante
> el que racional la hizo.
> ¡Víctor, víctor!

Because she is beautiful they envy her,
Because she is learned they compete:
For how many ages merits
Have been considered to be faults!
. . . .
By a woman they are convinced,
All the sages of Egypt,
By her proof that sex
Is not the essence of sense.
Bravo, bravo!
. . . .
She studies, argues, and teaches
And is of service to the Church,
For God doesn't want her to be ignorant
Since He made her a rational being.
Bravo, bravo!

(2:170–171)

The "Tenth Muse," as her contemporaries called her, even criticized Saint Peter in her defense of women. That criticism occurs in another *villancico*, in which the woman servant of Caiphas' house tells

Peter that she saw him with Jesus and he denies it. The poet sides with the woman because she speaks "science," that is, the truth. We can also understand her devotion to Saint Joseph, for he is, as Marie Cécile Bénassy says, the "antimachista" saint par excellence. The models of women that Sor Juana chose and with whom she identified are many and varied: from ancient Egypt there is the goddess Isis, the mother of the universe, the spirit of creation ("Is" represents the male essence; the word "Isis"—"Is" written twice—means the embodiment of the two sexes); Minerva, the Athenian goddess of knowledge, is another of her models.

In *Neptuno alegórico* (Allegorical Neptune) the poet commends Minerva on her victory over Neptune in a competition to determine the best gift for the human race: Minerva brought a twig of an olive tree, symbolizing peace and progress, which won over the horse, representing brute force, presented by the sea god. She brings forth many women of fortitude from the Old Testament, even the fallen ones like Eve. In a Latin poem to the Virgin Mary (2:35) "Eva" is turned to "Ave," vindicated by the Virgin Mary, the highest example of a woman, the one chosen to be the mother of God. She is presented in Sor Juana's *villancicos* as the teacher of the most intelligent beings in heaven, the angels. In the *auto sacramental* (religious allegory) *Divino Narciso* (Divine Narcissus) she is presented, with Jesus, as coredemptor of the human race.

Sor Juana's lifelong ambiguous social situation, due to being an illegitimate child and a woman, become even more serious for her during what Octavio Paz calls "el asedio" (the siege) of her final years. At some point after the publication of *Inundación castálida* in 1689, her confessor, Father Antonio Núñez de Miranda, who had been Juana's spiritual guide since before she entered the convent, pressed her strongly to avoid writing any poetry that was not rigorously serious. Thus began a long and painful period of profound self-searching and debate concerning her desire to devote herself to letters in a suffocating social atmosphere and under the vows that she had made as a nun.

Her self-confidence, her learning, and her firm belief in the intellectual equality of the sexes caused Sor Juana, at some point prior to 1690, to criticize the theological ideas of an important member of the clergy, the Portuguese Jesuit Antõnio Vieira (1608–1697). This great Luso-Brazilian figure had done admirable social work by fighting against the statutes of "blood purity" (which kept all persons of Jewish ancestry out of public office) in Portugal and against slavery in Brazil. The sermon that Sor Juana criticized had been delivered in the Royal Chapel of Lisbon in 1650 and had later been published in Portuguese and in Spanish translation. In it he questioned the ideas of three great church fathers and proposed an idea of his own as superior, a fact which seems to have provoked Sor Juana's critical spirit when she read the sermon. She was asked by an anonymous person to write up her critiques; she did so, hastily and provisionally, calling her ideas "meras bachillerias" (mere sophomoric wit). Her anonymous friend allowed the critique to be circulated in manuscript and, in its turn, to be praised and criticized. Some people took her essay to be an attack on the Jesuit order, to which Vieira, as well as Núñez de Miranda and the archbishop of Mexico, Francisco Aguiar y Seijas, belonged. The latter was a fanatical enemy of the theater and of fiestas, who fled from women as the source of sin. Battle lines were drawn up, and Sor Juana found herself in great difficulties that she had not foreseen, difficulties that were to mean the end of her career as an intellectual nun: a woman could not be allowed to engage in debate with a man at the high level of international theology.

The bishop of Puebla, Manuel Fernández de Santa Cruz, a friend and defender of Sor Juana, intervened on her behalf by publishing in Puebla, in 1690, her critical essay with the admiring title of *Carta athenagórica* (Athenagoric Letter; published later in the second volume of the nun's works with the title *Crisis sobre un sermón* [Judgment of a Sermon]). He appended a letter of his own, with the pseudonymous feminine signature "Sor Filotea de la Cruz," in which he praised her and urged her to stop writing profane works in order to concentrate on theology. Sor Juana's response to this letter constitutes the text of her *Respuesta*, signed in Mexico City on 1 March 1691: an eloquent autobiographical self-defense in which we can see ingenuously revealed the pathetic situation of an intellectual woman imprisoned by the society and culture of her times.

If in her *Dream* Sor Juana dramatizes the human soul as a thinking being, in her *Respuesta* she defends explicitly her own intellectual rights as a woman, and the rights of all women everywhere. How can we, then, explain her subsequent withdrawal from contact with the world? I believe that this decision, no matter how anguished, was voluntary. Sor Juana, facing the scandal provoked by her intervention in theological polemics, must have thought about the security of her religious vows, which gave a well-defined social recognition and status to a person like herself. For I do not believe that external pressures alone made her renounce the devotion to study that had been the driving force of her life. Probably Sor Juana saw herself, for the first time, through the eyes of others, and that made her give in.

Violent historical events in Mexico did contribute to her inner preoccupations. We find in her writings a growing sense of *desengaño* (disillusionment); in her *Dream* there is disillusion when the human mind embodied in her protagonist, the Alma (Soul), fails to comprehend the universe. Even the eminently Christian virtue of hope seemed to her merely a way of prolonging one's suffering; singly the senses deceive one, and one must be able to touch, as well as to see, things, for seeing to be believing.

One perceives in Sor Juana, a woman who has become identified with the baroque, clear examples of contradiction and plurality of meaning, of baroque paradox. This is what she tells us, not only in her lyric poetry, but in her prose *Respuesta*, when she speaks of parallel lines that seem to separate or converge in the distance, forming figures that are different from what they really are. Sor Juana, immersed in a closed world and criticized, doubled back on herself and decided to retreat to the convent. She was a product of her own times and, so as not to give up as a human being, she submitted voluntarily as a female intellectual, without implying that she rejected her own way of thinking. She then got rid of her books and scientific instruments, which had long been her beloved "friends," as Calleja calls them; she wanted no more possessions of any sort. Her decision to retire from the world led her to do penance and to renew her religious vows by signing them in blood. Sor Juana was a passionate extremist: once she made her decision to abandon writing and to be fully cloistered,

she showed the same energy in perfecting her virtue that she had formerly shown in defending her rights.

We must say, however, that she did not give up these rights, for the *villancicos* to Saint Catherine, mentioned before, were written and sung in Oaxaca and published when she probably was taking the decision that marked a turn in her life. Her inherent feelings of human compassion replaced her literary passion; and these feelings of sympathy took her to her death on 17 April 1695. According to Calleja, a highly contagious plague came to the convent of Saint Jerome. Sor Juana then devoted herself strenuously to taking care of her sisters in religion. While still young and beautiful, she contracted the fatal disease and, availing herself of the Church's last sacraments, she surrendered her soul with "serene acceptance" and "without the slightest clouding of her understanding."

HER WORKS

The literary life of the Tenth Muse developed within the literary currents that flowed to the New World across the Atlantic Ocean from the Iberian peninsula; it can be said that her works bring to a glorious close the baroque period of Spanish literature. She cultivated almost every genre of poetry and every metric style. We find in her works traces of influence from major and minor writers of Spain: Lope de Vega, Góngora, Quevedo, Gracián, in addition to Jacinto Polo de Medina, Francisco de Trillo y Figueroa, and Agustín de Salazar y Torres. The mental and linguistic ingenuity of *culteranos* (euphuists) and *conceptistas* (conceptists) seems to form the basis of her witty literary personality. But we also find in her poetry new and original rhymes and twists, precision and enthusiasm, as well as words that were unknown in the mother country. Her fresh innovations vie with her classical traditionalism. Her eminently intellectual poetry is at the same time, as Karl Vossler observed, permeated by a winningly ingenuous attitude toward reality. Thus, while her reputation has fluctuated with baroque and antibaroque vogues, her literary personality has always attracted readers.

Alfonso Méndez Plancarte, in Mexico, undertook in 1951 to celebrate the third centenary of the poet's birth by publishing an ambitious modern edition of her complete works. This was an important step toward the better understanding of Sor Juana's texts and toward recognition of her as a figure of the first magnitude in Hispanic literature. The original editions of her works, containing all but a few compositions, had been published in Spain during her lifetime or shortly after her death. They consist of three volumes. The first volume appeared in Madrid in 1689 with the baroquely suggestive title of *Inundación castálida*; seven subsequent editions and reprints, in various cities of the Iberian peninsula, have the colorless title of *Poemas* (Poems). The second volume (*Segundo volumen*, Seville, 1692) was published six times, changing its title to *Segundo tomo* (Second Volume) or *Obras poéticas* (Poetical Works). The third volume, always entitled *Fama y obras pósthumas* (Fame and Posthumous Works, Madrid, 1700), was published five times. The fact that her works were so frequently reprinted provides some idea of Sor Juana's fame in the seventeenth and eighteenth centuries. Her personal lyric poetry may be subdivided into four groups: occasional, philosophical, religious, and amorous. In addition, we have her *villancicos*, or carol sequences, her drama (*loas, autos sacramentales*, and full-length secular plays), and her prose works.

Personal Lyrics

Sor Juana's personal lyric poetry is the principal basis for her literary fame. It is highly reflexive, intellectually rational, and logical in structure, even when the themes derive from trivial social occasions such as birthdays. Courtly flattery is combined with astrology and science, mythology and history:

> *Vuestra edad, gran señor, en tanto exceda*
> *a la capacidad que abraza el cero,*
> *que la combinatoria de Kirkero*
> *multiplicar su cuantidad no pueda.*

> Let your age, my lord, so greatly exceed
> The capacity embraced by zero

That the *ars combinatoria* of Kircher
Are unable to multiply its quantity.

> (1:302)

Among the poems that Sor Juana devoted to the viceroys and vicereines, the many addressed to the marquis and marquise of la Laguna are often considered the best. In a language that suggests Renaissance hermeticism, in addition to expressions of devotion and respect, she uses stars, atoms, flowers, birds, numbers, and sand to express her wishes for an unending and cyclic life:

> *Si en una culebra el año*
> *figuraban los egipcios,*
> *que, unidos los dos extremos,*
> *junta el fin con el principio.*

> The Egyptians used to imagine
> The year in the shape of a snake,
> With its mouth and tail together
> Joining the end to the beginning.
> (1:133)

Sor Juana's portrait poems continue a Spanish tradition. They follow in an elaborate way a fixed order, reviewing a beautiful person's traits from head to foot, while the poet incidentally satirizes bad poets, analyzes musical structures, expresses feelings of love, and digresses in many other ways. The best known and most beautiful of her baroque literary portraits is the one she wrote for Lisi, the literary name of María Luisa Manrique de Lara, marquise of la Laguna and countess of Paredes. Each line begins with a word stressed three syllables from the end (*esdrújulo*, in Spanish), a tour de force that equals the extraordinary beauty of the marquise. The portrait is "painted," that is, written, on the blue skies with sun rays and stars, to match the everlastingness of Lisi's immaterial beauty.

Sor Juana's panegyric poetry is quite varied in themes and meter. Her praises are heavily charged with an erudition that often seems ironic. There are incidental autobiographical notes such as the following, as well as American touches, in the poem to the duchess of Aveiro, which begins "Grande Duquesa de Aveiro":

> *Que yo, señora, nací*
> *en la América abundante*

compatriota del oro,
paisana de los metales
    adonde el común sustento
se da casi tan de balde,
que en ninguna parte más
se ostenta la tierra, madre.

. . . .

    Europa mejor lo diga,
pues ha tanto que, insaciable,
de sus abundantes venas
desangra los minerales,

For I, my lady, was born
In an abundant America,
The compatriot of gold
And the countrywoman of metals,
    Where basic sustenance
Is provided so freely
That in no other place
Is earth so much our mother.

. . . .

    Let Europe say so,
For so long insatiably
Bleeding the minerals
From her abundant veins.

                    (1:102–103)

Sor Juana's six funeral poems are all sonnets. Three are on the death of the marquise of Mancera (Laura), and three on the duke of Veragua, an aged viceroy who died shortly after arriving in New Spain to take up his duties. The concision of the sonnet was perfectly suited to the interplay of form and logical concepts that belonged to the nun's scholastic mode of thought. The opposition between form and matter leads to a sublimation that is either Christian or pagan. Laura's lovely flesh is celestial and finds its own glorious element in heaven.

Sor Juana's philosophical poems are also predominantly sonnets, but there are also compositions based on shorter lines. One of the most famous sonnets is that concerning the poet's own portrait; its title helps clarify its complex argument.

    Éste, que ves, engaño colorido,
    que del arte ostentando los primores,
    con falsos silogismos de colores
    es cauteloso engaño del sentido;
        éste, en quien la lisonja ha pretendido
    excusar de los años los horrores,

y venciendo del tiempo los rigores,
triunfar de la vejez y del olvido:
    es un vano artificio del cuidado,
    es una flor al viento delicada,
    es un resguardo inútil para el hado,
        es una necia diligencia errada,
    es un afán caduco y, bien mirado,
    es cadáver, es polvo, es sombra, es nada.
        ("Procura desmentir los elogios que a
            un retrato de la poetisa inscribió
                la verdad, que llama pasión")

    This colored deception that you see,
Which, displaying the charms of art,
With its false syllogisms of color
Is a cunning deception of one's sense;
    This thing, in which flattery has attempted
To avoid the ravages of the years,
And by overcoming the cruelty of time
To triumph over old age and oblivion
    Is a vain contrived artifice,
Is a delicate flower exposed to the wind,
Is a useless defense against fate;
    It is a foolish, mistaken effort,
Is a failing eagerness and, rightly viewed,
Is a corpse, is dust, is shadow, is nothing.
    (She Tries to Refute the Praises Dedicated
        to a Portrait of the Poetess by Truth,
            Which She Calls Prejudice, 1:277)

The portrait, with its false colors, presents a triple deception. Anchored in Platonic and Aristotelian concepts, it first deceives the sense of sight, because it is a copy of the person, not the person herself. Second, in a deception at a deeper level, the portrait reproduces a body that, being mortal, will become a corpse and rot away into dust. And in a final deception, the canvas on which the portrait is painted will disintegrate some day.

There is a long tradition behind Sor Juana's most famous poem, which begins "Stupid men who accuse." It is in this same tradition—of the shepherdess who defends herself against the abuses of men in an idyllic environment—that we find the characters Marcela in Miguel de Cervantes' Don Quixote, Laurencia in Lope de Vega's Fuente Ovejuna (Sheep Well), and Camila, a shepherdess who defends her integrity against the erotic persecution of an old friend, in the Égloga II (Second Eclogue) written by

Garcilaso de la Vega. The theme of the poem finds its closest antecedents in the concepts developed by Jorge de Selvagia in Montemayor's *Diana* and the "Canto de Florisia" in Gaspar Gil Polo's pastoral novel *Diana enamorada* (Diana in Love), which attacks the arrogance of all men everywhere. The first stanza is well known throughout the Spanish speaking world:

> *Hombres necios que acusáis*
> *a la mujer sin razón,*
> *sin ver que sois la ocasión,*
> *de lo mismo que culpáis.*

> Stupid men who accuse
> Women without any grounds,
> Without seeing that you are the cause
> Of the very thing that you blame.
>
> (1:228)

If we ignore the carol sequences (*villancicos*), Sor Juana's religious poems (ballads and sonnets) are not numerous. There are New Testament themes, secular love themes "a lo divino" (that is, religiously parodied), and themes of Christian mystery expressed with baroque wit often used to defend women by analogy with the mother of God. Thus, on the Incarnation:

> *Que hoy bajó Dios a la tierra*
> *es cierto; pero más cierto*
> *es que bajando a María,*
> *bajó Dios a mejor cielo.*

> That God came down to earth today
> Is true, but truer yet,
> Coming down to Mary
> God found a better heaven.
>
> (1:162)

In lines written on the emblems of the "rose" and the "bee," representing Mary and Jesus, some of the symbols may seem to us to be obscure and in bad taste. But in other lines we find an authentically popular style. On Mary's virginity, for example:

> *Escuchen qué cosa y cosa*
> *tan maravillosa aquésta:*
> *un marido sin mujer,*
> *y una casada, doncella.*

Hear ye what a thing, a thing
So wonderful is this:
A husband with no wife
And a married virgin.

(1:164)

Sor Juana's love poems are numerous and varied. They are apparently not autobiographical. Love becomes a polemical theme, an occasion for surprise, for competition, for amazement. Passion merges with intellect, with theory, with set rhyme patterns. Her most original "mental" love sonnet is the following:

> *Detente, sombra de mi bien esquivo,*
> *imagen del hechizo que más quiero,*
> *bella ilusión por quien alegre muero,*
> *dulce ficción por quien penosa vivo.*
> *Si al imán de tus gracias, atractivo,*
> *sirve mi pecho de obediente acero,*
> *¿para qué me enamoras lisonjero*
> *si has de burlarme luego fugitivo?*
> *Mas blasonar no puedes, satisfecho,*
> *de que triunfa de mí tu tiranía:*
> *que aunque dejas burlado el lazo estrecho*
> *que tu forma fantástica ceñía,*
> *poco importa burlar brazos y pecho*
> *si te labra prisión mi fantasía.*
>
> ("Que contiene una fantasía
> contenta con amor decente.)

Halt, reflection of my elusive love,
Image of the charm I most adore,
Lovely illusion for whom I gaily die,
Sweet fiction for whom I sadly live.
If to the attractive magnet of your graces
My heart responds obediently like a needle,
Why do you woo me with flattery
If you later deceive me by fleeing?
But you can't brag, self-satisfied,
That your tyranny triumphs over me,
For, although you escape the tight noose
That bound your fantastic form,
It matters not that you escape my arms
If you're imprisoned within my imagination.
(Which Restrains an Amorous Fantasy,
Contenting It with Decency, 1:287)

Similar vocabulary can be found in Francisco de Quevedo and Pedro Calderón de la Barca. But Sor Juana's theme is radically original: the mind is capa-

93

ble of anything, even of restraining a lover who rejects. If he flees physically, the mind can retain him in fantasy.

Among the love poems by the Mexican nun, there is a group of sonnets about mismatched affections or circular oppositions of love, deriving from epigrams by Ausonius. They resemble the plot of a typical Spanish cloak-and-dagger play, pushing the triangle to its ultimate possibilities. The sonnets begin with:

> *Feliciano me adora, y le aborrezco;*
> *Lisardo me aborrece, y yo le adoro.*

> Feliciano adores me, and I abhor him;
> Lisardo abhors me, and I adore him.
> (1:288)

And they close with the poet's original and logical conclusion:

> *Pero yo, por mejor partido, escojo,*
> *de quien no quiero, ser violento empleo,*
> *que, de quien no me quiere, vil despojo.*

> But I, as the better alternative, choose
> To serve him whom I don't love, against my will
> Rather than be, of him who doesn't love me, the
> despised victim.
> (1:289)

One series of sonnets is devoted to faithful heroines, such as Lucretia ("¡O famosa Lucrecia, gentil dama!" [O Famous Lucretia, Gentle Lady!] 1:281), in which the poet deals with an idea we find in other poems with similar topics: the loss of honor itself is sufficient cause for death in a woman who is honorable.

Another theme is jealousy, which the poet must present as the final proof of sincere love, since she was taking part in a poetic debate in which her opponent had chosen the other alternative. More interesting is another poem in which the poet's voice makes a defense against ill-founded jealousy on the part of the beloved:

> *Porque te han informado,*
> *dices, de que mi pecho te ha ofendido,*
> *me has, fiero, condenado.*
> *¿Y pueden, en tu pecho endurecido,*

> *más la noticia incierta, que no es ciencia,*
> *que de tantas verdades la experiencia?*

> Because you've been told,
> You say, that my heart has offended you,
> You have fiercely condemned me.
> In your cruel heart, does a false report,
> Which is not science, have more power
> Than firsthand experience of great truth?
> (1:315)

But the most brilliant poem of jealousy is a sonnet in which the rhetoric of tears acquires new resonance:

> *Esta tarde, mi bien, cuando te hablaba,*
> *como en tu rostro y tus acciones vía*
> *que con palabras no te persuadía,*
> *que el corazón me vieses deseaba;*
> *y Amor, que mis intentos ayudaba,*
> *venció lo que imposible parecía:*
> *pues entre el llanto, que el dolor vertía,*
> *el corazón deshecho destilaba.*
> *Baste ya de rigores, mi bien, baste;*
> *no te atormenten más celos tiranos,*
> *ni el vil recelo tu quietud contraste*
> *con sombras necias, con indicios vanos,*
> *pues ya en líquido humor viste y tocaste*
> *mi corazón deshecho entre tus manos.*

> This afternoon, my love, as I was talking to you,
> Since I could see by your face and actions
> That I was not convincing you with my words,
> I wished that you could see my heart;
> And Love, who helped my efforts,
> Achieved what seemed to be impossible:
> For in my tears, shed in grief,
> I poured out my heart dissolved.
> Enough, my love, of your harshness;
> Be no longer tortured by tyrannous jealousy,
> Nor let low fears disturb your tranquillity
> With foolish imaginings, misleading evidence,
> For in a liquid humor you have seen and touched
> My heart, dissolved between your very fingers.
> (1:287)

The relation between heart and tears is reciprocal: tears arise from the heart's grief and flow down the face of the accused person; when seen and touched, they are tangible proof of true feelings and urge acquittal.

Another love theme is absence, expressed in silent writing:

> Óyeme con los ojos,
> ya que están tan distantes los oídos,
> y de ausentes enojos,
> en ecos, de mi pluma, mis gemidos;
> y ya que a ti no llega mi voz ruda,
> óyeme sordo, pues me quejo muda

> Listen to me with your eyes,
> Since your ears are so far away,
> And to my moans
> Of absent grief in the echoes of my pen;
> And since my crude voice cannot reach you,
> Listen in deafness since mutely I complain.
>
> (1:313)

The poetry written by Sor Juana is courtly in two senses of the word: it belongs to the court of the absent marquise of la Laguna, and it continues the themes of Provençal courtly love. Its intellectual character suggests that there is a distance between the poet and the feelings of love. This is abstract poetry, paradoxical and sublimated, the perfect playground for amorous fictions and total impossibilities:

> Ser mujer ni estar ausente,
> no es de amarte impedimento,
> pues sabes tú que las almas
> distancia ignoran y sexo.

> Neither being a woman nor absent
> Keeps me from loving you,
> For you know that souls
> Ignore distance and sex.
>
> (1:57)

Within Sor Juana's personal lyric poetry, the *Dream* is in a class by itself, her most important single work. Together with the *Respuesta*, it constitutes the basis for an understanding of Sor Juana as a person and as a poet. It is a long poem, consisting of 975 long and short lines, with a free pattern of rhyme. In it we find the whole range of Sor Juana's learning—mythology, theology, ancient and modern science, physiology, philosophy—subordinated to a vitally adventurous search for truth, for an understanding of the world's material reality. It was appreciated as a

baroque masterpiece when first published and again in the twentieth century, despite its almost hermetic difficulty, by Vossler and many others.

In *Respuesta*, Sor Juana draws special attention to the *Dream* (the title she gave the poem in that work, as well as the one Diego Calleja used twice in the biography he wrote of the nun in his "Aprobación") as her most authentic poem. Although it was first published in 1692, we do not know exactly when she wrote it, but it is obviously not an early work. The editor of the first edition relates it to Góngora's *Soledades*; it also has roots in Cicero's *Somnium Scipionis*, in Seneca's *Herculens furens*, in Statius' *Somnus*. The Spanish word *sueño* has, in fact, a double etymology, deriving from two Latin words: *somnium* (dream) and *somnus* (sleep). In this seventeenth-century *Dream* we find a variety of motifs belonging to a very long tradition: the mountain, the view from above and the precipitate plunge into the sea, the eagle, the tower over water, the beasts, the elk and the lion, somber birds of the night. In Spanish poetry the *sueño* theme represents both the sweet illusions of love and the warning of death. It reached a complicated dialectic in the circle life–dream–death. In poetry concerning dreams we find a basic structure that responds to three natural stages: exterior harmony that leads to sleep, dream, and waking. And this is the same structure we find in Sor Juana's *Dream*. The nun knew this whole rich tradition, as well as Calderón's *La vida es sueño*. (*Life Is a Dream*). In Callejas' "Aprobación" we find a summary of the poem's argument as follows: "When night came, I fell asleep. I dreamed that I was trying to comprehend, once and for all, everything of which the universe is made up. But I was not able to, neither in analytical categories nor yet as a synthetic individual. Disillusioned, at dawn I awoke."

Readers have suspected the influence of René Descartes, but Sor Juana's doubts do not constitute a systematic method. In her basically scholastic frame of reference, there are distinct traces of Renaissance neoplatonism and hermeticism. Consider, for example, this passage:

> Las pirámides fueron . . .
> . . . señales exteriores
> de las que, dimensiones interiores,

especies son del alma intencionales:

. . . .

así la humana mente
su figura trasunta,
y a la Causa Primera siempre aspira
—céntrico punto donde recta tira
la línea, si ya no circunferencia,
que contiene, infinita, toda esencia.

The pyramids were . . .
. . . external signs
Of the internal dimensions that are
Intentional faculties of the soul:

. . . .

Thus the human mind
Imitates their shape
And aspires ever to the First Cause
—The central point that fixes
The straight line, perhaps the circumference,
Which, infinite, embraces every essence.

(1:345)

While Sor Juana may not have read Descartes or Pico della Mirandola or Marsilio Ficino, she knew Andrea Alciati's emblems and Athanasius Kircher's works, as Vossler was the first to point out. The latter's *Oedipus Aegyptiacus* (The Egyptian Oedipus, 1653) was no doubt the source of her pyramid image. Kircher was also the source of her reference to the recently invented "slide projector":

Así linterna mágica, pintadas
representa fingidas
en la blanca pared varias figuras,
de la sombra no menos ayudadas
que de la luz.

Thus the magic lantern
Projects in fictive, colored form
On a white wall various figures,
No less dependent on shadow
Than on light.

(1:357)

Sor Juana's *Dream* is the only work in Spanish that develops fully the poetry implicit in science and technology, as Lucretius in *De rerum natura* (On the Nature of the Universe) had done long before her.

The poem begins with a traditional description of the invasion of night and sleep:

Piramidal, funesta, de la tierra
nacida sombra, al cielo encaminaba
de vanos obeliscos punta altiva,
escalar pretendiendo las estrellas.

A pyradmidal, funereal shadow
Born of the earth was aiming toward heaven
Its proud point of vain obelisks
Attempting to scale the stars.

(1:335)

Then sleep enters the poet's inner world: the body succumbs to the image of death, and only the Soul is still awake, ready in its dream voyage to be the protagonist of Sor Juana's philosophical adventure. The Soul is presented as an aspect of the mind, or human consciousness, with Aristotelian faculties such as the fantasy, which converts sensuous images into abstract concepts. The Soul rises above the stars, even above itself, seeing itself reflexively. From this high point, it attempts to grasp intuitively, in a neoplatonic style, the whole creation. But then it immediately subsides into defeat. The Soul recuperates and tries again to comprehend reality by using Aristotle's dialectical method, applying to each item the ten traditional categories, gradually moving from the simple to the more complex. In this slower process the Soul vacillates between optimism and pessimism:

Estos, pues, grados discurrir quería
unas veces. Pero otras, disentía.

Sometimes it tried to climb discursive steps,
But at other times dissented.

(1:353)

The poet's Soul finally reaches a state of total discouragement:

excesivo juzgando atrevimiento
el discurrirlo todo,
quien aun la más pequeña,
aun la más fácil parte no entendía.

Judging it to be excessive daring
To discourse upon everything
If even the smallest thing,
Even the easiest part was not understood.

(1:353)

Knowledge, then, is impossible; the comprehension of the universe is a mere dream. But the dream of knowledge was the very basis of Sor Juana's life, and she must understand its failure as somehow meaningful:

> y al ejemplar osado
> del claro joven la atención volvía
> —auriga altivo del ardiente carro—,
> y el, si infeliz, bizarro
> alto impulso, el espíritu encendía:
>
> . . . .
>
> que alas engendra a repetido vuelo.

> And the Soul turned its attention
> To the exemplary daring of that famous youth,
> The proud driver of the burning chariot,
> And took heart from that lofty impulse,
> Failing, yet spectacular,
>
> . . . .
>
> Begetting wings for repeated flight.
>
> (1:355)

Phaëthon, Apollo's son, is this chosen model: failure does not matter, because it is part of the human condition. But intellectual effort, bravery, and daring are in themselves enough to give meaning to life. This is the Faustian sense of the poem: intellectual problems are converted into poetry of great brilliance. The whole European cultural tradition was reenacted in Sor Juana's New World convent. The road to knowledge that the *Dream* represents is converted into dynamic movement: the effort is an activity that is constant and unending and does not reach its goal, but is the only way it can sustain itself. In the fatigue there is perpetual renovation. The effort itself explains life. It is in this way that the Tenth Muse, within the baroque period, advances toward later philosophical and literary concepts.

Carol Sequences

Villancicos have their roots in Arabic Spain. Sor Juana uses them as choir poems to be sung at matins on major feast days. She wrote a total of twelve sequences, between 1676 and 1691, for the cathedrals of Mexico City, Puebla, and Oaxaca. Each sequence consists of nine *villancicos* (or of eight plus the Te Deum). Sor Juana dedicated them to the following feasts: the Assumption, the Immaculate Conception, Saint Peter Nolasco, Saint Peter the Apostle, Christmas, Saint Joseph, and Saint Catherine. This literary genre was considered a humble one, so the Tenth Muse took advantage of the freedom and fluidity offered by its marginality. Some characters in her *villancicos*, as well as in her theater, pass from one role to another in suggestive metamorphosis. The comic traditions of the genre are also seen in the use of the substandard Spanish spoken by the lower classes and the macaronic Latin spoken by students. Sor Juana also presented Indians speaking Nahuat. In her treatment of black people, Indians, and other lower-class persons who appear in her *villancicos*, the poet was innovative. Sor Juana, being a woman, knew of unfair treatment; she established an artistic alliance with other marginal people, putting in the mouths of her blacks, for instance, sentiments of what we could call today "social protest." She brought forth the intimate preoccupations of these people, such as the Indians of her environment, presenting them as developing their abilities in a dignified way.

Each of the carol sequences has a central theme and variations. Thus, for example, the theme of the Apostle St. Peter's sequence is the denial of Christ and repentance. The Assumption has to do with Mary's ascent into heaven, elaborated upon in many ways: a fight between the body, which wants Mary to stay on earth, and the soul, which rises to heavenly glory; a parallel fight between earthly flowers and heavenly stars; Mary as an astronomer or as a scholastic professor with feminist touches:

> La soberana doctora
> de las escuelas divinas,
> de quien los ángeles todos
> deprenden sabiduría,
>   por ser quien inteligencia
> mejor de Dios participa,
> a leer la suprema sube
> cátedra de teología.

> The supreme female doctor
> Of the schools of heaven,
> From whom all angels
> Learn their wisdom,
>   Being the person who most fully

Participates in God's mind,
Goes up to be a professor
In the highest theological chair.
(2:6)

But she can also be a knight errant, a choir director,
a smart first-grade teacher, or a great astronomer:

> La astrónoma grande,
> en cuya destreza
> son los silogismos
> demostraciones todas y evidencias;
>
> . . . .
>
> no forma astrolabios,
> pues para más cierta
> cantidad, se sirve
> de los círculos mismos de la esfera.

> The great female astronomer,
> by whose skill
> all syllogisms become
> obvious demonstrations,
>
> . . . .
>
> constructs no astrolabes,
> for as more perfect
> measure, she uses
> the heavenly circles themselves.
> (2:65)

Saint Peter Nolasco was the French founder of the
Mercedarian order, which specialized in the ransom-
ing of captives. He is thus presented as a second
Redeemer. Sor Juana gives us in this sequence of
carols a view of a very healthy open mind, mingling
in a very Spanish way, the spiritual with the physical:

> Los enfermos visitaba
> con santo desinterés
> y su remedio buscaba,
> que, como era buen francés,
> del mal francés los curaba.

> He visited the sick
> So unselfishly,
> Seeking their health,
> That, being a good Frenchman,
> He cures them of the French disease [syphilis].
> (2:38–39)

The tone is always more comic than sentimentally
devout. The images are often ironic or learned or
witty. The four elements are entwined for the Assumption:

> Y haciendo dulce armonía
> el agua a la tierra enlaza,
> el aire a la mar abraza
> y el fuego circunda el viento.
> ¡Ay, qué contento,
> que sube al cielo María!

> And in sweet harmony
> Water binds earth,
> Air embraces sea,
> And fire surrounds wind.
> What joy, what joy,
> As Mary goes up to heaven!
> (2:93)

Sor Juana's carol sequences are among the best, if not
the best, in the whole Hispanic tradition: they are an
expression of religious joy, in a lighthearted, popular
vein, for the entertainment of large groups of people
of different classes and races gathered under the
domes of enormous Mexican cathedrals.

Theater

Sor Juana's loas are brief theatrical preludes of an
allegorical sort; she wrote a total of twelve. They tend
to be abstractly intellectual. Some of them are
autonomous, others are designed to accompany her
autos sacramentales, or full-length plays of religious
allegory. Her most original loa was written for the
auto Divino Narciso, a Calderonian mythological
work. This loa is entirely Mexican. In it a cannibal-
istic rite of the Aztecs, Teocualo (God-eaten), is
presented as a prefiguration of the Christian Eucharist, providing proof of the acute sense of sympathy
for a religious symbiosis that the nun shared with the
Jesuit fathers. Traits of this sort also appear in her
Virgin Mary sonnet to the Virgin of Guadalupe, in
which she explains the transfiguration of the "Rose of
Castile" into the "Mexican Rose."

Sor Juana's three autos sacramentales are El cetro de
José (Joseph's Scepter), based on a biblical story; El
Mártir del Sacramento, San Hermenegildo (St. Herme-
negildo, the Sacrament's Martyr), a saint's life; and
Divino Narciso, the best of her autos, based on the
classical myth of Echo and Narcissus. They all follow

the sophisticated theological models established in Spain by Calderón. Thus, Narcissus represents Jesus Christ, who rejects the shepherdess Echo's (Satan's) advances and falls in love with Human Nature, the image of God reflected in the waters of Grace. The death of Narcissus, drowned in his own bodily reflection, represents the Crucifixion of the Man-God. The fountain represents, in turn, Grace and the Virgin Mary. The Tenth Muse did not miss this opportunity to emphasize this very special woman. Sor Juana in her *autos sacramentales* competes successfully with her master Calderón.

Sor Juana's two full-length secular plays are comedies entitled *Los empeños de una casa* (The Tasks of a House) and *Amor es más laberinto* (Love the Great Labyrinth, first performed 1689). (The second was written in collaboration with Juan de Guevara.) They are typical cloak-and-dagger plays, complicated love plots, or labyrinths of Crete, which finally lead to happy marriages.

Los empeños de una casa takes place in a private home in Toledo, Spain. The most original character is the comic servant Castaño, a mestizo from Mexico. Sor Juana uses Castaño to make fun of sexual prejudices, reversing the usual device of a woman disguised as a man to disguise this man as a woman. He changes his clothes on stage, with exaggerated effeminate gestures. Then a handsome male character tries to win Castaño's love: this farce makes fun of the whole tradition of love intrigues on the stage. As Castaño says, as he finishes putting on his feminine garments:

> Ya estoy armado, y ¿quién duda
> que en el punto que me vean
> me sigan cuatro mil lindos
> de aquestos que galantean
> a "salga lo que saliere"
> y que a bulto se amartelan,
> no de la belleza que es,
> sino de la que ellos piensan?

> Now I'm all ready, and no doubt
> As soon as they see me
> Four thousand cute men will follow me,
> Those men who woo
> To find out what will happen,
> Who fall in love with shapes,

> Not of a real beauty,
> But of the beauty they imagine.

> (4:138)

Sor Juana criticizes those men who fall in love, not with the real woman but with the one they believe she is. This is the author's witty comment on the conventions of dramatic comedy and of Spanish life.

Discursive Prose

It was traditional in Mexico to follow the Roman custom of setting up triumphal arches to receive viceroys and other dignitaries. When in 1680 the marquis of Mancera entered Mexico as the new viceroy, the cathedral chapter commissioned Sor Juana to plan the allegorical arch and verses. She chose the figure of Neptune, god of the sea, and wrote her *Neptuno alegórico*, along with a detailed description of the arch. The text consists of three main parts: the dedication, which explains her reasons for choosing Neptune; an explanation of the structure, which provides a history of hieroglyphic emblems; and an explication of the arch, which describes in verse the paintings and mythological figures decorating it. The explication was probably distributed as a printed program on the day of the viceroy's triumphal entry. This was later combined with the other sections to form a souvenir volume, a monument to the Latin erudition of the nun and to Spain's viceregal power in Mexico.

Of greater interest are Sor Juana's *Crisis sobre un sermón* (later published as *Carta athenagórica*; 1690), and her closely related *Respuesta* mentioned before. The sermon referred to is one of the many published sermons written by the Portuguese Jesuit Father Antônio de Vieira. She read it and felt challenged by the Jesuit's ingenuity to answer its arguments with her own theological learning and wit.

Vieira's Maundy Thursday sermon is based on Jesus's command that "you, too, should wash one another's feet." As he speculates on Jesus's greatest favor to man in Holy Week, the Jesuit refutes three patristic arguments and reaches his own conclusion that "Christ's greatest favor was to make His love for us an obligation for us to love one another," not merely to love Him in return. The *Crisis* was Sor

Juana's response to Vieira's sermon. The nun begins by defending the church fathers that Vieira had refuted. She goes on to argue, in a very sophisticated way, that if God does not command us to love Him in return, it is to free us of the sin of ingratitude. His greatest favor would be in fact to do us no favors, to avoid putting us under obligation to Him, since we cannot repay Him.

Sor Juana's arguments circulated in manuscript form and were attacked and defended. Finally the bishop of Puebla, Manuel Fernández de Santa Cruz, published Sor Juana's critique, with his own appendix, a letter signed pseudonymously "Sister Philotea," in which Sor Juana was urged to devote herself more exclusively to theological studies. This gave the nun the opportunity to respond, in her *Respuesta*, with what is in fact the *apologia pro vita sua*.

José María de Cossio was the first to realize that we can see in the bishop of Puebla, not (as has been said) a severe critic of Sor Juana, but rather a good friend. If we take into account the whole ecclesiastical context, we realize that the bishop's intervention was his way of helping her in a moment of crisis, when she was being criticized by other clerics. For, although she says that her *Crisis sobre un sermón* (and later *Respuesta*) were to be read by the bishop alone, it is clear that she was modestly ignoring the possibility that they might be published, as they actually were, as a public self-defense. Her modesty is often so exaggerated as to be ironic, as when she protests at the end of her essay on Vieira's sermon:

> When we consider the lofty genius of the author, even giants seem to be dwarfs, to say nothing of a poor little woman. Although in antiquity a woman did wrest Hercules' club from his hands, a deed that was considered to be impossible . . . just for me to dare to criticize Father Vieira's sermon must be quite mortifying, for so famous a man . . . to see that an ignorant woman is so daring, a woman for whom theology is so alien a style of thought, so far removed from females; but Judith was not supposed to handle arms, nor Deborah to be a judge.
>
> (4:434–435)

Her exemplary females in each case cancel out her protests of modesty.

Sor Juana could not help feeling flattered that the bishop had taken the initiative in publishing her essay on Vieira's sermon. Since Vieira was one of the most famous Jesuit preachers of the period, to publish her critique was a way of applauding the nun and spreading her ideas, at the same time giving her an opportunity to defend herself against her real enemies, such as, probably, Father Francisco Aguiar y Seijas, the archbishop of Mexico, and Father Antonio Núñez de Miranda, her confessor. More indicative of this benevolent intention than the grandiloquent title (*Carta athenagórica*) that the bishop of Puebla gave to Sor Juana's critique is the fact that in answering her he himself assumed the name of a woman, of a nun. He thus identified himself with Sor Juana by recognizing implicitly that women, too, had spiritual authority. His feminine pseudonym, Sor Filotea, was a transparent disguise. Everyone knew that an important bishop had ambiguously assumed the role of a woman. His "fatherly" advice was simply to urge her to study more theology; in her *Respuesta* she, too, recognizes theology as the queen of the sciences.

Sor Juana took three months to write her *Respuesta*, an eloquent autobiographical document, full of personal life and intellectual vitality, designed to defend the rights of all women. No summary can do justice to this passionate document, which must be read in its entirety. What follows is a simple summary of some of its main points.

Sor Juana begins with courteous excuses for her delay in replying. She explains that she has never dared to devote herself to theology for fear of falling into heresy; that danger does not threaten purely secular literature, her usual genre, which the Inquisition tends to ignore. And she asserts that if she has written anything at all, it has been at the urging and request of others, for she herself was always satisfied simply to read and study and did not wish to write: "natural impulso que Dios puso en mí: Su Majestad sabe por qué y para qué." (God put the natural impulse in me, and only He knows why [4:444]). She explains her religious vocation in a negative way: she simply declared "la total negación que tenia al matrimonio" (a total opposition to matrimony). She goes back to her childhood: she learned to read at the age of three; she had wanted to go to the university, dressed as a man if necessary; she read the books in her grandfather's library; she always made great efforts to learn, even punishing herself if she did not; she learned Latin in less than twenty lessons. Finally, she entered the convent because she realized it was the most appropriate way to lead the life of study. And all of her studies would lead her eventually toward theology, the full comprehension of God's Creation.

The Mexican nun emphasizes the difficulty of studying on her own. She tells how she was frequently interrupted, whether deliberately or not, by fellow nuns and visiting friends. Her ability to write poetry came to her naturally and was a cause of envy. Using biblical texts she shows how any God-given ability can cause envy and even, in extreme cases, martyrdom. Nevertheless, her desire to know was so powerful that once, when a "muy cándida" (very innocent) mother superior ordered her not to study, even without printed books she could not help studying "en todas las cosas que Dios crió, sirviéndome ellas de letras, y de libro esta máquina universal" (every thing that God created: things were my letters, and the universe was my book [4:458]). She was aware of everything going on around her: geometric figures traced by children's toys, the combination of ingredients in a kitchen recipe, even the images appearing in dreams. "Si Aristóteles hubiera guisado, mucho más hubiera escrito" (If Aristotle had done cooking, he would have written even more, [4:460]), she says, claiming a superiority for women on the basis of the menial chores assigned to them. She concludes this section by saying that since her tendency to study was unavoidable, she should not be either praised or blamed for it.

The final section of the *Respuesta* is more argumentative. She makes a list of exemplary women from the Bible, heathen, Jewish, and Christian. And she explicates Saint Paul's famous precept, "Mulieres in ecclesiis taceant" (Let women keep quiet in church), by taking it quite literally: not only women, but men, too, should be silent and listen in church. But this does not mean that women are forbidden to study or give private lessons. In fact, the Christian community needs learned women, especially to instruct young girls, who might be led into sin by men, who tend to be heretics. One's sex has nothing to do with one's ability to understand the Bible. Hence she has the right to differ with Father Vieira. Her critics are wrong: if the church does not forbid her to express her theological opinions, her critics certainly have no right to do so. Nor is it sinful to write poetry: there is poetry in the Bible itself.

With these arguments she courteously closes her *Respuesta*; the rest, as Octavio Paz has said, is silence. Was this silence not, as I have suggested before, the result of a self-imposed decision? But this silence has carried abroad the voice of a Hispanic nun who, as a woman, embodies every human being that eagerly develops an enthusiastic and demanding intellectual life led among mechanical and musical instruments and books covering all branches of human knowledge. For Sor Juana is a compendium of European culture, brought to new life within a convent cell in a distant New World.

Sor Juana is unanimously recognized as the major lyric poet of colonial Spanish America, where baroque lyric poetry flourished for many years at a high level. Her superiority is obvious not only in her mastery of the tradition that she received from Spain, but also in her innovative originality and charming ingenuousness, as well as the special intellectual tone that she imparts to her works, particularly the major ones: *Divino Narciso, Dream,* and the *Respuesta*.

In the first of these three works, *Divino Narciso,* which is a play, she takes to a new poetic level the difficult genre of the religious allegory, surpassing the great Calderón in her invention of a new role for the mythological character of Narcissus and adding a personal note in her very Mexican prologue (*loa*). *Dream,* her major lyrical work, is not only the sole Hispanic poem devoted entirely to the question of scientific epistemology, but also transcends baroque *desengaño* (disillusion) by converting the shortcomings of the human mind into a constant effort that justifies the life of the mind in an existentialist mode anticipating Camus and Sartre. The *Respuesta,* her most important prose work, is an autobiographical letter in which Sor Juana sums up the meaning of all her writings: she expresses her rebellion against a world based on man's superiority to woman by asserting her belief in the absolute equality between the sexes and in the right of a woman to intellectual activity. The importance of this work is more obvious than ever today; Alberto G. Salceda calls it "la Carta Magna de la libertad intelectual de las mujeres de America" ("the Magna Charta of intellectual freedom for women in America," 4:xliii). And we need not limit her contribution to America: we can include women everywhere, since the Mexican nun refers to them all, without distinction of race, country, social class, or religious belief.

SELECTED BIBLIOGRAPHY

Original Editions

Individual Works

Villancicos,/ que se cantaron/ . . . *[a] la Purísima/ Concepción* . . . . Mexico City, 1676.

Villancicos,/ que se cantaron/ . . . *[a] S. Pedro Nolasco,/.* . . . Mexico City, 1677.

Villancicos,/ que se cantaron . . . */[al] Señor San Pedro./.* . . . Mexico City, 1677.

Villancicos,/ que se cantaron . . . */en honor de María Santísima/* . . . *en su/Asunción triunfante./.* . . . Mexico City, 1685.

Villancicos/ que se cantaron . . . */* . . . *en honor de María Santísima/* . . . *en su/Asunción triunfante./.* . . . Mexico City, 1686.

Villancicos/con que se solemnizaron/ . . . */* . . . */* . . . *los maitines del gloriosísimo/patriarca/Señor S. Joseph/.* . . . Puebla de los Angeles, Mexico, 1690.

Villancicos,/que se cantaron . . . */* . . . *[al] Señor/San Pedro,/.* . . . Mexico City, 1691.

Explicación succinta del arco triunfal . . . . Mexico City, n.d. A facsimile reproduction was published with the title of *Loa con la descripción poética.* . . . in Mexico City in 1952.

Neptuno alegórico, ... Mexico City, n.d.

Carta athenagórica, preceded by "Carta de Sor Philotea" Puebla de los Angeles, Mexico, 1690.

Auto sacramental del Divino Narciso. Mexico City, 1690.

Auto sacramental del Divino Narciso. Francisco Sanz: Madrid, n.d.

Amor es más labyrinto. Diego López de Haro: Seville, n.d.

Los empeños de una casa. Joseph Padrino: Seville, n.d.

_____. Viuda de Francisco de Leefdael: Seville, n.d.

_____. Herederos de Tomás López de Haro: Seville, n.d.

_____. Joseph Llopis: Barcelona, n.d.

Collected Works

Volume 1:

Inundación castálida. . . . Madrid, 1689. A facsimile edition was published in Mexico in 1962.

Poemas . . . . Madrid, 1690.

_____. Barcelona, 1691.

_____. Zaragoza, Spain, 1692.

_____. Valencia, Spain, 1709. 1st and 2nd eds.

_____. Madrid, 1714.

_____. Madrid, 1725. Reprinted, Madrid, 1725.

Volume 2:

Segundo volumen de las obras . . . . Seville, 1692.

_____. Barcelona, 1693. 1st, 2nd, and 3rd eds.

Obras poéticas . . . . Madrid, 1715.

_____. Madrid, 1725.

Volume 3:

Fama y obras pósthumas. . . . Madrid, 1700.

_____. Lisboa, 1701.

_____. Barcelona, 1701.

_____. Madrid, 1714 and 1725.

Modern Editions

Editions of the "Dream"

"*Primero sueño.*" Edited by Ermilo Abreu Gómez. *Contemporáneos* 1/3:272–313 and 2/4:46–54 (1928).

Die Welt in Traum. German version edited by Karl Vossler. Berlin, 1941. 2nd ed. Karlsruhe, 1946.

El sueño. Edited by Alfonso Méndez Plancarte. Mexico City, 1951.

Primero sueño. Edited by Gerardo Moldenhauer and Juan Carlos Merlo. Buenos Aires, 1953.

Il primo sogno. Italian version edited by Giuseppe Bellini. Milan, 1954.

Collected Works

Obras completas. 4 vols. Edited by Alfonso Méndez Plancarte and Alberto G. Salceda. Mexico City, 1951–1957. The only complete edition of the works of Sor Juana.

Partial Editions

Obras selectas de la célebre monja de México . . . . Edited by Juan León Mera. Quito, Ecuador, 1873.

Poesías escogidas de Sor Juana Inés de la Cruz. Edited by Antonio Elías de Molins, n.d. Pedro Henríquez Ureña believes the date is 1901.

Obras escogidas. Anonymous edition. Mexico City, 1938.

Poesías completas. Edited by Ermilo Abreu Gómez. Mexico City, 1940.

Poesías. Selected and with a prologue by Elena Amat. Valencia, 1941.

Sor Juana Inés de la Cruz. Edited by Clara Campoamor. Buenos Aires, 1944.

Poesía y teatro. Edited by Matilde Muñoz. Madrid, 1946.

Endechas. Edited by Xavier Villaurrutia. Morelia, Mexico, 1952.

Antología Sorjuanina. Edited by Giuseppe Bellini. Milan, 1961.

Poesía, teatro y prosa. Edited by Antonio Castro Leal. Mexico City, 1965.

Antología. Edited by Elias L. Rivers. Madrid, 1965.

Obras escogidas. Edited by Juan Carlos Merlo. Barcelona, 1968.

Antología clave. Edited by Hernán Loyola. Santiago, Chile, 1971.

Obras selectas. Edited by Georgina Sabat de Rivers and Elias L. Rivers. Barcelona, 1976.

Selección. Edited by L. Ortega Galindo. Madrid, 1978.

Sonetos y endechas. Edited by Rosa Chacel. With a prologue by Xavier Villaurrutia. Barcelona, 1980.

Inundación castálida. Edited by Georgina Sabat de Rivers. Madrid, 1982.

Lírica. Edited by Raquel Asún. Barcelona, 1983.

Obra selecta. Edited by Luis Sáinz de Medrano. Barcelona, 1987.

Translations

The Dream. Partially translated by Gilbert F. Cunningham. In "Sor Juana's *Sueño*—A Fragment in English Verse." *Modern Language Notes* 83/2:253–261 (1968).

A Woman of Genius: The Intellectual Autobiography of Sor Juana Inés de la Cruz. Translated by Margaret Sayers Peden. Salisbury, Conn., 1982. Translation of *Respuesta a Sor Filotea . . . .*

Biographical and Critical Studies

Abreu Gómez, Ermilo. *Sor Juana Inés de la Cruz: Bibliografía y biblioteca.* Mexico City, 1934.

———. *La ruta de Sor Juana.* Mexico City, 1938.

———. *Semblanza de Sor Juana.* Mexico City, 1938.

Aguirre, Mirta. *Del encausto a la sangre: Sor Juana Inés de la Cruz.* Havana, 1975.

Alatorre, Antonio. "Para leer la *Fama y obras pósthumas* de Sor Juana Inés de la Cruz." *Nueva revista de filología hispánica* 29/2:428–508 (1980).

———. "Un devoto de Sor Juana: Francisco Alvarez de Velasco." *Filología* 20/2:157–176 (1985).

Arenal, Electa. "Sor Juana Inés de la Cruz: Speaking the Mother Tongue." *University of Dayton Review* 16/2:93–105 (1983).

Arroyo, Anita. *Razón y pasión de Sor Juana.* Mexico City, 1952.

Bellini, Giuseppe. *La poesía di Sor Juana Inés de la Cruz.* Milan, 1954.

Bénassy-Berling, Marie Cécile. *Humanisme et religion chez Sor Juana Inés de la Cruz: La femme et la culture au XVII siècle.* Paris, 1982. It was translated into Spanish in Mexico in 1984.

Carilla, Emilio. *El gongorismo en América.* Buenos Aires, 1946.

———. "Sor Juana: Ciencia y poesía. (Sobre el *Primero sueño*)." *Revista de filología española* 36:287–307 (1952).

Castro López, Octavio. *Sor Juana y el "Primero sueño."* Xalapa, Mexico, 1982.

Chang-Rodríguez, Raquel. "Mayorías y minorías en la formación de la cultura virreinal." *University of Dayton Review* 16/2:23–34 (1983).

Chávez, Ezequiel. *Ensayo de psicología de Sor Juana Inés de la Cruz.* Barcelona, 1931.

Chinchilla-Aguilar, Ernesto. "El siglo XVII novohispano y la figura de Sor Juana Inés." *University of Dayton Review* 16/2:53–61 (1983).

Cossío, José María de, et al. "Homenaje a Sor Juana Inés de la Cruz." *Boletín de la Real Academia Española* 32:27–72 (1972).

Díaz de Ovando, Clementina. "Acerca de las redondillas de Sor Juana Inés de la Cruz." *Anales, Instituto de Investigaciones Estéticas* 4/13 (1945).

Durán, Manuel. "El drama intelectual de Sor Juana y el antiintelectualismo hispánico." *Cuadernos americanos* 22/4:238–253 (1963).

———. "Hermetic Traditions in Sor Juana's *Primero sueño.*" *University of Dayton Review* 16/2:107–115 (1983).

Fanchón, Royer. "Tenth Muse." *The Américas* 8/2:143–178 (1951).

Fernández, Sergio. *Homenajes a Sor Juana, a Lopez Velarde, a José Gorostiza.* Mexico City, 1972.

———. *Autos sacramentales de Sor Juana Inés de la Cruz ("El Divino Narciso"–"San Hermenegildo").* Mexico City, 1970.

Flynn, Gerard C. *Sor Juana Inés de la Cruz.* New York, 1971.

Galeano Ospina, Carlos E. *Juana de Asbaje: Aproximación a la autobiografía de la "Décima Musa."* Medellín, Colombia, 1976.

Gaos, José. "El sueño de un sueño." *Historia mexicana* 10/1:54–71 (1960).

Gates, E. J. "Reminiscences of Góngora in the works of Sor Juana Inés de la Cruz." *Modern Languages Association* 54:1041–1058 (1939).

Henríquez Ureña, Pedro. "Bibliografía de Sor Juana Inés de la Cruz." *Revue hispanique* 40:161–214 (1917).

Lavrin, Asunción. "Unlike Sor Juana? The Model Nun in

the Religious Literature of Colonial Mexico." *University of Dayton Review* 16/2:75–92 (1983).

Lazo, Raimundo. "Sor Juana Inés de la Cruz." *Boletín de la Real Academia Española* 1/1:78–94 (1952).

Leonard, Irving. "A Baroque Poetess." In *Baroque Times in Old Mexico*. Ann Arbor, Mich., 1959. Pp. 172–192.

Ludmer, Josefina. "Treatas del débil." In *La sartén por el mango*. Puerto Rico, 1984. Pp. 47–54.

Maza, Francisco de la, and Elías Trabulse. *Sor Juana Inés de la Cruz ante la historia*. Mexico City, 1980.

Menéndez y Pelayo, Marcelino. *Antología de poetas hispanoamericanos* 1. Madrid, 1893. Reprinted in his *Obras completas* 2. Madrid, 1911.

Moldenhauer, Gerardo. "Observaciones críticas para una edición definitiva del *Sueño* de Sor Juana Inés de la Cruz." *Boletin del instituto de filología* (Chile) 8:293–306 (1954–1955).

Monguió, Luis. "Compañía para Sor Juana: Mujeres cultas en el virreinato del Perú." *University of Dayton Review* 16/2:45–52 (1983).

Montross, Constance M. *Virtue or Vice? Sor Juana's Use of Thomistic Thought*. Washington D.C., 1981.

Nervo, Amado. *Juana de Asbaje*. La Plata, Argentina, 1946.

Pascual Buxó, José. *Sor Juana Inés de la Cruz en el conocimiento de su "Sueño."* Lecture delivered at the Universidad Nacional Autonoma de México. Mexico City, 1984.

Paz, Octavio. *Sor Juana Inés de la Cruz: O, Las trampas de la fe*. Barcelona and Mexico City, 1983.

———. *Sor Juana*. Translated by Margaret Sayers Peden. Boston, 1988.

Perelmuter Pérez, Rosa. *Noche intelectual: La oscuridad idomática en el "Primero Sueño."* Mexico City, 1982.

———. "La situación enunciativa del *Primero sueño*." *Revista canadiense de estudios hispánicos* 11/1:185–191.

Pérez, María E.. *Lo americano en el teatro de Sor Juana Inés de la Cruz*. New York, 1975.

Pfandl, Ludwig. *Sor Juana Inés de la Cruz. La Décima Musa de México: Su vida, su poesía, su psique*. Translated from the German by Juan Antonio Ortega y Medina. Mexico City, 1963.

Puccini, Dario: *Sor Juana Inés de la Cruz: Studio d'una personalità del baroco messicano*. Rome, 1967.

Ramírez España, Guillermo. *La familia de Sor Juana*. Mexico City, 1947.

Reyes, Alfonso. "Virreinato de filigrana." In *Letras de la nueva españa*. Mexico City, 1948. Pp. 87–118.

Ricard, Robert. *Une poétesse mexicaine du XVIIᵉ siècle. Sor Juana Inés de la Cruz*. Paris, 1953.

Rivers, Elias L. "Indecencias de una monjita mexicana." In *Homenaje William L. Fichter*. Madrid, 1971. Pp. 633–637.

———. "Diglossia in New Spain." *University of Dayton Review* 16/2:9–12 (1983).

Roggiano, Alfredo A. "Conocer y hacer en Sor Juana Inés de la Cruz." *Revista de occidente* (Madrid) 15:51–54 (1977).

Sabat de Rivers, Georgina. "Sor Juana y su Sueño: Antecedentes científicos en la poesía española del siglo de oro." *Cuadernos hispanoamericanos* 310:186–204 (1976).

———. *El "Sueño" de Sor Juana Inés de la Cruz: Tradiciones literarias y originalidad*. London, 1977.

———. "Sor Juana Inés de la Cruz y Gertrudis Gómez de Avellaneda: Dos voces americanas en defensa de la mujer." In *Homenaje a Gertrudis Gómez de Avellaneda*. Miami, 1981. Pp. 99–110.

———. "Sor Juana Inés de la Cruz." In *Historia de la literatura hispanoamericana. Epoca colonial* 1:275–293. Madrid, 1982.

———. "El Neptuno de Sor Juana: Fiesta barroca y programa político." *University of Dayton Review* 16/2:63–73 (1983).

———. "Biografías: Sor Juana vista por Dorothy Schons y Octavio Paz." *Revista iberoamericana* 132–133:927–937 (1985).

———. "Blanco, negro, rojo: Semiosis racial en los villancicos de Sor Juana Inés de la Cruz." In *Crítica semiológica de textos literarios hispánicos*. Madrid, 1986. Pp. 247–255.

———. "Sor Juana: La tradición clásica del retrato poético." In *De la crónica a la nueva narrativa mexicana*. Mexico City, 1986. Pp. 79–93.

———. "Autobiografías: Santa Teresa y Sor Juana." In *Texto Crítico*. Stillwater, Okla. Forthcoming.

———. "Lírica popular y lírica culta." In *Literatura hispanoamericana. La colonia* 2. Madrid. Forthcoming.

———. "Otra vez El Sueño: relectura feminista." In *"Y yo despierta": Toward a Feminist Reading of Sor Juana Ines de la Cruz*. Forthcoming.

Schons, Dorothy. *Some Bibliographical Notes*. Austin, Tex., 1925.

———. "Some Obscure Points in the Life of Sor Juana Inés de la Cruz." *Modern Philology* 24:141–162 (1926).

———. *Bibliografía de Sor Juana Inés de la Cruz*. Mexico City, 1927.

———. "Nuevos datos para la biografía de Sor Juana." *Contemporáneos* 9:161–176 (1929).

Schultz de Mantovani, Fryda. "La Décima Musa." *Sur* 206:41–60 (1951).

Scott, Nina M. "The Tenth Muse." *Americas* 30/2:13–20 (1978).

_____. "Sor Juana Ines de la Cruz: Let Your Women Keep Silence in the Churches." *Women's Studies in International Forum* 5/8:511–519 (1985).

Spell, Lota. *Cuatro documentos relativos a Sor Juana.* Mexico City, 1947.

Terry, Arthur. "Human and Divine Love in the Poetry of Sor Juana Inés de la Cruz." In *Studies in Spanish Literature of the Golden Age.* London, 1973.

Trabulse, Elías. *El hermetismo y Sor Juana Inés de la Cruz. Origenes e interpretación.* Mexico City, 1980.

Vossler, Karl. "La Décima Musa de México: Sor Juana Inés de la Cruz." In *Escritores y poetas de España.* Buenos Aires and Mexico City, 1947. Pp. 103–131.

Wallace, Elizabeth. *Sor Juana Inés de la Cruz: Poetisa de corte y convento.* Mexico City, 1944.

Xirau, Ramón. *Genio y figura de Sor Juana Inés de la Cruz.* Buenos Aires, 1967 and 1970.

Alonso Carrió de la Vandera

(ca. 1715–1783)

Raquel Chang-Rodríguez

The earliest writers in colonial Spanish America were captains and soldiers who wrote to describe the New World to the Spanish authorities and to tell of their exploits in the strange land discovered by Christopher Columbus. With their writings, these men often hoped to justify their misdeeds, explain their actions, and gain honor and wealth for services rendered to king and country. This literary tradition was continued in the seventeenth and eighteenth centuries by colonial officials sent to America by the crown and by literate *criollos* (sons and daughters of Spaniards born in the New World). By then, a minority of Indians and *mestizos* (people of mixed race) had mastered the art of writing and were familiar with European literary traditions. While colonial writers expressed themselves in several genres, of particular interest are works that combine history and geography, reality and fantasy, the general and the particular, the expected and the unexpected—works that challenge traditional classification while offering an all-encompassing vision of the New World. To this category belongs *El lazarillo de ciegos caminantes, desde Buenos Aires a Lima* (*El lazarillo: A Guide for Inexperienced Travelers Between Buenos Aires and Lima*, 1775), written by Alonso Carrió de la Vandera, a Spaniard appointed second postal commissioner and charged with inspecting and reorganizing postal service between Buenos Aires and Lima.

The title page of *El lazarillo* indicates that it was published "In Gijón [Spain]. At The Stolen [La Rovada] Printing Press. Year of 1773" and that its author was Calixto Bustamante Carlos Inca, alias Concolorcorvo (literally, The Dark-Colored). In spite of these details, the name of the printing press, La Rovada (The Stolen), with its humorous effect, was considered suspect by critics who asked: Who wrote the book, Carrió or Concolorcorvo? When and where was it published? Who really was Calixto Bustamante Carlos Inca? These questions have been answered in this century by the critics José J. Real Díaz and Marcel Bataillon, who have made available new documentation about Carrió's life. They established that *El lazarillo* was published, probably without a permit, by the printing press called Los Huérfanos (The Orphans), and definitely in Lima, Peru, toward the end of 1775 or the beginning of 1776. Emilio Carilla, a specialist on this work, favors the year 1775. This documentation confirmed beyond all doubt that the author of *El lazarillo* is Alonso Carrió de la Vandera and established that Concolorcorvo was his secretary for a period of ten months while they traveled from Córdoba, Argentina, to Potosí; Concolorcorvo received two hundred pesos for his services. Notwithstanding these clarifications, more questions were raised: Why was Carrió so deceptive about the date and place of publication? Why did he attribute the book to his secretary? To answer them properly, it is necessary to consider Carrió's biography.

Alonso Carrió de la Vandera was born in Gijón, Spain, in 1715 or 1716. Except for the names of his parents, Justo Carrió and Teresa Carreño Argüelles, nothing is known about him until 1736, when, perhaps for economic reasons, he sailed for Mexico, where he established himself as a merchant for ten years. By 1746, Carrió was in Lima; from there, his commercial ventures took him to Santiago, Chile, and Buenos Aires in 1748–1749. Carrió had enjoyed a certain measure of personal prestige; his marriage to Petronila Matute Melgarejo, a *criolla* from a distinguished family, allowed the author to climb higher on the social ladder and facilitated his appointment in 1752 as *corregidor* (magistrate) in two villages close to the city of Cuzco.

A restless man, the author of *El lazarillo* volunteered to escort to Europe members of the Jesuit order expelled in 1767 from all Spanish colonies, by order of Carlos III of Spain. In 1768, Carrió arrived in Cádiz; he later went to Madrid in order to seek at court a government position in Peru. It was precisely the time when the Spanish king had decided to make the existing postal service an official function of the crown. To begin this reorganization, José Antonio Pando was appointed postal administrator of the viceroyalty of Peru. Pando, who became an archenemy of Carrió, is criticized directly and indirectly in *El lazarillo*.

After several unsuccessful attempts at court, Carrió de la Vandera was finally appointed second postal commissioner in 1771. In February of that year, Carrió sailed for Montevideo, Uruguay. While on this voyage, he began to write a *diario naútico* (nautical journal), of which we know only a disputed fragment; there is no conclusive evidence to prove that it is indeed part of that document. Shortly after, he left for Buenos Aires and while there became a good friend of the first postal administrator of that city, Domingo Basavilbaso. The two officials organized and carried out a complete reform of the postal system, much to the irritation of Pando.

Carrió left Buenos Aires for Peru on 5 November 1771. After traveling 946 leagues in nineteen months, he reached Lima on 6 June 1773. His arrival there further fueled his quarrel with Pando. Anticipating more problems between the two men, Viceroy Manuel de Amat created a committee to look into their complaints. It was during the latter part of this period (1775–1776) that *El lazarillo* appeared in Lima. It is believed that a recurrent theme in the book, the riddle about the four *P*s, alludes to Pando and three of his backers, whose last names also begin with a *P*. The indirect criticism of the general postal administrator and others who did not follow Carrió's recommendations might explain the author's desire to conceal his name, attribute his book to Concolorcorvo, and change the place and date of publication. But Carrió soon went beyond the limits of discretion. In a public declaration in 1777, he launched a harsh attack against Pando, forcing him to sue for libel. As a consequence of this legal battle, Carrió was jailed and his property confiscated. Even though ultimately he was declared innocent and freed, these actions caused such a scandal that officials in Madrid, out of respect for his age and infirmities, ordered his immediate retirement in order to spare him further sanctions. The author of *El lazarillo*, however, did not resign himself to a life of isolation and anonymity. In 1782, shortly after Tupac Amarú's rebellion in 1780–1781 against Spanish rule, Carrió completed a *Plan de gobierno del Perú* (Government Plan of Peru), a document criticizing the colonial administration and offering solutions that would preserve the crown's supremacy. The author died in Lima in 1783.

Like many colonial Spanish-American books, *El lazarillo* is of both historical and literary interest. It is historically important because the author describes a long and unique journey that took him from Buenos Aires to Lima, thus providing a wealth of information about trade, roads, and demography. In addition, this Spanish official also comments on the diverse ethnic types, the attitudes of the people, and the attire and habits of the women. In these observations, he overestimates Spanish culture while making evident his prejudices against Indians, *mestizos*, mulattoes, and blacks. For Carrió, the miscegenation that had taken place in Spanish America throughout the colonial centuries had tainted the racial purity of the Spaniards. Surprisingly, he considered ideas about the intellectual inferiority of the *criollos* baseless (ch. 26). As one would expect, the author justified the Spanish conquest of America and further explained that abuses attributed to the *conquistadores* existed only in the propaganda launched by the enemies of Spain. Carrió felt that in order to "civilize" the native population, it was essential to make the learning of the Spanish language obligatory (chs. 16–18). In essence, he linked civilized behavior, that is to say, European ways, to the ability to speak Spanish (ch. 24). The inspector reserved his strongest criticism for the blacks, whom he judged to be inferior to the Indians because of the crudeness of their songs and customs (ch. 20).

The author of *El lazarillo* presents a very ungenerous view of colonial women. He criticizes the women of the mining city of Potosí who, after a licentious life, married almost anyone to secure a respected position (ch. 11). In other chapters, Carrió compares the women of Lima with those of Mexico and offers details about their manner of dress and customs (ch. 26). He takes time to describe the *tapadas* (veiled women) of Lima who covered their faces while coquettishly showing their small feet (ch. 26). In short, Carrió provides ample information about the appearance and status of colonial women in different parts of Spanish America. But, above all, he offers the most detailed analysis of mule traders in eighteenth-century Spanish America. These men and their animals were the main users of the roads described in *El lazarillo*. They also provided the only means of transportation within a harsh and vast territory that crisscrossed the Andes and extended from the Atlantic to the Pacific. *El lazarillo* is an important source of information about the commerce, geography, peoples, and customs in the immense territory that, a few decades later (1824), would proclaim its political independence from Spain.

When considering the literary importance of *El lazarillo*, critics have concerned themselves with the following points: its links to the Spanish-American novel; the influence of the picaresque genre; the author's ability to integrate diverse materials into the narrative; and the so-called double authorship. For some time, students of Spanish-American fiction

have viewed *El lazarillo* as an important source in the development of novelistic prose. For example, the Chilean critic Fernando Alegría judges it to be a forerunner of José Joaquín Fernández de Lizardi's *El Periquillo Sarniento* (*The Itching Parrot*, 1816), until recently considered the first novel written in Spanish America. In this connection, other critics have cited the influence of Spanish picaresque literature on Carrió's book. The title of his book resembles that of the novel which initiated the genre in Spain, the anonymous *Lazarillo de Tormes* (1554). But it is also similar to the title of guides for inexperienced travelers called *lazarillo de ciegos* prepared in Lima by the eighteenth-century physician and cosmographer Cosme Bueno. (The Spanish word *lazarillo* means a blind man's guide.) Carrió, a reader of Miguel de Cervantes' *Don Quixote*, of Francisco Gómez de Quevedo's poetry, and of François Fénelon's *Télémaque*, probably was well acquainted with *Lazarillo de Tormes*. Because he also admired Bueno's works, Carrió likely sought to blend the two traditions—picaresque and travel—while giving his book a distinct title.

But the influence of the picaresque on Carrió's masterpiece goes well beyond its title. It has the following hallmarks of the genre: it is a narration in the first person; it provides the detailing of an impure genealogy; it adopts a cynical, self-mocking attitude, most evident in Concolorcorvo's self-portrait (ch. 20); and it is episodic in nature, the chapters held together by the journey itself and by the travails of Carrió and Concolorcorvo. The picaresque frame also makes easier the inclusion of amusing, racy materials. But more than anything else, just as Lazarillo de Tormes wrote to explain his case to an unknown and respected figure, Carrió writes to inform the authorities of the things he has done for king and country, to defend himself against the criticisms of his enemies, and to gain privileges and recognition. In other words, writing is the pretext used by Carrió to be heard, to tell the tale that will present him as a loyal servant, and to narrate events that otherwise would go unrecorded. This is why the picaresque influence goes well beyond superficial elements. Viewed in this manner, the title was no casual choice. It reminds us of the Spanish *Lazarillo* and the tradition on which this book is based. It also sends us on a journey that goes well beyond geography and commerce and has literature at its core. The author is still dealing with a crucial question that had been central to early colonial writing—how to represent and explain to others a new and complex world.

While diverse materials are integrated into *El lazarillo,* the foundation of the book is the trip; Carrió wrote the book as his technical report as second commissioner of postal services. To this he added comments about how to use animals and plants, as well as observations on the improvement of roads and guesthouses for travelers. Carrió also availed himself of every opportunity to present and criticize a variety of customs and types. He provides many descriptions of the songs, attire, and behavior of the *gauderios,* as the *gauchos* (cowboys) of the River Plate region were then called (ch. 8). *El lazarillo* also incorporates humorous narrative materials, fulfilling the promise announced on the title page. The last chapters use a dialogue format to offer a justification of the Spanish conquest. Here again, the picaresque genre permits the integration of autobiographical segments, humor, and satire.

Several sections of *El lazarillo* explain how these diverse materials are integrated and to whom they should be ascribed. In fact, on the title page, we are made aware that Concolorcorvo was a scribe who extracted the information now included in *El lazarillo* from some memoirs written by Carrió. Statements in the prologue point to other possible collaborators in the task of writing—a neighbor, a friar—thus beclouding the issue of authorship. The diversity of possible collaborators lessens the importance of the first-person narrator Concolorcorvo. Further into the book, this process continues: Carrió's loud Spanish voice appears to prevail over Concolorcorvo's complaisant Indian voice. However, the conflicting opinions and judgments of the inspector and his scribe, who represent opposing cultures and values, create enough suspicion for the reader to question the prevailing narrator's, that is to say, Carrió's, perception and interpretation of the facts. The imperial vision that he tries to give and affirm quickly crumbles. Calixto Bustamante Carlos Inca—with his scornful questions, the only weapons that he can safely use—usurps Carrió's narrative authority and underscores the subjective nature of reality. Through this procedure, Concolorcorvo becomes the enlightened guide, the true narrator of *El lazarillo.* On this creative process, more than on anything else, rests the literary importance of this work. And because of it, *El lazarillo de ciegos caminantes,* a unique travel book, is closely tied to the development of the novel in Spanish America.

SELECTED BIBLIOGRAPHY

First Edition

El lazarillo de ciegos caminantes desde Buenos-Ayres, hasta Lima . . . Con Licencia. En Gijón, en la Imprenta de la Rovada Año de 1773.

Modern Editions

El lazarillo de ciegos caminantes desde Buenos-Aires hasta Lima. Edited by Martiniano Leguizamón. Buenos Aires, 1908.

_____. Edited by Ventura García Calderón. Paris, 1938.

_____. With an introduction by Antonio Portnoy. Buenos Aires, 1946.

_____. Edited by Juan Pérez de Tudela. With an introduction by José J. Real Díaz. Madrid, 1959.

_____. Montevideo, 1963.

_____. Edited and with an introduction by Emilio Carilla. Barcelona, 1973.

_____. Edited and with an introduction by Antonio Lorente Medina. Madrid, 1980.

_____. Edited and with an introduction by Antonio Lorente Medina. Caracas, 1985.

Translation

El lazarillo: A Guide for Inexperienced Travelers Between Buenos Aires and Lima. Translated by Walter D. Kline. Bloomington, Ind., 1965.

Biographical and Critical Studies

Álvarez-Brun, Félix. "Noticias sobre Carrió de la Vandera (autor del *Lazarillo de ciegos caminantes*)." *Caravelle* 7:179–188 (1966).

Bataillon, Marcel. "Introducción a Concolorcorvo y su itinerario de Buenos Aires a Lima." *Cuadernos americanos* 19/111:197–216 (1960).

Borello, Rodolfo A. "Alonso Carrió de la Vandera." In *Historia de la literatura hispanoamericana: Epoca colonial.* Coordinated by Luis Iñigo Madrigal. Madrid, 1982. Pp. 151–157.

Bose, Walter B. L. "*El lazarillo de ciegos caminantes* y su problema histórico." *Labor de los Centros de Estudio* (La Plata) 24:219–287 (1940–1941).

Carilla, Emilio. *El libro de los "misterios": "El lazarillo de ciegos caminantes."* Madrid, 1976.

Dunbar Temple, Ella. "Los Bustamante Carlos Inca." *Mercurio peruano* 243:283–305 (1947).

Johnson, Julie Greer. "Feminine Satire in Concolorcorvo's *El lazarillo de ciegos caminantes.*" *South Atlantic Bulletin* 45:11–20 (1960).

———. *Women in Colonial Spanish American Literature: Literary Images.* Westport, Conn., 1983.

Macera, Pablo. "Prólogo." In *Reforma del Perú.* Lima, 1966.

Mazzara, Richard A. "Some Picaresque Elements in Concolorcorvo's *El lazarillo de ciegos caminantes.*" *Hispania* 46/2:323–327 (1963).

Pupo-Walker, Enrique. "En el azar de los caminos virreinales: Relectura de *El lazarillo de ciegos caminantes.*" In *La vocación literaria del pensamiento histórico en América: Desarrollo de la prosa de ficción, siglos XVI, XVII, XVIII y XIX.* Madrid, 1982. Pp. 156–190.

Real Díaz, José J. "Don Alonso Carrió de la Vandera, autor del *Lazarillo de ciegos caminantes.*" *Anuario de estudios americanos* 13:387–416 (1956).

Soons, Alan. "An Idearium and Its Literary Presentation in *El lazarillo de ciegos caminantes.*" *Romanische Forschungen* 91:92–95 (1979).

Vargas Ugarte, Rubén, S.J. "En pos del verdadero autor de *El lazarillo.*" *Boletín del Instituto de Investigaciones Históricas* (Buenos Aires) 8:16–19 (1929).

———. "D. Alonso Carrió de la Vandera, autor de *El lazarillo de ciegos caminantes* y visitador de correos." *Revista histórica* (Lima) 26:17–112 (1962–1963).

Cláudio Manuel da Costa

(1729–1789)

Heitor Martins

With the exception of Alexandre de Gusmão, Cláudio Manuel da Costa is the earliest of all neoclassical writers born in Brazil. Many critics also consider him to be the most prominent among his peers.

Neoclassicism was born in the Portuguese linguistic milieu from the experience of a group of intellectuals who, from the beginning of the eighteenth century, showed a marked preference for French and Italian culture and an abhorrence for the Spanish tradition. French and Italian represented for these intellectuals a move away from the Counter-Reformation spirit that prevailed in the Iberian peninsula, which they deemed responsible for its cultural backwardness.

This group, which included at least two Brazilians (Gusmão and the playwright Antônio José da Silva, also known as "The Jew"), translated French authors (Boileau, Molière), accepted the possibility of atheistic thought, and philosophically defended a libertine position. Their ideas were not lightly dealt with (José da Silva was garroted and burned by the Inquisition in 1739), and the influence of Counter-Reformation ideology, although weakened, continued to be felt to the end of the century. Milestones in the disintegration of this traditional ideology were the publication in 1746 of *Verdadeiro Método de Estudar* (True Method of Study), by Luís Antônio Vernei—an extensive analysis of religious influence in the Portuguese school system and its negative results—and the foundation in 1756 of the Arcádia Lusitana, an association of poets who, under the motto *Inutilia truncat* (To trim useless things), were dedicated to cleansing Portuguese letters of any baroque vestiges. Finally, in 1761, secular power delivered the general of the Jesuits, Father Gabriel Malagrida, to the Inquisition for execution under the accusation of heresy and treason. The result of Father Malagrida's death at the stake was the end of both the Inquisition and the preeminence of the Jesuits in Portuguese society.

Cláudio Manuel da Costa entered this cultural world in 1749, when he enrolled at the University of Coimbra. Born on 5 June 1729, in Vila do Ribeirão do Carmo (Mariana, after 1745) in Minas Gerais province, Brazil, he was one of six children in a well-to-do family, whose wealth was probably very recent (his paternal grandfather was a Portuguese street peddlar of olive oil). Three of his brothers attended the University of Coimbra, where one died before graduation and two followed religious careers. Nothing is known of his two sisters. Cláudio studied under the guidance of his uncle, a priest, and at fifteen entered the Jesuit college in Rio de Janeiro, where he obtained a master of arts degree.

When he arrived at Coimbra he was still very committed to the defense of traditional values. His basic education had been religious. He planned on becoming a priest and even began the application procedures. His earliest known literary production, dating from that time, indicates his religious proclivity: *Munúsculo Métrico* (Little Metrical Gift, 1751) and *Epicédio* (Epicedium, 1753), both dedicated to D. Francisco da Anunciação, an Augustinian priest who presided over the University of Coimbra, and *Culto Métrico* (Metrical Cult, ca. 1751–1753), on the election of the prioress of Figueiró, Portugal.

The contact with new ideas seems, however, to have shaken some of these earlier inclinations. Abandoning the idea of priesthood, Cláudio graduated in law in 1753, and returned immediately to Brazil. He took up residence in Vila Rica (now Ouro Preto), then the administrative center of the Minas Gerais province, barely ten miles away from his birthplace (since 1745, the episcopal see of the province). He resided in Vila Rica for the rest of his life, following a career as both a lawyer and a public servant. He also owned several mines and was very active as a moneylender. He amassed a fortune that made him one of the richest men in the province at the time of his death. Continuing his early literary avocation, he translated the Italian poet Metastasio and composed a long poem on the birth of Christ, a mock-epic poem entitled *Cataneida,* and a few plays all in the Metastasian taste. None of these works survives.

In 1768 he published his major work, *Obras* (Works), and composed a musical drama, *O Parnaso Obsequioso** (The Courteous Parnassus, published in Rio de Janeiro, 1931). Following a fashion of the time, he signed these works with both his real name and his Arcadian name, Glauceste Satúrnio. Although tradition has it that he continued to be a practicing poet all his life, his only other known work is the epic *Vila Rica* (written ca. 1773, published in Ouro Preto, 1839). He never married but had two illegitimate daughters, whom he recognized and endowed modestly upon marriage.

*Modern spellings are used for titles in the text, while the original spellings have been retained for titles in the bibliography and for direct quotations from the works of Cláudio Manuel da Costa.

In 1789 he was accused of participating in the Inconfidência Mineira (the Minas Gerais Conspiracy), a plot to declare Minas Gerais independent from the Portuguese crown. Police records indicate that at the time of his arrest several manuscripts of his poetic works were confiscated. It was also rumored that he had translated Adam Smith's *An Inquiry into the Nature and Causes of the Wealth of Nations* (1776). None of this material ever surfaced afterward.

After a month in jail, he was interrogated and compelled to compromise his position and that of several of his named co-conspirators. Broken and remorseful, he committed suicide shortly afterward, on 4 July 1789. Although no documentation has been provided, some historians have contested the official version of his death, accusing the jailers of murder.

Cláudio Manuel da Costa suffered all his life from basic contradictions: raised as a baroque poet, he was faced with the need to adhere to neoclassical tenets; planning to pursue an ecclesiastical career, he ended up a bachelor with two illegitimate children; yearning desperately for the cultured life at Coimbra, he successfully pursued a bourgeois career in Vila Rica. He was aware of the dichotomy and analyzed it in one of his most curious poems, "A Lira—Desprezo/Palinódia" (*Obras*, pp. 262–269; To the Lyre—Despise/Palinode), where all the elements tend to emphasize his divided poetic voice: the superficial style is neoclassical, but the structure is baroque; the poetic statements are abstract, but the obligatory printing format (the parts of the poem are intertwined, and the stanzas face each other, with contradictory statements, on even and uneven numbered pages) requires a visual awareness of the text; the theme implies both negation and acceptance of the poetic creation.

Cláudio's neoclassicism is therefore tainted with baroque residues. In an erudite dissertation on his poetry, Melânia Silva de Aguiar analyzes chronologically some of the poet's compositional techniques and shows how slowly he freed himself from the elements of the past. Although a contemporary of other neoclassical poets (José Basílio da Gama and Tomás Antônio Gonzaga in Brazil; Pedro Antônio Correia Garção and Antônio Diniz da Cruz e Silva in Portugal), he has to be seen as an intermediary figure, the bridge between the two literary styles and world views.

Precisely because of that divided and contradictory self, the poetry of Cláudio represents the best of Brazilian neoclassicism, with all its problems and originality. In his poetry the nature of this literary period becomes explicit. On the one hand is a desire for naturalness, clarity, and rationality; on the other is a set of imitative procedures and decorous patterns, required by contemporary rhetoric. These latter tendencies cannot be entirely adjusted to the fact that the poets and their readers are in a non-European landscape in the Southern Hemisphere. The poet may speak of Arcadian paradises filled with shepherds and nymphs, frolicking in the spring of an eternal April among European garden trees, but he cannot totally avoid the craggy landscape and tropical vegetation of Minas Gerais and the weather references to the southern equinox, under which he and his readers lived.

Cláudio's first attempts at poetic composition are the common fare of the times. The poet uses only a ten-syllable blank verse quatrain, devoid of any special musicality. Mythological and historical clichés and over-repeated symmetrical structures abound, as in these lines from *Munúsculo Métrico* (p. 5): "Em bronze, em ouro, em mármores, em prata / Corintho, Potosi, Numidia, Memphis" (In bronze, in gold, in marbles, in silver / Corinth, Potosí, Numidia, Memphis).

If Cláudio's early publications are no more than competent but mediocre gratulatory verse in the baroque vein, his *Obras* make him one of the most respected lyrical voices in the Portuguese language. The book includes one hundred sonnets, three epicedia, one heroic romance, one fable, twenty eclogues, six verse epistles, four lyrical romances, three *canzonette* in Italian, two amoebean songs, and eight cantatas (two of which are in Italian).

The hundred sonnets are organized along the model of an epic poem. The series starts with a proposition and invocation: "Para cantar de Amor tenros cuidados / Tomo entre vós, ò montes, o instrumento. . . ." (To sing the tender cares of love / I seize, among thee, O mountains, the instrument [lyre]. . . .).

In the second sonnet (p. 2), he dedicates his work to the fatherland, represented by the river that runs through Mariana, the Ribeirão do Carmo, a constant motif in all of Cláudio Manuel da Costa's poetry: "Leia a posteridade, ò patrio Rio, / Em meus versos teu nome celebrado. . . ." (Let Posterity read, O fatherland's River, / Your name celebrated in my verses. . . .).

These first two pieces are followed by eighty love sonnets, one gratulatory piece dedicated to the king of Portugal, and fourteen compositions in Italian. In the first of the three sonnets of the closure, the poet ponders his own personality:

> *Destes penhascos fez a natureza*
> *O berço, em que nasci: oh quem cuidara,*
> *Que entre penhas tão duras se creara*
> *Huma alma terna, hum peito sem dureza!*
> (p. 50)

Nature made my cradle
From these cliffs: who would think
That among such hard crags could be born
A tender soul, a heart without hardness!

He then describes the destruction wrought upon nature by the death of his loved one; he addresses the Muses, saying farewell and stating (p. 51) that in spite of his present suffering, ". . . se o favor me dais, ao mundo attento / Em assumpto mayor farei espanto" (. . . if I have your favor, I will astonish / the attentive world with a greater subject).

Cláudio's eighty love sonnets are responsible for his standing as a major poet. Although marked in many places by traces of baroque redundancy and obscurity, they show an acute perception of the psychology of love, an awareness of the lyrical traditions of the language, a discerning ear for the particular music of Brazilian Portuguese, and a feeling for the landscape of his native Minas Gerais. In these sonnets we have, perhaps for the first time, the presence of a Brazilian poetic voice speaking to Brazilians. Moreover, it is a voice devoid of any consciousness of being either exotic or strange.

In the single fable of the volume, "Fábula do Ribeirão do Carmo" (Fable of the Ribeirão do Carmo), the poet attempts to write a "metamorphosis," in the Ovidian tradition, to explain the origin of the river of his native town. A young local shepherd woos and tries to abduct a virgin dedicated to Apollo. When the god foils his attempt, the shepherd commits suicide, and the flow of his blood creates the river. To ensure that the punishment is eternal, Apollo adds gold to the river, which in turn attracts a myriad of prospectors who will be dilacerating it forever.

This fable influenced the Portuguese Cruz e Silva, who later developed a whole series of "Brazilian metamorphoses" (As Metamorphoses, in his Poesias, vol. 4, Lisbon, 1814, pp. 89–156). Both the works of Cláudio Manuel da Costa and Cruz e Silva represent early versions of nativistic and Indianist poetry in the neoclassic vein.

O Parnaso Obsequioso is a short musical drama commemorating the birthday of the governor general of Minas Gerais. Apollo, Mercury, and the muses Calliope, Clio, Melpomene, and Thalia congregate on Mount Parnassus to praise the governor and his ancestors for their feats in Portugal and Brazil. The governor's presence in Minas Gerais will make precious stones burst forth from the earth; commerce will develop as never before; and all arts and sciences will flourish. A few poetic compositions accompany the drama. They follow the same style, are about the same subject, and were recited on the governor's birthday.

As if fulfilling his earlier promise to "astonish the attentive world with a greater subject," around 1773 Cláudio Manuel da Costa wrote Vila Rica, a long epic narrative in ten cantos, on the history of Minas Gerais. The poem is written in ten-syllable rhymed couplets. The theme was modest for an epic, the metric form is extremely monotonous in Portuguese, and the result is a long and mediocre exercise in nativistic verse. The influence of Voltaire's La Henriade (1723) is easily perceived, but the real inspiration of the poem was the recent work of a younger Brazilian poet, Basílio da Gama, whose O Uraguai (The Uruguay) was published in 1769 and caused a literary sensation. In it Cláudio Manuel da Costa found a model for the selection of a contemporary theme, and an interest in the Indian as an important participant in Brazilian history. In The Uruguay he also found the technical daring to abandon the tradition of Luís Vaz de Camões, which had dominated the epic form in Portuguese for two hundred years. Through Basílio da Gama, Cláudio came to know Voltaire and probably John Milton, to whom he dedicated an encomiastic ode. The examples of these poets encouraged him to try to compose an epic outside of this earlier tradition. The poet made no effort to publish Vila Rica in his lifetime, a fact that has led recent critics to suggest that he recognized the basic failure of his epic attempt.

Using a literary expression rooted in European culture, Cláudio Manuel da Costa described the new reality of Brazil. To achieve this he changed and enlarged this literary expression, adding dichotomies and contradictions that mirrored the ones that plagued his own soul. Both the empathy he felt for the reality of his native land and his success in expressing this feeling make him the founding father of Brazilian literature.

SELECTED BIBLIOGRAPHY

First Editions

Munusculo Metrico. Coimbra, Portugal, 1751.

Epicedio. Coimbra, Portugal, 1753.

Culto Metrico. N.p.,n.d. [Probably: Coimbra, Portugal, 1751–1753.]

Orbas [sic]. Coimbra, Portugal, 1768.

Villa Rica. Ouro Preto, Brazil, 1839.

O Parnazo Obsequioso. In O Inconfidente Claudio Manoel da Costa, edited by Caio de Mello Franco. Rio de Janeiro, 1931. Pp. 63–124.

Modern Editions

Obras poéticas. Edited by João Ribeiro. 2 vols. Rio de Janeiro, 1903.

Obras. Edited by Antônio Soares Amora and Ulpiano Bezerra de Meneses. Lisbon, Portugal, n.d. [ca. 1960].

Poemas. Edited by Péricles Eugênio da Silva Ramos. São Paulo, 1966.

Biographical and Critical Studies

Aguiar, Melânia Silva de. "O Jogo de Oposições na Poesia de Cláudio Manuel da Costa." Ph.D. diss., University of Minas Gerais, Belo Horizonte, Brazil, 1973.

Autos da Devassa da Inconfidência Mineira. 9 vols. Brasília and Belo Horizonte, Brazil, 1976–1982.

Cândido, Antônio. "No Limiar do Novo Estilo: Cláudio Manuel da Costa." In his *Formação da Literatura Brasileira* 1. 2nd, rev. ed. São Paulo, 1964. Pp. 93–111.

Castelo, José Aderaldo. "A Época Arcádica." In his *Manifestações Literárias da Era Colonial.* 3rd. ed. São Paulo, 1967. Pp. 131–188.

Coutinho, Afrânio. "From Baroque to Rococo." In his *An Introduction to Literature in Brazil.* Translated by Gregory Rabassa. New York, 1969. Pp. 66–118.

Dutra, Waltensir. "Cláudio Manuel da Costa." In *A Literatura no Brasil* 1, edited by Afrânio Coutinho. 2nd ed. Rio de Janeiro, 1968. Pp. 320–324.

Goldberg, Isaac. "Period of Autonomous Development." In his *Brazilian Literature.* New York, 1922. Pp. 53–71.

Inama, Carla. *Metastasio e i Poeti Arcadi Brasiliani.* São Paulo, 1961.

Lamego, Alberto. *A Academia Brazilica dos Renascidos—Sua Fundação e Trabalhos Inéditos.* Paris and Brussels, 1923.

Lange, Francisco Curt. *La Música en Villa Rica (Minas Gerais, siglo XVIII).* Santiago, Chile, 1967–1968. (Offprint from *Revista Musical Chilena,* nos. 102–103, pages numbered independently.)

Lapa, Manuel Rodrigues. *As "Cartas Chilenas": Um Problema Histórico e Filológico.* Rio de Janeiro, 1958.

_____. "Subsídios para a Biografia de Cláudio Manuel da Costa." *Revista do Livro* 9:7–25 (1958).

Lima, Jr., Augusto de. *Cláudio Manoel da Costa e Seu Poema Vila Rica.* Belo Horizonte, Brazil, 1969.

Lopes, Hélio. *Cláudio, o Lírico de Nise.* São Paulo, 1975.

_____. *Introdução ao Poema Vila Rica.* Muriaé, Brazil, 1985.

_____. "A Formação Política de Minas no Poema *Vila Rica.*" *Revista Brasileira de Estudos Políticos* 62:117–172 (1986).

Lousada, Wilson. *Para Conhecer Melhor Cláudio Manuel da Costa.* Rio de Janeiro, 1974.

Maxwell, Kenneth R. *Conflicts and Conspiracies: Brazil and Portugal, 1750–1808.* Cambridge, England, 1973.

Putnam, Samuel. "Arcady and the Rights of Man." In his *Marvelous Journey: A Survey of Four Centuries of Brazilian Writing.* New York, 1948. Pp. 81–95.

Silva, Domingos Carvalho da. "A Plêiade Mineira." *O Estado de S. Paulo* (literary supplement), 28 February 1959. P. 4.

José Joaquín Fernández de Lizardi

(1776–1827)

Nancy Vogeley

José Joaquín Fernández de Lizardi was born in Mexico City on 15 November 1776 and died there on 27 June 1827. He lived during the period of growing dissatisfaction with colonial rule that culminated in Mexico's independence. *El Periquillo Sarniento* (*The Itching Parrot*), the picaresque novel Lizardi published in 1816, when events pointed to the need for literary and cultural, as well as political, emancipation, has been singled out as the first Spanish-American novel. Although earlier colonial writers had attempted the genre, their efforts are usually regarded as semihistories or as inferior copies of European novels. Lizardi's novel is generally thought to be the first to be suitably imaginative in telling a uniquely American story.

In a society where Indians, blacks, and persons of mixed race formed the vast majority, Lizardi was a *criollo*, born to parents of Spanish blood. *Criollos*, persons of Spanish descent who were born in the New World, were to become the sector of the Mexican population most discontent with conditions in the colony. Often poor, they were customarily passed over for positions of importance. Lizardi's father was a physician at the Real Colegio de Tepotzotlán (Royal College of Tepotzotlán); in spite of his professional status, the family appears to have lived in reduced circumstances. Lizardi's identity as a *criollo*,

resentful of Spanish privilege in his own world yet still bound by blood and cultural loyalties to Europe, is an important clue to understanding the often conflicting perspectives found in his writing.

Having learned to read and write in Tepotzotlán, at the age of six, Lizardi was sent to Mexico City to study Latin. In *The Itching Parrot*, which draws on his own experience, Lizardi has Periquillo ridicule his Latin instruction: "I left with my head filled with rules, riddles, phrases, and false knowledge of Latin, but as regards intelligence in the purity and propriety of the language, not a word." Although there is no record that he completed his studies at the College of San Ildefonso where he enrolled in 1793, most of his biographers believe he received his *bachillerato* (college degree) there. In 1798 he completed a more advanced, yearlong course in rhetoric and enrolled in another brief course in the arts. Lizardi's formal education in rhetoric, logic, physics, and metaphysics appears to have been merely an exercise in memorizing impressive-sounding terms without understanding their meaning; the work of modern thinkers was systematically excluded from the curriculum, and classical writers were treated only superficially. Lizardi blamed the educational system for much of Mexico's corruption and backwardness.

Lizardi's true education came from his own reading. Subjects such as law, history, ethics, customs, education, theology, and the emerging sciences interested him to the extent that they could serve in solving pressing problems. Lizardi gives evidence in *The Itching Parrot* of a wide knowledge of classical and Spanish authors, as well as of French writers, whose ideas he uses, although he frequently omits mentioning their names throughout his writing. However, it is not clear whether he knew of these authors directly or only through popular digests of their works.

In 1798 Lizardi returned to Tepotzotlán. Thus began a mysterious ten-year period about which few facts are known, apart from his marriage in 1805 or 1806. Accounts by Lizardi's contemporaries reveal only that his father's death ended any plans for a professional career, and that during these years, Lizardi eked out a living as an amanuensis. Although Lizardi always kept silent about what he did during his early manhood, his vivid portrayal of the world of gamblers, thieves, beggars, and swindlers in *The Itching Parrot* suggests he had firsthand experience of that segment of life. A fact discovered among Inquisition records of the period provides further information about Lizardi's youth. In 1794 his father had reported him for possessing a deck of cards used in telling fortunes and off-color jokes. Although Lizardi's activities may have been relatively harmless in this case, the incident reveals an exasperated father who found it necessary to take his somewhat wayward son to public authorities.

Lizardi only gradually emerged from obscurity. In 1808 he published a nondescript poem. In 1810 he appears to have had his own printing press, leading Paul Radin to conclude in his annotated bibliography that at that time Lizardi was a maverick author cut off from conventional avenues of publishing. A contemporary historian wrote that Lizardi was at the time the head of a band of insurgents operating near Iguala, but this report has since been contested. Official records show that in 1810 Lizardi was acting as the viceroy's representative in Taxco when insurgent forces under José María Morelos y Pavón arrived. In a letter to the viceroy, Lizardi explained that he had been forced to turn over arms and ammunition out of concern for the townspeople. Colonial authorities did not accept his explanation, and he was imprisoned in January 1811. By spring of the following year,

he appears to have been free and living in the capital. Although controversy surrounded the Taxco incident during Lizardi's lifetime, it appears that in the early years of the insurgency Lizardi did not side with those fighting for independence. Lizardi's support of the insurgent factions came later, with his gradual recognition that the only way to improve conditions was for Mexico to break completely with Spain.

By 1811 Lizardi was writing more actively, choosing verse, the most prestigious literary form of the time, to express his ideas for social reform. His early poems were written to be sold as single sheets to Mexico's reading public. A rough idea of the market for this commercial literature may be derived from the subscription lists of the *Diario de México* (Mexican Daily), an important, privately published newspaper. In 1805 the *Diario* had 507 subscribers in the capital and 177 in the provinces. The *Diario* also sheds light on the success of Lizardi's publishing career; in late 1811 and early 1812, it published an exchange between Lizardi and several critics, one of whom took him to task for his unrefined language: "It is a shame that with the aptitude you have for poetry you do not take more care with the purity and dignity of the language, and in polishing your verses."

A newspaper culture formed around the *Diario* in the years prior to the famous Grito de Dolores of 16 September 1810. (The cry, or shout, was made by the priest Miguel Hidalgo as he led his Indian parishioners in revolt: "Long live Our Lady of Guadalupe! Long live Independence!") Members of the political, religious, military, and social elite who were its readers contributed letters to its pages, where they discussed how the ideas of the European Enlightenment could be adapted to the colony's needs; although they refrained from explicit mention of politics, that dimension was implicit in every topic. Even a man's language betrayed his political sympathies—whether he wrote in a formal manner, using Latin expressions and adhering to Spanish norms, or preferred a more colloquial style, sometimes incorporating Indian phrases and favoring Mexican usage. Colonials were becoming accustomed to reading a new kind of entertaining and informative literature—the newspaper—which, in its style and choice of subject matter, attempted to engage as many readers as possible.

In October 1812, when freedom of the press was decreed in New Spain (Mexico), many seized the opportunity to present political points of view as well as to make money by catering to the new taste for journalism. Lizardi, who had written in the *Diario* and had published separately some satirical pamphlets, began publication of his own newspaper, *El Pensador Mexicano* (The Mexican Thinker), a title he adopted as a pen name. The letters and essays of the newspaper, most written by Lizardi, attacked a broad range of monopolistic practices and corruption that characterized official Mexico. He continued to publish *El Pensador Mexicano* until 1814, even during a seven-month period when he was jailed for his writings. Unlike the members of the Arcadia de México (Mexican Arcadia), a group of colonial leaders who adopted pastoral pseudonyms and composed classically modeled poetry largely for the amusement of their own circle, Lizardi wrote for sale to as wide a readership as possible. In his newspaper writing, he began the experiments with different styles, imaginary characters, and popular stories that would mature into his novelistic style.

Lizardi became famous as a political journalist; and off and on until he died he published many newspapers whose life span varied according to the censors' wishes and readership interest. A list would include: *Las Sombras de Heráclito y Demócrito* (1815), *Alacena de Frioleras* (1815–1816), *Caxoncitos de la Alacena* (1815–1816), *El Conductor Eléctrico* (1820), *El Amigo de la Paz y de la Patria* (1822), *El payaso de los Periódicos* (1823), *El Hermano de Perico que Cantaba la Victoria* (1823), *Conversaciones del Payo y el Sacristán* (1824–1825), and *Correo Semanario de Mexico* (1826–1827). All were published in Mexico City. In addition to the newspapers he edited, Lizardi published more than 280 pamphlets during his lifetime. Most of these had a political or educational focus and were also printed by presses in Mexico City.

Beginning in February 1816, two chapters of a work called *The Itching Parrot* appeared each week. Lizardi projected four volumes, each to be composed of twelve chapters. His decision to augment the success of the newspaper with a novel reflected not only his awareness of the book's commercial possibilities but his sense of having discovered a proper form for continuing his social criticism. In the novel

Lizardi could dramatize specific truths his reader might not have understood if he had written more abstractly. The neoclassical aesthetic that Bourbon Spain had communicated to her colonies held that art must serve a social purpose, and Lizardi apparently shared this expectation. Identifying himself with the artisan class, he compared his task as a writer to that of a shoemaker, who serves society by carefully creating a useful product.

Between 1816 and 1820 Lizardi published three of the four parts of *The Itching Parrot*, his *Fábulas* (Fables, 1817), parts of two more novels—*Noches tristes y día alegre* (Sad Nights and Happy Day, 1818, 1819), and *La Quijotita y su prima* (Quijotita and Her Cousin, 1818)—and a collection called *Ratos entretenidos* (Entertaining Moments, 1819) that contained prose and poetry written by Lizardi and members of Mexico's literary elite. *Don Catrín de la Fachenda*, probably written in 1819, was his last novel and was published posthumously in 1832. It is true that Lizardi published much of his fiction during a period of press censorship. However, his four novels, fables, and several plays were not simply didactic pieces in disguise, nor were they potboilers cooked up merely to earn a living while his principal concern for reform was frustrated. The length and complexity of *The Itching Parrot*, in particular, reveal his awareness that solutions to Mexico's problems were not always simple and that imaginative literary constructs could sometimes set out better than reportorial writing the conflicts that thinking *criollos* were facing. His use of the more prestigious forms of the fable and the novel suggests that he wanted to elevate his writing to a level above that of journalism. Lizardi hoped recognition of his European-style novels would help legitimate his message: in the "Apology" he wrote for *The Itching Parrot* in 1819, he compared aspects of it with Cervantes' *Don Quixote*.

After May 1820, when freedom of the press was restored after a long period of suspension, Lizardi reverted to journalism, competing fiercely with other popular writers. These newly franchised colonial writers attacked everything and everyone. In March 1821, Lizardi was again jailed for several days for arguing that Mexico should be free of Spain, and on 22 February 1822 he was excommunicated from the Catholic church for his support of Freemasonry. He continued to be active in his last years in spite of the effects of extreme poverty and tuberculosis. Just before his death in 1827, he described his wasted body with characteristic ironic humor: "I'm a walking volume of the most complete osteology."

Lizardi's choice of the novel as the genre of his major work, *The Itching Parrot*, established the genre in the Americas. In the transplanting from Europe, two changes in the novel occurred that contributed to the production of a uniquely American product. The first change is the author's choice of subject matter; Lizardi justifies his focus on lowlife scenes and his use of incorrect and vulgar language on the grounds that these characters and their way of speaking were typically Mexican. In the "Apology" to *The Itching Parrot* he facetiously asked in response to a critic who chided him for not selecting the higher classes of society as more worthy subjects for literary treatment: "Why . . . should Periquillo hold up to ridicule an ambassador, a prince, a cardinal, a sovereign when . . . these people are not to be found here [in the colony]?" Lizardi's meaning is clear: in its dependent state Mexico knew only powerlessness, poverty, and corruption.

Having inherited the eighteenth-century preference for verisimilitude in literature, Lizardi avoided as much as he could the use of the word "novel" in describing his work. "Novel" suggested a trivial, often fanciful, work of the imagination, which only women read; whereas "history," "biography," "life," "confessions," or "letters" laid claim to the truth of actual, lived experiences. In the eighteenth century, only the picaresque novel, most notably Alain-René Lesage's *Gil Blas*, escaped this criticism. In that form, Lizardi saw possibilities for telling a story that was somewhere between fact and fiction. A Spanish invention, the picaresque mode emphasized the base and sordid aspects of man's material existence by telling the story of a boy, usually a guttersnipe or juvenile delinquent (*pícaro*). The unpleasant subject matter was embellished for the upper-class reader by means of a highly "artistic" literary style: that is, the use of wordplay and complex allusions that often restricted understanding to a few readers who thereby thought their training and intellect to be superior. Although Lizardi borrowed a well-established novel form from the European tradition in order to treat

colonial realities, he did not imitate the earlier writers' language.

The second change Lizardi worked upon the novel, thereby freeing it from European dictates and setting standards for its later development in Latin America, was shaped by his perception of the colonial reader. In the 1819 "Apology" he acknowledges having broken artistic precepts because he believes his reader is "ignorant" and therefore requires a different kind of writing. By "ignorant," Lizardi means a reader unskilled in interpretation, one who cannot disentangle the moral message from the story and who, therefore, needs explicit authorial comment and restatement. Rather than being naive or ingenuous, as the use of the word might imply, the colonial reader was probably simply unaccustomed to Lizardi's literary style. Trained in the pompous rhetoric of official language and baroque taste in literature, this reader needed instruction to appreciate the unadorned language. In *The Itching Parrot*, Lizardi innovated by presenting the peculiar speech of Indians, rustics, thieves, and beggars, among many others, alongside the high-flown jargon of charlatan doctors, teachers, lawyers, and noblemen. These he offset with his own clear and simple language, which simultaneously corrected and satirized that of the others. In a period of colonial dominance, his attempt to teach discrimination and to criticize empty or misleading language must be viewed as subversive in ways that anticipate the twentieth-century works of Carlos Fuentes, Julio Cortázar, Guillermo Cabrera Infante, and others, whose contributions to the "new Spanish-American novel" also derive from the recognition that Latin America must reject inherited norms. Like these later writers, Lizardi recognized that a renewal of the literary language, often through purposeful destruction, must accompany other efforts at self-conceptualization and self-determination.

Lizardi's story begins with Pedro Sarmiento, a reformed *pícaro*, telling his children: "I was born in Mexico, the capital of North America, in New Spain . . . around the years 1771 to 1773." The reader, cast in the role of one of the children, is immediately captured by the tone of experience and the story's seeming authenticity. Pedro describes his parents, who were neither very rich nor poor, as exemplars of kindliness, virtue, and wisdom. Rejecting their influence and wasting his inheritance, he leaves respectable society to enter another world. His misadventures in this new setting are meant to show the risks and dangers of that life. Now called Periquillo Sarniento, the defamatory name given to him by his schoolmates, he meets the honest poor, as well as those who prey on innocents, in the hospitals, jails, flophouses, and taverns of Mexico City. Dirty and often barely covering his nudity with a tattered blanket, Periquillo is constantly hungry; never knowing when he will eat next, at one point he so gorges himself that he vomits. Gamblers teach him their card tricks; beggars instruct him in duping gullible victims. Unprepared to earn an honest living and thinking he can survive by using these tricks, Periquillo is consistently outwitted and often beaten.

He enters the service of a series of characters who represent the fraudulence of Mexico's professions. For example, Dr. Purgante, whom he assists, mistreats many trusting patients because his medical knowledge consists of only a garbled sense of Latin terms. Dr. Purgante is Lizardi's equivalent of the stock character of the doctor from the European picaresque novel. In *Gil Blas* he was Dr. Sangrado, whose method of curing patients consisted of bloodletting; Lizardi's Dr. Purgante, as his name suggests, prescribes a laxative, or purge, in every case. In a larger political sense, the caricature of a doctor who drains life in this even more demeaning way goes beyond medicine to satirize the entire colonial system; Mexico's very life, the wealth of her mines, was being taken from her.

Periquillo's adventures take place largely in Mexico City. Although he makes brief journeys outside the city, the story moves mainly against an urban landscape easily recognized by Lizardi's original readers. In the fourth volume, which censors suppressed during Lizardi's lifetime, Periquillo sets sail for Manila; the long discussion of slavery with a black whom he meets there clearly provoked the censors' objections. The exchange exposes the premises on which the colonial system rested: What measuring stick proves that a people are inferior, thereby justifying their rule by another? Do the reciprocal relationships that are the result of living in society always mean dependence? Does the universality of family structures and educational systems suggest there are weak members who require governance by the strong? Does anarchy always result when the governed try to govern themselves? As pursued by Lizardi's protagonist, these questions troubled the colonials as well as the enslaved peoples.

Periquillo is shipwrecked on a Pacific island while returning from Manila, and the utopian society that he finds there contrasts with the ugly realities of Mexico. On the island everyone works. A citizen army exists, and no aristocracy pretends to defend the nation. Religious men are those who truly know God and can teach about his mysteries. Doctors really cure their patients. Lawyers are unnecessary because everyone has access to the law through engraved tablets, placed everywhere, that assign invariable sentences for crimes.

This ideal state is a government of impersonal laws; it is based on new definitions of human nature that, in declaring men to be essentially equal and rational, concede them the capacity to govern themselves. Thus Lizardi presents his reader with a contradiction. In the parts of the book that describe Mexico with literal realism, paternalistic structures based on personal relationships prevail. Periquillo transgresses by betraying his father's teachings; throughout his picaresque wanderings he meets older, wiser men whose advice he hears but shuns. But because the novel ends with Periquillo, now Pedro, proclaiming the validity of paternalistic wisdom, Lizardi seems to affirm the essential rightness of societal relationships that recognize inferiority and superiority. As a result, the inclusion of the utopian episode suggests more than criticism of Mexico's problems. In juxtaposing favorably two systems of government, Lizardi betrays the confusion he and other *criollos* were facing in proclaiming independence.

When *The Itching Parrot* first appeared, its lowlife scenes and vulgar language offended many academic critics. They conceded its popularity and even their enjoyment of the book, but these largely upper-class critics immediately distanced themselves from the work by deciding Lizardi was writing for the lower social classes in an attempt to correct their behavior. This was improbable because these persons could not read. Throughout the nineteenth century, it became fashionable to identify Lizardi with the ideals of the independence movement, and his tie to the people continued to be affirmed. His reputation grew to mythic proportions when Ignacio Altamirano called him "an apostle of the people" and described "his holy aureole as one of the martyrs of liberty and progress." In the twentieth century, members of Mexico's elite Ateneo de la Juventud (Atheneum of the Youth), in evaluating literary production of the independence movement for a centenary celebration, generally acknowledged his historical importance but described his influence as declining.

Like Argentina's *Martín Fierro* (1872) by José Hernández, *The Itching Parrot* is a symbol of nationhood. In the prologue to his edition of *El Pensador Mexicano*, Agustín Yáñez has lately seen its central character as a national type, a *pelado* (penniless person) rather than a *pícaro* (delinquent). Whereas the *pícaro* is often a coward who acts immorally in response to circumstances, the *pelado* is an individualist whose motives for challenging society are not malicious but rather are born out of a desire for freedom. Yáñez sees the pejorative term *pelado* as a corollary to the concept of *mestizaje* (crossbreeding of races and mixing of cultures) that so often characterizes Latin American society.

If *The Itching Parrot* lives in the popular imagination as a Mexican classic, Lizardi's later novel *Don Catrín de la Fachenda* is sometimes thought by academic critics to be technically superior. They argue that in the shorter *Don Catrín* Lizardi concentrated on the picaresque action, omitting the often tedious and erudite digressions of *The Itching Parrot*. Don Catrín represents another social type, the dandy (*catrín*). He alludes in the opening paragraphs to his friend, Periquillo Sarniento, and says that, although their stories are similar, his account of his life will gain even greater acceptance than Periquillo's because of these omissions. However, Lizardi's tone in *Don Catrín* is so ironic that one questions Lizardi's meaning in having his character describe such a stripped-down story as better told. Lizardi's second telling of almost the same picaresque story suggests either that he was trying to reach a more sophisticated reader or that his assessment of the colonial reader had changed. The switch from literal statement to irony's indirection may indicate Lizardi's growing awareness that, in order to express the disappointments Mexico faced in declaring independence, he required a more complex, and ultimately more cynical, form of literary address. When Don Catrín dies of dropsy at the end of the novel, too dissolute to be reeducated to decency and respectability, Lizardi suggests a darker historical outcome for the independence movement. If the picaresque tale of rebellion is an extended metaphor for the colonial experience, then the ending of Don Catrín's story may have seemed more likely to Lizardi than Periquillo's eventual rehabilitation.

Both novels are entertaining, even funny, books. Their humor depends to a great extent on the buffoonery of the characters and the slapstick situations. When Periquillo insults a barber's wife, she turns him out of her house by pouring a bucket of boiling water over his head, enacting a typical role from the farce tradition. In another incident, Chanfaina, whose name recalls the trickster (Chanfalla) of Cervantes' "Entremés del retablo de las maravillas" (The Wonder Show), is delightfully exposed when a perceptive lawyer reveals his fraud. However, much of the humor of *The Itching Parrot* also derives from the book's various language styles; when the pompous style of Chanfaina's bogus document is corrected by the serious speech of the lawyer, Lizardi's change of style reinforces the humor. In *Don Catrín*, the ironic tone persists throughout; Lizardi makes his style sufficiently broad to prevent his reader from drawing so near Don Catrín that he will find him sympathetic and adopt his point of view. An example is the flippant way Don Catrín describes some of the other fops in his circle of lazy young noblemen: "Then four or five ridiculous little gentlemen entered, in tails and capes, some very respectable and some respectable without the very." Although Don Catrín himself says these gentlemen were ridiculous and mocks their pretensions to respectability, Lizardi's racy, colloquial style prevents his reader from thinking that Don Catrín is much different.

In *La Quijotita y su prima*, Lizardi presents two female characters who in some ways approximate the bad Periquillo/Don Catrín and the good Pedro Sarmiento. As the title suggests, his principal interest is the wayward Quijotita and not her obedient cousin. The name Quijotita recalls that of Don Quixote; she is like him in that her antisocial behavior is somehow the result of a faulty education. Lizardi's two women are born into much the same family structure, but one is reared according to desirable moral standards and the other—nicknamed La Quijotita—is raised in an unwholesome and unacceptable way. Given over to a wet nurse at birth and neglected by both her parents, she is brought up by the ignorant Indian women who work in the kitchen. As a young girl, she imitates the poor example set by her mother; indeed the mother, Lizardi suggests, not only is responsible for her own destruction but bears much of the blame for her husband's death and her daughter's eventual tragedy. The mother follows the dictates of French fashion in lavishing money on clothes, engaging in frivolous social activities, and—most damaging of all—insisting that the gallant attentions men pay women mean that women are superior. Consequently, La Quijotita grows into a vain, capricious woman, respectful of no one and nothing.

Lizardi's treatment of the *pícara*, a female who falls from virtue, is far more restrained than that of most novelists; however, like most he describes his *pícara*'s foolishness and immorality in sexual terms. La Quijotita becomes pregnant out of wedlock, although the facade of respectability is maintained when she obtains an abortion. When she finally marries unwisely, her failure, like that of Don Quixote, is due to her lack of judgment. Her dreams of position and money have led her to choose a Spaniard whose claim that he is a *marqués* prove fraudulent. In the last chapter, Lizardi quickly concludes her story, describing her tragic end as a prostitute, without dramatizing it.

Much of the first part of *La Quijotita* is an attempt to adapt treatises on the education of women, which circulated widely in Europe during the period, to the taste of Mexican readers of fiction. The heavily didactic tone of these chapters has caused the book to be regarded more as a historical curiosity than as a novel. However, Lizardi's work is different from its European sources in several important ways. Political events made Lizardi aware of the importance the role of women had in an emerging society, and he appears confused by the way some women flouted established traditions and authority with successful results. In a later work, *Heroínas mexicanas* (Mexican Heroines, 1955), written in 1825, he would praise those extraordinary women who had fought alongside men for the cause of independence. The second part of *La Quijotita* was not published until 1832; internal evidence reveals that Lizardi did not write it until sometime after March 1821, when the fighting had stopped and a new government was in place. Consequently, Quijotita's story may be read as Lizardi's effort to think through the lessons of rebellion; the fact that he withheld its publication may also reveal an ambivalence on his part regarding its message of punishment.

Noches tristes y día alegre, Lizardi's fourth novel, was also published in two parts. The first edition (1818) contained only the *Noches tristes* section; a year later the second edition added the *Día alegre* ending. The most obviously literary of Lizardi's novels, it explicitly recalls the *Noches lúgubres* (Lugubrious Night, 1798) of the Spanish writer José de Cadalso y Vazquez and, less obviously, the *Night Thoughts* (1745) of the English poet Edward Young. However, Cadalso's eerie romanticism, in which a lovesick suitor disinters his beloved in a scene of dark despair, gives way in Lizardi's adaptation to a mood of despondency that is more socially explicable. Teófilo, in Lizardi's work, is an innocent man who is seized from his home one night by authorities. Although he protests, his house is searched, his family is terrorized, and he is thrown into prison. There, chains and the presence of death seem like a frenzied nightmare; when his jailer announces that the real criminal, also named Teófilo, has been found, he is suddenly freed. At this point, Teófilo voices a question that must have troubled many who suffered the uncertain policies of a desperate colonial regime and the unpredictabilities of internal fighting: "I'll live . . . but to what purpose? To be tomorrow the plaything of fortune or the object of man's ridicule."

In the rest of the short novel, Lizardi fictionalizes the crisis of faith that afflicted many Mexicans during that period. In incidents that occur over three ensuing nights, other characters show how the everyday problems of ordinary people often cause them to doubt the goodness of their Creator. Poverty, the death of a spouse, the failure of supposedly charitable persons such as doctors and priests to help—all illustrate the acute suffering of much of Mexico's population. Thus the use of foreign literary models allowed Lizardi to disguise his picture of cruelty and injustice in Mexico. (A measure of how much he altered the tender, artificial sentiment of Cadalso's work is the suggestion that the Mexican gravedigger, out of excessive need, would return the next day to rob the corpse.)

The dialogue format of much of the novel, in which doubter and believer parry, and the happy resolution of Teófilo's story imitate the structure of a catechism lesson. Again, Lizardi has taken a European literary mode, in this case the semiofficial form of the catechism, which the upper classes admired, and employed it to expose the realities of Mexican life. As in his other novels, the high style of literary language has been displaced as the proper vehicle for discussing the common man's existence.

The fables and plays Lizardi wrote also show his use of European forms. One fable was published in the *Diario de México* in 1812, but the rest (forty altogether) came out in 1817. Each fable was illustrated and published on separate sheets so that the person who could not pay at one time the book's price of three pesos could buy its contents piecemeal. Much less is known about the nine theatrical pieces. The dates of several are uncertain; two are known only through references; and there is no evidence that any of the works was ever performed.

Lizardi's plays and fables, some of which are written in poetry, show their author's concern for public instruction. In their frequent use of animal characters, the fables satirize human misconduct and present practical lessons; the down-to-earth stories convey with good humor such messages as the power of an ant to destroy an elephant and a task made easy if two mules cooperate in pulling a load. Although Lizardi was probably inspired to write fables by the example of French and Spanish writers such as Jean de La Fontaine and Tomás de Iriarte, his fables also draw on the tradition of anonymous satire that, during the late eighteenth and early nineteenth centuries, allowed citizens of New Spain to voice their discontent. Both oral and written, and often in rhyme, this satire often sounded like folk wisdom. It criticized the powerful in often shocking ways with its barnyard imagery, housewifely references, and childish sayings. In this anonymous tradition, the contributors, "the people," may have been members of the poor classes or wealthy persons disguising their protests.

The *Auto mariano para recordar la milagrosa aparición de Nuestra Madre y Señora de Guadalupe* (Marian Play to Remember the Miraculous Appearance of Our Mother and Lady of Guadalupe), variously dated 1813 and 1817, is a good example of Lizardi's theater. It is a simple retelling of the appearance of the Virgin Mary to the Indian Juan Diego, believed to have taken place on the hill of Tepeyac in 1531. When the archbishop of Mexico showed skepticism, Juan Diego brought him proof in the form of winter roses and the imprint of the Virgin in his cloak. The genre of the *auto* dates from the Middle Ages in Spain, where it was used to dramatize the beliefs of the church for the edification of the illiterate faithful. Lizardi's use of the form and his adaptation of the legend at this moment in Mexico's history are significant for several reasons. The insurgents had proclaimed the Virgin of Guadalupe as their patroness, thus making her almost a military symbol of national consciousness. Because the Virgin of Guadalupe had appeared to a humble Indian, this image also represented the interests of the lower classes in contrast to the cult devoted to the Virgin de los Remedios (Our Lady of Perpetual Help), the focus of wealthy royalist interests. Lizardi often criticized pious beliefs in such things as miracles, calling them superstitious inventions of the ignorant; but here, perhaps for political purposes, he appears to have sympathized with the believers. His portrayal of Juan Diego gave him the opportunity to create a character whose broken speech would draw admiration rather than laughter. Indian Mexico is gloriously vindicated when church authorities recognize Juan Diego to have been favored by a vision of faith.

In combining cultured and popular modes in his work, Lizardi attempted to draw together the diverse elements of his society. His efforts to redefine diversionary reading—to enhance his colonial reader's understanding of the world around him by making him truly see it—is a statement of faith that literature can be a powerful force for change.

SELECTED BIBLIOGRAPHY

First Editions

Novels

El Periquillo Sarniento. Mexico City, 1816.
Noches tristes y día alegre. Mexico City, 1818, 1819.

La Quijotita y su prima. Mexico City, 1818, 1832.
Don Catrín de la Fachenda. Mexico City, 1832.

Plays

El fuego de Prometeo. Mexico City, 1811.
Auto mariano para recordar la milagrosa aparición de Nuestra Madre y Señora de Guadalupe. Mexico City, 1813.
La Pastorela en dos actos. Mexico City, 1817.
El Unipersonal de Don Agustín de Iturbide, emperador de México. Mexico City, 1823.
El negro sensible. Mexico City, 1825.
El grito de libertad en el pueblo de Dolores. Mexico City, 1827.
La tragedia del padre Arenas. Mexico City, 1827.

Miscellaneous

Fábulas. Mexico City, 1817.
Ratos entretenidos. Mexico City, 1819.
Calendario histórico y político. Por el pensador mexicano. Para el año bisiesto de 1824. Mexico City, 1824.
Calendario para el año de 1825, dedicado a las señoritas americanas. Mexico City, 1825.
Calendario histórico y pronóstico político. Por el pensador mexicano. Para el año del Señor de 1825. Mexico City, 1825.
Testamento y despedida del Pensador Mexicano. Mexico City, 1827.

Modern Editions

Don Catrín de la Fachenda y Noches tristes y día alegre. Edited by Jefferson Rea Spell. Mexico City, 1959.
Heroínas mexicanas. Mexico City, 1955.
El Pensador Mexicano. With an introduction by Agustín Yáñez. Mexico City, 1962. Selections from Lizardi's newspaper.
El Periquillo Sarniento. Edited by Jefferson Rea Spell. 3 vols. Mexico City, 1949.
El Periquillo Sarniento. With a prologue by Jefferson Rea Spell. Mexico City, 1959.
Periquillo Sarniento. Edited by L. Sáinz de Medrano. 2 vols. Madrid, 1976.
La Quijotita y su prima. With an introduction by María del Carmen Ruiz Castañeda. Mexico City, 1967.
Testamento del Pensador Mexicano. Mexico City, 1963.

Collected Works

Obras 1: *Poesías y fábulas.* 2: *Teatro.* 3: *Periódicos: El Pensador Mexicano.* 4: *Periódicos: Alacena de Friole-*
ras/*Cajoncitos de la alacena*/*Las sombras de Heráclito y Demócrito*/*El conductor eléctrico.* 5: *Periódicos: El amigo de la paz y de la patria*/*El payaso de los periódicos*/*El hermano del perico que cantaba la victoria*/*Conversaciones del payo y el sacristán.* 6: *Periódicos: Correo semanario de México.* 7. *Novelas: La educación de las mujeres o la Quijotita y su prima; Historia muy cierta con apariencias de una novela. Vida y hechos del famoso caballero don Catrín de la Fachenda.* 8: *Novelas: El Periquillo Sarniento* (Vols. 1 and 2). 9: *Novelas: El Periquillo Sarniento* (Vols. 3, 4, 5); *Noches tristes y día alegre.* 10: *Folletos* (1811–1820). Mexico City, 1963–1981.

Translations

The Itching Parrot. Translated by Eugene Pressly. Edited and with an introduction by Katherine Anne Porter. New York, 1942.

Biographical and Critical Studies

Altamirano, Ignacio M. *La literatura nacional: Revistas, ensayos, biografías y prólogos 1.* Edited by José Luis Martínez. Mexico City, 1949. Pp. 39–44.
Bueno, Salvador. "El negro en *El Periquillo Sarniento:* Antirracismo de Lizardi." *Cuadernos americanos* 183: 124–139 (1972).
Cros, Edmond. "The Values of Liberalism in *El Periquillo Sarniento.*" *Sociocriticism* 2:85–109 (1985).
Dehesa y Gómez Farías, María Teresa. *Introducción a la obra dramática de José Joaquín Fernández de Lizardi.* Mexico City, 1961.
Franco, Jean. "La heterogeneidad peligrosa: Escritura y control social en vísperas de la independencia mexicana." *Hispamérica* 12/34, 35:3–34 (1983).
Godoy, Bernabé. *Corrientes culturales que definen al "Periquillo."* Guadalajara, Mexico, 1938.
González Obregón, Luis. *Novelistas mexicanos. Don José Joaquín Fernández de Lizardi (El Pensador Mexicano).* Mexico City, 1938.
González Peña, Carlos. "El Pensador Mexicano y su tiempo." In *Conferencias del Ateneo de la Juventud.* Edited by Juan Hernández Luna. Mexico City, 1962. Pp. 69–81.
Ibarra de Anda, Fortino, and Manuel A. Casartelli. *El Periquillo Sarniento y Martín Fierro: Sendas semblanzas sociológicas de México y Argentina.* Puebla, Mexico City, 1966.
McKegney, James C. "El Pensador Mexicano—Reactionary." *Revistas de letras* 3/9:61–67 (1971).

_____. "Some Recently Discovered Pamphlets by Fernández de Lizardi." *Hispania* 54/2:256–287 (1971).

_____. "Dos obras recién descubiertas de Lizardi." *Historiografía y bibliografía americanistas* 16:193–220 (1972).

Moore, Ernest R. "Una bibliografía descriptiva: *El Periquillo Sarniento* de J. J. Fernández de Lizardi." *Revista iberoamericana* 10/20:383–403 (1946).

Palacios Sierra, Margarita. *Estudios preliminares e índices del periodismo de José Joaquín Fernández de Lizardi.* Mexico City, 1965.

Pawlowski, John. "*Periquillo* and *Catrín*: Comparison and Contrast." *Hispania* 58:830–842 (1975).

Radin, Paul. *The Opponents and Friends of Lizardi.* San Francisco, Calif., 1939.

_____. *Some Newly Discovered Poems and Pamphlets of J. J. Fernández de Lizardi (El Pensador Mexicano).* Sacramento, Calif., 1939.

_____. *An Annotated Bibliography of the Poems and Pamphlets of J. J. Fernández de Lizardi: The First and Second Periods (1808–1823).* 2 vols. San Francisco, Calif., 1940.

_____. "An Annotated Bibliography of the Poems and Pamphlets of Fernández de Lizardi (1824–1827)." *Hispanic American Historical Review* 26:284–291 (1946).

Salomon, Noël. "La crítica del sistema colonial de la Nueva España en *El Periquillo Sarniento.*" *Cuadernos americanos* 21/138:166–179 (1965).

Spell, Jefferson Rea. "The Educational Views of Fernández de Lizardi." *Hispania* 9:259–274 (1926).

_____. "Fernández de Lizardi: The Mexican Feijoo." *Romanic Review* 17:338–348 (1926).

_____. "Fernández de Lizardi: A Bibliography." *Hispanic American Historical Review* 7:490–507 (1927).

_____. "Fernández de Lizardi and His Critics." *Hispania* 11:233–245 (1928).

_____. "The Genesis of the First Mexican Novel." *Hispania* 14:53–58 (1931).

_____. *The Life and Works of José Joaquín Fernández de Lizardi.* Philadelphia, Pa., 1931. The most valuable study available in English.

_____. "The Historical and Social Background of *El Periquillo Sarniento.*" *Hispanic American Historical Review* 36/4:447–470 (1956).

_____. "The Intellectual Background of Lizardi as Reflected in *El Periquillo Sarniento.*" *PMLA* 71/3: 414–432 (1956).

_____. "Mexican Society as Seen by Fernández de Lizardi." *Hispania* 8/3:145–165 (1925).

Vogeley, Nancy. "The Concept of 'the People' in *El Periquillo Sarniento.*" *Hispania* 70:457–467 (1987).

_____. "Defining the 'Colonial Reader': *El Periquillo Sarniento.*" *PMLA* 102:784–800 (1987).

Andrés Bello

(1781–1865)

Pedro Grases

Andrés Bello was born on 29 November 1781 in Caracas, the city that had been declared the capital of the Capitanía General (Captaincy General) of Venezuela only four years earlier. Situated at about 3,000 feet above sea level, in a beautiful valley extending to the foot of the Ávila Mountains, Caracas had a population of around 40,000 in 1780. Bello's maternal grandfather, Juan Pedro López, was a *caraqueno* (native of Caracas) and Venezuela's leading artist, painter, and sculptor of the eighteenth century. From his marriage to Juana Antonia de la Cruz Delgado he had twelve children, one of whom was Ana Antonia, born in 1764. She was married at the age of seventeen to Bartolomé Bello y Bello, born in Caracas in 1750. From this marriage came eight children, the oldest being Andrés Bartolomé Bello. Bartolomé Bello was a notable musician and a *clérigo de hábito talar*. He graduated from the university in civil law, and in 1789 he moved to Cumana, where he remained until his death in 1804.

Andrés Bello lived his first years in his maternal grandfather's house, located behind the Convent of the Mercedarians. The proximity to the convent was extremely significant to the young Bello, because its library represented his initial contact with books and reading. Furthermore, it enabled him to meet his future Latin teacher, Fray Cristóbal de Quesada, a noted authority on Latin literature and language. It was he who planted the seeds of classical humanism in Bello's soul. Fray Cristóbal died in 1796, while guiding the precocious fifteen-year-old Bello in the translation into Castilian of book 5 of Vergil's *Aeneid.*

In 1797 Bello began his studies at the Real y Pontificia Universidad de Caracas; he graduated with a bachelor's degree in the arts in 1800. He did not pursue more advanced studies in an institutional environment; rather, he devoted himself to the reading of good texts and decided to take up the independent study of first French and then English, the knowledge of which gave him an exceptional intellectual preparation in the Caracas of his day. In 1797 and 1798 Bello gave classes to the slightly younger Simón Bolívar, the future soldier, statesman, and revolutionary leader. Bolívar was later to characterize that period of instruction as the epitome of excellent teaching. By this time, Bello had initiated his own literary creations, which brought him increasing fame and prestige.

On 2 January 1800 Bello took part in Alexander Humboldt and Aime Bonpland's expedition to the summit of Mount Caracas, the so-called Silla del Ávila (Chain of Ávila). In 1802 Bello won an open competition for the newly created position of second official of the Captaincy General of Venezuela. From that date until 1810, the Captaincy General scarcely sponsored a cultural event or published a government document that did not in some way demonstrate the very visible presence of Bello. In April 1804 the "vaccine expedition" arrived in Caracas, headed by Francisco Javier Balmis. This event carried great significance, as smallpox epidemics had been a constant and terrible curse upon Venezuela since the sixteenth century. Bello participated in the general rejoicing by staging a drama in verse, *Venezuela consolada* (Venezuela Consoled), and by composing an extensive poem in assonant hendecasyllables, *A la vacuna* (To the Vaccine), perhaps the most vigorous composition of his early period.

In 1808 an extremely important event took place in Caracas: the introduction of the printing press. The local government agreed to begin the publication of an official newspaper for the Captaincy General, *La Gaceta de Caracas*, and Bello was logically selected as the paper's first editor. Toward the end of 1809 he undertook the direction of two projects: *El calendario manual y guía universal de forasteros de Venezuela* (The Manual Calendar and Universal Guide for Foreigners in Venezuela) and the noted journal *El Lucero* (The Star), of which only the prospectus appeared. *El calendario manual* contained the "Resumen de la historia de Venezuela" (Outline of the History of Venezuela), written by Bello. This article was the most important piece of prose he wrote before leaving Caracas; not only did it manifest an individualized style, but it also anticipated the themes of his best poetry, his *silvas* (verses of seven and eleven syllables), written much later in London.

Bello wrote several original and important works during his early years as a poet (the dates refer to first publication): a *romancillo* (a poem with verses of fewer than eight syllables) entitled *El Anauco* (The Anauco, 1870); the sonnets *Mis deseos* (My Desires, 1882), *A una artista* (To an Artist, 1881), and *A la victoria de Bailén* (To the Victory of Bailén, 1820–1823), an octave written upon the death of Bishop Francisco Ibarra; and a romance entitled *A un sáman* (To a Saman, 1881). The eclogue *Tirsis, habitador del tajo umbrío* (Tirsis, Inhabitant of the Shadowed Trail, 1882) and the ode *A la nave* (To the Ship, 1861) are perhaps most indicative of his poetic expression.

In his poetry Bello continued in the classical traditions of Latin culture and utilized the Castilian of Spain's best Golden Age writers, Garcilaso de la Vega, Francisco de Figueroa, Pedro Calderón de la Barca, and Lope de Vega.

The junta that formed in Caracas on 19 April 1810 sent Bolívar and Luis López Méndez as their envoys to England. The young Bello accompanied them as an aide, primarily because of his knowledge of English, but also because of the confidence and respect he had earned from his contemporaries. Bello's stay in London was intended to be brief. However, when Bolívar decided to return to Caracas to continue the fight for independence, López Méndez and Bello remained in London. When Venezuela's republican life was interrupted in 1812, the foreign diplomats were left bereft of financial support. This unforeseen turn of events was partially mitigated by the fact that they were at least provided with shelter at the residence of Francisco de Miranda, on Grafton Street. There, Bello experienced his first great discovery in London, namely, the world of his benefactor's library.

Nevertheless, the years 1812 to 1822 were difficult ones for Bello. It was not until he became acquainted with the Guatemalan Antonio José de Irisarri that his situation improved. As the ambassador from the Republic of Chile, Irisarri assisted Bello by appointing him secretary of the Chilean legation to London in 1822. The events of the ten years preceding this appointment, however, remain something of an enigma. In 1814 Bello married Mary Ann Boyland, who died seven years later. He aspired to return to South America and in 1814 unsuccessfully solicited the government of the provinces of the River Plate in an effort to be transferred to Buenos Aires. The next year he expressed his desire to the regime in Cundinamarca (a central department in present-day Colombia) to "establish himself in the only section of South America that still found itself independent." Irisarri, convinced of the exceptional worth of Bello, acted as his patron and tried to integrate him into the legation from Chile. Despite these efforts, Bello was removed from the legation by Mariano Egaña, an enemy of Irisarri. Shortly thereafter, though, a friendship and mutual respect arose between Egaña and Bello, based on common human understanding. When Egaña returned to his country, he became the most passionate defender of the idea of calling Bello to Chile. And it was primarily Egaña who ultimately influenced Bello to move to Santiago in 1829 with his second wife, Isabel Antonia Dunn, whom he had married in 1824. From the legation of Chile, Bello passed in 1825 to the legation of Great Colombia, where he remained until his departure for South America four years later.

While in London, Bello edited two great journals that were published by the Society of Americans, the spiritual leaders of which were Bello and Juan García del Río. In 1823 the *Biblioteca Americana* appeared and in 1826 *El Repertorio Americano* began publication. These two journals represented the epoch's most important manifestation of Latin American thought. Bello's intellectual life during the years from 1812 to 1822—a painful and dark period—was populated by a group of extremely interesting and, above all, profoundly human persons. The friendship between José María Blanco White and Bello, for example, was a strong and sustaining one. Blanco White, a priest in the Spain of Fernando VII, was a liberal Spaniard who moved to England in search of a free world and suffered a profound crisis of faith. He must have been a person of great nobility of feeling, for he tried to understand the South American struggle for autonomy. In the pages of *El Español,* the magazine that he published in London beginning in 1810, one finds the first attempt of a Spaniard to rationally interpret the Latin American world in rebellion. Blanco White extended a helping hand to Bello and saw him through some of his most difficult moments. Without his friendship, Bello might well have fallen into despair.

Another important relationship for Bello was that with Bartolomé José Gallardo, an Extremaduran of strong character and intelligence who was perhaps the man of his day most knowledgeable about Spanish culture. Several other Spanish émigrés formed the nucleus of Bello's circle. They included Vicente Salvá, a grammarian and biographer; Antonio Puigblanch, also a grammarian; and Pablo Mendivil, a critic and teacher. Bello and López Méndez enjoyed for a brief time a modicum of support from the English government. When this came to an end, they again fell upon hard times, and it was Mariano de Sarratea who approached the Argentine govern-

ment in search of support for Bello. During this period Bello participated in several intellectual undertakings, among which were his collaboration with a biblical society in London, his responsibility in deciphering the manuscripts of Jeremy Bentham, his study of the education system of Andrew Bell and Joseph Lancaster, and the many hours he spent in the British Museum every day.

Yet Bello's most eminent intellectual activity in London was his poetic creation. He wrote poetry during his entire stay in England. The works of greatest literary significance are his *silvas, La alocución a la poesía* (Allocution to Poetry) and *La agricultura de la zona torrida* (Agriculture in the Torrid Zone). Both works are segments of "América," a major poetic work that he never completed. The two smaller poems were published in *Biblioteca Americana* in 1823 and *El Repertorio Americano* in 1826, respectively.

Bello also began to publish in 1823 in these journals his great erudite scientific investigations and his critical and philosophical studies, particularly those dealing with medieval epic works, especially the *Poema del Mío Cid* (Poem of Mío Cid). However, his two great poems are the works by which he has earned his high status in Latin American literature. In the first, he invokes America's right to cultural independence. In the second, he sings the praises of nature in the tropics, with Horatian overtones, reaching levels of great inspiration. With a neoclassical air, but in a highly developed personal style, Bello played the role of the great poet of the era of Latin American literary definition. As for his other literary activities in London, he translated Lord Byron, Jacques Delille, and Matteo Maria Boyardo in excellent verse. His inquiries into the structure of rhyme, orthography, and medieval European literature were also published in the above-mentioned journals. The variety of Bello's pursuits is evident not only in his own works as a writer and in his insatiable appetite for study, but also in his diplomatic posts, the execution of which allowed him to become extremely well versed in a vast complexity of themes and problems, particularly in questions of international law. Yet the enduring object of Bello's meditations was America.

Bello changed deeply during his stay in London from 1810 to 1829. He was transformed by this period of studies and experience. By contemplating the world from London, he viewed the events of an epoch from an extraordinary and privileged vantage point. He participated in the violent transformations of the Western world in the first third of the nineteenth century, when romanticism swept through literature and when order was restored to the post-Napoleonic world. Without all of these concurrences in Bello's life between the ages of twenty-nine and forty-eight, he probably would not have reached the universal level that he did in his writings.

Taken as a whole, the works that Bello produced in England present us with characteristics different from those he had written earlier in Caracas. On the one hand, there is evidence of the maturity of years and the development of his meditations; on the other, the mastering of a personal style, as well as a considerable broadening of the horizons of his creative landscape. The process of the perfection of his literary aesthetic, begun in his early days in Caracas, is apparent in his language, which achieves a most unique literary expression. He was influenced by romanticism, the literary equivalent of the liberal doctrines then circulating in the political sphere.

Study and improvement had led to an obvious progression from his juvenile inquietudes. The future teacher as a creator or leader is glimpsed in everything written from the English capital. The distinct panorama of Bello's readings, his contact with people from other latitudes, and the greater depth of culture that London had to offer gave a new meaning to his literary work. Even in England, he was already a great poet who spoke for a continent. Likewise, there appeared in his prose writings, alongside the pleasure of investigation, a pedagogical purpose directed toward his South American compatriots, with full magistracy and authority. His literary task had already acquired its ultimate dimension, which he never abandoned: the education of his brothers in South America.

After his arrival in Chile, everything Bello wrote maintained that essential characteristic, but he added an important feature: an awareness of the value of culture as social action, as a formative medium for the peoples of South America, constituted in independent republics. Armed with a profound faith in civilization, achieved through the education of the masses, Bello advocated the study and cultivation of the arts and sciences. If he had remained in England, he would probably have been the initiator of modern Hispanic erudition.

In London he worked on and published his reflections on rhyme in Greek and Latin; the system of assonance in romance versification; a revealing commentary on J. C. L. Simonde de Sismondi, the greatest authority on literature during this period and the author of *De la littérature du midi de L'Europe* (*On the Literature of the South of Europe*, 1813); a proposal for orthographic reform; and research dedicated to writing a universal and philosophical grammar. The foregoing are works of singular learning and enormous wisdom, exceptionally profound monographs in very restrictive and precise fields.

The events that highlight the life of Bello in Chile are the following. In 1829 he was named *oficialia mayor* (undersecretary) of the Ministry of the Interior. The next year he initiated the publication of *El Araucano*, the newspaper for which he was the principal editor until 1853. In 1834 he began to carry out the function of *oficialia mayor* of the Ministry of Foreign Relations. In 1837 he was elected senator of the Republic until 1855. In 1842 the University of Chile was founded; Bello considered his participation in this event to be the most transcendental act of his life. In 1847 he published the first edition of *Gramática de la lengua castellana destinada al uso de los americanos* (Grammar of the Castilian Tongue for the Use of Americans). In 1851 he was designated an honorary member of the Royal Academy of the Spanish Language, and in 1861, a corresponding member. In 1852 Bello finished the preparation of *Código civil chileno* (The Chilean Civil Code), which was approved by Congress in 1855. In 1864 he was elected arbiter to settle a diplomatic difference between Ecuador and the United States. In 1865 he was invited to be the arbiter in a controversy between Peru and Colombia, a responsibility that he declined because he was gravely ill. He died in Santiago on 15 October 1865.

When Bello had returned to South America, instead of continuing the life of an erudite historian that he had begun in London, he shifted his orientation toward teaching. He wrote *Derecho de gentes* (Rights of Peoples, 1832) and *Cosmografía* (An

Astronomical Description of the World, 1848). He engaged in journalism and conducted classes. He elaborated a code of Roman law, *Derecho romano* (1843), because one did not exist in his country. His publication of the grammar of the Castilian tongue rendered it independent from the work of Elio Antonio de Nebrija (first published in 1492), which until that point had been considered the best in the Spanish language. He published *Ortología y métrica* (Orthography and Meter, 1835), a masterly work. Bello also dedicated himself to the elaboration of a civil code; he considered the regulation of social life an imperative.

What Bello had published in 1823 concerning the Poem of the Cid in *Biblioteca Americana* anticipated in many respects the much later writings of Manuel Milá y Fontans and Marcelino Menéndez Pelayo. He did not abandon poetic creation since it was the raison d'être for the humanist. He wrote original poems that displayed romantic tendencies, and translated and adapted works by poets such as Victor Hugo, in a process of admirable re-creation, as in the case of *La oración por todos* (*The Prayer for All*). Bello felt compelled to continue to cultivate the muses, and he was a poet to the end of his days. But upon returning to America, he seems to have applied himself to the needs of the new, politically independent nations, which required instruments of general education and orientation in the life of culture, in its widest sense. Thus he immersed himself in the multifaceted role of educator, involving himself with teaching manuals and other works of instruction, weekly articles for *El Araucano*, and suggestions on how to avoid the deterioration of Castilian. This erudite man had converted himself into an educator. Evidence of this process, begun in London, is found in the posthumously published *La filosofía del entendimiento* (The Philosophy of Learning, 1881) and in his reconstruction of the Poem of the Cid. Bello was the cultural conductor of independent Spanish America. London signified an alternate road, but if he had not lived for nineteen years in London, he would probably not have been prepared to become the "Maestro Americano."

In its entirety, the work of Bello, along with some areas now considered outmoded, contains a great deal that holds significance and relevance for our own times: philological thinking, civil law, poetry, and norms of education and their impact on civilization. Bello embodied, in his life and work, the definition of "humanist" as given in the dictionary of the Royal Academy of the Spanish Language: a person educated in *las letras humanas*. Bello, however, maintained a series of conceptual bases, and purposes that differed from those of his Renaissance precursors; building on the base of classical letters, he gave universal meaning to the fundamentals of American reality, constantly imbuing its spirit with the ennobling cause of liberty. He was the representative of a new culture that can be called liberal humanism, and indeed, he can be called the first humanist of South America.

Translated from the Spanish by David H. Nagel

SELECTED BIBLIOGRAPHY

First Editions

Individual Works

El Calendario manual y guía universal de forasteros en Venezuela para el año 1810. Caracas, 1810.

Principios del derecho de gentes. Santiago, Chile, 1832.

Principios de ortología y métrica de la lengua castellana. Santiago, Chile, 1835.

El incendio de la Compañía. Canto elegíaco. Santiago, Chile, 1841.

Análisis ideológico de los tiempos de la conjugación castellana. Valparaíso, Chile, 1841.

Instituciones de derecho romano. Santiago, Chile, 1843.

Discurso pronunciado . . . en la instalación de la Universidad de Chile el día 17 de septiembre de 1843. Santiago, Chile, 1843.

Proyecto de Código civil (1841–1845). Santiago, Chile, 1846.

Teresa. Drama por Alejandro Dumas, traducido por Andrés Bello. Santiago, Chile, 1846.

Gramática de la lengua castellana destinada al uso de los americanos. Santiago, Chile, 1847.

Cosmografía, o descripción del universo conforme a los últimos descubrimientos. Santiago, Chile, 1848.

Compendio de historia de la literatura. Santiago, Chile, 1850.

Compendio de gramática castellana escrito para el uso de las escuelas primarias. Santiago, Chile, 1841.

El Orlando enamorado del Conde Mateo María Boyardo. Traducido al castellano por Andrés Bello. Santiago, Chile, 1862.

Colección de poesías originales por Andrés Bello. Caracas, 1870.

Filosofía del entendimiento. Santiago, Chile, 1881.

Gramática castellana. Obra inédita. Santiago, Chile, 1937.

Modern Editions

Individual Works

Gramática de la lengua castellana destinada al uso de los americanos. Edited by Ramón Trujillo. Tenerife, Spain, 1981.

Gramática inédita de Andrés Bello. Edited by Josefa Dorta. Tenerife, Spain, 1982.

Collected Works

Obras completas. 15 vols. Santiago, Chile, 1881–1893.

Obras completas. 26 vols. Caracas, 1981–1986.

Translations

The Odes of Bello, Olmedo and Heredia. With an introduction by Elijah Clarence Hills. New York and London, 1920.

A Georgic of the Tropics. Translation by John Cook Wyllie. Charlottesville, Va., 1954.

Anthology of Andrés Bello. Compiled by Pedro Grases, with a foreword by Rafael Caldera. Translated by Barbara D. Huntley and Pilar Liria. Washington, D.C., 1981.

Philosophy of the Understanding. Translated by O. Carlos Stoetzer. With an introduction by Arturo Ardao. Washington, D.C., 1984.

Biographical and Critical Studies

Alvarez O., Federico. *Labor periodística de Andrés Bello*. Caracas, 1981.

Amunátegui (Aldunate), Miguel Luis. *Vida de Don Andrés Bello*. Santiago, Chile, 1882.

Balbín de Unquera, Antonio. *Andrés Bello: Su época y sus obras*. Madrid, 1910.

Bello y la América Latina. Cuarto Congreso del Bicentenario. Caracas, 1982.

Bello y Caracas: Primer Congreso del Bicentenario. Caracas, 1979.

Bello y Chile: Tercer Congreso del Bicentenario. 2 vols. Caracas, 1982.

Bello y Londres: Segundo Congreso del Bicentenario. 2 vols. Caracas, 1980–1981.

Brewer-Carías, Allan R. *La concepción del estado en la obra de Andrés Bello*. Madrid, 1983.

Caldera, Rafael. *Andrés Bello*. London, 1977.

Caro, Miguel Antonio. *Escritos sobre Don Andrés Bello*. Bogotá, 1981.

Chumaceiro Chiarelli, Fernando. *Bello y Viso, codificadores*. Maracaibo, Venezuela, 1959.

Comité Jurídico Interamericano. *Foro internacional sobre la obra jurídica de Andrés Bello*. Caracas, 1982.

Crema, Edoardo. *Trayectoria religiosa de Andrés Bello*. Caracas, 1956.

Durand, René L. F. *La poésie de Andrés Bello*. Dakar, Senegal, 1960.

España honra a Don Andrés Bello. Caracas, 1972.

Feliú Cruz, Guillermo. *Andrés Bello y la redacción de los documentos oficiales administrativos, internacionales y legislativos de Chile. Bello, Irisarri y Egaña en Londres*. Caracas, 1957.

———, ed. *Estudios sobre Andrés Bello*, 2 vols. Santiago, Chile, 1966, 1971.

Fernández, David. *Los antepasados de Bello*. Caracas, 1978.

Fernández Larraín, Sergio. *Cartas a Bello en Londres, 1810–1829*. Santiago, Chile, 1968.

Gaos, José, ed. *Filosofía del entendimiento de Bello*. Mexico City and Buenos Aires, 1948.

Grases, Pedro. *La épica española y los estudios de Andrés Bello sobre el Poema del Cid*. Caracas, 1954.

———. *Tiempo de Bello en Londres y otros ensayos*. Caracas, 1962.

———. *Los retratos de Bello: Notas históricas sobre las representaciones en vida del humanista*. 2nd. ed. Caracas, 1980.

Isaza Calderón, Baltasar. *La doctrina gramatical de Bello*. 2nd. ed. Madrid, 1967.

Lira Urquieta, Pedro. *Andrés Bello*. Mexico City and Buenos Aires, 1948.

———. *El código civil y el nuevo derecho*. Santiago, Chile, 1944.

Lynch, John, ed. *Andrés Bello: The London Years*. London, 1982.

Menéndez Pelayo, Marcelino. *Historia de la poesía hispanoamericana*. 2 vols. Madrid, 1911.

Orrego Vicuña, Eugenio. *Don Andrés Bello*. Santiago, Chile, 1935.

Prieto, Luis Beltrán. *Bello, educador*. Caracas, 1980.

Rodríguez Monegal, Emir. *El otro Andrés Bello*. Caracas, 1969.

Rosenblat, Angel. *Andrés Bello*. Caracas, 1967.

Silva Castro, Raúl. *Don Andrés Bello, 1781–1865*. Santiago, Chile, 1965.

Suárez, Marco Fidel. *Estudios gramaticales: Introducción a las obras filológicas de don Andrés Bello*. Madrid, 1885.

José María Heredia

(1803–1839)

Alfredo A. Roggiano

The Cuban poet José María Heredia was born in Santiago, Cuba, 31 December 1803 and died in Mexico City 7 May 1839. His father, who had immigrated from Santo Domingo, was a member of the Spanish juridical system in Cuba, Florida, Venezuela, and Mexico, and he took his family with him to his various postings. His son experienced a life full of change, uprooting, insecurity, and nostalgia for his distant native country, influences that were to form the background for the poet's concept of life and his ideological and literary themes. The death of his father in Mexico in 1820 left Heredia in charge of the family; as a result, he became burdened with a consciousness of responsibility, and his vision of his personal destiny worsened. In search of a quick and realistic solution, he returned to Cuba in 1821, and at the University of Havana, he obtained a law degree.

In 1823, accused of conspiring against the Spanish government in Cuba, he found it necessary to flee. He went to Boston and then to New York, where he suffered, during a year and a half in a boarding house in Brooklyn, from cold, loneliness, and poverty. He taught Spanish, with difficulty, because he knew little English. In New York, he wrote some of his best poems and published his first volume, *Poesías* (Poems), in 1825. In that year, a Spanish court in

Cuba sentenced him to death in absentia. The first president of newly independent Mexico, Guadalupe Victoria, invited the revolutionary and patriot poet Heredia to take up residence in that country's capital and to fight from there for Cuban independence.

In Mexico City, he married Jacoba Yáñez in 1827 and occupied important official positions, such as judge, minister of the Audiencia (court of common pleas), and president of the Mexican Institute, in addition to working in journalism (he was the director of *La miscelánea* [The Miscellany] in 1829) and teaching, as a professor of history and literature. Disillusioned by Mexican politics, he requested authorization from the Spanish governor of Cuba to return to his country, taking advantage of the 1836 amnesty. Under the strictest observation, Heredia was in Cuba from 14 November 1836 to 15 March 1837. Convinced that his country's colonialism was worse than Mexican anarchy, he returned to Mexico City and died there of tuberculosis in 1839.

After 1825, a new cultural literary tendency developed in Europe: romanticism, which Victor Hugo identified with libertarianism, as opposed to neoclassic rationalism, which was guided by the academies and based on norms and poetics designed to control the creative act. Other themes that formed the context of the romantic movement were: desolation and anxiety; attacks of adversity; man in disgrace and struggling against his destiny; the recurrence of instinct, sentiment, and fantasy; and a particular state of melancholy, which, according to Hugo, was "more than gravity and less than sadness." In general, the romantics attempted to overcome social abandonment and incomprehension, and the false, conventional, and hypocritical life of the bourgeois establishment; they became solitary rebels and, above all in Hispanic America, heroes struggling for a patriotic cause.

Heredia was a man of his period. In his short life, he experienced all of the forms of the *mal du siècle* (the illness of the century) in his vertiginous effort to freeze and place in his work the fugacity of time and the human destiny as a fatality. But he had a classical education, and he attempted to maintain his liberal, revolutionary, and patriotic convictions, sustaining them by relying on the humanistic tradition and channeling them according to the new ideals of equality and fraternity that were the basis for the modern democracies. Lomberto Diaz consider Heredia "the first Hispanic-American Romantic," and Manuel Pedro Gonzalez called him "the firstborn of Hispanic Romanticism."

Heredia's was not an academic philosophy, thought out and proposed as a theoretical system. He felt, suffered, and lived an existential romanticism, which he poured into his poems, mixed with ingredients from his readings of Ossian, Lord Byron, Alphonse de Lamartine, François René de Chateaubriand, Ugo Foscolo, Giacomo Leopardi, a little of Hugo, and quite a bit of the rhetoric of the Spanish poets of the eighteenth and the early nineteenth centuries, especially in his amorous poetry prior to 1825. A typical example of his romanticism that complains of misfortune in love is the autobiographical poem "En mi cumpleaños" (On My Birthday), written when he was nineteen:

> Desesperado,
> De fatal desengaño en los furores,
> Ansié la muerte, detesté la vida:
> ¿Qué es ¡ay! la vida sin virtud ni amores?
> Solo, insociable, lúgubre y sombrío,
> Como el pájaro triste de la noche,
> Por doce lunas el delirio mío
> Gimiendo fomenté.

> Desperate,
> With terrible disillusionment in furor,
> I desired death, detested life:
> What is, oh! life without virtue or love?
> Alone, unsociable, lugubrious and somber,
> Like the sad bird of the night,
> For twelve moons my delirium
> Crying I contrived.

In this, Heredia's most romantic specimen, the wounded heart, troubled and inconsolable, nourishes an "alma borrascosa" (turbulent soul), which pushes him to the "abismo" (abyss), but the poet appears to find some relief in the liberating act of writing poetry. In 1822, he wrote "En una tempestad" (In a Storm), in which nature is conceived as "estado de ánimo" (a state of mind, according to the critic and poet Henri Frédéric Amiel), and the poet identifies with it in searching for spiritual support and certainty:

> Al fin, mundo fatal, nos separamos:
> El huracán y yo solos estamos.
>
> ¡Sublime tempestad! ¡Cómo en tu seno,
> De tu solemne inspiración henchido,
> Al mundo vil y miserable olvido,
> Y alzo la frente, de delicia lleno!
> ¿Dó está el alma cobarde
> Que teme tu rugir . . . ? Yo en ti me elevo
> Al trono del Señor: oigo en las nubes
> El eco de su voz; siento a la tierra
> Escucharle y temblar. Ardiente lloro
> Desciende por mis pálidas mejillas,
> Y a su alta majestad tiemblo y le adoro.

> At last, terrible world, we are separated:
> The hurricane and I are alone.
>
> Sublime tempest! How in your breast,
> Swelled by solemn inspiration,
> The vile and miserable world I forget,
> And raise my forehead, full of delight!
> Where is the cowardly soul
> That fears your roar . . . ? I am elevated in you
> To the throne of the Lord: I hear in the clouds
> The echo of his voice; I feel the earth
> Listen to him and tremble: ardent tears
> Descend my palid cheeks,
> And before his majesty I tremble and adore him.

136

The search for support and ideal continuity is present in poems like "A la estrella de Venus" (To Venus' Star). Heredia addresses the "astro de paz" (star of peace), "luz apacible y pura de esperanza y amor" (peaceful and pure light of hope and love), a subject that he venerates because it inspires his meditations on love, virtue, goodness, and glory. In the poem "El desamor" (Lovelessness), the night, with its moon, "astro sereno" (serene star), is the saving refuge of his "triste corazón de penas lleno" (sad heart full of sorrows).

Nature as a symbol with which the poet identifies, in a unity of cosmos and human creature, gives the poem "Niágara" (Niagara) its reason for being and its lyric-existential strength. With a sorrowing tone, Heredia pours out, in a neoclassical ode composed of *octavas reales* (eight lines of eleven syllables) with rhetorical and resounding hendecasyllables, the desolation and anguish of his "alma estremecida y agitada" (suffering and agitated soul), which lives in "misero aislamiento" (impoverished isolation), in "lamentable desamor" (lamentable lovelessness), "desterrado, sin patria, sin amores" (expatriate, without a homeland, without love), but which looks for permanent liberation and affirmation in the example of the eternal renovation of the "torrente prodigioso" (prodigious torrent) of Niagara Falls. The poet invokes the natural wonder to ask that it revive his dead inspiration, that it allow him "mirar tu faz serena" (to look at [its] serene face) and that it fill his soul with "entusiasmo ardiente" (ardent enthusiasm). The turbulence and serene majesty of the torrent, as it falls, is undone and remade, as in Heraclitus' river, "arrebatado como el destino irresistible y ciego" (caught up as irresistible and blind destiny), confusing the poet's soul "en vagos pensamientos" (with vague thoughts); but "al contemplar la férvida corriente" (on contemplating the fervid current) that "al cielo cual pirámide inmensa se levanta" (rises to the heavens like an immense pyramid), in a complete destiny that integrates the cosmos, God, time, space, thought, and all humanity, the poet identifies with that mysterious force and recovers, as in a rite of mystical elevation:

> *El alma libre, generosa y fuerte*
> *Viene, te ve, se asombra,*
> *Menosprecia los frívolos deleites,*
> *Y aun se siente elevar cuando te nombra.*

> The free soul, generous and strong
> Comes, sees you, is astonished,
> Deprecates frivolous pleasures,
> Feels elevated even when it says your name.

In the example of that greatness and perfection of Nature, created by God, man is reborn purer and truer; he rejects the "error y fanatismo impío" (error and pitiless fanaticism) that flooded the world "en sangre y llanto" (with blood and weeping), with "infanda guerra" (infamous war) that was stirred up among brothers to "desolar frenéticos la tierra" (frenetically desolate the earth). In his philosophy, composed in part of the humanitarianism of the Enlightenment and the period following the French Revolution, and focusing on equality, fraternity, justice, peace, liberty, order, progress, and well-being for all, Heredia does not lose the opportunity to chastise the

> *. . . mentidos filósofos, que osaban*
> *Escrutar tus misterios, ultrajarte,*
> *Y de impiedad al lamentable abismo*
> *A los míseros hombres arrastraban.*

> . . . false philosophers that dared
> To scrutinize your [nature's] mysteries, insult you
> And who with impiety to the lamentable abyss
> Dragged miserable men.

Based on the example of Niagara Falls, Heredia appears to state that a renewed man is to be born for the well-being of humanity. As a poet, he wishes to continue writing poetry that embraces and celebrates the greatness he contemplates. He asks of Niagara:

> *¡Niágara poderoso!*
> *Oye mi última voz: en pocos años*
> *Ya devorado habrá la tumba fría*
> *A tu débil cantor. ¡Duren mis versos*
> *Cual tu gloria inmortal! Pueda piadoso*
> *Al contemplar tu faz algún viajero,*
> *Dar un suspiro a la memoria mía.*
> *Y yo, al hundirse el sol en occidente,*
> *Vuele gozoso do el Criador me llama,*

JOSÉ MARÍA HEREDIA

Y al escuchar los ecos de la fama
Alce en las nubes la radiosa frente.

Powerful Niagara!,
Hear my last voice: in few years
The cold tomb will have devoured
Your weak singer. Let my verses endure
Like your immortal glory! Piously,
On contemplating your face, may some traveler
Heave a sigh in my memory.
And may I, as the sun falls in the west,
Fly joyously to where the Creator calls me,
And, on hearing echoes of fame,
Raise in the clouds a glowing forehead.

In this poem and in other compositions, such as "Al Océano" (To the Ocean), "Al Sol" (To the Sun), "Himno del desterrado" (Hymn of the Exile), "La estrella de Cuba" (The Star of Cuba), "Vuelta al sur" (Return to the South), "Placeres de la melancolía" (Pleasures of Melancholy), Heredia is the first example of poetic precocity in Hispanic America. At the same time, he is the incarnation of the first image of the romantic hero in the New World, unfortunate, without a homeland, rebellious and liberal, trapped in an irremediable destiny. He searches for support in nature, in the abolition of an abominable past, and in the hope for a future more in keeping with the human condition. He is a creature disinherited by time and space, in a historical setting of alienation and impossibility, evading the present in a desire for affirmation, expression, and the search for himself.

Heredia overcame his confessed amorous misfortune (see "A Emilia" [To Emilia] and "A mi caballo" [To My Horse]), his sad destiny as an exile, and his inherent philosophical pessimism through the utopic and positivistic ideas of social affirmation that were common to the new religion of humanity expressed by the early romantics, such as Robert de Lamennais, in their desperate struggle to change life and man. In his form of composition, Heredia combined neoclassic continuities with the adjectives, verbs, and rhetorical turns of combative romanticism. His exaggerated sorrow and his eloquent counsel—the many examples he provides of what is negative and the many models for the triumph of goodness, utility, and beauty—give Heredia's poetry a vast and varied register, in terms of ideology and literary technique.

His work is lyric-sentimental, tragic-epic, civil, patriotic, nationalist, social, religious, political, very Europeanized, and frequently Americanist.

His most celebrated poetic composition, which some critics consider the highest achievement of early Spanish-American romanticism, is "En el teocalli de Cholula" (In the Teocalli of Cholula), written in December 1820, as the poet celebrated his seventeenth birthday. In *The Literature of Spanish America* (1966), the critic Ángel Flores has given an excellent synthetic interpretation of this poem:

In it moods and postures, frankly romantic, seem to converge: a twilight, a landscape in harmony with the poet, languor, ruins, night, a moon, a dream, and most significant, an elegiac meditation wherein past and present are compared—the bloody wars of the old Aztec emperors and the wars of the Mexican emperor Iturbide endeavoring now (1820) to crush the liberal revolution against Spain. Transcending the pictorial sunset, the socially conscious poet attacks "vile superstition and tyranny" and fulminates against man's egocentrism and destructive selfishness.

The poem consists of a description of sunset at the Mexican city of Cholula, site of a famous pyramid-temple, which the poet has come to admire and on which he meditates. Suddenly he goes to sleep:

> *Un largo sueño*
> *De glorias engolfadas y perdidas*
> *En la profunda noche de los tiempos,*
> *Descendió sobre mí. La agreste pompa*
> *De los reyes aztecas desplegóse*
> *A mis ojos atónitos.*

> A long dream
> Of glories engulfed and lost
> In the deep night of time,
> Came over me. The untamed pomp
> Of the Aztec kings unfolded
> Before my astonished eyes.

Afterward, he reflects on the civilization and culture of the Mexican forebears, who were, along with those from other New World regions, the foundation of the America that continues the Hispanic and European colonization. The poet rejoices that

Con su manto benéfico el olvido
Tu insensatez oculta y tus furores
A la raza presente y la futura.

With its benevolent cape, forgetfulness
Hides your foolishness and your furor
From the present race and the future.

He concludes with this admonition:

Muda y desierta
Ahora te ves, pirámide. ¡Más vale
Que semanas de siglos yazcas yerma,
Y la superstición a quien serviste
En el abismo del infierno duerma!
A nuestros nietos últimos, empero,
Sé lección saludable; y hoy al hombre
Que ciego en su saber fútil y vano
Al cielo, cual Titán, truena orgulloso,
Sé ejemplo ignominioso
De la demencia y del furor humano.

Mute and deserted
You stand now, pyramid. It were better
That for weeks of centuries you lie fallow,
And the superstition you served
Sleep in the depths of hell!
For our last grandchildren, however,
I know a healthy lesson; and today for man
Who, blind in futile and vain knowledge,
To heaven, as a Titan, thunders prideful,
I know an ignominious example
Of the madness of human furor.

Besides poems, Heredia wrote literary essays (*Poetas ingleses contemporáneos*, [Contemporary English Poets, 1832]); aesthetic theory (*Ensayo sobre la novela*, [Essay on the Novel, 1832]); history (*Lecciones de historia universal*, [Lessons of Universal History, 1831–1832]); translations and theatrical adaptations; stories, dramas, and discourses; and articles in his journals *El iris* (1826) and *La miscelánea* (1829–1832). His *Epistolario* (Letters, 1939) are an excellent psychological self-portrait. His *Últimos versos* (Last Verses, about 1839) are decidedly religious. And if Heredia was not a great poet—for his poetry varies in quality—he was a man of moral integrity, idealistic and with a final hope in human perfectibility. Heredia is one of the most representative figures in the

transition of colonial Latin American literature to the period of the Independence.

Translated from the Spanish by Bruce Stiehm

SELECTED BIBLIOGRAPHY

First Editions

Individual Works

Poesías. New York, 1825; 2nd, rev. ed., Toluca, Mexico, 1832.

Collected Works

Obras poéticas. Edited by Antonio Bachilles y Morales. New York, 1875.

Modern Editions

Antología herediana. Havana, 1939.
Poesías. Havana, 1965.
Poesías. Havana, 1980.
Poesías completas. Edited by E. de Leuchsenring. 2 vols. Havana, 1940–1951.
Poesías completas. With a study and notes by A. Aparicio Laurencio. Miami, 1970.
Poesías, discursos y cartas de José María Heredia. Edited by Maria Lacoste de Arufe. 2 vols. Havana, 1939.
Prédicas de libertad. Havana, 1936.
Revisiones literarias. Havana, 1947.
Trabajos desconocidos y olvidados. Madrid, 1972.
Versos: Selección. Havana, 1960.

Translations

A complete reference to Heredia's poetry translations may be found in: Francisco González del Valle's *Poesías de Heredia traducidas a otros idiomas*. Havana, 1940.
Blackwell, Alice Stone. *Some Spanish American Poets*. 2nd ed. Philadelphia Pa., 1937.
Hills, E. C. *The Odes of Bello, Olmedo and Heredia*. New York and London, 1920.
Walsh, Thomas. *Hispanic Anthology*. New York and London, 1920.

Biographical and Critical Studies

Augier, Ángel. "José María Heredia." In *Historia de la literatura hispanoamericano*, Madrid, 1987. Pp. 309–313.

Alonso, Amado, and Julio Caillet-Bois. "Heredia como crítico literario." *Revista cubana* 15:54–62 (1941).

Chacón y Calvo, José María. *Estudios heredianos.* Havana, 1939.

Diaz, Lomberto. *Heredia, primer romántico hispanoamericano.* Montevideo, 1973.

Esténger, Rafael. *Heredia: La incomprensión de sí mismo.* Havana, 1938.

García Garófalo y Mesa, Manuel. *Vida de José María Heredia en México, 1825–1839.* Mexico City, 1945.

González, Manuel Pedro. *José María Heredia: Primogénito del romanticismo hispano.* Mexico City, 1955.

González del Valle, Francisco. *Cronología herediana (1803–1839).* Havana, 1938.

Henríquez Ureña, Pedro. "La versificación de Heredia." *Revista de filologia hispánica* 4/2:171–172 (1942).

Mejía Ricarte, Gustavo Adolfo. *José María Heredia y sus obras.* Havana, 1941.

Páez, Alfonso E. *Recordando a Heredia.* Havana, 1939.

Rangel, Nicolás. "Nuevos datos para la biografía de José María Heredia." *Revista bimestre cubana* 25/2:161–179 (1930).

Robaina, Tomás F. *Bibliografía sobre José María Heredia.* Havana, 1970.

Rodríguez Demorizi, Emilio. *El cantor del Niágara en Santo Domingo.* Ciudad Trujillo, Santo Domingo, 1939.

Toussaint, Manuel. *Bibliografía mexicana de Heredia.* Mexico City, 1953.

Esteban Echeverría

(1805–1851)

Ester Gimbernat González

Esteban Echeverría, born in Buenos Aires on 2 September 1805, was a romantic poet and a liberal inspired by the new ideals of democracy. A study of his literary works has to be closely related to his civil and political activities and to those of his generation. As a young man, he studied at the recently opened Colegio de Ciencias Morales (College of Moral Sciences) of Buenos Aires. His attitude during that first period of his life showed an individualism, a desire for free will, and a passionate inclination against rules and conventions that were characteristic of the romantic movement. When his mother died in 1822, he felt guilty because of his licentious life, and became more serious.

At the age of twenty he went to Paris, where he studied for five years. During this second period of his life, he was acquainted with such significant literary figures as Victor Hugo, Alphonse Lamartine, Charles-Augustine Saint-Beuve, Comte Alfred-Victor de Vigny, Alfred de Musset, Johann von Schiller, Johann Wolfgang von Goëthe, Alessandro Manzoni, George Gordon, Lord Byron, and Sir Walter Scott. These were the years of the premiere of Hugo's *Hernani* (1830) and the romantic manifesto of Hugo in his preface to *Cromwell* (1827). Inspired by the literary and political excitement of the age, Echeverría wanted to write poetry. This desire led him to the study of the classic Spanish authors: Fray Luis de León, Miguel de Cervantes, Lope de Vega, Tirso de Molina, and Francisco de Quevedo. In addition to this literary interest, he read the political and philosophical works of Pierre Leroux, Johann Gottfried von Herder, and Victor Cousin. After a brief stay in England, and in poor health, he returned to his homeland in the early 1830's.

Echeverría found the realities in his country very distressing. All his hopes for liberty and freedom were lost. "I locked myself within myself, and from there were born infinite works." His illness broke out again, and the poet translated his worries about death into painful, tragic, and anguished poetry.

In 1832 he anonymously published *Elvira; o, La novia del Plata* (Elvira; or, The Bride of the River Plate), a poem written during his return trip from Europe. Elvira loves Lisardo with virginal purity. Lisardo promises to marry her, but she is worried by bad portents. Lisardo tries to charm her, but finally he comes to fear the bad omens. One night, when he goes to the country during a tempest, he has a series of macabre visions. After that fevered night, he learns that Elvira has died. The poem is a series of nightmares whose purpose seems to be the inclusion of the dance of death from the German tradition. Influences of Goëthe, Schiller, and Gottfried Bürger are present in this poem, but it is Hugo's *La ronde du sabbat* that has the greatest impact on the construction of the macabre dance. The poem *Elvira* was received with indifference at the time, a response that deeply hurt Echeverría's self-esteem. The work has special chronological significance: it was the first romantic expression in the Castillian lyric and the cornerstone of Argentine literature.

In 1834 Echeverría published *Los consuelos* (Consolations). His illness was worsening, and he was very sensitive to the political persecutions and circumstances under the government of Juan Manuel de Rosas. Since any form of tyranny enraged him, he hated Rosas and his Federalists. Romantic characteristics are accentuated in this new work, in which there is also more lyricism than in *Elvira*. The public received it warmly and enthusiastically. A well-known critic, Florencio Varela, said: "What a beautiful book! Echeverría is a poet, a poet! Buenos Aires has not seen anything like this for a long time; it probably has not been seen before!" Although romantic authors worldwide sought to represent social issues, for Echeverría and his generation social activism went beyond theory and philosophy. The historic moment required that Echeverría become involved with the political and historical reality of his country. By the time he published *Los consuelos*, he possessed a well-designed poetic theory, which had not shown clearly in the first works but which permeated the later ones. He thought that poetry had to be original and capable of reflecting the nature around the poet. Echeverría tried to attain these goals by presenting a lively picture of the national customs and expressing the dominant ideas of the country at the time of the revolution for independence (1810), in addition to revealing the passions and feelings that arose from the social consciousness that was part of the intellectual atmosphere of the time.

In 1837 he could see concrete evidence of his efforts; he participated in the underground literary salon held in the bookstore of Marcos Sastre, thanks to his close friends Juan María Gutiérrez and Juan Bautista Alberdi. He also published *Rimas* (Rhymes), a book of poems that reflected his poetic conceptions. With this work he changed the direction of his poetry. He had wanted to break away from the Spanish poets whose style he had been following, and his attempt was highly successful. The first poem of the book is *La cautiva* (The Captive Woman), the best exposition of his talent and the inauguration of the romantic era of writing about the Argentine landscape. It is a key work in Argentine literary history.

Echeverría knew he was introducing something different in *La cautiva*: romantic values in art of native features. The events were presented in plain and simple language, unlike the rhetoric of the neoclassical movement. He used octosyllable, the simplest and most traditional Spanish meter. The organization of the poem is well planned: there are nine parts and an epilogue. Each part coincides with a development in the plot, with a thematic presentation, or with a change in the discourse. The first part, "El desierto" (The Wilderness) is a detailed description of the solitary pampas of Argentina, an open space that is the most important element in the poem. Its presence is constant and overwhelming; every event in the plot is directly or indirectly provoked by the wilderness. The descriptions are sensuous and strongly pictorial, attempting to be both universal generalizations and a sentimental projection of the poet's soul. The poet selects the details and the effects that express the intimate emotions, without omitting those characteristic elements that permit recognition of a specific reality. The flow of time forms a constant and protagonistic presence. The days, hours, and minutes are insistently measured throughout the poem, underscoring the monotony of the landscape.

In "El desierto" the American reality became legendary. The pampas are shown in a double sentimental vision: as the ideal place both for the solitary ecstasy of the soul and for the fatal impulse toward chaos, desolation, and death. In that solitary area, Echeverría developed a world of opposite and intense passions. He could express both kinds of romantic emotions regarding nature: peace and dramatic disorder. The plot is very simple. A white woman named María, together with her family, is captured by the Indians. After the death of her son, she is able to free her husband, Brian. María leads their escape but is obliged to defend herself because Brian is so sick. After a short time he dies, and María wanders until a group of soldiers finds her. At that point she is delirious, and soon after she dies. The idea of fate as fatalism was common to the romantic mentality of that time. Both the scenery and the María-Brian story are pervaded by a desolation whose culmination is death. The protagonists are idealized examples of civilized people caught in barbaric Indian customs. With *La cautiva*, Echeverría initiated the dichotomy of civilization versus barbarism that has persisted in Latin-American literature.

The strong love of María and Brian is central to the plot of *La cautiva*, but at no point do the protagonists attain the importance of nature. The strength of their love is recounted in numerous passages of meditative poetry, reinforcing the romantic characteristics of the poem. The epigraphs, typical of the time, quote such European romantic masters as Lamartine and Hugo. It is possible to recognize the influence of François René de Chateaubriand and Abbé Prévost in the development of the plot.

La cautiva is composed in many poetic meters. The octosyllables alternate with lines of nine and ten syllables. Stanzas vary from decimas and sestinas to *pie quebrado* (tetrasyllables, or the equivalent, used in combination with the octosyllable) and romance. Echeverría was not very successful with the distribution of sounds and syllables and wrote only a few lines in perfect balance. Its metrical irregularity aside, the poem introduced into literature for the first time the Argentine pampas and the European-Indian confrontation. Echeverría initiated a new literary tradition that has been followed by several authors including Domingo Faustino Sarmiento and Rafael Obligado.

Fragments from *La cautiva* were read in the literary salon that met in the Marcos Sastre bookshop. That reading was especially noteworthy since the young men who met there talked not only about literature but about many political problems that afflicted their daily lives. The members of the salon intended to encourage the creation of a new historical consciousness that would bring together the youngest generation of Argentine intellectuals in a systematic and organized program for the future of the country. For Echeverría, the strong romantic influence from Europe was not limited to literary matters; it also motivated him toward an American ideal of revolution. His passion was to inaugurate a new kind of nation following the ideas of the May (1810) Revolution. His literary production tried to capture all those ideals of liberty, fraternity, and equality.

After discovering the tone and subject of the meetings, the repressive government of Rosas outlawed the salon. Echeverría formed an organization called the Joven Generación Argentina (Young Generation of Argentina), because he feared the government's measures would disperse the outstanding group of young intellectuals. The secret organization was founded in June 1838, and its members took oaths in July, expressing faith in the "Código o declaración de principios que constituyen la creencia social de la república Argentina" (Declaration of Principles That Constitute the Social Belief of Argentina). Echeverría, Alberdi, and Gutiérrez cooperated in the writing of this fundamental document, subsequently known as the *Dogma socialista* (1846), which was the first political manifesto of its kind in Argentina.

In 1839 Echeverría participated in an unsuccessful rebellion against the government, and he had to flee to Montevideo. Thus began the fourth and last period of his life: the exile. Because of his poor health, the scarcity of his resources, and his solitary and capricious artist's temperament, he could not take part in the armed action that was organized in Uruguay against the Rosas government. In 1843, he was one of the founders of the Historical and Geographical Institute of Uruguay. He prepared in 1846 the "Manual de enseñanza moral para las escuelas primarias" (Handbook for Moral Teaching at the Elementary Schools) and became in 1849 a member of the Superior Council of the University of Montevideo.

Since he always despised the use of literature for political propaganda, Echeverría was involved in many arguments with those who accused him of lack of political participation. He wanted to be a poet and write long and profound poems. During the eleven years in exile, Echeverría tried to create a colossal poem to fulfill the prophetic mission he felt he had as a poet. In an epic poem, he could present men, nature, society, and every facet of the life of his world and his time. The first part of this long poem was to be *La guitarra* (The Guitar), which was published in 1842; it was a two-thousand-line poem that was criticized as extravagant and ridiculous in its construction. The second part was to be entitled "La peregrinación; o, La civilización europea ante los ojos de un americano" (The Pilgrimage; or, European Civilization in the Eyes of an American); the third, "El idealismo, como resultado lógico y fatal de la segunda" (Idealism, the Logical and Fatal Result of the Second Part); the fourth, *El ángel caído* (The Fallen Angel, 1871); and the fifth, "El pandemonio" (Pandemonium). The hero of this epic would know the reality, the wounds, the pain of his contemporaries and would be able to proclaim their hopes and beliefs. *La guitarra* and *El ángel caído* were published, but the rest of the planned poem was not completed.

In 1849 Echeverría published *La insurrección del Sud* (The Southern Rebellion), a poem almost one thousand lines long, in which he commemorated the tragic events that had caused his exile. All the sadness and solitude of the exile is expressed with virile strength in this poem. He spent the last six years of his life working on *El ángel caído,* the longest of his poems. It was almost seven thousand lines long and was published twenty years after his death. Even though *El ángel caído* is a valiant lyric attempt, it fails completely. The Argentinized Don Juan of the poem is an unsuccessful combination of a crude political *caudillo* (leader) and a philosopher living in Paris. The poem lacks the local color of Echeverría's other work.

Some of Echeverría's prose writings, *El peregrinaje de Gualpo* (Gualpo's Pilgrimage, 1873) and *Cartas a un amigo* (Letters to a Friend, 1873), could be considered sketches for the cantos of his unfinished epic poem. He did not compose many prose works, even though *El matadero* (*The Slaughter House*) is one of the classics of nineteenth-century Argentine literature. Published in 1871 in *Revista del Río de la Plata,* it was probably written around 1839, judging on the basis of references in the text. The first publication incorporated an explanatory introduction by Gutiérrez, who tried to justify the crude realism of the piece by suggesting that it was a rough draft of an important literary work that Echeverría had never finished. Other critics have disagreed with Gutiérrez, calling *The Slaughter House* a fine piece of prose in which realism, *costumbrismo* (the depiction of regional customs and types), narration, and dialogue mingle in a subtle and powerful text.

Considered an explicit metaphor of the tyrannic government of Rosas, *The Slaughter House* represents the way in which political matters were controlled and the characteristics of the dictatorship and its procedures. After a brief introduction, Echeverría presents a detailed description of the prevailing conditions in Buenos Aires, including the painful circumstances that led to the shortage of beef during a Lenten season in the 1830's. For many days it has rained heavily, ruining the access roads to the slaughterhouse. Because beef is the main source of nutrition, the situation becomes unbearable, until the dictator Rosas authorizes the entrance of fifty steers. The arrival of the animals is powerfully described, and the filth and mire of the slaughterhouse is truthfully depicted in the realistic tradition of the Spanish picaresque. Everything follows the routine until the last animal, trying to escape the rope around its neck, pulls harder and the rope flies away, beheading a young boy watching the operation. The same animal runs over a group of black workers and an English gentleman, leaving them in the mud. Finally, the ferocious butcher Matasiete kills the steer, to the rejoicing acclamation of the poor people. When the butchers finish slaughtering the animals, they single out a rider passing by. Because of his beard, symbol of his affiliation with the opposition Unitarian party, the rider suffers different kinds of harassment until he dies.

The two parts of the story are very clear: the descriptions of the slaughterhouse, the mob, the poor black people, and the chaotic environment in the first portion serve as an introduction to the subsequent political struggle in which the Unitarian rider dies. Echeverría wanted to point out the infamy and barbarism of Rosas' government, and he did it successfully in *The Slaughter House*. This work is the best prose of Argentine literature during the nineteenth century and is included today among the outstanding classics of Latin American literature.

Echeverría died in Montevideo on 19 January 1851, receiving high honors from the Uruguayan government. He died knowing that his political and literary ideas had been an inspiration and a model for many young Argentines since 1832. Echeverría's works are significant as social and political documents and as literary achievements.

SELECTED BIBLIOGRAPHY

First Editions

Poetry

Elvira; o, La novia del Plata. Buenos Aires, 1832.
Los consuelos. Buenos Aires, 1834.
Rimas. Buenos Aires, 1837.
La guitarra. Montevideo, 1842.
La insurrección del Sud. Montevideo, 1849.
El ángel caído. In his *Obras completas* 2. Buenos Aires, 1871.

Prose Narratives

El matadero. In *Revista del Río de la Plata.* Buenos Aires, 1871.
El peregrinaje de Gualpo. In *Revista del Río de la Plata.* Buenos Aires, 1873.
Cartas a un amigo. In *Revista del Río de la Plata.* Buenos Aires, 1873.

Essays

Dogma socialista. Montevideo, 1846.

Collected Works

Obras completas. Edited by Juan María Gutiérrez. 5 vols. Buenos Aires, 1870–1874.

Translations

The Slaughter House. Edited and translated by Ángel Flores. New York, 1959.

Biographical and Critical Studies

Agosti, Héctor. *Echeverría.* Buenos Aires, 1951.
Arrieta, Rafael Alberto. "Contribución al estudio de Esteban Echeverría." In *Boletín de la academia argentina de letras* 9/33:437–472 (1941).
_____. "Echeverría y el romanticismo en el Plata." In *Historia de la literatura argentina* 2. Buenos Aires, 1958. Pp. 19–112.
Bogliolo, Rómulo. *Las ideas democráticas y socialistas de Esteban Echeverría.* Buenos Aires, 1937.
Borello, Rodolfo. "Notas a 'La Cautiva'." In his *Logos.* Buenos Aires, 1978. Pp. 13–14, 69–84.
Bucich, Antonio. *Esteban Echeverría y su tiempo.* Buenos Aires, 1938.
Chaneton, Abel. *Retorno de Echeverría.* Buenos Aires, 1944.
Cortázar, Augusto. *Echeverría.* Buenos Aires, 1946.
Ghiano, Juan Carlos. *"El matadero" de Echeverría y el costumbrismo.* Buenos Aires, 1968.

Gutiérrez, Juan María. *Sobre las rimas de Echeverría.* Buenos Aires, 1960.
Halperín Donghi, Julio. *El pensamiento de Echeverría.* Buenos Aires, 1951.
Jiménez Vega, E. *Esteban Echeverría.* Buenos Aires, 1951.
Jitrik, Noé. *Esteban Echeverría.* Buenos Aires, 1967.
_____. *El fuego de la especie. Ensayos sobre seis escritores argentinos.* Buenos Aires, 1971. Pp. 63–98.
Kisnerman, Natalio. *Contribución a la bibliografía de Esteban Echeverría.* Buenos Aires, 1960.
Knowlton, Edgar. *Esteban Echeverría.* Bryn Mawr, Pa., 1985.
Lafranco, Héctor. *Esteban Echeverría.* Buenos Aires, 1970.
Lamarque, Nydia. *Echeverría, el poeta.* Bueons Aires, 1951.
Mantovani, Juan. *Echeverría y la doctrina de la educación popular.* Buenos Aires, 1957.
Marianetti, Benito. *Esteban Echeverría: Glosas a un ideario progresista.* Mendoza, Argentina, 1951.
Martínez, Joaquín. *Esteban Echeverría en la vida argentina.* Buenos Aires, 1953.
Morales, Ernesto. *Esteban Echeverría.* Buenos Aires, 1950.
Moreno Davis, Julio. *Esteban Echeverría, su vida y su pensamiento.* Panama City, 1972.
Ortiz, Ricardo. *El pensamiento económico de Echeverría.* Buenos Aires, 1953.
Palcos, Alberto. *Echeverría y la democracia argentina.* Buenos Aires, 1941.
_____. *Esteban Echeverría.* Buenos Aires, 1951.
_____. *Historia de Esteban Echeverría.* Buenos Aires, 1960.
Petrocelli, Héctor. *El pensamiento de Echeverría y la interpretación de Mayo.* Rosario, Argentina, 1971.
Pina Shaw, Hilda. *Esteban Echeverría.* Buenos Aires, 1955.
Pupo-Walker, C. Enrique. "Originalidad y composición de un texto romántico: *El matadero* de Esteban Echeverría." In his *El cuento hispanoamericano ante la crítica.* Madrid, 1973. Pp. 37–49.
Rodríguez-Luis, Julio. "Civilización o barbarie en *El matadero.*" In his *La literatura hispanoamericana entre compromiso y experimento.* Madrid, 1984. Pp. 13–27.
Roggiano, Alfredo. "Esteban Echeverría y el romanticismo europeo." In *Actas del Sexto Congreso Internacional de Hispanistas.* Toronto, 1980.
Rojas Paz, Pablo. *Echeverría.* Buenos Aires, 1951.
Solari, Juan A. *Esteban Echeverría.* Mar del Plata, Argentina, 1949.
Sosnowski, Saúl. "Esteban Echeverría: El intelectual ante la formación del estado." *Revista iberoamericana* 114–115/293–300 (1981).
Weinberg, Felix. *Contribución a la bibliografía de Esteban Echeverría.* Santa Fe, Argentina, 1960.

Hilario Ascasubi

(1807–1875)

Georgette M. Dorn

Hilario Ascasubi, Argentine poet and best known for his depiction of *gauchos*, was born on 14 January 1807; his birth occurred under a covered wagon at the hamlet of Fraile Muerto (now Bell Ville), on the road from Buenos Aires to Córdoba. His mother was Cordoban and his father was Basque.

In a note at the beginning of *Santos Vega* (1872), Ascasubi described the *gaucho* as "a superb horseman and herdsman . . . generally poor, but free and independent . . . He is hospitable and possesses sharp intelligence and intuition, has a strong body, and is a man of few words. . . . He has a poetic side, is superstitious, but, above all, is extremely skilled in traveling through the immense deserted expanses of the country." Ascasubi's roots were in the countryside and its vast plains. Inspired by the Uruguayan *gaucho* poet Bartolomé Hidalgo, Ascasubi wrote about the life of the *gaucho* frontiersman in poems. He also chronicled the historical developments he witnessed during Argentina's protracted political turmoil, as his life spanned some of the most wrenching upheavals in his country's history. Owing to political conditions he spent many years outside of Argentina.

After early schooling under the Franciscans, Ascasubi ran away to sea at the age of twelve and traveled to Brazil, French Guiana, Portugal, California, and Valparaíso, a voyage he would describe years later in poems about a seafaring *gaucho* named Aniceto el Gallo (Aniceto the Rooster).

He began his literary career by founding the *Revista de Salta* (The Salta Review) in 1824, in the far north of Argentina, where he observed rural and urban *gauchos* firsthand. There he wrote his first political poem celebrating the Argentine rebels' decisive victory over the Spaniards at the Battle of Ayacucho (1824) in Peru, which finally ended the wars for independence.

Soon, however, Argentina was again torn by civil strife. The young poet volunteered for military service as a dragoon under the Unitarian General José María Paz, and henceforth Ascasubi's life would be intimately linked to political events. Argentina became increasingly polarized between Unitarians, who wanted a strong central government and rapid European-style modernization, and Federalists, who favored a loose federation of autonomous provinces and clung to the old colonial ways, regarding northern European ideas with suspicion. Ascasubi remained a staunch Unitarian throughout the half-century-long struggle between the two parties. Championing the Federalist cause, Juan Manuel de Rosas, *caudillo* (popular leader) and governor of Buenos Aires province, exercised hegemony over the other provincial *caudillos* and would rule the United

147

Provinces of the River Plate (today's Argentina) from 1829 to 1852.

Ascasubi was promoted to lieutenant in 1826 and met and fought against several Federalist *caudillos*, such as the legendary Juan Facundo Quiroga, who was later immortalized by Domingo Faustino Sarmiento in *Civilización y barbarie* (Civilization and Barbarism, 1845), an anti-Rosas work. Rosas crushed all opposition and defeated rival *caudillos* suspected of disloyalty. Imprisoned for a year by the Federalists, Ascasubi escaped in 1830, along with other Unitarians, and settled in Montevideo, the haven of most Argentines who had fled Rosas' despotic rule. Rosas tolerated no opposition, imposed strict censorship, and surrounded himself with henchmen who popularized the motto "Death to the Unitarian savages!"

In 1832 Ascasubi married the Uruguayan Laureana Villagrán, a descendant of José Artigas, Uruguay's founding father. The couple eventually had thirteen children, three of whom survived into adulthood.

Ascasubi devoted his long exile in Montevideo to fighting Federalist tyrants with his pen and his sword, running a bakery, writing political poetry, and publishing newspapers, devoted to his own poetry about the struggle against Rosas, such as *El Arriero Argentino* (The Argentine Herdsman, 1830), *El Gaucho en la Campaña* (The Gaucho on the Battlefield, 1839), and *El Gaucho Jacinto Cielo* (1841–1843). The poems, written in *gaucho* language, helped to build morale among Unitarian soldiers and exiles, and were also intended as psychological warfare against the Federalists. Copies of the newspapers and broadsides were smuggled into Federalist encampments, and sometimes they produced desertions.

By using the country language of the *gaucho*, Ascasubi could explain complex issues with wit and humor. Although the intellectuals and many merchants opposed Rosas and lived in exile, he still had many followers among the landowners, *gauchos*, Indians, and the poor. Ascasubi aimed his poems at Rosas' followers. In "La Refalosa" (The Slippery One), one of his most violent anti-Rosas poems, he depicted a decapitation in gruesome detail, comparing the victim to an animal in a slaughterhouse and the executioner to the butcher. Not even a Rosas henchman could have described the scene more vividly. In another poem, "Isidora la gaucha arroyera,

federala y mazorquera" (Isidora, the Federalist and Mazorcaist Gaucho), Ascasubi's female protagonist articulates the bitter and ferocious resentment that filled even many of Rosas' followers. (The Mazorca was Rosas' personal militia of terrorists.)

Ascasubi was also close to General Juan Lavalle and his armies fighting the Federalists. Lavalle's defeat and death (1841) dealt a serious blow to the struggle. Rosas tightened his grip on the Argentine provinces, continued terrorizing the population, and attacked Uruguay in an attempt to bring it back into the fold of the United Provinces, of which it had briefly been a part. The French and British began a blockade of the River Plate in retaliation against Rosas. Ascasubi, in addition to his pursuing his literary activities, turned his home and bakery into a haven for needy exiles and veterans from the campaigns. Some of the soldiers even wrote Ascasubi for help in the form of poems. As the popular bard of the civil wars, Ascasubi was honored by the writer José Rivera Indarte in a public ceremony in Montevideo in 1844. After two successful years of publishing the newspaper *El Gaucho Jacinto Cielo*, as well as writing poems for the Montevideo newspaper *El Correo del Plata*, Ascasubi created a memorable *gaucho* personality with the character Paulino Lucero, who began appearing in newspapers and pamphlets. So appealing was Paulino that Valentín Alsina, a Unitarian leader residing in Montevideo, published a poem in reply to Ascasubi, signing his name as Compadre Paulino. In 1853, Ascasubi collected most of his scattered poems in a volume entitled *Trobos de Paulino Lucero, o Colección de poesías campestres desde 1833 hasta el presente* (Paulino Lucero's Verses, or Collected Poems from the Countryside since 1833).

In 1848 the blockade of the river was lifted. In the same year Ascasubi published a long poem about the execution in Buenos Aires of the young Camila O'Gorman, daughter of a prominent landowner, entitled *Trovas y lamentos de Donato Jurado, soldado argentino a la muerte de la infeliz Da. Camila O'Gorman* (Verses and Lamentations by Donato Jurado, Argentine Soldier, at the Death of the Unfortunate Camila O'Gorman). Camila's execution was especially shocking because she was pregnant. The poem also portrayed widespread fear of random and unpredictable terrorism by the government. In

Montevideo a number of exiled Argentine writers were publishing works of fiction with Rosas' repressive regime as the main topic.

Ascasubi, having already published numerous poems about Rosas' regime, decided to produce a long epic poem that dealt with politics, entitled *Los mellizos, o Rasgos dramáticos de la vida del gaucho en las campañas y praderas de la República Argentina* (The Twins, or Some Dramatic Aspects of Gaucho Life on the Prairies of Argentina, 1850), in which he wrote in glowing terms about the *gaucho* and life on the *estancia* (large landholding) in early nineteenth-century Argentina. In a series of beautiful poems, he depicted the people of the plains, their horses and their animals, their relationship with nature, their love for song and poetry, their courage, and the breathtaking landscape. The work became an immediate success and brought favorable reviews by literary critics. He did not finish all the installments because he returned to the battlefield.

Across the river, opposition to Rosas gathered momentum and coalesced around the towering figure of the *caudillo* from the province of Entre Ríos, Justo José de Urquiza, who in an 1851 *pronunciamiento* (declaration), supported by many provinces, demanded Rosas' resignation. Ascasubi wrote a poem commenting on the declaration and was promptly invited by Urquiza to join his army in the final onslaught against Rosas. Ascasubi's old acquaintance, the writer Sarmiento, was also in the latest campaign, and they both issued reports from the battlefield. Ascasubi's reports in hendecasyllables proved more popular than Sarmiento's sober bulletins. Rosas was decisively routed at the battle of Monte Caseros.

Once the Federalist Urquiza entered the city of Buenos Aires, he quickly quarreled with the Unitarian leaders. Ascasubi broke with Urquiza and wrote poems disparaging the role of Urquiza's troops at Caseros. Buenos Aires seceded from the confederation, partly on the suspicion that Urquiza might become another dictator like Rosas. The wounds between Federalists and Unitarians were still raw, and the bitter enmity between Buenos Aires and the provinces worsened. In the turmoil over the secession, violence erupted once again in Buenos Aires, and Ascasubi sent his family back to the safety of

Montevideo. In 1853 he created the *gaucho* character Aniceto el Gallo, providing running commentary on the unfolding events through poetry that he published (1853–1859) in a newspaper called *Aniceto el Gallo.* He collected the poems in 1872 in a book of that title.

The city of Buenos Aires was in the throes of becoming a glittering capital and began fancying itself a nation-state. Ascasubi joined a group of investors who set out to build the Colón Theater and Opera House. As the monumental structure took shape, looming over the sprawling village that was Buenos Aires of the 1850's, wags began calling it The Rooster Aniceto's Comb, in reference to Ascasubi's character. At this time, another bird appeared in Buenos Aires, called Anastasio el Pollo (Anastasio the Chicken). Some thought it might be Ascasubi's newest character, but it was the brainchild of another gaucho poet, Estanislao del Campo, a follower of Ascasubi. A lively poetic dialogue ensued between the Rooster and the Chicken. From a newspaper published in the city of Paraná came a poem, offensive in tone, referring to Ascasubi as Aniceto the Turkey. The latter wasted no time in retorting with a poem steeped in vitriolic sarcasm. Poetic dialogues helped relieve the tension felt in 1859 in Buenos Aires, under siege from Urquiza's armies.

In 1860 Ascasubi embarked on the first of his many missions to Europe, chiefly Paris, in search of war materiel and mercenary soldiers, as Argentina was still sparsely populated and had vast uncharted frontiers. He was in Paris when the Battle of Pavón (1861) was fought and Argentina finally became a united nation under its first president, Bartolomé Mitre. Ascasubi undertook several missions on Mitre's behalf, furthering the outfitting of armies about to embark in the War of the Triple Alliance (1865–1870). Ascasubi also entertained the newly elected second president, Sarmiento, while in Paris. In *Viajes en Europa, Africa y América* (Travels in Europe, Africa and America, 1849–1851), Sarmiento wrote with admiration about Ascasubi, whom he considered a popular poet who had honed his talent on the battlefield and who depicted through widely celebrated poems the *gaucho* frontiersman.

Ascasubi spent most of his last years in Paris on government business. With all his activities in fighting dictatorship, he never managed to amass a large estate. During his lifetime he had been a poet, a soldier (he rose to colonel from ensign), as well as a printer, publisher, baker, merchant, and official Argentine envoy to Europe. When his health began to fail while in Paris—he died in Buenos Aires on 17 November 1875—he decided to complete his most ambitious literary project. The result, his most outstanding achievement, was *Santos Vega, o Los mellizos de la Flor* (Santos Vega, or The Twins from La Flor, 1872), which expanded the original poem, published in installments in 1850, from 2,022 to 13,180 stanzas. He also brought out an edition of his complete works in Paris, containing *Santos Vega, Paulino Lucero, Aniceto el Gallo,* and most of his scattered poetry.

The balladeer Santos Vega was a romantic *gaucho,* not the crude marginal being people were used to seeing every day. According to Jorge Luis Borges in *Otras inquisiciones* (1952), Santos Vega "is the totality of the pampas. The interminable adventures he related could happen anywhere in the country. His rhythm is smooth, easygoing, describing the empty but happy days where clocks are superfluous." José Hernández' *gaucho* epic *Martín Fierro* (1872) began selling in Buenos Aires the year before Ascasubi's *Santos Vega* arrived from Paris. Hernández' work overshadowed all other *gaucho* literature. While *Santos Vega* presented an idealized *gaucho* existence and held up life on the *estancia* as a model for society, Hernández' poems focused on the *gaucho* as a member of an underclass, relating the story of a man on the harsh Argentine frontier where life was constant struggle. *Martín Fierro* was an expression of social protest.

The publications of *Santos Vega* and *Martín Fierro* ushered in a golden age of *gaucho* literature, along with del Campo's *Fausto: Impresiones del gaucho Anastasio el Pollo* (1866), Antonio Lussich's *Los tres gauchos orientales: Coloquio entre los paisanos* (Three Uruguayan Gauchos: Conversations Between Countrymen, 1875), and Hernández' *La vuelta de Martín Fierro* (The Return of Martín Fierro, 1879). *Gaucho* literature was the first authentic Argentine literary expression, and its founders were Hidalgo and Ascasubi.

Like the other gaucho poets, Ascasubi was an educated urban author. He wrote first-person narratives, using poetry as an instrument in the maelstrom of struggle against Rosas and his Federalist allies. In one of the editions of *Paulino Lucero,* Ascasubi used the subtitle *Los gauchos del Río de la Plata cantando y combatiendo contra los tiranos de las Repúblicas Argentina y Oriental del Uruguay* (The Gauchos of the River Plate, Singing and Fighting Against the Tyrants of Argentina and Uruguay). His poetry was most effective and popular. Ascasubi inaugurated the defense of a whole social class, the outcast *gaucho,* and immortalized life on the *estancia* and on the vast, picturesque pampas in his classic work *Santos Vega.* Above all, he left a valuable document about the nineteenth century in the River Plate area.

SELECTED BIBLIOGRAPHY

First Editions

Poetry, Verse Tales, Epics

Paulino Lucero, o Dos gauchos de Entre Ríos. Montevideo, 1846.

Los mellizos, o Rasgos dramáticos de la vida del gaucho en las campañas y praderas de la República Argentina. Montevideo, 1850.

Trovas y lamentos de Donato Jurado, soldado argentino a la muerte de la infeliz Da. Camila O'Gorman. Concepcion, Uruguay, 1851.

Urquiza en la patria nueva, o Dos gauchos orientales platicando en los montes del Queguay en el 24 de julio de 1851. Concepcion, Uruguay, 1851.

Trobos de Paulino Lucero, o Colección de poesías campestres desde 1833 hasta el presente. 2 vols. Buenos Aires, 1853.

Aniceto el Gallo. Gacetero prosista y gauchi-poeta argentino. Extracto del periódico de este título . . . y otras poesías inéditas. Paris, 1872.

Santos Vega, o Los mellizos de la Flor. Rasgos dramáticos de la vida del gaucho en las campañas y praderas de la República Argentina. Paris, 1872.

Collected Works

Obras poéticas. Paris, 1872.

Modern Editions

Collected Works

Paulino Lucero. With a prologue by Manuel Mujica Láinez. Buenos Aires, 1945.

Paulino Lucero, Aniceto el Gallo, Santos Vega. Selección. With an introduction by Jorge Luis Borges. Buenos Aires, 1960.

Poesías para el pronunciamiento del Urquiza. Compiled and with a prologue by Manuel E. Macchi. Sante Fe, Argentina, 1956.

Biographical and Critical Studies

Ara, Guillermo. *La poesía gauchesca.* Buenos Aires, 1967.

Becco, Horacio. *Antología de la poesía gauchesca.* Madrid, 1972.

Borges, Jorge Luis. *Otras inquisiciones.* Buenos Aires, 1952.

_____, and Adolfo Bioy Casares. *Poesía gauchesca.* Mexico City, 1955.

Gallet de Kulture, Bénédict. *Quelques notes de biographie et un page d'histoire. Le colonel Hilario Ascasubi.* Paris, 1863.

Lanuza, José Luis. *Cancionero del tiempo de Rosas.* Buenos Aires, 1941.

Morales, Ernesto. *Lírica popular rioplatense.* Buenos Aires, 1927.

Mujica Láinez, Manuel. *Poetas argentinos en Montevideo.* Buenos Aires, 1943.

_____. *Vida de Aniceto el Gallo.* Buenos Aires, 1943.

_____. *Vidas de El Gallo y El Pollo. (Hilario Ascasubi y Estanislao del Campo).* Buenos Aires, 1966.

Sarmiento, Domingo Faustino. *Viajes en Europa, Africa y América.* Santiago, Chile, 1849–1851.

Sosa de Newton, Lily. *Genio y figura de Hilario Ascasubi.* Buenos Aires, 1981.

Tiscornia, Eleuterio. *Poemas gauchescos: Hidalgo, Ascasubi, del Campo.* Buenos Aires, 1940.

Trayectoria de la poesía gauchesca. Buenos Aires, 1977.

Weinberg, Félix. *La primera versión del "Santos Vega" de Ascasubi: Un texto gaucho desconocido.* Buenos Aires, 1974.

Yunque, Álvaro. *Poesía gauchesca y nativista rioplatense.* Buenos Aires, 1952.

Juan Bautista Alberdi

(1810–1884)

Delfín Leocadio Garasa

Juan Bautista Alberdi, born in Tucumán, Argentina, on 29 August 1810, was an important political thinker and an occasional literary writer. He lived most of his life out of his country, as an expatriate or on diplomatic missions. He was surrounded by constant and unceasing controversies that did not end with his death on 18 June 1884 but continue even today. During the terrible civil wars that followed Argentina's independence, his personality was always divided between artistic interests and meditation on political and legal themes, but in both activities he put his country at the center of his concern. The first struggle he worried about was the one between Unitarians, condemned by their blindness to the historical truths of the country, and Federalists, then led by the provincial *caudillos*, who were dominated by intentions and procedures that were not always clear. Afterward, there was the struggle between the supporters of the creation of a unified state ruled by a constitution and those who wanted to monopolize political and commercial hegemony in the port of Buenos Aires.

Alberdi was a man of weak health and clear intelligence. His father was a liberal Basque trader, a reader of the works of Jean-Jacques Rousseau and a friend of General Manuel Belgrano and of many of the delegates to the Tucumán Congress where, in

1816, Argentina's independence was declared. In his early youth, Alberdi went to Buenos Aires to study law. The city was full of young people enraptured by romanticism, and he became acquainted with a number of them. Afterward, he talked about the way in which he was moved by his reading of Rousseau's confessional novel *Julie, ou la nouvelle Héloïse* (*Julia, or The New Eloisa*, 1761). Like the author of *Du contrat social* (*The Social Contract*, 1762), Alberdi was a musician: he wrote minuets, a method to study the piano, and an essay entitled "El espíritu de la música" (The Spirit of Music, 1832).

He met Esteban Echeverría, who had experienced the romantic movement in Paris, as well as Juan María Gutiérrez, Vicente Fidel López, and other young intellectuals who wished to go beyond colonial neoclassicism. They usually got together in Marcos Sastre's bookstore, Librería Argentina, where they discussed the problems of those times of uncertainty. To supplement their university education, with its routine imperfection, these young men fed their spirits in the bookstores, where they could be in touch with the works of Montesquieu, Rousseau, Benjamin Constant, Jean Louis Lerminier, Félicité Robert de Lamennais, the Comte de Saint-Simon, Alexis de Tocqueville, Victor Cousin, and Sir Walter Scott. Marcos Sastre created the Salón Literario,

153

which was opened in 1837 with an event at which Sastre, Alberdi, and Gutiérrez delivered speeches. The salon was enthusiastically welcomed by many young people who felt disappointed about the intellectual apathy of the city, which in previous times had been called the Athens of the River Plate. In his autobiography, Alberdi declared: "In those times, I became closely connected with very distinguished young men, who had great influence in the later development of my studies and literary tastes" (*Escritos póstumos* 15, p. 294).

Those were not favorable times for political and literary activities in Buenos Aires. The authorities were suspicious of the Salón Literario, in spite of the fact that its habitués praised Gov. Juan Manuel de Rosas in every meeting. Alberdi in 1837 created the magazine *La moda,* which published comments on music, poetry, clothes, hairstyle, and other aspects relating to an elegant style of contemporary life. *La moda,* however, was condemned to a short existence: the authorities closed it a year after its birth, along with the Salón Literario. This left a great disillusionment in the young men who had created them, for now it was obvious that they must choose between exile and secrecy. In 1837, some of them founded the Asociacion de Mayo, where Echeverria was to read the *palabras simbólicas* (symbolic words)—built upon such concepts as association, progress, brotherhood, freedom, honor, sacrifice, and God—that would form his *Dogma socialista* (The Socialist Dogma, 1846), published in Montevideo during the years when Buenos Aires was ruled by terror and force.

Alberdi became a lawyer and later earned a doctorate in law with a thesis entitled *Fragmento preliminar al estudio del derecho* (Preliminary Project for the Study of Law, 1837), in which he studied juridical philosophy from a historical point of view, inspired principally by Lerminier's thought. Alberdi has described his feelings about his studies at this time: "Law became for me as attractive as the most biting phenomena of nature" (*Obras completas* 1, p. 104). He had already written *Memoria descriptiva sobre Tucumán* (Historical Memory of Tucumán, 1834), a book that reflects the romantic influence, with descriptions very like those of François Chateaubriand and Jacques Henri Bernardin de Saint-Pierre.

In the few numbers of *La moda,* Alberdi signed some articles with the pseudonym Figarillo. These works reflect his preference for Mariano de Larra, a Spanish satirical author who had commited suicide at the age of twenty-eight and who was the only writer Alberdi's Argentine generation exempted from its general hispanophobia. Alberdi and the other young intellectuals rejected everything that came from Spain. Alberdi had written in his thesis: "The day we exchanged slavery for freedom, we also replaced the Spanish authority with the French one." This rejection, which included language and Spanish literary models, was the cause of the carelessness evident in the romantic literature of the River Plate. Larra escaped this general condemnation because he was a sharp satirist of Spain. Published in *La moda,* Alberdi's *articulos de costumbres* (essays on mores), though they did not reach the Spanish author's literary quality, recorded with skill some ridiculous details of everyday life without attacking anyone personally, but with the obvious intention of denouncing certain Argentine habits. Alberdi showed this preference for satire all his life.

The presence of the banished Argentine intellectuals in Montevideo transformed that city's cultural life. Alberdi emigrated in 1838 and worked there as a lawyer and as a writer for *El iniciador* (The Initiator), a journal that had been founded by Andrés Lamas and Miguel Cané, Sr. In its pages Alberdi attacked the Buenos Aires government, which had become more and more cruel and tyrannical and was being defended by Pedro de Angelis, a mercenary Italian publicist. In 1841, on the occasion of a poetic contest held in commemoration of 25 May, the anniversary of the separation from Spain, Alberdi wrote a booklet, *Certamen poético* (Poetry Competition), to refute the ideas of Florencio Varela, a classicist emigrant of the previous generation and a supporter of academic neoclassicism. "Poetry must be the expression of the society that is being born in America and not of the one that is born in the Spain that withdraws" (*Obras completas* 1, p. 243). Alberdi was also a theater critic and the author of two plays, the unfinished *La revolución de mayo: Crónica dramática* (Dramatic Chronicle of the May Revolution, 1839), a historical-political evocation, and *El gigante Amapolas* (Giant Amapolas, 1842), a grotesque farce in which Rosas is presented as a straw puppet who overcomes his enemies without even moving. In this way, Alberdi joined the group of banished Argentines who cursed Rosas, as José Mármol did, or preached in favor of tyrannicide, like José Rivera Indarte, author of the booklet *Es acción santa matar a Rosas* (To Kill Rosas Is a Holy Deed).

In 1842, Alberdi embarked for Europe with Juan María Gutiérrez. During the journey, they avidly read Lord Byron's *Childe Harold's Pilgrimage* (1812); its influence can be traced in *El Edén* (The Eden, 1851), named for the steamer on which they traveled. Alberdi visited many countries in Europe, but he was nostalgic and in 1844 returned to America. He settled in Valparaiso, Chile, where he worked fruitfully as a publicist and stayed a long time, even after Rosas had been defeated by Justo José de Urquiza at the battle of Caseros (1852) and most other expatriates had gone back to Argentina.

In Chile, he wrote *Bases y puntos de partida para la organización política de la República Argentina* (Bases and Starting Points for Political Organization of the Argentine Republic, 1852), a fundamental work in which, in concrete terms, he dealt with Argentina's population, education, river navigation, and systems of industry and communication. He was in favor of the influence of European civilization in South America, rejecting a naive preference for Indian culture. He did not want to kill tradition but to improve it with foreign contributions. "In America, to govern is to fill the land with people," Alberdi believed. He wrote of his admiration for the way California was peopled, with persons from all over the world and of different religions; he supported equality of rights for foreigners, and thought that the predominance of Catholicism should not exclude other Christian sects. The book, published in several editions, was later corrected and expanded with a proposal for a constitution. The letters exchanged by the author and General Urquiza were added to the fourth edition. Alberdi's design clearly was the foundation upon which Urquiza attempted to create a constitutional organization of the Argentine Republic.

From that time on, Alberdi's contribution to political theory that addressed the problems of his country was never interrupted. He sometimes elicited rough opposition to his ideas, and he always replied with style. He defended Urquiza, who not only had

put an end to Rosas' tyranny but who also had wanted to create one country under a constitution to be written and discussed by representatives of all the provinces. Domingo Faustino Sarmiento and Bartolomé Mitre backed the supremacy of Buenos Aires and its exclusive right to collect customs revenues. Alberdi, who generally stayed in Quillota, Chile, for the summer, in 1853 sent letters to Buenos Aires in which, with tempered irony, he reproached Sarmiento—the author of *Civilización y barbarie* (Civilization and Barbarism, 1845)—for his contradictions and defended his view of the struggle between Buenos Aires and the other provinces that would reach bloody extremes in the battles of Cepeda and Pavón. Alberdi's letters, known as the "Cartas quillotanas" (Letters from Quillota), first appeared in the periodical *El Mercurio*, and then were published together as *Cartas sobre la prensa y la política militante de la República Argentina* (Letters on the Press and Activist Politics in the Argentine Republic, 1853) and *Complicidad de la prensa en las guerras civiles de la República Argentina* (Complicity of the Press in the Civil Struggles of the Argentine Republic, 1853). Sarmiento, always a touchy man, responded furiously to the "Cartas quillotanas" with the publication of *Las ciento y una* (The Hundred and One, 1853), in which he simply insulted his opponent. Alberdi replied in a tone of quiet sureness and compared Sarmiento's behavior and style with those of Rosas. The controversy was harsh and left them both with a bitter taste that never completely disappeared. Sarmiento later softened his tone, and Alberdi published *Sistema económico y rentístico de la Confederación Argentina* (Economic and Financial System of the Argentine Confederation, 1854), where he suggested reforms that would help to avoid the mistakes of the past, do away with bureaucratic barriers, and abolish Buenos Aires' colonial right to monopoly.

In 1855, Alberdi was appointed plenipotentiary minister of the Argentine Confederation (separate from Buenos Aires at that moment) to England and France; later, he performed the same role in the United States and Spain. During his long stay in Europe, he met outstanding figures of the political scene and fellow countrymen who were traveling or living in exile. He wrote important accounts of his conversations with Gen. José de San Martín during his first trip to France and later, in England, conversations with his past opponent Rosas, with whom he even got to share some federalist principles. His diplomatic missions ended in 1862, but he did not return to Argentina until 1879, when, under the presidency of Nicolás Avellaneda, he was elected representative of his province. He took part in the debates on the problem of transforming Buenos Aires into the capital city. But after forty years of being far away from his country, he was considered a foreigner; it may be that he himself felt that he was, in spite of the fact that he had never stopped thinking about the organization of the nation and contributing to it with his ideas. He finally chose to go back to Europe, where he died in 1884.

In Europe, Alberdi wrote one of his sharpest and most courageous works, polemic to the point of being forbidden in the Argentine schools. *El crimen de la guerra* (The Crime of War, 1915), a book that was never finished and that was published posthumously, was inspired by the antiwar campaign undertaken by many writers and thinkers after the Franco-Prussian War in the 1870's. Alberdi could not stop thinking about America and his own country's recent wars, like the one against Paraguay, of which he had been a firm opponent. In this book, he defines war as the legacy of the savage eras of human history, in frank contradiction of the brotherhood preached by Christianity. For Alberdi, it is a crime to attack a foreign country, in the same way that it is a crime to attack a fellow citizen. In both cases, the law that rules the relationships among men and people is being broken. War is legitimate only when it is undertaken in self-defense or to punish an aggressor. Alberdi considers that wars fought only to obtain geographical advantages or with the excuse of liberating other people, as if nations were judges, are simply criminal.

In South America, he says, wars have been caused by the ambitions of rulers, and they have only served to end lives, stop the economy, and lower moral values, as happened in Cepeda, Pavón, and Paraguay. Wars had brought only territorial losses to Argentina, and Alberdi abhorred leaders who organize wars without sharing the disagreeable tasks of killing and dying. He proposed that wars in South America should be put to an end by education, culture, economic development, material progress,

religious preaching, and, more than anything else, freedom. He suggested the creation of an international court that would have the power to intervene in cases of aggression. The citizens of any state where basic human rights were violated would be able to apply to the court, even if that meant being against their country's government.

Alberdi published in 1876 the biography of one of his friends in Chile, William Wheelwright, who represented for him the antithesis of the arrogant *caudillo* who had devastated South America. Wheelwright, an American born in Massachusetts, arrived in Buenos Aires in 1823; he later traveled to Chile, where he established a navigation service between Valparaiso and other ports on the Pacific Ocean and created a gas, lighting, and drinking-water service in several cities. He proved that the quickest road between the Pacific and Europe was not the Strait of Magellan but the Isthmus of Panama. He created the Pacific Steam Navigation Company connecting Panama, Chile, and England and planned the outline of a railroad that was to join several South American towns. Alberdi concludes from Wheelwright's life and achievements that "profit does not exclude morality, altruism, and glory for the manager of noble works." Wheelwright also undertook works in Argentina, in spite of the opposition of officials who considered that the promotion of the settlement of foreign companies in Argentina was unpatriotic. The Chilean Gonzalo Bulnes praised both Wheelwright and his biographer: "Both of them deserve America's attention, Wheelright as an untiring worker of every charitable undertaking and Alberdi as the deepest and most original thinker in today's Spanish America" ("Guillermo Wheelwright," *Revista chilena de historia y geographía* 5, 1876, p. 206).

In these later years, satire tempted Alberdi again, but this time it was more bitter in tone than what he had written as young Figarillo. In 1871 he published *Peregrinación de Luz del Día, o Viaje y aventuras de la Verdad en el Nuevo Mundo* (Daylight's Pilgrimage, or Truth's Adventures in the New World). In this work, Truth, tired of corrupt Europe, decides to travel to more favorable lands and disembarks in Buenos Aires. To her surprise, she finds European theater figures: first, Tartufo, Molière's hypocrite, with a mask not of devotion but of liberal education, yet the same opportunistic liar; afterward, she sees Don Basilio, Pierre Augustin Beaumarchais' and Gioacchino Rossini's character, who does not limit his slander to the salons of elegant society, but uses the press to spread his calumnies. In America, these characters have assumed different faces but are still the same. Alain-René Lesage's *pícaro*, Gil Blas, is another example. Gil Blas has become a political promoter without any scruples whatsoever. Truth does not take long to land in jail, for her presence is annoying. However, she has good company: there she finds Justice and Liberty, who are as despised as she is by this region of the New World, which has completely forgotten noble ideals. Yet another character is Don Quixote, who has founded in Patagonia a utopian republic, Quijotania, peopled by a group of sheep who constantly utter bleats of approval. In spite of the fact that the book too transparently contains allusions to well-known figures of the times, it was well received by the critics. Alberdi ended it by insisting on his praise of democracy and freedom.

We cannot consider Alberdi only as a literary writer. His main interests were not artistic ones. In his maturity, after having lived in Spain, he changed his attitude toward the Spanish language, accepted a diploma from the Real Academia de la Lengua (Royal Academy of the Spanish Language), and critized the rejection of the language by his friend Gutiérrez. Some of his sentences have become aphorisms of experience and meditation on basic themes; yet, although his doctrinal works are sometimes examples of accuracy and clarity, he was never an impeccable prose writer. A modern evaluation of Alberdi and his work must be deep and objective, and must avoid the hasty labels of polemic passion (he has been called a traitor). Such an evaluation should underline his visionary gifts, the loyalty he always had to his ideals, his intellectual honesty, and the complexities of his personality at a time in which it was not easy to distinguish goals from procedures.

SELECTED BIBLIOGRAPHY

Editions

Memoria descriptiva sobre Tucumán. Buenos Aires, 1834.

Fragmento preliminar al estudio del derecho. Buenos Aires, 1837. Reprinted 1942.

La revolución de mayo: Crónica dramática. Montevideo, 1839. Reprinted Buenos Aires, 1925.

Certamen poético de Montevideo. Montevideo, 1841.

El gigante Amapolas y sus formidables enemigos, o Sea fastos dramáticos de una guerra memorable. Valparaiso, Chile, 1842. Reprinted Buenos Aires, 1925.

Legislación de la prensa en Chile, o Sea manual del escritor, del impresor y del jurado. Valparaiso, Chile, 1846.

El Edén, especie de poema escrito en el mar. Valparaiso, Chile, 1851.

Bases y puntos de partida para la organización política de la República Argentina. Valparaiso, Chile, and Buenos Aires, 1852.

Cartas sobre la prensa y la política militante de la República Argentina. Valparaiso, Chile, 1853.

Complicidad de la prensa en las guerras civiles de la República Argentina. Valparaiso, Chile, 1853.

Organización política y económica de la Confederación Argentina. Besanzon, France, 1856.

Intereses, peligros y garantías de los estados del Pacífico en las regiones orientales de la América del Sud. Paris, 1866.

Peregrinación de Luz del Día, o Viaje y aventuras de la Verdad en el Nuevo Mundo. Buenos Aires, 1871. Reprinted 1916.

La vida y los trabajos industriales de William Wheelwright en la América del Sud. Paris, 1876.

Escritos póstumos de J. B. Alberdi. 16 vols. Buenos Aires, 1895–1901.

Grandes y pequeños hombres del Plata. Paris, 1912. Posthumous edition.

El crimen de la guerra. With an essay on Alberdi by José Nicolás Matienzo. Buenos Aires, 1915, 1934, 1947. Posthumous edition.

Estudios económicos: Interpretación económica de la historia política argentina y sud-americana. With an essay on the sociological doctrines of Alberdi by José Ingenieros. Buenos Aires, 1916, 1934.

Derecho público provincial argentino. Buenos Aires, 1917. New ed. 1927.

El imperio del Brasil ante la democracia de América. Articles written during Paraguay's war against the Triple Alliance. Asunción, 1919. Posthumous edition.

Collected Works

Estudios satíricos y de crítica literaria. With a prologue and notes by José A. Oría. Buenos Aires, 1945.

Ideario. Edited and with a prologue by Luis Alberto Sanchez. Santiago, Chile, 1941.

Juan Bautista Alberdi. Edited and with a prologue by Víctor Rico González. Mexico City, 1946.

La moda: Gacetín mensual de música, de poesía, de literatura, de costumbres. With a prologue and notes by José A. Oría. Buenos Aires, 1938.

Obras completas. 8 vols. Buenos Aires, 1886–1887.

Obras selectas. 18 vols. With an introduction by Joaquín V. González. Buenos Aires, 1920.

El pensamiento de Alberdi. Edited and with a prologue by Pablo Rojas Paz. Buenos Aires, 1943.

Modern Editions

Autobiografía: La evolución de su pensamiento. With a prologue by Jean Jaurés. Buenos Aires, 1927.

Cartas sobre la prensa y la política militante de la República Argentina. With a preliminary study by Horacio Zorraquín Becú. Buenos Aires, 1945.

Estudios sobre la constitución argentina de 1853. Buenos Aires, 1929.

Fragmento preliminar al estudio del derecho. With a preliminary study by Bernardo Canal Feijóo. Buenos Aires, 1955.

Luz del Día en América. With an introduction by Ricardo Rojas. Buenos Aires. 1916.

Sistema económico y rentístico de la Confederación Argentina, según su constitución de 1853. Buenos Aires, 1921, 1954.

Translations

The Crime of War. Translated by C. J. MacConnell. London, 1913.

The Life and Industrial Labors of William Wheelwright in South America. Boston, 1877.

Biographical and Critical Studies

Baqué, Santiago. *Influencia de Alberdi en la organización política del estado argentino.* Buenos Aires, 1915.

Biedma, J., and José A. Pillado. *Alberdi.* Buenos Aires, 1897.

Canal Feijóo, Bernardo. *Constitución y revolución: Juan B. Alberdi.* Buenos Aires, 1955.

Cárcano, Miguel Á. *Alberdi: Su doctrina económica.* Buenos Aires, 1934.

Carilla, Emilio. "Peregrinación de Luz del Día de Alberdi." In *Cervantes y América.* Buenos Aires, 1951. Pp. 47–57.

Carranza, Adolfo S. *Alberdi economista.* Tucumán, Argentina, 1919.

_____. *Alberdi y la liga de las naciones.* Buenos Aires, 1919.

_____. *¿Alberdi fué traidor?* Tucumán, Argentina, 1920.

Costa Álvarez, Arturo. "Alberdi y la lengua." In *Nuestra lengua.* Buenos Aires, 1922. Pp. 31–42.

Davis, Harold Eugene. *Juan Bautista Alberdi (1810–1884).* Gainesville, Fla., 1958.

Elizalde, Luis de. "Alberdi y el momento actual." *Sur* 248:39–53 (1957).

García Mérou, Martín. *Alberdi: Ensayo crítico.* Buenos Aires, 1890, 1916.

Groussac, Paul. "Las *Bases* de Alberdi y el desarrollo constitucional." In *Estudios de historia argentina.* Buenos Aires, 1918. Pp. 261–371.

Ingenieros, José. *La evolución de las ideas argentinas.* 2 vols. Rev. ed. Buenos Aires, 1951.

Matienzo, José Nicolás. *La política americana de Alberdi.* Buenos Aires, 1910.

_____. *Juan Bautista Alberdi, Antes y después de la constitución.* Buenos Aires, 1934.

Olleros, Mariano L. *Alberdi a la luz de sus escritos en cuanto se refiere al Paraguay.* Asunción, 1905.

Orgaz, Raúl. *Alberdi y el historicismo.* Córdoba, Argentina, 1937.

Oría, José A. "Alberdi 'Figarillo': Contribución al estudio de la influencia de Larra en el Rio de la Plata." *Humanidades* 25 (second part):223–283 (1936).

Palacios, Alfredo L. *Alberdi, constructor en el desierto.* Buenos Aires, 1944.

Popolizio, Enrique. *Alberdi.* Buenos Aires, 1946.

Posada, Adolfo. *Ideas políticas de Alberdi.* Buenos Aires, 1913.

Quesada, Ernesto. *La figura histórica de Alberdi.* Buenos Aires, 1919.

Rojas, Ricardo. "Vida y obras de Alberdi." In *La literatura argentina* 3. Buenos Aires, 1920. Pp. 505–535.

Rojas Paz, Pablo. *Alberdi, el ciudadano de la soledad.* Buenos Aires, 1941.

Rosa, José María. *La iniciación sociológica de Alberdi.* Santa Fe, Argentina, 1941.

Sáenz Hayea, Ricardo. *La polémica de Alberdi con Sarmiento.* Buenos Aires, 1926.

_____. "Juan Bautista Alberdi." In *Historia de la literatura argentina* 2, edited by Raphael A. Arrieta. Buenos Aires, 1958. Pp. 311–368.

Toledo, Antonio B. *Alberdi y la cultura espiritual.* Buenos Aires, 1935.

Domingo Faustino Sarmiento

(1811–1888)

Peter G. Earle

In *Recuerdos de provincia* (Provincial Recollections, 1850) Sarmiento remarked that his country and he were born within nine months of each other. He could have added that they grew up together; in the process he became Argentina's leading writer, educator, and politician of the nineteenth century. Between the first proclamation of independence on 25 May 1810 (formal independence was not gained until 1816) and Sarmiento's death in Asunción, Paraguay, on 11 September 1888, the viceroyalty of the River Plate—Spain's most isolated colony in the New World—developed into an economically flourishing republic. Domingo Faustino Sarmiento was the witness and embodiment of his country's growing pains. Of the New World's great leaders, only Thomas Jefferson is comparable to him in civic, educational, and political enthusiasms—and in romantic personal attachments. John Quincy Adams' impression of Jefferson could as appropriately be applied to Sarmiento: "He was a mixture of profound and sagacious observation, with strong prejudices and irritated passions."

Domingo Faustino Sarmiento was born in the small city of San Juan, in the western province of the same name, on 15 February 1811, the fifth child and only son among José Clemente Sarmiento Funes' and Paula Albarracín y Oro's six surviving offspring. Nine others died. His father fought with valor in General José de San Martín's battles against the Spanish loyalists in Chile. A good soldier and political organizer, José Clemente was for most of his life a restless and impractical man. During Domingo's childhood, he was often away from home and contributed little to the family's subsistence. By contrast his mother was a diligent and determined homemaker; she kept a vegetable garden, wove all the family's clothes, and maintained their humble brick house in livable condition.

José Clemente Sarmiento's shortcomings as a provider did not prevent him from encouraging his son to read or from seeking out scholarship opportunities for him later on. José Clemente and an uncle of Domingo's, José Eufrasio de Quiroga Sarmiento, taught the boy to read when he was four. From that point on, Domingo was always eager to learn. Concerned by his sometimes unruly behavior, his teachers were also impressed by his intellectual curiosity. From the beginning he sensed that life, for him at least, was an educative process. He was a pupil in the Escuela de la Patria (School of the Fatherland) in San Juan from its first year (1816) until its closing in 1825. Ignacio Fermín and José Jenaro Rodríguez had been sent by the Unitarian (liberal) governor of Buenos Aires to set up and direct the school. The two brothers were progressive educators in the best sense and cultivated an awareness of personal dignity in their students, each of whom by regulation was to be addressed as Señor, irrespective of social position. At an age not specified in his *Recuerdos de provincia* but in one of the earlier grades, Domingo was awarded by his teachers the honorary title of the school's First Citizen.

Of the several positive influences on Sarmiento in his formative years, probably the strongest was that of another uncle and priest, José de Oro. The Escuela de la Patria was forced to close in September 1825 because of local political turmoil. The new provincial government of San Juan banished José de Oro to the neighboring province of San Luis, and Oro proposed to take Domingo with him with a view to broadening his education. The boy's parents agreed, and for a year and a half Oro tutored him in Spanish grammar, Latin, the Bible, and oratory. In *Recuerdos de provincia* Sarmiento recalls, "My mind was shaped under the impression of his, and to him I owe my predilection for public life, my patriotism and love of freedom, and my dedication to the study of my country's culture, from which privation, exile and long years' absence could not distract me."

Sarmiento grew up in a rustic frontier environment during a period of rampant political anarchy. The governorship of San Juan province, for example, changed hands five times in a single year (1819–1820), and rural *caudillos* (chieftains) vied almost continuously for power for the next forty years. One of them was Juan Facundo Quiroga, protagonist of Sarmiento's best-known work, *Civilización i barbarie: La vida de Juan Facundo Quiroga* (Civilization and Barbarism: The Life of Juan Facundo Quiroga; published in English as *Life in the Argentine Republic in the Days of the Tyrants* [*Facundo*], 1845). Another was Friar Félix Aldao, the subject of a biographical essay by the author of *Facundo*, as the longer book is generally called, published three months before the latter. It is an unsubtle portrait of the "butcher priest" (a former priest, womanizer, and heavy drinker) who, like Facundo Quiroga, led an aggregation of *gaucho* (cowboy) soldiers under the banner of Juan Manuel Rosas' Federalist party. Rosas was the cleverest, cruelest, and most powerful of Sarmiento's enemies and the ultimate target of his portrait of Facundo.

Always in the background and often in the foreground of Sarmiento's life was Argentina's *gaucho* culture (vividly symbolized in José Hernández' narrative poem *Martín Fierro*, 1872 and 1879) and the civil unrest that it generated through most of the nineteenth century. Several historians have labeled the two decades dominated by Rosas as a gauchocracy of rural strongmen in continuous conflict among themselves. Together with a small group of liberal intellectuals who organized in 1838 and later identified themselves as the Asociación de Mayo, Sarmiento thought in terms of a broad liberation from the past and of a new nationalism. In the words of the Asociación's ideological leader, Esteban Echeverría, "the spirit of the times now moves all nations to free themselves, to achieve philosophical and literary as well as political independence."

The writings of the French educator and philosopher Victor Cousin were an important source for Sarmiento and his like-minded contemporaries, who were frequently in exile from the Rosas regime. In Cousin's work there was a confluence of G. W. F. Hegel's historical idealism, Thomas Reid's philosophy of common sense, and J. G. von Herder's theory of national cultures. Like Cousin, Sarmiento believed that history could be interpreted in social terms and redirected toward specific social ends. Cousin distinguished between unorganized "populations" and more civilized "peoples" who showed a consciousness of becoming unified in their beliefs and plans for the future. It was a population, wild and menacing, that Sarmiento thought of as he observed the entry into San Juan of Facundo Quiroga and his followers in 1827:

> I was standing in the doorway of my store [which belonged to an aunt; young Domingo was managing it], watching the six hundred ride by in a triumphal aura of dust and drunkenness. . . . We saw the thick cloud of dust advancing, filled with hoofbeats, shouts, curses and bursts of laughter; from time to time dirt-laden faces amidst unkempt hair and a suggestion of ragged clothes appeared in an amorphous image. . . . This was my vision on the Road to Damascus in my search for freedom and civilization. All my country's ills were revealed in that moment: Barbarism!
>
> (*Discursos populares*, in *Obras completas*, vol. 22, p. 238)

The experience had shown him, he later recalled, all he should have been fighting against, and two years later, during a brief imprisonment for refusing to continue service in the provincial militia as a second lieutenant, he assumed "political opinions." The opinions were vaguely consitutional (Unitarist), reflecting the recently attempted reforms by Bernardino Rivadavia's short-lived presidency of the United Provinces of La Plata (1826–1827), and concretely antiseparatist (anti-Federalist), anti-Spanish, and anti-*caudillo*. He joined the Unitarist forces as a lieutenant, had brief but intensive experience in battle against General Facundo Quiroga's army, was captured and held under house arrest in San Juan for four months, and, in February 1830, escaped for two months to Chile. Fighting flared anew and Sarmiento returned to San Juan. Once again Facundo Quiroga had the upper hand and in April 1831—this time with his father and a large contingent of Unitarist companions—Sarmiento again crossed the border into Chile.

In the next five years of exile (his mother obtained permission for him to return to San Juan in 1836) he taught reading, by a new syllabic method, in a small school in the town of Los Andes; sired, possibly with María de Jesús del Canto (documentary evidence is lacking), his first child, Emilia Faustina (born 18 July 1832); tended a store; studied English and read "all sixty volumes" of Sir Walter Scott in Valparaiso; and worked in a silver mine in northern Chile. Early in 1836 he contracted a severe case of typhoid fever and was allowed by the new Federalist governor of San Juan to come home, presumably to die.

But the prodigal son recovered and in his convalescence returned to reading and writing. His friend Manuel Quiroga Rosas had a fine library of modern European authors, many of them French romantics and social theorists, including Cousin. Of Sarmiento's studies in that phase of his life, Enrique Anderson Imbert, in chapter 8 of *Historia de la literatura hispanoamericana* (*Spanish-American Literature: A History*, 1954) has observed that he was more an intuitionist than a theorist, that his philosophy of history lacked systematic coherence, and that his originality is found in the fact that "his romantic philosophy of history was deeply fused with his idea of life itself as historical life. He sensed that his Self and his Country formed a single being committed to a historic mission in the mainstream of civilization."

In 1839 Sarmiento planned and inaugurated the Colegio de Santa Rosa de América in San Juan (a "School for Young Ladies") and together with Quiroga Rosas got permission to publish a weekly newspaper that, it was understood, would be apolitical. But it turned out that *El Zonda* assimilated and expressed the dangerously democratic ideals of the Asociación de Mayo, and Federalist Governor Nazario Benavídez forced it out of business after its sixth issue by raising the tax on newsprint. Soon after, Sarmiento was imprisoned for conspiracy and almost lynched by a Federalist mob. Governor Benavídez intervened at the last minute to save him and sent him into exile. On 18 November 1840, the date on which he again crossed the Andes—this time for his longest exile—he wrote in French on the wall of a shack he had built in the Zonda Valley, "On ne tue pas les idées" (Ideas cannot be killed). As the Federalist soldiers escorting him to the border did not read French, they let the message remain.

The prolonged exile that he began then marked the stage in Sarmiento's life that would raise him to permanent political and literary prestige, Over the next decade his three most readable works, *Facundo*, *Viajes por Europa, África i América* (1849 and 1851; a portion of this work was published in English as *Sarmiento's "Travels in the United States in 1847"*), and *Recuerdos de provincia* were written. Though composed in the relative powerlessness of exile, the three books exude hopefulness; Sarmiento had not returned to Chile in the spirit of defeat but with his mind set on overthrowing Rosas' coercive regime. Like Uruguay, Chile was then a refugee haven for Argentine liberals. Rosas' power had grown steadily since 1829, when he became governor of the province of Buenos Aires. In April 1835, he gained control of all the provinces. Two months earlier, Facundo Quiroga had been ambushed and killed in his covered wagon in the wilds of Barranca Yaco, an event commemorated in a poem by Jorge Luis Borges, "El general Quiroga va en coche al muere" ("General Quiroga Rides to His Death in a Carriage"). The victim had always been an ally of Rosas, but by this time (Rosas had sent him to Córdoba to mediate a dispute between two local *caudillos*) Facundo Quiroga's political strength was seen as a threat to the strongman in Buenos Aires, and many have suspected that the latter was involved in the assassination plot.

As a historian, Sarmiento viewed peoples and cultures through their representative men. Although he was of the colonial landed aristocracy, Rosas lived and worked among *gaucho* cowboys and learned their ways. He was an expert in the production of leather and salted meat (for the first half of the nineteenth century Argentina's only exports). He was a talented ranch administrator, and as a pathfinder he could tell where he was, day or night, by tasting the pampa grass. Sarmiento thought of him as the gauchocracy personified, the leader who could mold the unruly mass of plainsmen into a nation of plainsmen.

Essentially, that is what Rosas achieved. But the policies that consolidated his constituency were his ultimate undoing. In 1835 he enacted a sweeping tariff law against foreign imports. Ten years later, in response to a French blockade of the port of Buenos Aires, he ordered the River Plate literally chained off at a point just to the south of where the Paraná River flows into it. His purpose was to stop British and French vessels that had been plying their trade all the way up to Paraguay. The British and French, in turn, reacted with warships, destroying the chain barrier with cannon shot. That was the beginning of the end for the Rosas economy. A country that lived on its livestock and a rigid protectionist policy could not long survive chained off from the rest of the world.

In the early 1830's, Rosas had amassed a formidable following: the uneducated majority, the church hierarchy, the opportunistic, and the dispossessed. As a leader he was a heady mixture of the populist and the tyrant. In Facundo Quiroga, Sarmiento found the elements of psychological support that Rosas had been able to incite in virtually all his partisans: courage, cunning, distrust, and the *gaucho's* yen for freedom from civic obligation. In *Facundo*, the title figure appears as the phantasmagorical plainsman in the foreground, and Rosas as the calculating demon in the background. Thus, the "Vida de Juan Facundo Quiroga" ("Life of Juan Facundo Quiroga"), which begins in chapter 1 of part 2, is intended to be a vital cross-reference to the larger and further-developed phenomenon of Rosas' oppressive administration. In naturalistic terms,

Rosas' standing had been strengthened by Facundo's energy, and Rosas' propagandistic skill and massive repressions constituted an advance over Facundo's instincts and individualized cruelty. In Sarmiento's words, "what in him [Facundo] was only instinct, initiative, inclination, in Rosas became system, effect and result" (ch. 1, part 2).

Facundo is a work of fifteen chapters preceded by a vigorous introduction. It was written in considerable haste, as is often the case when a writer is moved by political urgency, and on 2 May 1845, it began appearing in serial form in *El Progreso*, a newspaper that Sarmiento had established in Santiago, Chile. Sarmiento's main purpose was to defeat Rosas ideologically (the civilized reformer versus the retrogressive despot) and politically (the pragmatic leader of the opposition who uses anecdote, symbol, and caricature as his principal weapons). To some degree, although he was not a foreign observer, Sarmiento aspired to become the Alexis de Tocqueville of Argentina, even though he was unlikely to achieve de Tocqueville's objectivity. In the introduction, he wrote:

> South America in general and especially the Argentine Republic have lacked a de Tocqueville who, forearmed with a knowledge of social theory like the scientific traveler with his barometers, sextants, and compasses, could acquire an insider's view of our political life, which is comparable to a vast, unexplored, and undocumented territory.

Sarmiento presented himself as an unabashed Europeanizer at a time (the 1840's) when "Americanism" in Argentina had a connotation of anarchy, violence, and persecution. One historian, Ricardo Rojas, has labeled the fifteen years that ended with Facundo Quiroga's assassination as the Argentine Middle Ages. The basic criterion for power and control during the Rosas years had little to do with legal principles, as José Luis Romero has shown in *Las ideas políticas en Argentina*; the main thing was the leader's ability to exact obedience, "the obedience he had earned on his own and which he enjoyed due to his innate ability as a commander." It was what at different times and cultural levels Napoleon, Genghis Khan, Rosas, and Pancho Villa had in common. "Egoism," Sarmiento wrote (part 2, chapter 2), "is the basis of almost all historical characters; egoism is the mainspring behind all memorable acts." Facundo, Rosas, and Sarmiento himself, as president from 1868 to 1874, seem to have confirmed that judgment.

Early editions of *Facundo* have three parts and are preceded by a ten-page introduction. The introduction and part 1 are a vivid panorama of Argentine culture and society in the first four decades of the nineteenth century. Part 2, the longest, is a biography of Facundo Quiroga that at some points gets entangled with observations of dubious relevance. Part 3, just two chapters, is a diatribe against Rosas and his regime. The book begins with an evocation of Facundo's "terrifying spirit" and ends on the satisfied note—even though Rosas was to remain in office another seven years—that all the groundwork of revolution has been done and that Rosas no longer governs "in the official sense of the word." Isolated in the presidential residence, he wages civil war, organizes intrigues, and directs his infamous secret police, the Mazorca (the word means "ear of corn," or corncob, and sounds like *más horca* [more gallows]). But, insists Sarmiento, the strongman has lost most of his support in Buenos Aires and throughout the provinces.

The most forcefully written sections are the introduction and part 1. In the introduction, the author laments that Argentine exiles in Chile have only "ideas, consolation, and encouragement" to offer their compatriots at home. He stresses that Facundo was a symbol and unknowing embodiment of the revolution and civil strife in Argentina, and that Rosas, far from being an aberration, was his country's natural representative and "a formula for the nation's way of life." Of humble rural origin and a natural creature of colonial life in the hinterland, Facundo was a "mirror" in which the progressive writer saw reflected "in colossal dimensions" the rough vitality of a turbulent historical era. As he reveals in the last paragraph of the introduction, the original (1845) edition was to consist of only two parts: the first the historical and environmental "stage," and the second the leading actor Facundo, "with his clothes, his ideas, and his manipulations." But by the time he had finished the rambling portrait that comprises part 2,

the author had warmed up for his inevitable barrage against the enemy still in control: Rosas.

In part 1 Sarmiento turns the near-empty expanses of Argentina into a symbolic map of barbarity. Its size is its "infirmity"; its landscapes suggest abstraction; jaguars abound on its plains; to the south and west of Buenos Aires fierce Indian tribes wait in ambush. The restless horsemen, lazy landowners (*estancieros*), and wild Indian hordes occupied a territory but did not constitute a nation: "there was no *res publica*." In these surroundings the *gaucho* developed physically but stagnated intellectually. Yet Sarmiento, who would profess until the end his official disdain for *gauchos* (and, by extension, the "Spanish race," which had proved to be "no more energetic" in the South American wilderness than in Spain, and also the *mestizos* and mulattoes of the New World), finds "poetry" in the *gaucho*'s way of life and habitat. "Solitude, danger, savages, and death. That is poetry."

Chapter 2 of part 1 describes four representative inhabitants of the pampas: the *rastreador*, the tracker with a detective's instincts; the *baqueano*, the pathfinder, who determines location through his knowledge of topography; the *gaucho malo*, the "outlaw, squatter, and peculiar misanthrope," who is feared but admired by the rest of society for his independent spirit; and the *cantor*, the ballad singer, whose songs about noteworthy events (kidnappings, acts of bravery, betrayals and killings—including Facundo Quiroga's own demise) are the main source of news in remote areas.

Chapter 3 is a perceptive analysis of a pastoral society whose basic elements were the horse, the knife, and leisure time in the *pulpería*, an establishment that combined the services of the general store and the Wild West barroom of the United States in the nineteenth century. The knife is seen as an organic extension of the *gaucho*'s personality. It was intended not for defense or attack but for the demonstration of the *gaucho*'s superior skill in "marking" an opponent, preferably on the face. "If an accident should occur [the spectators'] sympathies are all with the murderer." According to Sarmiento, Rosas had turned his home into "a sort of asylum for such murderers." Whether a *gaucho* as the result of his feats was to become a common criminal or a full-fledged *caudillo* depended on his nerve, his luck, and the rural judges' assessment of his bravery, a virtue not infrequently confused with aggressiveness.

The fourth and last chapter of part 1, "Revolucion de 1810" ("The Revolution of 1810"), purports to show how Argentina's war of independence from Spain deteriorated into a civil war. Sarmiento sees the first phase of that civil war as a reflection of the struggle between Spain and Europe—Europe, that is, as symbolized by an irrepressible Napoleon, one of whose armies had invaded Spain—and between an enlightened European culture (mostly French) and the retrograde Spanish tradition. In the second phase, civilization-hating *caudillos* took on the cities (mainly Buenos Aires and Córdoba). Briefly stated, "the cities triumphed over the Spaniards; and the rural areas, over the cities."

Part 2 is devoted principally to the wayward life of Facundo Quiroga. Perhaps more by impulse than design, the specific portrayal with which it begins moves into an increasingly diffuse discussion of Argentine political life; Sarmiento was obviously more interested in Facundo as a social manifestation than as a personage. The biography begins with the flight of the protagonist, unidentified on the first two pages; the authorities pursue him because he has just killed a man in a knife fight. His route is "The Crossing," a desert area between San Juan and San Luis also known as Los Llanos (The Plains). He soon realizes that a hungry jaguar is stalking him and, before it is too late, climbs a sapling tree to save himself. There he swings precariously for two anxious hours, until two companions who had agreed to catch up with him on horseback finally appear. Then the three of them, with the aid of lassos, subdue the jaguar and kill it with knives. "That's when I discovered what it is to be afraid," he often told his friends later on.

Probably with some exaggeration, Sarmiento stresses Facundo Quiroga's "evil character, poor upbringing, and bloodthirsty instincts," adding that he enjoyed terrorizing people, believed in no higher order, and resented "decent men." But he had a leader's genius, knew how to domineer, and how to discover guilt. Sarmiento attributes to him a feline evasiveness ("he'd never look a man in the eye") and a feline ferocity. The author claims to have substantiated the anecdote that one night, having failed to

secure a loan of money from his father, Facundo set fire to the thatched-roof house in which his parents slept.

The rest of part 2 abounds in anecdotes of that kind. Something had disappeared from a company of his soldiers; Facundo called them together, distributed sticks of equal length among them, and announced that the thief would be the one whose stick, the next day, turned out to be longer than the rest. At the next day's inspection, one soldier's stick was shorter than all the others, and Facundo immediately accused him of the robbery. The credulous *gaucho* had actually believed that his stick would grow overnight and had cut off a piece to compensate. Once, when angered by a junior officer who had done something he disliked, Facundo ordered six men to seize and tie him up, after which he ran him through several times with a spear. Such savagery notwithstanding, Sarmiento half excuses him, concluding that "Facundo was neither cruel nor bloodthirsty. He was just a barbarian who, once aroused, couldn't control his temper."

Sarmiento liked to include rural Argentina in a primitive category with the desert regions of Arabia and North Africa and to differentiate, for example, between terrorism as it was practiced in revolutionary France and the kind of terrorism employed by Rosas in Argentina in the 1830's and 1840's. The French kind, which reached its climax in 1793, was designed to eliminate the aristocrats and royalists as a political force; revolutionary action had led to that "result." In Argentina under Rosas, on the other hand, terror became the means of frightening the opposition into inaction; it was not a result but "an instrument." "Terror," he writes in part 2, chapter 4, is also contagious, "a sickness in spirit that afflicts entire populations, like the cholera, smallpox, or scarlet fever. No one's immune to it." Sarmiento was alert, as well, to color symbolism, particularly to Rosas' passion for blood-red, the color of the presidential coach, of the Federalist battle flags, of his wife's formal dresses, and of the ribbons worn by the citizenry as a sign of loyalty. Always the individualist, Facundo devised a battle flag of black with a white skull and crossbones in the center.

With *Facundo*, Sarmiento established himself as a writer of the first magnitude, having previously gained fame as an aggressive journalist and a rather awkward polemicist. The year 1845 was a pivotal one in his life. In 1840 Sarmiento had carried a letter of introduction from Argentina to an elderly Chilean resident of Santiago, Domingo Castro y Calvo, and visited his home frequently after that. Castro y Calvo had a twenty-two-year-old wife, Benita, who in 1844 became pregnant. In April 1845, she gave birth to a son, Domingo Fidel. Documentation is lacking, but persistent rumor pointed to Sarmiento as the father. In 1848 Sarmiento returned to Chile after a two-year inspection tour of educational systems in Europe and the United States, a tour sponsored by the Chilean government because Sarmiento had acquired a reputation as a talented educator and because the antagonistic articles he was publishing in *El Progreso* were becoming a source of embarrassment to the conservative administration of Manuel Montt. Castro y Calvo had died, and in less than three months after his return to Santiago, Domingo married the young widow Benita. From that time on, he treated Dominguito as his own son, which he probably was. The most tragic event in his life would be Dominguito's death in September 1866, in the bloody Paraguayan War; twenty years later he published a biography, *La vida de Dominguito* (The Life of Dominguito).

In the opinion of many critics, including his contemporary, Professor George Ticknor, Sarmiento's account of the trip that lasted from late 1845 to early 1848 (*Travels*) was his best-written work. France, from whose writers he had learned so much, was a disappointment; its leaders, including L. A. Thiers and F. P. G. Guizot, impressed him as hollow rhetoricians, and Baron Mackau, the Secretary of the Navy, as "an animal with two feet." In General Ramón María Narváez' Spain he saw mainly backwardness and political corruption quite similar to that against which he had been struggling in his native country. Bullfighting, which simultaneously repelled and attracted him, was symbolic of what was "barbarous" in Spanish culture: "a barbarous spectacle, yet strongly seductive and stimulating." His essay on the bullfight is sensitive and powerful; in it he recognizes that for Spaniards "danger is the pabulum of life." In North Africa he confirmed his preconception that *gaucho* primitivism had been transmitted from there to Argentina, at least in part, by the Spaniards. Before setting sail from Liverpool on a one-month voyage to New York, the inquisitive traveler had visited Italy, Germany, Switzerland, and many towns in England.

The United States was the country that impressed Sarmiento the most. He traveled on several important rivers, including the St. Lawrence, the Hudson, the Potomac, and the Ohio, as well as the whole length of the Erie Canal. He also took many train trips. Horace Mann, whose educational theories became a strong influence in Sarmiento's future work as minister of education and as president, received him in Boston. Mann's wife Mary, with whom he maintained a long correspondence, also translated *Facundo* into English and wrote a long biographical preface for it. Sarmiento's romantic capacity for surprise made North America easy for him to write about. He was dazzled by its well-made ships and riverboats, by its bustling commerce and efficient farming. By contrast, he asserted, "European monarchies are an amalgam of deterioration, revolution, poverty, ignorance, barbarism, and a degradation of the majority." Most of all, he was struck by the women, especially the unmarried woman, "or *man of feminine sex* [Sarmiento's emphasis], as free as the butterflies until she's imprisoned in the domestic cocoon to fulfill her social functions by marriage."

Sarmiento, as Allison Bunkley observed in chapter 24 of his biography, "analyzed the United States at the high point of its possibilities." Bunkley calls him "a positive de Tocqueville" and adds, "Sarmiento saw the optimism of the surface. De Tocqueville saw the pessimism of the undercurrent. Both are interesting to read as chronicles of an age. One is an inspiration. The other is a warning."

From 1850 on, Sarmiento became increasingly involved in the day-to-day work of politics and administration, and his writing became less literary and more specialized within the fields of public education, political speechmaking, and economic development. In the 1860's he had personal problems. At the same time that he was having an affair with Aurelia Vélez there were reports that his wife Benita was involved in an affair of her own. Whatever was actually going on, from about the end of 1862 he was separated from Benita. In that decade he was a senator, the governor of San Juan from 1862 to

1864, ambassador to the United States from 1865 to 1868, and president of the Argentine Republic from 1868 to 1874.

In 1883 Sarmiento published his last major (though unfinished) work, *Conflictos y armonías de las razas* (Conflict and Harmony in the Races). He had intended it to be a theoretical sequel to *Facundo*, but in it his thinking descends to an openly racist impressionism, including his assertion that primitive peoples "all tend to have the same size cranium and all think the same way; that is, they don't think, they only feel." He maintained that the United States was better off and more advanced than the rest of the Americas because it had not indulged in racial mixing and that Chileans had taken foolish pride in their Araucanian heritage. It is a flawed and disorganized book.

The tireless leader remained active in public life until his last three or four years. All his portraits and photographs until 1884 (a picture taken in Chile in 1884 shows him as sickly and aged) reflect the same intensity in his eyes, the same aura of persistence and will. From the time of his presidency, his political opposition had labeled him Don Yo (Mr. Ego). There is no doubt, if one thinks of his dynamic example, that great egos are likely to make history.

SELECTED BIBLIOGRAPHY

Many of Sarmiento's more specialized works on pedagogy, political administration, and military campaigns are not included; they can be consulted in his collected works (see *Obras,* below).

First Editions

Individual Works

The spelling in several of these titles was Sarmiento's own, in keeping with his strong convictions on the need for orthographical reform.

Mi defensa. Santiago, Chile, 1843.

Civilización i barbarie: La vida de Juan Facundo Quiroga i aspecto físico, costumbres, i ábitos de la República Arjentina. Santiago, Chile, 1845.

Viajes por Europa, África i América, 1845–1847. 2 vols. Santiago, Chile, 1849 and 1851.

Arjirópolis o la capital de los estados confederados del Río de la Plata. Santiago, Chile, 1850. A pamphlet in which the author proposes the foundation of a utopian republic with its capital on a small island near the mouth of the River Plate.

Recuerdos de provincia. Santiago, Chile, 1850.

Vida de Abrán Lincoln. New York, 1865.

Conflictos y armonías de las razas en América. 2 vols. Buenos Aires, 1883.

La vida de Dominguito: In memoriam del valiente i deplorado capitán Domingo Fidel Sarmiento, muerto en Curupaití a los veinte años de edad. Buenos Aires, 1886.

Collected Works

Obras. Edited by Augusto Belín Sarmiento. 52 vols. Buenos Aires and Santiago, Chile, 1885–1903. Volumes 1 through 7 were published in Santiago, Chile, from 1885 to 1889; the rest, in Buenos Aires in 1903.

Modern Editions

Argirópolis. Buenos Aires, 1938.

Conflictos y armonías de razas. With a prologue by José Ingenieros. Buenos Aires, 1915.

Facundo. Edited by Alberto Palcos. Buenos Aires, 1945. Rev. ed. 1961.

_____. Edited by Emma Susana Speratti Piñero. Mexico City, 1957.

_____. With a prologue by Noë Jitrik. Notes and chronology by Silvia Zanetti and Nora Dottori. Caracas, 1977.

Obras completas. 52 vols. Buenos Aires, 1948–1956.

Recuerdos de provincia. With a prologue by Jorge Luis Borges. Buenos Aires, 1944.

Viajes. With preliminary studies by Alberto Palcos, Norberto Rodríguez Bustamante, and Antonio de la Torre. Buenos Aires, 1955–1958.

Translations

Life in the Argentine Republic in the Days of the Tyrants (*Facundo*). Translated, with an extensive biographical introduction, by Mrs. Horace Mann. New York, 1868.

A Sarmiento Anthology. Translated by Stuart Edgar Grummon. Edited by Allison Williams Bunkley. Princeton, N.J., 1948.

Sarmiento's "Travels in the United States in 1847." The *Estados Unidos* portion of *Viajes.* Translated and with an introductory essay by Michael Aaron Rockland.

Princeton, N.J., 1970. Contains well-documented notes and Sarmiento's "Diary of Expenses," translated from Antonio P. Castro's facsimile edition, *Diario de gastos*. Buenos Aires, 1950.

Travels: A Selection. Translated by Inés Muñoz. Washington, D.C., 1963.

Biographical and Critical Studies

Anderson Imbert, Enrique. *Genio y figura de Sarmiento.* Buenos Aires, 1967.

Barrenechea, Ana María. "Notas al estilo de Sarmiento." *Revista iberoamericana* 21:275–294 (1956).

———. "Las ideas de Sarmiento antes de la publicación de *Facundo.*" *Filología* 5/3:193–210 (1959).

Becco, Horacio Jorge. "Bibliografía de Sarmiento." *Humanidades* (La Plata) 37/2:119–144 (1961).

Belín Sarmiento, Augusto [Sarmiento's grandson]. *Sarmiento anecdótico.* Buenos Aires, 1905.

Bunkley, Allison Williams. *The Life of Sarmiento.* Princeton, N.J., 1952. The best-documented biography of Sarmiento.

Carilla, Emilio. *Lengua y estilo en Sarmiento.* La Plata, Argentina, 1964.

Castro, Américo. "En torno al *Facundo* de Sarmiento." *Sur* 8/47:26–34 (1938).

Crow, John A. "Juan Manuel de Rosas: Tyrant of the Argentine" and "Sarmiento: Civilian President." In *The Epic of Latin America.* Berkeley, Calif., 1980. Pp. 580–603.

Cúneo, Dardo. *Sarmiento y Unamuno.* 2nd ed. Buenos Aires, 1955.

Earle, Peter G. "Sarmiento." In *Prophet in the Wilderness: The Works of Ezequiel Martínez Estrada.* Austin, Tex., and London, 1971. Pp. 36–65.

Franco, Luis. *Sarmiento y Martí.* Buenos Aires, 1958.

Gálvez, Manuel. *Vida de Sarmiento. El hombre de autoridad.* Buenos Aires, 1945. Lively and readable, but spiteful throughout because of Gálvez' strong anti-liberal sentiments.

Jones, C. A. *Facundo.* London, 1974.

Katra, William H. "Discourse Production and Sarmiento's Essayistic Style." In *El ensayo hispánico,* edited by Isaac Jack Lévy and Juan Loveluck. Columbia, S.C., 1984.

Leslie, John Kenneth. "Problems Relating to Sarmiento's *Artículos críticos i literarios.*" *Modern Language Notes* 61/5:289–299 (1946).

Lida, Raimundo. "Sarmiento y Herder." In *Memoria del Segundo Congreso Internacional de Literatura Iberoamericana.* Berkeley and Los Angeles, 1941. Pp. 155–171.

Lugones, Leopoldo. *Historia de Sarmiento.* Buenos Aires, 1911.

Martínez Estrada, Ezequiel. *Sarmiento.* Buenos Aires, 1946.

———. *Meditaciones sarmientinas.* Santiago, Chile, 1968.

Mazade, Charles de. "De l'Américanisme et des républiques du Sud (La société argentine, Quiroga et Rosas)." *Revue des deux mondes* 16:625–659 (1846). The first European commentary on *Facundo.*

Ocampo, Victoria. "Sarmiento." *Sur* 8/47:7–25 (1938).

Ottolenghi, Julia. *Vida y obra de Sarmiento en síntesis cronológica.* Buenos Aires, 1950.

Palcos, Alberto. *Sarmiento: La vida, la obra, las ideas, el genio.* 4th ed. Buenos Aires, 1962. The most perceptive biography of Sarmiento.

Rojas, Ricardo. *El profeta de la pampa. Vida de Sarmiento.* Buenos Aires, 1945.

Romero, José Luis. *Las ideas políticas en Argentina.* Buenos Aires, 1946. Translated by Thomas F. McGann as *A History of Argentine Political Thought.* Stanford, 1963.

———. "Martínez Estrada: Un renovador de la exegesis sarmientina." *Cuadernos americanos* 6/3:197–204 (1947).

Salomon, Noël. *Realidad, ideología y literatura en el "Facundo" de D. F. Sarmiento.* Amsterdam, 1984.

Sánchez Reulet, Aníbal. "La generación de Sarmiento y el problema de nuestro destino." *Sur* 8/47:35–46 (1938).

Sarmiento: Educador, sociólogo, escritor, político. Buenos Aires, 1963. Articles by eight scholars and critics, and an extensive bibliography.

Unamuno, Miguel de. "Domingo Faustino Sarmiento [1905]." In *Obras completas* 4. Madrid, 1968. Pp. 903–906.

Verdevoye, Paul. *Domingo Faustino Sarmiento: Éducateur et publiciste (entre 1839 et 1852).* Paris, 1963. A thorough, well-documented study.

Cirilo Villaverde

(1812–1894)

William Luis

Cirilo Villaverde is perhaps the most important novelist in nineteenth-century Hispanic American literature. Compared to other important works of the time, such as Jorge Isaacs' *María* (1867) and José Mármol's *Amalia* (1851–1855), Villaverde's *Cecilia Valdés* is a monumental work.

Villaverde's life and literary production can be divided into two stages: the first, his formative years in Cuba, during which he published a two-part short story "Cecilia Valdés" (1839) and the first version of the novel *Cecilia Valdés* (1839); the second, his political involvement in Cuba and exile to the United States, where he published the definitive version of *Cecilia Valdés* (1882).

Like many Cuban writers of the nineteenth century, Villaverde was an intellectual who pursued many interests; he was a novelist, a journalist, and a political activist. Born on 28 October 1812 in the region of Vuelta Abajo, Pinar del Río, Villaverde was the sixth of ten children. Of modest means, the Villaverde family lived on a sugar plantation where the father worked as a medical doctor. Since the plantation contained more than three hundred slaves, the young Villaverde was exposed to the evils of the slavery system.

At the age of eleven, Villaverde traveled to Havana, where he stayed with his father's widowed aunt and attended Antonio Vázquez' school. Villaverde later studied Latin with his maternal grandfather, a storyteller of sorts. In the introduction to *El penitente* (The Penitent, published in serial form in 1844 and in book form in 1889), Villaverde highlights the importance of this colorful figure; the grandfather converses with the author and even has the last word in the closing moments of the novel.

Villaverde returned to formal education by attending Father Morales' school and later studying philosophy in the Seminario de San Carlos, where he obtained a law degree in 1834. At the seminary, Villaverde befriended José Antonio Saco and other future Cuban notables. Simultaneously he studied drawing at the Convento de San Agustín. After briefly practicing law, Villaverde abandoned the profession because of corrupt lawyers and judges.

Villaverde taught at the Colegio Real Cubano and the Colegio Buenavista in Havana, and then at La Empresa in Matanzas. He pursued his interest in literature and published his first four short novels, *El ave muerta* (The Dead Bird), *La peña blanca* (The White Rock), *El perjurio* (The Perjury), and *La cueva de Taganana* (The Taganana Cave) in the magazine *Miscelánea de útil y agradable recreo* in 1837. *El ave muerta* narrates an incestuous relationship, a theme repeated in the definitive version of *Cecilia Valdés*.

These early works are not without flaws. The contemporary novelist Ramón de Palma had suggested that Villaverde's characters are not realistic and some of their behavior is never explained. However, Palma also recognized in those early works the excellent qualities seen later in *Dos amores* (Two Loves, published in serial form in 1843 and in book form in 1858) and *Cecilia Valdés*. Following Palma's romantic style, Villaverde wrote *El espetón de oro* (The Golden Skewer), published in *El Album* in 1838, preceded by Palma's introduction. *El espetón de oro*, reprinted in book form the same year, is considered the first book published in Cuba.

Villaverde was a member of the literary circle of Domingo del Monte, the most important cultural promoter of the time. Del Monte encouraged his friends to abandon romanticism and write in a realistic manner; he felt that the change in literary focus also represented a possible means of altering the Cuban slave society. Out of the Del Monte group emerged the Cuban antislavery novel. *Cecilia Valdés* was the last such work to be published before the emancipation of Cuban slaves in 1886.

By the time Villaverde returned from Matanzas to Havana in 1842, his literary career was under way. Of the works published in this first stage, the best known include *El guajiro* (The Peasant, published in serial form in 1842 and in book form in 1890), in which he documents the life of a Cuban peasant in the region of Vuelta Abajo. The story is a pretext for detailing the customs of an important sector of Cuban society. *El penitente*, based on Bernardo Gálvez' conquest of Florida, tells about the primitive early Cuban society as well as a frustrated love affair. *Dos amores* describes a woman's love for one man and her hatred for another; when the latter is not able to win her love, he forces her father into bankruptcy. *La joven de la flecha de oro* (The Young Woman with the Golden Arrow, published in serial form in 1840 and in book form in 1841) narrates a prearranged marriage that forces a woman to give up her love for a younger man. The nonfiction *Excursión a Vuelta Abajo* (Excursion to Vuelta Abajo) was first published in two parts, in the magazine *El album* in 1838 and in the newspaper *Faro Industrial de La Habana* in 1842. The two narrations, which were gathered in one volume published in 1891, describe the customs of the region and trace a journey that covered the limits of Guanajay to the Cape of San Antonio. Villaverde's picturesque narration recalls his introduction to Francisco Estévez' *Diario de un rancheador* (Diary of a Slave Hunter). Villaverde's father was one of Estévez' inspectors and had possession of the diary. The younger Villaverde intended to publish it to show the cruel acts of the slave hunter, but published only his introduction "Palenques de negros cimarrones" (Communities of Fugitive Slaves) in 1890.

In his mid thirties, Villaverde abandoned novelistic concerns in favor of political activities, although he did complete *Cecilia Valdés* in 1879. As he became more committed to Cuba's separation from Spain, Villaverde turned from fiction to a more politically oriented writing, which included journalism. In terms of adventure, some aspects of Villaverde's life rival his own fiction.

By 1847 Villaverde was a conspirator in the Club de la Habana, a group of well-to-do Cubans who desired not only the separation of Cuba from Spain but also its annexation to the United States. Although many members promoted annexation in order to preserve slavery in Cuba, others admired the democratic life of the northern states. Some simply preferred annexation to Spain's dominion over the island. Pablo, a character in *La joven de la flecha de oro*, who for eight years lived in the United States, best represents Villaverde's position. When referring to the United States, Pablo speaks highly of a civilization that respects the rights and liberties of both men and women. María Paulina, Villaverde's protagonist, consistently asserts her rights.

While in Cuba, Villaverde had joined General Narciso López in a failed uprising against the colonial government. López escaped to the United States, and Villaverde was captured and jailed on 20 October 1848. After a few months of detention, Villaverde escaped, with the aid of a guard and another prisoner, reaching Florida in April 1849. He traveled to New York and became López' secretary. With the help of Villaverde and others, López conducted three expeditions to Cuba, in 1848, 1849, and, the most successful one, in 1850. López invaded the island for the last time in August 1851; he was betrayed, captured, and executed in September. After López' death, Villaverde returned to journalism and teaching. Villaverde's annexationist ideas received another blow in a debate with José Antonio Saco. Unlike Villaverde, Saco favored independence but not annexation: he believed that United States citizens would take over the island; Cuba would not be annexed but absorbed into the Union. Villaverde answered Saco with his *El señor Saco con respecto a la revolución de Cuba* (Mr. Saco with Respect to the Cuban Revolution), published in New York in 1852.

Villaverde's involvement with the annexation movement ended with General López' death. As homage to him, Villaverde began (but never completed) the story of his life; the incomplete version was published under the title *General López, the Cuban Patriot* in New York in 1851. At the outset of the Ten Years' War, which lasted from 1868 to 1878 and marked the first of two stages of insurrection against the colonial powers—the second was from 1895 to 1898—Villaverde renewed his interest in politics. Rather than annexation, he now favored the independence of the island. In a document addressed to Carlos Manuel de Céspedes, entitled *La revolución de Cuba vista desde Nueva York* (The Cuban Revolution Seen from New York, 1869), Villaverde warns the Cuban patriot of the intent of the United States not to help the rebel forces.

Shortly after he arrived in New York, Villaverde collaborated in the separatist magazine *La verdad* (The Truth) and, in 1853, became its editor. That same year he founded and published the weekly *El Independiente* in New Orleans. Villaverde returned to New York in 1860 and published in *La América, Frank and Leslie's Magazine,* and *El avisador hispano americano.* He was also editor of *El espejo masónico,* from 1865 to 1873, *La Ilustración Americana,* from 1865 to 1873, *El Espejo,* from 1874 to 1894, and *El Tribuno Cubano* in 1878. He returned to teaching and opened a school in Weehawken, New Jersey, in 1874.

Villaverde made two brief trips to Cuba, the first from 1858 to 1860, and the second for two weeks in 1888. During the first trip, he acquired the publishing company La Antilla, and with the close collaboration of Francisco Calcagno, he founded the magazine *La Habana.* He also published Anselmo Suárez y Romero's *Artículos* and planned to publish his complete works in six volumes. Fearful of the power held by General José Gutiérrez Concha, the representative of Spanish authority in Cuba, Villaverde returned to New York. There he completed his last and most important work, *Cecilia Valdés.* He died on 20 October 1894.

The first and the last versions of *Cecilia Valdés* span Villaverde's literary career. Del Monte's influence and Villaverde's political involvement contributed importantly to the writing of *Cecilia Valdés.* The short story, which serves as the nucleus of the first volume, narrates the life of Cecilia, a ten-year-old orphan mulatto girl whose beauty is admired by the Gamboa family. After Cecilia visits the Gamboas, they joke about her resemblance to members of the family, including the father. The second part of the story is a conversation between Cecilia and her grandmother, Josefa, in which Cecilia relates her experience with the Gamboas. The grandmother is alarmed and pleads with Cecilia not to visit the Gamboas again, telling her a story about a girl like Cecilia, who was kidnapped by a student like young Leocadio Gamboa and literally swallowed by the earth. The short story ends with a vicious description of Leocadio, followed by Cecilia's disappearance and downfall and the grandmother's death.

There is no substantial difference between the short story and the first two chapters of the 1839 version of the novel although Leocadio's name is changed to Leonardo and Susanita, Cecilia's mother, becomes Rosario Alarcón. Both the short story and the first volume of the novel narrate the love relationship between Leonardo and Cecilia, but the theme of incest, important in the final edition of 1882, is never mentioned explicitly. Josefa's advice can be interpreted as a maternal concern for her granddaughter, and the resemblance between Cecilia and the Gamboas can be explained as coincidental. Blacks and the theme of slavery, so important in the definitive version of *Cecilia Valdés,* are not present in the short story and appear as only a marginal element in the novel. The only nonwhites mentioned in the versions of 1839 are urban mulattoes.

Forty-three years intervened between the first two versions of *Cecilia Valdés* and the final one. Except for stylistic and name changes, the short story and the first two chapters of the 1839 version coincide with the second and third chapters of the 1882 edition. Beyond these similarities, the versions of 1839 and

1882 are different. For example, the 1839 version ends with Leonardo's practical joke on Solfa, followed by Leonardo's conversation with Diego Meneses regarding Cecilia, Isabel, and Antonia. Unlike the 1839 version, volume 1 of the 1882 edition ends with the formal dance in which Cecilia encounters the Gamboa cook, Dionisio. Some events appear out of sequence and do not take place in the definitive version until volume 2. Although there is a coincidence in characters, the two works develop in completely different directions.

The three versions were written with different purposes in mind. If the short story narrates the demise of Cecilia's romance, the 1839 version takes up this theme but also documents the once popular Ferias del Angel. This is made explicit in Villaverde's dedication to Manuel del Portillo, a friend who inspired the author to write an account of the celebration. Villaverde included it in this version: more than three-quarters of the novel takes place during the day of the fair, 23 October 1831, the eve of San Rafael. The last edition of Cecilia Valdés is an antislavery novel and a political denunciation of the colonial government.

The 1882 edition rewrites the two earlier versions and places the action of the novel within the historical context of the administration of General Francisco Vives. Although the approximate age of Cecilia is the same as in the other versions, the dates have been changed to place the 1882 edition at the time of the corrupt Vives government. The first two versions mention that around 1826 or 1827 Cecilia was ten years old. This means that Cecilia was born either in 1816 or 1817. However, in the final version Cecilia was born in 1812, and in the second chapter she was eleven or twelve years old. This slight change in time situates the narrative time around 1823 and encompasses the Vives government which lasted from 1823 to 1832.

In the final version, 1812, the year in which Cecilia was born, is important not only because it was the same one in which Villaverde was born (also, they both have the same initials), but most significantly because it was the year of the Aponte conspiracy in which freed blacks, with the help of Haitians, attempted to liberate Cuban slaves; the conspiracy was suppressed in its early stage.

The definitive edition of Cecilia Valdés is an antislavery novel. The first volume shows how Cándido Gamboa enriches himself by trafficking in slaves, how slaves were thrown overboard, and how, piled one on top of the other, they suffocated in the bowels of ships. We are told the story of the former slave Dolores Santa Cruz whose hard work brought her freedom and enough money to buy a house and slaves. She lost everything, however, including her sanity, to the legal system that disputed her ownership of the house. This edition suggests that slavery for blacks is a hermetic system from which there is no escape, at least, not through legal means. Slavelike conditions existed even outside of the slavery system. Cecilia Valdés presents a vivid description of runaway slaves and the reasons for their daring actions. The life of the slave Pedro provides a disturbing account of a runaway slave who, after being bitten and captured by dogs, is placed in the cepo (shackle). He is later taken to the infirmary where he commits suicide by swallowing his tongue.

Perhaps the most significant addition to the 1882 edition is the increased presence of Doña Rosa, Leonardo's mother. A peripheral character in the first two versions, she has a more visible and important role and can even be considered one of the book's most powerful characters. She is the reason Don Cándido does not send Leonardo abroad to prevent his relationship with Cecilia, and although Doña Rosa has a weakness for her only son, it is she who controls him. She consents to and pays for the support of his mistress, Cecilia, and even tells him when it is time to end that relationship and marry Isabel, a white woman of his own class.

Cecilia Valdés calls into question the concept of motherhood in nineteenth-century white Cuban society. The black slave María de Regla, the maternal counterpart of Doña Rosa, is the "real" mother of all the children in the novel. She nursed her own daughter, Dolores, and was also the wet nurse of Cecilia and of Doña Rosa's daughter, Adela, and therefore their symbolic mother. Among the mothers in the novel, it is María de Regla, not Doña Rosa, Adela's mother, nor Rosario Alarcón, Cecilia's mother, who nurses her own child. Only the black wet nurse is described as performing the motherly act of nursing. María de Regla, whose name suggests both the Virgen María (Virgin Mary) and the Cuban black Virgen de Regla, is not only the mother of Adela, Cecilia, and Dolores, but the mother of the white, mulatto, and black races that her daughters represent. María de Regla opens and closes the book, and her presence is felt throughout the novel; it is she, and not Doña Rosa, who knows the secrets of Don Cándido's life.

In Villaverde's novel, Pimienta, Cecilia's frustrated mulatto lover, kills Leonardo Gamboa, an act that is a radical departure from other antislavery novels. Leonardo's death has broad implication; it suggests the end of the Gamboa family, of a mother who lived for her son and of a father who saw in his son a means of carrying on his recently received title of nobility. In addition, the death of Leonardo signals an end to a historical exploitation of black and mulatto women by white men. This pattern of exploitation had existed in Cecilia's family for generations. It began with Magdalena Morales, Cecilia's great-grandmother, and will end with Cecilia's daughter: both 1839 versions state that the exploitation will end in the fifth generation. This locates the beginning of the historical exploitation during the early part of the eighteenth century, possibly when Cecilia's family were slaves, and forecasts radical changes in the Spanish governments by the middle of the nineteenth century. Villaverde omitted this information from the 1882 edition because neither the emancipation of slaves in 1886 nor the liberation of Cuba from Spain in 1898 had occurred during the proposed fifth generation.

The ending of the novel never makes clear whether Pimienta was caught, allowing the possibility of his escape. Moreover, the killing has other positive implications. For example, Cecilia is reunited with her mother when she is detained in the Paula hospital.

Since its publication in 1882, *Cecilia Valdés* has met with great success and has been reissued numerous times in Havana, Barcelona, Mexico, Caracas, and New York. The novel has twice been translated into English. Since 1932, *Cecilia Valdés* has been performed as an operetta written by Gonzalo Roig. Habana Films published it as a film script in 1950. And in 1982 the Cuban Instituto de Arte e Industrias Cinematográficas brought it to the screen in a new version. *Cecilia Valdés* is indeed one of the greatest novels in Latin American literature.

SELECTED BIBLIOGRAPHY

First Editions

El espetón de oro. Havana, 1838.
"Cecilia Valdés." *La siempreviva* 2:75–87, 242–257 (1839).
Cecilia Valdés, o La loma del ángel. Havana, 1839.
Teresa. Havana, 1839.
La joven de la flecha de oro. Havana, 1841.
El librito de cuentos y las conversaciones. Havana, 1847.
General López, the Cuban Patriot. New York, 1851.
El señor Saco con respecto a la revolución de Cuba. New York, 1852.
Dos amores. Havana, 1858.
La revolución de Cuba vista desde Nueva York. New York, 1869.
Cecilia Valdés, o La loma del ángel. New York, 1882.
El penitente. New York, 1889.
El guajiro. Havana, 1890.
Excursión a Vuelta Abajo. Havana, 1891.

Modern Editions

Cecilia Valdés. With a prologue by Olga Blondet Tudisco and Antonio Tudisco. New York, 1971.
———. With a prologue by Raimundo Lazo. Mexico City, 1972.
———. With a prologue and chronology by Ivan A. Schulman. Caracas, 1981.
———. With a prologue by Emeldo Alvarez García. Havana, 1982.
Dos amores. Havana, 1980.
Excursión a Vuelta Abajo. Havana, 1981.
La joven de la flecha de oro y otros relatos. Havana, 1984.
La peineta calada. Havana, 1979.
La tejadora de sombreros de yarey. Havana, 1962.

Translations

Cecilia Valdés, or Angel's Hill. Translated by Sydney G. Gest. New York, 1962.
The Quadroon, or Cecilia Valdés. Translated by Mariano J. Lorente. Boston, 1935.

Biographical and Critical Studies

Arrufat, Antón. "Cirilo Villaverde: *Excursión a Vuelta-bajo.*" *Casa de las Américas* 2/10:133–140 (1962).

Baraona, Javier. "Itinerario de *Cecilia Valdés.*" *Carteles* 31 18–19:14–17, 14–28 (1950).

Barrera-Tomás, Pedro M. "La visión conflictiva en la sociedad cubana: Tema y estructura de *Cecilia Valdés.*" *Anales de literatura hispanoamericana* 5:131–153 (1976).

Bueno, Salvador. "Cirilo Villaverde, el creador de *Cecilia Valdés.*" In *Figuras cubanas: Breves biografías de grandes cubanos del siglo diecinueve.* Havana, 1964. Pp. 223–235.

Castellanos, José F. *Del Monte y Villaverde en "Cecilia Valdés."* Havana, 1947.

Cruz, Manuel de la. "Cirilo Villaverde." In *Cromitos cubanos.* Havana, 1892. Pp. 189–211.

Dorr, Nicolás. "*Cecilia Valdés: ¿Novela costumbrista o novela histórica?*" *Unión* 9/1:157–162 (1970).

Farinas, Lucila. "Las dos versiones de *Cecilia Valdés:* Evolución temático-literaria." Ph.D. diss., New York University, 1979.

Fernández de la Vega, Oscar. "La nueva traduccion de *Cecilia Valdés. Revista interamericana/Inter-American Review of Bibliography* 14:415–422 (1964).

Fernández Villa-Urrutia, Rafael. "Para una lectura de *Cecilia Valdés.*" *Revista cubana* 21/1:31–43 (1957).

Geada, Juan J. *Un novelista penareño: Cirilo Villaverde.* Havana, 1929.

Gomez y Martínez, Luis. *Cirilo Villaverde: Reflexiones a propósito de su personalidad literaria, resumida en su inmortal novel de costumbres "Cecilia Valdés."* Havana, 1927.

González Manet, Enrique. "Una incursión par *Cecilia.*" *Universidad de La Habana* 158:171–179 (1962).

Gutiérrez de la Solana, Alberto. "Ideas morales, politicas y sociales en dos novelas cubanas del siglo diecinueve." In *La literatura iberoamericana del siglo diecinueve.* (Instituto Internacional de Literatura Iberoamericana). Tucson, Ariz, 1974. Pp. 191–201.

Hernández de Norman, Isabel. "Cirilo Villaverde (1812–1894)." In *La novela criolla en las Antillas.* New York, 1977.

"Homenaje a Cirilo Villaverde." *Cuba en La UNESCO* 3–5 (1964).

Karras, M. Elizabeth. "Tragedy and Illicit Love: A Study of the Incest Motif in *Cecilia Valdés* and *Os Maias* [by José Maria de Eça de Queiroz]." Ph.D. diss., University of Colorado at Boulder, 1973.

Lamore, Jean. "Le thème de la traite negrière dans *Cecilia Valdés* de Cirilo Villaverde." In *Hommage des hispanistes français à Noël Salomon.* Barcelona, 1979. Pp. 455–463.

Leante, Cesar. "*Cecilia Valdés:* Espejo de la esclavitud." *Casa de las Américas* 15/89:19–25 (1975). Also in *El espacio real.* Havana, 1975. Pp. 27–42.

Luis, William. "*Cecilia Valdés:* The Emergence of an Antislavery Novel." *Afro-Hispanic Review* 3/2:15–19 (1985).

Martínez Bello, Antonio. "Cirilo Villaverde y la novela Cubana." *Carteles* 31/10:25–58 (1948).

Mesa y Suárez, Ramón. "Cirilo Villaverde." *Revista de la facultad de letras y ciencias de la Universidad de La Habana* 12:210–217 (1911).

Montero de Bascom, Berta. "*Cecilia Valdés.*" *Folklore americano* 21–22/17:182–188 (1972).

Nunn, Marshall E. "Some Notes on the Cuban Novel *Cecilia Valdés.*" *Bulletin of Hispanic Studies* 24: 184–186 (1947).

———. "Las obras menores de Cirilo Villaverde." *Revista iberoamericana* 14/28:255–262 (1948).

Padron, Elsie Corbera. "Un estudio sobre la mujer y el ambiente en *Cecilia Valdés* de Cirilo Villaverde." Ph.D. diss., Florida State University, 1980.

Rodriguez, Ileana. "*Cecilia Valdés* de Villaverde: Raza, clase y estructura familiar." *Areito* 18:30–36 (1979).

Rodríguez García, José A. "Sobre Cirilo Villaverde y su *Cecilia Valdés.*" *Cuba intelectual* (June 1909).

———. "La primitiva *Cecilia Valdés.* Edición del breve relato del que se deriva *Cecilia Valdés.*" *Cuba intelectual* (1910).

Ruiz, Gervasio F. "La navidad cubana en 1930 [*Cecilia Valdés*]. *Carteles* 36/51:182–183 (1955).

Sanchez, Guillermo. "Crónica." *Revista de la Biblioteca Nacional José Martí* 66/1:145–151 (1975).

Sanchez, Julio C. *La obra novelística de Cirilo Villaverde.* Madrid, 1973.

Santovenia y Echaide, Emeterio. *Cirilo Villaverde.* Havana, 1911.

———. *Personajes y paisaje de Villaverde.* Havana, 1955.

Torriente, Loló de la. *La Habana de Cecilia Valdés.* Havana, 1946.

———. "Cirilo Villaverde y la novela cubana." *Universidad de La Habana* 15/91–93:179–194 (1950).

Ximeno, José M. de. "Papeletas bibliográficas de Cirilo Villaverde." *Revista de la Biblioteca Nacional,* 2nd ser., 4/2:133–153 (1953).

Young, Robert J. *La novela costumbrista de Cirilo Villaverde.* Mexico City, 1949.

Gertrudis Gómez de Avellaneda

(1814–1873)

Elba Mata-Kolster

Gertrudis Gómez de Avellaneda, the most prolific woman writer of Hispanic America, was born in Camagüey, in Cuba's central region, on 23 March 1814. She was the daughter of Don Manuel Gómez de Avellaneda, commander of the Spanish fleet on the island, and Doña Francisca de Arteaga, of Spanish descent but a native of Cuba. Gertrudis had a happy childhood and was educated by tutors, as was customary at the time. At a very early age she showed signs of being a prodigy: in 1823 she published her first literary piece, a sonnet titled "A la muerte del Licenciado Don Manuel Gómez de Avellaneda" and in 1829, when she was only fifteen years old, she wrote her first drama, "Hernán Cortés."

The child's first sorrow was the death of her father in 1823. From that moment on Gertrudis became rebellious and independent, disliking domestic chores and stubbornly refusing to put away her books and spend more time with her friends. Her second grief was caused by the remarriage of her mother, scarcely ten months after the death of her father, to a Spanish army man, with whom Gertrudis was never able to establish an affectionate relationship. These two events deeply affected the child, who devoted herself even more to reading and writing as an escape for her emotions. Tula, as her friends called her, read French and was familiar with the works of Victor Hugo, Lord

Byron, José Quintana, George Sand, and others. She knew some of their works so well that she could recite and imitate them. The famous Cuban poet José María de Heredia was her tutor for some time, and had a profound and lasting influence on this exceptional woman.

In 1836 she fulfilled her longtime desire to travel to Europe when the whole family decided to leave Cuba. On the day of departure she wrote one of her most beautiful poems, "Al partir" (On Leaving), which shows a mature lyrical talent for a poet only twenty-two years old. On their way to Spain the family stopped at Bourdeaux, France, where Tula had many opportunities to visit the theater and the opera. But the memory of her native land saddened her, and once more she took refuge in writing; it is believed that she began her first novel, *Sab* (1841), at this time.

On leaving Bourdeaux Gertrudis decided to go to the province of Andalusia in Spain, to visit the home of her father, the town of Constantina de la Sierra. But the small village with narrow streets and very limited cultural activity soon disenchanted her, since she had imagined other landscapes and cultural climates. With her mother and her brother, Manuel, she settled in Seville, where winding streets, colorful carnations hanging from balconies, and the intense cultural life instilled new emotions and desires in her. Soon her extraordinary talent and rare beauty made her the center of attention, and the spacious house her mother had rented became a literary gathering place.

In 1839 Gertrudis met Ignacio de Cepeda y Alcaide, who became her only true love and the source of inspiration for much of her work, but also her constant source of despair and frustration. Cepeda was a law student at the University of Seville, a rich and charming man, but cold and indifferent to the poet's feelings. They became lovers, but with different perceptions, characters, and intentions. Undoubtedly, Cepeda felt a very strong attraction for Gómez de Avellaneda, but he feared her exceptional talent, her unconventionality, her ideas about freedom, and her liberty of conduct in her love life. Cepeda exercised a profound influence on her, having the power to lift her to brief moments of ecstasy and sink her into depression and melancholy. Among the most romantic works of Gómez de Avellaneda are her fifty-three letters to Cepeda, written over a period of fifteen years, 1839 to 1854. This correspondence was frequently interrupted because of his many trips throughout Europe, and it came to an end in 1854, when Cepeda married another woman. These letters reveal her uncontrollable passion for Cepeda, the bitterness that his indifference and abandonment caused her, and her internal struggle to control her feelings and protect her pride. Many of the themes are repeated in her plays, novels, and poems. The letters were carefully kept by Cepeda, and thirty-four years after Gómez de Avellaneda's death were published by Cepeda's widow under the title *Cartas de amor* (*Love Letters*, 1907).

Between 1839 and 1841 Gómez de Avellaneda, whom the literary circles began to call "La Avellaneda," published some poems in *La aureola*, a literary magazine in Cádiz, under the pen name of "La Peregrina." Soon her fame spread, and she received invitations from Málaga and Valencia to contribute to other publications. In Cádiz she met Alberto Lista, who introduced her to the Ateneo (Athenaeum) and gave her a letter of introduction for Juan Nicasio Gallego in Madrid. In Madrid Gómez de Avellaneda was welcomed in the literary circles; the beauty of her poetry and her admirable talent for writing in the best Spanish tradition amazed and captivated audiences. Juan Nicasio Gallego, José de Espronceda, Quintana, and other famous writers honored her at the Liceo. The poet José Zorilla welcomed Gómez de Avellaneda by reciting some of her poems, an event that officially marked her entrance into the literary world, proclaiming her the most outstanding woman poet of Hispanic letters. Some of the greatest literary figures of her time gathered at her residence to hear this tropical beauty recite her poems, and Gómez de Avellaneda inaugurated a series of poems dedicated to writers and people she admired with her poem "José María Heredia," about the author of *Niágara* (1825).

But Gómez de Avellaneda, an unconventional woman of determination and strong character, quickly aroused criticism and gossip. People were perturbed by her literary ambitions and independence, and compared her to George Sand. However, the two writers coincided only in their opinions about marriage, which both women attacked with very unorthodox ideas. For Gómez de Avellaneda, marriage itself was unimportant; the important element was love. She compared a bad marriage to a state of complete slavery and refused to accept the idea that marriage was a woman's only alternative. La Avellaneda, like Sor Juana Inés de la Cruz years before her, defended the right of woman to choose and forge her own destiny.

During the next twenty years Gómez de Avellaneda ventured into almost every literary genre: drama, comedy, novel, essay, legend, and, above all, lyric poetry. She became the first woman to compete with men in almost all literary endeavors. In 1840 she began her dramatic work with *Leoncia*, which had many elements of classical tragedy: jealousy, madness, incest, fatality, religion, friendship, and passionate love. In this early work we already find reflections of the poet's inner struggles and her tempestuous love for Ignacio de Cepeda. *Múnio Alfonso*, her second published play, was staged in 1844 and became her first dramatic success. The work is written in verse, and the source of its inspiration is medieval history. It tells the story of Prince Don Sancho of Castille, and of his love for Fronilde, the daughter of Múnio Alfonso. Gómez de Avellaneda skillfully combines elements of romanticism and classicism—Fronilde represents the romantic heroine, while Múnio Alfonso is the classical hero.

The same year, the drama *El príncipe de Viana* was presented; drawing again on medieval history, Gómez de Avellaneda built a plot around the familiar character of Don Carlos, the eldest son of Don Juan de Aragón. This drama did not receive the same warm ovation as *Múnio Alfonso*, but it is one of the best examples of the author's versifications. The biblical drama *Saúl* was presented at the Teatro Español in 1849. Literary critics consider it her closest approximation to Greek classical drama, and one of her best plays. The piece follows the biblical legend without any changes: Saúl represents rage, suicidal tendencies, and evil, while David represents humility and divine grace.

Baltasar (published in English as *Balshazzar*), her last dramatic work, has been judged indisputably the best of her plays. It seems to have been written in 1856, but was not produced until 1858. The source of inspiration for the work is *Sardanapalus* (1821) by Byron. The story portrays Baltasar as the powerful and corrupt king of Babylon, haughty and magnificent, but desperately searching for a great love to help him overcome the boredom of life. The success of *Baltasar*, the most romantic work of the Cuban writer, was without precedent. For the first time a play was on stage in Madrid for more than fifty consecutive days.

The dramatic production of Gómez de Avellaneda is impressive, even more so because the genre had been dominated by men until she began writing tragedies comparable in quality to those by long-established writers, such as Zorilla and the Duque de Rivas. Gómez de Avellaneda wrote sixteen dramas, twelve of them in verse; four dramas were successes, and her last one, *Baltasar*, is considered a masterpiece. Inspired by medieval history, Gómez de Avellaneda combined romantic and classical elements with a subtle touch of realism; her heroes and heroines are spiritually vulnerable, being surrounded by a materialistic world. However, Gómez de Avellaneda was first and foremost a romantic writer. She did not always follow the three unities of Greek tragedy, and she brought a new force into Spanish drama with the introduction of biblical themes. Many of the conflicts and frustrations of her tragedies

(as well as her poetry and prose) closely reflect the conflicts of her own personal life. One outstanding characteristic of her dramatic work is the mature quality of all her plays. From first to last, all give evidence of a mature artistic talent. Between 1850 and 1852 Gómez de Avellaneda wrote the following works: *Flavio Recaredo*, a drama in three acts; *La verdad vence apariencias* (Truth Is Stronger than Appearances), a drama in a less serious vein; *Errores del corazón* (The Mistakes of the Heart), her first comedy; *El donativo del diablo* (Gift from the Devil), a play based on a Swiss folktale; *La hija de las flores* (The Daughter of the Flowers), a comedy; and *La aventurera* (The Adventurer), a prose play in five acts. Three years later *Simpatía y antipatía* (Likes and Dislikes), *La hija del rey René* (The Daughter of King René), and *Oráculos de Talia* (Thalian Oracle) were produced. Partly due to the unfavorable reviews of some of these plays, she did not write for the theater again until 1858, when she wrote *Los tres amores*. Gómez de Avellaneda used her comedies to defend the right of woman to be free. In *La hija de las flores* she defends her right to choose her own destiny; in *La aventurera* and *Los tres amores* she exalts women who do not give in when threatened by power. Toward the end of her life, she wrote the comedy that posterity has considered her best, *El millonario y la maleta* (The Millionaire and the Suitcase), which was never put on stage.

In 1852, with a solid literary reputation, Gómez de Avellaneda asked the Royal Spanish Academy to grant her the privilege of occupying the chair left vacant by the death of her mentor, Juan Nicasio Gallego. But neither the time nor the country was ready to accept a woman as a member of the venerable academy, and though her literary work was equal, and sometimes far superior, to the work of many of its members, she was almost unanimously denied access.

Gómez de Avellaneda wrote six novels on varied themes—vengeance, poverty, disease, death, divorce—but with one constant element: passionate love. Only one novel, *Dolores* (1860), is historical; the others are contemporary. Her first novel was *Sab*; it is not exactly known if this work was begun in Cuba or Bourdeaux, but the vivid description of places and characters suggests that it was finished shortly after her arrival in Spain in 1840. *Sab* is the story of a black man born a free prince, and later bought as a slave. Some critics have considered *Sab* an abolitionist novel, but others have argued that the theme of slavery is no more important than the beautiful description of the Cuban landscape. *Sab* is the first Hispanic American novel written by a native, and the first to deal with the problem of slavery.

Espatolino was published in serial format in *El laberinto* of Madrid in 1844. The source of inspiration was an article published in Cuba years before, about an Italian thief who for years pillaged the provinces. *Espatolino* follows the romantic tradition but also has the humorous picaresque element of the "gracioso" of the Golden Age. *Guatimozín, último emperador de Méjico* (*Cuauhtemac, the Last Aztec Emperor*, 1846), is a historic novel with an American theme that describes the Aztec civilization and the character of Hernán Cortés. This work underwent extensive modification when Gómez de Avellaneda revised all her production for publication toward the end of her life. She even changed the title of the novel to *Una anécdota de la vida de Cortés* (An Anecdote of the Life of Cortés).

The novels of Gómez de Avellaneda have not been considered the best part of her work. More extensive study is necessary, however, before passing a definite judgment. Almost all her novels can be judged contemporary and romantic, and all share the conception that man cannot escape his fate.

The lyrical work of Gómez de Avellaneda is without doubt the most beautiful and important part of her work. She was above all a poet, and it is her poetry that has secured her a very special place in Hispanic American letters. Critics, often severe in judging her work, have unanimously agreed that her poetry is beautiful and almost flawless. Her first volume of poetry, *Poesías* (Poems), was published in 1841, with 54 poems. The second volume, also entitled *Poesías*, appeared in 1850 with 129 poems. However, her poetic work began in Cuba in 1836 when she wrote "Al partir." The theme of the poem is Cuba, and there are notes of pain, sadness, and fear of the unpredictable future. This poem contains all the elements that were to characterize the rest of her poetry. Twenty-four years later, when she returned to

Cuba, she wrote the poem "La vuelta a la patria" (The Return to the Fatherland), but this time her dreams and hopes were not what they had been in 1836. In this piece she speaks of the flora, the mountains, and the tropical sun of her Cuba, with nostalgia for the time that has irremediably gone by. In thirteen of her poems she extols unchangeable, eternal nature, which she compares with the brevity and futility of man's life. The infinitude of the ocean fills her spirit with apprehension ("Al mar"); but the beauty and coloring of the seasons ("La primavera") revive her hopes, and the songs of the birds ("A mi jilguero") bring back memories of her distant native land. In some poems she compares her emotional states with the seasons of the year. The hours of the day aroused in her profound and diverse emotions, especially the night, which she describes as a period of rest for body and soul. This seems a paradox, because Gómez de Avellaneda worked at night.

As the poet grew old her religious fervor increased. In her first volume of poetry she included one religious poem, and in her second volume twelve. After periods of crisis her thoughts always turned to religion, as she was in constant need of divine help. She was frequently affected with paralysis of will, periods of torpor from which she would emerge thanks only to her determination and faith in God. Her poetic output is a compression of neoclassical and romantic styles; while some of her poems follow the romantic tradition, others can be classified as neoclassical in form and content. Her mastery of meter and rhyme was such that she used the whole range of metrical and rhyme possibilities of the Spanish language. Her sources of inspiration are many; thematically her poems address Cuba, Spain, religion, public occasions, meditation, and especially love. Ignacio de Cepeda inspired many of her best poems: she wrote two poems with the same title "A él" (To Him). The first reveals an intense love, young and full of hope, and the second, a feeling of resignation and pain. Other poems that may be related to Cepeda are *El porqué de la inconstancia* (A Reason for Inconstancy) and *Amor y orgullo* (Love and Pride).

She also wrote a series of poems dedicated to writers and people she admired. This series began with her poem "A la muerte del célebre poeta cubana Don José María Heredia" (On the Death of the

Celebrated Cuban Poet Don José María Heredia), and includes "A la muerte del laureado poeta Señor Don Manuel José Quintana" (On the Death of the Poet Laureate Señor Don Manuel José Quintana), "A la muerte del joven y distinguido poeta Don José de Espronceda" (On the Death of the Young and Distinguished Poet Don José de Espronceda), and several poems dedicated to Queen Isabella II.

Love eluded Gertrudis Gómez de Avellaneda. The men who loved her were intellectually her inferiors and could not give her the passionate love she longed for. She married twice. When she was thirty-two years old and had already secured a reputation as a writer, she married Pedro Sabater, who died within three months of the marriage. In 1854 she married Coronel Domingo Verdugo, aide to the king and a gentleman of the chamber; the marriage was celebrated at the royal palace, for Gómez de Avellaneda had had friendly relations with Isabella II since 1843, when she wrote the queen a beautiful ode.

Gómez de Avellaneda returned to Cuba in 1859 with her husband, who had been appointed governor of the province of Cienfuegos. Cuba welcomed the illustrious poet with a crown of gold and laurel. In the four years she spent in Cuba she was as productive as in her years in Spain, despite the rapid deterioration of her health. She published a biweekly magazine, *Album cubano*, in which she included several articles in defense of women, reflecting the old pain and bitterness over the incident with the Royal Spanish Academy. She finished her last novel, *El artista barquero* (The Guiding Hand of the Artist, 1861), a story of love in tropical Cuba, and also wrote two legends, *El aura blanca* (White Halo, 1859) and *El cacique de Turmeque* (Chief Turmeque, 1859).

She returned to Spain in 1865, after the death of her second husband. But Spain was no longer the place she had left only a few years before. The country was in political turmoil, the reign of Isabella II was coming to an end, there were no more literary gatherings for Gómez de Avellaneda, and her name had been almost forgotten. Alone, she devoted herself to revising her works in five volumes—one of poetry, two of drama, and two of novels and other pieces. She accomplished this compilation in three years, 1869 to 1871.

Devastated by diabetes, she died in Madrid on 1 February 1873, at the age of fifty-nine. She died unknown in the country in which thirty years earlier she had been proclaimed the first poet of Hispanic America, and far away from the land where she was born, Cuba, the pearl of the sea.

SELECTED BIBLIOGRAPHY

First Editions

Poetry

A la muerte de Licenciado Don Manuel Gómez de Avellaneda. Havana, 1823.
Poesías. Madrid, 1841.
Poesías. Madrid, 1850.
El héroe de Bailén. Havana, 1853.

Prose Narratives

Sab. Madrid, 1841.
Dos mujeres. Madrid, 1842.
La Baronesa de Joux. Havana, 1844.
Espatolino. Havana, 1844.
Guatimozín, último emperador de Méjico. Madrid, 1846.
El aura blanca. Matanzas, Cuba, 1859.
El cacique de Turmeque. Matanzas, Cuba, 1859.
Dolores. Havana, 1860.
El artista barquero. Havana, 1861.

Plays

Leoncia. Madrid, 1840.
Múnio Alfonso. Madrid, 1844.
El príncipe de Viana. Madrid, 1844.
Egilona. Madrid, 1845.
Saúl. Madrid, 1849.
Flavio Recaredo. Madrid, 1851.
El donativo del diablo. Madrid, 1852.
Errores del corazón. Madrid, 1852.
La hija de las flores. Madrid, 1852.
La verdad vence apariencias. Madrid, 1852.
La aventurera. Madrid, 1853.
La mano de Dios. Matanzas, Cuba, 1853.
La hija del rey René. Madrid, 1855.
Simpatía y antipatía. Madrid, 1855.
Oráculos de Talia. Madrid, 1855.
Baltasar. Madrid, 1858.

Los tres amores. Madrid, 1858.
El millonario y la maleta. Madrid, 1869.

Letters

Autobiografía y cartas de la ilustre poetisa hasta ahora inéditas. Introduction by Lorenzo Cruz de Fuentes. Huelva, Spain, 1907.
Cartas de amor. Madrid, 1907.
Cartas inéditas y documentos relativos a su vida en Cuba de 1859 a 1864. Matanzas, Cuba, 1912.

Collected Works

Antología (poesías y cartas amorosas). Edited and with an introduction by Ramón Gómez de la Serna. Buenos Aires, 1945.
Obras de Doña Gertrudis Gómez de Avellaneda. Edited and with a preliminary study by José María Castro y Calvo. Vols. 272, 278, 279, 287, and 288 of the Library of Spanish Authors series. Madrid, 1974.
Obras literarias. 5 vols. Edited by Gertrudis Gómez de Avellaneda. Madrid, 1869–1871.
Teatro cubano del siglo XIX: Antología. With an introduction by Natividad Gonzalez Freire. Havana, 1975.

Modern Editions

Baltasar. Edited, with prologue and notes, by Carmen Bravo-Villasante. Salamanca, Spain, 1973.
Sab. Edited, with prologue and notes, by Carmen Bravo-Villasante. Salamanca, Spain, 1970.

Translations

Balshazzar. Translated by William Freeman Burbank. San Francisco, 1914.
Cuauhtemac, the Last Aztec Emperor. Translated by Mrs. Wilson W. Blake. Mexico City, 1898.
Love Letters. Translated by Dorrey Malcolm. Havana, 1956.

Biographical and Critical Studies

Aramburu y Machado, Mariano. *Personalidad literaria de Doña Gertrudis Gómez de Avellaneda.* Madrid, 1898.
Ballesteros, Mercedes. *Vida de la Avellaneda.* Madrid, 1949.
Bernal, Emilia. "Gertrudis Gómez de Avellaneda: Su vida y su obra." *Cuba contemporanea* 37 (1925).
Carlos, Alberto J. "La Avellaneda y la mujer." In *Actas del tercer congreso internacional de hispanistas. Mexico, 26–31 agosto 1968.* Mexico City, 1970.
Cotarelo y Mori, Emilio. *La Avellaneda y sus obras: Ensayo biográfico y crítico.* Madrid, 1930. Contains *Hortensia,* previously unpublished.
Lazo, Raimundo. *Gertrudis Gómez de Avellaneda: La mujer y la poetisa lírica.* Mexico City, 1972.
Marquina, Rafael. *Gertrudis Gómez de Avellaneda: La Peregrina.* Havana, 1939.
Pinera, Estela A. "El teatro romantico de Gertrudis Gómez de Avellaneda." Ph.D. diss., New York University, 1974.

Bibliography

Gertrudis Gomez de Avellaneda: Bibliografía y iconografía. Edited by Domingo Figarola-Caneda. Madrid, 1929.

José Mármol

(1817–1871)

Delfín Leocadio Garasa

Literary romanticism in Latin America was not merely an imitation or import of the cultural movement that shook Europe at the end of the eighteenth century. The two movements shared salient features: the predominance of imagination and feeling over reason, of freedom of expression over the imitation of classical models, of the emanation of subjectivity over universal ideas. These characteristics, in many cases, were accompanied by a yearning for the absolute, which, when frustrated, sunk romantics into melancholy, despair, and sorrow. Beyond these shared characteristics, romanticism in Latin America is usually associated as well with political independence from Spain and some of its tragic sequels, such as anarchy and despotism, which revealed the distance that separated idealism and the action of darker forces.

Romanticism developed in the River Plate region before emerging in Mexico or Peru. A tendency present in the minds of the younger generation was favored by the return in 1830 of Esteban Echeverría from Paris, where he had spent five years amid the fervent polemics of the romantics against classicism. Echeverría was the founder in 1837 of the Asociación de Mayo, a literary society whose members discussed historical and political themes; it was closed soon after by the government. Only exile remained as an alternative to the Young Generation of 1837, as it is called in histories of Argentine culture, which for fifteen years was forced to develop its activities in the Banda Oriental of Uruguay, in Chile, and in Bolivia.

The most representative poet of this period is undoubtedly Mármol, because of the force of his lyricism, which impregnates not only his poetry but also his dramas and his historical novel. Born in Buenos Aires on 2 December 1817, he attended the College of Moral Sciences. His rebellious temperament could not tolerate the arbitrary government of Juan Manuel de Rosas, an authoritative and intolerant leader who was popular among the lower classes. Rosas called himself the restorer of the laws, but he respected no law other than the imposition of his will. In 1839, Mármol, like many others, was sent to prison, where he remained for a short time; that unfortunate episode marked his life and his inspiration. He has described in "A Rosas (El 25 de mayo de 1843)" (To Rosas [25 May 1843]) how with burned sticks he wrote verses against the tyrant on the walls of his cell: "¡Bárbaro! nunca matarás mi alma / ni pondrás grillos a mi mente, no!" (Barbarian, you never will kill the soul / neither will you fetter the mind, no). In a later poem Mármol spoke of his "jail and chains." On leaving the prison, he lived in a more or less clandestine way, in the houses of relatives and friends, until in 1840 he could cross the River Plate into Uruguay. Exile was for many contemporary young men a kind of rite of initiation, an encounter with identity and destiny.

Mármol's life and works represent the struggle against the tyrant. Every 25 May, the anniversary of the date on which, in 1810, the freedom of the colony of the River Plate was proclaimed, the poet painfully evoked those ideals, frustrated in an Argentina oppressed by a merciless tyranny. Mármol's exaltation of liberty has as an inevitable corollary the hatred of Rosas, whose mere name scorned it. In "A Rosas" he writes: "¡Ah, Rosas! No se puede reverenciar a Mayo / sin arrojarte eterna, terrible maldición" (Ah Rosas, one cannot pay tribute to May / without thrusting an eternal terrible curse upon you). His sonorous stanzas, almost martial, are a personal confrontation with the despot. As if his own voice did not suffice, he begs the tempest to lend him its howling with which to curse Rosas. Domingo Faustino Sarmiento called Mármol the "poet of the curse." At times he reaches the electrifying vibration of the prophets of the Bible: "que entonces de ese Rosas que te abomina tanto / ni el polvo de sus huesos la América tendrá" (and then of that Rosas who so abominates you / not even his ashes will America hold). It is easy to imagine the echo that the fury of those bronze verses—published in *La Semana* of Montevideo, a newspaper he directed—would achieve among the exiles not only in Uruguay but also beyond the Andes or in the Altiplano (Bolivia).

Criticism has recognized the indignant force of his accent; its rancor exists by its own impetus, independent of history. Marcelino Menéndez y Pelayo, not always well disposed to the Latin American poetry of the period, has pointed out the Spanish roots of Mármol's poetry, unusual at a time and within a generation that rejected the Hispanic tradition. "In his imprecations against Rosas there is such an outburst, such vigor, such a sincere hatred, such a strange ferocity of thought, which although sometimes repugnant because of its monstrosity, at other times becomes gigantic enough to touch the sublime in its invective." He adds that the least passionate

reader cannot but feel inflamed with a similar fury, and that while Mármol does not always distinguish justice from vengeance neither does he isolate the patriot's fervor from the executioner's cruelty. The presence of some poetic exaggeration cannot be denied, but evidently the poet's hatred has drawn the historical image of many American autocrats.

The critic Calixto Oyuela complained that the power of those verses against tyranny threw a shadow over the delicacy of other of Mármol's works that are less compromised and strident but imbued with deep poetry. Many were collected in his book *Armonías* (Harmonies, 1851); the varied poems include religious and amatory compositions, as well as some poems of circumstance.

Mármol's most important lyrical work is *Cantos del peregrino* (Songs of the Pilgrim, 1847), published fragmentarily and now completed thanks to the erudition and diligence of Elvira Burlando de Meyer. In this work, Mármol created, under the confessed influence of Lord Byron's *Childe Harold*, poetic compositions of a different character and aesthetic value; its subject matter covers all the nuances of romanticism. It shows his skill in the employment of all kinds of poetic meters, although some of the poems are more outstanding for their sincerity than for their correctness.

Almost all of the writing in *Cantos del peregrino* is autobiographically inspired; like the Pilgrim, Mármol visited Rio de Janeiro, where he passed some happy moments, dazzled by its tropical exuberance. From there he sailed southward, aiming to reach Chile through the Straits of Magellan. A terrible storm prevented him from crossing Cape Horn and the captain decided to return to the port of departure. In the vision of the poem, this voyage acquired symbolic significance; the pilgrim was a deeply-rooted archetype (Ulysses, Sinbad, Ossian, Harold) resurrected by the romantics as a representation of the yearning for the infinite that inspired them. Mármol wrote in the preface of *Poesías completas* (1946–1947) that the poem is "a hymn in praise of the splendid nature of our continent" and "the history of the Argentine exile's heart."

Various of Mármol's poems are dedicated to American nature. The importance of nature shook the romantic soul intensely, and the natural elements became animated when contemplated by the poet, as if between nature and the poet's spirit a profound copenetration was established that transfigured both, impregnating spirit with cosmic power and nature with sensitivity. From the sea, the poet has a vision of the future of America, at that time a victim of disorder and oppression: in time freedom would come and law would prevail, just as the men who fought for independence had dreamed.

The romantic love that Mármol exalts in *Cantos del peregrino* has painful resonances; it even seems to delight in the suffering of its loss or the fear of losing it, although such feelings are punctuated with humor, reminiscences of home, and realistic descriptions of the crew and passengers. As the ship crosses the latitude of Buenos Aires, the poet cannot avoid nostalgia for the pampa. This longing for the unattainable country is typical of exiles and always occurs together with resentment against those responsible for the oppression and separation. His patriotic sentiments become stronger when the Pilgrim returns, after the failure of his journey; his gaze is directed to the evanescent coast bathed by the River Plate.

From a rigorously aesthetic point of view, it must be admitted that Mármol, rushed along by his facility for versifying, did not always correct formal, lexicographic, and syntactic weaknesses in his work; he let stand imprecisions, prosaisms, and even improprieties, many of them due to haste, a characteristic common to many romantic poets.

Mármol possessed an authentic theatrical vocation, but his wandering destiny and the surroundings in which he moved (Montevideo, under siege by General Oribe, a Uruguayan supporter of Rosas; Rio de Janeiro, where a different language was spoken) prevented him from consolidating himself as a playwright. His only two plays, *El poeta* (The Poet, 1842) and *El cruzado* (The Crusader, 1842) allow us to assume that his dramatic writing might have been similar in description and quality to that of the Duque de Rivas, García Gutiérrez, or even José Zorrilla. *El poeta* is a tragic love drama with an inevitable sad denouement. *El cruzado* takes place in Asia and deals with a complicated plot of love and jealousy, betrayal and perjury, developed against exotic scenery and in a grandiloquent style.

Amalia was first published in 1851 in the form of a weekly serial, like many works of that time. Mármol's purpose, as he describes in the preface to *Obras completas* (Complete Works, 1854), was to present "an ample picture of the political events during the last years of the dictatorship," although the action of the novel takes place in the course of only a few months. This contemporary approach prevents it from being grouped with the romantic historical novels influenced by Sir Walter Scott. Its plot revolves round Eduardo Belgrano's unsuccessful flight to Montevideo; he escapes wounded from an ambush, thanks to the help of his friend Daniel Bello, who takes him to the house of his cousin Amalia, a young widow who will shelter him from Rosist persecution. During Belgrano's convalescence, he and Amalia fall in love. Before they can move to a safer place in the north of the city and get married, they are discovered by the *mazorca* (the police), and their lives end in a bloodbath.

The real protagonist of the novel is Bello, a brilliant and astute young man, a sincere patriot who manages to fool official functionaries and act as an intermediary for the opposition. In *Amalia* one can clearly observe the characteristic polarization of romanticism. The men who confront one another in the novel, adversaries and supporters of Rosas, were not only opposed in their ideas and in the armed struggle, but also in their appearance, manners, and clothes, in the delicacy of some and the roughness of others, in terms of refined sensitivity versus coarseness, of elegance versus vulgarity. The description of Amalia's house, an oasis of refinement in the center of the dusty and muddy city, a prey to barbarism and terror, forms a functional part of the novel, as do the descriptions of the office of Rosas, who works in the late hours of night, among sordid and grotesque characters, and the house of his sister-in-law, María Josefa Ezcurra, who has organized a system of spying based on informers. In spite of this schematism, the novel provides sagacious observation and penetrating psychological wisdom. Details of plot and character are historically and autobiographically based.

Mármol has the capacity to narrate, and modern readers are still drawn to his novel, even though the writing sometimes shows signs of negligence. *Maria* (1867) by the Colombian Jorge Isaacs and Mármol's

Amalia are the most popular novels of Latin American romanticism.

The defeat of Rosas at the battle of Caseros in 1852 permitted the return of the exiles to their country. Many of them took up important functions (Sarmiento, Bartolomé Mitre, Juan María Gutiérrez), but not Mármol, who, although respected, reached a more modest destiny as director of the National Library of Buenos Aires.

Mármol was no revolutionary and did not form part of the Asociación de Mayo; he did not share the ideals of Echeverría as delineated in the *Dogma socialista*, an interpretation of the May Revolution's ideals. He remained faithful to the Catholicism of his ancestors and did not adopt the vague deism of his generation. In politics, he was convinced of the excellence of a unitarian government with power centered in Buenos Aires until the end of his life. There was an aristocratic quality about his spirit and bearing that kept him at a distance from political conflicts. For him romanticism was primarily an aesthetic attitude, and his rancorous opposition to Rosas was based on respect for human dignity rather than on the rejection of a political system. His poetic attacks against tyranny arose more as a result of repulsion than from principle. There lie his limitation and his great universality: his novel and poems separate themselves from their historical context, go beyond their time, and touch the oppressed everywhere.

José Mármol died in Buenos Aires on 9 August 1871.

SELECTED BIBLIOGRAPHY

First Editions

Cantos del peregrino. Montevideo, 1847.
Armonías. Montevideo, 1851.
Obras completas. Buenos Aires, 1854. Includes *Amalia*.
Obras poéticas y dramáticas. Paris, 1875.

Modern Editions

Amalia. Introduction and notes by Adolfo Mitre. 2 vols. Buenos Aires, 1944.
Cantos del peregrino. Edited and with an introduction by Elvira Burlando de Meyer. Buenos Aires, 1965.
Poesías completas. Edited and with an introduction by Rafael Alberto Arrieta. 2 vols. Buenos Aires, 1946–1947.

Translations

Amalia. Translated by Mary J. Serrano. New York, 1919.

Biographical and Critical Studies

Alberdi, Juan B. *Escritos póstumos* 15. Buenos Aires, 1900. Pp. 572–583.
Cuthberson, Stuart. *The Poetry of José Mármol*. University of Colorado Studies, General Series 22:2–3 (1935).
Giménez Pastor, Arturo. *El romanticismo bajo la tiranía*. Buenos Aires, 1922. Pp. 29–63, 132–145.
Menéndez y Pelayo, Marcelino. *Historia de la poesía hispanoamericana* 2. Madrid, 1913.
Oyuela, Calixto, *Poetas hispanoamericanos* 1. Buenos Aires, 1949–1950. Pp. 131–178.
Rohde, Jorge Max. *Las ideas estéticas en la literatura argentina*. Buenos Aires, 1921–1922. 1: Pp. 129–151; 2: Pp. 233–238.
Rojas, Ricardo. *Historia de la literatura argentina* 3. Buenos Aires, 1920. Ch. 15.

Antônio Gonçalves Dias

(1823–1864)

Almir C. Bruneti

Among all representative poets of Brazilian romanticism (1830–1880), Antônio Gonçalves Dias is surely the one whose name will remain inextricably linked with the emergence of a truly national Brazilian literature. He is also, thematically and technically, the best poet of the romantic period in Brazil. Being the natural son of a Portuguese immigrant and a Brazilian *cafuza* (a woman of mixed Indian and African blood), Gonçalves Dias incorporates in his person one of the most cherished myths created by postindependence nationalism: that of the three races (Indian, black, white) mingling harmoniously together to form a Brazilian nation free from all prejudices. This myth, elevated to the rank of active sociological and racial theory, is still prevalent among some segments of the Brazilian intelligentsia.

Soon after Gonçalves Dias' birth on 10 August 1823 in Caxias, Maranhão, João Manuel Gonçalves Dias, fearing the strong anti-Portuguese sentiments bred by independence, decided to return to Portugal for some time. He came back to Brazil to rejoin his companion, Vicência Mendes Ferreira, and their son in 1825. After four years of happy childhood in the company of his parents, Gonçalves Dias was confronted with the harsh reality of having to leave his mother, whom his father had "dismissed" in order to marry Adelaide Ramos de Almeida, and to go live with the new couple. In 1830 he began his education. At first he attended a private school and later was tutored by a cousin who worked at his father's store. His dedication to reading, probably a compensation for the lack of real warmth in a home dominated by a stern father and an antagonistic stepmother, so impressed the elder Gonçalves Dias that he was determined to give his son the opportunity for true education by enrolling him in another excellent private school and then taking him to Portugal to enroll in the University of Coimbra. The latter part of the plan was not carried out because João Manuel died in São Luís a few days before they were to embark for Portugal. The young Gonçalves Dias returned to Caxias, but did go to Coimbra a year later, in 1838, this time sent by his stepmother, who, at the urging of Gonçalves Dias' former teacher and other friends, had agreed to fulfill her late husband's desires.

In October 1838, Gonçalves Dias was already in Coimbra, enrolled in the College of Arts in courses that would allow him to register for the 1839–1840 academic year. This period of his life had a marked effect on the development of his artistic as well as personal temperament, above all because it was a period of economic hardship, which deepened his impression of himself as a beggar relying on charity in order to pursue his studies. It was only through the compassionate help of his Brazilian friends at the university that he was able to pay for his subsistence when his stepmother failed to send him money, and eventually (in 1845) he had to leave Portugal before completing his law degree and return home with passage to be paid on his arrival in Brazil. In a letter to his friend Alexandre Teófilo de Carvalho Leal, dated 1 May 1845 from Caxias, he says: "Sad was my life in Coimbra—for it's sad to live outside one's own country, climb other people's steps and sit at their table out of charity to eat . . . the bread of pity" (*Poesia Completa e Prosa Escolhida*, 1959, p. 799). His economic situation improved significantly only after the publication of *Primeiros Cantos* (First Songs) in 1847. But the Coimbra period was also important because his absence from country and family intensified in his soul the indefinable feeling of *saudades*, the nostalgia so essential to the best lyric poetry written in Portuguese. This circumstance, coupled with the fact that while at Coimbra he belonged to a group of youthful writers known as "the medievalists," accounts for the main themes addressed in his poetic work—childhood memories, the Indian (that is, the Brazilian "medieval knight"), nature, and love. "Love" figures prominently in all of Gonçalves Dias' works mainly because he was a great lover, possibly more in love with love than with the countless paramours he had throughout his lifetime. During his student years in Coimbra he fell "seriously" in love at least three times. In 1841 he almost married the daughter of the owner of the pension-house where he was staying in Lisbon. The poem "Inocência" (*Primeiros Cantos*) was inspired by one of the young ladies he courted in Coimbra.

Gonçalves Dias' first published poem dates from 1841; it appeared in a booklet entitled *Lede*, which contained five poems by different authors written to commemorate the crowning of Emperor Peter II of Brazil. The poem was recited by the poet himself at a celebration organized by the Brazilian students to salute the end of a very troubled period in national politics. Many of the poems later included in *Primeiros Cantos* were also composed during Gonçalves Dias' school years at Coimbra. First among these is the famous "Canção do Exílio" (Song of Exile), which was originally part of an autobiographical

novel called "Memórias de Agapito" (The Memoirs of Agapito), burned by the author because of personal references, and of which only a few fragments survive. It was also during this time that he wrote two of his four historical dramas—*Beatriz Cenci* and *Patkull*. (The latter deals with Johan Reinhold von Patkull [1660–1707], the Livonian patriot who fought against Swedish domination in a territory that is now part of the Soviet Union.)

In March 1845 Gonçalves Dias arrived in São Luís and a few days later departed for Caxias, where he lived with his stepmother until, forced by political hostility, he returned to São Luís in January 1846. He stayed with his dear friend Alexandre Teófilo, who obtained for him a free ticket to Rio de Janeiro, where he remained until June of the same year. During this time he wrote two poems inspired by Ana Amélia, the great frustrated love of his life, who was just a child then, and he finished his poetic prose composition "Meditação" (Meditation), the first piece in Brazilian letters to condemn slavery. In Rio he again relied on the kindness of his former university friends for support. At the same time he started to gather historical material for a host of literary projects, becoming an assiduous reader at the National Library. Soon, he contracted for the publication of *Primeiros Cantos* with the Laemmert publishing house. He had set his hopes for fame and fortune on the production of his drama *Beatriz Cenci*. But the censors of the Dramatic Conservatory, while praising the drama for its style and inventiveness, vetoed its presentation on the allegation that it was "immoral." In November 1846 Gonçalves Dias wrote to Alexandre Teófilo: "My *Beatriz* received maximum excommunication as a penalty, that is, it is forbidden to enter the Shrine of the Arts—scilicet—the Theater." In the same long letter he again refers to his play as "my sweet *Beatriz* . . . which was failed cum laude" (*Poesia Completa*, p. 802). Not discouraged, however, he immediately submitted *Leonor de Mendonça* (written in thirty days) to the conservatory. This time his play was approved, though it was not produced due to the refusal of the famous actor-director João Caetano to stage it.

The 1840's were possibly the most creative years of Gonçalves Dias' life. Along with an incredibly active social life, packed with dances, theater outings, visits, and, especially, romantic adventures of all types, he started to work on the poems that constitute most of the volume *Segundos Cantos* (Second Songs, 1848), and on "Sextilhas de Frei Antão" (Friar Antão's Sextets), published in the same volume. It is also at this time that he began work on the epic *Os Timbiras* (The Timbria Indians), of which only four cantos were later published in Leipzig (in 1857).

The critical reaction to the publication of *Primeiros Cantos* in January 1847 (with the title page bearing the date 1846) was slow in coming, but brought public acclaim with an article by Alexandre Herculano, dean of Portuguese romantic poetry, in the *Revista Universal Lisbonense* (Lisbon Universal Review) of 30 November. As early as April of the same year, when the first positive review appeared, Gonçalves Dias was conscious of having started a "kind of literary revolution" and saw that he was becoming the "first poet of Brazil." In September 1847 he was admitted as a member to the Brazilian Historical and Geographical Institute, and was appointed secretary and professor of Latin of the recently opened Liceu de Niterói (Niterói High School). May 1848 witnessed the publication of *Segundos Cantos*, received by the critics and the public with the same praise and enthusiasm that had been lavished on the first volume. That same month he requested a leave of absence from his teaching job in order to cover the debates of the Senate and the Chamber of Deputies for the newspapers *Jornal do Comércio* and *Correio Mercantil*; he held this assignment until 1850.

The year 1849 saw Gonçalves Dias' fortunes prosper. He was appointed professor of Latin and Brazilian history at the most prestigious school of that time, Colégio Pedro II, with a sizable salary. At the same time that he was executing a myriad of other functions—journalist, teacher, active member of the institute—he participated, together with his fellow writers Araújo Porto Alegre and Joaquim Manuel de Macedo, in the publishing of a new literary journal called *Guanabara*, whose first issue appeared on 2 December 1849. As it was the emperor's birthday, the three editors went to the palace to present a copy of the new publication to Peter II. When the emperor noticed that, unlike his colleagues, Gonçalves Dias did not display any decoration on his lapel, he had his name added to the list of newly appointed Cavaliers

of the Order of the Rose to be published that very day. The poet was not amused. According to Manuel Bandeira (*Poesia completa*, p. 27), he shunned the honor out of modesty, and said: "I do not want to be confused with some storekeeper or slave trader; it is enough that they already wrap the butter and sugar in the paper on which I write." However, a little further on Bandeira adds that "neither the emperor nor [Gonçalves Dias'] friends knew . . . how much pride there was under that 'inflexible mask,' under those modest manners." He was happier, however, with the theme the emperor assigned him to develop at the Historical Institute—a comparison of the Brazilian aborigines with those of Oceania. The long essay, titled "Brasil e Oceania," was read at several meetings of the institute between August 1852 and June 1853. It was published in *Obras Póstumas* (vol. 6) in 1869.

In 1850 Gonçalves Dias was taken ill with yellow fever, then one of the scourges of Rio. He did not remain inactive for long, though, and worked hard on *Boabdil*, a drama about the last Moorish king of Granada (Spain), during his recovery. He discontinued work with the Senate and the Chamber, but resumed collaboration with the press as soon as he could. At the same time he was working toward the publication of *Últimos Cantos* (Last Songs), which appeared early the following year. In June 1850, because of a rift with his fellow editors, he broke off with the journal *Guanabara*. In spite of the pessimistic tone of some of Gonçalves Dias' observations about his own work after *Últimos Cantos* appeared, this volume contains some of his best Indian poetry, such as "I-Juca-Pirama" (The One About to Die) and "A Canção do Tamoio" (The Tamoio Indian Song). It also includes the famous "O Gigante de Pedra" (The Giant of Stone), which became a symbol of Brazil's still unaccomplished potentialities.

In March 1851 Gonçalves Dias departed for the northern states of the country, charged by the government with the tasks of checking on the conditions of public instruction in those provinces and of gathering historical documents scattered in regional archives. It was during this trip that he re-encountered Ana Amélia at the home of his friend Alexandre Teófilo, who was her cousin and brother-in-law. She was now a charming young lady, and the poet fell helplessly in love. Anticipating a probable negative reply from her mother, Gonçalves Dias asked for Ana Amélia's hand in marriage at the last moment of his stay in Maranhão. He made his request in a letter in which, curiously, he tried to give the worst impression of himself. Among other things, he told Mrs. Ferreira do Vale that he had no ambition to figure prominently in Brazilian politics or to acquire great wealth (*Poesia Completa*, p. 811). The same scruples were iterated in another letter to Ana Amélia's brother, José Joaquim, some time later (p. 813). Gonçalves Dias' biographers are unanimous in stressing his sense of propriety and his pride, for he would marry his beloved only with the formal consent of her mother. Thus, when he received a negative response from Mrs. Ferreira do Vale (allegedly due to her racial and social prejudices), he declined to marry Ana Amélia in spite of her proposal that they should do so without her mother's permission. Manuel Bandeira says: "The man overruled the lover and the poet" (*Poesia Completa*, p. 31). Lúcia Miguel Pereira states that Gonçalves Dias' reaction to the refusal revealed "a noble character, completely devoid of rebelliousness, resentment, or selfishness" (*A vida . . .* , p. 162). They both accept the poet's statement in a letter to José Joaquim (referred to above) concerning the possibility of a negative reply: "I will not complain, nor will I have reasons to do so. . . . There will be nothing that will make me forget that I am your friend and a friend of the family's." Thus, this lack of action toward the fruition of his happiness is attributed to his sense of honor. This might very well have been the case, but Gonçalves Dias had countless love affairs without being able to remain faithful to anyone.

When he finally married Olímpia da Costa on 26 September 1852, if one is to believe his letter of May 1854 to Teófilo, it was only because of her persistence and her tricks. He eventually went so far as to blame her for the tuberculosis that he had probably inherited from his father. It goes without saying that theirs was an extremely unhappy marriage. In the last part of Gonçalves Dias' life they did not even live in the same house.

As the estrangement between him and his wife increased, Gonçalves Dias kept busy by participating in the meetings of the Historical Institute and by teaching. He was appointed to serve at the Foreign Office in December 1852, a post he held along with his chair at the Colégio Pedro II, now teaching only Brazilian history, from which he would soon request a leave of absence.

In June 1854 he departed for Europe in the company of his wife, who was pregnant, and his young sister-in-law. They were joined by his father-in-law later. The party visited Lisbon first, where Gonçalves Dias was received with enthusiasm. In November they were already in Paris, where his daughter, Joana, was born. She was a sickly baby and died in 1856. Gonçalves Dias was not happy with the birth of this child, the product of a loveless union. He even blamed his wife for the poor health of the unfortunate Joana.

In 1855 Gonçalves Dias traveled alone to England and then to Lisbon. There he met by chance Ana Amélia on the street one day. She had married a Portuguese businessman, Domingos da Silva Porto, who, according to António Henriques Leal, "was in the same unfavorable conditions of origin and birth" as Gonçalves Dias. Soon after the wedding, due to her husband's fraudulent bankruptcy, she had to accompany him to Lisbon, where Gonçalves Dias met her. This unexpected encounter inspired him to write the famous poem "Ainda uma Vez—Adeus!" (Once Again, Good-bye!, published in "Novos Cantos," 1860). On the whole, this unfulfilled romance with Ana Amélia resulted in Gonçalves Dias writing some of his best lyric compositions.

While in Portugal Gonçalves Dias was appointed to the commission in charge of representing Brazil at the International Exhibit in Paris. In March 1856 his wife returned to Brazil. Gonçalves Dias stayed in Europe until 1858, visiting Spain, Portugal, Belgium, Germany, and Austria. The highlight was his sojourn in Germany, where he contracted for an edition of his previously published work with the Brockhaus concern of Leipzig. The new volume, which appeared with the title *Cantos* (1857; 3rd ed. 1860), included new compositions under the name "Novos Cantos." The same firm also published the first four cantos of *Os Timbiras* and Gonçalves Dias' *Dicionário da Língua Tupi* (Dictionary of the Tupi Language, 1858). These European travels were interspersed with several love affairs and many bouts of disease.

In September 1858 the poet was back in Rio, ready

to start work as head of the ethnography section of the Commission for Scientific Exploration, created in 1856, to which he had been appointed in the same year. The commission left Rio in January 1859 to visit all of the states of northern Brazil. Gonçalves Dias returned to Rio only in December 1861, after an incredible voyage that took him to the Venezuelan border and was occupied by his amorous adventures and steadily failing health. The diary he wrote during this trip has been published as an appendix to Pereira's biography of the poet.

Although sick, Gonçalves Dias was famous now; everybody, including the emperor, tried to make things easier for him, especially at a time when he no longer lived with his wife. As his marital problems mounted and his health grew worse, he decided to go to his native Maranhão where he could find a better climate and the love and affection of Teófilo's family. He left Rio, which he would never see again, on 7 April 1862. His clinical condition could not have been more serious: he had been diagnosed as suffering from a heart condition, syphilis, chronic liver disease, and possibly cancer of the lungs. His biographers talk about tuberculosis, but since Gonçalves Dias was a chain smoker, one might assume cancer instead. Upon arriving in Recife, he became convinced that his only hope for improvement was a trip to Europe; he departed for France on 20 April. The diary he wrote during the crossing to Marseilles (transcribed by Pereira, pp. 339–349) is a dramatic account of how ill the poet was: he could hardly speak and had a severe cough and swelling of the body. When the ship arrived in Marseilles it had to be quarantined because of the death of a sailor on board. People assumed that the deceased was Gonçalves Dias, and the news of his death caused consternation all over Brazil.

Gonçalves Dias spent the rest of his stay in Europe pursuing all possible means of improving his health. He saw a great many doctors in Belgium, France, and Germany. In Belgium he even allowed a doctor to surgically remove his uvula in the hope of obtaining some relief. In spite of everything, he continued to do research and to work on his translation of Friedrich Schiller's *The Bride of Messina* into Portuguese, which he finished in Lisbon in 1863. Pressed by financial problems, and weary of medical treatments that produced no result, possibly even feeling that he was in his final days, Gonçalves Dias decided to go back to Maranhão. He embarked on the *Ville de Boulogne* at Le Havre on 10 September 1864. During the last weeks of the voyage his condition became almost hopeless. He could not eat; his meals consisted of only sugared water. When the ship first sighted the coast of Brazil on 2 November, he asked to be brought to the upper deck so that he could see his native land again. But because of the emotion or his extremely poor health, he fainted. The next day, on approaching São Luís, the ship struck some reefs at Atins, near the village of Guimarães. In the turmoil that followed, nobody remembered to assist the ailing poet: he was the only casualty of the disaster.

The Work

As is evident from his biography, Gonçalves Dias' fame rests mainly on his poetic labors, even though he was also a consummate playwright. For the purposes of discussion we will divide his poetic production into *saudosista* (nostalgic), Amerindian, lyric, and autobiographical poetry. His best-known poem, "Canção do Exílio," which is memorized by every Brazilian child early in primary school, was written in Portugal, as were most of the pieces included in *Primeiros Cantos*. It is the best example of Gonçalves Dias' *saudosista* production. In it, the poet laments his condition of exile, away from his native country and family. The poem is written in the *redondilha* meter, a seven-syllable line traditional in Portuguese since the Middle Ages. The melancholy tone of the lines is enhanced by the skillful manipulation of refrains and by the complete absence of adjectives.

> Minha terra tem palmeiras
> onde canta o sabiá;
> as aves, que aqui gorjeiam,
> não gorjeiam como lá.
>
> Nosso céu tem mais estrelas,
> nossas várzeas têm mais flores,
> nossos bosques têm mais vida,
> nossa vida mais amores.
>
> Em cismar, sozinho, à noite,
> mais prazer encontro eu lá;

minha terra tem palmeiras,
onde canta o sabiá.

Minha terra tem primores,
que tais não encontro eu cá;
em cismar—sozinho, à noite—
mais prazer encontro eu lá;
minha terra tem palmeiras,
onde canta o sabiá.

Não permita Deus que eu morra,
sem que eu volte para lá;
sem que desfrute os primores
que não encontro por cá;
sem qu'inda aviste as palmeiras,
onde canta o sabiá.
                    (Poesia Completa, 103)

My homeland has palm trees
where sings the *sabiá*;
the birds in this country
do not sing as in mine.

Our skies have more stars,
our fields have more flowers,
our woods have more life,
our lives have more love.

As I muse, alone, at night,
more joy I find over there;
my homeland has palm trees,
where sings the *sabiá*.

My homeland has charms,
which I cannot find here;
when I muse—alone, at night—
more joy I find over there;
my homeland has palm trees,
where sings the *sabiá*.

May God not let me die
before returning home;
without savoring the joys,
which I cannot find here;
without beholding afar the palm trees
where sings the *sabiá*.

"Canção do Exílio" is part of a group of seven poems designated by Gonçalves Dias as "Poesias Americanas" (American Poems). Of the other six

poems, two—"Caxias" and "O Soldado Espanhol" (The Spanish Soldier)—are stiff and unsuccessful, but the remaining four are excellent examples of his best "Indian poetry," as can be seen by the beginning stanza of the beautiful "A Canção do Tamoio":

Não chores, meu filho;
Não chores, que a vida
É luta renhida:
Viver é lutar.
A vida é combate
Que os fracos abate,
Que os fortes, os bravos,
Só pode exaltar.

Don't cry, my son;
Don't cry, for life
Is a tough struggle:
To live is to fight.
Life is a combat
Which only the weak can abate,
Which the mighty and the brave,
Can only exalt.

It is worth noting that *indianista* poetry was not Gonçalves Dias' invention. It had appeared already in the eighteenth century in the work of Santa Rita Durão and Basílio da Gama. Gonçalves Dias also gleaned his ideas from the works of many Frenchmen, from Michel de Montaigne to Jean-Jacques Rousseau, and Ferdinand Denis, who, using the Brazilian Indian as model, composed the archetype of the ideal "noble savage." It was Denis, an enthusiast of things Brazilian, who wrote the first prose narrative about the Brazilian aborigines—"Les Machakalis," included in his book *Scenes de la nature sous les tropiques* (Scenes of Nature under the Tropics, 1824). Paradoxically, one could say that Gonçalves Dias was repossessing something that was already Brazilian, even though he was doing it through European eyes. What makes his poetry characteristically Brazilian, then, is his feeling for the country, his Brazilian "condition," so to speak. Gonçalves Dias' Indian is the superman of the New World, ideally suited to subjugate the magnificent nature that surrounds him, and a worthy precursor of the noble heroes popularized by José de Alencar's fiction. In such poems as "O Canto do

Guerreiro" (The Warrior's Chant), "O Canto do Piaga" (The Shaman's Chant), and "Deprecação" (Deprecation), all from *Primeiros Cantos*, one can perceive through the epic, solemn tone and rhythm a great empathy for a people destined to be destroyed by the arrival of the white man. In *Ultimos Cantos*, the moving story of "I-Juca-Pirama," who begs his captors not to kill and devour him before he has the chance to return home to assist his old, blind father, is told in rhymed lines of varied accents which lead the reader through mounting tension to a climax of pity and sorrow. The old man, who had rejected his son's help because he thought the young warrior had come to him out of cowardice, receives in his arms the body of the brave youth. He had been killed by his enemies while wreaking havoc among them; since he had proved himself, he could now have the honor of being eaten by his foes. The same feelings can be experienced through the reading of "Marabá" (Half-Breed) or the moving "A Canção do Tamoio." In *Os Timbiras*, Gonçalves Dias' command of the unrhymed decasyllable infuses the poem with an epic grandeur seldom reached by other poets who have written in Portuguese.

Gonçalves Dias' best lyric poems are, to be sure, of an amorous nature. There are excellent examples in all his books. Antônio S. Amora says that few poets writing in Portuguese have ascended the heights reached by Gonçalves Dias in such compositions as "Seus Olhos" (Her Eyes) and "Amor! Delírio—Engano" (Love! Delirium—Deceit) of *Primeiros Cantos*, "Olhos Verdes" (Green Eyes) of *Últimos Cantos*, and "Se Se Morre de amor" (If It Is Possible to Die of Love) or "Ainda uma Vez—Adeus!" of "Novos Cantos."

The best examples of his autobiographical poetry are included in *Primeiros Cantos*—"Quadras da Minha Vida" (Stanzas of My Life) and "Minha Vida e Meus Amores" (My Life and My Loves)—and in *Ultimos Cantos*—"Desesperança" (Hopelessness).

A curious part of Gonçalves Dias' poetic output is "Sextilhas de Frei Antão," in which he shows his deep knowledge of the Portuguese language and its poetics by taking as his alter ego a sixteenth-century friar-poet who recounts, in the old meters, the legends and stories that Gonçalves Dias had gathered during his frequent visits to many archives and libraries. In his preface to *Segundos Cantos* Gonçalves Dias explained his voyage back in time, which was quite in accord with the medieval atmosphere of his years at Coimbra, by stating that the "Sextilhas" were

> a philological essay . . . in which I adopted as mine the phraseology and the ways of thinking of olden days, trying to write in a smooth and easy style, so that it would not displease the readers of today, and to color my thoughts with the strong shades of those times when faith and bravery were the cardinal virtues. . . . I strove to simplify my thoughts, to feel like the men of those days felt, and I put great effort into composing my poems in the language in which they could be best expressed— that of the trouvères—a language which was simple but stern, rhymed but easy, daring and harmonious without being pompous or arrogant.
>
> (Quoted by Montello, p. 251)

Tradition has it that Gonçalves Dias wrote the "Sextilhas" to show some critics (who had found fault with his vocabulary and meters in *Beatriz Cenci*) that his command of the language could not be criticized. The truth is that those "faults" indicated by the critics are part of the innovations that Gonçalves Dias introduced—part of his "Brazilianness." In 1847 Alexandre Herculano himself had criticized the poems of *Primeiros Cantos* in this regard. Gonçalves Dias paid no attention to such quibbles and never yielded to them. It is interesting to note, however, that as late as 1869 Luciano Cordeiro claimed Gonçalves Dias to be a "Portuguese" poet, rather than Brazilian. In his *Livro de Crítica, Arte e Literatura Portuguesa d'Hoje* (Book of Criticism, Art, and Portuguese Literature of Today), he says: "Gonçalo [sic] Dias— whom the Brazilians, in their monomania for having a literature . . . claim as theirs, as he himself thought he was. . . ." Cordeiro was certainly right if one considers only the "Sextilhas" and Gonçalves Dias' theatrical work.

Gonçalves Dias' plays, written when he was in his twenties, are all historical dramas that conform with the lessons and techniques (simplicity, conciseness) introduced by Almeida Garrett, the founder of modern Portuguese theater, as well as with the tenets of adherence to historical truth propounded by Herculano, the creator of the Portuguese historical novel.

In this sense Gonçalves Dias' plays are "Portuguese." His two earlier dramas, *Beatriz Cenci* and *Patkull*, and the last one, *Boabdil*, do not do justice to the scenic talent that bursts forth in *Leonor de Mendonça*, written when the poet was twenty-three. Had the play not been refused by João Caetano, who preferred the fashionable foreign melodramas of his day (his was a melodramatic style of acting), its production in Rio could very well have been (together with the many comedies of Martins Pena) the breath of fresh air needed to renovate the Brazilian theater. Unfortunately, it was presented much later (1848), in São Luís, capital of Maranhão state, which was located too far from the cultural center of the country to have any impact on the drama of the time. The somber, doleful story of the noble, innocent duchess of Braganza, mistakenly killed by her husband in order to avenge his honor, was much more influential in the 1960's when it was produced in São Paulo.

The importance of Gonçalves Dias for Brazilian literature can be summed up in the definitive words of Antônio Cândido Mello e Souza:

> In him, the new generations learned romanticism. From this point of view he was the decisive occurrence in romantic poetry; all the poets who followed him . . . presuppose (knowledge of) his work. After *Primeiros Cantos*, what before had only been a theme—nostalgia, melancholy, nature, the Indian—became something new and fascinating with its superior inspiration and excellence of formal techniques.
>
> (*Formação*, p. 83)

SELECTED BIBLIOGRAPHY

First Editions

Poetry

Primeiros Cantos. Rio de Janeiro, 1846.
Segundos Cantos. Rio de Janeiro, 1848.
Últimos Cantos. Rio de Janeiro, 1851.
Os Timbiras. Leipzig, 1857.
Cantos. Leipzig, 1857. 3rd ed. 1860, includes all the previously published works, plus sixteen poems under the title "Novos Cantos."
Obras Póstumas. 6 vols. Edited by Antônio Henriques Leal. São Luís (Maranhão), Brazil, 1868–1869. Includes all unpublished material—poetry, prose, and theater.

Prose

Dicionário da Língua Tupi. Leipzig, 1858.

Plays

Leonor de Mendonça. Rio de Janeiro, 1847.

Modern Editions

Obras Poéticas de Gonçalves Dias. Edited by Manuel Bandeira. São Paulo, 1944.
Poesia Completa e Prosa Escolhida. Includes "A Vida e a Obra do Poeta. A Poética de Gonçalves Dias," by Manuel Bandeira. Rio de Janeiro, 1959.
Poesias. Edited by Manuel Bandeira. Rio de Janeiro, 1960.
Poesias Completas. Edited by F. J. da Silva Ramos. São Paulo, 1950, 1957.

Biographical and Critical Studies

Ackermann, Fritz. *A Obra Poética de Gonçalves Dias*. Translated by Egon Schaden. São Paulo, 1940.
Amora, Antônio Soares. *O Romantismo, 1833–1838/1878–1881* São Paulo, 1967.
Bandeira, Manuel. *Gonçalves Dias*. Rio de Janeiro, 1952.
Bastide, Roger. *A Poesia Afro-Brasileira*. São Paulo, 1943.
Bosi, Alfredo. *História Concisa da Literatura Brasileira*. São Paulo, 1983.
Brandão, Roberto de Oliveira. "Entre o mítico e o profano." *Língua e Literatura* 6:235–243 (1977).
Cunha, Fausto. *O Romantismo no Brasil*. Rio de Janeiro, 1971.
Driver, David M. *The Indian in Brazilian Literature*. New York, 1942.
Haberly, David T. "The Songs of an Exile: Antônio Gonçalves Dias." In *Three Sad Races: Racial Identity and National Consciousness in Brazilian Literature*. Cambridge, England, 1983. Pp. 18–31.
Leal, Antônio Henriques. "Antônio Gonçalves Dias." In *Pantheon Maranhense 3*. Lisbon, 1874.
Lima, Henrique de Campos Ferreira. *Gonçalves Dias em Portugal*. Coimbra, Portugal, 1942.
Merquior, José Guilherme. *De Anchieta a Euclides*. Rio de Janeiro, 1977.
Montello, Josué. *Gonçalves Dias. Ensaio Bio-bibliográfico*. Rio de Janeiro, 1942.
————. "Ainda uma Vez Gonçalves Dias." In *Santos de Casa*. Ceará, Brazil, 1966. Pp. 177–300.

Nogueira da Silva, M. *Bibliografía de Gonçalves Dias*. Rio de Janeiro, 1942.

Pereira, Lúcia Miguel. *A vida de Gonçalves Dias*. Rio de Janeiro, 1943.

Ricardo, Cassiano. "Gonçalves Dias e o Indianismo." In *A Literatura no Brasil*, edited by Afrânio Coutinho. Vol. 1, no. 2. Rio de Janeiro, 1955. Pp. 659–742.

Salles, David. "Do sabiá na palmeira." In *Do Ideal às Ilusões. Alguns Temas da Evolução do Romantismo Brasileiro*. Rio de Janeiro, 1980. Pp. 17–25.

Sayers, Raymond. *The Negro in Brazilian Literature*. New York, 1956.

Souza, Antônio Cândido de Mello e. "Gonçalves Dias Consolida o Romantismo." In *Formação da Literatura Brasileira 2*. São Paulo, 1959. Pp. 81–96.

José de Alencar

(1829–1877)

José Aderaldo Castello

José Martiniano de Alencar was born in Ceará, Brazil, on 1 May 1829, just before the birth of the romantic movement, during which Brazilian literature sought its national identity after more than three centuries of Portuguese colonization. The movement began with *Suspiros poéticos e saudades* (Poetic Sighs and Longings, 1836), by Domingos Gonçalves de Magalhães, who founded the review *Niterói: Revista brasiliense* in Paris in 1836. Eight years later, the Brazilian novel was considered established with the publication of *A Moreninha* (The Little Brunette), by Joaquim Manuel de Macedo. Alencar, a student in the São Paulo Law School when Macedo's work appeared, was among the first to recognize it as a model of the genre in Brazil. A few years later, Antônio Gonçalves Dias, the great romantic poet of Brazilian Indianism, would make his debut. These distinctive works marked the emergence of a nationalistic and patriotic ideology, rooted in the independence period (1808–1822), which was to be sharpened and restated by Brazil's first romanticists. This ideology was fundamental to Alencar's formation. Its influence was revealed early in his life when he amassed information about the Brazilian oral tradition and landscape from the Northeast to the South and applied himself to the study of the colonial past. The role his relatives had played in the political

revolutions of 1817 and 1824 had an equally important impact on his development.

This background is reflected in Alencar's extensive activities as a politician, publicist, writer, lawyer, and public figure in three overlapping stages of development. The first stage, his childhood and adolescence, is marked by the presence of his father, who was involved in political and revolutionary struggles in Ceará, and in the royal court in Rio de Janeiro. During this period he moved from Ceará to Rio. The second stage includes Alencar's student days in the two major Brazilian intellectual centers in the nineteenth century, São Paulo Law School, from which he graduated, and Recife Law School in Pernambuco. The third stage begins with his work as a journalist and lawyer, which opened the way for his activities as a writer, politician, and public figure.

Alencar wrote a biography of his father, José Martiniano de Alencar, in which he pointed out three important moments in his father's career: his participation in the 1824 revolution (the writer's grandmother, Bárbara Pereira de Alencar, had been a heroine in the 1817 revolution); his role at the head of the so-called Ceará province; and his role as a senator of the empire. In his incomplete autobiography, *Como e porque sou romancista* (How and Why I Am a Novelist, 1893), Alencar discussed other close relatives as well as his childhood, trips, first readings, studies, and literary influences. He pointed out the impression made on him, in his studies in São Paulo, by Macedo, Alexandre Dumas, Alfred de Vigny, François René de Chateaubriand, Victor Hugo, Alphonse de Lamartine, and, above all, Honoré de Balzac, whose novels he considered "real life poetry." At that time he read old and classic writers of the Portuguese language and researched the colonial period as a source for both historical and Indian narratives. Interested in the changes in the Portuguese language in Brazil, which he saw as an identifying element both of the national literature and of his sense of himself, he set out to study the classic prose writers.

Alencar finished his college studies in 1850. The next year he returned to Rio de Janeiro, where he spent the rest of his life. As a journalist for the *Correio Mercantil,* he enriched his view of the court life; his training continued at another newspaper, the *Diário do Rio de Janeiro,* where he analyzed Brazilian social and political problems. A decisive event in his life was the publication of his *Cartas sobre "A confederação dos tamoios"* (Letters on "The Tamoio Confederation") in 1856, which launched a debate that was undoubtedly the most famous one in Brazilian romanticism. These letters were written in connection with the Indianistic poem *A confederação dos tamoios* (The Tamoio Confederation) by Gonçalves de Magalhães, published in 1856 in a luxurious "imperial edition." Leaving aside his criticism of the emperor's patronage, what really matters is Alencar's reappraisal of Indianism, an ideology stemming from nationalism, and its implications for romantic poetry. He would use this evaluation later when writing his first comprehensive preface to his own works, which had special significance for his Indian novels—*O Guaraní* (The Guaraní [Indian], 1857), *Iracema* (Iracema, 1865) and *Ubirajara* (Ubirajara, 1874). It would also inspire the outline of the poem "Os filhos de Tupã" (The Sons of Tupã, written in 1863 and published posthumously in 1910 and 1911).

These critical reflections initiated a debate that was the beginning of a career that moved between criticism and self-defense, both in literature and in politics. In the latter activity, which occupied his life beginning in 1861, he played a relevant and useful role, in spite of the annoyance it caused him, which was in great part aggravated by his sensitivity. Starting as a congressman representing his home province in 1861, he served as minister of justice from 1868 to 1870, and would have become a senator—he received the highest number of votes of recommendation for the office—had it not been up to the discretion of the emperor, Pedro II, who chose to disregard him. Alencar was, after all, one of the emperor's more aggressive opponents, which had been demonstrated by his criticism in *Ao Imperador: Cartas políticas de Erasmo* (To the Emperor: Political Letters of Erasmo, 1865) and *Ao Imperador: Novas cartas políticas de Erasmo* (To the Emperor: New Political Letters of Erasmo, 1866). However, it was in the literary field that Alencar experienced probably his worst difficulties, as a result of both envy and misunderstanding about what he was doing for the characterization and identity of Brazilian literature. Certainly, he received more praise than criticism, winning acclaim ranging from that of his contemporary Joaquim Maria Machado de Assis to the modernist Mário de Andrade, himself a great innovator. Two examples of the criticism Alencar received and his responses to it are representative of the works he felt compelled to write in his own defense. The first dispute was prompted by an article in the journal *Questões do Dia* written by the Portuguese writer José Feliciano de Castilho, who was visiting Brazil, in collaboration with the Brazilian novelist Franklin Távora. They appraised his novels one by one, contesting his romantic nationalism, mainly his defense of Brazilian literary language, which Alencar presented as model. Some time later, in 1875, in connection with Alencar's historical play *O Jesuíta* (The Jesuit, 1875), it was Joaquim Nabuco's turn to provoke Alencar's second literary dispute. Strict and unfair, Nabuco himself would later regret his excess and recognize "what is profound, national in Alencar—his Brazilianism."

"Bênção Paterna" (Paternal Blessing), a preface to the novel *Sonhos d'ouro* (Golden Dreams, 1872), was Alencar's response to the criticism of Feliciano de Castilho and Távora. It has been debated whether or not this preface can be taken as a kind of manifesto for the many works he had published. It does offer a clear and definite characterization of Alencar's past and future objectives and achievements. He begins by equating the works he had written up to that point with what he calls the "organic period" of Brazilian literature, which he breaks down into three phases. The first phase is that "of the legends and myths of both the wild and conquered lands." The second is represented by the "adaptation of the invaders to the American land," a time of mutual assimilation between "conqueror and the conquered," favoring the process of "slow gestation of the American people that would stem from Portuguese stock in order to continue in the New World the glorious traditions of their progenitors." The last phase, starting with Brazilian independence (1822), presents two aspects. One corresponds to "the infancy of [Brazilian] literature. . . . It is the persistence in their original purity, without any mixture, of our fathers' way of life, traditions, customs, and language, everything exhibiting a Brazilian brand." The other aspect shows the alterations the first was to undergo, that is to say, the changes that would occur within Brazilian society and be reflected in its literature.

> It is the consequence of the struggle between the spirit of the land and foreign invasion, inevitable in a society whose physiognomy was indefinite, vague, and manifold, which is so natural to the age of adolescence. . . . The influences come from various foreign nationalities: the English, the Italian, the Spanish, the American, but especially the Portuguese and French; all of them are superficial and gradually sink until they become part of the adoptive motherland and make up the new and great Brazilian nationality.

Beyond what he had already written, Alencar, in "Bênção Paterna," must have been thinking about what he would write later. He had considerably expanded upon the aesthetic reflections in *Cartas sobre "A confederação dos tamoios"* and in the outline for "Os filhos de Tupã," which were written at the beginning of his career.

To analyze Alencar's oeuvre effectively we must first reorganize the three stages into which he divided Brazilian literature. First, we fuse Alencar's first two stages, which are actually simultaneous and overlapping. Second, we allow for a new, prehistorical stage, which becomes our first, while the two in Alencar's classification, fused into one, become our

second. Thus, we begin with prehistorical America, free of any connections with European conquerors. Then comes the historical stage, starting with the European discovery and continuing through the domination of the natives; this stage encompasses the slow eradication of the native population either through miscegenation, which engendered the Brazilian prototype, or through extermination during battles in which the natives resisted colonization and exploitation. The second stage is historically expanded to reach the writer's time, which constitutes the third stage.

In our reordering, the classification of the works according to their chronology and the cyclical features suggested by Alencar becomes subordinate to a redistribution that seems more in tune with the writer's designs and objectives, whether accidental or deliberate. Thus, the prehistorical stage, which follows the historical romantic model, forms the background for the tale *Ubirajara*. This work is marked by the complete predominance of the Indianistic poetic style. On the other hand, the historical stage—the stage of formation characterized by the conquest and assimilation of the conqueror, conquered land, and natives, that is, the gestation of the South American people—engenders a kind of Indian-historical narrative and another kind that is predominantly historical. Representative of the former case are *O Guarani* and *Iracema*; of the latter, *As minas de prata* (The Silver Mines, 1862/1865–1866), *Alfarrábios: Crônicas dos tempos coloniaes* (Old Books: Chronicles of Colonial Times, 1873), *A Guerra dos Mascates* (The War of the Street Peddlers, 1873–1874), and the historical play *The Jesuit*.

In the prehistorical past, the Indian communities appear free in the wild landscape, fully in touch with nature. The Indian is man in his epic greatness, a simultaneous manifestation of the power, courage, and loyalty of the hunter, warrior, and lover. As the historical stage begins, the free natives are gradually dominated and destroyed by the power of foreign culture and civilization. The natives initially welcomed the invaders as long as their freedom was respected, but when this ceased to be the case, they became antagonists and enemies. Nevertheless, out of the historical view would come values, traditions, and cultural features differentiating the Brazilian prototype from both invaders and natives, whom the romanticists—led by Alencar and Gonçalves Dias—considered fundamental to this formation. We shall see how these seeds, acted upon by foreign influences after independence, determined changes mainly in Brazilian urban culture.

There were various influences and models for Alencar's development of the tales in the prehistorical and the colonial-historical stages. The Bible, especially the Book of Genesis (the style and rhythm of which are identifiable in *Ubirajara*), led Alencar to the legends and myths of man's racial division, his destruction in the universal deluge, and the repopulation of the world. All of this appeared as his initial inspiration in the outline for the miscarried "Os filhos de Tupã", from which would later come his lyrical epic tale *Ubirajara*. The two works previously published, *O Guarani* and *Iracema,* had already dealt with the first contacts between the settlers and the natives from a mythical viewpoint. They actually mark the beginning of the historical stage; that stage ends in independence, which would later be represented by works in which the settlers' action predominates—*As minas de prata, A Guerra dos Mascates, Alfarrábios: Crônicas dos tempos coloniais* and even the play *The Jesuit.* In these works Alencar searched for other sources of inspiration: Homer and the classical epic, John Milton, romantic historical novelists and their medieval legends, like Sir Walter Scott and Alexandre Herculano, and romantic French writers like Bernardin de Saint-Pierre and Chateaubriand. Another source of inspiration was the study of Indian languages, essential for the delineation of space, time, rhythm, and even the cosmogony of the Indian universe.

In romantic terms, the Indian novels show how Alencar gave literary and artistic form to scattered elements from continental and universal legends, and how he created myths to embody a collective, centuries-old memory, modified by imagination and folklore. The process of artistic recreation was nourished by the sensibility, sentimentality, and character that resulted from the fusion of the American man with the European, forecasting the Brazilian nationality. Thus, the romantic search for memory and national consciousness was completed.

Ubirajara can be seen as an effort to suggest the vast primitive space of the wild land to be conquered. Nothing is heaped up or cluttered in this landscape of primitive elements and human beings of towering epic beauty, whose rough features are softened by their loyal attitudes typical of their warring traditions and by the chosen woman's lyrical touch. The traditional hero concept of epic poems is fused with knightly ideals so as to focus on common values and feelings, such as courage, loyalty, and love. What happens to the human community is reflected in the landscape, in which the hero prevails as the summation of the qualities and dreams of his race. *Ubirajara* corresponds to a partial fulfillment of the plan for the epic "Os filhos de Tupã," insofar as it can be interpreted as the great introduction to the novels *O Guarani* and *Iracema,* which, although they preceded it, represent the following stage.

In *O Guarani*—a tale in which, within the tradition of Indian-historical fiction, the author foreshadowed the characterization of the hero in *Ubirajara*—Alencar presented a synthesis of a nation's collective dreams. In this picture of a wild, primitive nature, a new element appears. The values and ideals of the invaders are still bound to the remnants of a knightly tradition. It is an imaginary snapshot of the fusion of two cultures forming a new civilization. Here again we recognize the lyrical, epic vision in the surviving hero and heroine's fulfillment. Machado de Assis showed that Alencar, to suggest the fusion of values, traditions, and feelings, created one of the most beautiful allegories in Brazilian literature, one that is full of mythical and legendary notions concerning the repopulation of the earth and that calls to mind the Indian version of the universal deluge.

Chronologically, *Iracema* comes between *O Guarani* and *Ubirajara.* It comes third, however, in our revision because it represents the compression of the essential features of the other two tales and completes a cyclical trilogy. In *Iracema,* which focuses on the writer's native region, we readily recognize the presence of his innermost and strongest feelings: memories of the landscape, oral traditions, lyrical suggestions, and experiences accumulated in childhood—all of which support the feeling of nationality. Not exhibiting the ambitious proportions of *Ubirajara* or the historical concern of *O Guarani, Iracema* is poignantly written with fatalism, resignation, and nostalgia. Confined to the essentials but without any loss of epic or historical elements, which are as important here as in the first two novels, it is a moving narrative filled with lyrical inspiration. Torn from their community and projected alone into the landscape, the main characters are in unison with nature, which they make come alive in a dialogue of love, tenderness, and acceptance, whispered in a soft and musical common language. They incarnate a legend (the subtitle is *A legend of Brazil* . . .) that, from a certain historical moment onward, is taken as the deepest explication of the sentiments and destiny of a future hybrid nation. It is a romantic conception, emphasizing a moment of synthesis in which the character and sentimentality of those who die are taken up by those who are born. The legend is recreated out of scattered elements caught by the intuition and imagination of the artist, who moves back into the remote past in search of roots that may allow for a strongly lyrical understanding of the original moment when a new motherland was formed.

This first broad panorama of the native origins and hybrid formation of the Brazilian character is extended to colonial times with the inclusion of the remaining second-stage narratives, in which the historical narrative model prevails. These works are closely related to historical European romanticism. They are the already mentioned *As minas de prata, A Guerra dos Mascates, Alfarrábios,* and the play *The Jesuit.* Of course, we must recognize the inevitable influence of the sources and models of one subclass upon another; both were inspired by the nationalistic feeling generally typical of romanticism, which was concerned with the exaltation of a people's legendary past. We must always keep in mind that Indian, Indian-historical, and predominatly historical novels were produced simultaneously.

The second panorama is that of the novelist's time and corresponds to the third stage of his so-called organic period. In one sense, the bifurcation that he himself proposed refers to rural provincial Brazil and to the urban Brazil of Rio de Janeiro, home of the imperial royal court. The tales from this period are distributed in two groups. The first consists of rural social narratives: *O Gaúcho* (The Gaucho, 1870), *O tronco do ipê* (The Trunk of the Catalpa, 1871), *Til*

(Tide, 1872), and *O Sertanejo* (The Backlander, 1875). The second is that of narratives set exclusively in Rio de Janeiro: *Cinco minutos* (Five Minutes, 1856), *A viuvinha* (The Little Widow, 1860), *Lucíola* (1862), *Diva* (Goddess, 1864), *A pata da gazela* (The Gazelle's Hoof, 1870), *Sonhos d'ouro* (1872), *Senhora* (Lady, 1875), and *Encarnação* (Incarnation, posthumously published in 1893; first published in Alencar's lifetime as a serial in the newspapers *Folha nova* and *Diário Popular* in 1877). In addition to these novels, he wrote the plays *O demônio familiar* (The Familiar Demon, 1857), *O Rio de Janeiro: Verso e reverso* (Rio de Janeiro: Verse and Reverse, 1857), *As azas de um anjo* (The Wings of an Angel, 1860), and *Mãe* (Mother, 1862).

In the rural social narratives, Alencar also focused on legend and myth. However, what predominated was his intention of giving an accurate evaluation of both man and landscape in rural society. He attempted to be truly comprehensive, and occasionally explored the relationship between the rural and urban worlds. On the one hand, he attempted a study of characters (the *gaúcho* farmhand and the Northeast's cowboy), and he showed the relationship not only of man to the landscape but also of man to the animal. On the other hand, he searched for universal patterns and values in the society of the rural world, whose roots went back to the colonial formation of Brazil. But it is also clear that the geographical descriptions that form the settings of these novels are not sufficiently realistic for them to be called fully regionalistic. For Alencar, physical setting was a scene opening on three large dimensions: land, sky, and between them the measureless space of freedom for his heroes' impulses and actions, characterized by knightly deeds, fearlessness, generosity, and love.

Since Alencar's interpretations had their foundations in reality, it is possible to identify them. As for the rural narratives, we clearly see from the pampas of Rio Grande do Sul, the hinterland of São Paulo and Rio de Janeiro, and the backlands of Ceará, which are the settings for *O Gaúcho, Til, O tronco do ipê,* and *O Sertanejo.* At the two geographical extremes, Alencar portrayed roughness of traditions and customs; at the center, he presented a more developed, aristocratic atmosphere that shared the traditions and customs of a court undergoing changes. Alencar's view that the roots of the Brazilian way of life are embedded in the colonial past is so dominant in these novels that one of them, *O Sertanejo*, exhibits strong characteristics of the romantic historical novel. The original inspiration of the novel is the writer's childhood, when he would become emotionally carried away whenever he heard the popular verse narrative *Boi Espácio* (The Ox Espacio). In fact, it was Alencar who saved for posterity a version of that tale in the animal Boi Dourado (the Golden Ox), a sort of character in *O Sertanejo*. Looking for a theme in the collective memory, he went back to the seventeenth- and eighteenth-century practice of raising cattle in wild, open spaces. He thereby created a model that was to prevail in Brazilian fiction up to Hugo de Carvalho Ramos and João Guimarães Rosa. Indeed, his other country novels also could be models for this genre. In time they would be characterized as regionalistic, resulting from his treatment of the landowning and slaveholding rural patriarchs, who were usually supported by a small army of bandits.

All the novels of Alencar's fourth group, the social urban narratives, are quite elaborate. Portrayals of life, they are marked by the simplicity of the feminine profiles, drawn according to the romantic view of women's social and emotional behavior. Women stand out in the foreground of a changing society, whose colonial traits are gradually being eroded. It is a society undermined by the corrupting power of money and the desire for social status. It is, therefore, marked by the rise of honest and dishonest bourgeois traders and bankers, who rely on a rural economy to guarantee the permanence of their newly acquired aristocratic status. In both city and country, it is a society in which characters search for spurious titles of nobility or important positions in public offices or the professions; it is an atmosphere that favors idlers living for sensual pleasure and parasites ready to seize any financial opportunity. Predominant are the elegant, well-dressed people who use perfume from Paris and whose lives consist of attending the opera and family parties, strolling in the English fashion, and dining in plush hotels. Financial interests mingle with matrimonial objectives. But there exists an overall governing force—love, strong enough to restore the balance between the emotional ideal and society, and to redeem those who had been led astray by a debased social ethic. Along with a strong understanding of women's emotional independence— a kind of romantic feminism—the works of this group project an equally romantic psychology, which Alencar referred to as "physiology." It entails the vivid dissection of feelings, and equates temperament, personality, and individual behavior with good manners, social level, and social changes. Everything is subject to love's self-defining, restoring, and humanizing power, in which emotional truthfulness counts as much as moral balance, a conception that corresponded to the romantic ideal of morality.

For a better understanding of the novels with an urban setting, we must consider the importance of the serials, or weekly publications in the *Correio Mercantil*—*Cinco minutos*, *A viuvinha*, *Lucíola*, *Diva*, *A pata da gazela*, *Sonhos d'ouro*, *Senhora*, and *Encarnação*. Reflecting on and writing about the everyday life of Rio de Janeiro—worldly, intellectual, artistic, political—the serialist Alencar revealed his world vision, or rather, the existential position that controlled the representations of his fictional universe. He was in perfect keeping with romantic idealization, although in a very personal way, that is, according to his own sensibility, which he always cherished.

Later, Machado de Assis would take an identical stand, although his thought was informed by a philosophical background unknown to Alencar. Endowed with different sensitive natures but sharing a point of view regarding the effects of the passing of time and of life's continual and endless repetitions, both Alencar and Machado considered that man's existential vision had been reduced to dreams of love and glory, illusions that nourish our existence and motivate our behavior. Love and glory were seen either as mutually exclusive or coexisting in harmony. In the former case, they would come into conflict, causing tensions, primarily because one belongs to private life while the other involves social relationship. Would it be possible, in the latter case, to overcome conflicts, break tensions, and redress the balance? Each novelist provides his own answers.

Alencar's lyrical vision puts forward the idea of a regenerating and restoring love after the romantic fashion, producing in his characters conflicts and tensions sustained by their ambitions and desires for glory. Although this love becomes a somewhat nostalgic element, perhaps more in the writer than in his characters, it prevails in the novels as a result of its own regenerating and restoring nature. It both supports the reality that the novels project and extols an ethical system of ideal values and traditions, as distinct from the changes and transformations in the real society.

Within the still raw possibilities of the Brazilian fictional narrative, which very early turned to the observation and criticism of social structures, Alencar created a new model for the representation of social reality as part of tradition and the historical past. In the group of social novels with an urban setting, *Senhora* stands out as a real model, that is, a European romantic model that treats the past and present of Brazilian society, in a lyrical and ideal vision of life. And, as a first consequence of what Alencar did, Machado de Assis, a sincere admirer of his work, gave Brazilian literature a truly universal dimension. This influence is especially evident in Machado's early novels, where his vision of the human condition and his social criticism parallel much of Alencar's thinking.

When he died on 12 December 1877 in Rio de Janeiro, Alencar left in his fiction the most complete picture of Brazil yet produced by a writer, a picture corroborated by his reflections and critical studies. As the synthesizer of Brazilian romanticism, Alencar became the focal point upon whom all the efforts, theories, and criticism of preceding writers converged. From him came models and ideas that were doubly productive because they were both attacked and followed. He redefined Brazilian literature and, at the same time, pointed out its authentic nature, characterized from the remote past by its concern with reality—seen as diversity and as the essential unity of habits, customs, traditions—and a language already different from that of the settlers. Indeed, through a process of convergence and derivation, there exist in Alencar's works coordinate and constant topics and ideological positions that have marked his country's literature up to this day.

Before him, Indianism was descriptive and aimed at informing and protecting the Indians; Alencar's Indianism was a mythical vision of Brazilian origins and colonial past; after him came the Indianism of the modernists, which was a tool for studying the Brazilian national character. Indianism blends with the nationalism of colonial nativism, is restated by the romanticists (mainly by Alencar), and is revised by the modernists. And connected with both romantic Indianism and nationalism are the efforts to differentiate Brazilian Portuguese from the language of Portugal, to achieve a distinct Brazilian model. These were the concerns of the first romanticists and of Alencar; with his knowledge of tradition and the linguistic and philological theories of his day, he was the first great romantic scholar. He was a great example for the modernists, who were equally concerned with the questions of Indianism and national language. Finally, he suggested guidelines for the Brazilian narrative, focusing on contemporary reality with its contrasts and state of unbalance. In the social urban tales, Alencar presented the Brazilian reality from the point of view of Rio de Janeiro, since the attention of the Brazilian provinces converged on Rio and from Rio came national decisions and models. In the social tales that contrast rural provincial life with life at court (and later with life in the capital of the Republic) he restructured stratified layers of values and traditions, the marks of the inherited social structures that persist to this day throughout Brazil. Mario de Andrade left, in his original manuscript of *Macunaíma* (1928), the meaningful dedication: "To José de Alencar, father of the living, shining in the vast heavenly field."

Translated from the Portuguese by
Almiro Pisetta and Dennis Mahoney

SELECTED BIBLIOGRAPHY

First Editions

Prose Narratives

Cinco minutos. Rio de Janeiro, 1856. First published as a feuilleton in the *Diário do Rio de Janeiro* in 1856.
O Guarani. Rio de Janeiro, 1857. First published in the *Diário do Rio de Janeiro* in 1857.
A viuvinha. Rio de Janeiro, 1860. Partly published as a feuilleton in the *Diário do Rio de Janeiro* in 1857.
As minas de prata. Rio de Janeiro, 1862 and 1865–1866. The first two fascicles, dated 1862, form the first volume; publication resumed in 1865 and concluded the following year, with the addition of five volumes.

Lucíola: Um perfil de mulher. Rio de Janeiro and Paris, 1862.
Diva: Perfil de mulher. Rio de Janeiro and Paris, 1864.
Iracema: Lenda do Ceará. Rio de Janeiro, 1865.
O Gaúcho. 2 vols. Rio de Janeiro and Paris, 1870.
A pata da gazela. Rio de Janeiro and Paris, 1870.
O tronco do ipê. 2 vols. Rio de Janeiro and Paris, 1871.
Til. 4 vols. Rio de Janerio, 1872.
Sonhos d'ouro. Rio de Janeiro and Paris, 1872.
A Guerra dos Mascates. Rio de Janeiro and Paris. Vol. 1, 1873; Vol. 2, 1874.
Alfarrábios: Crônicas dos tempos coloniaes. 2 vols. Rio de Janeiro and Paris, 1873. Vol 1.: *O Garatuja;* Vol. 2: *O ermitão da Glória* and *A alma do Lázaro.*
Ubirajara: Lenda tupi. Rio de Janeiro and Paris, 1874.
O Sertanejo. 2 vols. Rio de Janeiro and Paris, 1875.
Senhora. 2 vols. Rio de Janeiro and Paris, 1875.
Encarnação. Rio de Janeiro, 1893. Posthumous edition.
O que tinha de ser. Rio de Janeiro, 1912. Posthumous edition.

Plays

O demônio familiar. Rio de Janeiro, 1857.
A noite de S. João. Rio de Janeiro, 1857.
O Rio de Janeiro: Verso e reverso. Rio de Janeiro, 1857.
As azas de um anjo. Rio de Janeiro, 1860.
Mãe. Rio de Janeiro, 1862.
A expiação. Rio de Janeiro, 1867.
O Jesuíta. Rio de Janeiro and Paris, 1875.

Chronicles

Ao correr da pena. São Paulo, 1874. Weekly chronicles published by the *Correio Mercantil* and the *Diário do Rio de Janeiro* in 1854 and 1855.

Essays and Polemics

Cartas sobre "A confederação dos tamoios." Rio de Janeiro, 1856.
Diatribe contra timonice do Jornal de Timon Maranhense à cerca da "História geral do Brasil" do senhor Varnhagen. Lisboa, 1859.

Biographies and Autobiographies

O marquês do Paraná: Traços biográficos. Rio de Janeiro, 1856. Published first in the *Diário do Rio de Janeiro* in the same year.
O marquês de Caxias: Biografia. Rio de Janeiro, 1867.

Como e porque sou romancista. Rio de Janeiro, 1893. Posthumous edition.

Politics

Carta aos eleitores da província do Ceará. Rio de Janeiro, 1860.
Ao Imperador: Cartas políticas de Erasmo. Rio de Janeiro, 1865.
Ao Imperador: Novas cartas políticas de Erasmo. Rio de Janeiro, 1866.
Ao povo: Cartas políticas de Erasmo. Rio de Janeiro, 1866.
Páginas de atualidade: Os partidos. Rio de Janeiro, 1866.
O sistema representativo. Rio de Janeiro, 1868.
A viagem imperial (Câmara dos Deputados. Sessão de 9 de maio de 1871). Rio de Janeiro, 1871.

Modern Editions

Individual Works

Cartas e documentos de José de Alencar. 2nd ed. Edited by Raimundo de Menezes. São Paulo, 1977.
Discursos parlamentares: Câmara dos Deputados. Brasília, 1977. Includes material previously unpublished in book form.
Iracema: Lenda do Ceará. Rio de Janeiro, 1948. With an introduction, notes, and appendix ("Alencar e a língua brasileira") by Gladstone Chaves de Melo.
_____. Rio de Janeiro, 1965. Centennial edition, with an introduction by Augusto Meyer.
_____. Rio de Janeiro, 1965. Critical edition, edited and with an introduction by M. Cavalcanti Proença.
Pareceres de José de Alencar. Rio de Janeiro, 1960.
A polêmica Alencar–Nabuco. Edited by Afrânio Coutinho. Rio de Janeiro, 1965.
A polêmica sobre "A confederação dos tamoios." São Paulo, 1953. Critical essays by José de Alencar, Manuel de Araújo Pôrto Alegre, Don Pedro II, and others, collected and with an introduction by José Aderaldo Castello.
Teatro completo. 2 vols. Rio de Janeiro, 1977. The first volume reproduces the full text of *Ao correr da pena* and the defenses that Alencar wrote to his plays *As azas de um anjo,* including remarks and the prologue from the first edition, and *O Jesuíta.* The second volume includes, besides the works published during Alencar's lifetime, two others not previously published: *O crédito* and *O que é o casamento?*

Collected Works

Obras de ficção. 16 vols. Rio de Janeiro, 1951. Illustrated by Tomas Santa Rosa and preceded by prologues, biographical studies, and criticism by various authors.
Obra completa. 4 vols. Rio de Janeiro, 1959.

Translations

Iracema: The Honey-lips. A legend of Brazil by J. de Alencar. Translated by Isabel Burton. London, 1886.
The Jesuit. Translated by Edgardo R. de Britto. In *Poet Lore* 30 (1919). Pp. 475–547.
Ubirajara: A Legend of the Tupy Indians. Translated by J. T. W. Ladler. São Paulo, 1922.

Biographical and Critical Studies

Araripe Júnior, Tristão de Alencar. *José de Alencar*. 2nd ed. Rio de Janeiro, 1894.

Broca, Brito. "Introdução biográfica." In *O Guarani*. Rio de Janeiro, 1951. Pp. 19–39.

Castello, José Aderaldo. "Bibliografia e plano das obras completas de José de Alencar." *Boletim bibliográfico* 13:37–57 (1949).

Eulálio, Alexandre, et al. *Boletim bibliográfico* 38 (1977). Commemorates the centennial of the death of Alencar.

Faria, João Roberto Gomes. "José de Alencar: A polêmica em torno da adaptação teatral de *O Guarani*." *Letras* (Curitiba, Brazil). 31:50–101 (1982).

Freixieiro, Fábio. *Alencar: Os Bastidores e a posteridade*. Rio de Janeiro, 1977.

Freyre, Gilberto. *José de Alencar*. Rio de Janeiro, 1952.

Girão, Raimundo. *Ecologia de um poema*. Fortaleza, Brazil, 1966.

———. *Botânica cearense na obra de Alencar e caminhos de "Iracema."* Fortaleza, Brazil, 1976.

Magalhães Júnior, Raimundo. *José de Alencar e sua época*. São Paulo, 1971. 2nd ed., revised, 1977.

Marçal, Heitor. *Martim Soares Moreno o "guerreiro branco" de "Iracema."* Rio de Janeiro, 1943.

Martins, Cláudio. *Cem anos depois*. Fortaleza, Brazil, 1977. Includes studies by Joaryvar Macedo, M. Cavalcânti Proença, Otacílio Colares, Raimundo de Menezes, Fran Martins, and Sânzio de Azevedo.

Melo, Gladstone Chaves de. "Alencar e a língua brasileira." In *Senhora*, by José de Alencar. Rio de Janeiro, 1951. Pp. 12–88.

Menezes, Raimundo de. *José de Alencar: Literato e político*. São Paulo, 1965.

Mota, Artur. *José de Alencar*. Rio de Janeiro, 1921.

Peixoto, Afrânio. *Martim Soares Moreno—fundador do Ceará, iniciador do Maranhão e do Pará, herói da restauração do Brasil contra franceses e flamengos—Nota à "Iracema."* São Paulo, 1941.

Proença, M. Cavalcanti. *José de Alencar na literatura brasileira*. Rio de Janeiro, 1966.

Viana Filho, Luís. *A vida de José de Alencar*. Rio de Janeiro, 1979.

Alberto Blest Gana

(1830–1920)

George D. Schade

Alberto Blest Gana was one of the most notable Spanish-American novelists of the nineteenth century. His long life, spanning much of that century, was intimately linked to the sociohistorical forces of the times. His contribution to the development of the Spanish-American novel was significant, as his works represented, more than those of most of his contemporaries, the transition from romanticism to realism, which reigned during the last half of the century. Blest Gana achieved fame as well in the world of diplomacy, serving his country brilliantly for many years in England and France. But, in the end, it is as a writer of novels that Blest Gana is especially renowned. In addition to his novels, of which half a dozen are major works, he published travel sketches and short pieces describing customs and manners, and made one attempt at drama. In all his work he emphasized certain social themes with a critical yet benevolent spirit.

Blest Gana was born on 4 May 1830 in Santiago, Chile, into a cultured family. His father, Dr. William Blest, had emigrated a few years earlier from Ireland as a young man; he soon married, had a large family, and set up a distinguished medical practice in Santiago. The doctor liked to read to his children from such classic English authors as Charles Dickens and Sir Walter Scott. Thus, Blest Gana very early on developed a taste for literature, as did one of his brothers, Guillermo, who later became a poet. As an adolescent, Blest Gana read many of the best European writers, but especially the novelists, who became his passion.

Blest Gana's mother came from a family of Basque origin who had settled in Chile in the eighteenth century; they were a family of wealth and property, and were given to the pursuit of arms. Indeed, this military tradition would predominate in the writer's youthful formation. When he graduated from a military school in Santiago in 1847, he was sent on his first trip abroad to France to continue his studies. He stayed four years in Europe, studying engineering and mapmaking as part of his military career.

During these impressionable years Blest Gana witnessed the fall of Louis Philippe and the proclamation of the Republic, and he attempted to reproduce some of these scenes in one of his earliest novels, *Los desposados* (The Newlyweds). He soon realized that his chief interest lay in literature and writing, so he abandoned his military vocation. On his return to Chile in 1851, Blest Gana began to collaborate in magazines, and in one of these, *El museo*, he published at the age of twenty-three his first novel, which carried the significant title *Una escena social* (A Social Scene, 1853). This work, like a series of others that followed in rapid succession, are novels of apprenticeship: *Engaños y desengaños* (Deceptions and Setting Things Right, 1855); *Los desposados* (1855); *El primer amor* (First Love, 1858); *Juan de Aria* (Juan de Aria, 1858); *La fascinación* (Fascination, 1858); *Un drama en el campo* (A Drama in the Country, 1859).

In 1860 the University of Chile in Santiago held a literary contest that Blest Gana won with *La aritmética en el amor* (The Arithmetic in Love), a novel that marks the beginning of his maturity as a writer. It is an obvious advance over his earlier novelistic efforts in terms of style and narrative construction. Its important subtitle, *Novela de costumbres* (Novel of Customs), indicates the work's strength as well as its nature. The judges certainly thought so when they declared that "the great merit of this composition is that it is completely Chilean. . . . The characters are Chilean and they are very like people we know, with whom we have shaken hands and conversed. . . . The entire novel is animated by a large number of sketches of customs filled with color and truth" (Manuel Rojas, "Prologue," in *Blest Gana: Sus mejores páginas*, p. 16).

The novel's felicitous title reflects society's greedy interest in money, a frequent theme in Blest Gana's works and reminiscent of the obsession of his chief European model, Honoré de Balzac. Blest Gana wanted to be the Chilean Balzac, and though he never really fulfilled this aim, he did succeed triumphantly in capturing in his best novels much of the human comedy of his epoch. The romantic posturings and false characterizations of his earlier novels give way essentially in *La aritmética en el amor* to believable characters and an admirably drawn environment: lottery players, rogues, bureaucrats, ladies of fashion, and many other types parade before us in lifelike form.

In rapid succession Blest Gana published several additional novels: *El pago de las deudas* (The Payment of Debts, 1861), *Mariluán* (Mariluán, 1862), *La venganza* (Vengeance, 1862), and, of prime importance, *Martín Rivas* (1862). The last work, which has brought him the greatest fame and popularity, has gone through almost forty editions and is probably the most widely read book of Chilean literature in Chile. In 1863, he brought out *El ideal de un calavera* (A Rake's Ideal), considered by some critics to be superior to *Martín Rivas* in technique and in the pleasing balance between its various parts. In 1864 he published a novel of rather inferior quality, *La flor de la higuera* (The Flower of the Figtree), and in that same year began to assume a series of government posts that left him no time for his writing.

In 1866 the Chilean government named him chargé d'affaires in Washington, D.C. A year later he was sent to London as ambassador to England, and in 1869 he was named ambassador to France. For two decades he was intensely involved in the world of diplomacy, representing his country at the most important courts of Europe. He witnessed wars and revolutions and defended Chile in dramatic circumstances, where he battled and triumphed. He established himself early on with his wife and children in Paris and never returned to his homeland, though he often thought of doing so.

After officially retiring from the diplomatic service in 1887, Blest Gana turned his attention back to literature and to writing novels; in his ripe years he produced some of his best work. Before leaving Chile he had begun a historical novel that he decided to finish. Dissatisfied, he destroyed it and started over, completely rewriting it. This immensely long novel, *Durante la reconquista* (During the Reconquest), which was concerned with the early years of Chile's struggle for independence from Spain, ran to well over a thousand pages in two volumes in its first edition, published in 1897 in Paris, thirty-three years after his last book had come out. Some critics consider *Durante la reconquista* his best work, though it has never enjoyed the wide popularity of *Martín Rivas* and was not published in his native Chile until 1933. In this novel Blest Gana displays all his powers of narrative invention, description of customs, and historical reconstruction to achieve a work on a grand scale.

In his old age Blest Gana continued publishing novels with mixed success. One of his best achievements was *Los trasplantados* (The Uprooted, 1904), in which he abandoned the history and customs of Chile and set the focus on rich, expatriate Spanish Americans who favored living in Paris. Dazzled by false values and the glitter of Parisian cosmopolitan life, these Latin Americans scorned their native countries, and in turn were scorned by the European aristocracy they aspired to join. *El loco Estero* (*The Madman Estero*, 1909) is one of Blest Gana's most attractive novels and certainly the most personal, containing a wealth of autobiographical material. In it he documents his childhood days in Santiago, focusing on the colorful personalities and customs of that era. Only his last novel, *Gladys Fairfield* (1912), which he published as an octogenarian, is a lamentable letdown from the two previous works of undeniable merit.

Blest Gana died on 9 November 1920 in France, where he had lived for over half a century, having enjoyed good health almost until the end and surrounded by his children and grandchildren, all of them French citizens. He was buried in the famous Parisian cemetery of Père Lachaise.

The majority of Blest Gana's novels reflect a fundamentally sentimental intrigue, describing the fluctuations and oscillations of love among and between his characters. But they also reflect the vicissitudes of society and abound in descriptions of typical manners and customs of the times. These descriptions are usually well incorporated into the weave of the novel, subordinated to the plot and narrative tension. And the author's eye, keenly observant of the custom, also gives a glimpse of the spirit lying behind the custom. Blest Gana underlines the social component in *Martín Rivas*, for example, with a somewhat cumbersome subtitle typical of the Spanish-American novel of the nineteenth century: *Novela de costumbres político-sociales* (Novel of Sociopolitical Customs). During the author's lifetime and slightly beyond—the first eight editions of *Martín Rivas*—this subtitle was faithfully maintained, but starting in 1925 it was often eliminated. However, in two recent editions, it has been brought out and dusted off to appear again, in order to capitalize on the sociopolitical aspect. One should not, therefore, play down the social element in the work, as some former critics have appeared to do, interpreting the novel as purely a good love story. Nor should one go to the other extreme, stressing only the sociopolitical inferences, as Marxist critics have insisted upon, forgetting that, after all, it is a most engaging sentimental novel.

Martín Rivas narrates the history of a young man from the provinces who goes to the big city. He lives with a rich family of high Santiago society and falls in love with the daughter of the house. Thematically, this relationship is at the core of the plot. Everything else seems to revolve around this love story and the hearts involved. And there are quite a few hearts, which makes for suspense, drama, and a good yarn, although the main focus never veers too far from Martín and Leonor Encina.

In all of Blest Gana's novels love is an omnipresent theme. The lovers are usually young, but quite frequently of different social class, status, and fortune. We encounter lovers who are faithful and those who are fickle or faithless, libertines like the protagonist of *El ideal de un calavera*. The theme of love seems to be the central knot tying everything together, and the narrator in these novels usually presents this theme in the form of love triangles. In *Martín Rivas* the main triangle consists of Martín, Leonor, and Edelmira. All three, but especially the two young women, are notable for their beauty or handsome appearance, and more important, for their moral stature. Another significant triangle is formed by Rafael, Matilde, and Adelaida. In contrast with the triangle formed by the protagonists and Edelmira, these three are weaker morally; they represent varying degrees of failure in regard to the sentiments of love. Continuing with this geometric symbology, one can cite Agustín, Matilde, and Adelaida, and Edelmira, Martín, and Ricardo Castaños as comprising other threesomes. In all of these, jealousy, misunderstandings, suspicion, and envy enhance the drama.

One of Blest Gana's principal devices in the novel, a significant structural element, is the use of letters written by the characters. The lack of true communication between lovers is often resolved in an epistolary fashion, as given the prudishness of nineteenth-century society it was difficult to say certain things in person. In *Martín Rivas* there are letters from Martín to Leonor, from Leonor to Martín, from Edelmira to Martín, from Rafael explaining his problems to his best friend, Martín, and so on. The rhythm of the novel accelerates considerably near the end, with a multiplicity of letters in which there are many explanations and declarations of love.

Ingredients of the nineteenth-century novel that Blest Gana shares with Dickens are a complicated and well-developed intrigue and moments of melodrama. The reader of *Martín Rivas* follows with interest the twistings and windings of its plot and encounters scenes with melodramatic overtones, like the one in which the lower middle-class Doña Bernarda de Molina seizes her daughter Adelaida by the hair and pulls her about in a fury, only to finally fall down unconscious when she learns Adelaida has an illegitimate child.

Martín Rivas contains all the aspects of a traditional nineteenth-century novel: social portraits, a cartography of love, animated dialogue, and character delineation. Its pages are crammed with the passions of the times; Blest Gana's use of the political uprising that took place in 1851 in Chile, described in the latter part of the book, is essential for its denouement, to bring the novel into action, and to resolve problems. Blest Gana observes society with a satiric eye, particularly the self-satisfied world of the upper classes. The obsession with money as the supreme goal in life is stressed over and over again, and characters like Fidel Elías and Amador Molina think of almost nothing else. They are active characters, constantly seeking money, and they contrast with the passivity of the already rich man, incarnated by Don Dámaso Encina, Leonor's father. The first significant dialogue of the novel—an opening scene that introduces two important members of the Encina household, the brother and sister Agustín and Leonor—emphasizes the importance of money, at least for Agustín, and thus sets the tone for much of the crass materialism to come.

Blest Gana not only captures the world of the upper-class, salon society with a gimlet eye; he also penetrates the world of the *medio pelo* (lower middle class in Chile), uncultured but with pretensions to rise in the world, especially in lengthy scenes describing the fiestas held at Doña Bernarda's house. Here the author holds society up to a mirror, and we see life not only in its ordinary light but also as being somewhat grotesque and deformed. His mirror reflects society's lack of culture, its brutal interest in money, and its conventionality. However, his tone is usually amiable and manages to soften the crudeness of the satire by incorporating it in certain comic situations or in some of the picturesque figures, such as Doña Bernarda.

The chief concern of most of the main characters, and some of the minor ones, is marriage, with its social and economic consequences. The destinies of the young characters seem to depend on who will marry whom, and this intrigue creates narrative suspense. Blest Gana gives the theme of matrimony various twists, including a false wedding between Adelaida and Agustín to ridicule the young Santiago dandy. The author insinuates that while it may be dangerous to marry for money, it also may be dangerous to marry just for love. Moreover, Blest Gana suggests that having sexual relations outside marriage is hazardous, because society will not condone them, even though society is very hypocritical in this regard. Though the traditional use of matrimony as raw material for the novel has largely been replaced by other themes, it is still provocative today, as marriage connotes certain fundamentals of human existence.

One weakness of *Martín Rivas* is Blest Gana's portrait of the protagonist. Martín is too good, too virtuous and heroic, too ingenuous sometimes, in spite of his intelligence, to convince us totally. For instance, he never seems to suspect the obvious passion that Edelmira feels for him, until she finally confesses it to him in a letter. But though his character lacks some credibility, his situation is quite believable: falling in love with the impossible. Martín symbolizes the young man from the provinces, pure and idealistic, and we are readily caught up in his situation.

Perhaps the lovers in *Martín Rivas* have an advantage over lovers in more contemporary novels. Restricted by nineteenth-century circumstances, they need to know their hearts well before they truly commit themselves. The obstacles in their paths reinforce their passion and force them to concentrate on solving their problems before they consummate their love. One character, the romantic Rafael San Luis, says in a moment of confidence to his friend Martín, "It's not a stupendous novel I'm going to tell you about. It's the story of my heart." Essentially, the novel is a series of situations in which one heart relates to another, which largely accounts for the book's perennial popularity. Rafael continues, "If you weren't in love, too, I would be very careful not to tell you about it, because you wouldn't understand, in spite of its simplicity."

Martín Rivas is also imbued with an appealing spontaneity and a genuine romantic sensibility, a portrayal not only of hearts expressing themselves, but also of a young country finding itself, with Blest Gana as interpreter. According to some critics, this would explain why readers relate to it so well: The romantic aura that transforms a young provincial's love for the lady of the privileged class is almost a symbol of an epoch, lending the book a fascination it still possesses. Martín rises from his humble beginnings through his excellent character and drive, winning the respect of all and the heart of the wealthy Leonor, whom he marries in the end. This contrived happy ending in marriage is also pleasing to much of the reading public and follows the convention of many nineteenth-century novels. But there is an interesting twist to the book beyond the conventional theme of the poor provincial youth getting the rich, beautiful girl. If one remembers that Dámaso Encina, Leonor's father, was originally Martín's father's partner in the mining venture that brought him riches, and that he accomplished this at Rivas' expense, one can say that Blest Gana applies a kind of justice. Through marriage, most of the Encina fortune will pass into Martín's hands.

Some critics have tended to fault Blest Gana for his lack of probing characterization; others have totally ignored this element in favor of other aspects of his work, such as plot, environment, customs, or satire. But though his characters are not drawn as deeply as one might like, many of them ring true. He is particularly skillful with certain female characters; indeed, the women in *Martín Rivas* generally are more interesting than the men. Doña Bernarda, matriarch of the lower middle-class family in *Martín Rivas*, is the most colorful and dynamic figure in the novel. Also admirable are the long-suffering, romantic Edelmira, who sacrifices herself to save her beloved Martín by marrying Ricardo Castaños; and Leonor's bluestocking aunt, Doña Francisca, also romantic and intelligent, who contrasts sharply with her stupid, materialistic husband and other members of the upper class to which she belongs.

But of all the women in the novel, the rich, imperious beauty Leonor is the character who most deserves our admiration. She holds complete sway over her family—parents and brothers—and her dominant personality seems to determine much of the plot and directs the actions of other characters. Despite or because of these qualities, the reader finds her sympathetic. Toward the end of the novel we come to grasp an interesting fact: Leonor, having so dominated the other characters, including the hero Martín, seems to have imposed herself on the author, too, so that she really comes to share the role of protagonist with Martín, if not to usurp it. Spoiled by her parents, aristocratic and haughty, Leonor is beautiful, elegant, proud, willful, and capricious. But she is also intelligent, decisive, serene, resolved, sensible, just, disinterested in money because she has plenty of it, and possessed of a very strong will, through which she exerts power and consequently controls her family, acquaintances, and admirers. This last essential quality is vitally important to the development of the plot, for it is through her will that Leonor saves Martín from the executioner, as he has been condemned to die for his part in the political uprising against the government.

While *Martín Rivas* portrayed the rise of a young man from his humble beginnings, *El ideal de un calavera* explores the plight of a young man of respectable family who has come down in the world. The protagonist, Abelardo Manríquez, has no money and consequently cannot fulfill his ideal of a perfect love; he cannot marry the woman he loves. Disillusioned, he decides to lead the life of a rake, carousing and seducing; he finally dies tragically, executed in the insurrection that took place in Chile in 1837. This novel brims over with colorful types and customs, and is graced with humor. Blest Gana draws his leading character in considerable complexity and psychological depth.

Several of Blest Gana's critics rank his long historical novel *Durante la reconquista* as his best or most artistic work. Though this dictum may be debatable—other candidates are *Martín Rivas* and perhaps *The Madman Estero*—still, this most ambitious novel has many merits. Set in Chile during the War of Independence against Spain, in the period between the disastrous battle of Rancagua of 1814 and the victory at Chacabuco in 1817, *Durante la reconquista* splendidly fuses history and fiction. Of the huge cast of characters, quite a few are taken from history, such as the patriot and hero Manuel Rodríguez, Sargeant Villalobos, the mulatto José Retamo, and the Spanish captain-general, Don Mariano Osorio. Blest Gana gives them new life, often creating very memorable portraits. He also introduces a host of well-defined fictional characters: Abel Malsira, his sister Trinidad, the Spanish widow Violante de Alarcón, and the rogue ño Cámara, among others. The action mainly revolves around scenes of battle and intrigue; love is significant in various secondary actions, as in the young patriot Abel Malsira's love for his cousin as well as for the tantalizing Spanish widow Violante, and in Trinidad Malsira's frustrated love for the Spanish colonel Laramonte. In *Durante la reconquista* love is not sentimentalized, as it was in earlier novels. *Durante la Reconquista* is a skillfully composed historical novel with a vast social milieu, authentic military trappings of battle and intrigue, dashing patriotic figures, and interesting love affairs. But its ponderous length and great wedges of material describing a bygone era slow down the narrative and probably appeal less strongly to the modern reader than do *Martín Rivas* or *The Madman Estero.*

In *Los trasplantados*, another mature Blest Gana novel, which runs to over eight hundred pages in two volumes, the theme is a variation on one from the works of Henry James: the cynical and impoverished European who courts the wealthy American woman for her fortune. Mercedes Canalejas, the protagonist, who may be counted among Blest Gana's most significant female characters, marries a European aristocrat at her wealthy family's urging and finally kills herself because she is really in love with Patricio, her countryman. Like Leonor in *Martín Rivas,* Mercedes battles against the false values of her family, who are convinced that they can buy anything, nobility included. In this bulky novel Blest Gana depicts again the fraudulent upper-class values of his Chilean characters, some of whom lead quite degenerate lives in the frivolous French capital. Here in Paris, as opposed to his novels set in Chile, the author concentrates almost entirely on high society, capturing it very aptly in all its tinsel and glitter, and heartbreak for some of the characters.

Blest Gana's amiable, rather unusual novel *The Madman Estero* displays the author's lighter touch. Its subtitle *Recuerdos de la niñez* (Childhood Memories) proclaims its theme of reminiscence. Here Blest Gana wistfully evokes his recollections of a time seventy years earlier in Santiago. He appears in the novel under one of his real names, Javier; his brother Guillermo and his father also take part as minor characters. The central plot revolves around a neighboring family, with the fictional name of Estero. The title is really a misnomer, for Julián Estero is neither crazy nor the main character. More important are his sister Manuela, a harridan; Carlos "el ñato" Díaz, the affable young man who courts Manuela's niece Deidamia; and the docile Matías Cortaza, Manuela's cuckold husband. The young lovers, opposed by the fierce Manuela, are united happily in the end, after Carlos Díaz helps to free Estero, who has been held a captive at home for many years because of his alleged madness. Julián Estero avenges himself on his cruel sister Manuela by giving her a blow on the head, from which she eventually dies. The plot, with its melodramatic and grotesque turns, unravels convincingly and is buttressed by a wealth of scenes involving customs, such as that of a kite-flying contest, an immensely popular pastime in Chile. In general, the characters are natural and full of vitality, especially the attractive young lovers, Díaz and Deidamia. Even the long-suffering, despised figure of the cuckold comes off as a rational and sympathetic person.

Blest Gana studied his social environment to gather material for his novels, but his realism never went beyond a certain point, for he was limited by a kind of temperamental timidity and modesty. Except perhaps in *Los trasplantados,* he did not incorporate the themes and points of view of the naturalist school of Émile Zola, with its emphasis on the sordid and the clinical, and on the power of sex and its corrosive action on human temperaments. For the last forty years of Blest Gana's life, naturalism powerfully influenced the Spanish-American novel. But the Chilean writer seemed content to stay within the bounds of his type of realism, and was at his best when writing about what one critic has aptly called domestic realism. He had a keen eye for local detail and captured the immediate reflection, like a photograph or a daguerreotype of his times.

Blest Gana studied various strata of society, indicating their flaws and weaknesses but also their strengths. In his works, the proletariat emerges less strongly than other groups; for example, in *Martín Rivas* there is only one scene, involving some street vendors, where the people make an appearance and speak a few lines. *Durante la reconquista* is the exception to this rule, for one of its leading characters, ño Cámara, is a sympathetic proletarian rogue. The people of Blest Gana's class, the wealthy bourgeoisie, are omnipresent in his works and are often portrayed as opportunistic, lacking in nobility, and ruled by gross economic passions. The intermediate classes, between rich and poor, are also well represented. The lower middle class, trying to rise in the world, is depicted well, for example, by the Molina family in *Martín Rivas*. And the middle class, which Martín and his friend Rafael belong to, seems the most favored by the author. Blest Gana's characters of this class often live on the edge of genteel poverty, but they have drive and energy, firm principles, and high moral standards.

Blest Gana's strong female characters often battle against social conventions and sometimes succeed in imposing their wills, like Julia Valverde in *La aritmética en el amor*, Leonor Encina in *Martín Rivas*, and Mercedes Canalejas in *Los trasplantados*. Though the author can scarcely be called a feminist in the contemporary sense, he did pay careful attention to the desires of the heart and went beyond convention in helping pave the way for portrayals of strong, passionate women in the Spanish-American novel.

Like Balzac, Blest Gana saw social life in cyclic terms of classes and stressed the importance of money. Although he attacks materialism throughout his work, his vision is pierced with a bourgeois morality that tends to respect social conventions and hierarchies. He looks at the lower classes with great sympathy and even understanding. But his narrators often possess a patriarchal view of society, though ideologically they may be kindled by the fires of liberal ideals. From his large output, we are left today with not only a sizable group of readable and entertaining works, but also several of major sociohistorical significance and considerable artistic proportions.

SELECTED BIBLIOGRAPHY

First Editions

Novels

Una escena social: Novela original chilena. In *El Museo* (1853).

Los desposados: Novela original. In *Revista de Santiago.* Santiago, Chile (1855).

Engaños y desengaños: Novela original. In *Revista de Santiago.* Santiago, Chile (1855).

La fascinación: Novela original. Valparaíso, Chile, 1858.

Juan de Aria. In *El Aguinaldo* (1858).

El primer amor: Novela original. In *Revista del Pacífico* (1858).

Un drama en el campo. In *La Semana* (1859).

La aritmética en el amor: Novela de costumbres. Valparaíso, Chile, 1860.

El pago de las deudas: Novela original. Valparaíso, Chile, 1861.

Mariluán. In *La Voz de Chile* (1862).

Martín Rivas. Novela de costumbres político-sociales. Santiago, Chile, 1862.

La venganza. In *La Voz de Chile* (1862).

El ideal de un calavera: Novela de costumbres. In *La Voz de Chile* (1863).

La flor de la higuera. In *El Independiente* (1864).

Durante la reconquista: Novela histórica. 2 vols. Paris, 1897.

Los trasplantados. 2 vols. Paris, 1904.

El loco Estero: Recuerdos de la niñez. 2 vols. Paris, 1909.

Gladys Fairfield. Paris, 1912.

Plays

El jefe de la familia. In *El Correo Literario* (1858).

Travel Books

De Nueva York al Niágara. Santiago, Chile, 1867.

Modern Editions

La aritmética en el amor: Novela de costumbres. Santiago, Chile, 1950.

Durante la reconquista. Prologue by Roque Esteban Scarpa. 2 vols. Santiago, Chile, 1952.

El ideal de un calavera. Barcelona, 1972.

El loco Estero. Prologue by Alfonso M. Escudero. Buenos Aires and New York, 1946.

El loco Estero. Prologue and bibliography by Jorge Román-Lagunas. Barcelona, 1977.

Martín Rivas. Prologue and bibliography by Jorge Román-Lagunas. Barcelona, 1977.

Martín Rivas: Novela de costumbres político-sociales. Introduction, "Alberto Blest Gana y su obra," by Guillermo Araya. Madrid, 1981.

Los trasplantados. Prologue by Hernán del Solar. Santiago, Chile, 1945.

Collected Works

Obras selectas. 3 vols. Prologue by Hernán Díaz Arrieta [Alone, pseud.]. 1: *La aritmética en el amor. Martín Rivas. El ideal de un calavera*. 2: *Durante la reconquista*. 3: *Los trasplantados. El loco Estero*. Buenos Aires, 1970.

Translations

The Madman Estero. Translated by Mrs. Charles Whitham. London, 1924.

Martín Rivas. Translated by Mrs. Charles Whitham. London, 1916.

Biographical and Critical Studies

Araya, Guillermo. "El amor y la revolución en *Martín Rivas*." *Bulletin hispanique* 77/1–2:5–33 (1975).

Astorquiza, Eliodoro. "Don Alberto Blest Gana." *Revista chilena* 34:345–370 (1920). Reproduced in *Atenea* 389:5–26 (1960).

Brushwood, John S. *Genteel Barbarism: Experiments in Analysis of Nineteenth-Century Spanish American Novels*. Lincoln, Nebraska, 1981.

Castagnaro, R. Anthony. "The First Master of Realism." In *The Early Spanish American Novel*. New York, 1971. Pp. 173–182.

Concha, Jaime. "*Martín Rivas* o la formación del burgués." *Revista chilena de literatura* 5–6:9–35 (1972). Reproduced in *Casa de las Américas* 15/89:4–18 (1975).

_____. "Prólogo." In Alberto Blest Gana, *Martín Rivas*, Caracas, 1977. Pp. ix–xxxix.

Díaz Arrieta, Hernán [Alone, pseud.]. *Don Alberto Blest Gana*. Santiago, Chile, 1940.

Durand, Luis. "Las mujeres en las novelas de Blest Gana." In *Alma y cuerpo de Chile*. Santiago, 1947. Pp. 179–206.

Edwards, Alberto. "Una excursión por Santiago antiguo. El *Martín Rivas* de Blest Gana y la sociedad chilena de 1850." *Pacífico Magazine* 2/38:115–128 (1916).

Fraysse Maurice. "Alberto Blest Gana et Balzac." *Caravelle: Cahiers du monde hispanique et luso-brésilien* 20:117–134 (1973).

_____. "La campagne chilienne et le 'huaso' dans les romans de Blest Gana." *Caravelle: Cahiers du monde hispanique et luso-brésilien* 28:91–103 (1977).

Goić, Cedomil. "Martín Rivas." In *La novela chilena: Los mitos degradados*. Santiago, Chile, 1968. Pp. 33–49, 184–187.

Lacham, Ricardo. "Blest Gana y la novela realista." *Anales de la Universidad de Chile* 112:30–46 (1958). Reproduced in *Ediciones anales de la Universidad de Chile* 20 (1959), and in *Antología: Crónica de varia lección*, edited by Alfonso Calderón and Pedro Lastra, Santiago, Chile, 1965, pp. 286–310.

_____. "Blest Gana y París." *El Diario Ilustrado* (31 July 1955). Reproduced in *Antología: Crónica de varia lección*, Santiago, 1965, pp. 311–317, and in *La literatura crítica de Chile*, edited by Raúl Silva Castro, Santiago, Chile, 1969.

Latorre, Mariano. "El pueblo chileno en las novelas de Blest Gana." *Atenea* 100:180–197 (1933).

Loyola, Hernán. "*Don Guillermo y Martín Rivas: visión paralela*." In Cedomil Goić et al., *La novela hispanoamericana: Descubrimiento e invención de América*. Valparaíso, 1973. Pp. 55–70.

Melfi, Domingo. "Blest Gana y la sociedad chilena." *Atenea* 100:168–173 (1933). Reproduced in *Estudios de literatura chilena*. Santiago, Chile, 1938. Pp. 23–47.

_____. "Una sombra en Blest Gana." In *El viaje literario*. Santiago, 1945. Pp. 46–51.

Phillips, Walter Thomas. "Chilean Customs in the Novels of Alberto Blest Gana." *Hispania* 24/4:397–406 (1943).

Poblete Varas, Hernán. *Genio y figura de Alberto Blest Gana*. Buenos Aires, 1968.

Rojas, Manuel. "Prologue." In *Blest Gana: Sus mejores páginas*. Santiago, Chile, 1961. Pp. 9–43.

Román-Lagunas, Jorge. "Bibliografía anotada de y sobre Alberto Blest Gana." *Revista iberoamericana* 46/112–113:605–647 (1980).

Rossel, Milton. "En compañía de Martín Rivas." *El Mercurio* (September 1962). Reproduced as "Pasado y presente de *Martín Rivas*." *Atenea* 396:93–102 (1962).

Salmon, Russell. "Alberto Blest Gana como retratista del roto." *Caravelle: Cahiers du monde hispanique et luso-brésilien* 20:135–148 (1973).

Schade, George D. "Notas sobre *Martín Rivas*: evaluación y vigencia." In *La literatura iberoamericana del siglo XIX: XV congreso internacional de literatura iberoamericana*. Tucson, 1971. Pp. 149–154.

Silva Castro, Raúl. *Alberto Blest Gana (1830–1920): Estudio biográfico y crítico*. Santiago, Chile, 1941. 2nd rev. ed., 1955.

_____. "Centenario de *Martín Rivas*." *Revista iberoamericana* 29/55:139–146 (1963). Reproduced in *Estampas y ensayos*. Mexico City, 1968. Pp. 9–16.

_____, and Homero Castillo. "Las novelas de don Alberto Blest Gana." *Revista hispánica moderna* 23/3–4: 292–304 (1957).

Valenzuela, Víctor M. *Chilean Society as Seen through the Novelistic World of Alberto Blest Gana*. New York, 1965.

Von Dem Bussche, Gastón. "Vigencia de *Martín Rivas*." In *Diez conferencias*. Concepción, Chile, 1963. Pp. 53–97.

Juan Montalvo

(1832–1889)

Alfredo Pareja Diezcanseco

In the nineteenth century Spanish America did not produce a better essayist than the Ecuadorian Juan Montalvo. Montalvo's linguistic mastery, the depth of his thought, and his skill as a polemist make Guillermo de Torre's opinion that "the essay is art plus studied reflection" a fitting description of Montalvo's work. From another perspective, Montalvo's writing satisfies the maxim of Edmond-Louis-Antoine de Goncourt that literature, more than a gift, is an acquired affliction.

Montalvo was a great student, a tireless scrutineer of the classics and of his European—especially French—romantic predecessors. He was also a true son of Michel de Montaigne, except that as humility was not his strongest virtue, he dared to answer the desperate, exasperating *"Que sais-je?"* of the essay's creator. Montalvo's masterpiece, *Siete tratados* (Seven Treatises), shows him likewise to be a literary descendant of Francis Bacon, at least in the purpose and titles of his essays: Bacon's "Of Truth," "Of Love," "Of Nobility," and "Of Beauty," are paralleled by Montalvo's "De la nobleza" (Of Nobility), "De la belleza en el género humano" (Of Beauty in the Human Species), and "Del genio" (Of Genius).

Montalvo's work foreshadows what Spanish prose would come to be, as exemplified by *El idearium Español* (1896) by Ángel Ganivet, precursor of the notable Generation of 1898. Montalvo, however, outshone Ganivet and his colleagues, with the exception of Miguel de Unamuno. Montalvo's advantage over Ganivet was the originality of the inspiration with which he mastered the torrent of ideas that came to him, at times confusedly, when he sat down to write.

Montalvo was born on 13 April 1832, in Ambato, Ecuador, then a small, backward Andean city. He spent his childhood on the beautiful little farm of Ficoa. A few years later, Montalvo studied in Quito, where, in May 1851, he graduated with a master's degree in philosophy. At that time, English free-trade policies opened the port of Guayaquil to world markets, thus ruining Quito's textile industry. This event sealed the capital's fate as a city of gloom in which any cry for liberty or democracy became a blasphemy against the divine order that had sustained its peaceful way of life for decades. Montalvo was oppressed in his yearnings to express himself freely and was almost considered a *malhechor* (wrongdoer), as were all opponents of the government. He lived in the home of Julio Zaldumbide, a liberal poet and *rara avis* whose own ideas would cost him his life. In 1857, Montalvo traveled to Europe as secretary of the Ecuadorian legation and in 1857 was assigned to Paris. He wrote to his brother, Francisco Javier, "I spend my days either in the woods on the city's outskirts, or in its museums and libraries; I almost always go to the Louvre, and I do not leave until the guards shout 'Messieurs, on va fermer'" (Rufino Blanco Fombora, *Montalvo*, Madrid, 1917).* One year later, after enthusiastic reflections on a trip to Italy, he visited Alphonse de Lamartine, who, financially ruined and deeply depressed, told Montalvo that he would have to sell his lands at Milly in order to survive. Montalvo, who was an admirer of Lamartine's work, invited the poet to visit the magnificent landscapes of the Andes.

In 1860, though not yet twenty-eight years old, Montalvo returned to Ecuador ill and, because of a swollen knee, on crutches, to find that the despot Gabriel García Moreno had seized power. Montalvo wrote in a letter to García Moreno that

> the nation needs renewal, and so do you. Your past behavior brings to light the atrociousness of your deeds. . . . Your actions were treacherous, have no doubt about it. . . . You have shown yourself to be excessively violent. . . . There is wisdom in moderation. . . . Do not let power corrupt you, Sir; call reason to your aid. . . . If I were ever to decide to participate . . . in the affairs of our country, you can be certain that you and anyone else . . . who opposed the freedom and rights of the people would have me as an enemy, and not an ordinary one, Sir. . . . You have the characteristics of both a hero . . . and a tyrant. . . . Relinquish . . . your absolute power. Does my frankness irritate you? You must understand clearly that I have more than enough courage to face the consequences of my candor.

This daring public letter did not receive an immediate reply, but "the fulfillment of this vow is, in terms of civic spirit and action, Montalvo's story" (Rodó, 1913). Later, in 1866, when the magazine *El cosmopolita* (The Cosmopolitan) appeared, García Moreno surprised Montalvo, its editor, by publishing two vicious sonnets. The title of the first, "A Juan que volvió tullido de sus viajes sentimentales" (To Juan, Who Came Back from His Sentimental Journeys Lame), reveals García Moreno's intention to ridicule his opponent by referring to his limp. The second tercet of the sonnet ends this way:

*All translations in this article are the work of its translator, Theodore Parks.

> *Y tras tanta fatiga y largos años,*
> *Regresar de cuadrúpedo a su tierra*
> *Quien, yéndose en dos pies, volvióse en cuatro!*
> (in Manuel María Polit Lasso,
> *Escritos y discursos de García Moreno*,
> Quito, 1923, p. 366)

And after so much fatigue and so many years
To return to your land a quadraped
You, who left on two feet but came back on four!

The second sonnet concludes with these words:

> *Si te viste tú mismo, yo discurro*
> *Que debiste también de ver un burro.*
> (*ibid.*, p. 367)

If you took a glance at yourself, I would say
What you would really see is an ass.

The fight between the writer and the tyrant ended only with García Moreno's death in 1875. Montalvo "had a prophetic voice, . . . a lyric loftiness and a dramatic emphasis, a cutting wit and an ethic based on moral rectitude" (Leopoldo Benites, *Ecuador: Drama y paradoja*, Mexico City, 1950, p. 226). Montalvo's rage was not aroused only against the tyrant but also against García Moreno's courtiers:

> Meddlesome and boisterous rabble, who purposelessly lie and prattle and flit foolishly about, a rude mob always in an uproar, an unimportant and ragged little crew, ignorant and hopeless riffraff. . . . And let García Moreno go to confession and take communion, . . . and let him go to hell with fifty or so pounds of communion wafer in his stomach to see if he can digest it there.
> (*El cosmopolita*, no. 1 [1860])

In *La dictadura perpetua* (The Perpetual Dictatorship, 1874), Montalvo declares that "García Moreno divided the Ecuadorian people in three equal parts: the first he sentenced to death, the second to exile, and the third to servitude." Exiled himself in 1869 to the Colombian town of Ipiales, Montalvo is said to have exclaimed upon learning of the despot's death, "My pen killed him!" Shortly after this, in his pamphlet "El último de los tiranos" (The Last of the Tyrants, 1875), Montalvo wrote,

Had García Moreno died in his bed, his people would have born forever the brand of slavery; he has died violently, however, and his victims can therefore claim a title of respect among free nations. . . . "My adversaries have the duty to kill me; if they do not, I shall exterminate them," he said. . . . To the Minister of Colombia the last time [they met], in violation of his own oath, he proclaimed himself dictator.

Around this time the devastating earthquake of August 1868 struck Imbabura, leaving the city of Ibarra in ruins. Montalvo immediately wrote Victor Hugo an elegiac description of the catastrophe:

You, poet of the heart, citizen of the universe, . . . would you not offer a glance toward these ruins, a sigh for these sighs, a tear for these tears? . . . And if you should happen upon an insignificant little barbarian who . . . has dared address himself to you, do not look at his intelligence, which is a minute thing, but see that, in his arrogance, he has overstepped his bounds to the extreme of measuring himself against you in his capacity for feeling.

Hugo answered him in this way:

Your precious letter has arrived late; in it you have made me an emotional plea. I shall seize the first opportunity I have to awaken the concern of all. . . . I have spoken against the scourge of despots; I shall not fail in my obligation likewise to speak against mankind's other tyrants, the elements of nature. . . . I am with you from the depths of my heart. I take your hand in my own. You are a noble spirit.

(in Roberto Agramonte, *Montalvo en su epistolario*, Puerto Rico, 1982, pp. 77–78)

In 1879, after spending seven of the last ten years in exile at Ipiales, Montalvo was able, with his friends' generous help, to leave again for Europe. In Ipiales he had had to sell his watch to eat and, offered more money than it was actually worth, had rejected the offer by saying "No, my watch is not worth more than twelve pesos," though these were days when he was persistently haunted by hunger. On his way to Europe, Montalvo stopped in Panama, where Eloy Alfaro, the great hero of liberalism, was living. Alfaro furnished him with money to support his publications and to help enable him to return to France.

Montalvo was, however, able to remain in Paris for only one year. Without great resources, and with the approach of the Franco-Prussian War, he returned to Panama, continued on to Lima, and returned to his exile in Ipiales.

The critic Enrique Anderson Imbert believes that "for [Montalvo] language is like a religion, with its rites, priests, and theologians" (Anderson Imbert, *El arte de la prosa en Juan Montalvo*, 1948, p. 49). Montalvo called Juan de Valdés, Covarrubias, and Don Diego de Clemencín the "Fathers of the Church of the Spanish Language" (*Siete tratados*, vol. 1, 1912, p. 348). When Marcelino Menéndez y Pelayo reproached Montalvo for his use of the French *roman* to mean "novel," Montalvo "kicked that frenchified foreigner out on his ear," and said "I am the first to take up arms and march in defense of this second religion that is called pure language, classic language" (*El espectador* [The Spectator], 1927, p. 233).

During the corrupt, dishonest, and chaotic dictatorship of José Ignacio de Veintemilla (1876–1883), Montalvo, who had begun the publication of *El regenerador* (The Regenerator, 1876–1878), was expelled from Ecuador and began the biting series *Las catilinarias* (1880–1882), whose first issues were financed by Alfaro in Panama. In 1881, Montalvo went to Paris again, where he lived until his death on 17 January 1889. The following passage from *Las catilinarias* provides an example of his indignation against "Ignacio de la Cuchilla" (Ignacio the Knife), as Montalvo called Veintemilla:

Laws? Why does he want laws? A tyrant, no problem; one can put up with a tyrant for fifteen years [the period García Moreno was in power]; but a villain? Ignacio de Veintemilla has never been and will never be a tyrant; his lack of brains is such that it is but a small step from him to a brute animal. His heart does not beat; it rolls around in a pool of slime. . . . Oh, God, and how he gobbles down the food! . . . Meat for the first dish, meat for the second, meat for the third; ten, twenty, thirty servings of meat. Is he full? Is he stuffed yet? He vomits in the stall, empties the waste bag, and continues eating in order to drink, and drinking in order to eat. . . . You who kill with the tongue and with the dagger; you who lie, . . . you who rob, rob, rob!

Unamuno, after hanging a commemorative plaque in the house at 26, rue Cardinet, where Montalvo lived for several years and in which he died, delivered a fervent defense of the great writer after Gonzalo Zaldumbide, the Ecuadorian diplomatic representative in Paris, had finished his opening address. Unamuno later extended this defense in the 1925 edition of *Las catilinarias*. "It was indignation," says Unamuno,

> that made [a man] who would have been no more than a man of letters with a passion for the study of Cervantes into an apostle, a prophet burning with poetic quixotism. I began to devour the *Catalinarias*. . . . I read them searching for their sharp, bleeding insults. The insults, yes! The insults that moved Montalvo's ardent and generous soul.

Answering Unamuno, Anderson Imbert says,

> Unamuno was unfair in his evaluation. . . . There is something more than insults in [Montalvo's] literature. Insult for the sake of insult added nothing to his work. . . . He had neither Rabelais' freedom nor his torrential and enumerative tongue, but . . . indignation saved him when his rhetoric began eating away at his prose. The insults came forth and were made into literature, came forth from . . . the conceptions Montalvo had of men, life, and history; and they were as well wrought as a metaphor or an allegory.
>
> (Anderson Imbert, *El arte de la prosa en Juan Montalvo*, 1948, p. 137)

Montalvo's masterpiece is *Siete tratados*. These "treatises" are essays, really, not pieces of systematic investigation of a scientific nature. However, his ethical-social values are also well represented in various pieces collected in *Páginas desconocidas* (Unpublished Pages), first published in Havana in 1936. Montalvo's social ethic is conveyed by the following passage:

> If my pen had the gift of tears, I would write a book entitled "The Indian," and I would make the world cry. . . . The Indians are . . . more civilized . . . than the whites in Ecuador: the whites are Negroes: García Morena will not be long in sending them to the coasts of the Congo and Guinea to be sold. Thus we will have traffickers in white slaves where until now there have only been traffickers in blacks. . . . Indians, noble Indians! Hunted with dogs as in Pizarro's time!

Agustín Yerovi's biographical essay tells us how Montalvo, gravely ill with pleurisy (he was probably suffering from tuberculosis), would not consent to anesthesia for the painful operation that the surgeon was to perform. Yerovi reports Montalvo's words: "Never have I lost consciousness of my actions. You will operate as if the knife produced no pain." Two days later, Yerovi tells us, he found Montalvo dressed in a formal coat and listened to his explanation of his formal attire: "The step into eternity is man's most serious." Yerovi then adds that, turning to a maid, Montalvo instructed her, "Do not forget my request. A corpse without flowers has always saddened me." Rufino Blanco Fombona, in his "Don Juan Montalvo" (in *Grandes escritores de América*, Madrid, 1917), adds, "They took him four carnations. . . . In winter, in Paris, and for five francs, it would have been impossible to fill the room for him with the roses and irises he would have liked."

Darío Lara's well-documented research (1983), however, proves that the "maid" referred to by Yerovi was, in fact, no maid at all, but rather Montalvo's lover and faithful companion of several years, Augustine-Catherine Contoux, a seamstress. Montalvo had a son by her, Jean Contoux-Montalvo, whose descendants still live in France. Neither is it out of line to admit that Montalvo was excommunicated by a dim-witted Quito bishop, José Ignacio Ordóñez, to whom he replied with a tremendous verbal lashing in *Mercurial eclesiástica* (1884). Nor is it too much to add that, despite the fame he had already attained in Europe and despite having friends like Juan Valera, Emilia Pardo Bazán, Campoamor, Gaspar Núñez de Arce, and Emilio Castelar to praise him, Montalvo was rejected for membership by the Spanish Academy of Language in 1883. A radical in that conservative institution—what a scandal it would have been! On learning of his rejection, Montalvo exclaimed, "I can exist without the Academy."

On 13 April 1919, to commemorate the day of Montalvo's birth in 1832, *El Condor* (The Condor), the newspaper of Ambato, the home town of the "cosmopolitan," reproduced the funeral invitation published in Paris on 18 January 1889. The invitation read this way:

> The countrymen of Mr. Juan Montalvo, who passed away in Paris on the seventeenth day of this month, . . . request that you honor with your presence the funeral

services that will take place at the Church of St. Francis of Sales, Bremontier Street, Sunday, the twentieth, at noon. The procession will begin at the home of the deceased at 26 Cardinet Street.

Unamuno's excessive admiration of Montalvo's insults and the paucity of attention he focused on the great master of the language can be pardoned if we remember that he too suffered exile at the hands of the Spanish dictator Primo de Rivera. One must remember, too, these beautiful words from Unamuno's prologue to *Las catilinarias*:

He was called mad, like Jesus, by his own, by his family. Like Jesus, according to the Fourth Gospel, he was crucified as unpatriotic. He was also mad like Don Quixote, who was blamed for the misfortunes of his country. And like these two Montalvo died, Christian, quixotic, poor, alone, and an outcast.

Translated from the Spanish by Theodore Parks

SELECTED BIBLIOGRAPHY

First Editions

Siete tratados. Besançon, France, 1882–1883. Includes "De la nobleza," "De la belleza en el género humano," and "Del genio."
Mercurial eclesiástica. Paris, 1884, 1895.
Capítulos que se le olvidaron a Cervantes. Besançon, France, 1895.
Geometría moral. Madrid, 1902.
Páginas desconocidas. Havana, 1936.

Later Editions

Capítulos que se le olvidaron a Cervantes. Quito, 1986.
El cosmopolita. Paris, 1927. Gathers together numbers of a serial originally published in Quito, 1866–1869.
El espectador. Paris, 1927. Gathers together numbers of a serial originally published in Paris, 1886–1888.
Geometría moral. Buenos Aires, 1968.
Las catilinarias. Bogotá, 1984. Gathers together numbers of a serial originally published in Panama City, 1880–1882.
Mercurial eclesiástica. Ambato, Ecuador, 1948.

Montalvo en su epistolario. Edited by Roberto D. Agramonte. Río Piedras, Puerto Rico, 1982.
Páginas desconocidas. Ambato, Ecuador, 1970.
El regenerador. Paris, 1929. Gathers together numbers of a serial originally published in Quito (nos. 1–3, 6–12); Guayaquil, Ecuador (no. 4); and Panama City (no. 5).
Selecciones. Puebla, Mexico, 1960.
Siete tratados. Paris, 1912.

Translations

Selections from Juan Montalvo. Translated by Frank MacDonald Spindler and Nancy Cook Brooks. Tempe, Arizona, 1984.

Biographical and Critical Studies

Actas del Colegio de Besançon Juan Montalvo en Francia. Paris, 1976. A compilation of the proceedings of a congress dedicated to Montalvo's work.
Agramonte, Roberto. *El panorama cultural de Montalvo.* Ambato, Ecuador, 1935.
———. *La filosofía en Montalvo.* Quito, 1972.
Anderson Imbert, Enrique. *El arte de la prosa en Juan Montalvo.* Mexico City, 1948. Medellín, Colombia, n.d.
Andrade, Roberto. *Montalvo y García Moreno.* 2 vols. Puebla, Mexico, 1970.
Blanco Fombona, Rufino. *Montalvo.* Madrid, 1917.
Carrión, Benjamin. *El pensamiento vivo de Montalvo.* Buenos Aires, 1961.
Crawford, W. Rex. In *A Century of Latin-American Thought.* Cambridge, Mass., 1963. Chapter 6.
Cultura. (Quito) 12 (1982). Special edition of this journal, marking Montalvo's sesquicentennial. With an introduction by Susana Cordero de Espinosa.
Darío, Rubén. "La *Mercurial* de Montalvo" and "Pro domo mea." In *Crónica literaria.* Madrid, n.d. Pp. 169–193.
García Calderón, Ventura. *Montalvo.* Madrid, 1920.
Jaén Morente, Antonio. *Juan Montalvo y Emilia Pardo Bazán.* Quito, 1944.
Jaramillo Alvarado, Pío. "Montalvo político." *América* (Quito) 8:49. This special issue was entitled *Homenaje a Don Juan Montalvo.*
Lara, Darío. *Montalvo en París.* 2 vols. Quito, 1983.
Naranjo, Plutarco. *Juan Montalvo.* Quito, 1966.
Reyes, Alfonso. "Sobre Montalvo." In *Simpatías y diferencias.* Madrid, 1921.
Rodó, José Enrique. "Montalvo." In *El mirador de Próspero.* Montevideo, 1913. Pp. 204–289. The essay also appears in Rodó's *Obras completas.* Madrid, 1957.

Roig, Arturo Andrés. *El pensamiento social de Montalvo.* Quito, 1984.

Rosenblat, Ángel. Introduction to *Capítulos que se le olvidaron a Cervantes.* Buenos Aires, 1944. Pp. 5–21.

Unamuno Miguel de. Prologue to *Las catilinarias.* Paris, 1925. Pp. ix–xxiii.

Valdano, Juan. *Léxico y símbolo en Juan Montalvo.* Otavalo, Ecuador, 1981.

Vásconez Hurtado, Gustavo. *Pluma de acero o la vida novelesca de Juan Montalvo.* Mexico City, 1944.

Vitier, Medardo. "Los *Siete tratados* de Montalvo." In *Del ensayo americano.* Mexico City, 1945. Pp. 75–94.

Yerovi, Agustín L. *Juan Montalvo, ensayo biográfico.* Paris, 1901. Ambato, Ecuador, 1932.

Ricardo Palma

(1833–1919)

José Miguel Oviedo

In nineteenth-century Peruvian literature, Ricardo Palma is the central, and perhaps sole, figure whose fame and prestige have spread throughout Spanish America and Spain to the extent of making him a classic of the republic's first century of literature. Although his works were many and varied, his popularity is mainly a response to his numerous *Tradiciones peruanas* (Peruvian Traditions).

Palma was born in Lima on 7 February 1833, twelve years after his country's declaration of independence. There are some unanswered questions concerning his background, whose details must have weighed heavily on him as both man and writer, faced with the prejudices of his time. The name he would make famous with his pen was not the one he received at birth. Christened "Manuel," he added "Ricardo" when he was fifteen and signed his first works "Manuel Ricardo Palma." According to his birth certificate, he is the natural son of Pedro Palma and Guillerma Carrillo, both *pardos,* or mulattos. However, it seems that Guillerma Carrillo was not really Palma's mother, according to the historian Raúl Porras Barrenechea, who found the birth certificate. Guillerma Carrillo could be the name of Palma's grandmother, and a woman named Dominga Soriano may well have been the writer's real mother.

In any case, Palma's parents, modest folk of limited means, lived with him for only a short time. On the one hand, Pedro Palma, although he married Dominga Soriano five years after the author's birth, lived apart from her until he died at the age of seventy-eight. On the other, his mother died when Palma was a child. There are no data on how many were in the family or how close they were, and there are no "true confessions" from Palma on this obscure aspect of his life.

Palma was born in the heart of Lima, an old city with a strong colonial flavor and deeply rooted customs barely altered by the change to the republican social organization. Palma's imagination was better trained in the lively, busy atmosphere of the street than in school; this orientation had a decisive influence on his work as a *tradicionista.* He lived his infancy and youth during years of great political turmoil and instability in Peru. Republican ideals frequently clashed with the chaos and disorder caused by the ambitions of the military's *caudillos,* or strong men. Palma's life often became involved with the trifling incidents of politics.

Although there was an active political and social life in nineteenth-century Peru, the literary ambience was meager and listless. The 1830's and 1840's were characterized by a transition from tenacious neoclassicism to the first notions of romanticism, and the limited public interest in literature was divided between academic expressions and popular, often anonymous, satire. In fact, Palma's generation, that of the 1830's, produced the first literary manifestations of the century that had the characteristics of a real movement. Romanticism arrived late in Peru, around 1850, and flourished in the years that followed, when the wave of romanticism in Spain and the rest of Spanish America was subsiding. Palma was, without doubt, the most visible personality in the group (although he soon separated himself from it), and it is still remembered by the name he gave it; he called the group "the bohemians," because of its disorderly and juvenile appearance on the contemporary literary scene.

In 1848, while a student just fifteen years old, Palma published his first poetry in Lima's newspaper *El Comercio*; at the same time he directed the satirical newspaper *El Diablo*, in an early indication of his literary leanings toward satire. Like many of the "bohemians," Palma tried to gain recognition first as a playwright. In 1851 and 1852 he staged three dramatic works; he published one of them, *Rodil* (1851), which deals with a historical theme. These works are nothing more than curiosities that later even Palma considered mere juvenile exercises. At the same time, he published his first romantic prose works and collaborated on various journals and newspapers; this journalistic activity continued throughout his mature life. In 1855, he published his first book of poetry entitled, simply, *Poesías* (Poems).

In 1860, as a result of his participation in a conspiracy against President Ramón Castilla (to whom Palma later became an ally and a friend), he was exiled to Chile, where he spent three years. His Chilean period was very important: it allowed him time to mature; to distance himself as a writer from the limited, local literary world of Lima; to collaborate on prestigious journals; and to develop a taste for history. When he returned to Peru, he brought from Chile the manuscript of the *Anales de la inquisición de Lima* (Annals of the Inquisition in Lima, 1863), which contained the germ of the idea that later gave rise to Palma's version of the *tradición*, an anecdotal, satirical, and vaguely idealized form that popularized historical motifs.

In 1864, Palma traveled through Europe, visiting Paris, London, and Venice. The following year he published his second book of poems, *Armonías* (Harmonies), in Paris. He then returned to his own country, which was facing a conflict with Spain and was also stirred by internal political strife, in which he actively participated. In 1868, when José Balta's revolution succeeded and Balta became president, Palma served as his personal secretary. Later Palma became both a representative and a senator in Congress for several terms. His third book of poems, *Pasionarias* (Passion Flowers), appeared in Le Havre in 1870.

In 1872, Palma collected the first series of *Tradiciones* in one volume, having published many in various newspapers. Its success was immediate. The same year, Palma retired from politics, worn out by the violence of recent events—which had culminated in the assassination of Balta—and devoted more of his time to his role as *tradicionista*.

In the years that followed, successive series of the *Tradiciones* appeared, cementing Palma's success as a writer. In 1876 he married Cristina Román; their two children, Clemente and Angélica, later became writers. In 1878, Palma was named a corresponding member of the Royal Academy of the Spanish language. The disastrous war between Peru and Chile (1879–1883) brought hard times for Palma. When Chilean troops burned his house in Miraflores, near Lima, the manuscript of what could have been a novel, "Los marañones" (The People of the Maranon), as well as books and many precious documents, were lost. During the Chilean occupation of Lima, Palma survived mostly on money from collaborations with foreign publications. In 1883 he was named director of the National Library and was charged with restoring it to its prewar state (it had been sacked and emptied by the Chileans). He initiated an international campaign that appealed to friends and colleagues for donations of books. He became known as the "begging librarian," a nickname that filled him with pride. The same year a set of the initial six series of *Tradiciones* appeared in a single edition for the first time, compiled by Carlos Prince.

During this period a new generation of Peruvian writers came to the fore. The most striking figure, Manuel González Prada, a refined poet and passionate prose writer, became the critical conscience of a Peru trying to recover from the ravages of war. González Prada accused the preceding generation of vain idealism and of defending outdated values. Palma was his favorite target for these aggressive judgments, since his *tradiciones* were models of national literature—models turned toward the past. With some irony, but showing just how much these attacks affected him, the subsequent series of *tradiciones* bore titles such as *Ropa vieja* (Old Clothes, 1889), *Ropa apolillada* (Moth-eaten Clothes, 1891), and *Cachivaches* (Junk, 1900).

Palma was aware that a literary age was coming to a close and that he now belonged to the past, to whose fictional reconstruction he had dedicated his life. His journey to Spain in 1892 contributed to his feeling of having given himself to a task not completely understood by others; although Spain's literary circles received him with respect and esteem, his dream of convincing the Royal Academy to include Spanish-American expressions in their dictionary was received with indifference. Palma published the fruit of his lexicographical efforts in two volumes: *Neologismos y americanismos* (Neologisms and Americanisms, 1896) and *Papeletas lexicográficas* (Lexicographical Index Cards, 1903).

Forbidden to write by his doctor and worn out from old age, Palma spent his last years in semiretirement. In 1911 his wife's death was a blow to his already delicate spirit. The same year, in Barcelona, his *Poesías completas* (Collected Poems) appeared. Amidst a scandal, one that once again brought him face-to-face with González Prada, he gave up his post at the library. In spite of repeated promises, he did not stop writing *tradiciones* and numerous letters to his friends up to the end. Palma died on 6 October 1919 at his Miraflores home, at the age of eighty-six. In recognition of his stature as a writer, the government arranged funeral services equivalent to those for a minister of state, occasioning a great display of public mourning. The year of his death, the important journal *Mercurio peruano* dedicated an edition in homage to him, the first of many, in which numerous friends and Peruvian writers collaborated, such as the historians Raúl Porras Barrenechea and José de la Riva-Agüero, and the critic Luis Alberto Sánchez.

Palma's relationship with Peruvian romanticism is both ambiguous and complex. On the one hand, he never stopped publishing poetry with clearly sentimental touches, inspired by motifs (freedom, love, exotic landscapes, and the motherland) characteristic of the romantic style. But he also produced works in a quite different vein, such as the poems in *Verbos y gerundios* (Verbs and Gerunds, 1877), in which he displayed witty, light, and derisive work vaguely inspired by the poetry of Heinrich Heine. Although minor, these texts constitute his most original contribution to the very modest body of Peruvian romantic poetry.

But Palma's "bohemian" stage was short-lived and not very significant; he always viewed it with self-irony, as if it were an amusing prologue to the discovery of his own literary path. This path led to a particular treatment of historical themes, a concern typical of romanticism. Strangely enough, Palma was the only "bohemian" seriously interested in exploiting the national historical vein further than the absurd "medievalist" imitations of some of his peers. In separating himself from the common attitudes of the "bohemians," Palma was actually more "romantic" than they, and his *tradiciones* represent a note of good sense and eclecticism within the literary canon adopted by the Peruvian romantics.

Palma's relationship with history is ambiguous and subtle. On the one hand, he wanted to be considered a historian, as we can see in his *Anales*. However, his more serious effort to be recognized as such, the short 1877 pamphlet entitled "Monteagudo y Sánchez Carrión" (about two figures associated with Peru's independence) provoked a hostile reaction from other historians. This convinced Palma that he had a unique place within the wide field of history, that of *tradicionista*, which allowed him to use facts from the past with freedom, humor, and imagination, all of which were native to his own temperament. The genre's success confirmed the demand for this kind of historical literature, both in and out of Peru; the *tradiciones*, as Palma said, hit "en la yema del gusto," a phrase that expresses the felicitous rapport that existed between the genre and the public's taste at the time.

Palma also claimed that he had "invented" the genre, which is not exactly true. The *tradición* was already common in the nineteenth century and was made fashionable by romanticism. Spread by means of journals, newspapers, and sometimes pamphlets, including the ever-favorite *feuilleton*, these little novels and reelaborations of legends and history were popular throughout Europe. The Spaniards imitated them and developed their own models, making use of the national predilection for *costumbrismo* (the depiction of local customs and types). The basic source of the *tradición* is the synthesis of the romantic legend in prose and the customs and manners article.

This heritage of historical tales, brought to Spanish America by romanticism, was vigorously taken up and adapted to new themes: the Indian, the epic of the Conquest, the legendary past. But among the Spanish-American *tradicionistas* of the time (including Palma's numerous imitators), Palma stands out with his very personal voice and vision. Although the sentimental legends, or "historical romances" with Incan themes, which he wrote at the beginning of the 1850's, cannot be distinguished at all from others that abounded at the time, shortly afterward he refined his historical intuition and his ability to express it in short, graceful lines. At the beginning of the *tradición* "Un virrey y un arzobispo" (A Viceroy and an Archbishop, 1874), whose first version, entitled "Debellare superbos," was published in *La revista de Lima* in 1860, Palma makes a programmatic defense of the genre:

the colonial age . . . is a source little used even by the American intellect. . . . In Spanish America the *tradición* barely survives. . . . Meanwhile, it is up to the younger writers to do something to avoid losing the *tradición* completely. So, we prefer to attract the public's attention to it by dressing the historical narrative in the trappings of romance.

Three things must be noted in this statement: his interest in the colonial past (which could be contradictory to a liberal spirit such as Palma's); his self-appointed role as a popularizer of history; and his right to invent upon a nucleus built up from documents and sources that attested to the past.

Palma would take a little longer to reach maturity as a *tradicionista* (his style was not defined until around 1864), an artistry that was, above all, either an ironic or charming depiction of what official history dryly tells us. If Palma did not invent the

genre, he did indeed develop a personal tone for it, a new way of telling history, which was as much reminiscent of the old, popular chronicle as it was of *criollo* satire or the Spanish picaresque novel. The *tradición* prolongs and aesthetically perfects the satirical vein of national *costumbrismo*, guarding and maintaining its popular flavor but granting it the grace of precise, suggestive, and colorful language. To a genre dominated by formal improvisation and carelessness, Palma brought the novelty of an unmistakable tone and a unique style.

Over and over, in letters to writers and personal friends (some also *tradicionistas*), Palma insisted that the essence of the *tradición* was its form, achieved only through deliberate effort; the form created a strong historical feeling (or "poetry of the past," as Palma called it) in the reader's imaginations. As he put it in a letter to Vicente Barrantes, dated 29 January 1890: "To my mind, a *tradición* is not something to be taken lightly; it is instead a work of art. I have the patience of a Benedictine for smoothing and polishing a sentence. It is form, more than content, that makes it popular" (*Epistolario* 1, p. 334). In another letter, dated 5 July 1875, to the Argentine romantic writer Juan María Gutiérrez, he explained:

I believe that the *tradición* depends above all on its form. It should be told as if it were a story. The pen should flow lightly and be frugal with details. The comments must be quick. The philosophy of the story or old wives' tale should make itself understood without the author having to say it. . . . At least, that is how I conceive the *tradición*.

(p. 20)

The importance Palma gave to form equaled the strength of his convictions regarding the chronicle's function as a historical genre and its relationship to the subject's truthfulness. Palma believed that the *tradición* acted as an auxiliary to history, as a lesser but gracious form that was the best means of educating people about their past: he gave them an idea of the great historical tapestry, seducing them with a fragment's brilliance, a dialogue's vivid color, or the humor of a minor situation. The chronicle served to provide the reader with a feeling of sharing a common past and, in fact, of belonging to a nation with old roots.

On the other hand, the chronicle's basically light or amusing character, a consequence of its narrative focus and language, allowed ample freedom for the treatment of historical truth. Unlike the erudite historian, the *tradicionista* could invent, fantasize, and interweave imaginary elements in order to complete the picture when certain data were lacking, while remaining faithful to the spirit and images evoked by the period in question. The realistic effect achieved was notable because it left a more persistent mark on the reader's imagination than did history itself. Always suspect as a historical source (although the great majority of his *tradiciones* are based on patient research), Palma was a remarkable storyteller. He based his authentic narrative technique on an artful style, a popular flavor, and a graceful eloquence.

Only occasionally did Palma choose a nonhistorical basis for a *tradición*. Some texts—like "La misa negra" (Black Mass), which Palma called "my grandmother's story," and other "little chronicles" about witches or old wives' tales from Lima—can almost be considered short stories. However, the author was quite reluctant to write without at least a minimal support of historical data. Significantly, when criticism was directed at Palma, he preferred to accept it as a creator rather than as a historical chronicler. When one of his *tradiciones* about Santa Rosa de Lima was challenged, Palma proudly declared his sources in a letter to Carlos Toribio Robinet dated 18 January 1878:

> I cannot understand how the gentlemen from *El Estandarte* can argue the literary absurdity that a writer cannot rightly deal with a theme already taken by someone else. Four volumes of *Tradiciones* have already been published, and two more will soon appear. In all of them there are no more than six legends whose plot belongs exclusively to me. From [el Inca] Garcilaso [de la Vega] and [Diego Fernández] El Palentino to the last conventual chronicler, the number of collaborators that I have had to string together in these poor pages of colonial history is infinite.

> (p. 76)

The nonpersonal origin of his anecdotes determined to an extent the structure of the *tradición*.

After presenting, in a rather general way, the mood or moment of the past in which the story occurred, Palma interrupted it with what he called "el consabido parafillo histórico" (the familiar little historical paragraph), in which he acknowledged his sources and provided the interested reader with more precise facts. This interpolation was a trademark of romanticism; it represented the discursive or digressive moment in which poets and writers of the time indulged. Then Palma continued his story and usually finished it off with a flourish, adding some element of comedy or surprise intended to show how false formal, official histories could be when their great protagonists acted like heroes rather than everyday people, as Palma wanted them to be perceived.

The *tradiciones* make up a collection of several hundred brief texts, whose variety of characters and thematic range is notable. From the Incas to the beginning of the twentieth century, from the most trivial detail to the most famous episode, they run the historical gamut of Peru. This diversity has at least two central points: Lima and the colonial world, especially the affluent, refined eighteenth century of Bourbon rule. Palma had a devotion to colonial times: approximately four hundred *tradiciones* deal with this period. The public came to identify the author with his themes; "colonialist Palma" was a charge that his critics, starting with González Prada, often used to attack him. This point is of interest and merits careful examination. Palma did not unrestrictedly idolize colonial Peru; it is easy to see that he cunningly made fun of it, wittily satirizing its customs and reproaching its habits. But his criticism was never bitter or cutting, and he never left the impression of an impossible rift between his republican ideals and his gentle colonial vision. He both mocked and revered colonial Peru; he criticized it, but he also grieved for it: his smile was accepting and nostalgic.

Palma was not so much a colonialist as he was an ambiguous, tolerant writer. The evils of the past in every case were lesser than those of the present, which he instinctively rejected when older. For him, "any past was better," as the Spanish poet Jorge Manrique had said, even if it was imperfect; the past was his psychological refuge when his own time wounded him with greed and a raw lack of charm. In

1872, after publishing his first series of *Tradiciones*, he wrote to the editor of the Buenos Aires newspaper *La Nación*, in which a favorable review of the book had appeared:

> The *Tradiciones* are my gift of love to my country and to literature. . . . I prefer to live in the past. In the past there was poetry, while today is just prosaic. . . , very prosaic. It is better to dress, adorn, and put together skeletons from colonial days. The work of the gravedigger, and nothing more, my friend; but tombs have their own kind of poetry.
>
> (p. 55)

Palma offered a courtly and complacent picture of colonial times, which corresponded fairly well to the traditional view of the national bourgeoisie that emerged after independence. Before Palma, this mentality had already made a myth of the Peruvian viceroyalty, raising it to the category of legend. Palma merely discovered the possibilities of this legend and made it into literature. In the people's imagination, the colonial era (and Lima, its most elegant center) was an arcadian time of luxurious splendor, a garden of delights, a bewitched court full of lover's trysts and quarrels, a fairy tale turned into reality. Three centuries of oppressive colonialization became almost honorable, even desirable.

The *tradiciones* earned the approval of the regressive element among the Peruvian petit bourgeoisie—a group who manifested a strange fixation with the past, consequence perhaps of the frustrated experience of the republican community. In the middle of the nineteenth century, when the remains of Spanish domination were still visible in Lima's customs, the light and frivolous evocation of the colonial city brought literature and the public into a new relationship.

Recognition of Palma's artistic consciousness, of the fact that he is the most refined of all Spanish-American satirists and *costumbristas*, should not prevent us from realizing, however, that his is, without doubt, a lesser art. Although the variety of topics and characters is great, Palma constantly repeats and imitates himself; his literary discoveries rapidly become patterns, even formulas. His inventive historical portraits are definitely amusing, but still monotonous and superficial. The plots basically do not differ; often only the words (countless proverbs, witty or picaresque verses added as picturesque brushstrokes, curiosities of dialect) change to give an impression of novelty. The anecdotes of offense and revenge, the conventual legends with the intervention of miracles or hoaxes, the forbidden idylls that end badly or destroy someone's honor, the fables of the repentant sinner or the seduced Don Juan—these are themes that systematically repeat themselves within the author's repertory.

Palma played with a certain number of stereotypes and worked them almost to exhaustion. His fondness for anecdotes sometimes created too much dispersion, too much miscellaneous chatter, under the indulgent assumption that the genre, as he said, was a *cajón de sastre* (bric-a-brac). Palma did not create in depth; he advanced through accumulation, scattering verbal humor and roguery, both essential to the story, in his opinion. He had a definite instinct for the expressive and picturesque line, for the graphic effect. His lexicographical passion led him to collect these lines in notebooks, which seem to be a depository of available techniques. Taking from here and there, he could "retouch" any little story and make it more tasty and interesting.

As a writer, Palma is a gallant and mystifying spirit, but he is also limited. His imaginary world presents a shiny exterior, where the strong and the weak, the famous and the anonymous, move as if dancers at a masquerade, but there is little to be seen underneath. His art is that of the miniaturist, in love with detail and hue but unable to paint the inner conflicts and real dramas of history. There are no deep tensions in the *Tradiciones*, no dilemmas that an opportune joke or ingenious trick cannot solve. We are offered an extensive gallery of characters and light, comic events, but almost never true human transcendence, since Palma's vision is foreign to problematical levels of reality. A fervid reader of colonial chronicles, such as those of the Inca Garcilaso de la Vega or Pedro de Cieza de León, Palma captured only what he found on the surface of those and other texts, reducing history to the level of gossip and tittle-tattle: history seen from a conformist's point of view.

Palma's frivolity flattered and soothed his public, confirming generally accepted myths and satisfying the need for historical topics. His *Tradiciones* contributed much to strengthen his country's historical consciousness. He also founded a literature authentically national in its roots, themes, and style, and with his fame he was able to gain aesthetic stature for Peruvian literature within the ample context of Hispanic letters, where he quickly became a "classic" thanks to his masterly handling of language. This unmistakably *criollo* spirit, so aware of Lima's popular and yet refined currents, was also a writer who yearned to be *castizo* (well-bred), accepted by contemporary Spanish academics and the great writers of Spain. He was both a Spanish-American writer and a purist, modern and archaic, and he gave the genre the international reputation it had lacked. His success and popularity say much about the function of historical literature and about the Spanish-American society of the time. His *Tradiciones peruanas* express and help define the Spanish-American consciousness as a new community during its formative period.

SELECTED BIBLIOGRAPHY

First Editions

Rodil. Lima, 1851. Drama in three acts with prologue.
Poesías. Lima, 1855.
Anales de la inquisición de Lima. Lima, 1863. Historical study.
Armonías: Libro de un desterrado. Paris, 1865. Poetry.
Lira americana. Collection of poetry by poets from Peru, Chile, and Bolivia, compiled by Ricardo Palma. Paris, 1865.
Pasionarias. Le Havre, France, 1870. Poetry.
Tradiciones. Lima, 1872. First series.
_____. Lima, 1874. Second series.
_____. Lima, 1875. Third series.
_____. Lima, 1877. Fourth series.
"Monteagudo y Sánchez Carrión." In *Documentos literarios del Perú* 11, edited by Manuel de Odriozola. Lima, 1877. Historical study.
Verbos y gerundios. Lima, 1877. Poetry.
El demonio de los Andes. New York, 1883. *Tradiciones* on the Conqueror Francisco de Carbajel.
Tradiciones. 6 vols. Lima, 1883. First to sixth series.
Enrique Heine. Traducciones. Lima, 1886. Poetry translations by Ricardo Palma.
Poesías. Lima, 1887.
Ropa vieja. Lima, 1889. Seventh series of *Tradiciones.*
Ropa apolillada. Lima, 1891. Eighth series of *Tradiciones.*
Tradiciones peruanas. 4 vols. Barcelona, 1893–1896.
Neologismos y americanismos. Lima 1896. Lexicographical study.
Recuerdos de España. Lima, 1899. Travel notes preceded by *La Bohemia de mi tiempo*, personal memoirs.
Tradiciones y artículos históricos. Lima, 1899.
Cachivaches. Lima, 1900. *Tradiciones* and miscellany.
Papeletas lexicográficas. Lima, 1903. Lexicographical documents.
Mis últimas tradiciones peruanas. Barcelona, 1906.
Apéndice a mis últimas tradiciones peruanas. Barcelona, 1910.
Poesías completas. Barcelona, 1911.

Modern Editions

Tradiciones peruanas. 6 vols. Madrid, 1923–1925. Edition sponsored by the Peruvian government.
Tradiciones peruanas completas. Edited and with a prologue by Edith Palma. Madrid, 1952. Reprinted 1957.
Tradiciones peruanas. With a bibliography by Raúl Porras Barrenechea. Lima, 1952.
Tradiciones en salsa verde. 2nd ed. Lima, 1973.

Collected Letters

Epistolario. 2 vols. Edited and with a prologue by Raúl Porras Barrenechea. Lima, 1949.
Diecisiete cartas inéditas con otras éditas cambiadas con Doña Lola Rodríguez de Tió (1894–1907). With a prologue, notes, and appendix by Luis Alberto Sánchez. Lima, 1968.
Cartas indiscretas de Ricardo Palma. Edited by César Miró. Lima, 1969.
Cartas a Piérola sobre la ocupación chilena de Lima. With a preliminary study and notes by Rubén Vargas Ugarte. 2nd ed. Lima, 1979.

Translation

The Knights of the Cape, and Thirty-seven Other Selections from the "Tradiciones peruanas" of Ricardo Palma. Selected, translated, and with an introduction by Harriet de Onís. Foreword by José Rollin de la Torre-Bueno y Thorne. New York, 1945.

Biographical and Critical Studies

Anderson Imbert, Enrique. "La procacidad de Ricardo Palma." *Revista iberoamericana* 18/36:269–272 (1953).

Arora, Shirley L. *Proverbial Comparisons in Ricardo Palma's "Tradiciones peruanas."* Folklore Studies 16. Berkeley and Los Angeles, 1966.

Bákula Patiño, Juan Miguel. "Don Ricardo Palma en Colombia. Tres de sus primeros impresos." *Fénix* 12:78–141 (1956–1957).

Bazin, Robert. "Les trois crises de la vie de Ricardo Palma." *Bulletin hispanique* 56/1–2:49–82 (1954).

Bonneville, Henri. "Ricardo Palma au présent." *Cahiers du monde hispanique et luso-brésilien* 39:27–47 (1982).

Carilla, Emilio. "Ricardo Palma y Casanova." *Cahiers du monde hispanique et luso-brésilien* 8:31–54 (1967).

Compton, Merlin D. *Ricardo Palma.* Boston, 1982.

———. "Las Tradiciones peruanas de Ricardo Palma: Bibliografía y lista cronología tentativa." *Duquesne Hispanic Review* 8/3:1–24 (1969).

Escobar, Alberto. "Tensión, lenguaje y estructura: Las Tradiciones peruanas." In *Patio de letras.* Lima, 1965. Pp. 68–140.

Feliú Cruz, Guillermo. *En torno a Ricardo Palma.* 2 vols. Santiago, Chile, 1933.

Flores, Ángel, ed. *Orígenes del cuento hispanoamericano: Ricardo Palma y sus "Tradiciones."* Mexico, 1979.

García Calderón, Ventura. "Nota preliminar." In his edition of *Tradiciones escogidas,* by Ricardo Palma. Paris, 1938. Pp. 7–12.

Leavitt, Sturgis E. "Ricardo Palma and the Tradiciones Peruanas." *Hispania* 34/4:349–353 (1951).

Mariátegui, José Carlos. "Ricardo Palma, Lima y la colonia." In *Siete ensayos de interpretación de la realidad peruana.* 13th ed. Lima, 1968. Pp. 193–200.

Martinengo, Alessandro. *Lo stile di Ricardo Palma.* Padua, 1962.

Miró, César. *Don Ricardo Palma: El patriarca de las tradiciones.* Buenos Aires, 1953.

Miró Quesada, Aurelio. "Noventa-dos cartas inéditas de Palma." In *Veinte temas peruanos.* Lima, 1966. Pp. 407–429.

Monguió, Luis. "Sobre un milagro en Meléndez, Palma y Barrios." *Revista hispánica moderna* 22/1:1–11 (1956).

Oviedo, José Miguel. *Genio y figura de Ricardo Palma.* Buenos Aires, 1965.

———, ed. Prologue and chronology, in his edition of *Cien tradiciones peruanas,* by Ricardo Palma. Caracas, 1977.

Porras Barrenechea, Raúl. *Tres ensayos sobre Ricardo Palma.* Lima, 1954.

Reedy, Daniel R. "Las Tradiciones en salsa verde de Ricardo Palma." *Revista iberoamericana* 32/61:69–75 (1966).

Riva-Agüero, José de la. *Del Inca Garcilaso a Eguren.* In *Obras completas* 2. Lima, 1963. Pp. 351–434.

Rodríguez-Peralta, Phyllis. "Liberal Undercurrents in Palma's Tradiciones peruanas." *Revista de estudios hispánicos* 15/2:283–297 (1981).

Rubman, Lewis H. "Ricardo Palma y el problema de la poesía romántica." *Revista iberoamericana* 32/61:113–120 (1966).

Salomon, Noël. "Las orejas del alcalde de Ricardo Palma: Un exemple de fabrication littéraire." *Bulletin hispanique* 69:441–453 (1967).

Sánchez, Luis Alberto. *La literatura peruana* 6. Asunción, 1951. Pp. 55–76.

———. "Ricardo Palma." In *Escritores representativos de América,* 1st series, 2. Madrid, 1963. Pp. 196–206.

Tanner, Roy L. "Ricardo Palma's Rhetorical Debt to Miguel de Cervantes." *Revista de estudios hispánicos* 17/3:345–361 (1983).

Thomas, Ruth S. "Las fuentes de las Tradiciones peruanas de Ricardo Palma." *Revista iberoamericana* 2/4:461–469 (1940).

Umphrey, George W., and Carlos García Prada. "Introducción." In *Flor de Tradiciones,* by Ricardo Palma. Mexico, 1943. Pp. vii–xxvii.

Winn, Conchita. "Más sobre las fuentes y documentos de información de que se sirvió Ricardo Palma: Sus lecturas en lenguas extranjeras." *Revista hispánica moderna* 34/3–4:799–809 (1968).

Xammar, Luis F. "Elementos románticos y antirrománticos de Ricardo Palma." *Revista iberoamericana* 4/7:95–107 (1941).

Estanislao del Campo

(1834–1880)

John F. Garganigo

The gaucho, legendary horseman of the pampas, is a social being indigenous to the River Plate region of Argentina, Uruguay, and Río Grande do Sul. This nomadic figure has inspired a great number of writers who have captured him in all his multifaceted aspects, covering a wide spectrum of views that range from the historical accounts of foreign travelers of the eighteenth century, to the fictionalized, highly romanticized literature of the nineteenth century. The literary gaucho exists even in our day. The influence of the historical gaucho was felt on the social, economic, and political planes from the second half of the sixteenth century to the end of the nineteenth century, when he finally succumbed to the forces of progress and became assimilated into society.

Characterized by a strong individualism and a rebellious nature, the gaucho held a particular mystique for the people of the River Plate. On a social level, the gaucho was a vagabond who profited from the illegal trade in hides of horses and cows, a practice that started in the colonial period and flourished until the end of the eighteenth century. This solitary individual also possessed many traits that were worthy of emulation. Like the North American cowboy, he was a master horse trainer and cattle hunter. He lived in direct contact with nature,

braving the elements without fear. He played an active role defending his country against the English invaders in 1806–1807 and fought valiantly against the Spanish and Portuguese forces during the wars of independence of 1810–1816.

The period following independence was chaotic; local and regional *caudillos* (military strongmen) participated in a number of civil wars in which they were aided by the blind allegiance of the gauchos. The struggle between the *unitarios*, the liberal, cultured individuals who favored a strong central government under the influence of Buenos Aires, and the *federales*, the conservative, traditionalist *caudillos* who clamored for a confederacy of independent, regional governments with political autonomy, polarized an emerging nation. The gauchos' support of the *caudillos* contributed significantly to the successful reign of Juan Manuel de Rosas, an enigmatic leader who ruled Argentina from 1835 to 1852.

The nineteenth-century Argentine politician and writer Domingo Faustino Sarmiento clearly defined this polarization as the struggle between civilization and barbarism, with the figure of the gaucho embodying the essence of the latter. Within a short period of forty years, the gaucho went from national hero to national disgrace.

With the advent of the great waves of immigration

that began during the latter decades of the nineteenth century and the modernization of the cattle industry, the gaucho's way of life became a thing of the past. While the real gaucho disappeared as a social entity, the literary gaucho, created by men of the city, continued to flourish. In their attempts to define autochthonous values, literary men of the city turned to the gaucho as the one individual who possessed many of the characteristics that they wanted to preserve. What emerged was a romanticized figure who bore little resemblance to the real gaucho. Writers felt a tie to this man of the pampas; they appreciated his rugged individualism, his ability to endure suffering, his perseverance, loyalty, and common sense. This mythmaking process culminated with the creation of Martín Fierro, the immortal gaucho made famous by José Hernández (1834–1886) in the poems *El gaucho Martín Fierro* and *La vuelta de Martín Fierro* (The Gaucho Martín Fierro, 1872, and The Return of Martín Fierro, 1879).

Estanislao del Campo is firmly entrenched within this literary tradition of gaucho poetry written by cultured men of the city. Their writings should not be confused with the oral, folkloric tradition of the *payadores,* wandering minstrels who improvised songs about the way of life of the inhabitants of the pampas. Although the subject matter is the same, the literary tradition did not evolve from the oral one. Gaucho poetry, written in a language akin to the spoken language of the man of the country, is totally a literary invention.

Gauchos, or *gauderios,* as they were called, first appeared in *El lazarillo de ciegos caminantes* (1773), a picaresque account of the travels of the main character, written by Calixto Bustamante, better known as Concolorcorvo. According to this writer, the *gauderios* were indolent men who lived in the most abject conditions. They composed earthy songs to be accompanied by the guitar, an instrument that they played not particularly well.

The gaucho then appeared in the works of the Uruguayan Bartolomé Hidalgo (1788–1822). His *Cielitos* (1811–1816) political songs whose main purpose was to incite patriots against Spanish and Portuguese enemies, employed the gaucho as a main character. The gaucho became the collective voice of those decrying injustice. In his *Diálogos* (Dialogues, 1821–1822) Hidalgo documented political reality, using the gaucho as a simple, rural being who is astounded when faced with urban situations. It is a point of departure for del Campo's masterpiece, *Fausto.*

Horacio Jorge Becco, who has studied the origins of gaucho poetry, attributes to Hidalgo the creation of basic formulae that later were adapted and developed most notably by del Campo and Hernández. Among them he includes the stock greetings between two gauchos, the offering of something tangible to the person recently arrived on the scene, how the gaucho's horses react to one another, remembrances of past, happy times, the gaucho's impressions of the city and his reactions to it, and the elimination of descriptive passages depicting nature.

Hilario Ascasubi (1807–1875) continued the tradition established by Hidalgo and wrote poems that were a direct indictment of Juan Manuel de Rosas. He created the pseudonymous character of Aniceto el Gallo (Aniceto the Rooster), who later inspired del Campo to create his own Anastasio el Pollo (Anastasio the Chicken). If Ascasubi was inspired by Hidalgo, del Campo in turn fashioned his writings after Ascasubi.

Estanislao del Campo was born in Buenos Aires on 7 February 1834. He died on 6 November 1880. Del Campo was a direct descendant of a patrician family with ties to the colonial viceroys of the River Plate. His father, Estanislao del Campo, fought against the dictatorship of Juan Manuel de Rosas. Young Estanislao became actively engaged in political matters from an early age. After the Battle of Monte Caseros (1852) and the fall of the Rosas regime, the provinces of Argentina united under the leadership of General Justo José de Urquiza, who invaded the Province of Buenos Aires. Del Campo defended the city against the troops of the Confederation under Urquiza.

Del Campo was considered by the elite of Buenos Aires society as a witty, intelligent young man who was more often than not the life of the party. He was not immune to playing an occasional prank on an unsuspecting victim. Underneath this playful nature, there was a more serious side to his personality. Del Campo became a newspaper writer and staunch defender of liberal causes. His combative, often vitriolic prose was frequently accented with touches of humor.

In 1855 he wrote a number of romantic poems typical of the age. These included love poems dedicated to young ladies of his time, as well as poems written with a deep religious fervor. The year 1857 saw the publication of "Décimas," gaucho poetry in the style of Aniceto the Rooster, pseudonym of Ascasubi. Del Campo signed his poems with the pen name Anastasio the Chicken.

As his literary career progressed, so did his military involvement. In 1861 he fought in the Battle of Pavón and was promoted to the rank of captain. In 1874 he reached the rank of colonel.

On 24 August 1866, del Campo witnessed the opening-night performance of Charles-François Gounod's opera *Faust* in the Teatro Colón of Buenos Aires. The events of that night have been documented by a number of critics. After the performance, del Campo recounted in a playful tone the details of the opera to a number of friends who had been with him in the theater. His account of the events, narrated in the typical language of the gauchos, produced laughter. Five days later, del Campo had produced a version of the opera that he gave to his friend, the noted Argentine writer Ricardo Gutiérrez. The result was *Fausto: Impresiones del gaucho Anastasio el Pollo en la representación de ésta ópera* (*Faust: Impressions of the Gaucho Anastasio the Chicken on the Presentation of This Opera*). The ingenious retelling of Johann Wolfgang von Goethe's work, adapted to the operatic stage by Gounod, and presented in 1866 in Buenos Aires with a libretto translated into Italian, was now retold by a simple, naive gaucho in del Campo's *Fausto*, one of Argentina's unquestioned literary masterpieces. The work was published on 30 September 1866 in the newspaper *El Correo de Domingo*, and on 3 and 4 October in *La Tribuna* of Buenos Aires. The definitive edition was published on 8 November 1866.

Enrique Anderson Imbert, the respected dean of Argentine criticism, has written extensively on *Fausto*. According to him, the seminal idea for the writing of *Fausto* came to del Campo when in 1857 he saw Giuseppe Verdi's opera *La traviata* and witnessed the saddened reaction of a young woman who empathized with the feelings of the protagonists. His observations gave rise to the poem "A unas lágrimas derramadas durante la presentacion de *La traviata*" (To Tears Shed During the Performance of *La traviata*).

Critics have also mentioned that del Campo might have been influenced by yet another performance; the recital by Emmy La Grúa in the opera *Saffo* by Giovanni Pacini, performed in Buenos Aires on 14 August 1857. Del Campo published a letter in *Los Debates* entitled "Carta de Anastasio el Pollo sobre el beneficio de la Señora La Grúa" (Letter from Anastasio the Chicken on the Benefit Performance of Madame La Grúa). The line between reality and fiction vanishes as the gaucho comments on the performance he has just witnessed.

In *Fausto*, rather than using the device of a letter, del Campo employs direct dialogue between two gauchos as his primary mode of expression. There are substantial reasons to believe that del Campo relied primarily on the Italian translation of the original French libretto as his source for *Fausto*, as well as the actual performance. Del Campo had worked on the Spanish translation of the libretto for the performance at the Teatro Colón.

Fausto is divided into six parts corresponding to the divisions of the libretto. It is a work of 1,278 eight-syllable verses in the popular *décimas* and *redondillas* stanzas. The *décima* is a ten-line stanza with a rhyme pattern of *abba, ac, cddc*. The *redondilla* is a four-line stanza with an *abba* rhyme pattern.

The dialogue between Anastasio el Pollo and his friend Laguna is the basis for this complex poem. Del Campo faithfully reproduces the simple dialect of the gaucho peasant. It is a language with many rustic images that reveal the charm and simplistic view of life of those who inhabit the countryside.

El Pollo greets his friend Laguna with a display of affection typical of the gaucho. As they embrace they exhibit a genuine feeling of affection that is contagious. Their two horses similarly nuzzle each other. The dialogue that follows reveals many nuances of gaucho life. Pollo begins telling the tale of his visit to Buenos Aires and alludes to an encounter with a gringo whom he considers inferior. This feeling of superiority on the part of the gaucho is typical of gaucho literature. The native son displays macho characteristics having to do with his capacity for drinking and his skill in games of chance.

In the course of the conversation Pollo mentions

that he had seen the devil in person, and after Laguna makes the customary sign of the cross to ward off the evil one, Pollo invites Laguna to sit down and enjoy the story that is about to unfold. Pollo and Laguna display their mutual friendship by sharing a bottle of gin. The motif of sharing food, a drink, or a cigarette acts to link the six parts of the poem.

In part 2, the poem assumes humorous characteristics as Pollo narrates his story. The humor is based on the parody of the story of Doctor Faustus. The sophisticated reader who comes to the text with complete cultural baggage is amused by the deformation of the details of the story as told by the simple, rustic gaucho. The gaucho might not be able to grasp the philosophical implications of the Goethean masterpiece, but his observations, aside from being humorous, reveal certain attitudes about his way of life.

The gaucho's attitude toward outsiders borders on racism. As Pollo joins the line waiting to enter the theater, he notices that someone has stolen his knife. His attitude is typical of the gaucho; some gringo must have stolen it. The same lack of respect for blacks and a general feeling of xenophobia is evident in *Martín Fierro*, Argentina's greatest gaucho poem. It was typical of an entire age.

Pollo's striking description of the devil is a vivid caricature based on literary tradition. The devil has "catlike claws, very thin countenance, a long sword, a plumed hat, cape, and a goatlike beard" (part 2, lines 1–4).

According to Pollo, Fausto does not want power or riches; all he desires is the love of the woman who has caused him so much pain. Margarita is compared to a virgin with lustrously smooth features, "golden hair, like the silk of new corn, white like milk curds, azure skirt, similar to the Immaculate Conception" (part 2, lines 3–5, 8). After cementing his pact with the devil, Fausto is changed from an old man to a handsome youth, his transformation captured in the image of a worm changing into a lovely butterfly.

In part 3 the plot is interrupted with a detailed description of nature, atypical of gaucho poetry. Del Campo's view that man's destiny is reflected in nature underscores a romantic aestheticism. This part ends with Margarita refusing to dance with her suitor and the devil promising that he has delivered women who were much more stubborn than the fair, blond maiden.

In part 4 Pollo sympathizes with Fausto in his repeated attempts to gain Margarita's favors. In a long digression, Pollo describes the effects of unrequited love. The suffering and pain are heightened by the constant presence of the loved one reflected in nature. A shift in the description of nature toward the end of part 4 prepares the way for Fausto's conquest of Margarita. As morning approaches and the entire countryside becomes alive, nature is resplendent in all its sounds and movements. Birds sing, the dew glistens, flowers gently sway and bend in the breeze, and as soon as the bud of a rose opens, a butterfly is ready to gather its nectar. All of this points to the eventual seduction of Margarita, alluded to in the text when the devil invites Fausto to enter her room and take advantage of the situation.

Part 5 of the poem deals with Pollo's reaction to Margarita's shame. Modern readers may be surprised by Pollo's defense of Margarita's honor. He denounces the double standard of the time, by which the woman is always made the victim, destined to suffer in shame. Had her brother been present to defend her, the results might have been different. Following a long tradition in Spanish poetry, Margarita's state is compared to that of a withered flower. "Not a trace was left of that rose-colored blonde. She was a withered carnation, a deflowered rose" (part 5, lines 1–4).

In part 6 Pollo continues the theme of the withered flower. Margarita's destiny is a cruel one. Like the flower whose fragrance and beauty is so captivating, woman is deceived into thinking that these attributes will last forever. As in the opera, Margarita kills her son, and as a result she is jailed. She dies, and Fausto, the cause of all her suffering, begs God's forgiveness; repentant, he asks God to receive her soul. In a scene reminiscent of romantic plays of the age, Saint Michael descends from heaven and defeats the devil. Margarita's soul is delivered from suffering and ascends into heaven. The poem ends with Pollo receiving his just reward for a story well told.

Despite the immense popularity of *Fausto*, critics have not been unanimous in its praise. Juan Carlos Gómez, Ricardo Gutiérrez, and Carlos Guido y Spano, contemporaries of del Campo, appreciated the poem for its social comments on gaucho life without understanding its full literary significance. Anderson Imbert, Leopoldo Lugones, and Ezequiel Martínez Estrada in our own century, in their attempts to place Hernández's *Martín Fierro* on a high pedestal, diminished the worth of *Fausto*. Critical battles aside, del Campo's poem stands out as a unique, original expression of Argentine literature. It is a work of art of great merit.

SELECTED BIBLIOGRAPHY

Editions

Fausto: Impresiones del gaucho Anastasio el Pollo en la representación de ésta ópera. Buenos Aires, 1866.

_____. With an introduction by Carlos Octavio Bunge. Buenos Aires, 1915.

_____. Facsimile edition. With an essay by Ernesto Mario Barreda and prologue by Raúl Quintana. Buenos Aires, 1940.

_____. With an introduction by Emilio Ravignani and an essay by Amado Alonso. Buenos Aires, 1943.

_____. With an introduction by Juan Bautista Aguilar Tórres. Buenos Aires, 1965.

Poesías. With an introduction by José Mármol. Buenos Aires, 1870.

_____. With an introduction by José Mármol. 3rd ed., enlarged, Buenos Aires, 1875.

Translations

Faust. Translated by Walter Owen. Buenos Aires, 1943.

Biographical and Critical Studies

Anderson Imbert, Enrique. *Análisis de Fausto.* Buenos Aires, 1968.

Assunção, Fernando O. *El Gaucho.* Montevideo, 1963.

Ayestarán, Lauro. "La primera edición uruguaya del *Fausto* de Estanislao del Campo." *Revista iberoamericana de literatura* 1:9–20 (1959).

Benítez, Rubén. "Una posible fuente española del *Fausto* de Estanislao del Campo." *Revista iberoamericana* 31/60:151–171 (1965).

Borges, Jorge Luís, and Adolfo Bioy Casares. *Poesía gauchesca.* 2 vols. Mexico City, 1955.

Mújica Láinez, Manuel. "Vida de Anastasio el Pollo." In his *Obras completas* 2. Buenos Aires, 1979.

Page, F. M. "*Fausto*, A Gaucho Poem." *Publications of the Modern Language Association* 11:1–62 (1896).

José Hernández

(1834–1886)

Antonio Pagés Larraya

Of all Argentine books, *Martín Fierro*, by José Hernández, is probably the most widely read. It has stirred considerable popular interest since its publication and has been translated into many languages. Despite the vast critical work that it has stimulated, *Martín Fierro* has never completely unveiled its secrets and continues to speak differently to different generations. Jorge Luis Borges, discussing Argentine literature, stated that "of the many books that make up . . . [gauchesque poetry], there is one, the *Martín Fierro*, that stands above the rest" (*The Spanish Language in South America—The Literary Problem*, London, 1964, p. 7). This poem, which probes deeply into the life of the *gaucho* with great inspiration and drama, is also, in its emotive sounding of the human condition, most universal. From the first, it was attacked by the intellectual leaders of the time, who stubbornly disdained it as antipoetic and wild; however, it eventually won the battle for acceptance, mainly on the strength of its own discourse, which reveals essential aspects of Argentine cultural history.

When the first part, popularly known as *La ida* (The Departure), appeared in 1872, Hernández was unknown to the small literary elite of Buenos Aires. His journalistic campaigns against the Unitarian partisans, particularly against Domingo Faustino Sarmiento, had awakened interest only in a small group of politicians, essentially his fellow Federalist sympathizers. Unitarians and Federalists were opposed in a political battle that led to a long civil war which was concluded with the Battle of Caseros (1852), where General Justo José de Urquiza defeated Juan Manuel de Rosas. Soon after Caseros the fight between the confederation presided over by Urquiza and Buenos Aires and its allies began. Hernández was a Federalist and President Sarmiento was his greatest political enemy. *La ida de Martín Fierro* was published when Sarmiento was president (1872). Nobody escaped the strong political attack posited by the poem. In Paraná, in 1863, he had published a brief work, *Rasgos biográficos del general Angel V. Peñaloza* (Biographical Traits of General Angel V. Peñaloza). Of no literary merit, this work was an exaltation of the *caudillo* (political leader) and a ferocious invective against Sarmiento. Hernández' political activities were carried out not in Buenos Aires but in the provinces of the Littoral, especially Santa Fe and Entre Ríos.

In 1875 the Chilean compiler José Domingo Cortés included a short sketch of Hernández in his *Diccionario biográfico americano* (American Biographical Dictionary), calling him "a writer of great inspiration and wit," and there is much other evidence that the book was widely read and the object of critical interest. In 1879, however, a curious and informed intellectual, Miguel Cané, wondered what kind of life Hernández had led "to be able to write such beautiful and truthful things that are not the result of pure abstract imagination but emerge from the lessons of life, acquired through the exchange of a part of oneself: the weak ones give their wool, like the ram; the strong ones, their entrails, like the pelican." Through the painful aspects of *Martín Fierro*, Cané intuited an existence he did not know about but whose suffering he could sense. Cané's ignorance of Hernández was typical of the Generation of 1880.

More proof of the silence enveloping Hernández, despite the constant reprinting of his poem, is to be found in *Recuerdos literarios* (Literary Remembrances, 1891), a detailed chronicle of the intellectual life of Buenos Aires, full of information on many, often minor, works, by Martín García Mérou, a sagacious critic with a genuine literary vocation. In this history, there is no mention of either Hernández or *Martín Fierro*. The *Anuario bibliográfico* (Bibliographical Annual) of 1880, directed by Alberto Navarro Viola, considered *Martín Fierro* "an epoch of crimes carefully passed as heroic deeds." The only exception to such attitudes of forgetfulness and scorn on the part of the Europeanized, specifically Frenchified, intellectuals of the 1880's, was the reaction of Carlos Olivera, a scholar, translator, and penetrating critic. Although he praised Hernández as an orator, politician, and journalist, Olivera centered on *Martín Fierro* as Hernández' irrevocable claim to glory: "The first and unique national poem born of this land speaks to us of our own things with the profundity of a thinker on the imponderable harmony of nature." Olivera pointed out the popularity of the book, its vigor in making evident the *gaucho*'s martyrdom, and its philosophic depth and expressive originality, qualities that "will overcome today's inexplicable coldness." He called *Martín Fierro* a seminal book, "a reflection of the Argentine spirit." Olivera's wise foresight is in contrast to the lack of appreciation of many of his contemporaries: "Foremost in inspiration, foremost in truth, foremost in the beauty of popular form, *Martín Fierro* covers and protects an immense zone of glory, in the center of which looms the modest yet firm figure of José Hernández."

In 1913, Leopoldo Lugones, the most original and influencial writer of Argentine *modernismo*, lauded *Martín Fierro*, declaring it superior to "purism and literature" and defending it from the contempt of "exquisite scholars." At the same time he wrongly maintained that in no work was "the phenomenon of unconscious creation" more perceptible than in Hernández'. This mistake has been refuted with ample evidence from Hernández' life, literary cultivation, and original political thought; the strong unity between the man's life and his poem has been established by the author's reflections on his book in numerous prologues and epilogues to *Martín Fierro* that have considered the poetics implicit in the poem and discoveries about the poet's life.

Hernández was sure that his name would go down in history on the strength of *Martín Fierro*: "el cantar mi gloria labra" (singing carves my fame), the poet sings in the prelude to The Departure (1.39).

> *Lo que pinta esta pince*
> *Ni el tiempo lo ha de borrar.*

> Not even time will erase
> what is painted by this brush

he announces in the prelude to *La vuelta* (The Return, 1.74–75). With pointed subtlety he refers to a region apart from worldliness and contingency:

> *Más que yo y cuantos me oigan,*
> *mas que las cosas que tratan,*
> *más que lo que ellos relatan,*
> *mis cantos han de durar.*

> My song will endure
> longer than I and those who hear me,
> longer than the things it deals with,
> longer than what it narrates.
> (1.97–100)

The thesis of "unconscious creation" is not supported by the numerous articles Hernández published in the Argentine and Uruguayan press (see the bibliography by Horacio J. Becco, pp. 316–338) and his speeches before the Buenos Aires legislature, as both a representative and a senator, collected in the three volumes of *Personalidad parlimentaria de José Hernández* (Congressional Personality of José Hernández, La Plata, 1937). *Martín Fierro* is a unique work of art because, among other things, its author possessed a vast cultivation, along with great sensibility and talent. He was a self-taught man with no education beyond that of elementary school; he never traveled to Europe, as many contemporary writers did, and he even turned down a well-paying commission that would have allowed him to travel around the world.

Hernández' knowledge was soundly based on his perusal of fundamental books. While the writers of his time avidly followed postromantic and naturalistic novelties, Hernández fed on the universal classics. In a 1881 letter to Florencio Madero (a physician), Nicolás Avellaneda (writer and president of Argentina, 1874–1880) remarked:

> What has Hernández studied? Before becoming acquainted with his literary habits and inspecting his library, I had my suspicions, later confirmed by him. Like Cervantes, he has studied the proverbs of every country and every language, that is to say, the voice itself of wisdom, as Solomon called them. He has imbibed the marrow of the human being.

Avellaneda went on to mention Confucius and Epictetus as Hernández' favorite authors, stressing his power to translate into the *gaucho* world this age-old, deep-rooted knowledge and flavor, which he expressed in a new, popular form. If these testimonies were not enough, the diversity and density of the poem would suffice to set aside the idea of a merely fortuitous creation. In 1879, in a well-known letter, Bartolomé Mitre, poet, historian, and president of Argentina (1862–1868), who objected to Hernández' social philosophy, emphasized, with acute aesthetic perception, the merits of *Martín Fierro*: "It has intent, philosophy, poetry, and descriptive beauty." Like every major literary piece, *Martín Fierro* is an unusual weaving of suffering and inventiveness. It is human substance transmitted into undying words.

A great part of *The Gaucho Martín Fierro* was written by Hernández between 1871 and 1872 in the solitude of a room on the first floor of the Hotel Argentino in Buenos Aires, on the Plaza de Mayo. A life of continual battle and danger had not afforded him the gifts of respite and creative leisure, and he lived in a kind of exile in his own land. Near the historical May Pyramid commemorating the revolution, near the Cabildo, where the seeds of the future republic had been planted, near the seat of the government of his archenemy Sarmiento, images and events assaulted his prodigious memory. Buenos Aires had still not recovered from the yellow fever epidemic of the previous year, which was responsible for the mournful notes that resound in the most melancholic passages of the poem. "Poor *Martín Fierro*," Hernández says in a letter that serves as prologue to The Departure, helped him to "defend himself from the nuisances of hotel life." On those long days, the writer, for the first time, cast a backward glance on the various stages of his dramatic life, beginning with his childhood in the Chacra de Pueyrredón, a small, agricultural, cattle-raising establishment.

Hernández was born on 10 November 1834 in what was known as Caserío de Perdriel, a small group of huts, during the eighteenth century. His father, Rafael Hernández, was eighteen years old; his mother, Isabel Pueyrredón, was twenty. When Isabel had to accompany her husband on a business trip to the far-off South, a rough zone threatened by Indians at that time, the boy was left in the care of a maternal aunt, Victoria Pueyrredón. In 1840, when he was six, José suffered the pain of separation when his aunt and uncle, persecuted by the Rosistas, had to flee to Buenos Aires. A strong feeling of orphanhood and helplessness engulfed him and was never to leave him. The characters Martín Fierro, his sons, and Picardía give sorrowful expression to the young Hernández' deep-rooted feelings. José also suffered, at an early age, the consequences of civil strife, a bloody war that was the result of what he later called the "politics of the dagger." Events soon determined another change of scenery, and José was next left to the care of his paternal grandfather, José Hernández Plata, with whom he lived in a house in Barracas near the Riachuelo. There, in the school of Don Pedro Sánchez, a teacher of renowned wisdom, the boy completed his short period of formal education.

Hernández lost his mother in July 1843, and suffering from a pulmonary disease, he was sent to live with his father. A new and surprising change of scenery awaited him in Camarones and Laguna de los Padres, where his father was in charge of vast cattle ranches. José was only ten, and the open and wild pampa was the vital center of his adolescence. It knew no limits:

> *Tendiendo al campo la vista,*
> *no vía sino hacienda y cielo.*

> Looking out across the land
> you'd see nothing but cattle and sky
> (The Departure, 2.215–216)

> *¡Todo es cielo y horizonte*
> *en inmenso campo verde!*

> All is sky and horizon
> on the immense green plain
> (The Return,
> 10.1491–1492)

There he became acquainted with *gauchos*, sat around the campfire with them, and listened to tales, songs, refrains, and counsel. His brother, Rafael Hernández, attributed "the patriotic *gaucho* genesis crystalized in *Martín Fierro*" to this early experience. He said that in those southern lands, young José "became a *gaucho*, learned how to ride a horse, participated in skirmishes repelling Pampa Indian raids, and witnessed the bulldogging of calves and the other tasks performed by his father" (*Pehuajó: Nomenclatura de las calles*, Buenos Aires, 1896, p. 81). In those days he must have heard the legend of Santos Vega and admired the art of the *gauchos* in the *payadas* (singing contests).

Events following the fall of Rosas, defeated at the Battle of Caseros in 1852, led to Hernández' recruitment as a soldier participating in the conflagration that almost destroyed the country. His uncle, Juan José Hernández, a colonel in the war for Argentine independence, died in the battle of Caseros, as a commander of Rosas' infantry. Hernández joined the ranks of the Federalists, against the Unitarians of Buenos Aires, as a soldier, politician, functionary, and journalist. At the age of thirty-seven, when he started working on *Martín Fierro*, Hernández had fought in the battles of Rincón de San Gregorío (1853) and El Tala (1854), the last Federalist stand led by Hilario Lagos. He also fought under Justo José de Urquiza against the army of Buenos Aires, participated in the victorious battle of Cepeda (1859), and

suffered in the defeat of Pavón (1861). The tragic impact of these battles left its mark on his writings. In his speech on the designation of Buenos Aires as the capital of the country, he bitterly alluded twice to the "nine terrible years" between Caseros and Pavón. This painful period corresponds to the ten years of Martín Fierro's peregrination.

The war never seemed to end. In 1868, Hernández took part in the armed resistance of Evaristo López, governor of the province of Corrientes. Two years later, after Urquiza's assassination, he joined the ranks of Ricardo López Jordán, *caudillo* of the province of Entre Ríos, participating in the fight against the national troops loyal to President Sarmiento up until the defeat at Ñaembé in January 1871. He accompanied the vanquished *caudillo* in his exile to Santa Ana do Livramento, in the Brazilian state of Rio Grande do Sul. There he came into contact with the life of the Brazilian *gauchos*, listened to their songs, and encountered the six-line stanza that may have served as inspiration for the sextet verse form of *Martín Fierro*.

Far from his country, in those peaceful days, Hernández began to forge this poem. Taking advantage of Sarmiento's decree of amnesty, he returned to Buenos Aires. His wife and four children had been on a ranch in Baradero since the yellow fever epidemic. There was nothing to disturb him. In anonymous solitude he pondered and wrote, scribbling lines on the white margins of newspapers, envelopes, any scrap of paper, giving vent to his indignation at the persecution of the *gauchos*. If there was sorrow in his life, he found consolation in his poetry. Thus he completed the thirteen cantos and the 2,316 lines of *The Gaucho Martín Fierro*, which came off the press at the end of 1872 and reached the market on 15 January 1873. The book's appearance marked a new direction in Hernández' life. The poet soon realized that the glory denied to him in his arduous fighting as a journalist and soldier could finally be expected from this work.

Besides his participation in the Argentine civil wars, many other events in his life up to 1872 had helped him to gain in experience and wisdom. In 1856, he began his career as a journalist with *La Reforma Pacífica*, an anti-Mitre newspaper that strongly defended the national Confederation directed by Nicolás Calvo. In 1857, when Hernández was twenty-three, he was deeply shaken by the death of his father, who was struck down by a bolt of lightning; his feelings of abandonment show up in the tenderness toward orphans seen in *Martín Fierro*. Along with Calvo, Hernández moved to Paraná, the seat of the Confederation Congress, in a show of support for the Federalist party. With no father or godfather, no formal education, poor and unknown, Hernández was forced to seek refuge as a clerk in a store.

After the battle at Cepeda, he worked as an accountant for the government. He learned shorthand and became the court stenographer of the famous Confederation Senate, where he met men famous for their patriotism and wide knowledge. His life became more settled, once again related to books and writing. He married in 1863 and took up journalism again, this time for *El Argentino* of Entre Ríos. He went to Nogoyá to live and there worked to reform the provincial constitution. From 1867 on, he collaborated in Corrientes with Governor López, a supporter of Urquiza. He was an attorney, minister, and teacher of Spanish literature in a provincial secondary school. From August 1869 to April 1870, Hernández directed *El Río de La Plata* in Buenos Aires, his most ambitious journalistic undertaking. His articles attacking frontier policies, defending the *gauchos*, and campaigning for institutional improvements are closely connected with the sociopolitical implications of *Martín Fierro*.

It is not difficult to see the links, often direct, between the journalistic discourse of Hernández' newspaper articles and the defense of the *gaucho* in *Martín Fierro*. It is the poem of a fighter who never knew truce, who, between wars and wanderings, found time for reflection, for the risky cultivation of literature, his heart and ear always attuned to the pain of the humblest peasant. In an eloquent summary of Hernández' life, his brother Rafael stated, "Always brandishing his sword and his pen, this warrior, revolutionary, journalist, and popular and prestigious orator worked a great deal but never enjoyed himself." This statement may not be altogether true. Many biographic references allude to his humor, his bantering manner, and even his childish carnival pranks.

Between *The Gaucho Martín Fierro* of 1872 and *La vuelta de Martín Fierro* of 1879, a fundamental change occurred in the life of Hernández, coinciding with the political modifications that took place between the end of Sarmiento's presidency and the new era initiated by Nicolás Avellaneda in 1874. Hernández had hardly started to enjoy the first favorable echoes of *Martín Fierro* in 1873, when, confronted with Sarmiento for having fought on the side of *caudillo* López Jordán, who was defeated at the Battle of Ñaembé, he went into exile in Uruguay to continue his journalistic battles at the head of *La Patria*, a Montevideo newspaper. His expatriation ended when Avellaneda became president.

Little by little, a new Hernández was born, quite different from the former tireless warrior. The changes in Hernández' life are reflected in the second part of the poem, which is longer (4,894 lines, thirty-three cantos) and more diversified than the first. The old Indian-like gaucho who returns to civilization from the Indian camp closely resembles Hernández settling in Buenos Aires and reconciling himself to the dictates of modern "order and progress." In 1875 Hernández met Avellaneda and became one of his firm supporters. He held several positions and was elected first representative, then senator. Hernández died, while fulfilling his duties as a senator, on 21 October 1886.

The second period of Hernández' life, after his return to Argentina, coincides with the second part of the history of his character, in that wandering and insecurity ceased to be dominant forces. In 1876 he opened a procurator's office, settled in Belgrano, then in the middle of the country, bought and sold land, and became a landowner himself. In the meantime, *Martín Fierro* became more and more successful. When the eleventh edition was published in 1878, 48,000 copies had been sold, apart from numerous clandestine editions. Hernández used his earnings to buy a ranch, which he named in honor of *Martín Fierro*, in Exaltación de la Cruz.

The year 1879 was highlighted by three events that had a profound influence on his life. First, he began his fertile and brilliant legislative career, which culminated in his speech on making Buenos Aires the national capital. In this speech he defended a position diametrically opposed to the one he had sustained in his youth. At the peak of his legislative career, Hernández was an accomplished orator and combatant. Second, he bought the La Plata bookstore, and third, through it he published The Return, this time not as a modest pamphlet like The Departure but as a modern book illustrated with ten plates by Carlos Clérice. Thus ended his literary career; his manual *Instrucción del estanciero* (Rancher's Guidebook) of 1882 and some minor poems have no aesthetic value.

"A man of pen and sword, of the outdoors and the salon, of the dais and the spur," according to his brother Rafael's accurate description, Hernández lived a great part of his life on the edge of danger, forced into endless wandering, unable to establish a permanent home until late in life. From an early age, he was thrust into orphanhood and had to withstand abandonment, a hard life on a still-wild pampa, the misery of war, and the biting rigors of penury. The hell alluded to in *Martín Fierro* with such dramatic insistence was often Hernández' own. He was saved from destruction by a stoic character, a soul capable of pity and resignation combined with an essential humanity and a love for song. It is important to comprehend the tragic and conflicting aspects of his life in order to fully understand the nature of *Martín Fierro*. Hernández succeeded in directing the contrasts of his agitated existence into creative channels, thus apprehending, from an outlook sensitive to the land and its people, the contrasts of a country that, in the course of its national incarnations, would find in this poem a path toward identity.

Hernández found the expressive vessel for his message. He situated himself within the context of the expectations generated by gauchesque poetry and defined his own creative space with fine artistic sensibility. In the letter that serves as a prologue to *The Gaucho Martín Fierro*, he made two observations that reveal his perception of his differences from his predecessors. In the first he expressed his divergence from the idea of poetry for the sake of entertainment: "Perhaps my undertaking would have been easier and more successful had I intended to make people laugh at the cost of their own ignorance, as was customary in this kind of composition." Hernández signaled an approach that he later explicitly contrasted with that of his predecessors Bartolomé Hidalgo, Hilario Asca-

subi, and Estanislao del Campo: "Martín Fierro does not go to the city in order to tell his friends what he has seen and admired at a patriotic celebration . . . but he relates his work, his misfortunes, the ups and downs of his *gaucho* life." This is the road Hernández chose. He himself said it was "more difficult than what many would suspect."

The poet sought to satisfy a generalized interest in the suffering and spoliation of the *gaucho*. He was also responding to concrete protests like that of Lucio V. Mansilla, who, in his *Excursión a los indios ranqueles* (Excursion to the Ranquel Indians) of 1870, criticized Argentine poets, who in singing of the *gaucho* "had only caricatured him." Two years later, Hernández would define new contents for gauchesque poetry; later, in the prelude to The Return, he would state his intention in his poetry:

> Yo he conocido cantores
> que era un gusta el escuchar,
> más no quieren opinar
> y se divierten cantando;
> pero yo canto opinando,
> que es mi modo de cantar.

> I have known singers
> it was a pleasure to listen to;
> they amuse themselves singing
> and refuse to give opinions;
> I sing giving opinions
> and that is my kind of singing.
> (The Return, 1.61–66)

Hernández' first critics noticed the difference from his predecessors. Cané pointed out that in his "very sad poetry" Hernández was not trying "to make the cultured person laugh at the *gaucho*'s language," as Ascasubi did. References to the sadness and the elegiac nature of the poem are frequent in the criticism on this work, and there is as well repeated mention of its break with the gratuitous character of previous gauchesque poetry. The warning remarks in the prologue to The Departure suggest the existence of a project of literary construction to offset the seemingly spontaneous flow of pure inspiration that the singer hints at when he says that the verses

> Las coplas me van brotando
> como agua de manantial.

spout from me
like water from a spring.
(The Departure,
1.53–54)

Hernández practices an original realism, divorced from the local-color school of the romantics, so that the poem's power of revelation does not get lost in the gingerbread.

While composing this work, Hernández realized that it would inevitably be compared to the gauchesque pieces by Hidalgo, Ascasubi, and del Campo. He also knew he was imposing a new direction on an apparently exhausted genre:

Yo he visto muchos cantores,
famas bien otenidas,
que después de alquiridas
las quieren sustentar;
rece que sin largar
cansaron en partidas

I have seen many singers
of well-merited reputation
who after they achieved it
were unable to maintain it;
it is as if they had tired in the trial runs
without ever having started the race.
(The Departure, 1.19–24)

Three days after the book's appearance, the 18 January 1873 issue of La Pampa, a Buenos Aires periodical, affirmed that the poem by Hernández could be favorably compared with previous gauchesque works.

The hero of the poem identifies himself almost completely with the figure of the singer presented by Sarmiento in his Facundo (translated as Life in the Argentine Republic in the Days of the Tyrants, 1845). For many critics the well-known episodes of the seventh and eighth cantos of The Departure constitute the generating nucleus of the poem: Martín Fierro kills a bullying black man at a dance and a provoking tough guy in a tavern. The coincidence is not only along general lines but also in the number of deaths: "The singer mixes into the heroic verses the narration of his own deeds. Unfortunately, he is not free from the long arm of justice. He has to account

for a couple of knife wounds he caused and one or two deaths he is responsible for."

Hernández used a centuries-old folklore tradition that he recreated even to the smallest detail, making a conscious identification between song and narration. Martín Fierro invokes the saints when he begins to "cantar mi historia" (sing my story; The Departure, 1.10). A little later he says

Me siento en el plan de un bajo
a cantar un argumento.

I sit in a hollow
to sing a story.
(1.43)

When he refers to his song he often uses the words historia (story) and relación (narration). The similarity to Sarmiento's work comes up again when the latter describes the "singer's original poetry," noting that it is "more narrative than sentimental." In the prelude to the payada with the black man in the thirtieth canto of The Return, Martín Fierro recalls his youth as a singer and takes the reader back to the initial moments of the poem:

Cuando mozo fuí cantor,
que es una cosa muy dicha,
más la suerte se encapricha
y me persigue constante:
de ese tiempo en adelante
canté mis propias desdichas.

As a young man I was a singer—
that's a thing that's often said—
but fate is fickle
and is always after me:
from that time on
I've sung my own sorrows
(30.3941–3946)

This evocative tone appears again toward the end of this personal remembrance:

Era la costumbre mía
cantar las noches enteras;
habia entonces dondequiera
cantores de fantasia.

241

I was used
to singing the whole night long;
anywhere you went in those days
there were fancy singers around.
(30.3967–3970)

At this point the protagonist has undergone a transformation. The plot is structured as a subtle counterpoint that sets up the *gaucho* who loves his work and his home against the bully, soldier, and deserter. It is his identity as a singer that finally elevates him to a dignity that transcends and overcomes the contradictory aspects of his personality. Just as Hernández became the poet-creator, thus finding his glory, Martín Fierro realizes himself definitively in the final counterpoint. The defeat of the black man vindicates Santos Vega, who had been defeated by the devil. At this juncture the poem takes on a meaning encompassing the wanderings of Martín Fierro, Cruz, their sons, and all the other characters. Thereby a poetic work rooted in reality acquires a new dimension that identifies speech with the human condition. This is "el don principal" (the principal gift) mentioned by the poet (The Return, 12.2011).

Martín Fierro has the capacity to speak differently to each epoch and to each reader. It is closely connected to the roots of Argentina. At the same time, it reveals with often overwhelming originality the extremes of anxiety and hope that give the *gauchos'* suffering an eternal magnitude. It is this, more than its representation of the typical, that accounts for its universal appeal.

From the moment *Martín Fierro* appeared, two currents—the text's spontaneous, popular reception and academic criticism—have fed each other. Hernández' poem is not sustained through time on the strength of the narrative of Fierro, Cruz, and their sons in the Indian camp, fort, and jail nor on the strength of the lyrical richness of many passages, the musicality of the verse, or its value as a social document. There is an open provocation in the text:

éste es un botón de pluma
que no hay quien lo desenriede.

This is a type of weaving
which no one can unravel.
(The Return,
33.4803–4804)

No critical reading will be able to exhaust its semantic wealth or be immune to its poetic vibration, which operates *more magico* (with magic procedures).

Nothing was further from Hernández' intention than the idea of presenting a testamentary image of the *gaucho*. Rather, he obsessively tried to give voice to beings who had been condemned to silence; he attempted to reveal their martyrdom and to offer Martín Fierro's fraternal bond to so many anonymous, forgotten men. The song finds unity in the search—flight and endless return—for the beloved country, which results in a hallucinatory nostalgia. Ten years of suffering and wandering

tres años en la frontera,
dos como gaucho matrero,
y cinco allá entre las indios

three years on the frontier,
two as an outlaw
and five in the Indian camps
(The Return,
11.1589–1591)

add to Martín Fierro's tribulations, but they cannot dry up the wells of his poetry. On his return he thanks the Virgin Mary and the Lord

Porque entre tanto rigor,
y habiendo perdido tanto,
no perdí mi amor al canto
ni mi voz como cantor.

because through so much hardship
and having lost so much
I did not lose my love for song
or my singing voice.
(The Return, 1.39–42)

This *gaucho* clearly acquires an orphic dimension as he returns to his own environs, "muy viejo" (very old) and "muy aindiao" (like an Indian; The Return, 11.1667–1668), shakes off his drowsiness and emerges into the light upon "al sentir la guitarra" (listening to the guitar; The Return, 1.11), and rises to the exigencies of the final *payada* with the black man.

Hernández—a fighter and politician engaged in the defense of the *gaucho*—was not by any stretch of the imagination attempting to wash away the blame of those who were responsible for the *gaucho*'s suffering and death. Hernández' exaltation of memory, that last recourse for the recuperation of the identity of the *gaucho*, together with the affirmation of a poetic based on a kind of song "opinando" (giving opinions; The Return, 1.65), reveals the poet's subtly critical awareness of how he differed from other writers who tried to gloss over the *gaucho*'s tragedy through the use of local color.

Martín Fierro is neither a romantic figure nor a Faustian character. He is just another *gaucho* who identifies with his fellow *gaucho*. But he was born with the gift of song. Hernández does not intend to set him apart as an egregious being because of this talent. Martín Fierro is one *gaucho* among many or all *gauchos* in one. Consequently, he indicts from within the system that exiles him. There is no room for mystification in this poem that is peopled by concrete beings and historical forces. *Martín Fierro* does not allow blame to hide in subterranean rivers. Hernández does not attenuate nor displace class responsibilities. Judges, landowners, army officers, merchants, mayors, and their factotums oppress and annihilate the *gaucho*. The poet exposes the vested interests that reify the gaucho and make him an exile in his own land. The poem is not comprised of petty anecdotes, pleasant events, insignificant occurrences. It is infused with a feeling of oppression, sometimes horror, haunting the reader and allowing no distraction or sentimental escape.

In conscious dissidence with the Argentine culture of his time, Hernández was closer to a barbaric, un-Europeanized Latin America tightly linked to its own three-hundred-year-old linguistic history. He did not romantically disfigure the *gaucho*. His men defy and confront the law, lie and cheat, get drunk, kill, desert the army, and are abandoned by their wives. Hernández strengthened the poem's veracity through two coinciding attitudes: he did not allow his meaning to be obscured in an exterior system of concrete historical references, nor did he allow the force of his message to be diluted in sentimentality or local color. The successive stories recreate experiences that, in their totality, make up an irrefutable testimony of the *gaucho*'s sacrifice.

Hernández did not set himself up as a privileged observer. Through his absence as a narrator, much

more perceptible in The Departure, he attained a perspective with no fractures or divisory lines. *Martín Fierro* does not possess the romantic flavor of adventure because its interest is not the result of amenity or suspense but of a reiteration of situations expressed by different voices. Observation is more frequent than judgment. The poem builds its world through many linguistic tonalities, including mannerism, as well as through the almost delirious apprehension of some situations: Fierro's arrival at his burned-down hut, Cruz's death in the desert, the second son's loneliness before the dead body of the old Viscacha. Hernández' writing maintains both the real and imaginary dimensions of beings who are as inaccessible as the pampas through which they rode and wandered. At times the writing reaches a strange level that transforms the poem into a universal visionary phantasmagoria.

The poem, focused on five basic tales by Fierro, Cruz, and their sons, is constantly enlarged by enriching episodes. The youngest son's confession incorporates a series of stories told in the first person by his tutor, old Viscacha. In Fierro's tale the *cautiva* (the woman captured by the Indians) tells her story. The black man acquires dramatic stature. Despite their brief appearance, characters like Barullo, La Bruja, El Ñato, or La Parda fully come to life. There is another group of anonymous people, mere *actantes*—judges, military men, witch doctors, grocers, Italian immigrants, Indians, local political bosses—as well as another group of less-well-defined characters—"a friend of mine," "an old friend of mine," "a friar," "a fool." The moving episode of the wall-eyed young boy drowned by the Indians "por causante de la peste" (for having caused the plague; The Return, 6.856) constitutes a good excuse to introduce all the inhabitants of the *gaucho*'s world. The defeated, the orphans, the children of penury are presented in a sympathetic light; their most abominable acts receive tacit justification. The bosses, chiefs, and tutors—those who rule—are faceless, as if Hernández wanted to present them in only one dimension: a hard, ferocious mask covers them all. *Martín Fierro* gives corporeal expression to that suffering, anonymous, poor world, which gains its identity through painful experience. Instead of negative complacence, the poem presents sorrow nourished by experience, inspiration, and wisdom.

243

A strong elegiac tone marks a great part of *Martín Fierro*. Only when the hero meets his sons again does the poem sound a note of happiness: "Yo me puse muy contento" (I was very happy; The Return, 11.1640). But it is only longing. "El viento de la desgracia" (The wind of misfortune; The Return, 3.365) blows painfully throughout the poem. There is no glimmer of hope in the final parting "para empezar vida nueva" (to begin a new life; The Return, 31.4590). The singer leaves his guitar behind and in absolute loneliness enters an impenetrable space, his own life already a legend. The poem's unsettling movement toward the intricate and the translucent forms its dialectic. *Martín Fierro* does not dwell in the peaceful haven of literary museums but in that ardent dimension where memory is not a balm. Hernández' words leave no room for fakery. The poem is the *gaucho*'s victory over suffering and silence. Intrinsically Argentine and universal at the same time, *Martín Fierro* probes deeply into the abysses of the human condition. Its inexhaustible meanings are subject to incessant transfiguration. Each reading, each semantic broadening, enriches the poem without crossing the frontier at which poetry triumphantly imposes the seal of its essential originality.

Translated from the Spanish by
Rolando Costa Picazo and Lea Fletcher

SELECTED BIBLIOGRAPHY

First Editions

El gaucho Martín Fierro. Buenos Aires, 1872.
La vuelta de Martín Fierro. Buenos Aires, 1879.

Translations

A Fragment from Martín Fierro (El Gaucho). Translated by Joseph Auslander. New York, 1932. The first twenty-six stanzas.
The Gaucho Martín Fierro. Adapted and translated by Walter Owen. Oxford, 1935. Complete poem.
The Gaucho Martín Fierro by José Hernández. Bilingual edition. Translated by C. E. Ward. Annotated and revised by Frank G. Carrino and Alberto J. Carlos. Coordinated and with an introduction by Carlos

Alberto Astiz. Albany, N.Y., 1967. Complete translation.
Martín Fierro: The Argentine Gaucho Epic. Translated and with an introduction and notes by Henry Alfred Holmes. New York, 1948. Complete translation.

Bibliography

Barbato, Martha J. "José Hernández y *Martín Fierro.* Nuevo aporte a su bibliografía." *Logos* (Buenos Aires) 12:259–318 (1972).
Becco, Horacio Jorge. "Bibliografía hernandiana." In *Martín Fierro, Un siglo.* Buenos Aires, 1972. Pp. 263–388. Completes and updates previous bibliographies.
Benson, Nettie Lee. *Catalogue of "Martín Fierro" Materials at The University of Texas.* Austin, Tex., 1973.
Cortázar, Augusto Raúl. *José Hernández, "Martín Fierro" y su crítica.* Buenos Aires, 1960.
Foster, David William, and Virginia Ramos Foster. "José Hernández: 1834–1886." In *Research Guide to Argentine Literature.* Metuchen, N.J., 1970. Pp. 103–109.
Maubé, José Carlos. *Itinerario bibliográfico y hemerográfico del "Martín Fierro."* Buenos Aires, 1943.
Sava, Walter. "José Hernández: Cien años de bibliografía. Aporte parcialmente anotado." *Revista iberoamericana* 38/81:681–774 (1972).

Biographical and Critical Studies

Aragón, Roque Raúl, and Jorge Calvetti. *Genio y figura de José Hernández.* Buenos Aires, 1972.
Astrada, Carlos. *El mito gaucho: "Martín Fierro" y el hombre argentino.* Buenos Aires, 1948.
Azeves, Ángel Héctor. *La elaboración literaria del "Martín Fierro."* La Plata, 1960.
Battistessa, Ángel J. "José Hernández." In *Historia de la literatura argentina 3*, edited by Rafael Alberto Arrieta. Buenos Aires, 1959. Pp. 119–259.
Borello, Rodolfo. *Hernández: Poesía y política.* Buenos Aires, 1973.
Borges, Jorge Luis. *El Martín Fierro.* Buenos Aires, 1953.
Canal-Feijóo, Bernardo. *De las aguas profundas en el "Martín Fierro."* Buenos Aires, 1973.
Carilla, Emilio. *La creación del "Martín Fierro."* Madrid, 1973.
Carretero, Andrés. *Ida y vuelta de José Hernández.* Buenos Aires, 1972.
Chávez, Fermín. *José Hernández: Periodista, político y poeta.* Buenos Aires, 1959.
Fernández Latour de Botas, Olga. *Prehistoria del "Martín Fierro."* Buenos Aires, 1977.

Halperín Donghi, Tulio. *José Hernández y sus mundos.* Buenos Aires, 1985.

Holmes, Henry Alfred. *"Martín Fierro:" An Epic of the Argentine.* New York, 1923.

Hughes, John B. *Arte y sentido del "Martín Fierro."* Princeton, N.J. 1972.

Jitrik, Noé. *José Hernández.* Buenos Aires, 1971.

Leumann, Carlos Alberto. *El poeta creador: Cómo hizo Hernández "La vuelta de Martín Fierro."* Buenos Aires, 1945.

Lugones, Leopoldo. *El payador.* Buenos Aires, 1916.

Martínez Estrada, Ezequiel. *Muerte y transfiguración de "Martín Fierro."* 2 vols., 2nd ed. Buenos Aires and Mexico City, 1958.

Pagés Larraya, Antonio. *Prosas del "Martín Fierro."* Buenos Aires, 1952, 1972.

Paoli, Pedro de. *Los motivos del "Martín Fierro" en la vida de José Hernández.* Buenos Aires, 1947.

Rojas, Ricardo. In *La literatura argentina 1: Los gauchescos.* Buenos Aires, 1917.

Scroggins, Daniel C. *A Concordance of José Hernández' "Martín Fierro."* Columbia, Mo., 1971.

Tiscornia, Eluterio. *La lengua de "Martín Fierro."* Buenos Aires, 1930.

Villanueva, Amaro. *Crítica y pico.* Santa Fe, Argentina, 1945.

Zorraquín Becú, Horacio. *Tiempo y vida de José Hernández.* Buenos Aires, 1972.

Jorge Isaacs

(1837–1895)

Enrique Pupo-Walker

In several aspects, the life and the literary career of Jorge Isaacs typify the paradoxical status of many prominent Latin-American writers. As with the Colombian novelist José Eustasio Rivera and the Mexican Mariano Azuela, Isaacs' literary fame rests mainly on one work, his novel *María* (Maria, 1867), the most popular romantic novel written in Spanish America. Literary fame, an intensely egocentric personality, and idealistic notions eventually propelled Isaacs into the turbulent political life of nineteenth-century Colombia. The descendant of well-to-do English Jews and Spanish immigrants who left Jamaica for Colombia in search of prosperity, Isaacs was born in Cali on 1 April 1837.

Isaacs was a controversial political figure who made enemies among leaders of different ideological persuasions, yet he became a diplomat and was chosen to represent his country in neighboring Chile. In his private life, Isaacs always struggled to maintain financial stability. He held a wide variety of bureaucratic positions for which he was ill suited and which inevitably brought him frustrations that outweighed the desired compensations. His greatest interest was literature, but a literary career in Colombia at that time was not a profitable endeavor. Perhaps because of the unsettled character of his life, Isaacs' literary production is rather small: a slim volume of poetry, a novel, an unfinished poem, some occasional political pamphlets, and early drafts of another novel. We know he envisioned a trilogy of novels that he was unable to complete. Undoubtedly, had he enjoyed more favorable circumstances, creative writing would have been the focus of his efforts.

The harsh economic realities of Isaacs' existence eventually led him to seek the legal protection of bankruptcy, an extreme measure that caused him considerable embarrassment and evoked the sarcastic attacks of his political enemies. These personal failures and the frustrations that Isaacs endured in public life brought a good deal of bitterness to his last years. On 17 April 1895, he died in Ibagué with definitely more notoriety than fortune. What he could not have anticipated is that literary historians and large numbers of readers all over the Spanish-speaking world would eventually confer upon him a position of great prominence in the history of Spanish-American literature.

Although Colombia has produced some of the finest poets of Latin America, Isaacs is not one of them. The small body of poetry he produced is gathered in *Poesías* (Poems, 1864). These are texts that dart unpredictably between personal confessions, moods of unrestrained melancholy, and satirical remarks. Many of these poems were written as occasional pieces and motivated by political and social events. "Al escudo de armas de N[ueva] G[ranada]" (To the Coat of Arms of N[ew] G[ranada]) is but one example. By and large, Isaacs' poetry reflects the early lyrical tendencies of multifaceted Spanish-American romanticism.

If much of Isaacs' poetry appears severely dated to the modern reader, many of his verses nevertheless retain a delicate, introspective gaze that covers the barren distances that often exist between feelings and meaning. His was not a powerful poetic intuition capable of discovering elemental forces or exquisite, secret bonds between human beings. Yet at times Isaacs could write with clear vision, expressing a deep affection for life. Although we recognize these refreshing qualities in Isaacs' earlier poetry, the fact remains that his poems are read mainly as suggestive antecedents of his famous lyrical novel, *Maria*. Indeed, at times the plot of the novel seems to exist as a pretext for displaying Isaacs' poetic inclinations.

There are, moreover, a multiplicity of thematic and anecdotal links between Isaacs' texts regardless of genre. His writings are also linked by a recurring autobiographical dimension that becomes even stronger in the later and more infelicitous stages of his production. It is fair to say that a good deal of the scholarship devoted to Isaacs has focused on the formal relationships between his descriptive poems and *Maria*. There are good reasons for this kind of inquiry, since Isaacs' best poetic writing is ultimately achieved not in his poems but in fiction. In *Maria*, Isaacs displays, with great range and feeling, his descriptive powers and his obvious gift for revealing the harmonious configurations of the lush Cauca Valley landscapes.

Although these are undeniable facts, Isaacs' brief descriptive poems, particularly those written between approximately 1860 and 1864, often employ subtle forms of syntactic condensation and a delicacy of nuance that can be delightful. This is particularly true of the poems centered on fond reminiscences and vivid sensual perceptions. In "Ve, pensamiento" (Go, Thought), there seems to emerge a distant and lyrical image of Maria, the central character of his novel:

y rosas muertas . . .
¡ que ya no adornan
sus negras trenzas! . . .
sobre el sepulcro
do la maleza
cubre la losa
ya cenicienta
que sollozantes
mis labios besan.

and wilted roses . . .
which no longer adorn
her black braids! . . .
upon the tomb
where the weeds
cover the slab
now gray
that my lips
kiss with a sob.

Perhaps even more effective are the poems in which he describes nature as a constant revelation of beautiful compositions. In "Elena" (Elena), Isaacs blends sensual memories and the natural context that frames them:

En las colinas verdes
del comarcano río
pasaba con Elena
la siesta de un Domingo.
Jamás tan complaciente
brindó a los labios míos
de mi emoción gozosa
sus labios purpurinos.
Siguióme hasta la vega
donde el raudal tranquilo
de las moreras moja
los maduros racimos.

On the green hills
near the river
I spent with Elena
much of Sunday afternoon resting.
In the most pleasing manner
she offered her lips to mine
her intensely red lips
brought to me feelings of joy.
She followed me to the meadow
where a soft stream
moistens the ripe mulberries.

Isaacs' poems tend to fall into two large categories, brief lyric poems and autobiographical compositions that include narrative sections. Particularly noteworthy is the specific and well-developed organization of longer narrative poems such as "La reina del campamento" (The Queen of the Army Camp), "La montañera" (The Mountain Girl), and "La vuelta del recluta" (The Return of the Recruit). One of Isaacs' more demanding projects was to compose a long epic poem to be entitled "Saulo." But as was often the case, he never managed to go beyond the first canto, which he published in March 1881.

The joy that Isaacs often found in contemplation and erotic reminiscences frequently turned, after 1875 or so, to melancholy, bitterness, and satirical moods. His later poems reflect his philosophical speculations and moments of dark remorse and regret. In "En las cumbres de Chisacá" (On the Summits of Chisacá) these moods tend to suffocate the bits of poetic inspiration:

> ¡Oh Patria! ¡Oh madre!
> . . . numen de mi vida,
> me oprimes sorda y cruel . . .

> Oh Fatherland, Oh Mother! . . .
> inspiration of my existence
> you oppress me cruelly and with indifference . . .

Isaacs was not a writer intimately attuned to the most refined forms of poetic writing. His abundant praise and admiration for the hollow Spanish poet Gaspar Núñez de Arce attests to the imbalances of Isaacs' literary preferences. Yet, the rather simplistic social and historical views of the poet have not diminished his prominent standing in the history of Colombian literature. Appraised in its totality, Isaacs' poetry (slightly over one hundred poems) is of interest to specialized scholars and to historians who have explored the links that have always existed in Spanish America between literary creativity and the political process.

The novel *Maria* is an important landmark of romantic fiction written in Spanish, although romantic fiction is not one of the richest areas of Hispanic letters. *Maria* has received a good deal of critical attention since it was first published. Nevertheless, much of what has been written—mainly in Colombia—amounts to overly lavish praise. In this context, the studies and the edition produced by Donald McGrady are of special interest and significance. McGrady was the first critic to show, with scholarly precision, that the novel had gone through at least four slightly different editions, a rather complex textual evolution determined mainly by the minute stylistic revisions that Isaacs made in successive editions. It is ironic, in any case, that the definitive edition published in Bogotá by Camacho Roldán and Tamayo in 1922 does not conform to the final manuscript elaborated by Isaacs. McGrady's critical edition resolves all the problematic features caused by the extended evolution of the text.

The plot of *Maria* evolves in a traditional fashion, with some digressions. Efrain, the narrator, tells of his love for Maria. He begins by reconstructing numerous episodes of his adolescence, mainly those that involve his separation from his family when he was sent to Bogotá for schooling. We learn that he and Maria had loved each other since the earliest years of childhood. Maria came to live with Efrain's family when she was three years old. Efrain states that any form of separation from Maria becomes intolerable, a pain that is aggravated greatly when his father insists on his leaving for Europe to study medicine. The highly idealized situations create an aura of sentimental tragedy that gradually increases.

Much of the narrative construct is clearly a distant literary parody of François René de Chateaubriand's *Génie du Christianisme* (The Genius of Christianity, 1802) and Jacques Henri Bernardin de Saint-Pierre's *Paul et Virginie* (Paul and Virginia, 1787), among other possible models. The noted Argentine scholar Enrique Anderson Imbert was the first to point out the precise links that exist between *Maria* and Saint-Pierre's novel. In some of the early chapters of the novel, specific references are made to *The Genius of Christianity*, particularly when Efrain reads aloud from several books, an activity that serves as Maria's only education. Shortly after these pleasant episodes, she suffers an epileptic seizure, the same ailment that caused the death of her mother. The premonitions of her death are many, and the fatal aura, so often bestowed on romantic heroines, gradually begins to surround Maria's fragile existence.

The overcharged atmosphere of sadness and gloom that prevails in the novel is countered by splendid descriptions of the landscape in the Cauca Valley. Another type of contrast is provided by the accounts of Efrain's hunting expeditions in the company of peasants and friends, in which he displays skill and courage in killing a jaguar. Financial disasters threaten the stability of Efrain's family, but he takes over some of the business affairs to alleviate the pressures on his father. In an environment filled with omens and sad premonitions, the separation of Efrain and Maria appears imminent.

Efrain finally leaves for London, but almost all references to his stay in England are muted. His thoughts are focused on Maria and the affairs of the family in Colombia, particularly since Maria's illness has worsened considerably since his departure. Efrain quickly returns to Colombia but learns from his mother of Maria's death. This news causes an intense illness that leaves him unconscious for several hours. Much of what remains to be told is a detailed and highly sentimental reconstruction of Maria's last days and Efrain's inconsolable sorrows, expressed through his frequent visits to Maria's grave.

Though there are disproportioned aspects in the general design of the novel, including digressions, interpolated material, and excessively elaborate descriptions of the landscape, the most enduring values of *Maria* are evident in the delicate lyrical framework of the plot. Detailed studies of the novel's sources, its textual evolution, and a variety of interpolated episodes (see chapters 40–43) have demonstrated the unexpectedly rich intertextual dimension of *Maria*. These facts in part explain the extraordinary impact of this novel on the development of Spanish-American fiction as well as its remarkable popularity among readers of all ages. Recent inquiries have thoroughly documented the many parodies and literary creations that have found in *Maria* their point of departure. Yet a truly demanding critical reading of the text remains to be done, one that would uncover the many uncentered and contradictory aspects lodged in the narrative sequence of *Maria*. Such a reading will lead as well to demystification of the novel and show how it assimilates and transforms some very complex and diversified textual traditions.

SELECTED BIBLIOGRAPHY

First Editions

Poetry

Poesías. Bogotá, 1864. Contains thirty poems.

Fiction

María. Bogotá, 1867.

Pamphlet

A mis amigos y a los comerciantes del Cauca [To My Friends and the Businessmen of the Cauca Valley]. Cali, Colombia, 1875.

Modern Editions

María. Edited by Donald McGrady. Barcelona, 1970. The only genuine critical edition of the novel.
Poesías. Edited by Armando Romero Lozano. Cali, Colombia, 1967. The best edition in every way.

Translations

Maria: A South American Romance. Translated by Rollo Ogden. New York and London, 1890. A deficient and incomplete translation.

Biographical and Critical Studies

Anderson Imbert, Enrique. "Prologue." In *María*, by Jorge Isaacs. Mexico City, 1951. Pp. vii–xxxiv.
Barta, John M. "La función estructural de los episodios costumbristas en *María*." In *La literatura iberoamericana del siglo XIX*, Memoria del XV Congreso Internacional de Literatura Iberoamericana, edited by Rosaldo Renato and Robert Anderson. Tucson, Ariz., 1971. Pp. 55–60.
Embieta, María J. "El tema del amor imposible en *María* de Jorge Isaacs." *Revista iberoamericana* 32/61:109–112 (1966).
Fein, John M. "*María*: La función de las digresiones." In *La literatura iberoamericana del siglo XIX*, Memoria del XV Congreso Internacional de Literatura Iberoamericana, edited by Rosaldo Renato and Robert Anderson. Tucson, Ariz., 1971. Pp. 51–54.
Magnarelli, Sharon. "*María* and History." *Hispanic Review* 49/2:209–217 (1981).

McGrady, Donald. *Jorge Isaacs.* Twayne's World Authors series no. 166. New York, 1972. The most complete and reliable study on the works of Isaacs.

Molloy, Sylvia. "Paraíso perdido y economía terrenal en *María.*" *Sin nombre* 14/3:36–55 (1984).

Moreno, Daniel. "Introduccion." In *María,* by Jorge Isaacs. Mexico City, 1966. Pp. xiii–xxxi.

Olivera, Otto. "*María:* Tema predilecto de Isaacs." *Symposium* 14/1:7–25 (1960).

Pupo-Walker, Enrique. "Relaciones internas entre la poe-sía y la novela de Jorge Isaacs." *Thesaurus* 22/1:45–59 (1967).

Tittler, Jonathan. "Tropos tropicales: Paisajes figurados en *María, La vorágine* y *El otoño del patriarca.*" *Discurso literario* 2/2:507–518 (1985).

Bibliography

McGrady, Donald. *Bibliografía sobre Jorge Isaacs.* Bogotá, 1971.

Joaquim Maria Machado de Assis

(1839–1908)

Afrânio Coutinho

Joaquim Maria Machado de Assis was a Brazilian poet, novelist, short story writer, essayist, playwright, and literary critic. A *mestizo* (person of mixed heritage), he was born on 21 June 1839 at the Livramento Hill, a very poor area near the docks of Rio de Janeiro. His father was a house painter, and his mother died when he was very young. After his father's death in 1851, his stepmother, Maria Inês, supported the family by working as a maid. Machado learned to read and write in a small school in his district. He was a clerk and later a typographer's apprentice at the National Press until 1858. He worked as a salesman and proofreader at the Paula Brito Bookstore and Typography, where he was in contact with several important Brazilian men of letters and began to read the great works of world literature.

Machado published his first poems, short stories, and essays in several periodicals, including *A Marmota Fluminense, Correio Mercantil, Diário do Rio de Janeiro, Jornal das Famílias,* and *Semana Ilustrada.* He soon gained a wide readership. In 1869 Machado married Carolina Augusta Xavier de Novais, the sister of his friend the Portuguese poet Faustino Xavier de Novais. In 1873 he began to work as a government employee at the ministry of agriculture. In 1888 he was granted the Order of the Rose by the Emperor of Brazil. He was director of the chamber of commerce in 1889 and executive officer of the ministry of transportation in 1892. In 1896 he founded the Brazilian Academy of Letters and was its president until he died on 29 September 1908. He is considered the greatest and most complete man of letters in Brazil.

That a writer of such high quality emerged in the middle of the nineteenth century, within a society that did not offer the minimal adequate conditions to its poorer members, is a mystery contrary to all the postulates of biological, social, and economic determinism. It can be explained only by the power of genius. Yet, if one can accept the Comte de Buffon's thesis that talent consists of a long work of patience, it is fair to say that, in the case of Machado de Assis, patience constituted half of his brilliance. Machado, an enemy of dilettantism and improvisation, had as a maxim the words "learning by investigation," and he studied with perseverance. He meditated upon the classical authors, through whom he learned the laws of literary art and improved his instrument of literary expression.

Machado de Assis disciplined his temperament, his inspiration, and his imagination. He never rushed, nor was he seduced by facility. He understood that "as one gets older, he acquires solidity, dominates art, increases his resources, and searches for perfection, which is the ambition and duty of all men who use writing to express ideas and sensations." He felt that the secret of art lies in classical equilibrium. He learned that originality and invention are not opposed to tradition; hence he never had an attitude of negation or iconoclasm. He believed that there was no difference between rejecting the past and idolizing it, and he fused tradition and originality. It was his sense of continuity that made him pay attention to the lesson offered by José de Alencar. Alencar managed very well to adapt the form of modern narrative to popular elements and national themes and to create a Brazilian style by combining literary and colloquial language. By following Alencar's methods as well as perfecting his own theory and style, both with respect to national themes and narrative technique, Machado strongly contributed to the establishment of a definitive Brazilian fiction. Indeed his works can be said to be the most genuine and thorough expression of the Brazilian spirit in literature.

The Evolution of a Writer

For a long time Machado's critics believed that his life and work could be distinctly divided into two phases, separated by the landmark year 1880. The novel Memórias Póstumas de Brás Cubas (Epitaph of a Small Winner), published in Revista Brasileira from March to December 1880 and printed in book form the following year, was felt to mark in shift of orientation, in terms of both narrative technique and the author's general attitude toward life. The works published before this date were considered to have been inspired by the romantic atmosphere predominant in Brazil, and the novel Iaiá Garcia (Iaiá Garcia, 1878) to have been the work that suggested that this transition was imminent.

There are decided differences in the author's aesthetic conception before and after Epitaph of a Small Winner. Machado underwent a personal crisis during the 1870's, as he approached the age of forty and the factors that determined his spiritual and aesthetic physiognomy converged. It was then that the multi-

ple, obscure, and complex influences that acted upon him harmonized to create the author's definitive way of being. These factors were of a constitutional, psychological, social, and cultural nature: the awareness of his physical shortcomings (epilepsy and stuttering); the conflict between his awareness of his low social position (resulting from his humble origins and his race) and his preoccupation with social climbing; and the doctrines inspired by the reading of his favorite authors.

The works constituting his initial phase include Crisálidas (Chrysalis, 1864), Falenas (Moth, 1870), Contos Fluminenses (Tales of Rio de Janeiro, 1870), Ressurreição (Resurrection, 1872), Histórias da Meia-noite (Midnight Tales, 1873), A Mão e a Luva (The Hand and the Glove, 1874), Americanas (American Poems, 1875), Helena (Helena, 1876), and Iaiá Garcia (1878). The writer, however, had not yet defined his identity. He was searching his way, investigating, trying several genres, seeking fulfillment.

Ultimately, one must reject the idea that there was a sudden change in his work. There was no abrupt rupture between the two phases. It is more accurate to state that the second phase was prepared for by the first and that there was continuity between the two. The difference was not an opposition but simply the result of a process of maturing. During this long process, Machado accumulated the experience that generated his spiritual and aesthetic creed and his concept of literary technique.

There are differences and similarities between the two phases. In both, one finds his psychological inclination and tendency to analyze customs. Humor is present in both, although in the first phase it was not associated with pessimism. It did not have the bitter tone, morbid melancholy, and disillusionment that he acquired later. The humor present in his first books is of a facetious, almost cheerful type. While his first phase was filled with the excessive romantic sentimentalism of that time, the eroticism and sensualism characteristic of his second phase were also present.

The seeds of the technical and stylistic devices developed and refined in his later works are present in the novels of Machado's first phase. His first novel, Ressurreição, contains introspection, linear plot development, interior monologue, a spirit of analysis,

254

and psychological penetration. The critic Barretto Filho stated that this novel was the one among his first books that had "the appearance of modernity," because "concern about the objective event was replaced by the study of characters" (*Introdução a Machado de Assis*, p. 111). Machado was closer here to the psychological novel to which he would later devote himself thoroughly. As he affirmed in the introductory note to his book, "I did not want to write a novel of manners; I tried to sketch a situation and to build up a contrast between two characters."

The author was struggling at that time between the novelistic pattern then predominant because of romanticism, and his intuition, which pointed in other directions. He knew that there was something new to try, another path to follow, and that was what he eagerly sought. Meanwhile, he continued to experiment, until he gained total control of his devices and established a definitive form for his aesthetic creed. Machado's works show him in a constant struggle to improve his artistic means. Some of his themes appeared first in essays, then in short stories, and finally in novels, and were frequently developed into two or three other forms in his search for perfection. He was a writer who constantly corrected and perfected himself. His meticulous craft was the product of diligence and a combination of experience, study, familiarity with the works of the great writers, and obedience to the rules of his *métier*.

Machado's phase of transition must be interpreted as a period in which two tendencies conflicted and were transcended: his own creative principles and the established literary traditions. His achievement was a consequence of his capacity to let his principles predominate over the rule of society. The individual talent, as T. S. Eliot defined it, creates a new tradition that imposes itself on the dominant one. By reacting against the romantic pattern, however, Machado was not seduced by the fallacies of naturalism. He did not follow any school in the strict sense. He instead absorbed the important concepts of various schools and incorporated them into his classical aesthetic ideal. He reacted against exaggeration, recognizing the vicissitudes of each school and selectively letting himself be influenced by all of them.

Machado's evolving process of awareness is apparent in the chronology of his publications, especially of his masterful short stories. In 1870 and 1873, *Contos Fluminenses* and *Histórias da Meia-noite* were published. The short stories composing these volumes had been published in the magazine *Jornal das Famílias*, from 1864 to 1869 and from 1872 to 1873, respectively. Barretto Filho was right when he wrote that "they were mediocre, unconvincing . . . works of a beginner, made out of a material arbitrarily chosen" (p. 83). Their value lay in the equilibrium Machado tried to establish between the romantic and the realistic treatment of the theme of love. His taste for psychological analysis was already present, and humor worked to neutralize excessive sentimentalism.

From 1875 on, there was a visible progress toward technical refinement in the short stories (some gathered in the volume *Papéis Avulsos* [Several Stories, 1882]), especially in the ones written in 1882 and 1883 (published in *Histórias sem Data* [Undated Tales, 1884]). Machado de Assis perfected his technique by constantly polishing his work—he was a precise and concise writer—and by exploiting all the possibilities of the genre selected. He reached the fullest expression of his creative artistry with *Dom Casmurro* (*Dom Casmurro*, 1899), although he added a new dimension to his method in *Esaú e Jacó* (*Esau and Jacob*, 1904), especially in his use of symbolic and mythical elements.

Yet, beginning with the short stories of 1875 and *Epitaph of a Small Winner*, he started establishing his artistic technique, and from that time on, the secret of his success was to exploit that style. The short story was the most fruitful laboratory for his experiments: he wrote more than two hundred. Some are masterpieces of the genre in any language. *Epitaph of a Small Winner* was not, then, the first and purest example of Machado's method. In 1875, he had already broken with the tradition of the romantic narrative. He had also abandoned the linearity of narrative and the abundant style of his predecessors by using a technique of conciseness and by eliminating any sort of excess in his art. Writing his short stories was a hard apprenticeship, through which he reached his mature method by subordinating the narrative to the analysis of his characters. His work then reveals a desire for accommodation, but also reflects an incessant search for something uncommon, different both from romantic sentimentality and from false naturalistic objectivity.

If for Machado artistic realization presupposed vocation and temperament, it was also a product of discipline, of meticulous effort, of technical consciousness, of study and meditation upon his literary models, of patient and obstinate research, practices that were in consonance with the classical attitude. Machado wrote in the introductory note to *Ressurreição*: "Reflection achieves its peak with time, and by that I also mean study, a condition without which the spirit remains in perpetual infancy." The art of Machado must be seen as the result of an obstinate, conscious process, in which reflection played the major role.

An examination of the criticism of his works gives further evidence that there was neither rupture nor antinomy between the phases before and after 1880. It reveals that the writer was in a process of constant evolution, always reflecting deeply upon the aesthetic problem. The critical essay "Instinto de Nacionalidade" (Instinct of Nationality), published in the New York journal *O Novo Mundo* (The New World) in March 1873, can be seen as the natural result of this long mental elaboration. Machado's statements about the question of national art, the influence of people on style, and the balance between nationality and universality, as well as his reflections on various technical aspects of the literary art of several genres, show how the artist was at that time entirely aware of his métier. As with most great artists, his theoretical consciousness awakened before his practical capacity. Although he knew what he wanted, he did not attain the means to achieve it until the second half of the 1870's.

Another example of Machado's theory can be found in his essay on José Maria de Eça de Queiróz' *O Primo Basílio* (The Cousin Basílio, 1878), published in April 1878. In this masterpiece of practical literary criticism, Machado expressed his conception of literary art, which would later be developed in the essay "A Nova Geração" (The New Generation, December 1879) and in the poem "O Almada" (The Almada, 1879). Machado went through a long process of evolution before reaching total mastery of his art. His critical works constituted the basis for the emergence of his creative spirit. He did not abandon

criticism for any extraliterary reason. What he really abandoned was militant criticism, that is, he did not wish to hurt or upset others, although he was always a severe critic of himself and his own works.

Realism and Symbolism

When interpreting Machado's works, some critics have difficulty in defining and classifying him according to the existing literary schools. Although Machado de Assis went through the romantic, naturalistic, Parnassian, and symbolist movements, he never belonged entirely to any of them. He lived the first years of his intellectual life during the romantic movement of the 1850's and 1860's, and he was so much influenced by the world view dominant at that time that he himself confessed: "Those who have sucked romantic milk can eat the naturalistic roast beef; however, when sensing the smell of the Gothic and oriental nipple, they abandon the best piece of meat to search for their infancy's drink. Oh! my sweet romantic milk!" (in "A Semana," *Gazeta de Notícias* [Rio de Janeiro], 25 December 1892).

Machado's romantic ideas can be better witnessed in his first writings in prose and verse. He also contributed to the romantic dogma of most prestige at the time in Brazil, the Indianist movement. Moreover, the movement's best-known followers, Alencar and Antônio Gonçalves Dias, were no doubt the Brazilian writers Machado most admired. He also was influenced by Manuel Antônio Álvares de Azevedo and such foreign romantic figures as Victor Hugo, François René de Chateaubriand, Giacomo Leopardi, Alfred de Musset, A. M. L. de Lamartine, Heinrich Heine, and Visconde de Almeida-Garrett.

The most typically romantic aspect of his works lay within the novelistic technique employed in his first writings. These consisted of linear narrations that were broken only now and then and were filled with sentimentalism. But romanticism was not present only in the books of his first phase. As Eugênio Gomes has affirmed, even in *Epitaph of a Small Winner* a heavy tribute is paid to romanticism.

Machado's attitude toward the realist movement was very similar to the one he expressed in relation to romanticism. In the aforementioned essay on the naturalism of Eça de Queiróz, he questioned, in a very incisive manner, the postulates of the school: "Let us face reality, but let us exclude realism, so that we do not sacrifice aesthetic truth" (*Crítica*, p. 83). "Reality is good, but realism is not worth anything" (p. 151). What was important for him, above all, was aesthetic truth, not to be confused with the photography of reality. Art was not a copy but a transfiguration of reality. That was why he remained in the *juste-milieu*, neither in romanticism, nor in realism: "I do not certainly want the obsolete portraits of decadent romanticism. On the contrary, there is something in realism that can be used to benefit imagination and art. However, the mere substitution of one excess for the other amounts to nothing at all" (p. 81).

The same holds true for Machado's practice. Although he refused the exaggerations of realism, he did not deny its contribution to artistic realization. In a study on Machado's aesthetics, Gomes has pointed out several aspects of realism present in his works: the persistence of formal, organic, metaphysical, and moral decomposition; the theme of dissolution; images and metaphors related to diseases, carnal deterioration, and death; death, illness, and physical misery in its most disgusting aspects; inferences of a scientific character; biological determinism and a mechanistic conception of life; and philosophical positivism (*Aspectos do Romance Brasileiro*, p. 103). In many cases, such as that of the short story "O alienista" ("The Psychiatrist"), Machado's intention was to satirize the exaggerations of the school. "In some way, . . . he paid a tribute to naturalism which was, perhaps, beyond his intentions" (*ibid.*), but he was certainly not overly influenced by it.

In the same way that Machado did not become totally involved with either romanticism or naturalism, he also maintained a critical detachment in relation to symbolism. Gomes has, however, pointed out the influence of the symbolic conception of art and the manipulation of myth during the writer's last phase, especially in *Esau and Jacob*.

The phase of Brazilian literature that followed naturalism, particularly in the first two decades of the twentieth century, only recently has been better understood by critics. After 1890, the objective and factual aesthetic of naturalism was exhausted. In its place came a wave of subjectivity and interiorization that caused a considerable transformation in literature, especially in prose writing. This aesthetic process, formed by the confluence of symbolism and naturalism, produced what is known today as impressionism.

In this respect, the work of Machado de Assis is extremely significant. As was stated above, Machado was initially a romantic, who then took part in naturalism in an independent manner, although he was influenced by many of its postulates and techniques, including autobiographical method, the observation of reality, dramatic narration, organic structure, and flexible plot. However, Machado was never a typical realist. His conception of art made him not so much a photographer of life as a re-creator of reality. For him, art and life were different. He conceived art as a set of symbols and conventions, without which the use of the elements of life is fruitless. Art was illusion, verisimilitude, transfiguration of reality.

Machado progressed toward this conception of art, which was accomplished in his late books. His tendency to interiorization and psychological analysis, his restless fantasy, and his tragic view of human existence were the substrata that led him to a transfigured realism, enlarged by symbolism and mythology, that is, an impressionistic realism. His last works were especially marked by this view and constituted a world of symbols and allegories. Thanks to his realistic technique, he extracted from everyday reality the life material he would transform into art. The *fait divers* (small news item) was, thus, transformed into fiction. However, the fact was altered, was rejected as a fact and transformed into aesthetic substance, into aesthetic truth, by means of which life revealed its deepest secrets. By not affiliating with any specific literary school, by keeping apart from false alternatives, by extracting from each the elements he considered useful for the formation of his aesthetic world view, Machado de Assis produced his works according to the classical ideal, to which he owes his permanence and universality.

The Transformation of Influences

When Machado de Assis affirmed that "one can use an alien spicery, but must season it with a sauce of his own making" (in Afrânio Coutinho, *Machado de Assis na Literatura Brasileira*, p. 31), he was stating his "theory of the sauce," of originality in literature. In another passage, he condemned Victor Hugo's imitators, who judged themselves poets just because they produced verses: "To be a disciple is something else: it is to learn with his master and to incorporate into his own spirit the spirit of the master" (*Crítica*, p. 35). He insisted: "No one will ever deny that the natural evolution of a thing modifies its appearance, its external feature; but there is something that links Homer to Lord Byron, something unchangeable, universal and common, which is important to all men and to all times" (p. 221).

Machado de Assis was a writer aware of his métier, and all his creative works were founded on a strong theoretical basis, on a general conception of art and literature, of the genres and the process of literary creation. The set of aesthetic principles on which Machado established his judgments of value are present in his essay on Eça de Queiróz and the realistic school. In this work he studied plot, structure, character development—everything that constituted an aesthetic, specific, or peculiar element in the construction of the novel—and revealed the literary nature of the genre. His criticism was thus of an aesthetic or poetic nature, in the manner of Aristotle, and not of a moral sort. The understanding of Machado's literary theory is fundamental to the interpretation of his narrative technique.

The influence of other writers on Machado's works is also of great importance. The study of sources and influences reveals the enormous debt he owed to ancient and modern foreign writers. He assimilated and transformed the material he absorbed through reading. What matters in art is not the material itself, but rather the way the material is treated. When Machado sought inspiration, suggestions, images, models, formulas, or solutions in alien sources, he never used them exactly as they were or reproduced them literally.

He employed the same procedure in handling the material he collected from the observation of reality. His view of life was transfigured into artistic material, and his experience of reality was transformed into aesthetic truth.

Nationalism

For a long time, Machado was accused of not being a typically Brazilian writer, of being inspired by foreign books, of not being intimately related to Brazil in terms of its subjects, settings, atmosphere, characters, topics, and style. The absence of landscape in his works was said to point up his lack of identification with the environment. Although Machado admitted some foreign influences in the development of his technique, his art, and his conception of life, the Brazilian character of his works is widely accepted today. Machado, a typical Brazilian *mestizo*, could not escape from the influence of his milieu; he was and he is a real Brazilian writer. His "theory of the sauce" is of great help in understanding both his process of creation and his Brazilian character. The artist provides a new treatment for themes and forms.

Everything, said T. S. Eliot, is renewed through expression. And this was exactly what Machado did: he gave a new treatment to themes and formulas that were frequently old and alien. By transforming, with his own sauce, raw material extracted from different sources, he attained his originality, his very personal formula. All his works reflect the environment in which he lived. The themes he employed were those of his time and place or were adapted to them by means of his process of seasoning the alien material. His imagination was filled with images and figures belonging to the reality around him, and the autobiographical element was of great importance in his works.

Machado was neither French nor English, as some critics once thought. He was a Brazilian in the full sense of the word, and Brazil recognizes him as such; hence, his increasing popularity. He expressed an "instinct of nationality" throughout his works. With his personal touch, he transformed his raw material into new and original works of a real Brazilian character. Through the use of Brazilian elements, he became a universal writer, like Miguel de Cervantes and William Shakespeare. The more national they were, the more universal they became.

Machado's works reflected his time and environment. His themes were extracted from the life of Rio de Janeiro at the time of the Second Kingdom in the nineteenth century. Without being chauvinistic, he was a national and popular writer. His works reflected the problems of his people, their customs, preoccupations, ideals, and difficulties. The national element is not opposed to the universal one. In order to reach the universal character, the writer has to be national and popular, since it is in the magma of his region, in the reality of his people, through the assimilation of the national legacy that he finds the nourishing blood that gives him greatness and universality.

Machado's method was to treat the Brazilian character in an indirect manner. This theory was well expressed in his critical works, mainly in the famous essay "Instinto de Nacionalidade":

> There is no doubt that a literature, especially an emerging one, should nourish itself with the themes of its region. However, we should not establish such absolute doctrines that may limit it. What one should demand from the writer is, above all, a certain intimate feeling that could make of him a man of his time and country, even when he is dealing with themes that are remote in time and space.
>
> (Crítica, pp. 13–14)

This doctrine was widely applied by Machado in his criticism. The criterion he employed to estimate the aesthetic value of literary works was an apt one: he subordinated local color to feeling when evaluating the "instinct of nationality." The same standard serves to describe his own works. This fact made Astrojildo Pereira characterize him as "the most national, the most Brazilian of all writers and, at the same time, the most universal one." (Machado de Assis, pp. 14–15). And if it is true, Pereira continued, that "other writers have depicted Brazilian scenery more closely, none of them revealed Brazilian men in a deeper manner" (p. 15). The same critic stressed the "intimate and deep consonance between the literary work of Machado de Assis and the meaning of the political and social evolution of Brazil" (p. 17) during a transition period in which literary stereotypes of the rural aristocracy were replaced by the portraits that Machado offered of the society of his time: conditions within the patriarchal family, which often held social conventions to be more important than love and frequently imposed marriages of convenience; the psychological and social consequences of slavery; the effects of war; the

political habits of the time; financial problems; the cultural changes caused by positivism and naturalism during the 1870's; and the literary search for national identity.

Machado's style was so much the expression of his time and milieu that, as far as language is concerned, no one may question his national character. In the same way that the tradition, the landscape, and the life of his time and milieu were present in his works, the language he employed was that used by his fellow citizens, that is, the old Portuguese idiom transformed under the impact of the new Brazilian geographical and social reality. He made this point clear in the final part of "Instinto de Nacionalidade."

Machado de Assis extended the vast nationalistic tradition that comes from Gregório de Matos to Gonçalves Dias, Alencar, and Antonio de Castro Alves, since he believed that literature was an expression of the national world view and that it played an important role in the development of the people and the unity of the country. Barretto Filho stated that "[Machado] became the central event of the Brazilian literary life, an isolated and peculiar expression of something important to our nation" (p. 230).

Machado's Pessimism

The main point, when judging an artist, consists of knowing whether or not he attained artistic fulfillment. One may disagree with his world view, his philosophical attitude, and the conception of art underlying his work. However, it is not the critic's duty to judge the artist's philosophy. In order to approach a work of art, the critic must have an attitude of "suspension of disbelief," as T. S. Eliot stated. The important thing for the critic is to verify if, regardless of the author's philosophy, he was successful in translating it, in transfiguring life into art, and to verify if the technique used was the most suitable for this purpose. This process of verification is the function of the critic. He should face the author and his work of art as they are and not as he believes they should have been. For the critic there is no right or wrong in art, nor is it his duty to morally condemn an author or attempt to correct him. Works of art are to be understood and judged aesthetically. Moral judgment and aesthetic judgment should not be confused, in the same way that moral truth and aesthetic truth are in essence different.

There are critics, however, who have condemned the philosophy of life implicit in Machado's works, a pessimistic and skeptical philosophy that sees man as an evil and corrupt being, dominated by selfishness, sensuality, ingratitude, meanness, lowness, villainy, and hatred. Machado's art has been viewed by some as existing only to torment his readers by means of a constant and systematic destruction and negation of values and themes of belief and hope, of faith in mankind, life, and God. There is no doubt that this is the philosophy present in his books. One may not agree with Machado's conception of life, but the critic should investigate only whether the writer was successful from an aesthetic point of view. Machado's pessimism was expressed in his artistic creations through a radical hatred for life and humanity, a total lack of sympathy and a distrust for man, an absolute indifference to man's suffering, and an overall feeling of bitterness and despair. This is the general tone of his works, the permanent note of his interpretation of the world—this lack of generosity in judging men and life.

Machado saw man's pure, noble, and altruistic acts as rare, and when he admitted their existence, the author always tried to unmask them, to reveal their selfish or sensual origin, the "cotton fringe of the silk mantle." He believed that there was always a secret cause to be looked for in human acts and that it was the task of the novelist to uncover it. In accordance with the dominant ideas of his time, Machado assented to a certain universal determinism. Thus he believed that evil things always happen and that it is not possible to change men, for each is born with a destiny that no education or discipline can alter. Machado's world view was shaded by pessimism and nihilism. He saw only the bad side of human nature.

The major intellectual source of Machado's pessimism was Pascal, whom he read very much since he was young, as he himself confessed in a letter to Joaquim Nabuco, on 19 August 1906, "not to amuse myself." Machado's pessimism, however, was more radical than Pascal's, since the latter, while he pointed out the essential contradiction of human nature, still had hope in a future life. Pascal did not believe in man and hated life, but he had confidence in God. Machado, on the other hand, did not trust men, did not love life, and did not hope for any future blessedness. Misery and pain, evil and suffering constituted the essence of life for Machado de Assis, who could not see, due to his private resentments, the good side of life. Such moral nihilism can be seen in the desolate final confession of Brás Cubas: "I had no children. Therefore I did not transmit to anyone the legacy of our misery." The problem of man and his fate, according to the Christian thesis of the Fall, which sees the earth as a valley of tears, is aggravated by Machado's distrust of future redemption, by his essentially negative and pessimistic ethic. Machado expressed, through a bitter and sardonic humor, the total misery of man and his impotence in the face of nature's laws.

In the genesis of this philosophy of life, there were antecedents and personal motivations of a social, psychological, and hereditary order, which gave the author an exaggerated consciousness of human miseries, a very refined taste for depicting the bad side of man, and a dark vision of social life. Machado was a very resentful person, although he often disguised this aspect of his personality. However, his private complaint against life was occasionally revealed. In a letter to Nabuco on 29 August 1903, for example, he reacted against the charge of pessimism assigned to him but confessed that it might be true, adding: "I sometimes attribute more justice to Nature, than Nature to man." His resentment was tied to his physical infirmities and to his race.

It is also important to insist, however, on the intellectual influence of other writers upon the works of Machado, especially those who provided him with his favorite readings. Machado's pessimism was in part a consequence of the reading and study of his favorite philosophers, who provided a philosophical framework for his natural tendencies.

Humor

Machado's pessimism and skepticism found artistic expression through humor, the instrument he used to express anguish and resentment caused by human cruelty and physical and moral suffering. Laughing at man's ridiculous acts was his way of disguising his own misery. Machado found his main source for humor in the English humorists, from whom he learned many of the technical and rhetorical devices employed in his works. Only in his maturity, after he had read the English humorists, were the traits of Machado's humor definitely established. However, while the role played by the English humorists was important in Machado's works, these influences complemented his innate tendencies.

In Machado, humor was associated with pessimism, bitterness, and hatred toward the human species. But, above all, what was essential and what constituted the peculiar trait that distinguished him from the English humorists was his moralistic preoccupation, his constant attempt to define man and his relations in society. Contrary to the pure humoristic purposes of many of those authors, amusement in Machado was always accompanied by a realistic idea of man, extracted from real, everyday life but related to the universality of the human condition. He was also a great psychologist, a conscious observer of man and human conduct. And since his judgment of man's nature was not very indulgent, he translated it into art through humor, the most appropriate expression for his temperament and view. In order to understand him, one must connect humor to melancholy and grief, to bitterness and tedium, to pessimism and hatred toward life.

Narrative Technique

Machado's craftsmanship can be seen through an examination of the technical devices of his fiction. Few works of art reveal so well the nature of fiction as a form of art; few workers were so conscious as Machado of the role played by craftsmanship. He paid great attention and gave importance to the diverse aspects of narrative technique and for that purpose he read the great works of literature. In the heroic-comic poem "O Almada," he confessed that he had studied the genre of the book before writing it. By knowing his métier, he was free to innovate. *Quincas Borba* (*Philosopher or Dog?*, 1891), for example, was polished so much that the final version was quite distinct from the first one, published in *A Estação* (The Season), between 1886 and 1891.

Machado was, above all, a great storyteller. He related his life experience to his personal view of the world, to a vigorous selection of subjects and themes, and to a capacity to capture the essential aspects of characters and situations. He employed fantasy and imagination when treating the observed material. He created an original style, as can be seen in his use of language and choice of words. Finally, he also carefully selected the technical devices he used to deal with problems such as plot, point of view, order of the narrative, presentation of the characters, creation of suspense, dramatization, movement of the narrative, and manipulation of time. Machado learned how to solve these and other problems by studying the great models of the genre since Homer.

In terms of point of view, the narrator, while reporting his story, may place himself inside or outside the limits of action. If inside, he narrates the story in the first person, assuming the personality of his character, be it the main or a secondary character, or even several different characters. Machado employed this method in *Epitaph of a Small Winner*, *Dom Casmurro*, and *Memorial de Aires* (*Counselor Ayres' Memorial*, 1908). In the first two books, the narrators are the main characters; they report the events of their own lives and are able to analyze themselves. The facts reported are limited to what the narrator has seen, heard, felt, or thought. In *Counselor Ayres' Memorial*, the narrator reports, in the format of a diary, events that occur around him. The narrator is not omniscient, because he has a limited view of the events observed. He is not an active participant, but a close observer, though in a position of relative independence. With this technique, the novelist accomplished a deeper psychological analysis, and the story gained in plausibility and emotional intensity.

In all his other novels, Machado used the external point of view. The narrator was a third person, outside the external limits of the action, kept apart from the events. He did not identity himself with the circumstances of the story. He was an impartial observer who watched the events and reported them objectively. Sometimes the narrator had a complete knowledge of the story; that is, he was omniscient, as

261

in the case of *Philosopher or Dog?* and *Ressurreição*. The narrator knew everything; he was everywhere, including within the characters' minds; thus he knew their thoughts and feelings, and guessed their desires and analyzed them mentally. In other cases, the observer limited his view to the external facts and did not worry about what happened in the characters' minds, allowing them to define themselves by means of their actions and behavior. This is the dramatic or visual narrative technique, so dear to Guy de Maupassant, that Machado frequently used, especially in his short stories.

One of Machado's characteristics, related to the issue of point of view, was the intrusion of the narrator in addressing the reader. He comments, interprets, or talks to the reader in the first person, referring to facts of the story in the manner of William Makepeace Thackeray. "Do you want the other side of the story, curious reader?" asks the third-person narrator of *Philosopher or Dog?* Placed outside the story, he gives the impression that the responsibility for the story is his own and that he knows it entirely.

By varying the point of view, Machado achieved objectivity and impersonality, demonstrating a rare mastery of this technical device. It is important to notice, also, that this technical control was perfected in his last works, in which, instead of a vague, omniscient narrator, he introduced an interested narrator who reports the story in the first person. The critic Dirce Côrtes Riedel shows how the problem of the point of view in Machado's last book (*Counselor Ayres' Memorial*) was complicated by the introduction of three levels of time—that of the report of the judge of the Court of Appeals, that of the counselor's report, and that of the events narrated—and how the author used the artifice of changing the perspective of the narrator. The importance of point of view in Machado's work can also be observed in his novel *Dom Casmurro*, a story of adultery that ends in an ambiguous manner, owing to the fact that it is reported by a person involved in the triangle—the heroine's husband.

The presentation of characters was a problem of narrative technique very well solved by Machado. One way of presenting the characters is the descriptive manner, by which the character is presented in a report or description. The character is introduced either at the beginning or as the narrative develops, through a progressive analysis in which the narrator frequently offers comments and explanations about the character's behavior. Machado used the latter method widely.

But the method in which Machado excelled was the dramatic or implicit one. According to this method, the character is revealed by means of his own acts and words and by the reports of other characters. Dialogues and monologues can play an important role. This method predominated in Machado's works because he preferred a dramatic tone for the narration. In *The Hand and the Glove*, the characters are introduced by means of their own dialogues. Later the narrator tells about their lives, thus complementing their self-characterization. This method was used by Machado especially in his short stories.

Machado's dramatic tendency is responsible for the fact that there are not many descriptions of characters or landscapes in his books. His interest was in the inner life of his characters and the effects of their consciousness upon their actions. As stated by Gustavo Corção in an article in *Diário de Noticias* on 6 June 1958, "a novel is the art of personalities, more than the narration of facts and events." The author himself declared, in his preface to *Ressurreição*, as if foreseeing the process he would later adopt in *Epitaph of a Small Winner*, "I did not want to write a novel of manners; I tried the sketch of a situation and the contrast between two characters." When criticizing Eça de Queiróz' *O Primo Basílio*, he revealed the mastery he had of the process of constructing characters: "Luisa is . . . a puppet" (*Crítica*, p. 63). Machado pointed out the futility of the heroine's character, her lack of moral substance. The psychological analysis of the characters had to be accompanied, for Machado, by a certain moral coherence, without which the former would become mere puppets.

The characters in Machado's first books were, with few exceptions, mere types that could be defined in a very generic manner. Barretto Filho compared some of Machado's female characters, so important in his works, pointing out the difference between Lívia (*Ressurreição*)—a figure of inaccurate and vague characterization—and the later Virgília (*Epitaph of a Small Winner*)—a complex and fascinating human being. Other complex female characters in Machado's later works are Sofia (*Quincas Borba*), Capitu (*Dom Casmurro*), and Flora (*Esau and Jacob*), all of them characters of great human dimension and highly representative of the Brazilian reality that served as his point of departure. Because of Machado's great ability in creating characters, his works contain a remarkable gallery of heroes and heroines, protagonists and antagonists, caricatures and types—a whole universe of characters moved by a tragic view of life.

When handling the elements of plot—complication, climax, resolution—Machado took special care with the creation and maintenance of interest and suspense. His short stories were extraordinary in this respect. But the finest example of maintenance of suspense is his novel *Dom Casmurro*. Machado also varied the chronological order of the narrative a great deal. *Epitaph of a Small Winner*, for example, begins with the death of the protagonist, that is, with the solution of the story. It is the dead man himself who hesitates, at the beginning of the narrative, about whether he should start the report of his memories from his early childhood or from the last part of his life; he finally chooses the second alternative. This is the Homeric way of narrating in flashback, used, for instance, in the *Odyssey*.

In many cases, as in his novel *Iaiá Garcia*, Machado used linear or chronological narrative, with no alterations or interruptions. The interruption of the narrative for a reflection or digression on the part of the author is very frequent, however, in his works. A typical example is chapter 130 of *Dom Casmurro*, in which the author excuses himself for breaking up the linearity of the narrative. Discontinuity and fragmentation of the narrative were in accordance with Machado's conception of art and were often employed in his last novels and short stories.

The problem of the order of the narrative is intrinsically connected with that of time, the treatment of which gave Machado the opportunity to demonstrate his technical mastery when dealing with a problem of major importance in modern fiction. This aspect of Machado's work has been analyzed by two of his critics, Riedel and Wilton Cardoso.

Professor Riedel demonstrates how Machado anticipated modern solutions for expressing psychological time in making use of an impressionistic technique by which time is delayed to represent the inner rhythm of life and to give way to the narrator's interferences. She points out that the treatment of time powerfully influenced the structure of Machado's novels and enumerates several aspects of this influence on his choices in terms of point of view, episodic structure, the use of humor, narrative order, the presentation of the characters, the novel's structure, plot development, and stylistic advances.

In Machado's works the past is expressed in an evocative and suggestive style, which confers upon his works an impressionistic resonance. Instead of faithfully copying reality, the author uses a suggestive tone of imaginative effect, which creates a subtle and vague atmosphere. Machado was not interested in mere intrigue, but rather in the psychological analysis of his characters. Thus, his narrative and plot are subordinated to the expression of the characters, and even the structure of the works and the order of the narrative are less important than the effects generated by his registering of feelings and emotions. Events are not ordered according to cause and effect. Rather, they are part of a subjective world and are evoked in an illogical, nonchronological manner. The narrator tries to capture the past moment and, even when reporting a subjective reality, does so in a vague and indirect manner, focusing especially on the impression of the moment. For this reason, there are not many descriptions of exterior reality in Machado's works. The narrator for him was the interpreter of a certain view of human nature. Hence the importance of pictorial and tonal effects on his works.

Machado's art was undoubtedly realistic, but his was a special kind of realism, an impressionistic realism. Not all of reality interested him. He selected from it what he needed in order to create the impression, the sensation, the emotion generated in his spirit by its presence. Hence we observe the relevant role that symbol played in his work and the importance of atmosphere, often the central element in the story, as in "Missa do Galo" ("Midnight Mass") and "Uns Braços" ("A Woman's Arms"). Impressions awakened by the senses are also common in Machado's works: vision, smell, taste, hearing, and touch register moments that are later recollected by the artist. They contribute to the atmosphere of voluptuousness and sensuality that is present in some of his short stories and novels.

Machado was a highly imaginative writer who reached the reader both emotionally and intellectually. His writings were predominantly of a psychological sort, and his rare power of evoking past impression, thus creating present and enduring emotion, is the secret of the permanence of his works. The art of suggestion and impression demanded special techniques of language and style. Some of Machado's major stylistic traits are a simple, exact, and clear syntax; a *brisé* and *saccadé* rhythm; short, discontinuous, fragmented sentences, deprived of élan and rhetorical effects, of symmetries, subordinations, and coordinations. Machado's evocative intention called for the use of the imperfect indicative, which, as Augusto Meyer has observed, was sometimes converted into the present tense—a psychological present tense, not just an imitation of the historical present. Another device frequently used by the novelist was indirect speech, a technique by means of which he hid himself behind his characters.

In order to transmit his emotions and sensations, the impressionist writer makes abundant use of rhetorical figures. Machado had an outstanding command of metaphor and simile, and thanks to it, he often transmitted his impressions so well that the reader could perceive them as if they were his own. Unusual metaphors were of special interest for him, mainly those that focused on sensations. Machado's style, however, was basically characterized by its conciseness. It was this aspect, above all, that was responsible for its greatness.

Themes

The study of themes in Machado's works—and their persistence and repetition—is extremely significant for the understanding of his aesthetic conception. Machado often first outlined a theme or an idea in an essay and later developed it in a short story or a novel. He was a patient writer who sometimes experimented repeatedly with an idea. This iterative process may have been a consequence of his morbid personality or the result of his struggle for perfection.

The most extensive and widely used of Machado's themes were those that dealt with his tragic view of existence, his intrinsic pessimism, and his existential restlessness. They include a preoccupation with death and the relativity and the transitory nature of life; the existence of evil; the essential contradictions of man; the absurd character of life; the instability of human judgment; insanity and cruelty; the ambiguous nature of man; human ingratitude; the predominance of evil over good; tedium; the dualism of pleasure and disillusionment; the longing for perfection and immortality; vanity and selfishness; the misleading nature of love; the precariousness of scientific theories and philosophical systems; and the contrast between infancy and death, abundance and misery.

Another important theme in Machado's works concerns the financial condition of the characters. No one works in Machado's fictional world, as a consequence of his pessimistic view. Laziness is the rule among Machado's characters, since life is not worthy of effort. Many of his characters live on family fortunes, retirement pensions, legacies, loans, suspicious business dealings, or lotteries. Financial preoccupation is constant in Machado's works, in compensation for the general absence of regular work.

Social themes were important in Machado's works, which were a faithful mirror of the society of his time, a social picture of the Second Kingdom in Brazil. He was a novelist of his time and place, of the small bourgeois world and the society around him. Social background and position are depicted in his books through the use of articles of adornment and wardrobe, personal possessions, houses, modes of transportation, and honorific titles.

Aesthetic and Critical Beliefs

Underlying Machado's artistic creation was a code of aesthetic values and a critical doctrine. Criticism, for him, had the function not only of regulating literary production in general, but also of serving as a guide for his own creative activity. His idea was that of a didactic kind of criticism, out of which good literature would spring. Hence his affirmation: "Do you want to change this distressing situation? Then, you should establish criticism" (*Crítica literária*, p. 12). This is the same thought James Russell Lowell had regarding American literature: "Before we can think of having an American literature, we must have an American criticism." This topic was later developed by Machado in the essay "Instinto de Nacionalidade," in which he spoke out in favor of a doctrinaire and normative type of criticism that would improve taste and stimulate invention, that is, work that would be simultaneously criticism and self-criticism.

Self-criticism played a decisive role in Machado's literary creation, so decidedly characterized by discipline and a strong sense of responsibility. Machado's aesthetic conception was in accordance with the classical tradition. For the ancient writers, art was the result of a formal regulation of the subject, impossible without a code of rules. Machado's rule was to complement creativity with the study of poetics. He was for the autonomy of art; for him, aesthetic and ethical truth were two different things.

Having distinguished art and moral, aesthetic and historical truth, we must consider again the problem of realism. As stated earlier, when Machado condemned realism, he did not disregard reality. The realistic technique, he declared, "is the very negation of the principles of art," since "there is an unsurpassing limit between reality, according to art, and reality, according to nature." For this reason, art is not "the faithful reproduction of things, men and facts" (*Crítica literária*, p. 188).

> If the novelist's mission was to copy facts the way they are in reality, art would be worthless; memory would substitute for imagination. . . . The mere narration of a fact does not constitute a novel; it would, at best, make a section of a newspaper. It is the poet who takes life events and transfigures them with art's magic hand. Criticism should not judge the nature of this or that individual, but rather that of the characters depicted by the poet and should discuss less the feelings of people than the skill of the writer.
>
> (*Crítica literária*, pp. 62, 64)

Machado's position was clear: one should turn to reality, but should exclude realism, in order not to sacrifice aesthetic truth. He considered art not an imitation but rather a transfiguration of reality. His works, therefore, should be judged and understood according to this concept of objective criticism, in light of which "it is not enough to read an author; it is necessary also to compare and question his truth" (*Crítica literária*, p. 13). This means that the critic should adopt the author's point of view, apprehend his truth, and then verify if the work done was faithful to such truth. This way of thinking was especially important in 1859, a time when romanticism still glorified the author as a hero and when the writer's biography often attracted more interest than his literary work. It was only in the twentieth century that the work itself recovered its importance for criticism.

A final aspect of great importance for Machado's aesthetic creed is that of the nationality of art, of which his works were an example and a lesson. To affirm the national character in literature is not to list names of flowers, fruits, and animals typical of the country from which they spring. National character should not be confused with local color. It consists, rather, of "a sort of intimate feeling that can make of the writer a man of his time and place" (*Crítica literária*, pp. 134–135). This deeper kind of nationalism reconciles the outer society in which the author lives, and "a more elevated order of ideas," so as to attain a condition of universality. This fusion of nationality and universality was successfully achieved in Machado's works, and he is unanimously recognized in Brazil as the national writer par excellence.

Translated from the Portuguese by
Maria Lúcia Rocha Coutinho

SELECTED BIBLIOGRAPHY

Editions

Novels

Ressurreição. Rio de Janeiro, 1872.
A Mão e a Luva. Rio de Janeiro, 1874.
Helena. Rio de Janeiro, 1876.
Iaiá Garcia. Rio de Janeiro, 1878.
Memórias Póstumas de Bras Cubas. Rio de Janeiro, 1881.
Quincas Borba. Rio de Janeiro, 1891.

Dom Casmurro. Rio de Janeiro, 1899.
Esaú e Jacó. Rio de Janeiro, 1904.
Memorial de Aires. Rio de Janeiro, 1908.

Plays

Queda que as Mulheres têm para os Tolos. Rio de Janeiro, 1861.
Desencantos. Rio de Janeiro, 1861.
Teatro (O Caminho da Porta, O Protocolo). Rio de Janeiro, 1863.
Quase Ministro. Rio de Janeiro, 1864?
Os Deuses de Casaca. Rio de Janeiro, 1866.
Tu, Só Tu, Puro Amor. Rio de Janeiro, 1881.
Teatro (O Caminho da Porta, O Protocolo, Quase Ministro, Os Deuses de Casaca, Tu, Só Tu, Puro Amor, Não Consultes Médico, Lição de Botânica). Rio de Janeiro, 1910.

Poetry

Crisálidas. Rio de Janeiro, 1864.
Falenas. Rio de Janeiro, 1870.
Americanas. Rio de Janeiro, 1875.
Poesias Completas. Rio de Janeiro, 1901.

Short Stories, Essays, and Literary Criticism

Contos Fluminenses. Rio de Janeiro, 1870.
Histórias da Meia-noite. Rio de Janeiro, 1873.
Papéis Avulsos. Rio de Janeiro, 1882.
Histórias sem Data. Rio de Janeiro, 1884.
Várias Histórias. Rio de Janeiro, 1896.
Páginas Recolhidas. Rio de Janeiro, 1899.
Relíquias de Casa Velha. Rio de Janeiro, 1906.
Crítica. Edited by Mário de Alencar. Rio de Janeiro, 1910.
Outras Relíquias. Edited by Mário de Alencar. Rio de Janeiro, 1910.

Collected Works

Adelaide Ristori. Edited by Barbosa Lima Sobrinho. Rio de Janeiro, 1955.
O Alienista. Lisbon, 1941.
Cartas de Machado de Assis e Euclides da Cunha. Edited by Renato Travassos. Rio de Janeiro, 1931.
Casa Velha. Introduction by Lúcia Miguel Pereira. São Paulo, 1944.
Conceitos e Pensamentos. Edited by Júlio Cesar da Silva. São Paulo, 1925.
Contos. Edited by José Osório de Oliveira. Lisbon, 1948.

Contos Avulsos. Edited by R. Magalhães Júnior. Rio de Janeiro, 1956.
Contos e Crônicas. Edited and with a preface by R. Magalhães Júnior. Rio de Janeiro, 1958.
Contos Escolhidos. Rio de Janeiro, n.d.
Contos Esparsos. Edited and with a preface by R. Magalhães Júnior. Rio de Janeiro, 1956.
Contos Esquecidos. Edited by R. Magalhães Júnior. Rio de Janeiro, 1956.
Contos Recolhidos. Edited by R. Magalhães Júnior. Rio de Janeiro, 1956.
Contos sem Data. Edited and with a preface by R. Magalhães Júnior. Rio de Janeiro, 1956.
Correspondência de Machado de Assis. Edited by Bernardo Neri. Rio de Janeiro, 1932.
Crônicas de Lélio. Edited and with a preface by R. Magalhães Júnior. Rio de Janeiro, 1958.
Dialogos e Reflexões de um Relojoeiro. Edited and with a preface by R. Magalhães Júnior. Rio de Janeiro, 1958.
Estante Clássica. Vol. 2: *Machado de Assis.* Edited by Laudelino Freire. Rio de Janeiro, 1921.
Histórias Reais. Edited by Fernando Góis. São Paulo, 1958.
Idéias e Imagens de Machado de Assis. Edited by R. Magalhães Júnior. Rio de Janeiro, 1956.
Machado de Assis. Edited by Otávio Mangabeira. Rio de Janeiro, 1954.
Machado de Assis Romancista. Edited by Armando Correia Pacheco. Washington, 1949.
Novas Relíquias. Edited by Fernando Neri. Rio de Janeiro, 1932.
Obra Completa. Edited by Afrânio Coutinho. 3 vols. Rio de Janeiro, 1959.
Obras Completas. Rio de Janeiro, 1937–1955.
Páginas Esquecidas. Edited by Elói Pontes. Rio de Janeiro, 1939.
Pensamento Vivo de Machado de Assis. Preface by Helio Sodré. Rio de Janeiro, 1942.
Pensamentos de Machado de Assis. Rio de Janeiro, 1923.
Poesia e Prosa. Edited and with a preface by J. Galante de Sousa. Rio de Janeiro, 1957.
A Semana. Edited by Mário de Alencar. Rio de Janeiro, 1914.

Translations

Counselor Ayres' Memorial. Translated by Helen Caldwell. Berkeley, Los Angeles, and London, 1972.
Dom Casmurro. Translated by Helen Caldwell. New York, 1953. 2nd ed. Berkeley and Los Angeles, 1966.
Epitaph of a Small Winner. Translated by William L. Grossman. New York, 1952.

_____. New York, 1978.

Esaú and Jacob. Translated by Helen Caldwell. Berkeley and Los Angeles, 1965.

The Hand and the Glove. Translated by Albert I. Bagby, Jr. Lexington, Ky., 1970.

Helena. Translated by Helen Caldwell. Berkeley, Los Angeles, and London, 1984.

The Heritage of Quincas Borba. Translated by Clotilde Wilson. London, 1954.

Iaiá Garcia. Translated by Albert I. Bagby, Jr. Lexington, Ky., 1977.

Philosopher or Dog? Translated by Clotilde Wilson. New York, 1954. Reprinted 1982.

The Psychiatrist and Other Stories. Translated by William L. Grossman and Helen Caldwell. Berkeley and Los Angeles, 1963.

Yayá Garcia. Translated by R. L. Scott-Buccleuch. London, 1976.

Biographical and Critical Studies

Abreu, Modesto de. *Biografos e Críticos de Machado de Assis.* Rio de Janeiro, 1939.

Almeida, Heloísa Lentz de. *A Vida Amorosa de Machado de Assis.* Rio de Janeiro, 1939.

Aranha, José Pereira da Graça. *Machado de Assis e Joaquim Nabuco.* São Paulo, 1923. 2nd ed. 1942.

Ataíde, Tristão de. *Três Ensaios sobre Machado de Assis.* Belo Horizonte, Brazil, 1941.

Barretto Filho. *Introdução a Machado de Assis.* Rio de Janeiro, 1947.

Belo, José Maria. *Retrato de Machado de Assis.* Rio de Janeiro, 1952.

Brandão, Otávio. *O Niilista Machado de Assis.* Rio de Janeiro, 1958.

Broca, Brito. *Machado de Assis e a Política e Outros Estudos.* Rio de Janeiro, 1957.

Caldwell, Helen. *The Brazilian Othello of Machado de Assis.* Berkeley and Los Angeles, 1960.

_____. *Machado de Assis.* Berkeley, Los Angeles, and London, 1970.

Cardoso, Wilton. *Tempo e Memória em Machado de Assis.* Belo Horizonte, Brazil, 1958.

Casasanta, Mário. *Machado de Assis e o Tédio à Controvérsia.* Belo Horizonte, Brazil, 1934.

_____. *Minas e os Mineiros na Obra de Machado de Assis.* Belo Horizonte, Brazil, 1938.

Castelo, José Aderaldo. "Ideário Crítico de Machado de Assis." *Revista de História* (São Paulo) 11 (1952). Pp. 93–128.

Coutinho, Afrânio. *A Filosofia de Machado de Assis.* Rio de Janeiro, 1940. 2nd ed. 1959.

_____. *Machado de Assis na Literature Brasileira.* Rio de Janeiro, 1960.

Gledson, John. *The Deceptive Realism of Machado de Assis.* Liverpool, England, 1984.

Gomes, Eugênio. *Influências Inglesas em Machado de Assis.* Salvador, Brazil, 1939.

_____. *Aspectos do Romance Brasileiro.* Salvador, Brazil, 1958.

Grieco, Agrippino. *Machado de Assis.* Rio de Janeiro, 1959.

Jucá Filho, Cândido. *O Pensamento e a Expressão em Machado de Assis.* Rio de Janeiro, 1939.

Machado, José Betencourt. *Machado of Brazil: The Life and Times of Machado de Assis.* New York, 1933.

Magalhães Júnior, R. *Machado de Assis Desconhecido.* Rio de Janeiro; 1955; 2nd ed. 1955; 3rd ed. 1957.

_____. *Ao Redor de Machado de Assis.* Rio de Janeiro, 1958.

_____. *Machado de Assis: Funcionário Público.* Rio de Janeiro, 1958.

Maia, Alcides. *Machado de Assis: Algumas Notas sobre o Humor.* Rio de Janeiro, 1912.

Matos, Mário. *Machado de Assis: O Homem e a Obra, Os Personagens Explicam o Autor.* São Paulo, 1939.

Meyer, Augusto. *Machado de Assis.* Pôrto Alegre, Brazil, 1935.

Moog, Vianna. *Heróis da Decadência.* Rio de Janeiro, 1934.

Nunes, Maria Luisa. *The Craft of an Absolute Winner.* Westport, Conn., 1983.

Pati, Francisco. *Dicionário de Machado Assis.* São Paulo, 1958.

Peregrino Júnior. *Doença e Constituição de Machado de Assis.* Rio de Janeiro, 1938. 2nd ed. 1976.

Pereira, Astrojildo. *Machado de Assis.* Rio de Janeiro, 1959.

Pereira, Lúcia Miguel. *Machado de Assis: Estudo Crítico e Biográfico.* São Paulo, 1936.

Pontes, Eloi. *A Vida Contraditória de Machado de Assis.* Rio de Janeiro, 1939.

Pujol, Alfredo. *Machado de Assis.* São Paulo, 1917. 2nd ed. Rio de Janeiro, 1934.

Revista do Brasil (Rio de Janeiro) June 1939. On the centennial of Machado de Assis' birth.

Ribeiro, João. *Crítica: Clássicos e Românticos Brasileiros.* Rio de Janeiro, 1952.

Riedel, Dirce Côrtes. *O Tempo no Romance Machadiano.* Rio de Janeiro, 1959.

Rodrigues Pereira, Lafaiete. *Vindiciae.* Rio de Janeiro, 1899.

Romero, Sílvio. *Machado de Assis: Estudo Comparativo de Literatura Brasileira.* Rio de Janeiro, 1897. 2nd ed. 1936.

Silva, H. Pereira da. *A Megalomania Literária de Machado de Assis.* Rio de Janeiro, 1949.

Vale, Luís Ribeiro do. *A Psicologia Mórbida na Obra de Machado de Assis*. Rio de Janeiro, 1917.

Vítor, Nestor. *A Crítica de Ontem*. Rio de Janeiro, 1919.

Bibliographies

Galante de Sousa, J. *Bibliografia de Machado de Assis*. Rio de Janeiro, 1955. Includes information about pseudonyms, editions, translations, manuscripts, records, and adaptations into movies, theater, and radio.

_____. *Fontes para o estudo de Machado de Assis*. Rio de Janeiro, 1958. 2nd ed. 1969. A chronological list of references and critical works.

Exposição Machado de Assis (1839–1939). Rio de Janeiro, 1939. Includes biographical references, facsimiles, letters, photographs, and a bibliography.

Eugenio Cambaceres

(1843–1889)

George D. Schade

Eugenio Cambaceres emerged on the scene during the last decade of his short life, at a crucial moment in Argentine literary history. He formed part of the significant Generation of 1880, an innovative and forward-looking group of writers celebrated for their style and humor, and for their miscellaneous prose writings: memoirs, travel books, essays, and short stories. Cambaceres stands somewhat apart from the rest of this generation as the only important novelist and also as the most enthusiastic and gifted exponent of naturalism, though his admiration for Émile Zola was tempered by sardonic humor and bitter satire. Cambaceres believed, as all naturalist writers do, that literature must have social significance. For the French master and many of his followers in Europe and the Americas, the novel seemed the ideal instrument for social reform, and this tended often to have a deleterious effect on novelistic technique: plots sometimes became as sprawling as life; themes concentrated on the typical but frequently went further to stress the sordid in experience; and characters represented standard types. Unlike Zola, however, Cambaceres usually does not offer social guidance or emphasize a moral approach in his novels. In his best work, Cambaceres' narrative technique reaches a high degree of artistry.

Cambaceres played an important role in the development of the novel, not only in his native Argentina, but in all of Spanish America. He not only introduced Zola's naturalism into Spanish American literature, but in his best work, *Sin rumbo* (Without Direction, 1885), he made great technical strides over his predecessors. Consequently he is a forerunner of the modern Spanish-American novelist. Pilloried during his time as a "pornographic" writer by many of his contemporaries, one of whom, for example, found his earliest work to be "a water closet carpeted with Persian rugs," today he is rightly esteemed as a significant figure in the development of the Argentine and the Spanish-American novel, one who in his best moments knew how to write extremely well and without vulgarity.

Until recently, confusion has surrounded certain important details of Cambaceres' life, such as the date of his death—some historians incorrectly placing it in Paris in late 1888, instead of six months later in Buenos Aires on 14 June 1889—and the fact that this "perennial bachelor," who is variously called misogynist and misanthrope, actually married an Italian woman, a former opera singer, shortly before he died. Though his relatively brief life does not offer as many concrete facts as one might expect, certain biographical details are well known. His father was a Frenchman of considerable means who immigrated in the early 1830's to Argentina, where he bought up large ranches and soon became a powerful landholder. He married into an established Buenos Aires family and had two sons, both of whom made names for themselves: the elder, Antonino, became a distinguished senator and cofounder of the famous Jockey Club; the younger, Eugenio, born 24 February 1843, became a novelist.

Like other young men of fortune, Eugenio Cambaceres traveled a good deal to Europe, where he made Paris his headquarters and enjoyed the status of man-about-town. Witty, graceful, and amusing in conversation, his love affairs seemed to be short lived. He relished the company of beautiful women and was wont to escort actresses and singers, notably the prima donnas of the opera company that each season visited the Colón Theater in Buenos Aires.

Cambaceres also took a law degree, and during the 1870's engaged intensively in Argentine politics. Two events in his short political career demonstrate the independent thinking that later shows up in his novels. In 1871, as a delegate to the convention of the province of Buenos Aires, he daringly proposed the separation of church and state. His project was rejected by the scandalized majority in forthright terms, bringing down upon his head a rain of invective; he was called impious and accused of being an atheist and a Freemason. In 1874, as a congressman, he publicly denounced his own party for election fraud and thus sealed his doom in political affairs. He wisely decided to retire from politics and turn his attention to writing novels, where he fared much better, though here, too, he was fiercely attacked for his ideas and the way he expressed them.

During the 1880's, relatively late in life, Cambaceres feverishly began to publish. He produced four novels in the short span of six years: *Potpourri* (Hodgepodge, 1882), *Música sentimental* (Sentimental Music, 1884), *Sin rumbo* (1885), and *En la sangre* (In the Blood, 1887). All are rather short, the last two quite succinct and pithy, not at all the typically voluminous novel of the nineteenth century. Just when this production was flowing freely, it was truncated in 1889 when the author died of tuberculosis, in his mid-forties.

Cambaceres gave his first novel a French title, *Potpourri*. As in so many naturalistic works, the stress is on biting social criticism. The second part of the title word, *pourri*, which originally meant "rotten" in French, takes on new significance, for the author emphasizes all the rottenness and degradation of society. The novel's subtitle, *Silbidos de un vago* (Whistlings of a Vagabond), adds an interesting dimension. In several later editions of the novel, the subtitle is substituted for the title itself, and when Cambaceres brought out his second novel, *Música sentimental*, two years later, curiously he gave it the same subtitle as *Potpourri*. "Whistlings of a vagabond" seems quite appropriate as a subtitle for these two works, because "whistlings" suggests their loose configurations and "vagabond" hints at the narrator's situation: an idle life with no need to work. Cambaceres explains more clearly in the narrator's opening lines in chapter 1 of the second edition of *Potpourri*:"I live on my income and have nothing to do. I cast my eyes about to kill time, and I write. The least intellectual effort prostrates me. I live for the sake of living, or better, I vegetate." The marginal quality Cambaceres gives to his narrator helps prepare for the ironic point of view and the sarcastic criticism that follow in the book itself.

Potpourri is cast in the spirit and substance of the naturalistic novel. The narrator/protagonist recounts in the first person the story of an adulterous love affair, and while doing so, introduces a series of mordant political allusions and stabs at society; the humor is acrid. *Potpourri* first appeared anonymously, for the Argentine reading public was not used to this kind of virulence and not ready to accept the censure. The narrator is a dispassionate spectator, relating one episode after another to show the corruption of Buenos Aires society. Politicians and people of important rank file by; we listen in on conversations at the Jockey Club and on the promenades. But the passive narrator takes action only when he discovers the adulterous affair of his best friend's wife.

Cambaceres is still grappling with form here, and for many readers this first novel seems not to take on much novelistic shape. The plot is weak and rambling, and the story is filled with digressions. But as one critic has aptly remarked, this lack of organization may well not be exclusively due to disorder;

it may reflect a deliberate attempt to superimpose one scene upon another instead of juxtaposing them in the traditional way, a common technique of twentieth-century novelists. Cambaceres abandoned this method or lack of method in his subsequent works and followed a chronological scheme, one his contemporaries could comprehend.

Nevertheless, waves of indignation greeted *Potpourri* and Cambaceres' later novels alike. Scandalized readers and critics lambasted them not only for their naturalistic ideas and typical situations; they were also incensed and disconcerted by the language the author used. In *Potpourri* Cambaceres sprinkled his text with a mixture of colloquial expressions; he inserted gallicisms and even whole phrases in French and reproduced the speech of certain Italian immigrants. This indiscriminate use of language infuriated the purists, and there are in fact some syntactical slips in the book, probably owing to the author's lack of experience. Nonetheless, Cambaceres was gifted with verbal talent; he had an unusual way with words. In *Sin rumbo*, especially, he managed to employ all kinds of language with brilliant effect. The educated and cultured Argentines he wrote about knew French well, they babbled the Italian of the popular operas, and they often were in close contact with country folk on their haciendas and with immigrants.

Cambaceres gives full rein to the deterministic tendencies of naturalism in his second novel, *Música sentimental*, where men and their actions are seen and judged solely as products of heredity and environment. Following the precepts of Zola's canon, sex plays a predominant role: one of the protagonists is a prostitute, and the other, a dissolute young Argentine leading a life of dissipation in Paris. Some of the characters become completely degraded in *Música sentimental*: they drink excessively, gamble away fortunes, make love promiscuously, fight and despair, suffer the agonies of syphilis, and die wretchedly. The title of this second novel is laden with irony.

Música sentimental tells the story of Pablo, a wealthy young Argentine who goes to live in Paris and Monte Carlo. Shortly after his arrival in the French capital, his friend, the narrator (the author, thinly disguised), introduces him to Loulou, a young prostitute. They form a liaison that remains unbroken until Pablo's death, although he also seeks sexual adventures elsewhere, notably with a countess, whose husband challenges him to a duel. Pablo kills the count in the duel, but he, too, is wounded. Loulou has fallen deeply in love with Pablo and tenderly nurses him. As Pablo's syphilis does not allow the wound to heal, his condition worsens. He goes blind and finally dies. Loulou suffers a miscarriage of Pablo's child and, after her recovery, goes back to her life of prostitution.

The narrator of *Música sentimental* witnesses the action from the outside. He is a pessimistic spectator, just like the narrator friend in *Potpourri*, and with a similar scorn for women. Nonetheless, Loulou is treated quite sympathetically and comes off much better than Pablo. This fallen woman pathetically desires to be redeemed in the eyes of the world. Her love for Pablo awakens in her a sense of shame and repentance; she is the typical whore with the golden heart. But in the end, when her lover dies, she returns to her old profession. Time, nature, heredity, and environment perform their customary roles, as the narrator dryly comments.

In *Música sentimental* Cambaceres pays stricter attention to narrative form than in his first novel. This book unfolds with more clarity and organization; the style has become more taut and firm, showing that he has taken careful pains with his material. But in this second novel we also find more emphasis on the squalid aspects of behavior and environment. There are several clinical scenes of special crudeness near the end of the book. The influence of naturalism is paramount as Cambaceres describes the effects of syphilis on Pablo's skin, which has become all blotched and splotchy, full of reddish spots. This ruthless description awakens our compassion, but we are also repelled by it. Much worse a little farther on, in chapter 31, is a passage in which Pablo attempts to possess Loulou in his state of advanced disease. Here Cambaceres uses grotesque imagery from the animal world to convey Loulou's fears, to suggest the fatal threat that contact with him holds. She escapes as one fleeing from death, from "the poisonous fang of the viper," "the black spittle of the octopus." Cambaceres has outdone Zola in this scene, approaching the realm of Charles Baudelaire, who sought to find beauty and love in the ugly, deformed world of the grotesque. However, with *Música sentimental* Cambaceres captures the cosmopolitan low-life Parisian atmosphere extremely well, and its air of fatality clearly coincides with the tenets of French naturalism.

The scientific approach of naturalism is still plainly evident in Cambaceres' third novel, *Sin rumbo*, with more than one scene stressing the clinical and the sordid. The author, perhaps inspired by Zola, even inserted a subtitle, *Estudio* (A Study), which in later editions was dropped as superfluous. The plot is simple. Rich, cynical, and world-weary at age thirty, the protagonist Andrés finds momentary pleasure in seducing Donata, an innocent country girl who lives on his ranch. This brief idyll over, Andrés returns to Buenos Aires for the winter, leaving her pregnant. After a frenzied affair in the city with a visiting opera star, he finally returns to his country estate. There he finds that Donata has recently died in childbirth, leaving him a daughter. Two years afterward, the little girl falls ill and dies, and Andrés, in despair, kills himself.

Through most of the book Andrés suffers from fits of pessimism that lead him inexorably to suicide. Cambaceres again remains faithful to determinism as a conducting strand in his work. But *Sin rumbo* transcends naturalism in many of its best moments, chiefly as a result of the dynamism of its narrative art. Cambaceres achieves great technical mastery and intensity in this work, with a unity of design and reiterated motifs more commonly found in the mid-twentieth-century novel.

Sin rumbo is a short novel of about 150 pages, divided into very brief chapters, ranging from a half page to eight pages in length. It has two parts. The first has thirty-two chapters and can be divided in terms of setting in the following manner: chapters 1 through 13 are set in the country on Andrés' large hacienda; chapters 14 through 26 take place in the city of Buenos Aires (thirteen chapters). The first part of the book closes with chapters 27 through 32, back in the country again (six chapters, or almost half of thirteen). The second part of the novel continues in the country and comprises chapters 33 to 45 (thirteen chapters again). These divisions cannot be completely casual; they seem to obey a rigorous formal symmetry. When we carefully examine the interior structure of the work, we find that the novel continues to yield interesting and unexpected parallels and symmetries.

One of the most remarkable of these parallels is found in the opening and closing scenes of the novel. In the initial scene, Andrés' farm workers are shearing sheep in a large shed on his ranch. One might simply take this for a typical nineteenth-century description of local customs, but actually it is a foreshadowing of two tragedies, one near the end and the other at the finale of the novel. On the first page of his book, Cambaceres focuses directly on the sheep—shears snipping away the wool, plunging into the fleece, piercing at times through their skins: "Their flesh, cruelly cut into, showed wide, bleeding wounds." The motif of the bloody sheep is repeated with sinister force in the penultimate chapter when Andrés' little girl, deadly ill with diphtheria, is operated on by the country doctor, her throat cut open, reminding her father "of a lamb with its throat slit." After his daughter dies, Andrés has nothing to live for and in the closing scene commits hara-kiri, cutting open his stomach in the form of a cross, slashing "from top to bottom and side to side." Thus the novel is framed between these scenes, the bleeding sheep at the beginning, and the bloody little girl and the dramatic suicide at the end.

Action, violence, and tension characterize *Sin rumbo*. The novel's dynamism is largely due, as well as to the violent action, to language filled with imagery of movement, which contributes a texture of high tension and drama. The plot is spun together with images of movement, from which emerges a design of repeated motifs having to do with violence and, secondarily, the theater. From the opening scene to the tragic suicide that ends the book, everything seems geared toward movement. This movement is depicted with various words—roads, directions (or lack of them, as in the title), voyages, journeys—and these words are employed especially in relation to Andrés' actions. Dynamic motion prevails, despite Cambaceres' insistence at times on a lack of movement, on the protagonist's spiritual inertia in moments of feeling "without direction" in his life, when he is plunged into one of his states of depression.

The lexicon favored by the naturalists—with its

scientific, clinical flavor—does not predominate in *Sin rumbo*. What does stand out in the novel's language is its expressive vitality. The accelerated pace of the book is due in great part to the often violent, often elliptical language in which verbs prevail, particularly in the descriptions of hunting, fights, and violent confrontations between Andrés and other characters, especially the peon Contreras. This rhetoric reinforces and harmonizes with the novel's conflictive theme and reflects the nervous and volatile state of mind of the protagonist.

Repeated theatrical motifs occur throughout the chapters devoted to the months Andrés spends in Buenos Aires. During that period, in which his tempestuous love affair with the opera star Marietta Amorini is described in some detail, appearance and reality seem to fuse together and the novelistic world takes on theatrical characteristics. In chapter 13 the narrator comments on Andrés' life in Buenos Aires, saying, "He looked for a refuge . . . in gambling, in the theater, in the facile love affairs behind the scenes . . . where the living farce is nothing more than a gross repetition of the farce being presented on the stage." Farce is a word repeated various times in the text, helping to reinforce the idea of theatricality and giving a certain burlesque tone to this part of the novel. The most theatrical scene in the book occurs in chapter 20, after Amorini proposes to Andrés that they make love in his theater box, exclaiming, "What a fine farce for the rest! A pity the theater isn't full!" Despite Andrés' protests, the diva realizes her caprice in a scene that in turn becomes farcical, with the suspicious husband pounding on the door of the theater box and the unfaithful wife fleeing over the rail.

The nervous, staccato style lends strength to the novel's drama. Cambaceres has even sprinkled in his pages phrases that function to set a scene just as if the text were a drama: "a short distance away," "to the left," "to the right," "farther off." The first scene in the city, which contrasts violently with the primitiveness and simplicity of the country and the rustic Donata, takes place in the Colón Theater during a rehearsal of the opera *Aida*. Brusquely, Cambaceres thrusts his protagonist into this milieu of farce and artificiality in chapter 14, which is the longest in the novel, necessary not only for the introduction to the world of urbanity and theatricality, but also to prepare for the love affair with Amorini and to present the secondary personages of the theater who surround the diva.

The characters of *Sin rumbo* are mainly types with unchanging characteristics and qualities, typical of the nineteenth-century novel in Spanish America and of the naturalist novel in particular. Andrés, however, is an exception, for he seems to undergo a remarkable change in the second part of the novel. From an essentially egotistical hedonist, he becomes almost overnight a self-denying father. But this is quite in character, for Andrés seems to typify obsessive passion in one extreme or another; he shifts from egotism to exaggerated paternal love.

In the first part of the book, Andrés lacks motivation for living, but in the brief second part, he emerges for a time from the spiritual abyss into which he has been floundering. His small daughter, Andrea, becomes his reason for living. She teaches him to love others and to seek out the good in them. In the child's presence, he feels purified, capable of all virtues, accessible to kindness. This situation, though of short duration, contrasts sharply with Andrés' sense of the futility of life in most of the book. The first thirteen chapters unfold in the country on Andrés' hacienda at the end of springtime; when Andrés returns from Buenos Aires to his country estate, it is again spring. This spring may also be interpreted as spiritual, for the birth of his daughter has renewed him. When the second part of the book commences, two years have passed, and again it is spring. Andrés feels optimistic, full of plans for his daughter's future—but his happiness is brutally cut short with the child's death.

In *Sin rumbo* there is scarcely a chapter or scene in which the focus is not on Andrés. We see him successively angry, violent, passionate, nervous, cynical, skeptical, and filled with an overpowering ennui in response to city life. In the second part, we see him momentarily happy and tender with his daughter, spoiling her outrageously, then frenzied during her illness. Sometimes he is extremely active, at other moments in a state of boredom, and in the end, in complete despair, a suicide. His impulsive and violent nature destroys him and the others who have the misfortune to become involved with him, like poor Donata and her trusting old father.

The reader of *Sin rumbo* is doubtless well prepared for the final suicide, for he has seen Andrés sunk in black moods off and on throughout the book. Beginning with the symbolic title, Cambaceres lets us know that something is not going well. In the text itself, the expression "without direction" is repeated several times in describing Andrés and his actions. As we advance in the novel, in addition to telling descriptions of Andrés' weariness with life, we come upon direct references to suicide, in which the protagonist toys with the idea of killing himself. These reiterated premonitions of the tragic end serve the double purpose of creating an effect of tension while preparing the reader for the inevitable final suicide. What will undoubtedly surprise the reader is the way Andrés accomplishes this aim, slashing open his abdomen in the form of a cross, with blood and intestines pouring out. This may have satisfied followers of naturalism or those who wish to see a Christian symbolism in the cross. Cambaceres does fulfill here the precepts of fatalism of the naturalist school. But this frightfully brutal scene against a background of billowing smoke (for Contreras has set fire to the sheep shed that we saw in the opening scene, and all of Andrés' wealth is being destroyed) swiftly gives way to the rapid strokes of the denouement. Cambaceres displays admirable narrative economy and forcefulness of language.

The author is also adept at character portrayal in a few words. Almost all the minor characters in *Sin rumbo* are determined by their heredity, environment, and temperaments in the naturalist style, and, in addition, some are characterized onomastically. An obvious example is Amorini ("Cupids" in Italian, and from the Latin *amor*, "love"). Others who bear symbolic names are Donata (from the Latin *donare*, "to present") and Contreras (suggesting *contra*, "against"), Andrés' antagonist. Marietta Amorini and her husband are types, almost caricatures. She is the egotistical, voluptuous, capricious, and melodramatic prima donna, and—as we discover when Andrés and we get to know her a little better—she is extremely vulgar. Andrés tires of her very soon. His admiration becomes aversion, and the beautiful woman turns ugly in his eyes. The narrator describes her in a naturalistic passage in chapter 24, focusing cruelly on her defects, with consequent grotesque

effects: "Her eyes were sunk into the nape of her neck, the point of her nose went a little sideways, her ears were poorly made, her mouth too big, her arms skinny, and her legs hairy like a man's." Cambaceres looks at all the secondary theater characters derisively, in contrast with his usually brief but sympathetic treatment of the country folk, like Donata, Donata's father, or the foreman Villalba.

Besides the rather deforming view of life we get from the theater scenes, a memorable episode near the end of the first part of the book is also clearly grotesque. Cambaceres devotes chapter 28 entirely to reproducing the monstrous images of a dream Andrés has when he flees from the city to find solace in the countryside, apprehensive about the child Donata is going to bear him. As commonly happens in dreams, the main image goes through constant metamorphoses. In this instance his "son," large and powerful, suddenly assumes the shape of a dwarf, then turns into a pig, then a frog—nightmarish chimeras that fit in well with the oneiric atmosphere and typify grotesque deformation. Cambaceres employs the grotesque as a creative element, to evoke the atmosphere, charged with tension and anguish, in which Andrés lives.

Sin rumbo, then, goes far beyond its naturalistic surface dotted with pessimistic quotes from Arthur Schopenhauer. Cambaceres has attained a real artistry and powerful dramatic sense in his narrative style. This taut volume, filled with dynamism, has achieved the status of a classic, and its superb narrative art is not equaled in the Spanish-American novel until well into the twentieth century with Mariano Azuela's masterpiece *Los de abajo* (The Underdogs, 1916).

Cambaceres' last novel, *En la sangre*, does not quite measure up to the high artistic achievement of *Sin rumbo*; for many critics, this final work has been a letdown. What seems to have irked them especially is the novel's devoted filiation to the naturalist canon, which insinuates itself in the very title. *En la sangre* does adhere more closely to naturalist ideas than any other Cambaceres work, and there are perhaps too many passages stressing the concept of the impossibility of escaping the influence of one's heredity and environment. References to man's bestiality, another motif frequently found in the works of Zola, are also plentiful here, with characters, especially the protagonist Genaro, compared to the fox, the snake, the bat, and the vulture.

Nonetheless, the author at times displays in this work the narrative flair we have witnessed in *Sin rumbo*. A fine example of his technical prowess is found in the opening sentence of the novel, which describes Genaro's father, a humble Italian immigrant. Cambaceres sketches the features of his face in grotesque, animalistic terms, stressing his rapacity, a trait his son Genaro will inherit: "With a large head, flat features, hooked nose, jutting lower lip, in the wicked expression of his small sunken eyes there was a vulture's rapacity." One may shrug off this sort of description as a lopsided Dickensian characterization typical of the nineteenth-century novel and its exaggerations; still, it has a dramatic force, and it aptly sets the tone for the entire book.

En la sangre focuses unswervingly on its leading character, Genaro, as was the case with Andrés in *Sin rumbo*. With greater detail than in previous works, Cambaceres depicts the life of this first generation Argentine of lowly Italian parents, following his footsteps relentlessly from birth and the privations of his childhood to his marriage with a millionaire's daughter. Zola's penchant for documentation is here, but Cambaceres knows how to select the revealing minutiae that illuminate lives rather than giving us mountains of fact and flat, literal detail. We get a brief sketch of Genaro's street-urchin days, which abruptly change after his miserly father suddenly dies when the boy is ten, leaving him and his mother with enough to live on. Next we find Genaro at school, passing his exams by cheating and continuing his struggle for a better social status. He sends his ailing and doting mother, of whom he is very ashamed, to Italy to visit relatives so he can dispose of her money; and by scheming and calculation, he manages to court, seduce, and impregnate a beautiful and wealthy young woman. After they marry, he squanders her money, and when her father dies, Genaro appropriates to himself most of the family fortune, going through it in a dizzying series of stock-market gambles. At last, he turns again to his wife, Máxima, for a loan, but she refuses to help him out of his financial ruin. The novel closes with a dramatic confrontation between the two, Genaro striking her and threatening to kill her.

Unlike Andrés in *Sin rumbo*, Genaro seems to have hardly any redeeming features. He is avaricious, cowardly, cynical, stupidly pretentious, unscrupulous, immoral, and even indifferent to the welfare of his small child. Still, there are fleeting moments when he seems to feel some remorse for his actions, and we can feel a touch of pity for him along with the more pronounced reaction of repugnance he inspires. As a child he did not have much of a chance, with his brutal father and a miserable environment of petty crime and idleness on the streets. Later we can comprehend his wishes, as a youth and young adult, to rise in the social scale, his efforts to be somebody, his pitiful desire to join the Jockey Club, where he is blackballed by conservative members with their rigid rules and prejudices. But as the novel progresses, we come to heartily dislike the way he behaves with his wife. Making Genaro so repellent, Cambaceres really seems to despise him, but one must note that the author was expressing a xenophobia, strongly felt at that time, toward the enormous intrusion of Italian immigrants on Argentine soil. This was a serious problem that was treated also in other novels of this period, and shortly afterward in the dramas of Florencio Sánchez.

In *En la sangre* Cambaceres uses a third-person narration similar to the one employed in *Sin rumbo*, and the novel unfolds with naturalness and with attention to the interior design, repeating certain motifs. Cambaceres uses a variety of techniques for his narration, among them, entering the minds of Genaro and Máxima. Thus he is able to create a work of considerable psychological drama as well as a naturalistic portrayal of reality.

Cambaceres broke the taboos of his day and presented the misery and violence of society in a harshly realistic manner. His "slice of life" naturalistic approach made reality more convincing, though less agreeable than the idealization rampant in earlier romantic novels. Though to some he may seem the archetype of the naturalist writer in Spanish America, the focus in his best work, *Sin rumbo*, is on man's inner conflicts as well as on the brutal realities of the external world; Andrés' essential solitude and suffering are poignantly presented. At his best, Cambaceres' narrative art and technique far transcend the one-dimensional naturalist mold.

SELECTED BIBLIOGRAPHY

First Editions

Novels

Potpourri. Silbidos de un vago. Buenos Aires, 1882.
Música sentimental. Silbidos de un vago. Paris, 1884.
Sin rumbo: Estudio. Buenos Aires, 1885.
En la sangre. Buenos Aires, 1887.

Modern Editions

En la sangre. With a prologue by Teresita Frugoni de Fritzsche. Buenos Aires, 1968.
En la sangre. With an introduction by Noemí Susana García and Jorge Panesi. Buenos Aires, 1980.
Música sentimental: Silbidos de un vago. With a prologue by Arturo Giménez Pastor. Buenos Aires, 1924.
Sin rumbo. With an introduction by María Luisa Bastos. New York, 1971.
Sin rumbo. With an introduction by Liliana Ponce. Buenos Aires, 1980.

Collected Works

Obras completas. With a prologue by E. M. S. Danero. Santa Fe, Argentina, 1956.

Biographical and Critical Studies

Bastos, María Luisa. "Introducción." In *Sin rumbo,* by Eugenio Cambaceres. New York, 1971. Pp. 7–29.
Beck, Phyllis Powers. "Eugenio Cambaceres: The Vortex of Controversy." *Hispania* 46/4:755–759 (1963).
Blanco Amores de Pagella, Angela. "La lengua en la obra de Eugenio Cambaceres." *Universidad* (Santa Fe, Argentina) 45:97–115 (1960).
Blasi, Alberto Oscar. *Los fundadores: Cambaceres, Martel, Sicardi.* Buenos Aires, 1962.
Borello, Rodolfo. "Para la biografía de Cambaceres." *Revista de educación* (La Plata, Argentina) 5/1–2:1–10 (1960).

Castagnaro, R. Anthony. *The Early Spanish American Novel.* New York, 1971. Pp. 119–129.
Epple, Juan. "Eugenio Cambaceres y el naturalismo en Argentina." *Ideologies and Literature* 3/14:16–50 (1980).
García Merou, Martín. "Las novelas de Cambaceres." In *Libros y autores.* Buenos Aires, 1886. Pp. 71–90.
Giusti, Roberto Fernando. "Un novelista porteño: Eugenio Cambaceres." In *Siglos, escuelas, autores.* Buenos Aires, 1946. Pp. 321–328.
———. "La prosa de 1852 a 1900." In *Historia de la literatura argentina* 3, by Rafael Alberto Arrieta. Buenos Aires, 1959. Pp. 393–397.
Guillén, Héctor. "El realismo de Eugenio Cambaceres." *Revista nordeste* 5:191–211 (1963).
Jitrik, Noé. "Cambaceres: Adentro y afuera." In *Ensayos y estudios de literatura argentina.* Buenos Aires, 1970. Pp. 35–54.
Leumann, Carlos Alberto. "Prólogo." In *Sin rumbo,* by Eugenio Cambaceres. Buenos Aires, 1949. Pp. vii–xxiii.
Lichtblau, Myron I. "Naturalism in the Argentine Novel." In *The Argentine Novel in the Nineteenth Century.* New York, 1959. Pp. 164–173.
Rojas, Ricardo. "Prólogo." In *Sin rumbo,* by Eugenio Cambaceres. Buenos Aires, 1924. Pp. v–x.
Schade, George D. "El arte narrativo en *Sin rumbo.*" *Revista iberoamericana* 44/102–103:17–29 (1978).
———. "Lo grotesco en la literatura argentina del siglo XIX." In *Estudios de literatura argentina.* Buenos Aires. 2nd series. 7:191–215 (1982).
Solero, F. J. "Eugenio Cambaceres: Primer novelista argentino." *Contorno* 5–6:5–7 (1955).
———. "Eugenio Cambaceres y la novela argentina." *Ficción* 3:105–124 (1956).
Uhlír, Kamil. "Cuatro problemas fundamentales en la obra de Eugenio Cambaceres." *Philologica pragensia* 6/45:225–245 (1963).
Vergara de Bietti, Noemí. *Humoristas del Ochenta: Eduardo Wilde, Eugenio Cambaceres, Lucio López, Bartolomé Mitre y Vedia, y José S. Álvarez (Fray Mocho).* Buenos Aires, 1976. Pp. 39–56.
Viñas, David. *Literatura argentina y realidad política.* Buenos Aires, 1964.
Williams Álzaga, Enrique. "Aparición de la pampa en la novela *Sin rumbo,* de Eugenio Cambaceres." *La Nación* (20 May 1951). Reproduced In *La pampa en la novela argentina.* Buenos Aires, 1955. Pp. 149–158.

Miguel Antonio Caro

(1843–1909)

Carlos Valderrama Andrade

Miguel Antonio Caro was born in Bogotá on 10 November 1843 to the poet José Eusebio Caro and Blasina Tobar. Because his father was exiled and died at an early age, Caro was left to the protection of his maternal grandfather, Miguel Tobar, a learned jurist and Latin scholar who exerted a definite influence over the boy, guiding his thought and shaping his character. The English professor Thomas Jones Stevens, residing in Bogotá, served as Caro's tutor and also helped to form his strong personality.

Caro was a student of the Jesuits at the Colegio de San Bartolomé from 1859 to 1861, at which time they were expelled from the country. Caro was then forced to take refuge in the solitude of his home, where he dedicated himself to perfecting his English under the tutelage of the erudite Samuel Stuart Bond, who also wrote Latin verse.

Caro came of age under the power of the radical constitution of Rionegro, established in 1863. He became a journalist, contributing to the conservative Catholic newspapers *La Caridad* (Charity), *La Fe* (Faith), and *La República*. This was a notable period in Caro's life, as he had the good fortune to befriend men venerable in all senses of the word, such as General Joaquín Posada Gutiérrez, an officer in the Liberator Simón Bolívar's army, whose memoirs would be published because of Caro's interest; his

father's contemporary, the poet José Joaquín Ortíz; and José María Vergara y Vergara, an intimate friend and the first historian of Colombian literature. From journalism, Caro entered politics.

Caro's public life began in 1868, when he joined the legislature as representative from the state of Tolima. However, political agitation led him to concentrate instead on literature and poetry; he produced excellent pieces that in 1866 and 1867 appeared in *La Prensa* (The Press), a Bogotá newspaper. With his friend Rufino José Cuervo, he wrote *Gramática de la lengua latina* (Grammar of the Latin Language, 1867). His *Tratado del participio* (Treatise on the Participle) appeared in 1870.

El Tradicionista (The Traditionist), a newspaper intended to speak for the *Partido Católico* (Catholic party), first appeared on 7 November 1871. Intellectually and politically, it was almost exclusively the work of Caro, and its appearance marks one of the most important and decisive moments of his life. The project sprang to life vigorously and combatively; it came to an end in August 1876 with the expropriation of the newspaper and the economic ruin of the Caros. The life of *El Tradicionista* was always turbulent; in October 1873 it was at the point of being closed because of the opposition of religious groups who took a dim view of lay people speaking for the church. In 1873, Caro married Ana Narváez Guerra, a happy union blessed with seven children, most of whom, however, died prematurely.

In 1875 Caro joined the senate of the republic as deputy for the state of Tolima. He had been elected the previous year to represent the Partido Conservador, the Conservative party. A difficult time, one of open persecution, afflicted Caro, his family, and *El Tradicionista*. Because he represented the interests of the Catholics and conservatives, he suffered dispossession, harassment, and financial ruin as a result of the attacks by the Partido Liberal, the radical party that came to power in 1876.

A persecuted politician, Caro retired to his home and dedicated himself fully to the literary and philological works that would earn him distinction as the greatest intellect of the time in Colombia. In 1878 he opened the Librería Americana (the Americana Bookstore), which came to have great importance to the intellectual circles of Bogotá. He later became a distributor of such sought-after books as those published by Roger and Chernovitz, of Paris, and Appleton, of New York.

During the years 1873–1876, Caro published the translation of the *Obras de Virgilio* (Works of Vergil) in three volumes. This work brought Caro recognition not only in Colombia but also in other Spanish-speaking countries, particularly Spain, where the versatile and erudite Marcelino Menéndez Pelayo rivaled Caro in his love of Latin letters, though he preferred Horace, whose works he translated, over Vergil.

The civil war of 1876 opened the way for political changes that became concrete reality in 1878 with the presidency of General Julián Trujillo, a liberal. After Trujillo came Rafael Núñez, and with him the victory of the Regeneration, the political movement in which Caro was Núñez' right arm. The two men were of distinct ideological persuasions: Núñez tended to a positivist philosophy and radical liberalism, while Caro was more traditional and conservative. The result of this fusion was called the Partido Nacional (National party).

Caro, who since his youth had been involved in culturally oriented endeavors and who in 1871 had been among the founders of the Colombian Academy, was called upon by Núñez to direct the national library. There he accomplished important bibliographical work, some of the first to be undertaken in the country, as he methodically compiled catalogs and acquired new collections.

But Caro's masterpiece was the constitution of 1886, which replaced the radical one of 1863 and which followed Núñez' reelection to the presidency in 1884 and the civil war of 1885. Here, in distilled form, appeared Caro's deep knowledge of constitutional law he had developed through many years of public activity. Though the constitution was inspired by the thought of Núñez, the Regenerator, it was really conceived by Caro, who in writing it and defending it in the council of delegates was able to provide it with balance, moderation, and the ability to adapt perfectly to the Colombia of the past and of the present. In the new constitution, the juridical romanticism of the federal era was replaced by a centralist conception of the state, respect for the rights of the church, affirmation of presidential power, and concrete expression of civil rights and social guarantees. Caro's document continues in force today, more than a century later.

Caro's legislative activity, which Núñez called "the first enlightenment and the first virtue of Colombia," did not end in the council of delegates but continued in the constitutional council that succeeded it; his activity continued further, in a new capacity, on the state council. He also returned to journalism in 1888, as director of *La Nación*, mouthpiece of the Regeneration, which that November paid him extraordinary tribute on the occasion of his saint's day. He produced a volume of *Traducciones poéticas* (Poetic Translations, 1889). Politics sought him out: On 26 November 1891, he was elected as vice-president to Núñez.

Ill and in retirement, Núñez, who would die in 1894, never assumed his post, and Caro took charge of the government beginning in August 1892. His administration, which lasted until 1898, saw times of true agitation. In early 1893, one of the first social outbursts interrupted the tranquillity in which his administration had begun; the conspiracies of his political enemies led to the civil war of 1895, which was repressed by General Rafael Reyes; in 1896 Caro retired from the presidency, but seeing the direction events were taking in the hands of his appointee,

Guillermo Quintero Calderón, he returned to his post in five days. Regarding electoral prospects, the conservatives were divided between the "históricos" and the nationalists, and the great movement headed by Núñez and Caro struggled to survive, apparently victorious but actually mortally wounded.

Caro retired from the presidency on 7 August 1898. The events that followed could not have been more unfortunate: the coup against his successor Manuel Antonio Sanclemente on 31 July 1900, the Thousand Days' War (1899–1902), and the loss of Panama (1903).

Caro came to the Colombian senate in 1903 as senator from the department of Antioquia. The difficult debates over the Herrán-Hay Treaty (1903), which had been hastily signed by the government of José Manuel Marroquín on 22 January 1903, set the scene for Caro's last public action. He contested the treaty's approval because he considered it detrimental to Colombia's national interests. The separation of Panama was consummated on 3 November 1903. Caro returned to the senate in 1904, performing brilliantly, opposing any arrangement with the United States that might be intended to heal Colombia's bruised dignity with dollars.

Thereafter he seldom left his home and his only public action was to censure the excesses of the dictatorship of General Reyes, during the years 1905 to 1909. The death of his wife in April 1909 was a blow from which he would never recover. On 5 August of that year, Caro died in Bogotá.

Caro's prodigious intellectual activity ranged through and within a number of fields: philosophy, apologetics, education, politics, law, international affairs, economics, history, literature, linguistics, and philology. His philosophical career began in 1867, when he became professor at the National University, in the College of the Rosary and in the Conciliar Seminary of Bogotá. While he taught there, he wrote *Estudio sobre el utilitarismo* (Study on Utilitarianism, 1869), "Informe sobre 'Elementos de ideologia' de Destutt de Tracy" (Report on 'Elements of Ideology' by Destutt de Tracy, 1870), and original pieces such as his "Ligera excursión ideológica" (Light Ideological Excursion), published in 1872 in *El Tradicionista*. These were doctrinal works, in which he attacked the advances of utilitarianism and sensualism in Colombia, personified by Jeremy Bentham and Antoine Destutt de Tracy; Caro's position was based on a traditionalism that owed much to Joseph de Maistre, Louis de Bonald, Jaime Luciano Balmes, and Juan Donoso Cortés.

Caro was a champion of the Catholic cause against the excesses of radicalism. In 1864, initiating his work of writing for the public, he refuted the work of Ernest Renan, which was applauded in secular newspapers. Connected to the Society of Saint Vincent de Paul (1865) and later to the Catholic Youth of Bogotá (1871), Caro conceived of the Catholic party, in support of which he founded *El Tradicionista*. From that rich enterprise came such valuable pieces as *El darwinismo y las misiones* (Darwinism and the Missions, 1887), "San Cirilo de Alejandría" (Saint Cyril of Alexandria, 1887), and *Galileo* (Galileo, 1888). He translated the letters of Father Lacordaire (1868–1870) and the encyclical *Humanum genus* (1884) of Pope Leo XIII.

In addition to teaching at the institutions mentioned above, Caro had ties to the College of the Holy Spirit, where he delivered a famous lecture on 15 November 1880. Most outstanding among his works on educational problems is the series of essays titled *La religión y las escuelas* (Religion and the Schools), published in *El Tradicionista* in 1872.

A born politician, Caro greatly influenced the course of the nation through his enormous journalistic production during the years 1871–1909. It could not be said that Caro was a militant or partisan of the Conservative party. Certainly he was linked to it in principle, but he found its structure too constricting. In 1871, he tried to establish the Catholic party, an undertaking that met with neither understanding nor success. In 1885, with Núñez, he founded the National party, whose members were the driving force of the Regeneration movement and the instigators of the constitution of 1886. The incomprehension and opposition on the part of liberals and conservatives alike would cause the failure of the party, which ceased to exist following the coup of 1900 and the Thousand Days' War.

Caro revealed himself as the consummate constitutionalist upon taking his seat in the council of delegates on 11 November 1885. He presented a draft of the constitution on 13 May 1886 and, through the course of many busy sessions, carried it forward. His proposals addressed a number of important issues: territorial division, classification of Colombian nationals, unconstitutional laws, the definition of crime, copyright, the confiscation of property, the inviolability of certain rights, the election of senators, the powers of the house of representatives, congressional immunity, presidential powers in relation to the army, jobs that could be held by senators and representatives, extraordinary powers, presidential immunity, presidential reelection, amendments to the constitution, citizenship, electoral power and how it should be exercised, suffrage, the electoral system, and the confirmation of certain acts of executive power. As an experienced jurist, Caro wrote *Libertad de imprenta* (Freedom of the Press, 1888).

Caro's interest in international matters, obvious during the life of *El Tradicionista* and reaffirmed during the years in which he directed *La Nación* or contributed to it, was manifested in his studies on the problems of mediation and other complex cases. He was also consul to Ecuador in Bogotá for many years. His speeches at diplomatic receptions during his presidency exemplified timeliness and high-mindedness. But his most brilliant action in the international arena was during the senate sessions (1903–1904), in which the Herrán-Hay treaty with the United States was debated and when matters came to a head regarding the independence of Panama.

Just as valuable were his contributions to the clarification of such economic problems as external debt, interest, paper currency, credit, loans, and fiscal rates. It was by the efforts of Caro and Núñez that Colombia adopted paper money, against the resistence of those who thought that only coins could serve as currency.

Caro was not a professional historian, but he was wise enough to understand the importance of such studies in the life of a nation. Thanks to his work, the *Memorias histórico-políticas* (Historico-Political Memoirs) of General Joaquín Posada Gutiérrez, an officer in Bolívar's army, were published in 1864 and 1881. He edited the work of his father, writing an exemplary and definitive biographical sketch for the volume, which was published in 1873. In a library

published by the press of *El Tradicionista*, in which the book on his father appeared, he included, also in 1873, the work of José Manuel Groot, along with his biography. He wrote the prologue to his edition of Lucas Fernández de Piedrahita's *Historia general de las conquistas del Nuevo Reino de Granada* (General History of the Conquest of the New Kingdom of Granada, 1881). He authored an extensive study titled "Menéndez Pelayo y la ciencia española" (Menéndez Pelayo and Spanish Science, 1882–1883). He also wrote the "Noticia biográfica de Julio Arboleda" (Biographical Note on Julio Arboleda), which opens the edition of that author's volume of *Poesías* (Poetry, 1883). He produced many other pages on various topics of historical interest.

Caro's contributions as a literary critic were invaluable not only in the area of Colombian letters but also in that of Spanish and Spanish-American, as well as foreign, literature. Perhaps his greatest contribution was made to Latin studies, with his thoughtful studies of Vergil and other Roman authors. To cite a few examples: "Virgilio y el nacimiento del Salvador" (Vergil and the Birth of the Savior, 1865), the preliminary study to Vergil's *Obras completas* (complete works, 1873), translated by Caro, "Olmedo: La Victoria de Junín" (Olmedo: The Victory of Junín, 1879), *Virgilio en España* (Vergil in Spain, 1879), and the preface to the *Poesías de Andrés Bello* (Poetry of Andrés Bello), in the Spanish edition of 1882.

Caro made significant contributions to the field of linguistics, in *Gramática de la lengua latina*, *Tratado del participio*, the essay *Americanismo en el lenguaje* (Americanism in Language, 1878), the *Contradiálogo de las letras* (Counterdialogue on Letters, 1880), and the speech *Del uso en sus relaciones con el lenguaje* (On Custom in Its Relations with Language, 1881).

Caro was an outstanding and prolific poet. As a very young man, he published a beautiful little book of sentimental poetry entitled *Horas de amor* (Hours of Love, 1871). In 1883, he wrote and published the lovely ode *A la estátua del Libertador* (To the Statue of the Liberator), perhaps his greatest work in poetry. He was also a fine translator, not only of the works of Vergil but also of other Latin, French, English, and Italian authors.

Caro's work in Latin includes both original works and translations of his own poems and those of many

Colombians, Spaniards, Spanish Americans, and poets of other languages. Of particular note is his annotated edition of Rodrigo Caro's *Canción a las ruinas de Itálica* (Song to the Ruins of Itálica, 1888). The multifaceted personality of Miguel Antonio Caro and his political and intellectual influence on Colombian life are realized in the constitution of 1886 and the continuing work of the Caro and Cuervo Institute in Bogotá.

Translated from the Spanish by Jane A. Johnson

SELECTED BIBLIOGRAPHY

Editions

Collected Works

Obras completas. 8 vols. Bogotá, 1918–1932.
Obras poéticas, 3 vols. Bogotá, 1928–1933.
Obras. 3 vols. Bogotá, 1962–1980.

Modern Editions

Discursos y otras intervenciones en el Senado de la República, 1903–1904. Bogotá. 1979.
Escritos sobre don Andrés Bello. Bogotá, 1981.
Oda a la estatua del Libertador. 1984.
Epistolario de Ezequiel Uricoechea con Rufino José Cuervo y Miguel Antonio Caro. Bogotá, 1976.
Epistolario de Rafael Núñez con Miguel Antonio Caro. Bogotá, 1977.
Epistolario de Rufino José Cuervo con Miguel Antonio Caro. Bogotá, 1978.
Epistolario de Miguel Antonio Caro, Rufino José Cuervo y otros colombianos con Joaquín García Icazbalceta, Bogotá, 1980.
Epistolario de Cecilio Acosta, con Miguel Antonio Caro, Rufino José Cuervo y otros colombianos, Bogotá, 1981.
Epistolario de Miguel Antonio Caro y otros colombianos con Joaquín Rubió y Ors y Antonio Rubió y Lluch. Bogotá, 1982.
Epistolario del beato Ezequiel Moreno y otros agustinos recoletos con Miguel Antonio Caro y su familia. Bogotá, 1983.
Epistolario de Miguel Antonio Caro y Rufino José Cuervo con Rafael Angel de la Peña y otros mexicanos. Bogotá, 1983.
Estudios virgilianos. 2 vols. Bogotá, 1985–1986.
Estudios constitucionales y jurídicos. 2 vols. Bogotá, 1986.

Biographical and Critical Studies

Arrubla, Juan Manuel. *Caro y Sully Prudhomme*. Bogotá, 1930.
Bonilla, Manuel Antonio. *Caro y su obra*. Bogotá, 1948.
Caro, Victor E. and Augusto Toledo. *Bibliografías de Don Miguel Antonio Caro y de Don Rufino José Cuervo*. Bogotá, 1945.
Hernández de Mendoza, Cecilia. *Miguel Antonio Caro: diversos aspectos de un humanista colombiano*. Bogotá, 1943.
Hernández Norman, Isabel. *Miguel Antonio Caro: Vida y obra*. Bogotá, 1968.
Instituto Caro y Cuervo, Bogota, Colombia. *Miguel Antonio Caro y Cuervo: Actos celebrados en su honor en la ciudad de Roma*. Bogotá, 1965.
López de Mesa, Luis. *Miguel Antonio Caro y Rufino José Cuervo*. Bogotá, 1944.
Rivas Sacconi, José Manuel. "Los escritos latinos de Miguel Antonio Caro." *Abside* XII/1:21–42 (1948).
Robledo, Alfonso. *Don Miguel Antonio Caro y su obra*. Bogotá, 1912.
Torres, Carcía, Guillermo. *Miguel Antonio Caro: Su personalidad política*. Madrid, 1956.
Torres, Quintero, Rafael. *Caro, defensor de la integridad del idioma*. Bogotá, 1979.
Valderrama Andrade, Carlos. *El pensamiento filosófico de Miguel Antonio Caro*. Bogotá, 1965.
_____. *El centenario de "El Tradicionista."* Bogotá, 1972.
_____. *Un capítulo de las relaciones entre el Estado y la Iglesia en Colombia, Miguel Antonio Caro y Ezequiel Moreno*. Bogotá, 1986.
Zuleta Alvarez, Enrique. *Lengua y cultura de Hispanoamérica en el pensamiento de Miguel Antonio Caro*. Bogotá, 1977.

Manuel González Prada

(1844–1918)

Eugenio Chang-Rodríguez

Manuel González Prada, who often signed his literary works with the abbreviated name Manuel G. Prada, was one of the most liberal thinkers in the Peru of his time. His contributions to poetry and prose occupy a special place in the history of Latin American literature. He was born on 5 January 1844 in Lima, the third child of a conservative and religious aristocratic family. Baptized by the archbishop of Lima, he was godfathered by an army general upon receiving the sacrament of confirmation. Manuel attended a primary school in Lima and an English school in Valparaiso, where he learned English and German. He was not a good student even in high school; chemistry and mathematics were the only subjects that attracted his attention, as he dedicated most of his time to writing romantic poems. When his mother vetoed his plan to study chemistry at a Belgian university, he reluctantly remained in Lima to study law. Several years later, he dropped out and never returned to school.

In his twenties, González Prada continued composing poems, some of which were published with various pen names. Playwriting was also one of his favorite occupations, even though his works were never staged. Dissatisfied with what he wrote, he translated into Spanish several classic German literary pieces. Although fully devoted to writing, he rarely published his articles, and when he did he used a pen name. Visits to the Andean regions awakened his interest in the exploited. The suffering of the poor and the pathetic lot of the Indians moved him profoundly.

From 1870 to 1879, González Prada lived some sixty miles south of Lima at Tutumo, one of his family's largest farms. There he dedicated himself to farming and laboratory experiments with several species of indigenous starchy plants. Rural life allowed him to spend many hours reading literature in various languages. It was during this time of semi-retirement that this solitary writer began to compose ballads with Indian themes, most of which were to be published posthumously. On the day in 1879 that the news that Chile had declared war on Peru reached Tutumo, González Prada rushed to his family in Lima; a few months later, he joined the army. The decisive battle for the defense of his hometown ended with the victory of the invading forces. Immediately after the Chilean army entered Lima in January 1881, González Prada withdrew to his home to dedicate himself to writing verse and prose: sonnets, triolets, ballads, epigrams, plays, and articles. When in 1884 the occupying army was still withdrawing from Lima, by virtue of the humiliating Treaty of Ancón imposed on Peru in 1883, González Prada came out of retirement. This time, as a transformed man, he determined to denounce the misgovernment and immorality that had contributed to the nation's defeat.

When, after the war, the Literary Club was reorganized in 1885, González Prada was elected its second vice-president in recognition of his contributions to the institution he had helped to found twelve years earlier. In 1887, he married Adriana Verneuil, a French friend of the family, then twenty-two years old. The ceremony took place scarcely four months after the death of his mother, who had repeatedly opposed the marriage. From that day on, Adriana became the writer's inspiration and his inseparable companion. In the same year, González Prada was elected president of the Literary Circle and became famous for his cry "The old to the cemetery, the young to work!" which had been part of an address he made to a patriotic gathering. At the close of 1889, he wrote the essay "Propaganda y ataque" (Propaganda and Attack). This title was later used for one of his posthumously published books. The ruling circles offered González Prada high positions in the government: the editorship of a newspaper, a seat in the senate, and an important diplomatic post; he refused them all.

Early in 1891, González Prada presided over the conversion of the Literary Circle into the National Union, a political party for which he wrote the declaration of principles. Partly because he was anguished by three deaths in his family, González Prada decided to travel to Europe. Although the news of the trip did not please those who considered him an irreplaceable leader, he and Adriana left for Europe in June 1891.

In Paris, González Prada attended the Collège de France to listen to lectures by Ernest Renan, experts on positivism, distinguished sinologues, and professors of Arabic and Hebraic inscriptions. After his son Alfredo was born in October 1891, he resumed his cultural search, going to classical plays, the opera, and famous museums. In response to requests from Lima, a selection of his articles, essays, and speeches was published in Paris in 1894 with the title *Pájinas libres* (Free Pages). The book introduced an orthography that defied the standard spelling as prescribed by the Royal Academy of the Spanish Language. In the title, for example, he used *j* instead of *g*. When

copies of this publication reached Peru, conservatives attacked its author violently, and in Arequipa, a paid crowd burned him in effigy. After visiting Belgium and the southern part of France for a few weeks, the family spent the winter of 1896–1897 in Barcelona. Afterward they settled in Madrid until they began their trip home on 26 March 1898.

Back in Lima, González Prada resumed his leadership of the National Union, which had experienced some disappointing desertions, partly because of dishonest internal politicking. Writing and delivering speeches kept him busy once again. In 1901, after six months of patient labor, Adriana and their son, Alfredo, printed at home on a small press one hundred copies of *Minúsculas*, González Prada's first book of verses. The frustrating battles within the National Union forced him to resign from that party on 2 April 1902. Disappointed by the intellectuals, González Prada became very close to the manual workers, and his conversion to anarchism was accelerated. Notwithstanding his new philosophy, he was proposed as a candidate for the first vice-presidency of the nation on the National Union–Liberal party ticket. He declined the nomination, as he was already fully embarked on attacking clericalism, militarism, dirty politics, and immorality in the government, while defending the exploited masses, particularly the Indian population.

Advised by his wife, in 1908, González Prada put together several of his essays and articles, and published them in book form with the title *Horas de lucha* (Hours of Battle). Three years later, *Exóticas* (Exotica), a new volume of poetry, was ready for circulation in Lima. In March 1912, he accepted an appointment as director of the National Library, a position he held until his death on 22 July 1918, except during the year that Colonel Oscar R. Benavides served as *de facto* president of the country.

Just as tensions between his liberalism and his popular religiosity stirred up his anticlerical convictions, the corrupt sociopolitical atmosphere in Peru sharpened González Prada's penetrating critical sense and stimulated him to analyze the country's decaying structure. His intellectual rebelliousness and moral integrity in facing the frightening reality made him a mixture of Marcus Porcius Cato and Jean Jacques Rousseau. Like the Roman critic, González Prada identified the causes of corruption in order to unmask mercenary politicians, decadent aristocrats, and the undiscerning masses, incapable of challenging the reactionary clergy, the shameless army, the avaricious landlords, and the venal politicians who ruled the land. Very appropriately, he counseled: "Let us break the infamous, tacit pact of speaking in a whisper. Let us leave the intersection and take the true road, let us do away with ambiguity and speak frankly and directly with precise language" ("Discurso en el Teatro Olimpo," in *Páginas libres*, 1946).

Battling hours of depression and consuming pessimism, González Prada managed to feel optimistic in order to advise his disciples about what to do physically and morally to reconstruct the country. Yet he did not bequeath a program of systematized action, nor did he formulate a philosophical or political doctrine for the new Peru. He was neither a politician nor a philosopher. He was simply a man of letters with great sensibility and patriotism, deeply troubled by the plight of his people.

González Prada widened the scope of the social struggle in Peru. Twelve years before the Russian Revolution started, he expressed his fears that an uprising fought only on behalf of the workers would not fulfill its just purposes and would be similar to the Praetorian Revolt and other rebellions of the past. He feared that, once in power, the workers would impose the dictatorship of the proletariat with a tyrannical force as evil as that of the bourgeoisie whom they had sought to overthrow—the oppressed would become the oppressors. Because of these reservations, González Prada placed his confidence in the ultimate triumph of a worldwide revolution that would bring freedom to all men of all races and creeds: "Christians keep a heaven for some and reserve a hell for others; true revolutionaries seek an earthly paradise where all may find room, even their implacable enemies" ("Fiesta universal," in *Anarquía*).

Furthermore, González Prada emphatically observed that since social inequities were based on force, the oppressed were completely within their right to use violence to gain justice. The people had only one recourse: revolution, to cut the knot with a single saber blow, as Alexander the Great had done. Using Marx's comparison of social revolution and childbirth, González Prada asserted that true liberty is born bathed in blood, and that the advent of justice for the people is like a tempestuous illumination: the more pain experienced, the better the child brought into the world. With an apocalyptic vision, he predicted: "Peru is today a plain dried by the sun; a spark, a sole spark will ignite the entire nation: the first to be destroyed will be the leaden soldiers" ("Varsovianas," in *Prosa menuda*).

González Prada's best essay with an Indian theme is "Nuestros indios" (Our Indians). In it the author observed that the Peruvian republican period was simply a continuation of colonial times. The Indians were still victims of the old order based on the exploitation of man by man. In fact, the living conditions of the native population were worse at the time of his writing than they had been centuries ago. González Prada was the first to point out that the Indian problem was more than a pedagogic issue, that it was a social and economic matter. He favored teaching the Indians to be proud and rebellious so that when conditions were ripe, they could act on their own.

González Prada's prose has the flavor of Francisco Gómez de Quevedo, the freshness of Voltaire, and the enthusiasm of Rousseau. His graphic sentences summarize a profound philosophy and are charged with deep emotional feeling. His best critics have been the Peruvian essayist Antenor Orrego and the North American professor John A. Crow. Orrego called him a man of subtle talent and creative genius, a free and courageous citizen, a fervid apostle, the first ideological agitator in Peru. Crow, on the other hand, pragmatically affirmed that González Prada dynamited the perplexing forest of Peruvian politics to open furrows for others to plant new seeds. Both were right, because González Prada was the precursor of the architects of the new Peru, the herald of revolution.

González Prada ranks among the best Latin American essayists, along with José Martí, Juan Montalvo, Eugenio María de Hostos, and José Enrique Rodó. His themes follow the general trend of Spanish America's literature of ideas, preoccupied with the fundamental question of national identity. His search for national identity is evident in his sociopolitical criticism; in considering the importance of aesthetic sustenance, he differs from the point of view that regards literature as the slave of ideology, as well as from the attitude that holds ideas in subjection to the beauty of expression. This is true in his anticlerical and sociopolitical essays, as well as in his writings on anarchism and the Indian. He believed in balancing critical ideas with literary expression.

In the last fifteen years of his life, González Prada became the most important anarchist writer in Spanish America. He was not a theoretician but a mere defender of anarchist philosophy as conceived by Pierre Joseph Proudhon, Mikhail Bakunin, and Pyotr Kropotkin. He was definitely not a revolutionary with a bomb in his hand and a dagger between his teeth. As a true anarchist, he was more against domination than against government. González Prada dreamed of an egalitarian society, in which government would be reduced to its minimum expression. With Bakunin, he postulated that power corrupts; therefore he struggled for a total social change leading toward a future society formed by an independent association of free men. As a faithful anarchist, he had many objections to Marxism and advocated instead the alliance of manual and intellectual workers. He understood anarchism as a doctrine of love, piety, and humanitarianism.

During his youth, after overcoming his romantic impulses, González Prada excelled as a precursor of the so-called modernist literary movement of Spanish America that existed from 1876 to 1916. In 1871, before the Cuban Julián del Casal and the Colombian José Asunción Silva, he showed modernist characteristics in his poetry. That same year, his poems were included in the anthology *Parnaso peruano* (Peruvian Parnassus), published in Santiago, Chile, and avidly read throughout Latin America. When Spanish metrics could not express his dynamic thoughts and profound feelings, he resorted to the versification patterns of other languages or created new forms: he adopted the German ballad, the French rondel and triolet, and the Italian rispetto. He was even fond of Persian and Malayan poetry. His masterful command of the rules of versification and his desire for change and for perfection of poetic form led him to formulate the important theory on poetry included in his introduction to *Exóticas*. If we agree with Immanuel Kant in considering poetry's main characteristic to be the transformation of concepts into aesthetic ideas,

then it is in González Prada's poetry that we should search for the most artistic elements of his writings.

González Prada's style resists being placed in a single school. It is true that his inclination to eclecticism and ingenious innovation places him more in the modernist camp than in any other literary movement, even though he rejected exoticism and art for art's sake. He was too much of an individualist to submit himself to a single political ideology or literary current. The romantic rejection of all kinds of rules was his hallmark. González Prada's prose, patiently elaborated, exudes the aggressiveness of those who want to propagandize an ideology. However, he always presented his ideas and criticized man's aberrations using a simple, clear, and stimulating language. His political caricatures and essays on national events are expressed with cutting sentences, satirical in tone. His articles on literary criticism and essays on philosophical, sociological, and historical themes are witty. In them mordacity is softened by an expert application of literary devices. A powerful will is evident in González Prada's style. It shapes a firm determination to invent, adapt, transform, adopt, and re-create a literary language to be used as a comfortable, swift, efficient, and suitable linguistic vehicle. In a way, González Prada's language became an extension of his thinking and feeling.

According to González Prada, an original prose has to be powerful, proper, correct, harmonious, exact, and plastic. For him, as for Alphonse de Lamartine, the writer's mission is to spread the truth to the people with a spontaneous, clear, and convincing prose. He preferred a language easily understood, one that does not send the reader to the dictionary repeatedly. His recommendations on the art of writing are found in several essays, especially in "Propaganda y ataque" and "Notas acerca del idioma" (Notes About Language, 1889). González Prada practiced what he preached. He always tried to offer the greatest number of ideas with a minimum number of words. His sentences contain rich thoughts, even when they are short, simple, coherent, and of varied syntactic structure. A dexterity in the exact use of nouns, adjectives, and verbs adds agility to the expression and eloquence to the conclusions. González Prada's sentences are shorter than those used by his contemporaries: they average twenty words. On the other hand, his paragraphs are made up of approximately eight sentences. The different parts forming his essays have no subtitles. They are preceded by roman numerals. An expert handling of comparisons and similes and a rich metaphorical system illuminate a logical presentation of ideas that stimulate sympathy. González Prada's art of writing easily reaches the consciousness and unconsciousness of the reader. He accomplished this by the clever use of hyperbole, antithesis, synecdoche, exclamation, gradation, interrogation, irony, and phrases preceded by a colon. He knew exactly what effect he wished to produce in his reader. Despite his limitations, Manuel González Prada is indeed the precursor of the architects of contemporary Peru and one of the most important writers of Latin America.

SELECTED BIBLIOGRAPHY

First Editions

Essays

Pájinas libres. Paris, 1894.
Horas de lucha. Lima, 1908.
Bajo el oprobio. Paris, 1933.
Trozos de vida. Paris, 1933.
Anarquía. Santiago, Chile, 1936.
Nuevas páginas libres. Santiago, Chile, 1937.
Figuras y figurones. Paris, 1938.
Propaganda y ataque. Buenos Aires, 1939.
Prosa menuda. Buenos Aires, 1939.
El tonel de Diógenes. Mexico City, 1945.
Optometría: Apuntes para una rítmica. Lima, 1977.

Reports

Nota informativa acerca de la Biblioteca Nacional. Lima, 1912.
Memoria del director de la Biblioteca Nacional. Lima, 1917.

Poetry

Minúsculas. Lima, 1901.
Presbiterianas [published anonymously]. Lima, 1909.
Exóticas. Lima, 1911.
Trozos de vida. Paris, 1933.
Baladas peruanas. Santiago, Chile, 1935.
Grafitos. Paris, 1937.
Libertarias. Paris, 1938.
Baladas. Paris, 1939.
Adoración. Lima, 1947. Included in the 4th edition of *Minúsculas.*
Poemas desconocidos. Lima, 1973.
Letrillas. Lima, 1975.
Cantos de otro siglo. Lima, 1978.

Modern Editions

Individual Works

Baladas peruanas. Lima, 1966.
Horas de lucha. Callao, Peru, 1924. Callao, Peru, 1935. Buenos Aires, 1946. Lima, 1969.
Minúsculas. Lima, 1909, 1928, 1947.
Páginas libres. Madrid, 1915. Arequipa, Peru, 1934. Lima, 1946. Lima, [1969].
Pájinas libres y Horas de lucha. Caracas, 1976.

Collected Works

Antologia poetica con traduziones all'italiano. Edited and translated by P. Ferrari. Lima, 1942.
Florilegio. Lima, 1948.
González Prada. Prologue by Andrés Henestrosa. Mexico City, 1943. Anthology of his prose.
González Prada: Antología poética. Edited and with an introduction by Carlos García Prada. Mexico City, 1940.
Manuel González Prada. Edited and with an introduction by Luis Alberto Sánchez. Mexico City, 1945.
Manuel González Prada en el veintisiete aniversario de su fallecimiento. Edited by Manuel Beltroy. Lima, 1945. Articles and reflections.
Obras. With prologues and footnotes by Luis Alberto Sánchez. 4 vols. Lima, 1985–1986.
Páginas libres. With an introduction by L. G. Leguz. Mexico City, 1944.
Pensamientos. Edited and with an introduction by Campio Carpio. Buenos Aires, 1941.
Pepitas de oro. Quito, 1938.
Poesías selectas. Edited and with an introduction by Ventura García Calderón. Paris, n.d.
Sobre el militarismo: Antología. Bajo el oprobio. Edited and with an introduction by Bruno Podestá. Lima, 1978.

Biographical and Critical Studies

Basadre, Jorge. "El significado de la actuación inicial de Manuel González Prada . . ." In *Historia de la República del Perú, 1822–1933.* Lima, 1983. Pp. 157–170.

_____. "Ubicación sociológica de González Prada." In Perú: Problema y posibilidad. Lima, 1931, 1971, 1978. Pp. 156–170.

Belaúnde, Víctor Andrés. "González Prada, escritor de combate." Mercurio peruano 1:65–69 (1918).

Beltroy, Manuel R. "González Prada, el versificador." Mercurio peruano 1:78–81 (1918).

Blanco Fombona, Rufino. Crítica de la obra de González Prada: Apéndice de José Carlos Mariátegui. Lima, 1966.

Calcagno, Miguel Ángel. El pensamiento de González Prada. Montevideo, 1958.

Campos, Jorge. " Manuel González Prada." In Diccionario de literatura española. Madrid, 1949. Pp. 585–586.

Carrillo, Francisco. "La temática indigenista de 'Las baladas peruanas.' " In Baladas peruanas, by Manuel González Prada. Lima, 1966. Pp. 5–10.

Chang-Rodríguez, Eugenio. "El ensayo de Manuel González Prada." Revista iberoamericana 42/95:239–249 (1976).

_____. La literatura política de González Prada, Mariátegui y Haya de la Torre. Mexico City, 1957.

_____. "González Prada y el anarquismo." In Opciones políticas peruanas. Lima, 1985. Pp. 67–89. Lima, 1987. Pp. 69–92.

Cometta Manzoni, Aída. "Manuel González Prada, vocero del indigenismo." In El indio en la poesía de América española. Buenos Aires, 1939. Pp. 220–224.

Cossío del Pomar, Felipe. "González Prada, el maestro." La nueva democracia 20/3:18–21 (1939).

_____. "Prosa menuda." Cuadernos americanos 4/4:170–172 (1942).

Crawford, William Rex. "Manuel González Prada (1848–1918) [sic]." In A Century of Latin-American Thought. Cambridge, Mass., 1944. Pp. 108–115. Cambridge, Mass., 1961. New York, 1966. Pp. 173–182.

Crow, John A. "Manuel González Prada." In An Outline History of Spanish American Literature. New York, 1941, 1944. Pp. 108–109. New York, 1968. Pp. 105–107.

Goldberg, Isaac. "A Peruvian Iconoclast." American Mercury, November 1925. Pp. 330–333.

González Prada, Adriana de. Mi Manuel. Lima, 1947.

González Prada, Alfredo. "Manuel González Prada: A Son's Memories." Books Abroad 17/3:201–207 (1943).

Halperin, Maurice. [Review of Anarquía] Books Abroad 15/4:463–464 (1941).

Haya de la Torre, Victor Raúl. "Mis recuerdos de González Prada." In Obras completas 1. Lima, 1977. Pp. 219–224.

Hernández, J. M. [Review of Grafitos] Books Abroad 12/2:227 (1938).

Jones, Willis Knapp. [Review of Nuevas páginas libres] Books Abroad 12/2:228–229 (1938).

Mariátegui, José Carlos. "González Prada." In Seven Interpretative Essays on Peruvian Reality. Translated by Marjory Urquidi. Austin, Tex., and London, 1971. Pp. 203–213.

Mead, Robert G. "Manuel González Prada: Peruvian Judge of Spain." PMLA 68/4:696–715 (1953).

Mejía Valera, Manuel. "El pensamiento filosófico de Manuel González Prada." Cuadernos americanos 12/5:122–135 (1953).

Orrego, Antenor. "Prada, hito de la juventud en el Perú." Amauta 16:1 (1928).

Sánchez, Luis Alberto. Don Manuel: Biografía de don Manuel González Prada . . . Santiago, Chile, 1937.

_____. "Manuel González Prada and Peruvian Culture." Books Abroad 14/1:9–13 (1939–1940).

_____. Mito y realidad de González Prada. Lima, 1976.

_____, ed. Documentos inéditos sobre la familia González Prada. Lima, 1977.

Zum Felde, Alberto. "González Prada y el movimiento indigenista en el Perú." In Índice crítico de la literatura hispanoamericana 1. Mexico City, 1954. Pp, 271–288.

Antônio de Castro Alves

(1847–1871)

David T. Haberly

Antônio de Castro Alves is usually regarded as one of Brazil's greatest poets, the "Condor Bard" whose lofty vision and limitless talent enabled him to soar far above his contemporaries. In addition to his literary reputation, however, Castro Alves is esteemed as a fearless champion of freedom and the spiritual leader of the movement to abolish slavery, and has in fact become a kind of saint in the civil religion of patriotism—the Brazilian counterpart of Abraham Lincoln.

The reality of Castro Alves' life and work is often at variance with his heroic image, an image which was already firmly established at the time of his death. The apostle of abolitionism appears to have been a slaveowner, there is no concrete evidence that his poetry directly influenced the campaign to abolish African slavery in Brazil, and the heroic martyr died of complications after shooting himself in the foot. Such contradictions, however, in no way diminish Castro Alves' stature or his importance; the poet himself would have argued that they in fact proved his greatness. He was not concerned with reality but with the creation of images transcending reality, and his greatest creation was his enduring image as a genius, hero, and martyr.

Antônio de Castro Alves was born on 17 March 1847, in a small town in the interior of the province of Bahia. He was raised in Salvador (or Bahia), the provincial capital, where his father was a prominent physician; his maternal grandfather was one of the heroes of Brazil's independence from Portugal. Castro Alves was educated at one of Brazil's finest secondary schools and published his first poems at the age of thirteen. In 1862, when he was fifteen, Castro Alves was sent to Recife to study at one of Brazil's two faculties of law, but he failed the entrance exams, enrolled in a cram school, and was not admitted to the faculty until 1864. He detested the law, hated his classes, and cut them regularly; he wrote a friend that all he did in Recife was lie "in a hammock, staring at the ceiling, reading a little, smoking too much." At the time of his death in 1871, he had managed to complete only three of the six years required for a law degree.

Academic success, however, was not Castro Alves' goal. Like many of his contemporaries in Recife and at other faculties, he saw higher education as a parentally enforced vacation from responsibility, bourgeois morality, and reality. This was a time to experiment with sex, alcohol, tobacco, opium, and hashish; to read forbidden books and think forbidden thoughts; to rebel, in nonviolent and nonthreatening ways, against parents and against the Empire (Brazilian monarchy, 1822–1889). It was clearly understood, however, that eventually these new doctors of medicine or law, having sown their wild oats, would return to their families and to society, accepting the careers and the wives their parents had chosen for them.

The rebelliousness of Castro Alves and many other students in the faculties was therefore largely superficial. They sought to offend the older generation in particular through the symbolism of dress and appearance, affecting styles their parents regarded as effeminate; they were clean-shaven, and they often polished their nails, carmined their lips, and wore wristwatches. Castro Alves was one of the most extravagant young dandies of Recife, thanks to the generous support of his family, and his reputation as a student leader was further enhanced by his success as a poet.

The poems Castro Alves wrote during this period in Recife frequently reflected his absolute confidence in his own gifts and in the potential power of poetry itself. He declared, at the age of seventeen, in "Mocidade e Morte" (Youth and Death), which appeared in the collection *Espumas Flutuantes* (Floating Foam, 1870), that

> Eu sinto em mim o borbulhar do gênio
> Vejo além un futuro radiante:
> Avante!—brada-me o talento n'alma
> E o echo ao longe me repete—Avante!—

> I feel my genius bubble up in me.
> I see a radiant future there beyond:
> Go on! cries out the talent in my soul,
> And far away the echo calls, Go on!

New versions of the patriotic odes he had composed as a boy in Salvador, declaimed in the extravagant oratorical style he was developing, were big hits among the students in Recife, and this success convinced Castro Alves that verse could serve as the vehicle for fundamental social change in Brazil. Through poetry, a few highly talented individuals could express the loftiest ideals of the nation, unify and educate the people, and change the course of history. The other genre Castro Alves cultivated during this period—love poetry—appears to have been equally successful, for he achieved a considerable reputation among his peers as a Don Juan.

That reputation was enormously enhanced by Castro Alves' greatest conquest, which ensured his acclamation as the supreme idol of Brazilian students everywhere. In 1866 he became the lover of a well-known Portuguese actress, Eugênia Câmara, who stopped briefly in Recife on one of her Brazilian tours. Castro Alves was barely nineteen years old; Eugênia claimed to be thirty, but a contemporary photograph shows a grim, plump, and rather plain woman of at least forty.

Eugênia Câmara is one of the most interesting of the dozens of foreign actresses who came to Brazil in the nineteenth century. She appears to have been very effective on stage and also published two volumes of her own verse. These poems are of particular interest because they are our only firsthand account of what it meant to be an actress at that time. Eugênia is enthusiastic at length about the glory of her chosen career and about her God-given talent to move audiences to tears or to laughter, but she is also very open about the ambivalence of what she calls her "sad mission": applauded on stage, but scorned by society and religion because she was required to sell her body between performances. As an English visitor to Brazil in 1870 noted, "an actress who is not a prostitute would be shunned as unfit for the boards of the theaters." Eugênia Câmara and all the other leading actresses of the day were expected to entertain wealthy landowners and businessmen in every city and town they played. A few of these foreign actresses saved the payments and presents they received and managed to return to their own countries as wealthy women. Eugênia was not so fortunate; she slipped slowly into full-time prostitution and died, in 1874, of encephalitis brought on by chronic alcoholism.

In 1866, however, Eugênia was viewed by the students of Recife as the epitome of beauty, sensuality, and sophistication, and Castro Alves' conquest of her favors was seen by his contemporaries as a generational triumph and as proof of his uniqueness. Castro Alves lived with Eugênia Câmara for more than two years, touring with her to Bahia, Rio de Janeiro, and São Paulo. He wrote a play for her and regularly rose to declaim poetic tributes to her talents during intermission, but there is also some evidence that he was accused of serving as her pimp. When the couple reached São Paulo, Castro Alves enrolled in the faculty of law there and attended a few classes. Once again he became the idol of the student population, and retained this status even after Eugênia threw him and all his belongings out into the street in September 1868.

Castro Alves responded by writing a few bitter poems, attacking Eugênia as extravagantly as he had praised her. In November, he discharged his shotgun into his left foot while hunting. Gangrene forced the amputation of the foot in 1869, and the shock revived the tuberculosis Castro Alves had contracted as a child and which had killed his mother. He returned to his birthplace in the Bahian interior, and there finally began to work seriously on collecting his poems; many of his works had been performed in public, but only a very few had appeared in newspapers and magazines. Castro Alves completed one collection of verse, *Espumas Flutuantes*, which he published in Salvador in 1870. He also started organizing a volume of his abolitionist poetry, *Os Escravos* (The Slaves, 1883), and completed a third book, *A Cachoeira de Paulo Afonso* (The Paulo Afonso Falls, 1876). Castro Alves moved to Salvador in September 1870, but his health continued to deteriorate. He died on 6 July 1871, about four months after his twenty-fourth birthday. His admirers in Bahia and elsewhere in Brazil mounted a campaign to collect enough money to publish all of the poet's works but rather quickly lost interest in the project. As a result, many of Castro Alves' poems did not appear in print until 1921, fifty years after his death.

Ironically, the unavailability of a very considerable portion of Castro Alves' poetic production in no way retarded the growth of his reputation; in fact, it can be argued that it increased his fame. Castro Alves was above all an oral poet. Many of his works, designed for performance, do not transfer well to the printed page. With relatively few published texts available, the cult of Castro Alves, in his own lifetime and in the decades that followed his death, relied heavily on oral tradition—on the memories of his friends and admirers and on the recollections of those who had been moved by the power of his theatrical recitations of his poetry.

The nature of this oral tradition, then, emphasized one of the key elements in Castro Alves' philosophy of poetry and of the poetic life—the link with the theater. Castro Alves unhesitatingly defined himself as a genius. Within this category of superior beings, he recognized two subdivisions, actors and poets. Undoubtedly influenced by Eugênia Câmara's experiences and perceptions, Castro Alves saw actors and actresses as individuals uniquely able to present texts written by others in a form that could move audiences, shifting melodramatically from laughter to tears within a few short lines. The recompense for this ability was applause and adulation. But in Castro Alves' universe, every extreme was balanced by its antithesis. Therefore, the cheers and curtain calls that rewarded actors and actresses on stage were balanced by poverty, dependency, and social marginality.

The Poet—and Castro Alves almost always capitalized the term—was simply an actor on a far vaster stage, the stage of the world. It was the Poet's function and glory to capture divine inspiration and to communicate his vision of the universe and of humanity to lesser mortals. In order to accomplish this task, it was not enough for the Poet simply to write; he was also required to live the poetic life. The Poet was destined to receive the admiration he deserved, but he was also condemned to poverty, to suffering, and to the early and tragic death which appeared to Castro Alves and other Romantics to be the ultimate proof of literary merit. The poetic life, with its antitheses of fame and tragedy, was the Poet's greatest creation, designed to communicate the balance of the universe far more powerfully than mere words.

Castro Alves never wanted to be a lawyer, and it should not surprise us that he never finished his studies. His one ambition was to be a Poet. He created that role for himself, and he played it throughout Brazil with enormous success—enjoying the adulation of his audience but always insisting, as in "Ahasverus e o Gênio" (Ahasverus and the Genius), in *Espumas Flutuantes*, that he was really a tragic figure, the reincarnation of Ahasverus, the Wandering Jew:

> O Gênio é Como Ahasverus . . . Solitário
> Invejado! a Invejar os Invejosos.

> The Genius, like Ahasverus, is alone,
> Envied! But jealous of those who envy him.

Ahasverus' tragedy was that he could not die; the tragedy of the true Poet, as Castro Alves defined himself, was that he was doomed to die young.

Castro Alves reinforced this tragic image in his public performances by dressing only in black and by using rice powder to make his face deathly white. All the accounts of his contemporaries stress the enormous effectiveness of his recitations at the theater: "Everyone who heard him got goose pimples of astonishment," according to Afrânio Peixoto, and idolized him as "more demigod than poet, less poet than prophet" (*Castro Alves*, pp. 19–20). In São Paulo, writes Pedro Calmon, "shouts, delirium, cheers, frenzy—such was the overwhelming reaction to every line; every idea, every thought caused a sensation in the audience" (*Castro Alves*, p. 197).

As we read Castro Alves' poems it is often difficult to understand how they could have inspired the adulation described by those who first heard them. Today, in the second half of the twentieth century, we do not associate such audience frenzy with poets but rather with rock stars—the inheritors of the Romantic mantle of the rebellious, marginal, and often tragic genius. Carrying this analogy one step further, reading Castro Alves is as unsatisfactory as trying to recreate a Grateful Dead concert by studying the sheet music to their songs. The typography of Castro Alves' poems—the forests of question marks and exclamation points, the constant dashes and ellipses—attempts to represent his dramatic gestures, his theatrical shifts in pitch and volume, but it is obviously a very poor substitute for an experience that cannot be duplicated.

Moreover, Castro Alves' audiences had expectations very different from our own. Those who attended his recitations, first, wanted to witness poetic genius firsthand. Improvisation on the part of the poet, whether real or simulated with the help of a good memory, was something very close to a religious experience for audiences who believed that what they were seeing and hearing was the brief moment of contact between divine inspiration and the genius of the true Poet.

Castro Alves' audiences also wanted to be moved to an intense emotional catharsis, and his contemporaries' descriptions of the pandemonium that accompanied his recitations make it clear that the poet

filled this need. Antithesis was not only the basis of Castro Alves' vision of the universe and of his role as Poet; it was also his basic technique for accomplishing this desired catharsis. Using a quite simple vocabulary, Castro Alves endeavored to make his listeners feel a number of basic emotions (love, fear, anger, happiness, or sorrow, for example) or visual, tactile, or spatial sensations (height, depth, light, darkness, warmth, cold, and so on). The trick was to juxtapose antithetical emotions and sensations very closely and very rapidly, as in this description of the martyred missionaries of colonial Brazil:

> Dor—tu és um prazer!
> Grelha,—és un leito! Brasa—és uma gema!
> Cravo—és um cetro! Chama—um diadema!
> O' morte—és o viver!
>
> Pain,—purest pleasure!
> The rack,—but a bed! Hot irons,
>   —jewels so bright!
> The stake,—is a scepter! The fire,
>   —but a gem!
>   Oh death,—you are life!
>   ("Jesuita" [Jesuits],
>   in *Espumas Flutuantes*)

Such rapid-fire antitheses, when reinforced by Castro Alves' verbal talent, charismatic presence, and theatrical gestures and changes in pitch, could so disorient his audiences that they dissolved into a frenzy of shouting, weeping, and fainting.

Castro Alves' enormous success in creating and playing the role of the ultimate Poet, however, is only part of his enduring image. He is also the "Bard of the Slaves," the great apostle of abolitionism in Brazil. He wrote his first poem attacking slavery in 1863, when he was sixteen, but did not systematically devote his talents to the cause until the spring of 1865. He wrote at least sixteen abolitionist poems during the next six months or so, but few of these works were published. He then stopped writing anti-slavery poems until 1868, when he was in São Paulo. At that time he added a few new texts to the collection of political and abolitionist poems he planned to publish under the title of *Os Escravos*. Those plans were sidetracked by his health problems and by his eagerness to get the largely apolitical *Espumas Flutuantes* into print, and Castro Alves' last letters do not even mention his antislavery book. Only six of the thirty-four poems now generally accepted as belonging to *Os Escravos* were printed, in periodicals, before the poet's death in 1871. Fewer than a dozen other texts from *Os Escravos* were published before Brazil abolished slavery in 1888, and the rest of the collection—half the poems—appears to have remained unknown until 1921.

This chronology might appear to cast some doubt on Castro Alves' reputation as the great literary champion of the slaves. Nonetheless, it is important to recognize that his abolitionist works, when compared to other texts in the campaign against African slavery in Brazil, represent fundamental changes in ideology and approach.

Millions of slaves were imported into Brazil from the first decades of the sixteenth century until 1850, and African slavery was an essential part of the economy and society of every area of the nation until the institution was abolished in 1888; as a result, the regional differences in attitudes toward slavery that characterized the United States in the decades before the Civil War simply did not exist in Brazil, where almost all educated men and women accepted the institution without question.

Because of this national consensus in favor of slavery, very few abolitionist works were written in Brazil before 1888. From the early eighteenth century on, the humanitarian crusade against the Atlantic slave trade in Europe and North America produced thousands of tracts, poems, plays, and works of fiction. No similar literary campaign ever developed in Brazil, where the abolition of the slave trade in 1850 was entirely the result of pressure from the British government, enforced by the Royal Navy. Nor did abolitionism have much of an impact on Brazilian literature after 1850, as the nation slowly began to consider freeing the slaves already in Brazil. Thus, while Castro Alves' antislavery works—his long dramatic poem *A Cachoeira de Paulo Afonso* and the thirty-four poems included in *Os Escravos*—may not seem like much when set against the massive abolitionist bibliography created by Henry Wadsworth Longfellow, James Russell Lowell, Harriet Beecher Stowe, and hundreds of lesser North Amer-

ican writers, his small corpus is nonetheless the largest collection of antislavery poems by a single Brazilian author and in fact makes up a significant percentage of *all* the abolitionist works written in Brazil before 1888.

Castro Alves' antislavery works are important qualitatively as well as quantitatively. Most of the abolitionist works written by other Brazilians in the nineteenth century lie entirely outside the European and North American concern with the humanity, even the nobility, of the slaves and the immorality of their enslavement. Within this Brazilian context, slavery was wrong simply because the nature of the institution forced naturally good white men and women into close daily contact with those of African descent, beings viewed as inherently violent and immoral beasts. The physical and moral survival of white Brazil, it was argued, required the separation of the races, and this separation could only be accomplished through abolition.

Almost all of Castro Alves' antislavery poems depart from this Brazilian tradition, and are far closer to the humanitarian, moralistic abolitionism of Europe and North America. What is most surprising about his works, however, is the degree to which he identifies with his slave characters. This identification is extraordinarily intense and represents a clear departure from both the hostility toward nonwhites found in much Brazilian abolitionism and the often patronizingly self-righteous pity characteristic of European and North American writers.

It is difficult, at least at first glance, to explain Castro Alves' ability to identify with Brazil's slaves. Some critics have suggested a genealogical explanation for the phenomenon, but there is no evidence of his possible African ancestry, and it is clear that the poet's contemporaries perceived him as the wealthy and privileged scion of one of Bahia's leading—and very white—families. Some of Castro Alves' admirers have explained his abolitionism by imagining a great and tragic passion for a slave girl or free woman of color, but no hard facts back up this theory. Moreover, Castro Alves' biography at times belies his ideology; he appears to have had a personal slave, the son of his wet nurse, for much of his life.

Such contradictions, however, would not have troubled Castro Alves or his contemporaries, for contradiction and antithesis were central to his ideology and his image as a Poet. And it is within his definition of himself as a Poet that the roots of his abolitionism can be found. As an adolescent in Recife, Castro Alves—like all the other students—sought to rebel. His early abolitionist works, which tend to describe slave characters rather than identify with them, are at one level simply a form of rebellion against an institution which was central both to the Empire as a whole and to the fortunes of his own family. The rebelliousness of these early poems, however, like all the protests of Brazil's students, is more symbolic than concrete, more philosophical than political.

It is also evident, at a slightly deeper level, that Castro Alves was endeavoring to use the cause of the slaves to validate his self-definition as a Romantic and as a Poet. He therefore does not treat Brazilian slavery as a local problem but as one facet of the universal struggle of freedom against tyranny and oppression, and he thereby defines himself in the image of the greatest heroes of his generation, the true Poets who had fought for similarly noble causes: Lord Byron and Greek independence, Adam Mickiewicz and Polish independence, Louis Kossuth and Hungarian independence.

Castro Alves' equation of Brazilian abolitionism and Greek or Polish independence was revolutionary, but its practical effect was undercut by his ideology. The true Poet needed a great and noble cause, and Castro Alves had chosen abolition, but the antithetical nature of the universe and the poetic life required that the glory of the Poet's struggle for freedom and humanity be balanced by the tragic failure of that struggle. To champion abolition, therefore, was simultaneously to admit its impossibility, at least in the short run.

If Castro Alves' abolitionism, in its early stages, was both a noble cause worthy of a true Poet and a token of his adolescent rebelliousness, it eventually became more central to his vision of the world and of his function than he could have anticipated. His chosen role as Poet fulfilled all of his adolescent ambitions: to be famous, to be loved by an actress, to be admired and envied by his fellow students. However, Castro Alves' poems and correspondence show little evidence that he was able or willing to look beyond these short-term goals to marriage, to a career, to life after graduation from the faculty of law. This narrowness of vision should not surprise us, since it was implicit in his definition of the nature of the true Poet, a definition that was the focus of his self-image but that he increasingly came to view as a dead end rather than as a source of liberation.

Castro Alves had no trouble accepting, on an intellectual level, the typical Romantic vision of the Poet as a solitary and uniquely talented individual whose glorious literary triumphs had to be balanced by the failure of his chosen cause, by social marginality, by sickness and physical pain, and, in the end, by an early and tragic death. But it was a far more difficult matter indeed to accept this destiny literally. Castro Alves had played his chosen role as Poet with resounding success everywhere in Brazil, but ultimately he saw no way to escape from the tragic and inevitable consequences inherent in his definition of that role, which had become as much a prison as the humdrum future of family and career responsibilities against which he had originally rebelled.

This sense of being trapped, whether by society or by his role as Poet, lay at the heart of Castro Alves' abolitionism and was the key to his ability to identify with Brazil's slaves or "captives," his preferred term for them. In Castro Alves' antislavery poems, the slaves are above all victims of entrapment; their status as captives overshadows both their race and their color. The color of the slaves was relatively unimportant to Castro Alves, in part because it did not fit neatly into his antithetical cosmology of light and darkness, good and evil, which was fundamental to his poetic method. He frequently finessed this potential conflict between complexion and cosmology by describing his slave characters as light-skinned or even *pálidos* (pallid), and by making their white oppressors swarthy or deeply tanned. The race of the *cativos* (captives), their African origins, merely established their symbolic value as the children of Ham and of Hagar, icons of eternal bondage. For Castro Alves, then, the enslavement of those of African descent was ordained by history and geography and was as inevitable as his own entrapment by society and by the poetic destiny.

In short, Castro Alves was not writing about the reality of slave life in nineteenth-century Brazil but about himself. Slavery was a metaphor for his own situation, and Castro Alves found it difficult to formulate a political program that would lead to abolition precisely because he was so convinced of the inevitability of his own captivity. He had no reason to expect that Brazil would abolish slavery, at least in the near future, because he saw no way to escape from the crisis of his own life.

Modern readers have often been puzzled by Castro Alves' most famous abolitionist work, O Navio Negreiro (The Slave Ship, 1880), which he wrote in São Paulo in April 1868. The poem's conclusion vehemently demands that Brazil stop importing African slaves—a step which British pressure had actually accomplished in 1850, eighteen years earlier. O Navio Negreiro therefore seems to be a curious anachronism, divorced from the reality of Brazil in 1868. Castro Alves' abolitionism, however, was always philosophical and psychological rather than realistic and political. In O Navio Negreiro and in his other major antislavery works, the young poet endeavored to create symbolic structures drawn from his own experiences and from the traditions of Brazilian Romanticism, which could enable him to use the nation's African "captives" as metaphors for his own captivity.

In Castro Alves' poetry, these symbols are centered around a handful of literary commonplaces, the standard last refuges of Truth and Hope and Beauty to which despairing, world-weary poets sought to escape: the Brazilian landscape itself, the realm of natural beauty, innocence, and freedom from constraint; memories of childhood and of maternal love and protection; the boundless liberty of the sea, the ultimate symbol of escape; and the interior of Brazil, like the area around the poet's birthplace in Bahia, which for Castro Alves signified security, freedom, and the pure joy of childhood.

Castro Alves designed his major antislavery works as methodical and very effective descriptions of the destructive impact of the institution of slavery on such places of refuge. The gradual loss of liberty and of the possibility for escape, which is one of the primary consequences of this destructive impact, paralleled and symbolized the erosion of options Castro Alves perceived in his own life. Slavery, the poet insists, is alien to the Americas, imported by a decadent Europe. Its presence, however, has permanently stained the Brazilian landscape, and even the wild condor, one of Castro Alves' favorite symbols of the freedom once possible in the New World.

> Condor, que transformara-se em abutre,
> Ave da escravidão
>
> The condor has become a vulture,
> The bird of enslavement
>   ("Vozes d'África [Voices of
>   Africa], in Os Escravos)

Slavery also pollutes and ravages the refuge of family life in "Tragédia no Lar" (Tragedy on the Hearth); when a slave woman's infant child is taken from her to be sold, the grieving mother goes mad. And in O Navio Negreiro the almost incomprehensible suffering of the Africans contaminates both the sky above and the ocean below; the once-proud Brazilian flag, which flies above the ship, is stained by the horror beneath it and becomes a shroud.

Castro Alves' most ambitious abolitionist work was his long dramatic poem A Cachoeira de Paulo Afonso, which he completed in 1870. The poem idealizes both the interior of Bahia and the two slaves, Maria and Lucas, who inhabit that naturally pure and beautiful landscape. But Maria is raped by the white son of their master, and this violent act, a symbol of the slave system as a whole, transforms the peaceful landscape of the interior into place of suffering and brutality. Lucas longs to avenge Maria's dishonor, but the noble slave, like Castro Alves himself, is not a man of action but an emblem of suffering. The slave couple tries to escape, but their canoe is swept over the well-known falls of the poem's title. All of Nature joins in a ritual that is both wedding and funeral:

> As estrelas palpitam—São as tochas!
> Os rochedos murmuram! . . . —São os monges!
> Reza um órgão nos céus!
> Que incenso!—Os rolos que do abismo voam!
> Que turíbulo enorme—Paulo Afonso!
> Que sacerdote!— Deus. . . .
>
> The stars above twinkle!—like torches!
> The cliffs murmur low!—like monks!
> A celestial organ prays!

Doves rise from the depths!—as incense!
From the censer—the crashing Falls!
The priest!—is God Himself. . . .
("Loucura Divina" [Divine Insanity])

Death, then, became the final refuge, for the Bahian poet as for his slave characters, and it might well seem that Castro Alves was a failure. Despite his talent, he did not advance the noble cause in any concrete way. Despite his obvious sincerity and his identification with the captives, his antislavery verses were not calls to action but appeals for pity and paeans to resignation. To conclude that Castro Alves failed, however, would be entirely and very ironically wrong. In the final analysis, the poet's basic assumptions about his mission turned out to be correct: symbol was in fact more important than substance, and the verses the true Poet produced were but one aspect of his most sublime and enduring creation— the poetic life and its necessary corollary, the poetic death. At least half of Castro Alves' antislavery poems remained unpublished when the Golden Law of 1888 freed Brazil's slaves, but this did not really matter. As abolitionism finally developed as a political movement in the decades following Castro Alves' death in 1871, the poet's image provided a suitably heroic focus for the campaign—the saintly image of the tragic young genius who had, in some nebulous and totally unexplained fashion, sacrificed his life for the slaves. Castro Alves' apotheosis as nothing less than the martyred "Christ of the Slaves" did a great deal to make abolitionism respectable for white Brazilians and undoubtedly contributed to the final victory of the cause he had championed in his poems.

SELECTED BIBLIOGRAPHY

First Editions

Poetry

Espumas Flutuantes. Salvador, Brazil, 1870.
A Cachoeira de Paulo Afonso. Salvador, Brazil, 1876.
Vozes d'África—Navio Negreiro. Rio de Janeiro, 1880.
Os Escravos. Rio de Janeiro, 1883.

Plays

Gonzaga ou a Revolução de Minas. Rio de Janeiro, 1875.

Collected Works

Obras Completas de Castro Alves. Edited by Said Ali. 2 vols. Rio de Janeiro, 1898.
_____. Edited by Afrânio Peixoto. 2 vols. Rio de Janeiro, 1921. 2nd ed. São Paulo, 1942. 3rd ed. São Paulo, 1944.

Modern Editions

Individual Works

Os Escravos. São Paulo, Brazil, 1972.
Espumas Flutuantes. Edited by Sonia Brayner. Rio de Janeiro, 1974.
Gonzaga ou a Revolução de Minas. Rio de Janeiro, 1972.

Collected Works

Antologia Poética. Rio de Janeiro, 1971.
Correspondência, Inéditos e Dispersos. Salvador, Brazil, 1956.
Os Mais Lindos Poemas. Rio de Janeiro, 1974.
Os Melhores Poemas. Edited by Lêdo Ivo. São Paulo, 1983.
Obra Completa. Edited by Eugênio Gomes. Rio de Janeiro, 1960. 2nd ed. Rio de Janeiro, 1966. 3rd ed. Rio de Janeiro, 1976.
Poesias Completas. Edited by Jamil A. Haddad. São Paulo, 1952. 2nd ed. São Paulo, 1953.
_____. Edited by Manuel Bandeira. Rio de Janeiro, 1969. Reissued 1972, 1980.

Translations

El navío negrero y otros poemas de Castro Alves. Translated by Francisco Villaespesa. Madrid, 1930.
Tres poetas románticos. Spanish translations of Castro Alves, Gonçalves Dias, and Sousândrade. Translated by Washington Delgado, Arturo Corcuera, and Javier Sologuren. Lima, 1984.

Bibliographical and Critical Studies

Amado, Jorge. A.B.C. de Castro Alves. São Paulo, 1941.
Braga, Thomas. "Castro Alves and the New England Abolitionist Poets." Hispania (U.S.A.) 67:585–593 (1984).

Calmon, Pedro. *Castro Alves: O Homem e a Obra.* Rio de Janeiro, 1973.

_____. *Para Connecer Melhor Castro Alves.* Rio de Janeiro, 1974.

Cavalcanti Proença, Ivan. *Castro Alves Falou.* Rio de Janeiro, 1979.

Haberly, David T. "Eugênia Câmara: The Life and Verse of an Actress." *Luso-Brazilian Review* 12:162–174 (1975).

_____. *Three Sad Races.* New York, 1983. Pp. 51–69.

_____. "Heine and Castro Alves: A Question of Influence." *Romanische Forschungen* 97:239–248 (1985).

Haddad, Jamil A. *Revisão de Castro Alves.* 3 vols. São Paulo, 1953.

Hill, Telênia. *Castro Alves e o Poema Lírico.* Rio de Janeiro, 1978.

Horch, Hans Jürgen. *Antônio de Castro Alves, 1847–1871.* Hamburg, 1958. In German.

Passos, Alexandre. *O Humanismo de Castro Alves.* Rio de Janeiro, 1965. Rev. ed. Rio de Janeiro, 1971.

Peixoto, Afrânio. *Castro Alves, o Poeta e o Poema.* 2nd ed. São Paulo, 1942. 5th ed., São Paulo, 1976.

Putnam, Samuel. *Marvelous Journey.* New York, 1948. Pp. 123–135.

Sayers, Raymond S. *The Negro in Brazilian Literature.* New York, 1956. Pp. 112–117.

Tolman, Jon M. "Castro Alves, Poeta Amoroso." *Luso-Brazilian Review* 12:241–262 (1975).

Bibliography

Horch, Hans Jürgen. *Bibliografía de Castro Alves.* Rio de Janeiro, 1960.

Eduardo Acevedo Díaz

(1851–1921)

Jorge Ruffinelli

Eduardo Acevedo Díaz was born in Montevideo, Uruguay, on 20 April 1851. He died in Buenos Aires, Argentina, on 18 June 1921. He lived and wrote near the end of one of Uruguay's most convulsive historical periods, a time when two antagonistic political parties (the White party and the Red party) emerged from civil wars, and the country started to move toward a peaceful, institutional period.

Acevedo Díaz was first of all a novelist, and the first Uruguayan novelist to establish successfully his identity as a writer. His literary activities were always subjected to his political interest, for two reasons. First, he could dedicate himself to writing only during relatively peaceful periods, that is, when he was in exile in Argentina. Second, the real subjects of his novels were history and politics. Acevedo Díaz created within Uruguay's literature the genre of the historical novel at the very moment when the national consciousness was being formed.

During the second half of the nineteenth century, Latin American literature was intimately linked to political ideas and activities. At the same time that they were intellectuals, novelists, and poets, writers frequently took up arms, joining in revolution against established governments. For example, from an early age, Acevedo Díaz took part in such battles, and when he was twenty years old, he joined the forces of Timoteo Aparicio against the government of Lorenzo Batlle. This kind of insurgent movement typically ended with the signing of a peace treaty that would last until a new period of violence broke out. Within this context, separation of literature and politics was not possible. It was not until the end of the nineteenth century, with the advent of modernism, that a cult in favor of literature and art "for art's sake" started. That period also marked the beginning of professionalism in literature.

Acevedo Díaz' importance within the history of Uruguay's literature is based on the historical tetralogy made up of *Ismael* (Ismael, 1888), *Nativa* (Native, 1890), *Grito de gloria* (Cry of Glory, 1893), and *Lanza y sable* (Lance and Saber, 1914). The four books, which span the years 1808 to 1825, define Acevedo Díaz as a realistic writer concerned with the epic cycle of his country's liberation from Spanish power and the resistance against later Portuguese and Brazilian invaders until the achievement of total independence. Although the literary merit of the novels in the tetralogy is uneven, the forcefulness with which the author delineates his characters, whether real or fictitious, shows his great talent in making history come alive. His ability to make use of the historical and political background adds to the importance of the novels, since they help define the complex polemics that remain alive today.

Although he was influenced by Sir Walter Scott, Acevedo Díaz did not think of the historical novel as a genre dedicated to the reconstruction of the past, as in the Spaniard Benito Pérez Galdós' *Episodios nacionales* (1873–1912). More than that, Acevedo Díaz was interested in finding in Uruguay's past a rising national spirit that achieved nationhood and was at the same time a result of it. Independence meant self-determination for the *criollos*, the direct descendants of the Spanish. It meant the breaking away of a colony that had been dependent on a European power. From the time of the conquest until the war of independence, fundamental changes took place in the mentality of the *criollo* that resulted in Uruguayan nationalism. Acevedo Díaz tried to find and express this consciousness within its historical context. This meant that the writer could not be merely a well-informed conservative in love with the past. Acevedo Díaz' historical perspective and insight were sharpened by his participation in the political life of the country.

A student of law and a journalist, Acevedo Díaz started publishing articles in the newspaper *La Revolución* around 1870. In 1872, he founded *La República* and collaborated in several other newspapers. (Both the White and the Red parties made use of newspapers to express their ideologies.) Acevedo Díaz' ability as a journalist, his extraordinary gift as an orator, and his experience in other political activities were decisive when he became the leader of the White party. But, eventually, his political militancy meant persecution and exile, and he spent long periods in Buenos Aires, where he published at least six books.

The most significant incident of Acevedo Díaz' political career occurred in 1903, when his support of José Batlle y Ordóñez (Lorenzo Batlle's son) was decisive in the latter's election as president. In time, Batlle became the greatest statesman in the history of Uruguay, but at this time, because Batlle was the leader of the opposition, this meant that Acevedo Díaz was banished from his own party. From that time on, Acevedo Díaz gave up politics in favor of diplomacy, representing Batlle's government in the United States, Mexico, Argentina, Paraguay, Italy, Switzerland, and Austria-Hungary.

Some of Acevedo Díaz' novels (*Brenda* [1886] and *Grito de gloria*, for example) were first published in installments; serialization was common at that time. To keep his reader's interest, Acevedo Díaz traced his plots carefully and at the same time maintained a direct and unadorned literary style, both of which were integral to the success of his novels. Such a traditional form of writing meant that he had to use certain literary elements—such as dialogue, descriptive passages, narratives—sparingly. The same held true regarding content—love stories, episodes of war, political affairs, and so forth. This might well have led to Acevedo Díaz' principal weakness as a writer: an excess of romanticism; he never overcame it, especially when he wrote about his characters' love affairs. In his historical novels this tendency stands in contrast to the forceful prose of his war episodes and his rural scenes depicting the rough life of the *gauchos*.

In the novels about intimate relationships, the romanticism led to failure. *Brenda* and *Minés* (Minés, 1907) demonstrate that his talent was not in the genre of the romantic novel, to which he contributed hardly anything original. These novels are merely love stories; needlessly complicated, they center on characters from the upper class of an urban society. The books were never well received by readers or by critics. His magnificent historical novels, on the other hand, made up for his few failures.

Ismael, probably Acevedo Díaz' best novel, undertakes a revision of the history of his country. Combining fact and fiction, the author sets up characters and stories that never were, such as Ismael and his hardships, alongside others who really existed, for example, the patriot José Gervasio Artigas. This truly historical novel describes the personal hardships of Ismael within the wider historical context of the country; within that frame, Ismael's story is kept to only the most essential facts: his luckless love affair, his persecution, and his killing of his antagonist, Almagro.

The character Ismael is the prototype of the young *gaucho montonero* (fighting cowboy), rough and daring, and at the same time capable of tenderness and sensuality. The novel starts with a love triangle: Ismael, Felisa, and the Spaniard Almagro. Almagro is in love with Felisa, but his unrequited love leads to tragedy. First there is the knife duel between Ismael and Almagro over Felisa's love, then Felisa's accidental death at the hands of Almagro, and, as a sort of poetic justice, Almagro's death at the hands of Ismael. Acevedo Díaz' skill consists in creating, from a simple, credible plot, an ambience charged with passion, but not necessarily love; this is the kind of passion aroused by antagonistic political parties and by war.

Ismael has been considered a great novel since the moment it was published. Better than any historical document, it narrates the past in a multifaceted fashion, filled with emotion. Acevedo Díaz commented on the advantages of the novel form, for the purpose of describing a vivid past, over the dry, brief style of historiography:

> The novelist is able to recover the past, with greater ease than a historian, by means of a convincing tale. History gathers much data, coldly analyzes events, operates on a cadaver, and searches for the secret of the life that was. The novel assimilates the historian's patient endeavor and, like a god, with a wisp of inspiration, revives the past.
>
> ("La novela histórica," *El Nacional*, 29 September 1895)

Ismael covers the years from 1808 to 1811, a time when the provinces of the River Plate region were trying to wrest their independence from Spain; Uruguay and Argentina did not yet exist as such. At the beginning of the novel, these historical aspects are presented in dialogue; later they are portrayed dramatically as revolutionary struggles that end with the banishment of the Jesuits from the Plaza Fuerte of Montevideo in 1811.

The second novel in the tetralogy, *Nativa*, covers events between the years 1823 and 1825, the so-called Cisplatina period, denoting the time when the country was occupied by Portuguese and Brazilian forces and Uruguay was considered a province of Brazil. (Acevedo Díaz did not record the years between 1811 and 1822, years that were decisive in the history of Uruguay. It was then that José Gervasio Artigas' troops were defeated, putting an end to his plans of establishing a federation.) *Nativa* and *Grito de gloria* could well have been written as one novel because they share the same setting and characters;

from a historical as well as a literary point of view, *Nativa* is less important than *Grito de gloria*.

The historical background of *Grito de gloria* is important because of the crusade of the thirty-three *orientales*, a group of revolutionaries who invaded the territory and became victorious after battles at Rincón de las Gallinas and Sarandí. A number of events and battles in this novel reveal Acevedo Díaz' great artistic sensibility. His characters are forceful and precise, and his descriptions sometimes have been compared to the pictures of Juan Manuel de Blanes, the famous Uruguayan artist who portrayed the same period with great beauty. The historical figures José Fructuoso Rivera and Manuel Oribe represent the conflicting interests and opposing political ideas that gave rise to the White and the Red parties. Acevedo Díaz tries to reflect certain attitudes that later in history would spark bitter political strife.

The novels *Ismael*, *Nativa*, and *Grito de gloria* are notable because although history is used as a means to support his fiction, Acevedo Díaz never lets the former overshadow the plot. The main characters— Ismael in the first novel and Luis María Berón in the other two—are fictitious; nevertheless, they blend in with the historical characters without affecting the novel's verisimilitude.

On the other hand, in *Lanza y sable*, which covers the years between 1834 and 1838, the inordinate amount of attention given to the character Fructuoso Rivera upsets the novel as a whole, making it unbalanced. Before it was published as *Lanza y sable*, Acevedo Díaz referred to the novel as "*Frutos*" (a shortened form of Fructuoso), revealing the importance of the *caudillo* (military commander) in the author's mind while he was writing. The novel tells about the uprising of the rebel Fructuoso Rivera (a former president) against Manuel Oribe (then president of Uruguay). Although written eighty years after the events, Acevedo Díaz' description is forceful and dramatic, and remarkably, those same events have continued to influence the country. Political discussions between Uruguay's two parties revolve around the same themes that provoked their formation. To this day Rivera and Oribe are the symbols of the ideas and attitudes of these parties and are the subject of endless polemics. The historian Alberto Zum Felde has summarized this phenomenon as follows:

"Uruguay doesn't have a history, everything revolves around politics." Rivera and Oribe "remain very much alive. They are part of Uruguay's political strife" (*Proceso intelectual*, p. 184).

In addition to his historical novels and his two romantic novels, Acevedo Díaz' short story "El combate de la Tapera" (The Fighting of the Tapera, 1892) and the novel *Soledad* (Soledad, 1894) provide evidence of the extraordinary skill of Acevedo Díaz as a writer. They are still his most widely read and praised works. "El combate de la Tapera" unfolds in 1817 during the Portuguese invasion and is remarkable in its perfection. It tells about the retreat of the natives after a battle against an enemy superior in numbers as well as weaponry. *Soledad* has been considered a masterpiece; Zum Felde called it a "prose poem." The rough and violent country life is the setting of this love story. This time Acevedo Díaz is not carried away by romanticism even though he makes use of a familiar scheme: a love triangle complicated by a tragedy that resolves it. Soledad, the female protagonist, represents the primitive country: the vastness of the land and the feelings it awakens in the people.

The novels of Acevedo Díaz were a founding premise for Uruguayan narrative. Although they never reach any kind of perfection and are at times a mixture of journalistic discourse and artistic narration, they generally achieve their lofty goals, one among them to provide the national culture with a portrait of the country, a portrait that is profound and essential since it came from an examination of the roots of the nation.

The work of Acevedo Díaz evolved from romanticism to realism. He stopped being merely romantic after *Brenda*, but he never became a naturalist/positivist in the tradition of Émile Zola, Guy de Maupassant, and Edmond and Jules de Goncourt.

Alejandro Magariños Cervantes, author of *Caramurú* (1865), was Acevedo Díaz' most immediate predecessor in Uruguayan literature. Acevedo Díaz was well aware that he had superseded Margariños Cervantes' descriptions of rural settings, in which prototypical characters were drawn up with excessive romanticism. His narrative had become much more realistic. In a letter to Alberto Palomegue, Acevedo Díaz compared his work with that of Magariños Cervantes: "My unkempt taciturn gauchos can never be identified with his sentimental gentleman gauchos. Neither can my tough heroines be compared to his angelic women, nor my fierce wild love affairs to his chaste encounters" (*El Siglo*, 25 March 1893). Acevedo Díaz was much more concerned with writing about the inner strength of a people, a strength that ultimately comprises the history of a country. In defining the aesthetic and philosophical purpose of his novels, he refers to them as "the history of the instincts": "All peoples, however modest they may be, have heroic moments. Heroic moments are nothing less than the natural source that has to be exploited in order to tell the history of instincts that have been worn out . . . by more than half a century of revolutionary action" (prologue to *Lanza y sable*).

Acevedo Díaz' major literary contribution was to keep alive these instincts, which were about to disappear because of a people's exhaustion by war. He recaptured and recorded these instincts in his novels, and in some essential way, they urged thousands of men and women to cherish their newly born national identity.

SELECTED BIBLIOGRAPHY

First Editions

Novels

Brenda. Buenos Aires, 1886.
Ismael. Buenos Aires, 1888.
Nativa. Montevideo, 1890.
Grito de gloria. La Plata, Uruguay, 1893.
Soledad. Montevideo, 1894.
Minés. Buenos Aires, 1907.
Lanza y sable. Montevideo, 1914.

Essays

Ideales de la poesía americana. Buenos Aires, 1884.
Índole de los partidos: Criterio histórico y político. Montevideo, 1895.
Arroyo Blanco, rememoración en el "Club Nacional." Montevideo, 1898.

Canal Zabala de riego, navegación y fuerza motriz. Montevideo, 1903.
Carta política. Montevideo, 1903.
L'Uruguay: l'elevage et l'agriculture. Rome, 1909.
Epocas militares de los países del Plata. Buenos Aires, 1911.
El mito del Plata. Buenos Aires, 1916.

Modern Editions

Grito de gloria. With an introduction by Emir Rodríguez Monegal. Montevideo, 1964.
Ismael. With an introduction by Roberto Ibáñez. Montevideo, 1953.
Ismael. With an introduction by Francisco Espínola. Montevideo, 1966.
Lanza y sable. With an introduction by Emir Rodríguez Monegal. Montevideo, 1965.
Nativa. With an introduction by Emir Rodríguez Monegal. Montevideo, 1964.
Soledad y "El combate de la Tapera." With an introduction by Francisco Espínola. Montevideo, 1954.

Biographical and Critical Studies

Acevedo Díaz, Eduardo (Jr.). La vida de batalla de Eduardo Acevedo Díaz. Buenos Aires, 1941.
Alegría, Fernando. Breve historia de la novela hispanoamericana. Mexico City, 1959. P. 275.
Ardao, Arturo. Racionalismo y liberalismo en el Uruguay. Montevideo, 1962. Pp. 235–281.
Barbagelata, Hugo D. La novela y el cuento en Hispanoamérica. Montevideo, 1947. Pp. 113–121.
Castagnaro, R. Anthony. "History and Fiction: The Powerful Art of Eduardo Acevedo Díaz." In The Early Spanish American Novel. New York, 1971.
Darío, Rubén. "La novela en América: Eduardo Acevedo Díaz." Revista Nacional 146:175–178 (1951).
De Medina García, Lorenzo. "El hombre del campo uruguayo en las novelas de Eduardo Acevedo Díaz, Carlos Reyles y Javier de Viana." Revista Nacional 209:387–426 (1961).

Deus, S. Eduardo Acevedo Díaz, el caudillo olvidado. Montevideo, 1978.
Espínola, Francisco. "Ensayo sobre la personalidad del gran novelista oriental." El País (20 April 1951). P. 5.
Etcheverry, José Enrique. "Acevedo Díaz: Aportes para el estudio de su ideario estético." Marcha 582 (1951).
Gallinal, Gustavo. "Grito de Gloria." Mundo Uruguayo 1270:4–5 (1943).
Garganigo, John F. El perfil del gaucho en algunas novelas de Argentina y Uruguay. Montevideo, 1966. Pp. 19–37.
Lasplaces, Alberto. Eduardo Acevedo Díaz. Montevideo, 1931.
Palomeque, Alberto. Eduardo Acevedo Díaz. Montevideo, 1901.
Paternain, Alejandro. Eduardo Acevedo Díaz. Montevideo, 1980.
Pereira Rodríguez, José. Ensayos 1. Montevideo, 1965. Pp. 111–128.
Rama, Angel. Ideología y arte de Eduardo Acevedo Díaz. "El combate de la Tapera." Montevideo, 1965.
Rodríguez Monegal, Emir. Vínculo de sangre. Montevideo, 1968.
Roxlo, Carlos. Historia crítica de la literatura uruguaya 2. Montevideo, 1912–1916. Pp. 530–565.
Tinker, Edward L. The Cult of the Gaucho and the Creation of a Literature. Worcester, Mass. 1947.
Torres-Ríoseco, Arturo. La novela en la América Hispana. Berkeley, Calif, 1939. Pp. 213–214.
Verani, Hugo J. "Realismo y creación artistica en Soledad de Eduardo Acevedo Díaz." Revista de la Biblioteca Nacional de Montevideo 24:9–18 (1986).
Zum Felde, Alberto. Crítica de la literatura uruguaya. Montevideo, 1921. Pp. 83–106.
_____. Proceso intelectual del Uruguay y crítica de su literatura 1. Montevideo, 1930. Pp. 275–307.
_____. Indice crítico de la literatura hispanoamericana. La narrativa. Mexico City, 1959. Pp. 111–124.

Bibliography

Rela, Walter. Eduardo Acevedo Díaz: Guía bibliográfica. Montevideo, 1967.

Clorinda Matto de Turner

(1852–1909)

Efraín Kristal

Clorinda Matto de Turner is, with Ricardo Palma and Manuel González Prada, one of the major literary personalities of nineteenth-century Peru. She wrote novels, books of legends and historical tales, a play, and numerous essays on topics ranging from the emancipation of women to the literary and historical relevance of Latin America's indigenous languages.

Clorinda Matto de Turner was not, as it is commonly held today, the originator of *indigenismo*—the literary depiction of the contemporary Indian in the rural setting. The first work in this style, Narciso Aréstegui's *El Padre Horán,* appeared as early as 1848. Nevertheless, Matto's first novel, *Aves sin nido* (*Birds Without a Nest,* 1889), is certainly a landmark in the genre.

Clorinda Matto de Turner was born in Paullu, Cuzco, on 11 November 1852. When her mother died in 1862 she was sent to a boarding school in Cuzco; she stayed there for six years until she was called back home to take care of domestic chores for her father and two brothers. In 1871 she married John Turner, a British entrepreneur who lived in Tinta, a small village about 100 miles from Cuzco.

In Tinta Clorinda Matto became interested in the *Tradiciones peruanas* of Ricardo Palma (1833–1919), the most distinguished Peruvian writer of his time. The *tradición,* Peru's contribution to Latin American romanticism, is a short literary piece that includes anecdotes, stories, poems, or refrains, and makes allusions to historical documents. Ricardo Palma defined the genre he invented as a configuration of beautiful lies of a poet and a dreamer based on some historical truth.

Clorinda Matto wrote *tradiciones* set in Cuzco and its outlying areas from colonial times through independence. She wrote anecdotes about viceroys, archbishops, and nuns; and stories about the Spanish Inquisition and the hidden treasure of the Incas. Some of her *tradiciones* were devoted to national heroes, including Simón Bolívar, who led many Latin American nations to their independence.

In one of her best *tradiciones,* "El señor de la capa roja" (The Gentleman in the Red Cape), a beautiful woman from Tinta suspected of sin is escorted home after a religious festival by a gentleman in a red cape. The woman accidentally trips and inadvertently exclaims the names of Jesus and the Virgin Mary. The caped man cringes back and an angel appears to inform the woman that her escort is the devil himself. The woman abandons her companion and decides to lead a pious life. The narrator remarks that one can still detect the devil's anger at the loss of this beautiful woman on the anniversary of the religious observance of El Día de San Nicolás.

When Matto first came to Lima, on a visit with her husband in 1877, she had not yet published a book but she was a well-known literary figure. Indeed, her *tradiciones* were being printed in Peruvian and other Latin American journals. Some had been translated into English and published in the *Times* of London. Juana Manuela Gorriti, the Argentine writer then living in Peru, hosted a literary evening in her honor. It was attended by some of the most prominent contemporary writers, including her revered *maestro* Ricardo Palma.

On her return to Tinta her life as a writer was interrupted by the war between Peru and Chile (1879–1883). She participated in the resistance raising funds, turning her home into a military hospital, and writing patriotic articles including praise for Peru's most successful general, Andrés Avelino Cáceres. She also took control of her husband's business interests when he died in 1881. Several years later, in 1884, she left Tinta in dire financial straits, with contempt for small-town living.

Matto moved to Arequipa, where she spent two productive years as editor-in-chief of *La Bolsa*, a daily newspaper. She published her first book, *Tradiciones cuzqueñas* (Tradiciones from Cuzco), with a prologue by Ricardo Palma, in 1884, and, later the same year, she published a literary anthology for women with edifying and educational themes, *Elementos de literatura. Según el reglamento de instrucción pública. Para el uso del bello sexo* (Elements of Literature. According to the Rules of the Public Instruction. For the Use of the Fair Sex). Her play *Hima-Sumac*, based on Juana Manuela Gorriti's novel *El tesoro de los incas* (The Treasure of the Incas), was also staged in 1884. Hima Sumac is an Indian princess, a descendant of the Incas and keeper of their legendary hidden treasure. She is engaged to Tupac Amaru (the hero of the Peruvian emancipation who led Indian uprisings in the eighteenth century), but she falls in love with a Spaniard eager to loot the treasure. Although her character is weak, she finds a measure of inner strength in her dying moments and does not reveal the location of the treasure even while being tortured to death.

In 1886, after her successful stay in Arequipa, Clorinda Matto decided to settle in the Peruvian capital. In Lima her *Tradiciones cuzqueñas* received a new edition; she gave important and well-publicized lectures, hosted a literary salon, and ran a literary press. In 1889 Matto became the editor of *El Perú ilustrado*, an influential journal where she published new Latin American writers such as the poet Rubén Darío. In her articles and literary pieces in the journal one could detect a change in her literary sensibility: although she did not abandon the *tradición*, she began turning away from embellishing historical events to embrace the project of accurately representing Peruvian reality in order to change it. Her turn to naturalism is manifest in her three novels, *Aves sin nido* (*Birds Without a Nest*, 1889), *Índole* (Character, 1891), and *Herencia* (Heredity, 1895).

Although each novel can be read on its own, the plot lines of the three are interconnected, the central theme is shared, and the characters are informed by Manuel González Prada's political thought. In his first essays and lectures González Prada (1844–1918) argued that enlightened Peruvians should educate the ignorant but powerful landowners and public officials in order to liberate the Indians from servitude and to integrate them into the Peruvian mainstream.

Matto's application of the concepts of ignorance and servitude to create characters and situations separates her brand of *indigenismo* from that of her predecessors. In *Birds Without a Nest*, Matto presents a situation of degradation and brutal exploitation of the Indians in the Peruvian provinces where their labor is poorly remunerated; they lack legal protection; and local priests sexually abuse the women. The plot is set in motion with the arrival of an enlightened couple who witness the depravation of Kíllac, a fictional town in the Peruvian Andes fashioned after Tinta. The couple attempts to improve the situation of a few Indians and to become role models for the local whites. The novel concludes dramatically when an Indian girl and the son of the mayor's wife are unable to marry because they discover that they have the same father, a priest.

Birds Without a Nest leaves an enigma unresolved. Although the sexual exploitation of the Indians occupies a central place in the novel, priestly seduction of upper-class women remains a mystery. *Índole* explores the struggles of a respectable woman whose priest attempts to seduce her. *Herencia*, the third and final novel of the cycle, focuses on the end point of an Indian's integration into civilized society. Margarita, the Indian orphan brought to Lima by the enlightened couple of *Birds Without a Nest*, becomes fully adapted to Limean society and marries a respectable young man.

The reception of Matto's works depended in part on the ideology of those who judged them. Soon after the publication of *Birds Without a Nest*, President Cáceres, the military hero, wrote Matto a letter. He praised her accurate depiction of Andean society, pledged to work against corruption, and promised to discuss the sexual exploitation of Indians by priests with the archbishop of Lima. Her popularity ebbed in 1891, when a short story by the Brazilian writer Henrique Coelho Netto, in which Jesus is willing to have an affair with Magdalen, appeared in *El Perú ilustrado*. Even though she tried to distance herself from that story, claiming that it was published without her knowledge or permission, she was fired from the magazine and persecuted by Peru's highest religious officials, who banned her journal, put her books on censured lists, and excommunicated her. Once the proclerical Nicolás de Piérola toppled Cáceres in a military coup in 1895, Matto lost the support of political and literary personalities. When her house and press were sacked she felt compelled to go into exile.

She moved to Argentina, where she was received warmly. She taught in two schools for women in Buenos Aires and edited a literary journal, *El búcaro americano*. She published a grammar textbook for school and translated the gospels of Luke and John into Quechua, the most widely spoken indigenous language in the Andean region.

Before she died she took her only trip to Europe, which she summarized in her last book, *Viaje de recreo* (A Voyage of Recreation, 1909), published posthumously. She was granted an audience with Pope Pius X, which vindicated her earlier condemnation by leaders of the Peruvian Catholic Church.

Clorinda Matto published several books that brought together material previously published in journals, newspapers, and pamphlets: *Bocetos al lápiz de americanos célebres* (Pencil Sketches of Renowned Americans, 1890), a book of biographical pieces including her essay on Cáceres; *Leyendas y recortes* (Legends and Clippings, 1893), which includes *tradiciones*, short stories, and an eulogy for Juana Manuela Gorriti, whom she called the Victor Hugo of Latin America; and *Boreales, miniaturas y porcelanas* (Northern Lights, Miniatures and Porcelains, 1902), a collection of essays and lectures from the Argentine exile. In these books she expressed her views on the emancipation of women.

Clorinda Matto believed that women should not reject religion, although they should be cautious about confession. She wrote that women were meant for motherhood but that that does not preclude their useful participation in society. Denouncing the pervasive tendency to see women as either servants of their men or as exchange commodities, she exhorted them to make it clear that their bodies are not merchandise. She also complained about Peruvian freethinkers like González Prada, who reduced the emancipation of women to a struggle of men against priests for the control of women's minds and souls. Clorinda Matto understood emancipation as overcoming the barriers to a woman's self-development. She believed in marriage as an institution whose aims should include the education of women. She longed for the day that women would be judged for their accomplishments rather than for their attachments, and she regretted living in a society where men tended to disregard educated, independent women.

The political vindication of Clorinda Matto took place publicly in 1924 during Augusto B. Leguía y Salcedo's second administration, when the president requested the repatriation of her body from a cemetery in Argentina through official diplomatic channels. This act did not redeem her in the cultural arena. She had been viciously attacked by conservative critics, and José Carlos Mariátegui (1895–1930), who praised writers' attempts to vindicate the Indian even when he disagreed with their political ideas, did not include Clorinda Matto in his well-known essay (1927) on Peruvian literature where he coined the term *indigenismo* as a literary category. Mariátegui's omission of Clorinda Matto de Turner was symptomatic of the contempt for women's contributions to Peruvian culture by the turn-of-the-century intellectuals.

Clorinda Matto was reintegrated into Peruvian

literary history after the Puerto Rican critic Concha Meléndez underscored her importance in Latin American letters in an influential essay published in 1934. The full dimension of her contribution to Latin American letters, however, has not yet been assessed, although such recognition would be appropriate. After all, she was the key Peruvian writer in the transition from romanticism to naturalism, and the only Peruvian novelist to have commanded an international reputation until Ciro Alegría in the 1940's.

SELECTED BIBLIOGRAPHY

First Editions

Novels

Aves sin nido. Lima, 1889.
Índole. Lima, 1891.
Herencia. Lima, 1895.

Plays

Hima-Sumac; drama en tres actos y en prosa. Estrenado en el Teatro de Arequipa el 16 de oct. de 1884 y representado en el Olimpo de Lima el 27 de abril de 1888. Lima, 1892. Includes "Crítica a *Hima Sumac*" by Gerardo Chavez.

Essays

Tradiciones cuzqueñas. With a prologue by Ricardo Palma. Arequipa, Peru, 1884. Includes "Apuntes biográficos" by Julio F. Sandoval.
Bocetos al lápiz de americanos célebres. Lima, 1890. Includes "Apuntes de viaje; Clorinda Matto de Turner" by Abelardo Gamarra.
Leyendas y recortes. Lima, 1893. Includes "Clorinda Matto de Turner; Lectura hecha por Joaquín Lemoine en el Palacio de la Exposición de Lima en el solemne aniversario de la instalación del 'Círculo Literario'"; and "Una nota crítica sobre la autora" by Nicanor Bolet Peraza.
Boreales, miniaturas y porcelanas. Buenos Aires, 1902.

Nonfiction

Elementos de literatura. Según el reglamento de instrucción pública. Para el uso del bello sexo. Arequipa, Peru, 1884.
Analogía. Segundo año de gramática en las escuelas normales, según el programa oficial. Buenos Aires, 1897.

Apostulcunac ruraskancona panan chis Clorinda Matto de Turner castellanonanta runa sim iman Hicrasccan. Buenos Aires, 1901. Translation of the gospels of Luke and John into Quechua.
Cuatro conferencias sobre la América del Sur. Buenos Aires, 1909.
Viaje de recreo: España, Francia, Inglaterra, Italia, Suiza, Alemania. Valencia, Spain, 1909.

Modern Editions

Aves sin nido. Lima, 1973.
_____. With a prologue by Luis Mario Schneider. Mexico City, 1981.
Herencia. With a prologue by Antonio Cornejo Polar. Lima, 1974.
Índole. With a prologue by Antonio Cornejo Polar. Lima, 1974.
Tradiciones cuzqueñas completas. Selected and with a prologue by Estuardo Núñez. Lima, 1976.

Translations

Birds Without a Nest. A Story of Indian Life and Priestly Oppression in Peru. Translated by J. G. Hudson. With a preface by Andrew M. Milne. London, 1904.

Biographical and Critical Studies

Alegría, Fernando. *Nueva historia de la novela hispanoamericana.* Hanover, N.H., 1986. Pp. 72–74, 78–79.
Cáceres, Andrés Avelino. "Carta a Clorinda Matto de Turner." *El Perú ilustrado* 156:1802 (1890).
Carrillo, Francisco. *Clorinda Matto de Turner y su indigenismo literario.* Lima, 1967. Includes a bibliography of articles Clorinda Matto published in newspapers and literary journals.
Castro Arenas, Mario. *La novela peruana y la evolución social.* 2nd ed. Lima, 1967. Pp. 105–112.
Cornejo Polar, Antonio. "*Aves sin nido*: Indios notables y forasteros." In *La novela peruana; siete estudios.* Lima, 1977. Pp. 7–32.
_____. *La novela indigenista.* Lima, 1980. Pp. 38–44.
Cuadros, Manuel E. *Paisaje i obra. Mujer e historia. Clorinda Matto de Turner.* Cuzco, Peru, 1949.
Franco, Jean. *An Introduction to Spanish American Literature.* London, 1969. Pp. 101–103.
Garcia Calderón, Ventura. *Del romanticismo al modernismo; prosistas y poetas peruanos.* Paris, 1910. Pp. 283, 330.
Gutiérrez de Quintanilla. "*Aves sin nido*, novela peruana por Clorinda Matto de Turner; juicio crítico." Lima,

1896. This essay is the prologue to the Spanish edition of *Aves sin nido*. Valencia, Spain, 1908(?).

Meléndez, Concha. *La novela indianista en hispanoamérica, 1832–1889*. Madrid, 1934. Pp. 171–178.

Miller, John C. "Clorinda Matto de Turner and Mercedes Cabello de Carbonera: Societal Criticism and Morality." In *Latin American Women Writers: Yesterday and Today*, edited by Yvette E. Miller and Charles M. Tatum. Pittsburgh, 1977.

Riva Agüero, José de la. *Carácter de la literatura del Perú independiente*. Lima, 1905. Reprinted in his *Obras completas 1*. Lima, 1962. Pp. 255–257.

Rodríguez-Luis, Julio. "Clorinda Matto." In *Hermenéutica y praxis del indigenismo. La novela indigenista de Clorinda Matto a José María Arguedas*. Mexico City, 1980. Pp. 17–55.

Tauro, Alberto. *Clorinda Matto de Turner y la novela indigenista*. Lima, 1976.

José Martí

(1853–1895)

Ivan A. Schulman

José Martí was a revolutionary writer in every sense of the word. Born of Spanish parents in colonial Cuba on 28 January 1853, he witnessed the oppressive measures imposed on the island by the Spanish colonial administration. Early in his life he made the decision to fight for the liberation of Cuba and similarly oppressed Antillean countries. But he was not merely a political revolutionary; he was also a revolutionary in literature. Martí gave expression to the emerging ideas and emotions of a modernizing world in a language and style that perplexed and fascinated many of his contemporaries. Manuel Gutiérrez Nájera, for example, wrote of the Cuban that at times he could not follow his ideas, "because his ideas have sturdy wings, strong lungs, and rise inordinately. . . . [In his] magic style we lose ourselves from time to time, like Reynaldo in the garden of Armida" (Nájera, *Obras* 1, Mexico, 1959, p. 372).

Martí's conscious resolve to devote himself to revolutionary political and literary ideals became clear shortly after the first Cuban war against Spain in 1868. During this period he participated in the publication of clandestine newspapers and circulars, including *El Diablo Cojuelo* (The Limping Devil) and later *La Patria Libre* (The Free Fatherland). In the latter in 1869 he published a dramatic poem, "Abdala," in which the main character sacrifices his life to defend his country against its oppressors. For a while the colonial regime took no action against Martí. But in 1869 when he and a friend, Fermín Valdés Domínguez, signed a letter questioning the political behavior of one of their classmates, Martí was accused of being unfaithful to the Spanish colonial regime. He was tried and condemned to six years of hard labor in the quarries of San Lázaro in Havana.

The San Lázaro experience is recorded in a political essay, "El presidio político de Cuba" (The Political Prison in Cuba, 1871), that is both moving and revealing: moving, because it records an adolescent's reactions to the harsh, sometimes nightmarish conditions of a forced labor camp; revealing, because it is an early essay that foreshadows the expressive force of the mature writer. "El presidio político de Cuba" is directed to the Spanish authorities. It is a plea for humanity and reform in the administration of the island. But it is also a milestone in the evolution of prose in a period of metamorphic change called *modernismo* in Latin American literature and culture. "El presidio político" was followed by a companion piece entitled "La república española ante la revolución cubana" (The Spanish Republic Faced by the Cuban Revolution, 1873), written in Spain where the young Martí had been exiled following the commutation of his forced labor sentence.

Martí's Spanish exile marked the beginning of a lengthy period of peregrination through Spain, Mexico, Guatemala, Venezuela, and, finally, the United States. The Cuban spent his final fifteen years in the United States, a productive period during which he wrote, spoke to Cuban and Hispanic revolutionary and cultural societies, and organized the invasion of colonial Cuba in 1895.

Martí received his formal education in Spain. At the universities of Zaragoza and Madrid he earned degrees in philosophy and law. Late in 1874, he left Spain for Mexico, after a brief stay in France. Mexico proved to be a hospitable environment for Martí. He participated widely in the country's cultural life, wrote for the *Revista universal*, helped found the Sociedad Alarcón, debated the merits of spiritualism and materialism in a national forum, and wrote a play entitled *Amor con amor se paga* (Love Is Repaid with Love, premiered in 1875). It was in Mexico that he met Carmen Zayas Bazán, who was to become his wife and subsequently the symbol of a painful, frustrated domestic life. The rise of the dictator Porfirio Díaz caused Martí to leave Mexico in 1876, to return for a short term in 1877, and then renew his wanderings in search of a place where he could work with personal freedom. He returned briefly to Cuba, responding to the pull of family and a desire to resettle in his homeland.

Guatemala was the next place on Martí's itinerary. His stay there also proved to be brief. He was named to the faculty of the Central School of Guatemala, where he taught French, English, German, and Italian literature as well as the history of philosophy. For a while, life seemed prosperous and serene. He married Carmen Zayas Bazán, contributed to Guatemala's developing cultural life, and wrote of his gratitude to Guatemala in a slender volume entitled *Guatemala* (1878). But a shift in political factions made life there untenable for him. Once again Havana drew him. But in 1879, while working in the Havana law offices of Miguel Viondi, his revolutionary activities resulted in his second deportation to Spain.

Instead of staying there, he left almost immediately, going first to France and then to the United States. While in New York, he met Charles A. Dana, who invited him to write for the *New York Sun*. But

New York was not to become Martí's home until he had attempted life in Venezuela. In 1881 he went to Caracas with the hope of finding refuge and solace in "Our America," as he called the Hispanic countries of the New World. Things went well in Venezuela, but for an extremely short period. Nevertheless he succeeded in founding an important modernist magazine, the *Revista venezolana*. In its second issue (15 July 1881), he defended his magazine's style and, in the course of this defense, developed one of modernism's early manifestos:

> Some of the "simple" pieces that appeared in our last issue have been tagged polished and exquisite. What follows is not a defense, but a clarification. Private speech is one thing; passionate, public discourse, another. Bitter polemics speak one language; quite another serene biography. . . . Thus, the same man will speak in a different language when he turns his searching eyes to past epochs, and, when, with the anguish and ire of a soldier in battle, he wields a new arm in the angry struggle of the present age. . . . The sky of Egypt ought not to be painted with London fogs; nor the youthful verdure of our valleys with the pale green of Arcadia, or the mournful green of Erin. A sentence has its adornments, like a dress, and some dress in wool, some in silk, and some become angry because their dress is wool and are displeased to see another's is silk. Since when has it become a defect to write in polished form? . . . It is essential that notice be taken of the following truth about style: Writers should paint just as the painter does. There is no reason for one to use different colors from the other.
>
> (*Obras completas*, 1946; vol. 2, pp. 431–432)

When Martí left Venezuela for New York, he resumed his writing for the *Sun*. New York was to be Martí's permanent home until he returned to Cuba, just prior to his untimely death fighting for Cuba's liberation, on 19 May 1895. In New York, which both attracted and repelled Martí, he wrote his best prose and poetry. Amid the din and clatter of an industrializing society that was plagued by labor strikes, anarchist terrorist attacks, and racial and religious conflicts, Martí peered into the future of a capitalist society. From that confusing vantage point, he drew conclusions that he described in his prose pieces about life in the United States, written for Latin America's major newspaper, *La Nación* (Buenos

Aires). His association during 1883 with this newspaper was followed by invitations from others, among them, *La República* (Honduras), *La Opinión Pública* (Uruguay), and *El Partido Liberal* (Mexico).

To earn money for survival, this extraordinary writer became a versatile professional. He worked as a translator for Appleton Publishers, as a clerk for the New York commercial firm Lyon and Company, and as consul for Uruguay in 1887 and for Argentina in 1890. Writing and political organization took up the rest of his energy and time. Martí immersed himself in the careful planning of the Cuban revolutionary process. He organized patriotic clubs not merely in the New York area, but all along the eastern seaboard, especially in Florida among the tobacco workers of Tampa and Key West. Before these groups of workers, he spoke with a passion and fervor that transfixed his audiences. Unfortunately, many of these speeches have been lost. A few that have survived, such as "Los pinos nuevos" (The New Pines), show a writer of learning and passion in command of a rhythmic prose, an accomplished political tactician who skillfully swayed his audience.

With the generals of the revolutionary forces, Máximo Gómez and Antonio Maceo, Martí organized and monitored the exile groups. In 1884 he had a falling out with the generals, especially Gómez, but later he worked with them again to raise the funds and provide the organization and arms for the invasion of the island of Cuba in 1895. It was hoped that this invasion, carefully planned in the United States and the Dominican Republic, would liberate Cuba from Spanish rule and bring independence to the island. Martí's herculean task was superior to his dwindling physical strength, vitiated years before by lesions and diseases contracted in the quarries of San Lázaro. Yet such was his determination to see the liberation of his homeland that will and desire sustained a calendar of activities that would have sent more robust souls to an early grave.

Patriotism and self-sacrifice in the cause of Cuba and Puerto Rico consumed his being. Writing and his faith in the revolution kept him alive. To be sure, Martí often experienced moments of despair. His knowledge of human cruelty was such that at one point he wrote: "It is with horror that one looks within many intelligent and attractive men. One

leaves in flight, as from a lion's den" (30:106). * This modern Machiavellian analyst wrote: "Men like to be guided by those who abound in their own shortcomings" (30:18). Cognizant of human foibles, but committed to social redemption, he noted: "Man is ugly, but humanity is beautiful." Martí's was an eighteenth-century faith in the perfectability of mankind, in social progress, and in the feasibility of socioeconomic reform. And like the thinkers of the Enlightenment, he needed to be persuaded of the inevitability of violent change, which he espoused only when all other viable channels were exhausted.

Martí found temporary release from anguish in poetic creation. Poetry had a double interface for him: "To create beautiful poetry one has only to turn one's eyes outward: to Nature; and inward: to the soul" (19:76). Nature was an enchantress who consoled, fortified, and soothed. By contrast, internal suffering purified inspiration and provided an alternative to the oppressive realities of everyday existence. Pain, said Marti, "matures poetry. . . . Man needs to suffer. When he lacks real pain, he creates it. Pain purifies and prepares" (27:217). Convinced that suffering engenders art, the poet poured his personal anguish into his verses.

Martí wrote three major books of poetry: *Ismaelillo* (1882), *Versos sencillos* (Simple Verses, 1891), and *Versos libres* (Free Verses, 1913). A fourth volume, entitled *Flores del destierro* (Flowers of Exile, 1933), is somewhat loosely organized, and some of its poems traditionally have been included in other volumes, a problem in textual criticism that has yet to be solved. *Ismaelillo* and *Versos sencillos* were published in New York during the poet's lifetime; he read the proof for both works. *Versos libres* was first published posthumously, having been transcribed inaccurately from complex manuscripts; it has recently been corrected by the present writer. The volumes have one element in common, which Karl Vossler described as the characteristic of all poets of intense fantasy: a capacity for liberating themselves from the norms of the linguistic community. By passing under or over words, such poets create works by means of notes, melodies, rhythms, images, gestures, and dances. This is the case

* All quotations of Martí's work are from *Obras completas*, edited by Gonzalo de Quesada y Miranda, unless otherwise noted.

with Martí and that of other modernist poets of his generation; they were subjective creators, attentive to internal flux. In this connection, Fina García Marruz finds syllabic groupings of suffering in *Versos libres*, and Cintio Vitier senses the voice of a poet of light and movements who creates a baroque, obscure, foaming, volcanic, abrupt, and strange world. Martí's is a highly original verse, in which there is both innovation and tradition, a paradoxical admixture common to the poets of the Age of Modernity, intent upon recasting the past to express an unstable present.

Ismaelillo is a free, luminous volume, written largely in Caracas and published in New York. Its imagery is so singular that the poet felt compelled to comment on its oneiric quality in a letter to Diego Jugo Ramírez on 23 May 1882:

> I've seen those wings, those jackels, those empty goblets, those armies. My mind was the stage, and on it all those visions were actors. My work, Jugo, consisted of copying. There isn't one single mental line there. And how should I be responsible for the images that come to me without my calling them? I have done nothing more than put my visions into verse.
>
> (p. 1336)

The volume is dedicated to the poet's absent son. The poet occupies the center of a visionary space in which the perils of modern life assault the poet/narrator. "Espantado de todo, me refugio en tí" (Frightened by everything, I take refuge in you [p. 1340]), he writes to his son in the brief introduction. The absent son is ever-present in verses whose levels of reality and dreams reach beyond the limits of nineteenth-century positivism and reason. "Yo sueño con los ojos / Abiertos . . ." ("I dream with open eyes" [p. 1341]) reads the beginning of "Sueño despierto" ("I Dream Awake"). The visionary quality is sometimes surrealistic, as in "Amor errante" ("Errant Love"):

> *Y sobre el dorso*
> *De aves gigantes*
> *Despiertan besos*
> *Inacabables.*
> (p. 1346)

> And on the backs
> Of giant birds

> Endless kisses
> Awaken.

Through a process of inversion, a metamorphosis is effected by filial love. The father conjures up the vision of the son and in this vision is reborn through the son:

> *¡Hijo soy de mi hijo!*
> *¡El me re hace!*

> I am the son of my son!
> He remakes me!

This identification of father and son orchestrates and unifies the metaphoric "eruptions" of a volume that, at bottom, is a musical concert centering around three motifs, filled with chaotic, tender, and troubled leaps to a loosely associated poetic space. *Ismaelillo's* motifs are the poet, the son, and the world. The leaps are executed in the form of voyages in which traditional concepts of time and space are unhinged so that the poet/son can move freely outside the limitations of a traditional Logos. In "Musa traviesa" (Mischievous Muse), he writes:

> *Yo suelo, caballero*
> *En sueños graves,*
> *Cabalgar horas luengas*
> *Sobre los aires.*
> *Me entro en nubes rosadas*
> *Bajo a hondos mares,*
> *Y en los senos eternos*
> *Hago viajes.*
> (p. 1342)

> Often a rider
> In momentous dreams,
> I ride long hours
> Through the air.
> I pierce rosy clouds,
> I fathom deep seas,
> And in the eternal bowels
> I travel.

In these travels the poet/son/seer comes upon battles, visions of martyrdom, caves, dances, erotic scenes, heights of idealism, and depths of materialism. It is a confusing world the narrator captures, reflecting the frightening realities of modern life. We witness torments, confused scenes, temptations, moments of disarray, and spirited battle. It is a spectacle of "splendid transformations" that boils, creaks, bites, and assaults the agonists of modern life. In keeping with these decentered, fragmented visions, the son is Ismael, Jacob, the object of pleasure, love, tenderness, the heart, the soul of the father, and finally not merely his reflection but his very being. Thus this volume is more than the lyric prayer book the Nicaraguan modernist Rubén Darío found it to be; it is more than the "Art of Being a Father" that he saw in it. It is rather a voyage that encarnates a modern mythic sense of experience and existence.

Equally personal and equally anguished are the poems of *Versos libres*. Darío said of them that they were free verse produced by a free man. Martí called them "my irritated Free Verses," "my rough hendecasyllables, born of great fears, or of great hopes, or of an unbridled love of liberty, or of a painful love of beauty" (*Versos sencillos*). In his preface, Martí insisted once again, as in *Ismaelillo*, upon the visionary quality of his verses, visions that he "copied" and for whose strangeness, singularity, and passion he alone was accountable. These are verses written "not in academic ink, but rather in my own blood," an image used by the poet to refer to the personal quality as well as to the aura of sacrifice and martyrdom that pervades so many of the poems. Their key words are *love, liberty, unconquered, passionate, natural,* and *vigorous*. To this linguistic base, José Olivio Jiménez adds another that centers around the terms *circumstance, nature,* and *transcendence,* and three concepts: *love, suffering,* and *duty.* The originality of these poems consists in their anguish. It is a poetry of existence in which the poet/narrator confronts the imperative to transmit an authentic, sincere, necessary reality. "What matters in poetry," he wrote, "is to feel, regardless of whether it resembles what others have felt; and what is felt anew, is new" (12:222).

Images of nature, often traditional in origin, appear in this volume as in others by Martí, but it is man, not nature, that occupies the center of his poetic discourse. It is a poetry that speaks of daily cares, experiences, existences. It radiates in circular patterns, reaching toward the upper spheres, that is, toward a quality of transcendence, noted by Jiménez,

that in spatial form points to the fundamental idealism of Martí's philosophy. Yet, by contrast, Martí's poetic vision is fundamentally realistic. It is based upon specific, concrete circumstances: those of his life and of the emotions of his existence. Miguel de Unamuno called Martí's words "acts." But when the Cuban poet harnessed his words to his thoughts, he created novel structures that even today surprise us by dint of their modernity.

The visionary quality of his first volume persists in *Versos libres*. Present also are the dualities of experience, the antithetical images that constitute Martí's assumption of the contradictions of modern life and the aspirations of perfection and idealistic placement of his visionary poetics. The dualities sometimes represent a truncated world or the poet's split vision of life: "He vivido: me he muerto . . ." (I have lived: I have died . . .) (*Versos libres*). The poet in his anguish wishes to sacrifice himself for his fellow man, for that is his mission in life. At times, he feels useless, unable to realize the martyrdom that will release him from his earthly struggle and allow him, finally, to seek an undefined solace in a vaguely expressed afterlife.

Less anguished, at least at first glance, are the poems of *Versos sencillos*. Their apparent serenity is linked to their traditional, popular metrics and to the poet's insistence upon more direct and unencumbered forms of expression than those that made up the volcanic "eruptions" of the previous volumes. In this volume there is an emphasis upon the harmony of life and philosophy, upon a system of transformation from crass, material forms to noble, ideal objects. This search for and belief in idealism and harmony lends the volume a placid quality that has disquieting moments, for the *Versos sencillos* are poems born of pain and anguish: "My friends know how these verses were born in my heart. It was in that winter of anguish, in which out of ignorance, or due to fanatic faith, or fear, or courtesy, that the Spanish American republics met in Washington, in the shadow of the dreaded eagle" (p. 1350), wrote Martí in the introduction. Martí represented Uruguay at the Monetary Conference in Washington, D.C., called by the United States to standardize currency in Latin America. Martí led the opposition of the Latin American countries to the plans of the United States to impose a silver standard.

Elsewhere the poet explained that "Without profound pain, man never produced truly beautiful works" (33:146). The poet's anguish is personalized. The verses speak of his individual view of the world, as the poet/seer turns his eyes upon the universe, internalized, and describes its external and internal structures. The poet has assumed the universe, and from a symbiotic stance, he offers new insights into its meaning. Martí's experience is broad. It includes the divine spirit, the terrestrial clamor of voices, envy, hate, human ugliness, materialism, idealism, and the metamorphosis of reality. Commentary on the writing of poetry is also present here as in previous volumes. But unlike these, experience is expressed from the viewpoint of a compendium, seen, to be sure, from the interior world ("I know," "I've seen," "I hear," "I am,") of the creator in search of harmony:

> *Todo es hermoso y constante,*
> *Todo es música y razón,*
> *Y todo, como el diamante,*
> *Antes que luz es carbón.*
> (p. 1351)

> All is beautiful and constant,
> All is melody and reason,
> And all, like a diamond,
> Is dark before light.

In this volume one finds the most frequently cited Martí verses: section 9 is devoted to "La niña de Guatemala" ("The Girl From Guatemala"), and section 10 to "La bailarina española" ("The Spanish Dancer"). Other sections may be less musical and more anguished, but all point to the future in modern poetry. In sections 8 and 11 the poet carries on a dialogue with his doubles: a dead friend and a page/skeleton. In the end a conversation is established between the poet and his verse in which he declares:

> *Verso, o nos condenan juntos*
> *O nos salvamos los dos!*
> (p. 1363)

> Either they will condemn us together, Poetry,
> Or they will save both of us.

The reputations of the poet and the poetry have survived. In addition, Martí is considered one of Spanish America's most original prose writers. "Verses," he said, "can be improvised, but not prose; prose style comes with maturity" (22:84). His early prose works, mentioned above, were followed by a voluminous opus of imaginative, rhythmic, chromatic pieces that found their way into the cultural and literary life of his period through a network of contemporary artists and the columns of the most prestigious newspapers of both North and South America. It is perhaps as a *cronista*, a chronicler of contemporary events—political, social, and literary—that Martí is best known. He read accounts of current events voraciously. And such was his imagination that he was capable of creating visions of events as they occurred even when he was not a witness to them.

His account of the opening of the Oklahoma frontier in 1889, for example, appears to have been written by a journalist who observed at firsthand the excitement and violence of the events. His moving account of the 1886 earthquake in Charleston, South Carolina, captures the shrill cries, the emotional despair, and the fervent, frightened prayers of the residents, as if the chronicler himself had experienced the tragedy. Martí wrote with vision, compassion, uncanny perception, and a highly developed, innovative style on subjects as diverse as European monarchs, American anarchists, elevated railways in New York City, urban tenements, violent crimes, St. Valentine's Day, Buffalo Bill, Walt Whitman, Ralph Waldo Emerson, American technology, and agricultural and floral exhibitions. On all of these and others too numerous to mention, Martí informed his Latin American readers. He was especially careful to show them the advantages as well as the dangers of life in a modernizing, capitalist society such as the United States, hoping to interest his fellow men in technical innovations while helping them to avoid the social, racial, and political strife he observed in New York. For American readers of the *New York Sun*, he wrote mainly of life in Europe, signing with a pseudonym, M. de S.

Another of Martí's major undertakings while in New York was *La edad de oro: Publicación mensual de recreo e instrucción dedicada a los niños de América*

(The Age of Gold: A Monthly Magazine of Entertainment and Instruction Dedicated to the Children of Spanish America). He contributed his own writing to the magazine as well as selecting articles for translation, and *La edad de oro* became a milestone in Spanish children's literature.

Less known and less studied are Martí's letters. His epistolary art fascinated Unamuno and continues to attract devoted readers. Next to his poetry, the medium in which Martí most frequently expressed his intimate thoughts are his letters, especially those to his closest friends and confidants. The letters to his friend Manuel A. Mercado, to his daughter María, and to his mother are filled with the deep tenderness and anguish of his *Versos libres*. In his letters, Martí dared to bare his soul and allow the solitude and suffering of a mission-driven artist and revolutionary to surface. The prose of these epistolary pieces is sometimes baroque, sometimes limpid; it ranges from being convoluted to being succinct, even telegraphic. He once complained: "Words I cannot." The reader at such moments is placed in the role of having to add, interpret, complete.

Martí wrote one novel, without great enthusiasm, as a favor to a friend. She had agreed to write the work for a New York magazine but could not. Under the pseudonym of Adelaida Ral, Martí composed the novel in her place in seven days. Its format followed the prescriptions laid down by the editor: lots of love, a death, many young girls, no sinful passions, nothing that might offend priests or fathers of families, and a Spanish-American setting. The narrative was not Martí's favorite genre, because, as he put it, one had to feign the existence of people, scenes, and dialogues. The revolutionary in him preferred writings "beautiful but useful." Yet this work, variously entitled *Amistad funesta* and *Lucía Jerez* (1885), has proved to be a milestone in the evolution of the modern Spanish-American novel.

Originally viewed as a melodramatic narrative, its reexamination by Enrique Anderson-Imbert and M. P. González has shown *Amistad funesta* to be a lyric novel composed in what might be termed lengthy stanzas or sequences, with spatial movement provided not through traditional chapter divisions but by the repeated symbolic use of a white magnolia from Lucía's garden. The dialogues often reach the reader with discordant tones, with superimpositions that sound illogical and unexpected in the background. Geography and narrative space are unspecified, internalized, or characterized in impressionistic and expressionistic images. Actions become symbolic; objects turn animate. The emotional impact of music and art acquires the substance of a reality more significant than the material realities of the world, subsumed into a lyric vision of life or contorted with the irrationality of Lucía's pathological jealousies. It is a truly experimental novel in the tradition of both modernist and vanguard literature.

In this narrative, and in his other prose pieces, poetry, letters, and journals, Martí understood that at the end of the nineteenth century man stood at the crossroads of an entirely new world order, the Age of Modernity. He understood its metamorphic qualities. He often felt anguished about their influence over man and kept the socioeconomic progress of Latin America and the liberation of Cuba and Puerto Rico always uppermost in his mind. He saw and understood the falling away of traditional institutions—religious, social, and economic—and the cultural and ideologic void that would result. This visionary writer was thus able to write as early as 1882: "There are no permanent works, because those that are the product of reframing and recasting are by their very essence mutable and restless; there are no constant roads; the new altars, great and open as the woods, are barely visible" (20:51). Though they were invisible to most people, Martí was able to see and foresee, to write and speak the signs of both his age and the future, scanning the past and linking its universal values to an unstable, chaotic present.

SELECTED BIBLIOGRAPHY

First Editions

Amor con amor se paga: Proverbio en un acto. Mexico, 1876.
Guatemala. Mexico, 1878.
Ismaelillo. New York, 1882.
Amistad funesta. Published under the pseudonym Adelaida Ral. New York, 1885.
Versos sencillos. New York, 1891.

Ismaelillo, Versos sencillos, Versos libres. Vol. 11, *Obras del Maestro.* Havana, 1913.

Flores del destierro (versos inéditos). Edited by Gonzalo de Quesada y Miranda. Havana, 1933.

Adúltera: drama inédito. Havana, 1935.

Translations by Martí

Antigüedades clásicas 1: Antigüedades griegas, by J.S. Mahafy. New York, 1883.

Antigüedades clásicas 2: Antigüedades romanas, by A. S. Wilkins. New York, 1883.

Mistero . . . (Called Back), by Hugh Conway. New York, 1886.

Nociones de lógica, by William Stanley Jevons. New York, 1886.

Ramona, novela americana, by Helen Hunt Jackson. New York, 1888.

Modern Editions

Poetry

Poesías completas. Edited by Rafael Esténger. Madrid, 1953.

Poesías de José Martí. With a prologue, selection, and notes by Juan Marinello. Havana, 1928.

Versos de amor (inéditos). Collected and edited by Gonzalo de Quesada y Miranda. Havana, 1930.

Versos sencillos. Prologue by Gabriela Mistral. Havana, 1939.

Prose

Amistad funesta. Edited by Gonzalo de Quesada y Aróstegui. Vol. 10, *Obras del Maestro.* Leipzig, 1911.

Artículos desconocidos. With a prologue by Félix Lizaso. Havana, 1930.

Cartas a Manuel A. Mercado. Mexico City, 1946.

Epistolario de José Martí. 3 vols. With an introduction, selection, and notes by Félix Lizaso. Havana, 1930–1931.

Nuevas cartas de Nueva York. Edited by E. Mejía Sánchez. Mexico City, 1980.

Obras escogidas. Selection, prologue, and notes by Rafael Esténger. Madrid, 1953.

Collected Works

Obras del Maestro. 16 vols. Edited by Gonzalo de Quesada y Aróstegui. Havana, 1900–1933.

Obras completas de Martí. 8 vols. Edited by N. Carbonell. Havana, 1918–1920.

Obras completas de José Martí. 2 vols. With a prologue by Armando Godoy and Ventura García Calderón. Paris, 1926.

Obras completas. 8 vols. With a prologue by Alberto Ghiraldo. Madrid, 1925–1929.

Obras completas de José Martí. 2 vols. Paris, 1926.

Obras completas. 74 vols. Edited by Gonzalo de Quesada y Miranda. Havana, 1936–1953.

Obras completas. 2 vols. With a prologue and biography by M. Isidro Méndez. Havana, 1946.

Obras completas. 28 vols. Havana, 1963–1973.

Obras completas. 1 vol. Havana, 1983–.

Translations

The America of José Martí: Selected Writings. Translated and edited by Juan de Onís. New York, 1953.

Inside the Monster by José Martí. Writings on the United States and American Imperialism. Translated by Elinor Randall, with additional translations by Luis A. Baralt, Juan de Onís, and Roslyn Held Foner. Edited, with an introduction and notes by Philip S. Foner. New York, 1975.

Major Poems. A Bilingual Edition. Translated by Elinor Randall. Edited and with an introduction by Philip S. Foner. New York, 1982.

Martí on the U.S.A. Selected, translated, and with an introduction by Luis A. Baralt. Carbondale, Ill., 1966.

On Education: Articles on Educational Theory and Pedagogy and Writings for Children from "The Age of Gold" by José Martí. Translated by Elinor Randall. With an introduction and notes by Philip S. Foner. New York, 1979.

Biographical and Critical Studies

Agramonte, Roberto. *Martí y su concepción del mundo.* Río Piedras, Puerto Rico, 1971.

Antología crítica de José Martí. Edited by Manuel Pedro González. Mexico City, 1960.

Anuario del Centro de Estudios Martianos. Havana, 1978–.

Anuario Martiano. 4 vols. Havana, 1969–1978.

Archivo José Martí. 6 vols. Havana, 1940–1953.

Armas, Emilio de. *Un deslinde necesario.* Havana, 1978.

Atlas histórico: biográfico José Martí. Havana, 1983.

Augier, Ángel. "Martí poeta y su influencia innovadora en la poesía de América." In *Vida y pensamiento de Martí* 2. Havana, 1942. Pp. 265–333.

Cantón Navarro, José. *Algunas ideas de José Martí en relación con la clase obrera y el socialismo.* Havana, 1970.

Carbonell, Néstor. *Martí, carne y espíritu.* 2 vols. Havana, 1951–1952.

Darío, Rubén. "Martí, poeta." In *Antología crítica de José Martí.* México, 1960. Pp. 3–11.

En torno a José Martí. Edited by Noel Salomón. Bordeaux, 1974.

Estudios martianos. Río Piedras, Puerto Rico, 1974.

Esténger, Rafael. *Vida de Martí.* Santiago, Cuba, 1934.

Florit, Eugenio. "Notas sobre la poesía en Marti." *Revista iberoamericana* 4/8:253–266 (1942).

———. "José Martí: Vida y obra, versos." *Revista hispánica moderna* 18:20–71 (1952).

García Marruz, Fina. "Los versos de Martí." *Revista de la biblioteca nacional "José Martí"* 59:3–39 (1968).

Ghiano, Juan Carlos. "Martí, poeta." In *Poesía,* by José Martí. Buenos Aires, 1952. Pp. 7–52.

González, Manuel Pedro. *José Martí, Epic Chronicler of the United States in the Eighties.* Chapel Hill, N.C., 1953.

Gutiérrez Nájera, Manuel. "La edad de oro." *Revista azul* (Mexico), 8 September 1895.

Homenaje a José Martí en el centenario de su nacimiento. Boletín de la Academia Cubana de la lengua 1/4:481–787 (1952).

Homenaje a José Martí en el centenario de su nacimiento. Anales de la Universidad de Chile 111:1–165 (1953).

Homenaje a José Martí en el centenario de su nacimiento. Revista cubana 29 (1951–1952).

Homenaje a Martí. Boletín del Archivo Nacional (Havana) 39/1–6:5–317 (1940).

Homenaje a Martí. Número (Montevideo) 5/22:3–4, 38–67 (1953).

"José Martí: Vida y obra." *Revista hispánica moderna* 18:1–161 (1952).

Iduarte, Andrés. *Martí, escritor.* Havana, 1951.

Jiménez, José Olivio. *José Martí: Poesía y existencia.* Mexico City, 1983.

José Martí: Antología di testi e antologia critica. Rome, 1974.

Kirk, John M. *José Martí: Mentor of the Cuban Nation.* Gainesville, Fla., 1983.

Lazo, Raimundo. *Martí y su obra literaria.* Havana, 1929.

Lizaso, Félix. *Pasión de Martí.* Havana, 1938.

Mañach, Jorge. *Martí, el apóstol.* Buenos Aires, 1942.

———. *El espíritu de Martí.* Havana, 1952.

Marinello, Juan. *Once ensayos martianos.* Havana, 1964.

———. "Martí: Poesía." *Anuario martiano* 1:117–165 (1969).

Martínez Estrada, Ezequiel. *Martí: El héroe y su acción revolucionaria.* Mexico City, 1966.

———. *Martí revolucionario.* Havana, 1967.

Memoria del Congreso de Escritores Martianos. Havana, 1953.

Mistral, Gabriela. *La lengua de Martí.* Havana, 1934.

———. "Los 'Versos sencillos' de José Martí." *Crónica; Revista mensual de orientación y cultura* (Havana) 3/20: 16–17 (1953).

Pensamiento y acción de José Martí. Santiago, Cuba, 1953.

Rama, Ángel. "Indagación de la ideología en la poesía (Los dípticos seriados de *Versos sencillos*)." *Revista iberoamericana* 46/112–113:353–412 (1980).

Reyes, Alfonso. "Comentario a *Ismaelillo* y *Versos sencillos* por José Martí." *Cuadernos: Revista trimestral del Congreso por la Libertad de la Cultura* (Paris) 2:5 (1953).

Roggiano, Alfredo A. "Poética y estilo de José Martí." *Humanitas* 1/1:351–378 (1953).

Schulman, Ivan. *Símbolo y color en la obra de José Martí.* Madrid, 1960, 1970.

———. *Génesis del modernismo: Martí, Nájera, Silva, Casal.* Mexico City, 1966, 1968.

———. *Martí, Darío y el modernismo.* Madrid, 1969. Written with Manuel Pedro González.

———. "Introduction." In *Versos libres,* by José Martí. Barcelona, 1970. Pp. 11–54.

Unamuno, Miguel de. "Sobre el estilo de José Martí." *Germinal* (Cuba) 2:2–4 (1921).

———. "Carta sobre Martí." *Archivo José Martí* 2:10 (1947).

———. "Sobre los *Versos libres* de José Martí." *Archivo José Martí* 4:7–9 (1947).

———. "Cartas de poeta." In *Obras completas* 8. Madrid, 1958. P. 573–577.

Vida y pensamiento de Martí. 2 vols. Havana, 1942.

Vitier, Cintio. *Los versos de Martí.* Havana, 1969.

———, and Fina García Marruz. *Temas martianos.* Havana, 1969.

Bibliographies

Blanch y Blanco, Celestino. *Bibliografía martiana* (1954–1963). Havana, 1965.

González, Manuel Pedro. *Fuentes para el estudio de José Martí.* Havana, 1950.

Peraza Sarausa, Fermín. *Bibliografía martiana (1853–1953).* Havana, 1954.

Ripoll, Carlos. *Archivo José Martí.* New York, 1971.

———. *Indice universal de la obra de José Martí.* New York, 1971.

Manuel Zeno Gandía

(1855–1930)

Aníbal González-Pérez

Manuel Zeno Gandía is Puerto Rico's preeminent turn-of-the-century novelist and, along with the grand old man of Puerto Rican romanticism, Alejandro Tapia y Rivera (1826–1882), one of the founders of Puerto Rico's modern novelistic tradition. Physician, scholar, journalist, poet, politician, and novelist, Zeno was one of the most lucid members of the Puerto Rican Creole elite during a critical period in the island's history. In his novels, Zeno produced trenchant analyses of Puerto Rican society that continue to enlighten scholars. Today he is revered as a classic figure of Puerto Rican letters, and recently his reputation has begun to spread throughout the Hispanic world as new editions and translations of his masterpiece *La charca* (Stagnant Waters, 1894; translated as *La Charca*) have been published in New York, Spain, Cuba, and Venezuela, and as critics have once again become interested in other Spanish-American writers of naturalist fiction, such as the Cuban Miguel de Carrión, the Chilean Alberto Blest Gana, the Peruvian Clorinda Matto de Turner, and the Mexican Federico Gamboa, among others. Zeno was not unknown outside Puerto Rico during his lifetime; he was a well-traveled, cosmopolitan person who had many important friends and acquaintances in Cuba, Spain, and the United States. Zeno's oeuvre marks one of the high points in the "increase in quantity and importance" that Max Henríquez Ureña notes in the Spanish-American novel of the 1880's. Puerto Rican critics have written abundantly about Zeno's life and works, although a great deal more remains to be written in both areas.

Manuel Zeno Gandía was born in 1855 in the town of Arecibo, on the northern coast of Puerto Rico, to well-to-do parents. Like other members of his family, he decided on a career in medicine, and after his first years of study on the island, he was sent to Madrid. As a young medical student in the Spanish capital, Zeno began writing poems and plays, many of which have remained unpublished to this day. Among the literary figures of the time with whom Zeno was acquainted in Madrid was the Cuban José Martí, who had recently been exiled to Spain for his political activities and who would become one of the founders of Spanish-American *modernismo* as well as of his country's independence.

Zeno returned to Puerto Rico in the late 1870's and began to practice medicine in the city of Ponce, on the island's southern coast. There he continued to write poetry, including the positivist verses of *Al microscopio* (To the Microscope, 1879), as well as the philosophical verses in *Abismos* (Abysses, 1885), and the more frivolous ones in *La señora duquesa* (My Lady the Duchess, 1888). Almost all of Zeno's production during those years appeared in Puerto Rican journals and newspapers, in which Zeno was an assiduous collaborator. Indeed, for nearly a half century Zeno combined a considerable journalistic output with his literary and scientific endeavors. Beginning in the late 1870's, his work appeared in such journals as *La azucena, La página, La revista puertorriqueña, La revista de Puerto Rico*, and the *Revista de las Antillas*. In 1890, Zeno purchased the large San Juan daily *La Correspondencia de Puerto Rico*, which he directed for twelve years; in 1892 he founded and directed the liberal newspaper *El Estudio*, and in 1900, the political newspaper *La Opinión*.

Zeno's narrative production began in 1889 with the short novel *Rosa de mármol* (The Marble Rose), followed in 1890 by *Piccola* (both works published in the *Revista puertorriqueña*). He continued to publish short stories in the newspapers and journals; these were collected posthumously, in 1958, in a volume titled *Cuentos* (Stories). But the culmination of Zeno's literary career came with the publication of a series of novels written in a realist and naturalist vein, conceived under the general title of *Crónicas de un mundo enfermo* (Chronicles of an Ailing World): *La Charca, Garduña* (Marten; published in 1896, though it was written before *La Charca*), *El negocio* (The Business, 1922), and *Redentores* (The Saviors, serialized in the newspaper *El Imparcial* in 1925 and published as a book in 1960). Zeno is said to have written a fifth novel, "Hubo un escándalo" (There Was a Scandal), which is presumed lost, and he left unfinished a manuscript for another, "Nueva York" (New York), considered a prefiguration of the later narratives about Puerto Rican emigrant life in New York during the 1950's and 1960's by authors like José Luis González, Pedro Juan Soto, and José Luis Vivas Maldonado.

The twenty-six-year hiatus between *Garduña* and *El negocio* was occupied in Zeno's life by the sociopolitical crisis that resulted from the United States' invasion of Puerto Rico in 1898. Zeno, a liberal under the Spanish regime, became a fervent believer in the need for Puerto Rico's independence after the United States' occupation of the island. He traveled to Washington in 1898, along with Dr. Julio J. Henna and the great Puerto Rican intellectual Eugenio María de Hostos as part of a commission to set

before President William McKinley Puerto Rico's right to freely determine its destiny as a nation. But the United States was determined to keep for itself those territories it had taken from Spain as spoils of war, and Zeno's delegation did not succeed in convincing the Americans to honor the ideals they had proclaimed in their own Declaration of Independence. Zeno, Hostos, and Henna then published a summary of their arguments in *The Case of Porto Rico* [sic] (1899). After this episode, Zeno devoted himself to Puerto Rican politics; he was one of the founders, in 1904, of the Puerto Rican Union party, in representation of which he served in the Chamber of Delegates. He later broke with the party when it left independence out of its platform. One of Zeno's last writings, left unpublished at his death, was a work on the prehistory and history of Puerto Rico, titled "Resumpta indo-antillana." Manuel Zeno Gandía died in 1930 at the age of seventy-five, after a long illness. His last words, uttered in delirum on his deathbed, seemed to reflect Zeno's deep-seated preoccupation with the fate of his country, which had been ruled for several decades by American generals and American civilians appointed by Washington: "Solicito del General de los Estados Unidos una noche de sueño" (I request of the general from the United States a good night's sleep).

Although Zeno wrote formally correct poems whose possible connections with his prose works (as is the case with *Abismos*) are interesting, it is his novels that have made him a key figure in Puerto Rican literary history. Chronologically, *Garduña* is the first novel written by Zeno. *Garduña* is the name of a scheming lawyer who attempts to deprive the young Casilda, the natural daughter of a rich landowner, of her inheritance. The action occurs in an imaginary Puerto Rican town called, significantly, Paraíso (Paradise). Critics of Zeno have observed how little there is of "naturalism" in this novel. Certainly, in *Garduña* Zeno seems to have opted for a more traditionally "realist" approach laced with strong allegorical elements, in a manner reminiscent of the Spaniard Benito Pérez Galdós' early novel (and one of his best) *Doña Perfecta* (1876).

Whenever one attempts to bring to bear upon Spanish-American literary history critical concepts that belong to European literature, problems arise, and the concept of naturalism is no exception. Even within a European and North American context, to place under the heading of naturalism the work of such different writers as Émile Zola (the "father" of naturalism), Giovanni Verga, Emilia Pardo Bazán, and Theodore Dreiser implies an oversimplification of each author's work. In order to avoid such gross categorizations, one must go beyond the naive understanding of naturalism as a sort of intensified realism that delights in portraying the seamier side of human nature (from this perspective, medieval authors such as Boccaccio or Chaucer might qualify as naturalists), or as the use of scientific concepts in narrative description (Jules Verne did this, and he is not a naturalist). Instead, one should see the literary movement of naturalism as a set of narrative strategies through which authors have sought to systematically explore the relationship among people, society, and the laws of nature as they are understood at a particular time.

What is specific to late-nineteenth-century naturalism is the privilege given to science. Naturalist fiction seeks to use science as a model for narrative writing at almost every level of the text. The branch of science exalted by each naturalist writer can vary. Zola, for instance, sought to model his series of novels about the Rougon and Macquart families principally on the biological sciences, particularly on his own reading of Charles Darwin's theory of evolution and on the medical ideas of Claude Bernard. The French philosopher of science Michel Serres has argued that underlying Zola's obvious biologism was an even deeper model: thermodynamics, the branch of physics that studies how matter changes state (from solid to liquid or gas and vice versa). It is important to remember that Zola himself preferred to use the term *experimental novel* to refer to his work, stressing his novels' attempts to mimic the process of scientific inquiry. The use of scientific discourse in the naturalist novel was primarily designed to give legitimacy and authority to the social and political criticism that was the naturalist novelists' ultimate aim. A thorough and penetrating critical reading of Zeno's novels, particularly of his masterpiece, *La Charca*, virtually demands this more refined view of naturalism.

While the action in *Garduña* is set in the sugar-producing lowlands of Puerto Rico, *La Charca* takes place in the mountains of the island where, at the end of the nineteenth century, coffee was king and thousands of landless peasants toiled in the coffee haciendas that belonged to a few landowners, many of whom were wealthy Majorcan or Corsican immigrants to Puerto Rico. The plot of *La Charca*, befitting a novel dominated by metaphors of water, is as meandering as the course of a mountain stream: the most coherent sequence of events has to do with the scheme by the peasant Gaspar and the escaped convict Deblás, with the aid of the former's wife, Silvina, to rob the merchant Andújar, the owner of the only "general store," who exploits the peasants mercilessly. Gaspar and Deblás are moved not by class hatred but by simple greed. Little do they know that Andújar has already been warned of their plot by the peasant Marcelo and has run off to the lowlands with his saddlebags full of money, leaving his coffers empty inside his house. The night of the attempted robbery, in their confusion and nervousness, Gaspar and Silvina kill Deblás, whom, in the darkness, they take for Andújar. The consequences of the crime will involve not only Gaspar and Silvina but also Silvina's lover, Ciro, as well as Marcelo and Silvina's mother, Leandra. In the midst of this story, long passages are devoted to the solitary musings of the wealthy and honest landowner Juan del Salto about the evils of the island's socioeconomic situation, and to the conversations of del Salto with his friends Dr. Pintado and Father Esteban, in which various projects to reform Puerto Rico's society are proposed and compared. While some conservative critics view Juan del Salto as the novel's main character (thus showing a certain class prejudice), it is more accurate to say that Zeno features two women, the peasant Leandra and her daughter Silvina, with whom the novel opens and closes.

Zeno's greatest achievement in *La Charca* is his portrayal of the depressed economic and social situation of what at that time comprised a large and significant sector of Puerto Rico's population, without falling into the crude and mechanical determinism of Zola's brand of naturalism. Zeno seems to have derived his curiously contemporary-seeming version of nonmechanistic materialism from the writings of the Roman Epicurean philosopher Lucretius, who wrote his famous poem *De rerum natura* (*The Nature of the Universe*) around 55 B.C., and who may be considered one of the earliest naturalist authors in the most literal sense of the word, since he explicitly dealt with the relationship between science and literature. One way in which Zeno differs from and implicitly criticizes Zola's naturalism is in his rejection of a biological model to structure his novel; instead, the physical science on which Zeno bases his picture of Puerto Rican life is the one on which Lucretius also based his work: the older discipline of hydraulics, a branch of physics that deals with liquids and their flow. Because liquids are made up of loosely bound particles that do not react uniformly when force is applied to them, the science of hydraulics, unlike that of mechanics, which deals with the movement of solids, requires an analysis based on probability and differential calculus. It is thus a branch of physics that is more open to the operation of chance and less likely to fall into a gross determinism.

In *La Charca*, water images abound and the novel itself takes place in a geographic setting in which water is omnipresent, even in the clouds, which collide with the mountaintops and turn into the streams and rivers that flow to the sea. The opening and closing scenes of *La Charca*, in fact, take place next to a mountain stream. Zeno often describes his characters as "atoms" or "particles" caught in a whirlpool of socioeconomic circumstances they cannot control. With its aquatic metaphors and its recourse to hydraulic physics (with all it implies in terms of the role of chance in the narrative), *La Charca* is probably one of the most sophisticated naturalist novels ever written, despite the fact that, unlike most naturalist works, its action takes place in the countryside and not in the city. (For this reason, *La Charca* has been seen by some critics as a prefiguration of the *novelas de la tierra*, the telluric novels of the 1930's such as the Venezuelan Rómulo Gallegos' *Doña Bárbara* [1929].) Also, unlike the often dogmatic novels of Zola and his epigones, *La Charca* is a profoundly skeptical, critical text that tends to avoid the authoritarian tone common to most realist narratives. In his novels, Zeno is more concerned with finding a way to faithfully describe and diagnose in all their complexity and ambiguity the social illnesses

that plague his country rather than with prescribing solutions to them.

In his next two novels, *El negocio* and *Redentores*, Zeno continued his systematic portrayal of Puerto Rican society in the same Lucretian vein of naturalism he had developed in *La Charca*. The action in *El negocio* takes place in the city of Ponce, on the southern coast of the island. Zeno tended to avoid imposing preconceived models on his description of Puerto Rican reality; he preferred instead to try to derive his models from real-world situations. Because the environment is now urban, Zeno seems to return to a more traditional kind of realism, in which thermodynamics and economic theory serve as the basis for the novel's structure (significantly, the novel begins with the arrival of a steamship to the port of Ponce). *El negocio* and *La Charca* are linked not only in the fact that two characters, Andújar and Galante, had already appeared in the latter novel, but also in the fact that the commercial life of the big port city of Ponce was intimately connected to the coffee plantations that were *La Charca*'s setting; indeed, as historians like Fernando Picó have shown, the coffee plantations and the commercial interests in the coastal cities of Puerto Rico formed parts of a single system of economic exploitation that reached as far as the large European and North American trading centers in Madrid, Paris, and New York. Like *La Charca*, *El negocio* has several interweaving plot lines, none of which seems to predominate over the others, and numerous characters. One of the most interesting is the skeptical, alcoholic intellectual Camilo Cerdán, who observes all the economic, political, and personal activities around him dispassionately, and who nevertheless in the end acts discreetly to help some of the novel's characters. Camilo is, along with the archbishop in *Redentores*, the closest thing in Zeno's narrative to an authorial alter ego; both characters serve as mouthpieces for Zeno's Epicurean view of reality, and their presence in their respective novels probably reflects Zeno's increased personal political involvement after the American invasion.

In *Redentores*, Zeno turns his attention to the capital, San Juan, and to the conflict between the Puerto Ricans and their new masters after 1898, the Americans. As is typical of Zeno, this novel also has more than one plot line; there is a rather allegorical one, in which the evil American Elkus Engel, the governor's secretary, tries to corrupt the innocent Puerto Rican girl Piadosa Artante. Another plot line concerns the machinations of the American authorities to help an opportunistic Puerto Rican politician who once had proindependence leanings, Aureo Sol, to become the island's first native governor. Critics have not failed to notice Zeno's prescience in this last regard, because this was indeed what happened in Puerto Rico's political history some twenty-seven years after the novel's publication. (Luis Muñoz Marín was elected governor in 1949.) Zeno attempts to balance his portrayal of the Americans by means of the character of Madelón, a progressive young American woman who vainly tries to save her beloved Aureo Sol from betraying his people. Images of water once again appear frequently in this novel, indicating Zeno's desire to portray Puerto Rico's perennially turbulent colonial situation through a model that would faithfully reflect its complexity.

Manuel Zeno Gandía left Puerto Rico a rich and profound novelistic legacy. Indeed, he was the first Puerto Rican novelist to significantly influence a group of other writers: the naturalist novelists Matías González García (1866–1938), José Elías Levis (1871–1942), and Ramón Juliá Marín (1878–1917) all followed his example. Today, Zeno's legacy may still be seen in the contemporary best-seller *La guaracha del macho camacho* (*Macho Camacho's Beat*, 1976), by Luis Rafael Sánchez, which is, in many ways, a parodic homage to *La Charca*.

SELECTED BIBLIOGRAPHY

First Editions

Poetry

Abismos. Ponce, Puerto Rico, 1885.
La señora duquesa. Ponce, Puerto Rico, 1888.

Prose Narratives and Novels

La charca: Crónicas de un mundo enfermo. Ponce, Puerto Rico, 1894.

Garduña: Crónicas de un mundo enfermo. Ponce, Puerto Rico, 1896.
El negocio: Crónicas de un mundo enfermo. New York, 1922.
Redentores: Crónicas de un mundo enfermo. In *El Imparcial.* San Juan, 1925.
Cuentos. New York, 1958.

Essay

The Case of Porto Rico. With J. J. Henna and Eugenio María de Hostos. Washington, D. C., 1899.

Collected Works

Obras completas: Crónicas de un mundo enfermo. 3 vols. San Juan, 1955. These so-called complete works include only three of Zeno's novels: *La charca, Garduña,* and *El negocio.* Probably for political reasons, *Redentores* was not published in this edition.
Obras completas: Crónicas de un mundo enfermo. Prologue by Francisco Manrique Cabrera. 2 vols. San Juan, 1973. Again, this is not a truly complete set, but it includes *Redentores,* along with the three novels featured in the 1955 edition. Neither Zeno's short stories nor his poems and essays are included in this edition.

Modern Editions

Redentores. San Juan, 1960. First publication in book form.
There are numerous modern editions of Zeno's masterpiece, *La charca;* following are the most recent and interesting ones.
La charca. Havana. 1965. A Cuban edition, prepared by Casa de las Américas, with a prologue by Salvador Bueno.
La charca. Río Piedras, Puerto Rico, 1973. This is the widely available Editorial Edil edition, used as a text in high-school and university Puerto Rican literature courses. The Editorial Edil series reproduces the text of each novel's first edition but provides no critical apparatus or scholarly prologue.
La charca. Caracas, 1978. The most recent edition, prepared for the Venezuelan Biblioteca Ayacucho, with a prologue and chronology by Enrique Laguerre.
The following three novels also belong to the Editorial Edil series.
Garduña. Río Piedras, Puerto Rico, 1973.
El negocio. Río Piedras, Puerto Rico, 1973.
Redentores. Río Piedras, Puerto Rico 1973.

Translations

La Charca. Translated by Kal Wagenheim, with an introduction by Juan Flores. Maplewood, N.J., 1982.

Biographical and Critical Studies

Aponte Alsina, Marta. "Notas para un estudio ideológico de las novelas de Manuel Zeno Gandía." *Sin nombre* 10/1:23–46 (1979).

Arce de Vázquez, Margot. "Bibliografía de Manuel Zeno Gandía." *Asomante* 4:72–74 (1955).

Barradas, Efraín. "La naturaleza en *La charca*: Tema y estilo." *Sin nombre* 5/1:30–42 (1974).

Beauchamp, José Juan. "Manuel Zeno Gandía y la interpretacion naturalista." In his *Imagen del puertorriqueño en la novela*. Río Piedras, Puerto Rico, 1976. Pp. 29–69.

Cabrera, Manrique. "Manuel Zeno Gandía: Poeta del novelar isleño." *Asomante* 4:19–47 (1955).

Colón, José M. "La naturaleza en *La charca*." *Asomante* 5/2:50–59 (1949).

Gardón Franceschi, Margarita. *Manuel Zeno Gandía: Vida y poesía*. San Juan, 1969.

González, Aníbal. "Turbulencias en *La charca*: De Lucrecio a Manuel Zeno Gandía." *MLN* 98/2:208–225 (1983).

González, José Luis. *Literatura y sociedad en Puerto Rico*. Mexico City, 1976. Pp. 193–202.

Laguerre, Enrique. "El arte de novelar en Manuel Zeno Gandía." *Asomante* 11/4:48–53 (1955).

Quiñones, Samuel R. "Nuestro novelista de la tierra, Manuel Zeno Gandía." *Indice* 2/12:183 (1930).

Rivera de Alvarez, Josefina. "Manuel Zeno Gandía." In *Diccionario de la literatura puertorriqueña*. San Juan, 1974. Pp. 1631–1638.

Zeno de Matos, Elena. *Manuel Zeno Gandía: Documentos biográficos y críticos*. San Juan, 1955.

Juan Zorrilla de San Martín

(1855–1931)

Rubén Benítez

In the second half of the nineteenth century, Uruguay produced two important writers of Hispanic postromanticism, José Enrique Rodó and Juan Zorrilla de San Martín. Although they represent opposing currents of idealism, their works are related. Rodó's best-known book, *Ariel* (*Ariel*, 1900), called for the creation and preservation in Spanish America of an intellectual aristocracy to withstand the materialistic impact of the United States, identified as Caliban. Zorrilla discusses these ideas in his posthumous book *Las Américas* (The Americas, 1945), describing at the same time his own thought, which penetrates all his literature and political activity. For him, Spanish America is not an expression of spiritualism, or *arielismo*, nor is English America the epitome of materialism. On the contrary, whereas after 1914 a new religious fervor arose in the United States, in Spanish America both lack of faith and materialism increased. Zorrilla defines his thought as "evangelical idealism," which he summarizes in the following manner: The universe is the manifestation of God, and the history of civilization is the gradual achievement of religious truths. Because of its missionary origins, Spanish America represents a promised land for the dissemination of Christianity and the future realization of human perfection. He tends to agree with Miguel de Unamuno, with whom he maintained a brief but intense correspondence, in his belief that religious feeling is the crux of modern spiritual reform. On the political plane, Zorrilla led the Uruguayan neo-Catholic movement that claimed as its own the indulgence Pope Leo XIII predicated in his encyclical letters of 1878.

Zorrilla was born in Montevideo on 28 December 1855. His father, a Spaniard of blemish-free religious faith, entrusted his son's education to the Jesuits of Montevideo and Santa Fe, Argentina, after the death of his wife. The poet was to maintain constant respect and admiration for the order's work in education, about which he wrote in his 1879 pamphlet *¡Jesuítas!* (Jesuits). After completing high school, the young Zorrilla moved to Santiago, Chile, where he earned a degree in law. By 1877, he had become known in Chilean Catholic circles as a writer of poetry, legends in both prose and verse, and journalistic articles. That same year, he published *Notas de un himno* (Notes for a Hymn, 1877). The following year, he returned to Montevideo and founded *El Bien Público* (The Public Good), the newspaper in which he published the first version of *La leyenda patria* (Legend of the Fatherland, 1879) and the prologue to *Tabaré* (1879).

These were difficult years in Uruguay. In 1855, the dictator Lorenzo Latorre came to mistrust the Chris-

327

tian Democrats; his successor, Máximo Santos, removed Zorrilla from the university post he had assumed in 1880 and forced him into exile in Brazil and Argentina. In 1886, Zorrilla took part in the thwarted Quebracho revolution; Santos, his power weakened, resigned at the end of the year. But Máximo Tajes, the new president, refused any promise of freedom, and Zorrilla stayed in Argentina until 1887, when he returned to Uruguay and was elected deputy to the congress, serving for three years. *Tabaré*, known until then only partially through such periodical publications as *El Bien Público* and *La Tribuna Popular* (The Public Tribune, 1886), was finished in the same year and appeared in Paris in 1888; many editions with fundamental changes followed the first one until the definitive text was given in the edition of 1923.

The poem's international success, along with the author's patriotic attitude, made Zorrilla one of the most influential men in Uruguay. In 1891, President Julio Herrera y Obes, whose liberal government he supported, appointed him ambassador to Spain, Portugal, France, and the Vatican. In Spain, Zorrilla gave several lectures, including "Descubrimiento y conquista del Río de la Plata" (Discovery and Conquest of the River Plate Region), which were widely acclaimed for their positive appraisal of the spirit of the conquest and for its anti-indigenism. Zorrilla participated in social gatherings in Madrid, where he met Marcelino Menéndez y Pelayo, Ramón de Campoamor, Gaspar Núñez de Arce, and Rubén Darío. In France, he associated with Anatole France, Maurice Barrès, Jules Supervielle, and other enthusiastic readers of *Tabaré*. In Parisian cafés, he observed the bohemian life of the avant-garde poets, such as Paul Verlaine, of whom he wrote a striking portrait. Zorrilla recounted his impressions of these years in a series of prose sketches, *Resonancias del camino* (Sounds from the Road, 1896). Of special interest is the description of his interview with Pope Leo XIII.

In 1897, Zorrilla was unjustly deprived of his diplomatic post by the new president of Uruguay, Juan Lindolfo Cuestas, and, soon after, the poet returned to Uruguay. He continued directing *El Bien Público* and held some classes at the university; his lectures on the theory of art formed the basis of his last work, *El libro de Ruth* (The Book of Ruth, 1928).

Zorrilla, however, no longer felt at home among either the young Catholics, who resented his propensity toward liberalism, or the extreme liberals. Little by little, he was excluded from a number of activities, among them the direction of his newspaper, with which he ceased to be associated in 1905. He was left only with an honorary post at the Banco Central. During this period, he wrote *La epopeya de Artigas* (Artigas' Epic, 1910) and other historical studies. In 1926, the Chilean government, supported by the Uruguayan and other Hispanic governments, submitted his candidacy for a Nobel Prize, but to no avail. A year before his death on 3 November 1931, Zorrilla received a warm tribute from his fellow countrymen when the congress sponsored the sixteen-volume edition of his *Obras completas* (Complete Works).

Many of Zorrilla's writings in the *Obras completas*—journalistic articles, speeches, lectures—have only incidental value. Although his prose has been less studied than his poetry, in his greater works—*Resonancias del camino, El libro de Ruth,* and *Huerto cerrado* (Closed Orchard, 1900)—there are many pages of captivating beauty. Zorrilla is one of the great Hispanic prose writers; his translucent, graceful style is reminiscent of both biblical literature and sixteenth- and seventeenth-century Spanish religious prose. But even his less important books, such as *Las Américas, El sermón de la paz* (The Peace Sermon, 1924), or the unfinished *La profecía de Ezequiel* (Ezekiel's Prophecy, published only partially in 1938), contain sound information, precise, serious arguments, and flowing style.

La epopeya de Artigas, his best-known prose work, is of uneven value. It was intended as a report to foreign sculptors who, charged with submitting sketches of a monument to José Gervasio Artigas, knew little about the life and importance of the hero. But it was an overly enthusiastic portrayal that seemed to join with the attempts of others to make the life of the *caudillo* into a national myth, an archetype of the evangelical virtues of the national spirit (Unamuno considered it the book more of a pettifogger than of an artist). For some critics, *La epopeya de Artigas, La leyenda patria,* and *Tabaré* constitute the triptych through which "the poet of the fatherland" exalted the nationality of his people from the very roots.

Zorrilla's poetic work fits easily into the Hispanic

postromantic literary framework: it becomes intimate and subjective; time and space, interiorized, attain symbolic dimensions; verbal expression is enriched through plastic images and musical rhythms. It is not surprising that Zorrilla's poetry has been likened to that of the Spanish poets Gustavo Adolfo Bécquer, Ramón de Campoamor, and Gaspar Núñez de Arce, all great masters of the modernist generation. Most profound is the influence of Bécquer, whose *Rimas (Poems)* and *Leyendas (Legends)* were introduced to Spanish America in 1871. Six years later, Zorrilla paid homage to the Spanish poet using a line from Bécquer's poetry as the title to his first book, *Notas de un himno*. Both Bécquer and Zorrilla considered poetry a "sonorous echo," after the expression coined by Victor Hugo: an echo of the enormous and mysterious hymn of creation. But, as Zorrilla contends in the poem "Bécquer," the Spanish poet listens only to the "sensual and not sensitive" music of this divine song, endowing human love with an excessive worth, coloring his rich sensitivity with too much eroticism. Zorrilla proposes instead the transcription of the universe's "virgin psalmodies," which resound in the landscape, history, and spiritual physiognomy of his people; that is to say, Zorrilla would make use of Becquerian sensitivity for religious and patriotic poetry. The first book was only a youthful expression of romantic lyricism written in old-fashioned style, full of sentimentality and false oratory. Traces of a new style can be found in but few of the poems: *El ángel de los charrúas* (The Angel of the Charruas), for example, a verse legend included in the book that anticipated themes and techniques in *Tabaré*. *La leyenda patria*, the extensive poem that in 1879 secured Zorrilla his position as national poet, was still the work of an immature artist. On the one hand, it is a tiring rhetorical evocation of national glories, while, on the other, it offers some magnificent descriptive moments. The imagery—of the river, the riverbank woods, the Uruguayan flora, the times of day, and the twilight in the pampas—is entirely reminiscent of Bécquer; in this framework, legendary and historical figures lose their reality in deference to a symbolic dimension.

These values culminate in *Tabaré*, which is to some degree an extension of *La leyenda patria*. The first manuscript had the subtitle *Epopeya lírica* (Lyric Epic). In one of the notes added to *Tabaré*, Zorrilla explained his concept of *epopeya*: "The incarnation of mysterious laws in human events is called epic creation"; he referred more to the religious epics of, for example, Dante or John Milton than to the medieval epic. *Tabaré* dramatically presents the spiritual conflict of the conquest, the symbolic battle between Christianity's evangelical message, ordered by Providence, and the mysterious New World reality. America as a whole has the ill-fated mark of crossbreeding as its original sin. The vagueness of Zorrilla's intended message reminds us of the more comprehensive aim of Hugo's *Légende des siècles* (or *Petites épopées*, the first general title of the collection, used later in one of the sections), the work of the "second Hugo," according to critics. Whereas Zorrilla initially aimed to describe the geological history of the entire American continent, he fortunately limited this goal later on. Among the influences the poet and his critics recognized in *Tabaré* (Homer, Aeschylus, William Shakespeare, Miguel de Cervantes, Ossian, Johann Wolfgang von Goethe, Friedrich von Schiller, José Zorrilla, and Friedrich Halm), preeminent is that of Bécquer, creator of the *leyenda lírica* (lyric legend), but in prose, not in verse, as are Zorrilla's legends.

The narrative thread of *Tabaré*, as described by Enrique Anderson Imbert, reproduces the typical frontier story whose most remote antecedent is Chateaubriand's *Atala* (1801). Indeed, characteristics typical of Chateaubriand appear in Zorrilla's work not only in the transcendental qualities of the landscape, but also in the characterizations of the protagonists. Tabaré, like Cháctas in Chateaubriand's novel, is the victim of the historical destiny of a race; Blanca, the symbol of Christian virtue and beauty. The story is quite naive, as Zorrilla himself admits: Tabaré, a handsome *mestizo*, sad and alone, falls in love with young Blanca, sister of the Spanish *conquistador* Gonzalo de Orgaz. The latter fears for his sister's safety and orders Tabaré exiled. During a raid by the last of the Charruan Indians, the indomitable Yamandú kidnaps Blanca, claiming her as part of his booty. Tabaré kills Yamandú and recovers the captive Blanca. When he returns to the stronghold with Blanca in his arms, Gonzalo, convinced of Tabaré's guilt in the matter, kills him unfairly.

During the ten years it took to write the poem, Zorrilla studied chronicles as well as anthropological and linguistic sources in order to accurately reproduce the life, customs, and language of the Charruan Indians. In this, too, he proceeded in the manner of Chateaubriand, as well as other masters of romantic exoticism, inserting customs and typical speech without achieving a sense of reality. Yet there is a certain dramatic strength (reminiscent even of Shakespeare) in the descriptions of the Indians, especially Caracé, Sapicán, and Yamandú, that surpasses all Hispanic models, such as Esteban Echeverría's *La cautiva* (The Captive Woman, 1837). The figure of Don Gonzalo, whose violent and unpredictable personality unleashes the plot, seems derived from the chronicles, for few of his attributes coincide with the values Zorrilla recognized as typical of Spanish *conquistadores*. The evangelical feeling is embodied in Father Esteban, a composite portrait by which Zorrilla pays tribute to his Jesuit masters. It was Francisco Enrich, a Chilean Jesuit, who, when he related a Chilean *boroan* tale of an Indian with light eyes, provided Zorrilla with the germ of *Tabaré*.

Neither historical veracity nor portraiture matters for the characterization of the protagonists: mere expiatory victims of their historical and personal destinies, they are symbols, not beings. Nonetheless, Blanca communicates a human shiver of fear when she senses Yamandú's proximity and a stirring of her body when she is in Tabaré's strong arms. Tabaré's character is merely an absence, a flash of light, a shadow. His very name indicates his alienation from all human contact: in the alphabetical index added by Zorrilla to the edition of 1888, he indicated that Tabaré in the Tupi language means "he who lives alone, distant or removed from people." The hero is then a mysterious silhouette who darts through the poem framed between shadows and lights, without contours. We see only his blue eyes, symbols of baptism, which, for Anderson Imbert, hold the key to the poem.

The greatest worth of *Tabaré* rests in its style and not in its action or character portrayal. Zorrilla managed to reproduce Bécquer's fundamental blueprint for literature: detailed and subtle analysis of the finest of sensations along with the imprecision of mystery, placed within an almost mathematically perfect structure. The models for both these poets are to be found in music rather than literature.

Tabaré was organized musically and operatically, even before it was converted into an operatic libretto. The introduction and the three "books" constitute an overture and three acts. The poet, whether we think of him as an Ossianic bard or Provençal troubadour, has the gift of song and the magical power of evocation. Before our eyes, he presents a virginal landscape, an Eden disturbed by the demonic presence of the Indians, the story of the primordial couple whose sin is paid for by the sacrifice of their son, and the shadow of the main character, "dreamlike," an "impalpable image," the incarnation of "our America." But this singer-poet has above all the gift of hearing and reproducing the mysterious sounds of the jungle: the chirping of birds, the bubbling of rushing water, the creaking of branches.

Tabaré is a poem to be both seen and heard. Some images (Yamandú lying over Blanca's moribund body, Tabaré carrying Blanca in his arms) suggest Pre-Raphaelite paintings or Aubrey Beardsley's aquarelles. Juan Manuel Blanes and other American and European painters portrayed some of these scenes on canvas: Tabaré standing in the forest, Blanca in Tabaré's arms, the death of the *mestizo*. The colors and the symbolic transformation of the landscape recall paintings by Pierre Puvis de Chavannes, a painter preferred by the modernists. Zorrilla considered the poem's musical quality to be a product of his very deliberate process of composition. The leitmotiv that ties the three books together, "a flower dropped into the river," has a songlike quality. Many Guarani and Tupi words are inserted in the rhythmical structure of a popular song, imitating sometimes the poetic dirges of Paraguay called *nenias*. But the musicality also derives from Bécquer's *Poems*, echoes of which resound from time to time in the overriding symphony that is the poem.

In *Tabaré*, these techniques take on yet another meaning and a still-deeper dimension. Darío saw it, as he says in a letter, as a symbolist poem, in which Bécquer's harp played like a distant echo in a symphony interpreted by "an organ made with the cane and bamboo of the American jungle." Zorrilla, before Darío, had wandered in the sacred jungle, bringing from it harmony (compare Darío's *Cantos de vida y* esperanza [Songs of Life and Hope, 1905]), harmony that is still the religious psalm and the celestial music of Fray Luis de León.

SELECTED BIBLIOGRAPHY

Editions

First Editions

Notas de un himno. Santiago, Chile, 1877.
La leyenda patria. Montevideo, 1879 (published in *El Bien Público*).
¡Jesuítas! Montevideo, 1879.
Tabaré. Paris, 1888.
Resonancias del camino. Paris, 1896.
Huerto cerrado. Montevideo, 1900.
La epopeya de Artigas. 2 vols. Montevideo, 1910.
El sermón de la paz. Montevideo, 1924.
El libro de Ruth. Montevideo, 1928.
La profecía de Ezequiel. Montevideo, 1938 (published in *Revista nacional*).
Las Américas. Montevideo, 1945.
Maris Stella. Montevideo, 1951 (limited edition of two hundred copies).

Complementary Works

Correspondencia de Zorrilla de San Martín y Unamuno. Edited by Arturo Sergio Visea. Montevideo, 1955.
Páginas olvidadas de Zorrilla de San Martín, insertas en "La estrella de Chile" (Santiago, 1874–1877). Edited by Alfonso M. Escudero. Montevideo, 1956.

Maris Stella. Edited by Raúl Blengio Brixto. Montevideo, 1981.

Collected Works

Obras completas. 16 vols. Montevideo, 1930.
Obras escogidas. Madrid, 1967.

Translation and Operatic Version

Tabaré: An Indian Legend of Uruguay. Translated by Walter Owens. Foreword by Enrique Anderson Imbert. Washington, D.C., [1956].
Bretón y Hernández, Tomás. *Tabaré: Drama lírico en tres actos.* Madrid, 1913.

Biographical and Critical Studies

Anderson Imbert, Enrique. "La originalidad de Zorrilla de San Martín." In *Los grandes libros de Occidente y otros ensayos.* Mexico City, 1957. Pp. 121–163.
Anido, Naïade. "*Tabaré*: Mythe stigmatique de l'indigénisme uruguayen et réalité génétique dans la société 'rioplatense.' " In *Culture et société en Espagne et en Amérique latine au XIXᵉ siècle.* Edited by Claude Dumas. Lille, France, 1980. Pp. 167–199.
Bordoli, Domingo L. *Vida de Juan Zorrilla de San Martín.* Montevideo, 1961.
Crispo Acosta, Osvaldo [pseud. of Osvaldo Lauxar]. *Juan Zorrilla de San Martín.* Montevideo, 1955.
Ibáñez, Roberto. *La leyenda patria y su contorno histórico.* Montevideo, 1959.
Seluja, Antonio, and Alberto Paganini. *Tabaré: Proceso de creación.* Montevideo, 1979.
Suiffet, Norma. *Análisis estilístico de "Tabaré."* Montevideo, 1960.
Valera, Juan. "*Tabaré*: Carta a Don Luis Alonso (1889)." In *Nuevas cartas americanas,* in *Obras completas 3.* Madrid, 1958. Pp. 386–397.

Aluísio Azevedo

(1857–1913)

David T. Haberly

The standard dictionaries and histories of Brazilian literature uniformly describe Aluísio Azevedo as the nation's leading naturalist novelist. While there is some truth to this description, the reality of Azevedo's career and of his literary production is far more complex. Of the eleven novels Azevedo wrote during his relatively brief literary career (from 1879 to 1895), only four in any way conform to the model of French naturalism established by the brothers Edmond and Jules Goncourt and by Émile Zola. One of those four, *O Cortiço* (published in English as *A Brazilian Tenement*, 1890), is Azevedo's masterpiece and one of the greatest Brazilian books of the century, but many of his other novels are very seriously flawed and are almost unreadable today.

The diverse nature of Azevedo's fictional production is directly related to the economics and politics of literature in Brazil during the last quarter of the nineteenth century. While he claimed that he wrote "because it is my fate, just as I would limp if I'd been born lame," there are few convincing indications of any creative imperative at work in his life (quoted in Menezes, p. 183). Azevedo wrote not because he felt compelled to self-expression, but because literature was a career chosen after careful consideration of its potential economic and social benefits.

Aluísio Tancredo Gonçalves de Azevedo was born in the northeastern coastal city of São Luís, the capital of the province of Maranhão, on 14 April 1857. São Luís was then a provincial city of fewer than 20,000 inhabitants; less than a third of those inhabitants were classified as white, and black slaves made up as much as 40 percent of the city's population.

São Luís, despite its often suffocating tropical heat and its nonwhite masses, was the most Portuguese city in Brazil. The small landholding aristocracy was intensely proud of its pure Portuguese descent, retaining this purity by intermarriage or by carefully arranged alliances with a few of the more recent immigrants from Portugal who had come to dominate much of the commercial life of the province. Most of these immigrants, from small towns in Portugal, arrived in Maranhão without capital and without much education. Because the province's landowners were loath to soil their hands with the vulgarity of buying and selling, the immigrants filled this void. Many of them prospered through hard work, extreme thriftiness, and close economic cooperation within their own group.

This background is important, both for Azevedo's own family history and for the plot development of several of his major naturalist novels. The novelist's mother, Emília Amália Pinto de Magalhães, was born in Lisbon around 1818. Her parents later immigrated to São Luís, where her father became a successful trader. When she was seventeen, Emília's parents arranged her marriage to another prosperous Portuguese merchant, whose interests complemented those of her father. This marriage appears, from her later accounts of it, to have been a total disaster. Her husband mistreated her and was openly unfaithful with his female slaves.

Emília appears to have been more sophisticated than other upper-class young women in São Luís— among other things, she was literate and had read a sufficient number of romantic novels to have very clear ideas about what love and marriage were supposed to be—and she shocked and astonished the province by leaving her husband. She and her infant daughter took refuge with powerful and wealthy friends. Her life was threatened, she and the family who helped her were instantly cut off from polite society in São Luís, and she was not able to go out in public for months. Emília's husband was so humiliated by her desertion that he sold his business and moved to Rio de Janeiro, where he died some years later.

After the intensity of the scandal died down, Emília met one of the most eligible young men in São Luís, David Gonçalves de Azevedo, the vice-consul of Portugal in the city. He was handsome, wealthy, and highly respected as the official link between the large Portuguese colony in Maranhão and the government in Lisbon. Creating yet another scandal, Emília moved in with him. The couple had three sons (Artur, Aluísio, and Américo) and two daughters. All were considered illegitimate until 1864, when David de Azevedo recognized them as his heirs.

Aluísio Azevedo's childhood was a comfortable and happy one, despite this background. He was raised in one of the largest and most beautiful of the tile-faced colonial townhouses in the center of São Luís. His brother Artur, born in 1855, was writing plays by the age of nine; Aluísio showed considerable artistic precocity, and built and painted the scenery for Artur's household productions.

Neither boy was particularly successful in primary school in São Luís, and both were sent off, at about the age of thirteen, to work as clerks in warehouses owned by their father's friends. Artur and Aluísio detested commerce, and both dreamed of life in Rio de Janeiro, a sophisticated city of more than 400,000 inhabitants, the cultural and administrative center of the Brazilian empire. Artur left for Rio in 1873; Aluísio followed him in 1876. By that time, Artur had begun to establish himself as a journalist, humorist, and dramatist. With his brother's help, Aluísio found a position as a caricaturist for several newspapers and enjoyed considerable success. When David de Azevedo died in 1878, however, Aluísio felt it his responsibility to leave Artur in Rio and settle his father's affairs in São Luís.

Back in Maranhão, Azevedo threw himself into local journalism, proclaiming his anticlerical and antiestablishment ideas and rapidly acquiring a reputation as an irritating young radical. After members of the provincial assembly turned down a request that it underwrite his artistic studies in Italy, Azevedo turned his hand to writing fiction. He was convinced that success as a novelist would allow him to escape the squalor and pettiness he so hated in his hometown. His first attempt at the genre, *Uma Lágrima de Mulher* (A Woman's Tear), written in 1878 and published in 1879, was a banal romantic tale set in southern Italy. It sold well in São Luís, where Azevedo advertised it heavily, putting up posters on every bare wall in the city, but it was far too traditional and commonplace to win him any sort of reputation outside his native province.

His second novel, *O Mulato* (The Mulatto), written in 1880 and published in 1881, was designed to attract both local notoriety and national attention. Its scandalous theme, explicit sexuality, and obvious utilization of ideas and techniques taken from European naturalism made it an instant best seller in São Luís, where several thousand copies were sold within a few weeks. This level of sales was almost unknown in nineteenth-century Brazil. The novel, also widely read and reviewed in Rio de Janeiro, established Azevedo's reputation as an important and innovative writer; it enabled him to return to Rio in 1881.

Between 1881 and 1895, Azevedo continued to write and to promote his novels. He also collaborated, with Artur and others, on a few plays. He was convinced, at first, that the nation's economic and cultural progress had finally made it possible for a

Brazilian writer to make a living by writing, and he was determined to do so. One of the ironies of Azevedo's career is that while many of his works violently attack capitalism, commercial activity in general, and the profit motive itself, he clearly viewed the production and sale of those same works as above all a commercial enterprise, and was aggressive in contract negotiations with publishers and in advertising his novels.

Azevedo did manage a fairly comfortable life for himself in the cafés and salons of Rio de Janeiro, perhaps with a little financial assistance from family and friends. However, the charms of bohemianism began to pale after he reached his thirties, and his complaints about literature as a career became increasingly bitter. Writing did not seem to him all that different from the life he had left São Luís to escape: "I describe an episode or a landscape, I develop a dialogue, just as I would have cut up yard goods or slabs of dried meat if I had wound up in business" (quoted in Menezes, p. 183). It now seemed absurd to have tried to make a living as a writer in a nation of illiterates. "There are a few pedants here who read French novels," he complained, "and there are businessmen who read foreign exchange rates and customs tariffs; everyone else is ignorant" (p. 146).

His new goal was a sinecure in government service, and his aggressive pursuit of financial security was finally rewarded with an appointment to Brazil's consular service in 1895. When a friend congratulated him on the appointment and on the leisure for writing that it would provide, Azevedo exploded: "What? Novels and stories? You're out of your mind. I'm going to be a consul; nothing more. I've had it up to here with literature" (p. 256).

Azevedo served the Brazilian government in Vigo (Spain), Yokohama (Japan), Salto (Uruguay), Cardiff (Wales), Naples (Italy), Asunción (Paraguay), and Buenos Aires (Argentina). He complained bitterly about every post and about consular life in general. He never married, although his will left part of his estate to his Argentine housekeeper and her two children. Azevedo died in Buenos Aires, of a heart attack, on 21 January 1913. As he had sworn, Azevedo had written no more novels during the last seventeen years of his life, and he appears to have bitterly regretted the time he had devoted to literature. "Just between you and me," he told a friend in 1910, "the only books that count are checkbooks."

Azevedo's many complaints about his penury, about the sorry state of literature in Brazil, and about the exploitation of writers by publishers, however, express something more than his ironic capitalist yearnings. Through these complaints he was also constructing a rationalization and a justification for the diversity of his own novelistic output. He wanted very much to convince his friends—and himself—that his failure to live up to the promise of O Mulato in any consistent fashion was the direct result of financial pressures. Many of his novels were romantic potboilers, written for daily serialization in the newspapers of Rio de Janeiro, and he often insisted that he wrote such works only to put food on his table.

In reality, however, Azevedo wrote his many romantic novels simply because they were easy—for him and for his readers. Despite the pressures of daily serialization, Azevedo seems to have been able to turn out such novels almost effortlessly, utilizing the tried and true formulas of Brazilian romantic fiction to create highly complex, and highly unrealistic, plots. While several of Azevedo's novels that attempted to conform to the naturalist model were no less formulaic, the formulas were not as clear in his mind and not nearly as instinctive; nor was he at all certain where the limits of his readers' taste—and tolerance—lay.

Azevedo's literary career, alternating between romanticism and naturalism, brings into sharp focus an extraordinary anomaly in the literary history of nineteenth-century Brazil: the virtual absence of realism, as a movement, until well after 1880. Azevedo's abrupt transition from the romantic Uma Lagrima de Mulher, written in 1878, to the composition of his naturalistic O Mulato one year later simply duplicated, at the individual level, what happened to Brazilian fiction as a whole between 1850 and 1880.

Realism, a movement infinitely more influential than naturalism in the history of the novel in Europe and North America, never took root in Brazil during this period. The one early Brazilian novel sometimes described as realist, Manuel Antônio de Almeida's Memórias de um Sargento de Milícias (Memoirs of a Militia Sergeant, 1854–1855), is in fact the late flowering of a typical romantic subgenre, the picaresque novel of local color. The early fictions of Joaquim Maria Machado de Assis, considered by many the greatest Brazilian novelist, reflect his dissatisfaction with the formulas of the romantic novel. But Machado did not move from romanticism to realism with the publication of his revolutionary *Memórias Póstumas de Brás Cubas* (The Posthumous Memoirs of Braz Cubas; published in English as *Epitaph for a Small Winner*) in 1881, but to something so personal and so utterly original that the *Memórias Póstumas* and his later works fall entirely outside the standard categories of nineteenth-century fiction in both Europe and the Americas.

Perhaps the most intriguing aspect of this anomalous history is the fact that the major French exponents of the realist novel, particularly Honoré de Balzac, were widely read and admired in Brazil. Why is it, then, that realism found admirers but not disciples? One explanation is chronological; the speed with which European movements and even individual works crossed the Atlantic to Brazil increased dramatically in the second half of the nineteenth century. The romantic novel took so long to develop in Brazil that José de Alencar's *O Guaraní* (The Guarani [Indian]), the first successful fusion of romanticism and nationalistic Indianism, appeared in 1857, the same year Gustave Flaubert published *Madame Bovary*. And two of the most important Brazilian romantic novels, Alfredo d'Escragnolle Taunay's *Inocência* (Innocence, 1872; published in English as *Inocência*) and Bernardo Joaquim de Silva Guimarães' *A Escrava Isaura* (The Slave-Girl Isaura, 1875), appeared just as educated readers in Rio and elsewhere began to discover the naturalist novels of Zola.

Chronology, however, is not the only reason for the absence of realism in the development of the Brazilian novel. Above all, realism, as a movement, must have seemed totally foreign to the social reality of Brazil in the second half of the nineteenth century. The central focus of European realism was the middle class—its ideals and aspirations, its passions and ambitions, the simplest details of its daily existence in the city and countryside. Brazilian society, sharply divided between the wealthy and literate few and the illiterate masses of the poor and the enslaved, was a very different world indeed.

The France of Balzac and Flaubert was racially homogeneous. By contrast, Brazil was inhabited by whites, blacks, and Indians—and by every possible combination of the three races. And, most important of all, the novels of the major European realists portrayed a world in which change and progress were facts of life, for individuals, families, and society as a whole—an ideology and a reality both alien and threatening to educated Brazilians. It is easy to understand, within this context, why Brazilian writers were uncertain whether European realism could—or should—be successfully assimilated into the nation's literature.

Naturalism, on the other hand, was extremely attractive to Azevedo and to other Brazilian writers between 1880 and about 1895. As it was understood in Brazil, naturalism was not a negation of romanticism, but a reformulation of romanticism on the basis of detailed observation and sound scientific principles. In this view, Brazilians came very close to the ideas of a leading American naturalist, Frank Norris, who made a distinction between accuracy and truth. Accuracy, he suggested in 1901, was typical of realism but provided an incomplete vision of reality; truth was the big picture, the perception and depiction of eternal verities that romanticism had sought to achieve. Naturalism, the best of both worlds, synthesized truth and accuracy.

Accuracy, for Brazilian naturalists, meant the careful description of the details of life. Such description was not, however, an end in itself, an attempt to reproduce reality through the written text. Detailed descriptions of settings, of characters, and—most strikingly—of the sexual activities of those characters were designed to reinforce, at the level of the text, the naturalists' assertions of the scientific validity of the larger truths they were expounding. Zola's famous essay "Le roman expérimental" ("The Experimental Novel," 1880) explicitly linked naturalism and the scientific method, but neither he nor his French disciples were as frank, in their descriptions of sexuality, as the Brazilians. When Azevedo's *A Brazilian Tenement* was translated and published in the United States in 1926, the text had to be heavily censored for the North American audience. While this explicitness often approached hard-core pornography, the Brazilian naturalists insisted that it was designed to inform and to warn, not to titillate.

Moreover, no European or North American naturalist went as far as the Brazilians in endeavoring to adapt the vocabulary of science to fiction. The most extreme example of these efforts is Rodolfo Teófilo's novel *A Fome* (Hunger, 1890); this description of starving refugees during the great drought in the state of Ceará in 1877 is typical of his style.

> Functional disorder, in these organisms, had become total. Their hearts beat heavily and irregularly, due to low blood density and to an excessive proportion of leucocytes, causing them terrible pain. Systole and diastole had become fragmentary, the velocity of the circulatory system had accelerated, and their valves functioned poorly; as a result, those valves allowed a portion of the blood supply, already severely diminished, to back up in the heart, bringing about cerebral anemia and causing both vertigo and the loud buzzing in their ears that tortured them constantly.

Accuracy, in the form of detailed description, alternates with the enunciation of truths. In the weakest Brazilian naturalist novels, that enunciation is explicit and tendentious; in the best, it is implicit in the events described. There are three central truths in Azevedo's naturalist novels and in other works of the school in Brazil: change is impossible—or, at the very least, the consequences of change are invariably negative; the sex drive is the single most important imperative in human existence; and genetic inheritance and environmental conditioning wholly determine the character and the behavior of human organisms.

Despite the scientific and pseudoscientific trappings with which naturalism sought to invest these truths, these were not new ideas. In fact, they were to a large extent reformulations of central truths found in the novels of Brazilian romanticism: the stability provided by home and family and by acceptance of one's proper place in society is the source of human contentment; true love conquers all; physical beauty and purity of character prevail among the right sort of people, whether well-bred young Brazilians or naturally noble Indians; rural life is healthier and happier than city life.

Many of these truths can be found in Azevedo's first novel, the romantic *Uma Lágrima de Mulher*. He declares, for example, that upward social mobility is invariably destructive: "There is nothing so disastrous and dangerous as a sudden change in status" (ch. 2). Love—indistinguishable from lust—is "savage, gross, egotistical, since delicacy, civility, and social character are the creations of man or mere social conventions, while passion is an antediluvian monster, the creation of Nature" (ch. 8). The city is the cradle of misery, greed, exploitation, and cruelty, while out in the countryside "feelings are open and true, souls stronger and more human" (ch. 1). Because "the character of a place is always transmitted, through the air, to those who live and breathe there, just as a wet nurse passes on all her physical ills and moral weaknesses to the child she suckles" (ch. 3), so those upright and happy individuals who live in the country "have good stomachs and pure blood. A healthy stomach is the basis of each and every possible happiness" (ch. 2). In the metropolis, however, urban vices, "both the delight and the attraction of the great cities, start by destroying the stomachs of their citizens, and wind up laying siege to their souls, which are weakened, eroded, corrupted, and rotted" (ch. 2).

Azevedo's use of science in his naturalist novels became a good deal more sophisticated than this early emphasis on the importance of a healthy digestive tract, but his basic truths did not change. And while those truths derived from romantic verities, the underlying spirit and purpose of his works were very different indeed from the romanticism of Alencar. Alencar had sought to use the novel to glorify the past and future of Brazil, and to convey both national pride and boundless optimism. Azevedo and his contemporaries, writing in very different times, responded to the feelings of pessimism and fear that began to affect many educated upper-class Brazilians after about 1870. The long stability of Pedro II's empire began to crumble, endangered by church-state conflicts, by the rapid growth of the armed forces during the Paraguayan War from 1865 to 1870, and by the political and economic consequences of the abolition of slavery, a long and gradual process that began in 1871 and ended with full emancipation in 1888. All of these changes were to culminate, in 1889, with Pedro II's exile, the end of the empire, and the proclamation of the republic.

If many of Azevedo's readers felt a general disquiet

about all of these changes, they also saw themselves specifically and personally threatened. As members of the traditional national elite, they were witnessing the increasing presence and potential economic and social power of two previously marginal groups. One consisted of the recent immigrants from Europe, particularly from Portugal, and the other, of the free blacks and mulattoes whose numbers were about to swell enormously with abolition. These two types—the Portuguese immigrant and the freedman—are central figures in Azevedo's naturalist fiction. Their characteristics and function are most clearly visible, perhaps, in his first naturalist novel, O Mulato, and in his masterpiece, A Brazilian Tenement. In both these works, native-born white Brazilians are reduced to the level of minor characters, bystanders on the fringes of the action.

Raimundo, the hero of the first of these novels, is hardly a typical mulatto in appearance; he "would have been the perfect [white] Brazilian type were it not for his blue eyes, inherited from his father" (ch. 3). The free, illegitimate son of a Portuguese merchant and a slave woman, Raimundo was sent to Europe as a child. He returns to São Luís a university graduate and a handsome, polished young gentleman. He is quite unaware of his ancestry, and entirely unprepared for the violent passions his return will ignite in the squalid and petty world of São Luís.

Raimundo stays in his uncle's house, where his white cousin, Ana Rosa, falls madly and hysterically in love with him. He agrees to marry her but courteously seeks to bow out when he learns the truth about his past. To keep Raimundo, Ana Rosa seduces him and becomes pregnant. Ever the decent and proper young man, Raimundo feels obliged to ask for her hand, but her family indignantly refuses. The totally corrupt Canon Diogo, the family's spiritual adviser, conspires with a young and ambitious Portuguese clerk to arrange Raimundo's assassination.

O Mulato has sometimes been described, in the years since its publication, as an abolitionist novel. In fact, however, the text does not directly criticize slavery, and Azevedo clearly intended it as an anticlerical tract, focused on the treacherous Canon Diogo. Within the peculiar context of Brazil's late-blooming literary campaign against slavery, however, it is easy to see why Brazilians read O Mulato as an abolitionist text. Central to its plot is the basic argument of Brazilian abolitionism: slavery is wrong not on humanitarian grounds, but because it forces white Brazilians into close contact with those of African descent, beings defined as inherently violent and contagiously immoral.

That argument was reinforced, as naturalism and abolitionism flowed together after about 1880, by the assimilation of theories of genetic and environmental determinism. Raimundo's impact upon São Luís shows the triumph of genetic determinism over the environmental advantages of education and manners. There is something about Raimundo that awakens lust, some animal aura of temptation that surrounds him and violently inflames the white women of the city. It is this unconscious, genetic force that compels Ana Rosa to seduce him, setting off the chain of events that leads inevitably to his death.

Once Raimundo is removed from the scene, life returns to normal. Ana Rosa marries the Portuguese clerk, and the two appear to live happily ever after. The Portuguese have triumphed over the freedmen, in short, and the society of São Luís is quietly pleased with the removal of the threat Raimundo represented to the white Brazilian world. "Ability?" asks one of the minor characters in the novel; "Talent, I tell you. This mixed race is the smartest in all Brazil. If those people ever get a little education and decide to start something—well, I feel sorry for the whites; that would be the end of everything" (ch. 14).

These themes are even more evident, and more forcefully and deftly presented, in A Brazilian Tenement. There are two plots in the novel, involving three sets of major characters. The first plot charts the relationship between João Romão and the Miranda family. Romão is the archetypal Portuguese immigrant, who comes to Rio with nothing and works and saves and cheats his way to wealth. He purloins building supplies to construct and expand the tenement he rents out, and overcharges in his store. His mistress, Bertoleza, is an unattractive black slave who is convinced that Romão used her life's savings to purchase her freedom; in fact, the Portuguese invested the money in his tenement, and keeps her around only because she is a good cook and works for nothing.

The Miranda family lives next door, their town

house besieged by Romão's ever-expanding empire of shacks, laundry facilities, stores, and stone quarry. Miranda, a Portuguese immigrant of good family, married a wealthy Brazilian girl to advance his career. He and his wife detest each other but are held together by social convention and by the sporadic lust that not only overwhelms their mutual hatred but is in fact intensified by it. Miranda despises Romão at first, but comes to admire his drive and prosperity, treats him as an equal, and finally accepts him as a son-in-law. First, however, Romão must dispose of Bertoleza. When her owner's son comes to retrieve her, Bertoleza commits suicide rather than return to slavery. The fusion of Romão and the Mirandas, of tenement and town house, symbolizes social change, but that change is built upon the shattered bodies and ruined lives of almost all those it touches.

At the center of the novel's second plot is the one character who combines strength of character, intelligence, and basic human goodness. Jerônimo is yet another Portuguese immigrant, poor but hardworking, faithful to his wife, Piedade, to their daughter, and to his homesick memories of Portugal. Jerônimo and Piedade are slowly working their way out of poverty. They have some decent furniture and are paying for their daughter's education in a boarding school.

Within the squalor of the tenement, however, Jerônimo meets Bahian Rita, a beautiful and overwhelmingly sensuous mulatto temptress. Rita's seduction of the Portuguese is not intentional; temptation is a genetic imperative for her, as it was for Raimundo. Beyond her personal attraction, moreover, Rita is Brazil itself: beautiful but destructive and ultimately vicious. Her power leads Jerônimo to murder his rival for her affections, to desert his family, destroying their future, and to give up work and ambition—to become, in Azevedo's pessimistic view, a typical Brazilian.

The combination of total pessimism and apathy found in A Brazilian Tenement is typical of Brazilian naturalism and sets it apart from its French models. Zola devoted much of his life to concrete efforts to improve the conditions his novels described. In those novels, moreover, there are always at least a few characters who symbolize the hope and nobility of human beings able to survive even the most terrible cruelties. Azevedo's depiction of slum life in Rio is not a plea for improvement, nor did he ever show the slightest interest in political matters. His novel is, above all, a rationalization for inaction: environmentally and genetically maimed, the inhabitants of the tenement are largely beyond redemption. They are victims of life, captives of society and of the omnipresent Brazilian lust that seems to seep from fruits and flowers, that hangs heavy in the hot air—the smell of masses of animals in heat, as Azevedo describes it.

The Little Dove, another Portuguese immigrant in the tenement, can remain innocent and free only so long as she does not reach puberty. She has the promise of a good marriage, enabling her and her mother to escape poverty. Corruption and menstruation arrive simultaneously, however, as she is seduced by a wealthy and beautiful prostitute, Leonie. Little Dove goes through with her arranged marriage, but she has been fatally touched by the all-pervasive, all-destructive lust of Brazil, and she quickly leaves her husband to work with Leonie. Her mother, whose one dream was to someday achieve respectability, ends her days as a servant in the whorehouse. The only survivor in the novel, in fact, is João Romão, whose pathological greed is the only force capable of neutralizing lust.

The fate of Little Dove is symbolic of one of the most depressing aspects of A Brazilian Tenement, its treatment of children. In 1885, Azevedo sketched out his master plan for a series of naturalist novels, with the general title "Brazilians Then and Now." This collection of five volumes, starting with the novel that was to become A Brazilian Tenement, would trace the future of several of its characters over more than a generation. The other four novels were never written, however. This was in part because Azevedo found it easier to turn out romantic entertainments, in part because he was tired of the stresses of literary life, but above all because, as A Brazilian Tenement suggests, he could not envision a future worth describing. Despite the lust that hangs heavy over all his characters, no next generation is conceived, and those children who already exist are systematically maimed and corrupted and killed.

This pessimism, reinforced by the stylistic and philosophical trappings of science, reflected Brazilian attitudes at the end of the nineteenth century. Through naturalism, literature placed itself at the service of fear, fear of abolition and of open competition from freedmen and mulattoes, and fear of the aggressive capitalism and technological progress defined as the province of European immigrants. It was widely argued, among many Brazilian intellectuals during the next twenty years, that the nation itself was doomed, like naturalism's characters, by genetics and by environment. The large nonwhite population, the heat of the tropics, the immoral heritage of slavery, the easy and weak-willed life that tropical abundance fostered—all of these factors, it was claimed, cheated Brazil of its future.

Naturalism, as a literary movement, began to fade from popularity around 1895, as educated readers tired of its heavy-handed theses and its repetitive scenes of sexuality. It did not disappear, however, but simply went underground, particularly in the Northeast; its attitudes and some of its stylistic quirks were to resurface, decades later, in a new guise—the northeastern "new novels" of the 1920's and 1930's, written by such figures as Rachel de Queiroz, José Lins do Rêgo, Graciliano Ramos, and Jorge Amado. And, despite all the differences between modern Brazil and the world Azevedo described a century ago, his best naturalist novels are regularly reissued and sell well. The continuing popularity of these works suggests, finally, that at least some of his readers today feel, or fear, that Azevedo's vision of their society still holds true.

SELECTED BIBLIOGRAPHY

First Editions

Novels

Uma Lágrima de Mulher. São Luís do Maranhão, Brazil, 1879.
O Mulato. São Luís do Maranhão, Brazil, 1881.
Memórias de um Condenado. First serialized in A Gazetinha (Rio de Janeiro), 1882. First book edition (with same title), Ouro Preto, Brazil, 1886. Second edition (with title A Condessa Vésper), Rio de Janeiro, 1902. Second title used in subsequent editions.

O Mistério da Tijuca. First serialized in A Folha Nova (Rio de Janeiro), 1882. First book edition (with same title), Rio de Janeiro, 1883. Second edition (with title Girândola de Amores), Rio de Janeiro, 1900. Second title used in subsequent editions.
Casa de Pensão. Rio de Janeiro, 1884.
Filomena Borges. Rio de Janeiro, 1884.
O Homem. Rio de Janeiro, 1887.
O Cortiço. Rio de Janeiro, 1890.
O Coruja. Rio de Janeiro, 1890.
A Mortalha de Alzira. Rio de Janeiro, 1894.
Livro de uma Sogra. Rio de Janeiro, 1895.

Stories and Essays

Demônios. São Paulo, 1893.
Pegadas. Rio de Janeiro, 1897.

Modern Editions

Individual Works

Casa de Pensão. São Paulo, 1977.
O Cortiço. São Paulo, 1983.
O Coruja. São Paulo, 1973.
O Mulato. São Paulo, 1983.

Collected Works

Obras Completas. Edited by Nogueira da Silva. 12 vols. Rio de Janeiro, 1937–1941.
_____. 12 vols. São Paulo, 1959–1961.

Translations

A Brazilian Tenement [O Cortiço]. Translated by Harry W. Brown. New York, 1926. Reprinted 1976.

Biographical and Critical Studies

Brayner, Sônia. A Metáfora do Corpo no Romance Naturalista. Rio de Janeiro, 1973.
_____. Labirinto do Espaço Romanesco. Rio de Janeiro, 1979.
Brown, Donald F. "A Naturalistic Version of Genesis: Zola and Aluísio Azevedo." Hispanic Review 12/4:344–351 (1944).
_____. "Azevedo's Naturalistic Version of Gautier's La

morte amoureuse." *Hispanic Review* 13/3:252–257 (1945).

Gomes, Eugênio. *Aspectos do Romance Brasileiro.* Salvador, Brazil, 1958.

Loos, Dorothy S. *The Naturalistic Novel of Brazil.* New York, 1963.

MacNicoll, Murray Graeme. "*O Mulato* and Maranhão: The Socio-Historical Context." *Luso-Brazilian Review* 12/2:234–240 (1975).

Magalhães Júnior, Raimundo. *Artur Azevedo e Sua Época.* 4th ed. São Paulo, 1971.

Marotti, Giorgio. *Il Negro nel Romanzo Brasiliano.* Rome, 1982.

Menezes, Raimundo de. *Aluísio Azevedo: Uma Vida de Romance.* 2nd ed. São Paulo, 1958.

Mérian, Jean-Yves. "Un roman inachevé de Aluísio Azevedo." In *Manuel Bandeira, Aluísio Azevedo, Graciliano Ramos, Ariano Suassuna.* Poitiers, France, 1974. Pp. 97–116.

———. "Structure et signification du roman de Aluísio Azevedo: *O Mulato.*" *Nouvelles Études Portugaises et Brésiliennes* 7:83–121 (n. d.).

Miguel-Pereira, Lúcia. *Prosa de Ficção de 1870 a 1920.* 3rd ed. Rio de Janeiro, 1973.

Preti, Dino. *Sociolinguística.* São Paulo, 1974.

Sales, Herberto, ed. *Para Conhecer Melhor Aluísio Azevedo.* Rio de Janeiro, 1973.

Sant'Anna, Affonso Romano de. *Análise Estrutural de Romances Brasileiros.* Petrópolis, Brazil, 1973.

Sayers, Raymond S. *The Negro in Brazilian Literature.* New York, 1956.

Sodré, Nelson Werneck. *O Naturalismo no Brasil.* Rio de Janeiro, 1965.

Tomás Carrasquilla

(1858–1940)

Kurt L. Levy

Tomás Carrasquilla was born in Santo Domingo, Colombia, on 17 January 1858 and died in Medellín on 19 December 1940. He never left Colombia and only twice traveled outside his native Antioqueño mountains, on both occasions to Bogotá. His life, he tells us, was devoted entirely and wholeheartedly to three pursuits: reading, writing, and chatting informally with his family and friends. Little reliable information is available about his childhood. His father, a mining engineer, had a busy professional schedule, usually away from home. Thus the children's upbringing remained largely the mother's task, and Carrasquilla acknowledges repeatedly, in both his correspondence and creative writings, the importance of the maternal influence during his formative years.

To say that young Carrasquilla's scholastic record was singularly undistinguished may be an understatement. The one and only school report that has come down to us provides the evidence, as it details an array of average and below-average marks. However, what makes this report a memorable document is not the scholar's mediocre achievement, but rather a succinct handwritten note appended by the principal of the school that deplores the fact that "the constant reading of novels has harmed this student greatly." In 1876, Carrasquilla enrolled in the Law School of the Universidad de Antioquia in Medellín, but his studies were short-lived due to the outbreak of a civil war that precipitated the closing of all institutions of learning. He did not return to his law books but concentrated instead on readings more to his taste and tried his hand at writing.

Carrasquilla's earliest creative effort was a short story entitled "Simón el mago" (Simon Magus, 1890), which he "dashed off," to use his own description, to satisfy the entrance requirements of a literary circle, the Literary Casino, in Medellín. Similarly, the genesis of his first full-length novel *Frutos de mi tierra* (Fruits of My Homeland, 1896) is closely linked to the activities of the same cultural institution. Carrasquilla first visited Bogotá in 1895 in order to make arrangements for the publication of the novel. The family moved to the provincial capital, Medellín, and Carrasquilla wrote two short novels, *Dimitas Arias* (Dimitas Arias, 1897) and *El padre Casafús* (Father Casafús, 1899), as well as "Herejías" (Heresies, 1897), his first literary criticism. A civil war, the War of the Thousand Days, which ravaged Colombia between 1899 and 1902 and which prompted one of Carrasquilla's best-known short stories, "A la plata" (Money Talks, 1901), was followed in short order by a massive crash of the People's Bank in Medellín. Carrasquilla, who saw his

TOMÁS CARRASQUILLA

savings all but wiped out, found himself compelled, for the first time, to abandon his bohemian existence and to look for gainful employment. A vacancy in the supply store of the San Andrés mine, near the village of Sonsón, seemed to provide the answer; Carrasquilla moved to that area and remained there for three years. While his letters from San Andrés reflect a profound distaste for the monotony of the daily routine, his prolonged contact with the mining milieu was to bear rich fruit in some of the climactic stories of his later, mature works.

When Carrasquilla returned to Medellín, his life resumed the bohemian flavor that he enjoyed and that stimulated his continuing dialogue with the local literary milieu. The novel *Grandeza* (Grandeur, 1910) is a product of that period. In September 1914 the capital beckoned once again and Carrasquilla accepted a minor civil service position in the ministry of public works. His return to Medellín in 1919 marked the beginning of the final two decades of his long life. It was a period of severe physical and psychological stress as circulatory inadequacies impaired his movement and cataracts deprived him of his sight. Yet, in terms of literary achievement, it proved a most fruitful period, during which he wrote such mature novels as *Ligia Cruz* (1926), *El Zarco* (The Blue-Eyed Boy, 1925), *La Marquesa de Yolombó* (The Marchioness of Yolombó, 1928), all published first in periodicals and later in book form, and *Hace tiempos* (Long Ago, 1935–1936). The last-mentioned trilogy dates from a time when Carrasquilla was entirely blind and had to dictate, so he tells us, "those thousand pages . . . not to a skilled secretary but to any member of the family at any possible moment." Carrasquilla succumbed to arteriosclerosis in 1940.

In two secular "Homilías" (Homilies), issued in 1906, Carrasquilla formulated a guiding principle of his literary craft, urging the new generation of writers to steer clear of affectation and shallow brilliance, to be true to themselves and give voice to "the hymn of real life." Three major themes in his writings focus on the individual and on concerns that he describes as "vulgares y cotidianos" (everyday and commonplace), unfolding in a humble everyday setting: the impact of single ideas and all-embracing obsessions; the child mind during its formative period; and the

living regional folklore involving prominently topics "de tejas arriba" (above the rooftops). A scrutiny of representative individual writings will help identify these themes and discern the author's fascination with psychological issues which, though in regional attire, clearly transcend the limits of the local setting and take on a universal dimension.

The short story "Simón el mago" was Carrasquilla's *coup d'essai*. Autobiographical in form, the unpretentious story derives its unity from the central character of the black servant Fructuosa Rúa, Frutos for short, and her totally uncritical affection for the boy narrator, who can do no wrong as far as she is concerned. That relationship comes under scrutiny as Frutos' unquestioning devotion breeds the narrator's blind trust in her authority. Fantastic tales of witchcraft assume the appearance of gospel truth, and the sensitive boy becomes obsessed with the possibility of emulating supernatural powers and flying into space. Disaster is narrowly averted at the moment of crisis, and the magic jump into space ends in humiliating defeat. The moral of the tale is conveyed by a village luminary who provides the author's cautioning message: "You see, my young friend, anyone who seeks to soar too high easily comes to grief." This story, which may be considered a light preamble to the author's literary production, not only testifies to the skill of the born storyteller but also introduces in embryonic form two thematic elements that remain central to the author's narrative art: an abiding and affectionate understanding of child psychology and, above all, the recognition that "soaring too high" may invite disaster. Finally it presents for the first time the figure of the mentor, to whom Carrasquilla returns repeatedly.

Frutos de mi tierra was Carrasquilla's first full-length novel, and the Literary Casino in Medellín played a significant part in its origin. One of its meetings, Carrasquilla recalls, witnessed a heated debate on whether the province of Antioquia could provide a milieu conducive to the writing of novels. A majority of those present voiced their doubts; only Carrasquilla and Carlos E. Restrepo, later to become president of the republic, upheld the affirmative, and Carrasquilla was assigned the task of supplying documentary proof for the optimistic thesis. *Frutos de mi tierra* was Carrasquilla's response to this challenge. It is a story in which the main plot is one of stark

344

realism verging on naturalism, while the subplot injects strongly romantic traits.

The Alzate family is motivated by greed pure and simple; sordid materialism guides their wretched lives. Agustín, the head of the household, suffers from an acutely inflated sense of self-importance. His world is purely external, totally devoid of spiritual values. When the son-in-law of a woman whom Agustín had consistently verbally abused decides to thoroughly thrash the bully, his universe crumbles, and the shell reveals its essential hollowness. He had tried to soar too high; his destination is no less melancholy than the pigpen into which the little boy in "Simón el mago" descends unceremoniously. Filomena is her brother's equal in material concerns and economic skills. But her situation is complicated by the fact that an ill-fated urge to marry assails her at the mature age of forty-five. This urge blinds her to the performance of a consummate trickster, César, from Bogotá, who "arrives, sees, and triumphs." Filomena's downfall is no less drastic and definitive than her brother's. Neither one recovers, and, given their psychological equipment, the sequence of events is quite logical.

The secondary plot of the novel, which provides relief from the consistent sordidness of the unholy Alzate trinity, tells of the turbulent courtship of Martín Gala and Pepa Escandón. He is a romantic student who prefers to read Byron rather than attend his classes; she is a charming but equally unstable young lady who delights in leading on her suitors, only to reject them when the mood suits her. She seems to approve the adage that "all is fair in love and war" and acts accordingly. The skirmishes between Martín and Pepa make entertaining reading, but her whimsical behavior (which is sweetened by a delightfully distinctive laugh) backfires eventually, and she capitulates, acknowledging that this time at last she had been unable to play her customary game with impunity. Reality, both sordid and romantic, was the author's domain, and his exploration of the human heart became increasingly intense and less monolithic as he matured. *Frutos de mi tierra*, though possibly the best known of Carrasquilla's novels outside of Colombia, lacks the subtle psychological shading that the author was to provide later in his career.

The next story is full of autobiography transformed into an adventure in fiction. In his "Autobiografía" (1915), Carrasquilla recalled: "My first teacher was 'The Cripple' by Antonomasia, later the protagonist of some tale of mine." *Dimitas Arias* is the tragic account of the "teacher without pupils," a rural schoolmaster permanently disabled in an accident and confined to a wheelchair, whose magnificent obsession is teaching and the daily contact with the young that it provides. In fact, faced with his infant son's death and the haunting fear that he would have no heir, Dimas seeks to fill the human gap vicariously. The decrepit schoolhouse and its undisciplined inhabitants turn into his lifeline and indeed an obsessive raison d'être. When the unfeeling school board removes him from his post in the name of progress, his lifeline is broken, existence loses its meaning, and he seeks comfort in a strange illusion, as the statue of the Christ Child assumes a real-life dimension, becoming identified with the son, Dimitas, who had died. *Dimitas Arias* remains a moving tribute to a tragic figure consumed by a great obsession and a searching psychological document. Its human interest is spelled out in universal terms.

El padre Casafús, published two years after *Dimitas Arias* and originally entitled *Luterito* (Little Luther), at first suggests a subject matter somewhat alien to Carrasquilla's literary art. The issue is religion and its impact on politics. Carrasquilla did not approve of the thesis novel as a vehicle for literary expression. The ideological flavor evoked by the historical context of the war of 1876 (the civil strife that cut short Carrasquilla's law studies) is therefore less important to the author's literary purpose than is the enquiry into human beings and the motivations for their actions. Pedro Nolasco Casafús is one more individual who soars high and comes to grief because he is obsessed with his position and refuses to compromise. The novel *El padre Casafús* pits two fanatics against each other; failure to compromise and blind intransigence are portrayed as human failings that, with the best of intentions, prove counterproductive in the end. Politically a staunch liberal who advocated tolerance and flexibility, Carrasquilla rejected the novel as a medium for making his ideological views known.

Entrañas de niño (A Child's Heart, 1906) returns to

his favorite theme of child psychology. In a letter to a friend, Carrasquilla, the avowed bachelor, once declared defiantly: "I have no wife, I have no children and, God willing, I shall never have any." Yet he devoted a substantial section of his creative work to searching and affectionate scrutinies of small people and to the molding of his characters' personality patterns in terms of emotions, intellect, and taste. *Entrañas de niño* coincides with Carrasquilla's venture at the San Andrés mine. Paco, the youthful protagonist, is obsessed with beauty and repelled by the ugly side of life. Because toads exemplify the latter, Paco sadistically roasts them, which results in paternal retribution and the boy's temporary departure from the parental home. The key to Paco's personality is the nebulous search for beauty that guides his behavior, nurtures his superiority complex, and sets him aside from his everyday environment. In exploring the diverse facets of Paco's human relationships, the author detects mild condescension for his father, utter scorn for his brothers, affectionate respect for his mother, and total adoration for his grandmother. When the latter dies, Paco reacts with stunned disbelief to God's inexorable will. His "neurosis of grandeur" brings to mind, in a very different context, the unsavory "fruits of my homeland," Agustín and Filomena Alzate, and clearly announces the central psychological concern in *Grandeza*.

If teaching and contact with the young are overwhelmingly obsessive forces in *Dimitas Arias*, and the boy in "Simón el mago" is irresistibly—almost fatally—drawn to magic, *Grandeza* tackles a very different kind of obsession; it is the story of a woman whose love for her daughters is her sole raison d'être. Juana Barrameda is obsessed with her daughters' happiness—at least her definition of their happiness—and she will make every sacrifice to that end. In short, "the love for her daughters was virtually madness." The grandeur that she considers essential for her daughters' marital bliss and that makes her assail the social ladder with almost indecent haste backfires eventually, and her own son falls victim to his mother's ill-conceived maneuvers. *Grandeza*, which contains one of Carrasquilla's most enchanting characters, Magdalena Samudio (intended as a tribute to one of his closest friends, Susana Olózaga de Cabo), takes the reader into Medellín's upper middle class and satirizes, more or less gently, a social group that prizes social brilliance and attaches inordinate importance to material possessions. There are marked points of comparison between *Grandeza* and *Frutos de mi tierra*. Both portray aspects of Medellín society and both are frankly critical of abuses by the monied aristocracy. *Grandeza*, while less entertaining, is the more mature work. It displays greater human variety and more subtle psychological shading.

A decade later, after his second visit to the capital, the author produced a short novel of astonishingly broad psychological dimensions. *Ligia Cruz* is the study of an obsession that develops into a mental aberration. The heroine, not unlike Emma Bovary (a female Don Quixote), has erected for herself a rose-colored dream world, after devouring romantic novels in immense quantities. Her readings serve as a protective mechanism against her primitive surroundings. When her parents send her to Medellín to further her education, she credits Providence with sponsoring the move. Infatuated with the photograph of a handsome young doctor, Mario, the son of her godfather, her romantically overheated imagination envisions Mario as a further link in a grandiose scheme designed by Providence to shape her future in some mysterious manner. Most important, the illusion that colors her vision gives rise to a misunderstood relationship. What she interprets as unmistakable symptoms of love at first sight—"he devors her with his eyes when their paths cross"—is in reality the fascination of the scientist with the emotional responses of a supremely unstable girl: "erotic hysteria" is the term that Mario applies to Ligia's condition. Yet when tragedy strikes—Ligia's radiant exterior conceals an advanced case of tuberculosis—the moment of crisis produces an astonishing metamorphosis in the young man. And that is what the novel is basically about: Mario's transition from unfeeling scientific enquiry to human understanding, which enables him to nurture her beautiful dream to the end. *Ligia Cruz* is a profound book, unique among the author's writings. Because of its psychological depth and human complexity it stands at the threshold of the final and most mature phase in Carrasquilla's literary career.

El Zarco has been called "Carrasquilla's most intense and laboriously shaped work." There are obvious similarities between this book and *Entrañas de niño*: both intermingle reminiscences with fictional material; both are built around a sensitive boy and the shaping of a personality and therefore merit the label bildungsroman. Yet *El Zarco* is by far the more complex work, not only because of the protagonist's distinctive physical and psychological traits but particularly because of the variety of impressions and sensations that crowd the susceptible imagination of "the blue-eyed boy," El Zarco, and bring forth his emotional responses. The boy's basic problem—he is a foundling of unknown parentage—is compounded by the irrational hostility of some members of his foster family. When one of them inflicts physical injury on the boy, his foster mother confronts the attackers in a memorable scene that leaves no doubt about her position in the controversy. In this final period of Carrasquilla's literary career, the psychological probing that was central to the author's narrative art is most organically integrated with regional ambience and detail.

La Marquesa de Yolombó is the culminating product of Carrasquilla's pen. Published in serial form in 1926, it did not appear as a book until 1928, when the author was seventy years old and confined to a wheelchair "like my hero *Dimitas Arias.*" The gestation of this important novel, as the author reveals in a letter written shortly before his death, spanned three decades and involved stimuli by one of his great-grandfathers as well as distinct nudgings from his maternal grandfather, who suggested the topic. Bárbara Caballero, although not beautiful, is an appealing woman whose pioneering feminist extravaganzas perplex, and even shock, male-dominated society; nicknamed "Perseverance," she is untiring in challenging male monopolies. Yet this born leader has one tragic flaw, a fanatical devotion to the mother country, Spain, and its monarch. That obsessive loyalty, with its deeply personal dimension, eventually overshadows all other concerns and brings about Bárbara's downfall at the hands of an unscrupulous impostor posing as a Spanish nobleman. Surrounding the heroine and the other principal characters, many of whom are based on the author's ancestors, is a cross section of society made up of peasants, miners, workers, and domestics. *La Marquesa de Yolombó* is the only historical novel among

Carrasquilla's writings, and he skillfully succeeds in capturing a piece of colonial history in all its throbbing vitality. Historical events in this case are filtered through the hopes and fears—and one all-embracing, disaster-breeding obsession—of an ordinary human being, within the context of everyday humble reality. The integration of characters, historical events, and regional milieu is successfully achieved.

The trilogy *Hace tiempos*, dictated to family members and friends while the author was entirely blind, is Carrasquilla's valedictory. Its initial volume, entitled *Por aguas y pedrejones* (Among Rivers and Rocks), was to bring him the Vergara y Vergara National Prize in 1936. The author reverts in his swan song to two favorite themes, a child's heart and mind, and the potential influence of a mentor. There is no comparison between, on the one hand, a playful sketch like "Simón el mago" and such related approaches to the theme as *Entrañas de niño* and *El Zarco*, and, on the other, *Hace tiempos*; there is an unmistakable evolution and an increasingly defined psychological focus and complexity in the latter. The *Memorias de Eloy Gamboa* (Memoirs of Eloy Gamboa), the subtitle of *Hace tiempos*, is a tribute to Antioquia's past and is the author's most mature set of recollections. Autobiography is intertwined with fiction, and a whole period is brought to life along with the factors that shape an individual personality. The three volumes focus in turn on the boy's moral, spiritual, and intellectual awakening. The first volume and the second, *Por cumbres y cañadas* (Amid Peaks and Ravines), continue the integration of narrative technique, psychological enquiry, and milieu found in *El Zarco* and, most successfully, *La Marquesa de Yolombó*. The third volume, *Del monte a la ciudad* (From the Mountain to the City), is anticlimactic, devoid of the structural unity and the human immediacy of the first two.

The *cuento* provided another potent release for Carrasquilla's creative talents. "Blanca" (1897) and "Rogelio" (1926) address the question of mysticism and its salutary potential in a shallow society that all too easily loses sight of the region "above the rooftops." Blanca's great obsession is the Virgin Mary, and the charming initial scene sets the mood for the events that follow. Blanca's healing ministry is cut short by her drowning as she loses her life in pursuit of a dream that has assumed obsessive proportions. Carrasquilla did not like the story, describing it as "pretty bad and insignificant" and deploring the fact that his temperament was not in tune with the delicacy of the subject matter. In returning to the same theme some thirty years later in "Rogelio," he must have felt more sure of his spiritual ground. No autocriticism of the story is extant; Carrasquilla, in dedicating the story to a friend, refers to it as "rugged in appearance, mystical in essence." The author's sympathetic understanding of a deeply personal religious experience is evident, as he pinpoints the decisive moment of conversion in the life of an eleven-year-old boy who triumphs over physical and spiritual handicaps and the most barren of environments. While Rogelio's crisis involves a genuine religious experience, "San Antoñito" (Little Saint Anthony, 1899) depicts a religious fraud, showing the hazards of mass hypnosis and the potential dangers of wishful thinking. The unsavory machinations of a young Antioqueño "Tartuff," which go undetected for two years, make for a perfect short story that holds the reader's interest until the unexpected denouement.

"Salve, Regina" (Hail, Regina), commissioned for a charity function in Medellín in 1903, displays some of the finest examples of Carrasquilla's narrative prose. The conflict between love and duty provides the theme and occasions the heroine's frustrating dilemma. Carrasquilla was so pleased with the story that he praised it as the only one among his works that appeared good to him.

The War of the Thousand Days is the grim setting for "A la plata." Longas' reluctant departure for the war and his return to a broken home capture the painful experience of many a conscript. The story's stark approach to reality is naturalistic; the accent is on the stench of the human garbage heap, where emotions are a low priority. The father's warped concept of honor gives the ending a grotesque twist and demonstrates how adhering to paternal authority may have unforeseen consequences.

Other *cuentos* define the impact of the single idea and of obsession in human relationships: "El rifle" (The Toy Gun, 1915), "La mata" (The Plant, 1915), and "Superhombre" (Superman, 1920). "El rifle" is one of the very few pieces by Carrasquilla that is set in Bogotá. The universal message is built around an anonymous donor, a youthful recipient, and a Christmas gift of small material value and overwhelming human significance. When Tista's stepmother, in an ill-tempered outburst, destroys the gun, life loses its meaning for the shoe-shine boy.

Similarly, "La Mata" is based on a humble object that redeems, at least temporarily, a wretched existence. The essence of María Engracia's melancholy story is as common as it is distressing. Having been abused by an unscrupulous Don Juan who overcame her small-town inexperience by sweet promises and promptly deserted her, the girl leads a squalid existence and is scorned by everyone. She acquires a shoot that grows into a plant and soon begins to bridge the gap that had set her apart from her surroundings. Human contact is restored when passersby stop to admire the plant, stimulating her urge to overcome her physical and spiritual isolation. The plant, like the toy gun, performs a life-giving function. When the unfeeling landlord (echoing the callous stepmother) destroys the plant, he snuffs out the mainspring of her wretched existence. In a merciful vision during her final delirium, María Engracia's plant, splendidly restored, ushers her into paradise.

Fraud and despotism are called into question in "Superhombre." Ceferino Guadalete is a spellbinder and the hypnosis of his oratory has distinct points of similarity to the spectacular skills of "San Antoñito." At another level, there are echoes of Agustín Alzate, whose glittering shell crumbles when the bully's authority is challenged, revealing the essential hollowness underneath. Carrasquilla is unimpressed with bullies and does not condone dictatorial abuses.

The most beloved of all of Carrasquilla's tales, "En la diestra de Dios Padre" (In the Right Hand of the Father, 1897) illustrates the author's affectionate concern with the colorful folklore of his region. It dates from the year that saw the publication of *Dimitas Arias*, "Blanca," and the essay "Herejías."

"En la diestra de Dios Padre" is another piece of which the author approves, though he describes it modestly as "a folklore that depicts our people." The theme is a traditional one: a poor man, Peralta, is granted five wishes to reward his selflessness, and he confounds his supernatural benefactors by the strange nature of his requests. When his card game with the devil nets Peralta an inflationary number of lost souls, along with the theological dilemma of how to cope with them, he avails himself of the counsel of Saint Theresa and Saint Thomas. Finally, there remains only one wish: one that particularly perplexes his visitors. But Peralta knows what he wants and in the closing lines of the *cuento,* one of the most frequently cited passages among Carrasquilla's writings, Peralta "grows tinier and tinier until he had turned into a three-inch Peralta and forthwith with the nimbleness that is given to the blessed, he lept into the world that the Father holds in His right hand. He made himself thoroughly at home and embraced the cross. There he remains for all eternity." Carrasquilla's narrative charm endows a time-honored folkloric theme with literary autonomy. The pronounced humor is particularly noteworthy when viewed in the context of the Latin American literary panorama that until quite recently has been known to "smile infrequently."

Chronicles, essays, and sketches of customs and manners make up the remainder of Carrasquilla's creative work: they are tied largely to the middle period in the author's career, when he wrote a newspaper column that required regular contributions on themes of regional interest. Literary theory and criticism prompted the essay "Herejías" as well as the two "Homilías," with the novel genre under review in the former and poetry scrutinized in the latter. He wrote only one poem and vowed never to repeat that exercise. His one and only attempt at drama proved abortive when, according to his confession, the five characters in the play turned out to be "five Carrasquillas."

Narrative fiction, then, remained his almost exclusive domain. His literary and human commitment resulted in a corpus of novels and *cuentos* that, with very few exceptions, focus on individuals. Taking into consideration that the trilogy is subtitled *Memorias de Eloy Gamboa,* only two of his major works carry titles that do not refer explicitly to female or child characters: *Frutos de mi tierra* and *El padre Casafús.*

Carrasquilla's pages breathe autobiography. In noting that "recordar es vivir" ("to remember is to live"), he acknowledged the organic bond that ties his writings to his life and circumstance. His charac-

ters, both principal and secondary, bring a picturesque region to life. His perceptive probing into their hopes and fears, not to mention their single ideas and obsessions, endowed them with universality. Yet the author made it clear, in one of his theoretical asides, that "ideas belong to everyone . . . only the expression of those ideas is an individual's very own" (which inevitably brings to mind the often cited formula "le style c'est l'homme"). The application of this adage to Carrasquilla's unique style shows a mode of expression that fuses harmoniously the literary and the popular. His narrative wealth and mastery of linguistic resources caused the distinguished Spanish literary historian Julio Cejador y Frauca to exclaim in wonderment: "As far as Tomás Carrasquilla's language is concerned, any praise is inadequate. . . . he is the most authentic and popular among the Castilian writers of the nineteenth century."

Recognition was slow in coming to this master of Colombian prose fiction. Following an initial period of neglect, there has been, since the 1950's, a renewed interest in his writing, the extent of which is suggested by two distinguished pioneers in the teaching of Hispanic American literature in the United States. Federico de Onís was unequivocal in exalting Carrasquilla in 1952 as a "writer . . . of unique worth" and a "brilliant precursor, unsurpassed, of American literature subsequent to *modernismo.*" Arturo Torres Rioseco voiced his belief in 1965 that "the name of the Colombian novelist is growing and soon his fame will be universal in our tongue."

SELECTED BIBLIOGRAPHY

First Editions

Novels

Frutos de mi tierra. Bogotá, 1896.
Grandeza. Medellín, Colombia, 1910.
El padre Casafús. Medellín, Colombia, 1914.
Entrañas de niño. Medellín, Colombia, 1914.
El Zarco. Bogotá, 1925.
Ligia Cruz; Rogelio. Bogotá, 1926.
La Marquesa de Yolombó. Medellín, Colombia, 1928.

Hace tiempos: Memorias de Eloy Gamboa. 3 vols. Medellín, Colombia, 1935–1936.

Novelas. Bogotá, 1935.

Entrañas de niño. Salve, Regina. Bogotá, 1946.

Short Stories

Salve, Regina. Medellín, Colombia, 1903.

Dominicales. Medellín, Colombia, 1934.

De tejas arriba. Medellín, Colombia, 1936.

Cuentos de Tomás Carrasquilla. Medellín, Colombia, 1956.

Seis cuentos. With a prologue by Carlos García Prada. Mexico City, 1959.

Cuentos. Medellín, Colombia, 1964.

Cuentos. Medellín, Colombia, 1968.

Later Editions

Individual Editions

Frutos de mi tierra. Edited and with a study by Seymour Menton. Bogotá, 1972.

Grandeza. Medellín, Colombia, 1935.

La Marquesa de Yolombó. With a prologue by Rafael Maya. Buenos Aires, 1945.

La Marquesa de Yolombó. Buenos Aires, 1946.

La Marquesa de Yolombó. Buenos Aires, 1957.

La Marquesa de Yolombó. Bogotá, 1958.

La Marquesa de Yolombó. Bogotá, 1960.

La Marquesa de Yolombó. Medellín, Colombia, 1968.

La Marquesa de Yolombó. Critical edition by Kurt L. Levy. Bogotá, 1974.

Complete Works

Obras completas. With an introduction by Federico de Onís. Madrid, 1952.

Obras completas. Edición Primer Centenario. 2 vols. Medellín, 1958.

Biographical and Critical Studies

Arango Ferrer, Javier. *Dos horas de literatura colombiana.* Medellín, Colombia, 1963.

Bejarano Díaz, Horacio. "Tomás Carrasquilla: Novelista del pueblo antioqueño." *Universidad de Antioquia* 31/122:400–422 (1955).

Cadavid Restrepo, Tomás. "Tomás Carrasquilla." *Anuario de la Academia Colombiana* 8:487–503 (1940–1941).

Cadavid Uribe, Gonzalo. *Presencia del pueblo en Tomás Carrasquilla.* Medellín, Colombia, 1959.

Curcio Altamar, Antonio. *Evolución de la novela en Colombia.* Bogotá, 1957.

Englekirk, John E., and Gerald E. Wade. *Bibliografía de la novela colombiana.* Mexico City, 1950.

González, José Ignacio. "La novela y el cuento en Antioquia." In *El pueblo antioqueño.* Medellín, Colombia, 1942. Pp. 329–348.

Levy, Kurt L. *Tomás Carrasquilla.* Boston, 1980.

Maya, Rafael. *Los orígenes del modernismo en Colombia.* Bogotá, 1961.

Menton, Seymour. *La novela colombiana: Planetas y satélites.* Bogotá, 1978.

Ramos, Oscar Gerardo. *De Manuela a Macondo.* Bogotá, 1972.

Sanín Cano, Baldomero. *Letras colombianas.* Mexico City, 1944.

Sylvester, Nigel. *The "Homilies" and "Dominicales" of Tomás Carrasquilla.* Liverpool, 1970.

Torres Rioseco, Arturo. "Sobre Tomás Carrasquilla." In *La hebra en la aguja.* Mexico City, 1965. Pp. 113–115.

Wade, Gerald E. "An Introduction to the Colombian Novel." *Hispania* 30/4:467–483 (1947).

Manuel Gutiérrez Nájera

(1859–1895)

Ivan A. Schulman

Manuel Gutiérrez Nájera was a major nineteenth-century Mexican writer and a prime mover in the development of the innovative styles of writing associated with the modernist period of Latin American literature (1875–1925).

The modernist writers, from within an enclosed, interior world, produced works in which the vision of reality was both fragmented and subjective. As Gutiérrez Nájera put it in 1894, "Carlos [Díaz Dufoo] and I are the intimate friends and the incurable lovers of Beauty. We both feel fortunate in our lives because we have a home, and at home we have good people and good books to read" (*Obras* 1, 1959, pp. 533–534). From this protected world, centered around the reading of literature—principally French literature—Gutiérrez Nájera wrote poetry, essays, short stories, and *crónicas*, interrupted constantly by the implacable tyranny of newspaper and magazine deadlines.

Gutiérrez Nájera's biography is a recounting of trivialities. The writer, always sensitive but sentimental, embellished them with elegant flourishes of fantasies unfulfilled. He was a Parisian, wrote Max Henríquez Ureña, the historian of Hispanic modernism, yet he never visited Paris. He was a dreamer of exotic landscapes, of imaginary lives, and of unspoken dialogues, but he never traveled outside his native Mexico and hardly ever left Mexico City,

where he had been born on 22 December 1859. His subjective transmigrations to other realities were a compensation for the limitations of the prosaic life he lived. But escape, though imaginary, was not always easy, and sometimes he had second thoughts about evading his humdrum life through literature and about the exasperating demands of journalism, whose ball and chain he once said was an illness in which he and others of his coterie reveled.

Gutiérrez Nájera's father was a journalist, editor, poet, and dramatist who saw one of his works performed at Mexico City's National Theater in 1862. His mother, a devout Catholic, instilled in her young son a religious fervor; when it waned over the years, in an age of positivism, Gutiérrez Nájera experienced a dramatic crisis of values that threatened to undermine a life of serenity and "quiet desperation."

The young Gutiérrez Nájera taught himself to read and write. He occasionally took classes in French, math, Latin, and physics from private tutors. Some biographers have erroneously stated that he attended French schools, when in fact his intense interest in reading classic and contemporary writers was a self-generated habit, one that was formed early and that stood him in good stead in his later life as a journalist. His initiation in that profession came at the age of sixteen with an article signed "Rafael," one of Gutiérrez Nájera's numerous pseudonyms. The pen names that he used throughout his creative life were both picturesque and practical. Mr. Can-Can, Nemo, Omega, El Duque Job, XX, and Crysantema are only a few examples of the names he invented to shield the identity of a writer condemned, without respite, to earn his living by constant writing. The author's varied but methodical use of the pseudonyms allowed him to answer his economic needs by reusing and adapting texts, signing them with the name that suited the quality and the style of the prose.

E. K. Mapes has demonstrated that almost all of Gutiérrez Nájera's prose pieces appeared four or five times with minor variants, such as stylistic retouchings or major structural bridges that joined pieces of two previously separate works. The resultant prose pieces were similar in content to the originals, yet distinct enough in quality to stand on their own. More than fifteen hundred *crónicas* were produced in this fashion, penned with passion and compassion amid the hurried events of the writer's life. Luis G. Urbina, a contemporary colleague and literary figure, recalled Gutiérrez Nájera's public description of his creative process. He confessed to simply letting his imagination, aided by his memory, run unbridled through fields and forests of fantasy.

Gutiérrez Nájera's work is divided into three genres: verse, short stories, and *crónicas,* the latter constituting the largest corpus. The *crónica,* an intermediate prose genre, was derived from the French *chronique* and was cultivated extensively by Spanish-American writers of the modernist era.

The physical and emotional pivots of Gutiérrez Nájera's life were Mexico City and his domestic life. In Mexico City he was born, and there he lived his entire existence except for a brief residence in Querétaro, two political trips to Veracruz, a honeymoon in Michoacán, and occasional visits to the family *estancia* (farm) in the state of Puebla. He yearned to see foreign landscapes but never realized his dream.

Recordable events were few in his life. In 1888 he was appointed deputy to the national congress from Texcoco (Veracruz), a position that provided sufficient income to smooth the way for his marriage to Cecilia Maillefert. From that moment on, his wife, his two daughters (Cecilia and Margarita), his jour-

nalism, the magazine he founded (*La revista azul*), and the newspaper he directed (*El Partido Liberal*) formed the bulk of his existence. In 1895, the Associated Press of Mexico named him president, but he became ill and died on 3 February before he could occupy this post. "By dint of scribbling so much I'm beginning to hate the ink I use," he once wrote in a letter to José Martí. Life's exasperations and limitations created an overwhelming sense of tragedy in a "life without major biography," to use Carlos Gómez del Prado's characterization.

It has been traditional to consider Gutiérrez Nájera a major poet and to place less importance on his production in prose. As more and more of the prose reproduced on photographic plates years ago by E. K. Mapes is published, Gutiérrez Nájera's stature as a writer of prose continues to increase, as does his central role in the development of the styles of modernism. Spanish-American modernism was a revisionist period of style, its development intertwined with and driven by the early stages of Latin America's socioeconomic modernization. Its fin-de-siècle identity crises—both cultural and personal—were associated by Federico de Onís with contemporary Western symptoms of social malaise. Intuitional, subjective, antidoctrinaire, and countercultural statements on literature and life characterized the writing of this stage of Spanish-American literary history.

In Gutiérrez Nájera's works, representative theoretical modernist ideas are expressed in his insistence that his journal, the *Revista azul,* had no specific slant and moreover eschewed models of "archaic beauty"; it was, by way of contrast, "fundamentally modern" and searched for "expressions of modern [that is, new] life," in their most accentuated and "chromatic" forms.

Subservience to rhetoric and to classic models was abandoned by Gutiérrez Nájera and his peers. Writing no longer reflected life but became the very measure of life. Literature was no longer mimesis; it was reality itself, self-sufficient as well as individualistic and subjective. Poetry became an act of externalizing automatic, internalized sensations: "I don't write my verse; I express it within myself" (*Obras* 1, p. 277). Gutiérrez Nájera's poetry came not as a reflection from the increasingly materialistic world of a modernizing Latin American bourgeois society but from a separate spiritual universe of "poets and angels" whose utterances, he held, flickered but a moment "like fireflies" and then vanished.

An elegiac sense of frustration and pain was a constant in Gutiérrez Nájera's work; not surprisingly, in his theoretical writings he insisted that "suffering created art." His modernism is not entirely free of an ambivalent traditionalism, which he sometimes accepted, sometimes rejected. This duality is structurally and stylistically expressed in a spatially organized metaphorical system with a traditional idealistic typology—wings, stars, sky—and the chromatic equivalents of ethereal, pure, and noble values—white, blue, gold. Gutiérrez Nájera's ideal world was tied to an aesthetic/modern counterstatement to the materialistic world.

In examining the development of modern Hispanic literature and Gutiérrez Nájera's place in its evolution, M. P. González, B. G. Carter, and the present writer have demonstrated that with highly individualistic and often distinct concepts, Gutiérrez Nájera and the Cuban José Martí were the initiators of a revisionist prose. Both modernists, like the later Rubén Darío of Nicaragua, experimented first with prose rather than verse. Gutiérrez Nájera developed, from 1875 forward, a delicate, emotionally charged expression that Justo Sierra, his contemporary, described as full of grace (*gracia*). It was a prose fashioned of traditional imagery used in an innovative manner, chromatic metaphors, and literary impressionism; it incorporated French and English vocabulary into an expanded literary language, as well as foreign names and places, contributions from nineteenth-century Parisian boulevard culture, and an ambience described as escapist and European-centered. An alternative reading of Gutiérrez Nájera's texts shows a Francophilia that was in fact a Mexican elitist vision, oriented toward European and French forms of modern culture. "Today," wrote Gutiérrez Nájera in the *Revista azul* on 9 September 1894, "every artistic publication . . . must take its main source of provisions from France, because today in France artistic life is more intense than in any other country." At the same time, he recognized the importance of tradition. In addition, he felt that reading French literature helped break restrictive molds, but that Spanish, Greek, and Latin literature

ought not to be overlooked. His idea was that "we [Mexicans and Latin Americans] must show our individuality, but within our literary tradition."

The titles of Gutiérrez Nájera's early short story collections reflect the new forms of writing; they contain imaginative correlations and synaestheses that later become conventions: *Cuentos frágiles* (Fragile Stories, 1883), and *Cuentos color de humo* (Smoke-Colored Stories, 1898). Similarly entitled, in keeping with the new modernist style, are the several series of *crónicas*: *Crónicas color de rosa* (Rose-Colored Chronicles), *Crónicas color de lluvia* (Rain-Colored Chronicles), *Crónicas color de oro* (Golden Chronicles), *Crónicas de mil colors* (Myriad-Colored Chronicles). These series have served as sources for organizing later collections of the author's short prose. The process by which short stories are derived from *crónicas* is typical of the breakdown of traditional genre distinctions in modernist writing. A similar sense of deconstruction in the literary universe of these short narratives is evident not merely from the adjectives in the titles—*fragile* stories, *smoke-colored* stories—but in the narrator's reality and the language of the dialogues.

In the best-known short stories—"La mañana de San Juan" (The Morning of St. John's Day), "La novela del tranvía" (The Novel in the Streetcar), "Los amores del cometa" (The Loves of the Comet), "Historia de un peso falso" (History of a False Peso), and "Juan el organista" (John the Organist)—there is a prevailing sense of melancholy born of a tragic view of life that the contrasting notes of joviality never succeed in masking. In these short stories, the unfulfilled lives of women and children create a highly charged, compassionate sense of identification in the reader that has been described as sentimental in the romantic tradition. But Gutiérrez Nájera's concern with the unprotected, abandoned, sick, unhappy, and luckless is more than a literary convention; it is a sincerely expressed statement consistent with a transitional writer's response to a modernizing society that has trapped vulnerable urban dwellers in an inextricable web of tragic circumstances. The patterns of antithesis, life-death, and joy-tragedy in an uncentered, unhinged social structure are characteristic (for example, the death of Bebé indoors in "La balada de año nuevo" [The Ballad of the New Year], amid the celebration in the streets). At times, the narrators of the short stories dream of an ideal world, a "rose-colored limbo," as in "La odisea de Madame Théo" (Madame Théo's Odyssey):

> Limbo is a rose-colored land very distant from earth. There are only children and flowers there. . . . In this happy land there is no legislative chamber, no government, no municipality. . . . No pedestrian is robbed of his watch, because there are no watches. . . . Even the wine is pure. . . . Neither children nor birds have invented gunpowder, and the river waters are as blue as the eyes of the angels and the tiny leaves of the forget-me-nots.
>
> (*Cuentos completos y otras narraciones*, p. 179)

The diminutive, decorative, sentimental qualities of Gutiérrez Nájera's narrative are also evident in his poetry. His search for a sheltered, alternative, romantic, and often idealized reality has been characterized as an illustration of the modernists' search for evasion. However, more than escaping, Gutiérrez Nájera and his contemporaries were empowering a separate reality that can be seen as the antithesis of and the negation of a materialistic, modernizing reality that engulfed them and created their anguish.

Their material world was more often than not seen with distorted vision (for example, the "rose-colored limbo"). In Gutiérrez Nájera's *crónicas*, the criticism is tempered with good-natured humor; undoubtedly, the writer feared the consequences of blatant antagonism under Porfirio Díaz' dictatorship. In describing Mexican culture in this period of political repression, material development, and foreign influences, Gutiérrez Nájera expressed admiration for European culture. But he also was aware of the limits of a model based on a "prostituted Europe" whose decadence he rejected ("El arte y el materialismo" [Art and Materialism]) in favor of "hymns to noble sentiments of the human heart" (*Obras* 1, p. 63).

His *crónicas* are too numerous and varied in scope to be characterized succinctly. They deal with art, literature, cultural problems, national identity, theatrical performances, political and social questions (especially his "Plato del día" [Special of the Day]). His vision was broad; his compassion for those who suffered was consuming. He was impatient with violence, aggression, and injustice, although his protests against them were tempered with humor and geniality. Many of the *crónicas* are expressed in a relatively terse, uncomplicated style. Others are difficult to separate from the "literary" style of the short stories, rich in imagery, in uncommon syntactic structures, in chromatic and impressionistic passages. Their accessibility is complicated by their dispersal. Of the many collected by Mapes and held and published later by Carter, a significant number, still unpublished, are in the archives of the Institute of Hispanic Studies at Texas Tech University. Those published are in *Escritos inéditos de sabor satírico: "Plato del día"* (1972), *Obras 1: Crítica literaria* (1959), *Obras 3: Crónicas y artículos sobre teatro 1* (1974), and in the first editions of Gutiérrez Nájera's prose.

Gutiérrez Nájera's verse is more easily available and certainly more widely read and cited than his innovative, modern prose. His poetry is equally significant in the development of a Spanish-American modernist discourse. Like his prose, his verse is tied to romanticism, conceptually and emotionally. At the same time, its stylistic and metric experimentations, its existential anguish, and its alternative, subjective realities have created for it a lasting place in the evolution of early modernist literature. In verse as in prose, French influence is evident, especially from Théophile Gautier, Alfred de Musset, Theodore de Banville, and Catulle Mendès, sufficiently so that Justo Sierra remarked that Gutiérrez Nájera wrote "French thought in Spanish verses." But if one reads the texts and their intertexts carefully, even in "La duquesa Job" ("The Duchess Job"), considered the most "French" of Gutiérrez Nájera's poems, the "French" elements are tied to an expression of Franco-Mexican culture, the legacy of Maximilian and Carlota's imperial regime and the elitist, boulevard, "Parisian" ambience in Mexico during the second half of the nineteenth century.

Pain, suffering, and a deeply felt existential anguish are present everywhere in Gutiérrez Nájera's verse. These constants are personified in "Mis enlutadas" (In Mourning), in which the poet accepts torment, actually inviting its presence and philosophizing on it as a basic element of existence. Life's agonies are compensated for in dreams, in the remembrance of things past, in moments of abandon, love, and passion. Death, in the classic Hispanic tradition, is the leveler that eases us from a life of affliction. Stoicism also makes life bearable, as in "Pax animae" (Peace of the Soul, translated as "Pax Animae"):

> ¡y ve, poeta, con desdén supremo
> todas las injusticias de la vida!
> (*Poesías completas* 2, p. 223)

> Poet, look with supreme disdain
> upon all life's injustices.

Life is short, and like Pierre de Ronsard in his sonnets to Helen, the poet suggests that we

> Corta las flores, mientra haya flores,
> perdona las espinas a las rosas . . .
> ¡También se van y vuelan los dolores
> como turbas de negras mariposas!
> (p. 227)

> Gather flowers, while there are flowers,
> forgive the roses their spines . . .
> Pain also disappears and takes flight
> like bands of black butterflies.

The antithesis of the black butterflies is the exploration of the realities of white in "De blanco" (On White), which has been linked to Gautier's "Symphonie en blanc majeur" (Symphony in White Major) and a later poem by Darío that is a composition in gray. The three poems display a related concern with the crossover of the arts and the use of their separate resources in the modernist's construction of a new literary language and style. Gutiérrez Nájera's poem is a paean to all that is ethereal, virginal, ideal:

> ¿Qué cosa más blanca que cándido lirio?
> ¿Qué cosa más pura que místico cirio?
> ¿Qué cosa más casta que tierno azahar?
> ¿Qué cosa más virgen que leve neblino?
> ¿Qué cosa más santa que el ara divina de gótico altar?
> (p. 167)

What is whiter than the lilies' immaculate white?
What is purer than tapers with mystical light?
What more virginal than mist as it drifts soft and fine?

What more chaste than the blossoms that orange-trees wear?
What more holy than stones on the altars that bear the White Host, food divine?

The tension between reality and desire, between material and ideal, does not simply course beneath the surface of Gutiérrez Nájera's poetic texts. The poet himself was conscious of creative limits, which often led to a failure to forcefully express the inspiration he felt. In "Non omnis moriar" (I Shall Not Perish Altogether), he speaks of "unknown tears" and the deceptions of creation:

> Era triste, vulgar lo que cantaba . . .
> ¡mas, qué canción tan bella la que oía!
> (p. 302)

> What he sang was sad, vulgar . . .
> but what a beautiful song he heard.

The search, the desire for language to express what was new in a metamorphosing, modernizing world was a conscious, ever-present act for Gutiérrez Nájera and his modernist contemporaries.

SELECTED BIBLIOGRAPHY

Editions

Poetry

Poesías. Mexico City, 1896.
Poesías. Paris, 1897.
Amor y lágrimas. San José, Costa Rica, 1912.
Sus mejores poesías. Madrid, 1916.
Poesías escogidas. Mexico City, 1918.
"Manuel Gutiérrez Nájera. Poesías inéditas recogidas de periódicos de México." Collected by E. K. Mapes. *Revista hispánica moderna* 8/4:334–355 (1942); 9/1–2:79–99 (1943).
Poesías completas. 2 vols. Mexico City, 1953.

Prose

Cuentos frágiles. Mexico City, 1883.
Obras de Manuel Gutiérrez Nájera 1: Prosa. Mexico City, 1898.

Obras de Manuel Gutiérrez Nájera 2: Prosa. Mexico City, 1903.

Hojas sueltas: Artículos diversos. Edited by Cecilia Maillefert. Mexico City, 1912.

Cuentos de Manuel Gutiérrez Nájera. Cultura (Mexico) 1/3 (1916).

Cuaresmas del Duque Job. Paris, 1922.

Cuentos, crónicas y ensayos. With a prologue and selection by Alfredo Maillefert. Mexico City, 1940.

Cuentos color de humo. Mexico City, 1942.

Obras inéditas de Gutiérrez Nájera: Crónicas de Puck. Collected and edited by E. K. Mapes. New York, 1943.

Cuaresmas del Duque Job y otros artículos. Selected and with a prologue by Francisco González Guerrero. Mexico City, 1946.

Cuentos completos y otras narraciones. Selected and with a prologue and notes by E. K. Mapes. Mexico City and Buenos Aires, 1958.

Obras 1: Crítica literaria. Researched and collected by E. K. Mapes. Edited and with notes by Ernesto Mejía Sánchez. Mexico City, 1959.

Escritos inéditos de sabor satírico: "Plato del día." Edited and with a prologue and notes by Boyd G. Carter and Mary Eileen Carter. Columbia, Mo., 1972.

Obras 3: Crónicas y artículos sobre teatro (1876–1880) 1. Edited by Alfonso Rangel Guerra. Mexico City, 1974.

Biographical and Critical Studies

Carter, Boyd G. *Manuel Gutiérrez Nájera: Estudio y escritos inéditos.* Mexico City, 1956.

———. *En torno a Gutiérrez Nájera y las letras mexicanas del siglo XIX.* Mexico City, 1960.

———. "Gutiérrez Nájera y Martí como iniciadores del modernismo." *Revista iberoamericana* 28/54:295–310 (1962).

———. "Manuel Gutiérrez Nájera en Hispanoamérica." *Revista de bellas artes* 1:81–85 (1965).

———. "Manuel Gutiérrez Nájera, primer teorizante del modernismo." *Sembradores de amistad* 212:18–21 (1969).

———. "Manuel Gutiérrez Nájera y el arte." In *Del arte: Homenaje a Justino Fernández.* Mexico City, 1977. Pp. 135–145.

Castagnaro, R. Antonio. "Bécquer and Gutiérrez Nájera—Some Literary Similarities." *Hispania* 27/2:160–163 (1944).

Contreras García, Irma. *Indagaciones sobre Gutiérrez Nájera* Mexico City, 1957.

———. "Apuntes para una bio-bibliografía." *Boletín de la Biblioteca Nacional* 1/1–2:32–38 (1962).

Crow, John A. "Some Aspects of Literary Style." *Hispania* 38/4:393–403 (1955).

Díaz Alejo, Ana Elena, and Ernesto Prado Velázquez. *Indice de la "Revista azul" (1894–1896).* Mexico City, 1968.

Durán, Manuel. "Gutiérrez Nájera y Teófilo Gautier." *Universidad de México* 8:6–7 (1954).

Gómez Baños, Virginia. *Bibliografía de Manuel Gutiérrez Nájera y cuatro cuentos inéditos.* Mexico City, 1958.

Gómez del Prado, Carlos. *Manuel Gutiérrez Nájera: Vida y obra.* Mexico City and East Lansing, Mich., 1964.

González Guerrero, Francisco. *Revisión de Gutiérrez Nájera.* Mexico City, 1955.

González, Manuel Pedro. "El conflicto religioso en la vida y en la poesía de Manuel Gutiérrez Nájera." *Estudios sobre literaturas hispanoamericanas: Glosas y semblanzas.* Mexico City, 1951. Pp. 121–132.

Gutiérrez Nájera, Margarita. *Reflejo: Biografía anecdótica de Manuel Gutiérrez Nájera.* Mexico City, 1960.

Kosloff, Alexander. "Técnica de los cuentos de Manuel Gutiérrez Nájera." *Revista iberoamericana* 19/38:333–357 (1954); 20/39:65–93 (1955).

Lonné, Enrique Francisco. "Lo nocturnal en la poesía de Manuel Gutiérrez Nájera". In *Estudios literarios.* La Plata, Argentina, 1966. Pp. 53–127.

Mapes, Erwin Kempton. "The First Published Writings of Manuel Gutiérrez Nájera." *Hispanic Review* 5/3:225–240 (1937).

———. "The Pseudonyms of Manuel Gutiérrez Nájera." *Publications of the Modern Language Association* 64/4:648–677 (1949).

———. "Manuel Gutiérrez Nájera: Seudónimos y bibliografía periodística." *Revista hispánica moderna* 19/1–4:132–204 (1953).

Martínez Peñalosa, Porfirio. "*La revista azul.* Notas para interpretación de un color." *Trivium* 9–10:11–16 (1949).

Mejía Sanchez, Ernesto. *Exposición documental de Manuel Gutiérrez Nájera: 1859–1959.* Mexico City, 1959.

Novo, Salvador. "Evocación de Gutiérrez Nájera." *Letras vencidas.* Universidad Veracruzana. *Cuadernos de la facultad de filosofía y letras* 10:33–65 (1962).

Oberhelman, Harley D. "*La revista azul* y el modernismo mexicano." *Journal of Interamerican Studies* 1/3:335–339 (1959).

———. "Manuel Gutiérrez Nájera, His 'Cronicas' in the *Revista azul.*" *Hispania* 43/1:49–55 (1960).

Pérez Trejo, Gustavo. "Bibliografía de Manuel Gutiérrez Nájera." *El libro y el pueblo* 12/3:129–136 (1934).

Puga y Acal, Manuel. *Los poetas mexicanos contemporáneos.* Mexico City, 1888.

Schulman, Ivan A. "Función y sentido del color en la poesía de Manuel Gutiérrez Nájera." *Revista hispánica moderna* 23/1:1–13 (1957).

———. "José Martí y Manuel Gutiérrez Nájera: Iniciadores del modernismo." *Revista iberoamericana* 30/57:9–50 (1964).

———. "El modernismo y la teoría literaria de Manuel Gutiérrez Nájera." In *Studies in Honor of M. J. Benardete: Essays in Hispanic and Sephardic Culture,* edited by Izaak A. Langnas and Barton Sholod. New York, 1965. Pp. 227–244.

Walker, Nell. *The Life and Works of Manuel Gutiérrez Nájera.* The University of Missouri Studies 2/2 (1927).

João da Cruz
e Sousa

(1861–1898)

Raymond S. Sayers

The son of a father who was a slave and a mother who was a freed slave, João da Cruz e Sousa not long after his death began to be recognized in his own land as an extraordinary poet and to receive the praise of foreign critics like Rubén Darío and Maurice Maeterlinck. Yet, in spite of his achievements in verse and prose, Cruz is remembered as a tragic figure. Following some brief happiness during his childhood, his life was a succession of battles against powerful odds: poverty, his wife's and his own illnesses, and lack of recognition by the reading public and many of the respected critics. The first black of pure African heritage (there had been many distinguished literary figures of mixed race), he suffered from the misunderstanding and hostility of other Brazilians of lighter color to the point that he came to think of himself as a stranger in his own land. His symbolist poetry did not help his situation. Symbolism was too abstract, too unusual, its music too new for it to be accepted by readers whose taste had been formed by the romantics and the Parnassians. Cruz was ahead of his time as an artist; he was very much part of his time as a black struggling to advance in a society that was not ready to accept the great changes brought about by the abolition of slavery in 1888 and the overthrow of the monarchy in 1889.

Cruz e Sousa was born on 24 November 1861 in Desterro (now Florianópolis), the capital of the southern state of Santa Catarina. As there were only a handful of blacks in this area, he stood out physically. He also stood out intellectually, for he spoke French, wrote for newspapers, gave speeches against slavery, and organized abolitionist clubs. A wealthy couple had reared him and sent him to an excellent school where he had studied languages, science, and mathematics, and where he had become the firm friend of students who were white. However, as he grew up he was forced to realize that there was no place for a black like him in the southern province, although if he had been of mixed race he would have been able to use his talent and his friendships to find a good position with the provincial government. In 1890 he left for Rio de Janeiro, hoping to become a journalist and to write poetry, but he was unable to find any sort of permanent employment until 1893, when he was made a minor clerk for the government railway.

He continued to write poetry, as he had been doing since his adolescence, but he did not begin to reach his potential as a poet until he became involved in the symbolist movement, which at the end of the 1880's had begun to spread into Brazil from France. In 1893 his first collection of symbolist poetry, *Broquéis* (Shields), was published. Reactions to the book were generally unfavorable, as they were to *Missal* (Missal), rhapsodic prose poems and essays published later that year. These were his only books to be published during his lifetime, with the exception of *Tropos e Fantasias* (Tropes and Fantasies, 1885), a small volume in which he had collaborated with a friend.

In 1893, in spite of his having found work, his difficulties increased after his marriage to a beautiful but unstable young black woman, Gavita Rosa Gonçalves, who was to bear him four children. His increasing poverty, the poor reception of his books, and his feeling that there was no way that he could struggle against social prejudice depressed him to the point that he began to avoid people and even to shun his friends. His hostility and anger increased during the few years of life that remained to him. Even though he had to depend increasingly on others for help and intellectual stimulus, he refused to flatter successful writers who might have been happy to aid him. In "Ritmos da Noite" (Night Rhythms) in *Missal*, he sneeringly referred to them as "imbeciles gilded with easy popularity." In "Emparedado" (Walled In) in *Evocações* (Evocations, 1898), he called them men for whom art is "a deceitful, tricky game to be played to gain influence and prestige." He realized that his mental instability was another reason for his being an outsider. Again in "Ritmos da Noite," he wrote about the disturbance that he felt after he passed a café frequented by men of letters: "Finally I enter my room, agitated, with a thousand ideas, impressions, and doubts in my head, and I reflect deeply. I have such mental monologues that I almost hallucinate."

Turned in upon himself, he sought refuge in the world of dreams and in the blackness of night, and read Arthur Schopenhauer in his despair. He died on 19 March 1898. Later that same year *Evocações*, the last collection that he had organized, was published. Still about half of his work remained to be collected and published. In 1900 *Faróis* (Beacons) and in 1905 *Últimos Sonetos* (Last Sonnets), both volumes of poetry, were brought out. *Obras Poéticas* (Poetic Works), edited by José Candido de Andrade Muricy, which was the first comprehensive collection of his verse, appeared in 1945. It contains many previously uncollected and even unprinted poems, among them the famous "Crianças Negras" (Black Children). The *Obra Completa* (Complete Work, 1961), also edited by Andrade Muricy, contains additional poems as well as much uncollected prose, to which the editor gives the titles of *Outras Evocações* (Other Evocations) and *Dispersos* (Miscellanea).

Cruz e Sousa produced his first great poetry as a symbolist, although he had begun as a romantic of the school of Antônio de Castro Alves, had tried his hand briefly at realism, and then had written some good poems under the aegis of the Parnassian school. During the 1880's, the years of the last abolitionist campaign in Brazil, he wrote antislavery poems and prose, in which he showed his preoccupation with social issues, a concern that he carried with him through the rest of his career. Influenced by the Parnassians, he developed a keen sense of formal values and the idea that the artist must consider himself a fine craftsman. Through his education, with its strong emphasis on science, the classical languages, and philosophy, he acquired a vast vocabulary as well as a skeptical view of the world. However, it was only when he read Charles Baudelaire and other symbolists that his poetry reached maturity. His writing then entered a mystical, highly abstract phase, in which his vision of earthly human experience was transcended by a striving for freedom of the spirit, release from material bonds, and absorption into nirvana. It was only through symbolism that he obtained the means for the expression of his desire for eternal truth, an expression that pervades his poetry.

Baudelaire sought to extend the limits of human perception and of the artist's subject matter. The symbolists stressed that the world of dreams and of the unconscious were worthy subjects of poetry, and broadened the definition of the beautiful to include organic corruption and decay. They accepted the existence of sin and perversion and made a cult of Satanism. Baudelaire's doctrine of *correspondances*—a theory of interrelation among the senses that allowed the poet to see perfumes as colors and colors as sounds—infinitely enlarged the scope of poetry. Cruz applied all that he learned from Baudelaire, including the understanding of what a poem in prose is, in his developing art and in his choice of subject matter.

Certain standard themes and subjects continued through the poems of the last seven years of his life (the poems appeared in different volumes, but their affinity is such that they may be treated as a whole). One is the note of social criticism as in "Crianças Negras" (Black Children) and "Consciência Tranqüila" (A Clear Conscience), which first appeared in *Obras Poéticas* and *Obra Completa* in 1945 and 1961 respectively. They cry out against the wretched treatment of black children and against that of black slaves. His themes also include the Baudelairean doctrine of the artist as humanity's prophet; the concept of ideal beauty; the existence of the poem; appreciation of the human body, as in "Braços" (Arms) in *Broquéis*; physical decay; and the anti-Christ, as in "Cristo de Bronze" (The Bronze Christ) in *Broquéis*. These poems project the poet's reactions subjectively and indirectly, but the greater number of Cruz's poems are the direct expression of his feelings. He conveys his sexual attraction toward women as well as his alienation from society, from other writers and men of his intellectual level because of his color, and from others of his own race because of their primitiveness. In fact, he communicates his alienation from himself, for in himself he sees the physical characteristics of the crowds of blacks whom he rejects. He writes about his desperate situation in life, his desire for death, and his inner confusion. He can be overwhelmingly, explicitly sensual, but he can also admire white chastity and black beauty. Sometimes he is morbid and even macabre, as in "Anho Branco" (The White Paschal Lamb) in *Evocações*, which is tinged with sexual sadism.

The symbols of which this abstract poetry is composed are also abstract in their representation of emotional states. Cruz used many and repeated symbols of whiteness: the pale moon, snow, fog, lilies, dead and dying white virgins, and many others. They represent a desire for cold, distant countries far from Brazil and a deep, unconscious desire to be free of his own blackness. Similarly his poetic vocabulary contains a surprising number of nouns and adjectives that relate to whiteness. With these literary tools, Cruz achieved startling effects:

> *Braços nervosos, brancas opulências,*
> *Brumais brancuras, fúlgidas brancuras,*
> *Alvuras castas, virginais alvuras,*
> *Lactescências das raras lactescências.*
>
> ("Braços")

Nervous arms, white opulences,
misty whitenesses, shining whitenesses,
chaste albescences, virginal albescences,
lactescences of rare lactescences.

The other color that appears with some—but less—frequency is black, the color of night, night that brings sleep and annihilation, nirvana. It was also the color of Cruz's own race, which, after his rejection by the whites, he felt was his only refuge. White was the color of white women and unattainable sexual experience. Black was the color of his sexual fulfillment. The basic statement of his sexual appreciation of the black woman is in "Núbia" (Nubia) in *Missal*, dating from the year in which he married Gavita. His is a fleshly love for a beautiful woman sculptured in Florentine bronze, a woman beneath whose skin flows warm blood. Núbia was blackness. Núbia was the Africa about which he knew nothing, a tortured continent that was the only refuge left for his tortured soul.

The poems in *Broquéis* and in *Missal* did not shock their first readers so much by their sexual reference and symbology, their sensuous language, and their irreverence and possible blasphemy—all of which were to be found in the writings of the naturalists—as by their frequent unintelligibility. Their abstruseness was due to the use of archaic and rare words, the novel syntax, and the new, powerful, hypnotic music that Cruz e Sousa employed. After the poet's death, Sílvio Romero, the greatest critic of the time, remarked that in vague, apparently disorganized phrases and by some unknown, interesting, and curious magic, Cruz e Sousa was able to draw the reader's thoughts to indefinite distances and to hypnotize the imagination. Other critics attributed his music to his African heritage. One said that his music came from his primitive ancestors and echoed the sounds of the African jungles. There is, however, nothing African about the magic of Cruz e Sousa; it is the art of a supreme verse technician who was instinctively a musician. He achieved his aural magic through repetition and selection of words, and his harmonies are not only musical but also associative.

The repetition includes that of word endings, rhyme, assonance, alliteration, and rhythmical beat, as well as that of words and phrases. All the poems are in rhyme, and almost without exception the rhymes are feminine, that is, formed by an accented syllable followed by one or two unaccented ones. Cruz e Sousa much preferred, especially for his sonnets, the ten-syllable line (Portuguese versification), which accents the tenth syllable and admits the addition of one or two unaccented syllables, producing an eleven-syllable line, the uneven number that was recommended by the French symbolists. He showed great ability in manipulating polysyllabic, unusual, and archaic words, as well as archaic forms of familiar words, and in avoiding the frequent use of monosyllables. These qualities are exemplified in a stanza from "Violões que Choram" (Weeping Guitars) from *Faróis*:

> Vozes veladas, veludosas vozes,
> Volúpias dos violões, vozes veladas,
> Vagam nos velhos vórtices velozes
> Dos ventos, vivas, vãs, vulcanizadas.

> Veiled voices, velvet-soft voices,
> Voluptuous violins, veiled voices,
> Wander wild, willful, volcanized
> In old swift whirling winds.

The verses move in sustained sweeps, frequently flowing from one line into another, without stopping, through three or four lines. This enjambment and the use of groups of polysyllabic words, as well as alliteration and other kinds of repetition, may be observed in the sonnet "Pés" (Feet), from *Faróis*

> Pés que o fluido magnético, secreto
> Da morte maculou de estranha e maga
> Sensação exquisita que propaga
> Um frio nalma, doloroso e inquieto.

> Feet that the magnetic, secret fluid
> Of death has maculated with a strange, magic
> And mysterious sensation diffusing
> A dolorous, restless cold in the soul.

No less magical are the effects achieved in the prose poems, many of them obtained by the same means. The most finely orchestrated is the tumultuous "Emparedado," in which the poet gives way to complete despair as he contemplates his life and the lives of his fellow blacks in Brazil and Africa. It is the last testament of this proud man, this symbolist who did not remain in an ivory tower but who fought against society's indifference to social problems, of this handsome black whose dreams of justice were never to be realized. At the end of this long piece, he hears a voice that tells him so. He is of the race of Ham, he is from Africa, the land of marvelous solitudes and spasms of despair, and he will never be able to pass through the portals of the great world of civilization, which has walled him into the prison of his race, piling stone upon stone.

> And more stones and more stones will be placed above the stones already heaped up, more stones and stones . . . Stones from these odious, ridiculous, and wearisome Civilizations and Societies . . . More stones and more stones! And the strange walls shall rise—long, black, terrifying! They shall rise, rise, rise, mute, silent, up to the Stars, leaving you forever, irremediably maddened and walled in within your Dream.

SELECTED BIBLIOGRAPHY

Editions

Tropos e Fantasias. Desterro, 1885. In collaboration with Virgílio Várzea.
Broquéis. Rio de Janeiro, 1893.
Missal. Rio de Janeiro, 1893.
Evocações. Rio de Janeiro, 1898.
Faróis. Edited by Nestor Vítor. Rio de Janeiro, 1900.
Últimos Sonetos. Edited by Nestor Vítor. Rio de Janeiro, 1905.

Collected Works

Cruz e Sousa: Obras Completas. Edited by Nestor Vítor. 2 vols. Rio de Janeiro, 1923–1924.
Cruz e Sousa: Obra Completa. Edited by José Candido de Andrade Muricy. Rio de Janeiro, 1961. An edition containing much prose and poetry that had not been published in the collection of 1923–1924. Includes the verse collected in *Obras Poéticas* (edited by Andrade Muricy, 1945) and additional poems and prose under the titles *Outras Evocações* and *Dispersos*.

Biographical and Critical Studies

Bastide, Roger. "Quatro Estudos Sobre Cruz e Sousa: 'A Nostalgia do Branco,' 'A Poesia Noturna de Cruz e Sousa,' 'Cruz e Sousa e Baudelaire,' 'O Lugar de Cruz e Sousa no Movimento Simbolista.'" In *Estudos Afro-Brasileiros*. São Paulo, 1973. Pp. 61–92.

Haberly, David T. "The Black Swan: João da Cruz e Sousa." In *Three Sad Races*. Cambridge, England, 1983. Pp. 99–122.

Magalhães Júnior, Raimundo. *Poesia e Vida de Cruz e Sousa*. 3rd ed., revised. Rio de Janeiro, 1975.

Muricy, José Candido de Andrade. *Para Conhecer Melhor Cruz e Sousa*. Rio de Janeiro, 1973.

Pauli, Evaldo. *Cruz e Sousa: Poeta e Pensador*. São Paulo, 1973.

Portella, Eduardo. *Nota Prévia a Cruz e Sousa*. Rio de Janeiro, 1961.

Sayers, Raymond. "The Black Poet in Brazil: The Case of João Cruz e Sousa." *Luso-Brazilian Review* 15 (supplementary issue):75–100 (1978).

Translations

The only translations, which are excellent, are contained in Haberly's essay, mentioned above. They are of four sonnets, part of a longer poem, and short prose selections.

Julián del Casal

(1863–1893)

Robert Jay Glickman

Julián del Casal was one of the principal initiators of the modernist movement, which brought widespread change to Spanish-American literature in the latter decades of the nineteenth century. At that time, change was coming quickly to every corner of the Western world and was difficult to govern. Even in Cuba, which was still politically bound to Spain, it was a trying age in which to live. "Wretched times! . . . age of turmoil and of pain," excalimed José Marti. "No one's faith is safe these days . . . No work is permanent . . . no road is constant . . . there's something like a breakup of the human mind . . . what once seemed noble now begins to be a crime. . . ." Such was the world of Julián del Casal.

Born in Havana on 7 November 1863, José Julián Herculano del Casal y de la Lastra was the third child of Julián del Casal of Santurce, Spain, and María del Carmen de la Lastra of San Marcos de Artemisa, Cuba, who had married in Havana in 1860. Doña Carmen died when Julián was five. The demise of his mother caused Casal intense grief and left a mark upon him all his life. In childhood, this abandonment caused him to feel guilty of some unspeakable sin. Later it inspired fears that he would be despoiled of everything he loved. Casal's father seems to have done little to brighten his son's outlook. He was a somber, sermonizing man, more inclined to reprove than to encourage and at odds with the spirit of modernity.

Casal received a diet of somber sermonizing, too, at the Real Colegio de Belén, where he studied from 29 September 1873 until 6 June 1879. His one-year stay at Havana University's Faculty of Law was much too short to neutralize the effects of this childhood education. Working as a clerk in the government's treasury department and publishing a series of articles on Havana Society in *La Habana Elegante* did not help much either. In the end, these experiences actually increased the darkness within his soul: when he made some indiscreet comments about Governor General Sabas Marín in the first of the "Sociedad de la Habana" (Havana Society) articles on 25 March 1888, not only did he lose favor with the sponsors of *La Habana Elegante*, but he lost his treasury job, as well. In order to put his troubles behind him, Casal sold a piece of property he had inherited and, in November 1888, went off to Spain.

After landing in Santander, Casal proceeded to Madrid, where he saw the sights, visited museums, and mingled with artists and writers. In a few weeks, his funds were gone and, in the words of his friend Enrique Hernández Miyares, he returned to Cuba "dejected, emaciated, with a new load of disappointments, and 'propertyless.'"

To help maintain himself after his trip to Spain, Casal worked briefly on two Havana newspapers: *La Discusión* and *El País*. Neither job was to his liking, a fact that readers easily sensed from the bitter tone of his articles. In order to release the public and himself from further anguish, he gave up first one position, then the other, and found a job so obscure that scarcely anyone would notice him. This is what Casal preferred. Although he had a bright and playful side that sought the company of others, he felt most comfortable in a world of shadow illumined by dreams of his own making.

Deep down, Casal was prone to self-abasement. In his own eyes, he was a poisonous flower, a living being who was dead inside. Betrothed to sadness and accompanied by discontent, he assiduously cultivated his ills, yet wished to escape them, like the nihilist Giacomo Leopardi, by "dissolving in the bosom of nothingness." Afflicted by what he described as his "neurosis," Casal experienced antithetical pulls on his mind and his emotions. Longing to be ardently religious, but unable to dispel the skepticism that chilled his soul; impulsive in his feelings, but immobilized by indecision, he went through life in great distress. For him, the world was filled with "hidden reefs," "steep slopes," "desolate fields," "gloomy spaces," and "stormy nights." It was a place where innocence was a constant target of attack, and disillusion was the promise every journey held. For this reason, suffering was man's surest expectation. If there was any safety to be had, it could come only through steadfast rejection of material temptations and heroic fidelity to one's dreams.

Casal's boredom with Cuba's tropical sameness kept him from finding solace in nature. His disgust with Havana's dirt and noise caused him to look to exotic lands where he could delight his imagination: Africa, Asia, the South Pacific, and halcyon regions of eternal snow. His apprehensiveness regarding women (he feared that they would leave, betray, or bore him) discouraged him from risking marriage or cohabitation and led him to give his skittish heart to "ideal ladies," like the singer Ina Lasson and the actress Jeanne Samary whom he could worship from afar. His hatred of crowds, and of the vulgar and self-satisfied, caused him to restrict his social life to a small group of Cuban friends and to correspond with an elite group who lived abroad. Among the latter were Luis G. Urbina, Manuel Gutiérrez Nájera, Rubén Darío, Enrique Gómez Carrillo, Pedro II of Brazil, Judith Gautier, Paul Verlaine, Joris-Karl Huysmans, and Gustave Moreau.

The letters of Moreau (one in Spanish, eleven in French) tell much about Casal. They reveal a man familiar with contemporary literature and art, and able to read and write in French, although imperfectly. They show a man devoting his life to beauty; filling his soul with appreciation of the works of a "divine master" in a distant land; proving he could be "the most faithful, loyal, and passionate admirer" of that exalted being; composing quickly with a graphic flair, yet representing himself only as "a sick dreamer of little worth." This tendency toward self-deprecation was produced, in part, by Casal's strict upbringing, which frowned on vanity and by the absence of a mother's love. His battle with tuberculosis also played a part. This complex malady left Casal so weak and dispirited that he wanted only "to be alone, hidden, without speaking."

Casal sought to escape life's rigors in several ways. One of the most pleasurable for him was reading. As a boy, he studied the classics, the writings of the church, and Spanish literature. Later, guided by the fashions of the day, he familiarized himself with works by modern authors of the Western world. Most of these were French.

Casal sought escape through writing, too. He published verse as early as February 1881. But it was only after his father's death in 1885 that he began to publish poems with regularity, his main outlets being *La Habana Elegante* and *El Fígaro*. By the spring of 1890, he had a fair portfolio of poems. Selecting forty-nine, he brought them out as a book entitled *Hojas al viento* (Leaves in the Wind).

This first collection, which went on sale around 5 May, reveals a lot about Casal in the early stage of his career. At that time, he was still very much a part of the world in which he lived. For example, "A los estudiantes" (To the Students), "Adiós al Brasil del emperador don Pedro II" (Emperor Pedro II's Farewell to Brazil), and "La perla" (The Pearl) show him responding to contemporary topics and events, while the ten poems tagged as "imitations" or "paraphrasings" show him touched by European authors popular in his day: Victor Hugo, François Coppée, Théophile Gautier, José Maria de Hérédia, Louis Bouilhet, Heinrich Heine, and Lorenzo Stecchetti. Despite all this, Casal's main focus was on himself: how deeply death had hurt him in his youth, his loss of religious faith, his lack of trust in women, and his hope that art would free him from his cares. As far as his poetic progress is concerned, *Hojas al viento* reveals that by the age of twenty-six Casal could write respectably in three modes: the romantic, the Parnassian, and the decadent. And the detailed changes that we find in successive printings of his poems disclose his deep commitment to the perfection of his art.

Buoyed by the publication of the book, Casal sent copies to acquaintances in Cuba and abroad; among the latter were Urbina, Gutiérrez Nájera, and Darío. Although Enrique José Varona, the dean of local critics, asserted that *Hojas al viento* contained elements quite foreign to Cuba's history and other critics perceived within it echoes of the European decadence, almost everyone, including Varona, applauded the book. It was a work that showed sincerity, imagination, originality of expression, and a facility for handling imagery and rhyme—a commendable start by a poet of promise.

The year 1890 was a financially difficult one for Casal, and a time of increasing problems with his health. In spite of this, he persisted in the cultivation of his art. More poems came out in periodicals, and as early as October 1890, it was clear that, in his mind, they were being grouped into categories, like paintings to be hung in different galleries of an art museum. The result was a collection consisting of an introduction in verse and five discrete parts: fifty-four poems in all.

The five poems of "Bocetos antiguos" (Antique Sketches) were based on pagan and Judeo-Christian themes. The twelve poems of "Mi museo ideal" (My Ideal Museum)—eleven of them sonnets—were inspired by the art of Gustave Moreau, a number of whose works Casal had seen in photographic reproduction. And the three sonnets of "Cromos españoles" (Spanish Prints) were word pictures of well-known Spanish types. These works were mainly of Parnassian cast. The following section, "Marfiles viejos" (Old Ivories), focused on Casal's most inti-

mate concerns. Its sixteen sonnets contained reflections on the pain of living, the fear of dying, and the need to vitalize his soul. "La gruta del ensueño" (The Grotto of Illusion) came last. It was a catchall for seventeen poems that, because of subject or form, did not fit in any other group.

By the spring of 1892, Casal was ready to send his work to press. Seeing himself as spiritually chilled by the winds of doubt that filled his age, emotionally chilled by "the glacial boredom of existence," physically chilled by his proximity to what he called "the winter without end," and convinced that his poetry, like precipitation on a winter's day, would not endure, he chose *Nieve* (Snow) as the title of his book. Although a variety of literary influences could be discerned within it, *Nieve* contained no direct imitations or paraphrasings of the work of other writers. Its poems were original creations by an author becoming more and more mature.

Nieve went on sale around 20 April 1892. As he had done with *Hojas al viento* Casal liberally distributed copies to acquaintances in Cuba and abroad. Darío saw the book in July when he visited Havana en route to Spain. Moreau, Huysmans, Hérédia, and Verlaine were sent copies through the mail. In the opinion of Verlaine, *Nieve* was "beautiful" in its composition, "but too even," too Parnassian. As for Casal, he was "a solid, fresh talent," though "poorly trained." If this "beautiful singer" would only steep himself in "contemporary mysticism," he might one day win a crown of laurel for his poems.

In contrast to Verlaine, critics in Havana, Varona among them, thought Casal had already immersed himself too deeply in decadentism. They reproached him for his gloom, his nihilism. They censured him for excessive enumeration, for repeating the same motifs with undesirable frequency, for using a strange vocabulary, for going beyond the bounds of decency, and for being more concerned with writing than with meaning. Encouraged by all this, Ciriaco Sos Gautreau, using the pseudonym César de Guanabacoa, wrote a critique designed to give Casal what he called the coup de grace. It came out in 1893 as a pamphlet entitled *Julián del Casal o un falsario de la rima* (Julián del Casal, or A Counterfeiter of Rhyme). This savage attack was offset by an event that took place in Mexico the same year. Favorably impressed by what

Casal had done, Urbina reprinted *Nieve* with his own flattering review of its contents as an afterword. Because the original edition was already out of print, Urbina's initiative helped bring Casal to a larger audience than might otherwise have been the case.

Casal began preparing his third book even before *Nieve* went to press. By the end of September 1893, he had composed some forty-five new poems. From these, he chose forty-one that seemed appropriate to issue as a collection. His illness, however, was becoming more acute, and, as he wrote Darío on 7 October, he doubted he would live to see the book in print. Casal's doubts were justified. He died on the night of 21 October 1893. Casal's demise made it necessary for his friend Hernández Miyares to complete production of the book. The resultant publication later that year differed from the two earlier volumes in that it contained prose as well as verse. Its dual nature was reflected in its title, *Bustos y rimas* (Busts and Rhymes). The Latin words "ARS RELIGIO NOSTRA" (Art Is Our Religion) were inscribed on its cover.

Rimas was more extreme than *Nieve* in terms of content. It opened with an epigraph from Baudelaire's "Bénédiction" and had many features inspired by the decadents: startling images, novel sound patterns, abnormal characters in shocking situations—"the necrophiliac king who embraces dead illusions . . . the courtesan who suffers from emotional anemia . . . the murderess who finds herself a prey to the sanguinary vulture of remorse . . . the hermit who seeks consolation in the caresses of a snake. . . ." (*The Poetry of Julián del Casal* 2, p. 298).

In his effort to set his spirit free, Casal introduced change quite readily in the content of his poems. Yet, with regard to form, he was not extremely radical. Although at times we find enneasyllables, decasyllables, Spanish alexandrines, monorhymed tercets and rondeaux, we discover that, in general, Casal preferred the more common forms of composition. For example, of the 157 poems now extant (144 in his books, plus 13 uncollected works), more than one-third are sonnets; the hendecasyllable predominates over all other meters, and no really novel stanza form exists. We discover, too, that the major expressive tools he used were rather standard for the time: accumulation, repetition, comparison, and many forms of contrast, such as chiaroscuro, spatial polarity, temporal opposition, and antithesis of concept and value.

If this is so, then why study Casal the poet? First, because he shows in miniature what Spanish-American modernism as a whole was doing in its initial stage: developing a new sensibility in reaction to the growing complexities of life; stressing cosmopolitanism above nationalism; turning toward a new religion, Art; capriciously combining diverse aesthetic modalities in order to express the new sensibility and ethic; exploiting a virtually limitless variety of inspirational sources; exploring such marginal realities as the worlds of neurosis, drugs, and fantasy; experimenting with form as well as content; and braving venomous attack for the sake of an ideal. Casal deserves attention, too, because among the works he wrought, there were some truly fine examples of the poet's craft. Because they were few in number, we might apply to him the words he used about Ricardo del Monte, another Cuban of his day: "In order to enter the temple of glory it is unnecessary to carry enormous trunks filled with every kind of object; it is enough to have a tiny chest of precious wood, artistically carved, that contains a few black diamonds."

Casal's prose is as fascinating as his verse. Its history begins in earnest in the spring of 1887 with his publication, in *La Habana Elegante*, of five of Baudelaire's *Petites poèmes en prose* in Spanish translation. Casal continued publishing translations until May 1890. In addition to pieces by Baudelaire, he wrote versions of stories by Catulle Mendès, Louis Ulbach, and Guy de Maupassant. This was the same period during which he was writing the paraphrasings and imitations in verse he subsequently brought out in *Hojas al viento*. After May 1890, as happened with his verse, he put aside translation and published only original pieces.

Among the themes touched on in the original compositions are love of people and of things; maternal abnegation; the demands of art; alcoholism and infidelity; vice and neuroticism; the torment of living and the complexities of dying. In these tales the focus is more on human essence than on events, more on person than on plot. The aim is to tantalize the reader who finds voluptuousness in suffering and stimulation in the bizarre. Unfortunately, Casal never published these stories in a book.

Another book he never published was to be entitled "La sociedad de la Habana." This overview was to deal with subjects like the upper classes, the demimonde, the arts, the press, and sports. Only the introduction, five chapters, and two additional segments ever went to press. The first chapter, which was devoted to Governor General Sabas Marín, caused Casal to lose his job with the government. A few months later, he made his trip to Spain and left the book unfinished.

After returning to Cuba, Casal worked on two Havana newspapers. He wrote more than one hundred articles for *La Discusión,* under the pseudonym Hernani, between November 1889 and July 1890. Then he moved to *El País* where, between October 1890 and February 1891, he penned columns entitled "Crónica semanal" (Week in Review) and "Conversaciones dominicales" (Sunday Conversations) under the pseudonym Alceste (from Molière's *Le misanthrope*). He touched on many subjects: music and art; the theater and the circus; parties, balls, and weddings; the latest women's fashions. He quoted foreign press reports and gossip from abroad. And within the trivia he embedded his ideas on things that really mattered: *fin-de-siècle* sadness, the noble "good old times," the sick new generation, the search for cures to illness, the heroism of suicide. Casal did not publish any of these pieces in a book.

The only prose compositions he did collect were the sketches he called *Bustos.* Although through the years he had written important essays on foreign luminaries like Manuel Reina, Francisco A. de Icaza, Darío, and Huysmans, here he profiled only Cubans: seven living, two recently deceased. This focus on his homeland may seem strange for a man who was neither a patriot nor a nationalist, yet it must be said, in fairness, that Casal had a keen concern for Cuba's progress. As he saw it, the key to that progress lay with people: people such as the nine "extraordinary beings" depicted in *Bustos*—people who embodied that superior quality of mind, heart, and spirit that would be the nation's most valuable resource as it embarked on its challenging journey into the future.

Like his poetry, Casal's prose is very instructive insofar as the cultural development of Spanish America is concerned. It allows us to see how rapidly people, goods, and creations of the human mind were moving through the region in the final decades of the nineteenth century. It helps reveal the role of periodicals in making such movement possible and in documenting it, as well. It brings to our attention some of the strains that the advent of unregulated change engendered in the individual ("a breakup of the human mind," Martí had said). It illustrates some of the major effects of intellectual free trade and artistic crossbreeding upon verbal communication. It allows us to be present as a new kind of elite was coming into being: sensitive, freedom-loving, ruggedly individualistic—the "brotherhood" of modernism, staunchly committed to their art.

SELECTED BIBLIOGRAPHY

First Editions

Hojas al viento. Havana, 1890.
Nieve. Havana, 1892.
Bustos y rimas. Havana, 1893.

Modern Editions

Poetry

Poesías completas. Edited with a preliminary essay and notes by Mario Cabrera Saqui. Havana, 1945.
Poesías. Edited by the Consejo Nacional de Cultura. Havana, 1963. Reproduces Cabrera Saqui's text, notes, and preliminary essay, and Ciriaco Sos Gautreau's *Julián del Casal o un falsario de la rima.* Contains other important materials.
The Poetry of Julián del Casal: A Critical Edition. Edited by Robert Jay Glickman. 3 vols. Gainesville, Fla., 1976–1978. All of Casal's poems, in Spanish, are contained in vol. 1; a detailed critical study of his poetry, in English, appears in vol. 2; and 14 computer-produced word indexes are found in vol. 3. The most reliable sourcebook for research into Casal's poetry. Essential for scholars doing linguistic and stylistic analysis.

Prose Narratives

Prosas. Edited by the Consejo Nacional de Cultura. 3 vols. Havana, 1963–1964. Indispensable for scholars wishing to do research on Casal's prose.

Prosa. Compilation, prologue, and notes by Emilio de Armas. 2 vols. Havana, 1979. More manageable and slightly more complete than the Consejo Nacional edition but contains fewer extensive notes.

Biographical and Critical Studies

Figueroa, Esperanza, ed. *Julián del Casal: Estudios críticos sobre su obra.* Miami, 1974. Contains articles by various critics on important aspects of Casal's life and works.

———. "Julián del Casal y Rubén Darío." *Revista bimestre cubana* 50/2:191–208 (1942).

———. "Julián del Casal y el modernismo." *Revista iberoamericana* 31/59:47–69 (1965).

Fontanella, Lee. "Parnassian Precept and a New Way of Seeing Casal's *Museo ideal.*" *Comparative Literature Studies* 7/4:450–479 (1970).

Geada de Prulletti, Rita. "El sentido de la evasión en la poesía de Julián del Casal." *Revista iberoamericana* 32/61:101–108 (1966).

Glickman, Robert Jay. "Julián del Casal: Letters to Gustave Moreau." *Revista hispánica moderna* 37/1–2:101–135 (1972–1973).

González, Aníbal. "Arqueologías: Orígenes de la crónica modernista." In *La crónica modernista hispanoamericana.* Madrid, 1983. Pp. 61–120 (see, especially, pp. 108–120).

Henríquez Ureña, Max. "Julián del Casal." In *Breve historia del modernismo.* 2nd ed. Mexico City and Buenos Aires, 1962. Pp. 115–134.

———. *Panorama histórico de la literatura cubana 2.* San Juan, 1963. Pp. 232–250 and *passim.*

Hernández Miyares, Julio E. "Los cuentos modernistas de Casal: Apuntes para un estudio." In *Festschrift José Cid Pérez,* edited by Alberto Guitérrez de la Solana and Elio Alba-Buffill. New York, 1981. Pp. 237–241.

Monner Sans, José Maria. *Julián del Casal y el modernismo hispanoamericano.* Mexico City, 1952. A valuable study of Casal's life, style, and role in modernism. Followed by an anthology of 112 poems and an appendix consisting of twelve pieces about Casal.

Pearsall, Priscilla. "A New Look at Duality in Julián del Casal." *Chasqui: Revista de literatura latinoamericana* 8/3:44–53 (1979).

———. "Julián del Casal: Modernity and the Art of the Urban Interior." In *An Art Alienated from Itself: Studies in Spanish American Modernism.* University, Mississippi, 1984. Pp. 11–39.

Porrata, Francisco E., and Jorge A. Santana, eds. *Antología comentada del modernismo.* Sacramento, Calif., 1974. Pp. 131–181. Reproduces some of Casal's best-known poems. The majority of these are critically analyzed. Each of the eight critics represented has a different approach to the study of poetry.

Portuondo, José Antonio. "Angustia y evasión de Julián del Casal." Reprinted from *Cuadernos de historia habanera* (1937), in *Prosas 1,* by Julián del Casal. Havana, 1963. Pp. 42–68.

Schulman, Ivan A. "Casal's Cuban Counterpoint of Art and Reality." *Latin American Research Review* 11/2:113–128 (1976).

———. "La *Salomé* de Julián del Casal y Guillermo Valencia: *Transposición y Werden.*" In *Estudios: Edición en homenaje a Guillermo Valencia, 1873–1973,* edited by Hernán Torres. Cali, Colombia, 1976. Pp. 67–84.

———. "Las estructuras polares en la obra de José Martí y Julián del Casal." *Revista iberoamericana* 29/56:251–282 (1963).

Vitier, Cintio. "Casal como antítesis de Martí." In *Lo cubano en la poesía.* Havana, 1958. Pp. 242–268. Also reproduced in *Prosas 1,* by Julián del Casal. Havana, 1963. Pp. 90–111.

Federico Gamboa

(1864–1939)

Seymour Menton

Mexico's most outstanding prerevolutionary novelist, Federico Gamboa has not yet received full recognition in Mexico, because of his participation in the counterrevolutionary government of Victoriano Huerta (1913–1914) and because of his opposition to the anticlerical policies of the postrevolutionary governments of the 1920's and 1930's. On the international literary front, his reputation has suffered because of his explicit adherence in his principal works to the now-unfashionable naturalistic school of Émile Zola. Nevertheless, his six novels, three plays, one collection of short stories, and several autobiographical volumes make him one of the most important Mexican literati of the late nineteenth and early twentieth centuries. His various posts in the diplomatic service during the last twenty years of the Porfirio Díaz dictatorship, his brief but highly significant tenure as Huerta's minister of foreign affairs (July–September 1913), and his opposition to the ensuing revolutionary governments make him a fascinating subject for a yet-to-be-written biography.

Gamboa's father, a general, had fought bravely against the invading Americans in 1847, had been governor of Jalisco, and in 1862, before Federico was born, had fought on the side of the invading French in support of the Mexican conservatives. On his mother's side, Federico's uncle was José María Iglesias, vice-president under Sebastián Lerdo de Tejada (1872–1876). At the age of sixteen, Federico spent one year in New York with his father, who was serving on the board of directors of the Tehuantepec railroad. Because of both his father's experiences with the Yankees and his own, Federico developed a fierce patriotism which showed up in several of his literary works as well as in his diplomatic career. He entered his country's foreign service in 1888 as second secretary to the legation in Guatemala. By March 1905 he was acting ambassador in Washington and three months later was appointed minister to Guatemala. In that capacity, Gamboa gained international recognition in 1906 for his staunch opposition to Leslie Combs, the United States delegate to the Central American Peace Conference held aboard the USS *Marblehead*. Gamboa objected to a clause in the treaty supported by Guatemalan dictator Manuel Estrada Cabrera involving the prompt delivery of political refugees, and refused to sign the treaty until Combs removed the clause. Between 1908 and 1910, Gamboa served as vice-minister of foreign affairs before being appointed minister to Belgium and Holland.

He sailed for Europe in January 1911, two months after the Mexican Revolution had broken out. The resignation of the eighty-one-year-old dictator Díaz in May 1911 left Gamboa in a precarious situation. Nonetheless, he remained in Brussels as President Francisco Madero's minister to Belgium until July 1913, when he was named minister of foreign affairs by the counterrevolutionary government of Huerta, who had seized power after having President Madero and Vice-president José María Pino Suárez shot. In August 1913, Gamboa once again stood fast against the United States, objecting to Woodrow Wilson's officious attempts to make peace among the warring revolutionary factions. When Huerta called for a presidential election for October 1913, the gullible Gamboa accepted the nomination of the Catholic party, not realizing that Huerta was planning to declare the election void on the grounds that no candidate had received a sufficiently large number of votes.

When, soon thereafter, the triumphant constitutional armies entered Mexico City, Gamboa was forced to flee. He spent a year in Galveston and San Antonio, Texas, earning his living as a translator before rejoining his wife and son in Cuba. He was not allowed to return to Mexico until late 1919. The final twenty years of his life were devoted to the teaching of literature. From 1923 on, he presided over the Academia Mexicana de la Lengua. Although his literary accomplishments were widely recognized in Mexico during the 1920's and 1930's, the anticlerical nature of the regimes of Álvaro Obregón, Plutarco Elís Calles, and Lázaro Cárdenas created a political climate that was hostile to Gamboa and prevented him from reentering public service.

Gamboa's literary fame rests primarily on the novel *Santa* (Santa, 1903), one of the best-known novels in all of Spanish America. In addition to its high sales record during the period 1903 to 1950, *Santa* has been the subject of three films, a popular ballad, and two theatrical productions. In the early 1930's, two streets of the formerly small village of Chimalistac, Santa's childhood home and by then an integral part of rapidly expanding Mexico City, were named after the novel's two main characters, Santa and Hipo.

Santa is considered by some to be Gamboa's masterpiece because in this work he achieves a perfect fusion of the four elements that constitute the core of all his novels and short stories: an erotic theme; a naturalistic method; a Mexican setting, replete with customs and social problems; and a rich, sophisticated style. Although *Santa* has often been labeled a Mexican version of Émile Zola's *Nana* (1880), it actually bears greater similarity to Edmond de Goncourt's *La fille Elisa* (Elisa the Prostitute, 1877), which Gamboa specifically mentions in the dedication of the novel, and to Leo Tolstoy's *Resurrection* (1899–1900), which Gamboa read, according to his published diary, at the time that he was writing *Santa*. Nevertheless, the book is by no means an imitation of its European predecessors. It surpasses them because of the author's thorough familiarity with and sincere compassion for his protagonist and his keen observation of details, which permitted him to recreate the world of the prostitutes in Mexico City.

In the prologue Gamboa traces the story of his protagonist from her birth to her autopsy. As in all of Gamboa's novels, love in both its physiological and psychological aspects is the principal motivating force. Santa, the beautiful eighteen-year-old pride of her working-class family, falls in love with a dashing young soldier and allows herself to be passionately wooed. After succumbing to his charms, she finds herself pregnant and, shortly thereafter, abandoned by her lover. A miscarriage reveals her disgrace to her family, and she has no alternative but to accept an invitation to move to a high-class Mexico City brothel. As she inevitably descends from the pinnacle of success to death by cancer, her relationships with different men are sufficiently individualized to make for real human-interest stories. At the height of her career, Santa falls in love with a jealous Spanish bullfighter. Their passionate love affair ends when he surprises her in the act of seducing his friend. Santa is miraculously saved when the backward thrust of the bullfighter's drawn dagger knocks over a small statue of the Virgin Mary. She later becomes the mistress of a wealthy married Mexican until he terminates the affair because of her growing alcoholism. Hipo, the blind piano player in the brothel, never stops idolizing her and takes her in after she is expelled from one of the lowest brothels in the city because of her terminal illness. The grateful Santa would like to satisfy Hipo's lust but pain prevents her from doing so. Other less-developed but nonetheless significant love relationships involve the sixteen-year-old student who takes the drunken Santa to a cheap hotel room and the lesbian prostitute who confuses the then relatively innocent Santa by kissing her body passionately.

As conceived by Zola, the naturalistic novel was like a chemical experiment. By combining certain hereditary and environmental factors, the "chemist"-author determines the inevitable "chemical reaction" and fate of his characters. In the case of Santa, Gamboa's lip service to heredity is totally gratuitous. He would have the reader believe that Santa quickly adjusted to the nocturnal life of Mexico City because of the vice of some unknown ancestor. On the other hand, his presentation of the environmental factors involved in Santa's fall are not only plausible but actually taken from many real-life cases. In addition to his deterministic philosophy, Gamboa reveals his naturalistic bent by including many detailed descriptions of the cruder, more sordid, and more morbid aspects of life. The various passages describing the brothels, the butcher shop, the factory, the police station, the hospital, the cemetery, and the stagnant water and garbage in the fountains and sewers are in the best Zolaesque tradition. Santa's first indications of puberty, her seduction by the officer, and her miscarriage, as well as some of her encounters in the brothels, are narrated with pseudoscientific objectivity and precision.

Despite its crude naturalism, *Santa* is an edifying, moral novel. The narrator does not blame his character for becoming a prostitute; she is the victim of circumstances. Although her career as a prostitute leads to her inevitable illness, alcoholism, and death, the narrator sympathizes with her as he does with the blind pianist. He places the blame for prostitution, illegitimate children, and the high incidence of blindness squarely on the shoulders of the men whose machismo demands that they have a mistress, frequent the brothels, or both.

The novel ends on a religious albeit incongruent note. *Santa* would be a better book if it ended with the description of the indifferent animals, birds, insects, and wildflowers that profane Santa's grave. However, in the final three pages, Gamboa injected his own reconversion to Catholicism by describing how the blind pianist unexpectedly prayed at Santa's grave; the prayer "soared up to the heavens, fading away into the glorious firmament." Nonetheless, these final three pages are inconsequential when weighed against the complete and artistic development of the entire work.

In addition to a rather thorough presentation of a prostitute's life, comparable but superior to Zola's *Nana*, Gamboa's *Santa* is enriched by a select number of typically Mexican scenes. Particularly outstanding is his description of the Grito de Dolores ceremony (a reenactment of Father Manuel Hidalgo's 1810 independence proclamation) on the eve of Mexican Independence Day in the capital's *zócalo*, or main square. In this as well as other descriptions, Gamboa distinguishes himself from other Mexican novelists of the period by his use of a more sophisticated style, including a more extensive vocabulary, and an artistic appeal to the auditory and visual senses. In this respect, he was not surpassed in Mexico until the publication in 1947 of Agustín Yáñez' *Al filo del agua* (*The Edge of the Storm*).

Santa represents the midpoint, as well as the peak, of Gamboa's novelistic career. His three preceding novels, *Apariencias* (Appearances 1892), *Suprema ley* (Supreme Law, 1896), and *Metamorfosis* (Metamorphosis, 1899), were written completely within the precepts of naturalism, while his final two, *Reconquista* (Reconquest, 1908) and *La llaga* (The Wound, 1913), reflect the rebirth of Gamboa's faith in religion and in work, and were modeled after Zola's *L'oeuvre* (*The Masterpiece*, 1886) and *Travail* (*Labor*, 1901), the latter reflecting Zola's own repudiation of naturalism. Of the first three novels, the best is clearly *Suprema ley*. In some respects, it even surpasses *Santa*. The story of a tubercular law clerk who allows his uncontrollable passion for a beautiful prisoner to ruin his family life is skillfully narrated, with emphasis on the psychological conflicts of the leading characters. The title refers to love, which is the basic theme and the dominant force in the lives of a variety of major and minor characters. Unlike Gamboa's other novels, *Suprema ley* was not patterned after or directly inspired by any foreign novel, which may be one of the explanations for its superior characterization. It is also the most Mexican of his novels in that it presents in a most convincing manner a relatively broad panorama of Mexico City's social classes in a variety of typical scenes. The family excursions on Sundays to Alameda Park, with the shrill whistle of the balloon vendors in the background; the trips to the Dolores Cemetery on the trolley car packed with lower-class people, with the view of the urban landscape from the *zócalo* to Chapultepec Park and beyond; and the very Mexican outdoor banquet that celebrates the judge's saint's day on the outskirts of the city—these are among the best *costumbrista* (local color) scenes in all of Mexican literature.

Although Gamboa's last novel, *La llaga*, may not be as original or spontaneous as *Suprema ley*, it does contain sharp criticism of some of the social and political abuses characteristic of the defunct Díaz regime. The vivid and detailed descriptions of the horrible conditions surrounding the prisoners on the island fortress of San Juan de Ulúa, although they resemble those of Dostoyevsky's *House of the Dead* (1862), emerged from Gamboa's own notes and photographs taken during his several visits to the malaria-stricken island opposite the port city of Veracruz.

Oddly enough, Gamboa's most outspoken denunciation of the Díaz dictatorship, directed against the semifeudal hacienda system, was a well-attended play, *La venganza de la gleba* (The Revenge of the Masses, premiered in 1905). Although the play is marred by the characters' excessively long speeches and its melodramatic ending, the contrast between the cavalier attitude of the absentee landowner and the human suffering of the peasants constituted a warning for the upper classes that reforms in the system were long overdue. Although Gamboa is unjustly considered a relatively minor figure in the history of the Mexican theater, this play, along with the little-known *La última campaña* (The Last Campaign, 1894) and *Entre hermanos* (Among Brothers, 1928), are important for having introduced contemporary Mexican problems and characters to the Mexico City theater, where, as late as the first decade of the twentieth century, audiences were still applauding *zarzuelas* (operettas) and translations of French farces.

Whereas the Latin American theater, like the novel, did not come into its own until the 1950's, the most important pioneers in both genres deserve better treatment than they have been accorded by students, professors, and critics. Gamboa was one of the very few professional novelists and playwrights in the late nineteenth and early twentieth centuries in Mexico and Latin America in general. It is likely that at some point his antirevolutionary stance of the 1920's will be forgotten and that his works will receive the recognition they deserve.

SELECTED BIBLIOGRAPHY

Editions

Prose Fiction

Del natural: Esbozos contemporáneos. Guatemala City, 1889.
Apariencias. Buenos Aires, 1892.
Suprema ley. Paris and Mexico City, 1896.
Metamorfosis. Mexico City, 1899.
Santa. Barcelona, 1903.
Reconquista. Mexico City and Barcelona, 1908.
La llaga. Mexico City, 1913.
"'El evangelista,' novela de costumbres mexicanas." *Pictorial Review* (New York) March–April 1922.

Plays

La última campaña. Guatemala City, 1900.
La venganza de la gleba. Guatemala City, 1907.
Entre hermanos. Mexico City, 1944.

Essays

La novela mexicana. Mexico City, 1914.

Memoirs

Impresiones y recuerdos. Buenos Aires, 1893.
Mi diario. Series 1, Part 1 (1892–1896). Guadalajara, Mexico, 1908.
_____. Series 1, Part 2 (1897–1900). Mexico City, 1910.
_____. Series 1, Part 3 (1901–1904). Mexico City, 1920.
_____. Series 2, Part 1 (1905–1908). Mexico City, 1934.
_____. Series 2, Part 2 (1909–1911). Mexico City, 1938.

Collected Works

Diario de Federico Gamboa (1892–1939). Mexico City, 1977.
Novelas. Mexico City, 1965. Contains *Apariencias, Suprema ley, Metamorfosis, Santa, Reconquista, La llaga, Del natural.*

FEDERICO GAMBOA

Biographical and Critical Studies

Carreño, Alberto María. "Federico Gamboa." *Abside* 2/12:18–38 (1938).

Fernández MacGregor, Génaro. "Federico Gamboa como diplomático." *Revista de literatura mexicana* 1:30–53 (1940).

González Peña, Carlos. "Las bodas de oro de un novelista." *Letras de México* 2/10:6–7 (1939).

Homenaje a don Federico Gamboa. Mexico City, 1940.

Hooker, Alexander C. *La novela de Federico Gamboa.* Madrid, 1917.

Jiménez Rueda, Julio. "Federico Gamboa." *Revista iberoamericana* 1/2:361–363 (1939).

Menton, Seymour. "Revalorización de Federico Gamboa." In *Memoria del sexto congreso del instituto internacional de literatura iberoamericana.* Mexico City, 1954. Pp. 205–211.

_____. "Influencias extranjeras en las obras de Federico Gamboa." *Armas y letras* 1/3:35–50 (1958).

_____. "Federico Gamboa: Un análisis estilístico." *Humanitas* 4:311–342 (1963).

Moore, Ernest R. "Bibliografía de obras y crítica de Federico Gamboa, 1864–1939." *Revista iberoamericana* 2/3:271–279 (1940).

Niess, Robert J. "Federico Gamboa: The Novelist as Autobiographer." *Hispanic Review* 13/4:346–351 (1945).

Rosenberg, S. L. M. "El naturalismo en Méjico y don Federico Gamboa." *Bulletin hispanique* 36/4:472–487 (1934).

Salado Álvarez, Victoriano. "*Suprema ley.*" In *De mi cosecha.* Guadalajara, Mexico, 1899. Pp. 69–74.

Urbina, Luis G. "Federico Gamboa." In *Hombres y libros.* Mexico City, 1923. Pp. 151–160.

José Asunción Silva

(1865–1896)

Lily Litvak

The author Miguel de Unamuno, in his prologue to the 1908 edition of *Poesías* by José Asunción Silva, commented,

> How is it possible to reduce to ideas a pure poetry, one in which the words taper, thin, and fade to the point of becoming cloudlike, whirled about by the wind of sentiment and forced to kneel before the sun, which at its height whitens them and in its setting covers them in its golden aura? . . . To comment on Silva is like explaining the movements of Beethoven's symphonies to an audience while the notes fall upon their ears. Each individual will find in them his own sorrows, desires, and feelings.

The words of Unamuno aptly characterize the writer Silva, one of the most accomplished modernist poets and one who, more than any other poet before him, sought the most quintessential form of poetry. Silva was one of the greatest craftsmen of the Spanish language, providing it with a previously unknown scale of subtle suggestion. He was, at the same time, as his friend Baldomero Sanín Cano expressed, "analytical and coldly scrutinizing." Because of those qualities, Silva was able to reveal his entire self within his works.

According to his birth certificate, José Asunción Silva was born in Bogotá, Colombia, on 26 November 1865. The oldest of five brothers, he came from a rich and aristocratic family. His parents were Ricardo Silva and Vicenta Gómez. Among his forefathers, descendants of noble Spanish lineage, were adventurers, soldiers, scholars, nuns, and preachers.

The boy was intellectually precocious, affected by an innate sadness and a special love for all that was beautiful. A withdrawn child, he spent long hours reading in the silent, lonely house in Bogotá. He studied in various private schools, first in the institute headed by Luis M. Cuervo and later in the one directed by the celebrated costumbristic writer Ricardo Carrasquilla. At age sixteen, he left his academic work and joined his father in the administration of the family store.

Bogotá was at that time a fairly self-contained city of some seventy thousand inhabitants. It was a pure-blooded town, gray, and far from the sea and the commercial shipping lanes. Silva himself described it in the following manner: "In Bogotá, everyone knows everyone else. The primary preoccupations are religion, the vices of a neighbor, and the arrival of mail from Europe" (Alberto Miramón, *José Asunción Silva*, 2nd ed., p. 42). The city, patriarchal and isolated, might also have been considered prudish and hypocritical. Between 1880 and 1900 the echoes of Nietzscheanism, positivism, and symbolism began to be felt in the poet's environment, both in his father's store and in the Silvas' home, a gathering place for discussions about literature, politics, and news from abroad.

The house of Don Ricardo provided the city of those years with a singular element of elegance and refinement. It was, as Alberto Miramón, Silva's biographer, tells us, "noteworthy not only for its social status and the unquestionable culture and beauty of the people who frequented it, but also for its almost exaggerated luxury and refinement, or, more aptly put, for its excessive pomp. There, the furniture, the tableware, everything was unusual and unique" (p. 45).

Silva was a cultured youth. He was self-taught and possessed startling powers of assimilation, which he dedicated almost fanatically to reading. Between the ages of ten and eighteen, the boy composed his first poems. He wrote some in the albums of the girls he courted and read others to his parents and colleagues.

These adolescent verses can be placed under the sign of the Spanish poet Gustavo Adolfo Bécquer, whose influence was always to be felt in the work of Silva. From Bécquer, Silva adopted vagueness, subtlety, and musical words, pregnant with suggestion, although Silva was never as sentimental or colorist as Bécquer.

Yet even in those early years, Silva wrote poems that display his originality. In "Crisálidas" (Cocoons) and "La voz de las cosas" (The Voice of Things), the future author of "Vejeces" (Old Things), "Los maderos de San Juan" (The Ships of San Juan), and the poem that he named simply "Nocturno" (Nocturne) is already apparent. The latter poem, which begins "Una noche . . ." (One night . . .), is considered by some to be the poet's finest achievement. Silva's early material reveals the infinite yearning, the love for the past, and the obsession with death that clearly haunt his later writings.

At the age of eighteen, nourished with romantic literature from France and Spain, Silva realized one of his great dreams: to visit Europe and, above all, Paris. He visited the City of Light with his heart deeply longing for beauty and perfection. He remained in Europe for two years, a Europe that was filled with uncertainties and doubts, with political and religious rumblings. During his stay Silva became

even more familiar with literature, developing his taste for Charles Baudelaire, Edgar Allan Poe, Alfred de Musset, Johann Gottfried von Herder, and the brothers Grimm. He began studies in the positivist theories of Hippolyte Taine, Auguste Comte, and Herbert Spencer. Friedrich Nietzsche and Gabriele D'Annunzio gave him a longing for the heroic, Paul Verlaine the love of soft music, and Pierre Loti the taste for the exotic and the bizarre. Arthur Schopenhauer intensified his sadness and dejection, and Marie Bashkirstev his yearning for the world beyond.

Silva returned to Colombia submerged in a deep melancholy. He had become a dandy, refined and delicate, with an extraordinary sensibility. The perfect aristocratic creole, alienated and unadapted to his world, he felt repelled by its sordid and vulgar materialism and nauseated by the growing bourgeoisie. Using a word from his contemporary society, he was a decadent. Silva possessed great physical beauty: an oval face, black hair, a sharp nose, thin lips, and long hands that were nervous and expressive. He dressed with extreme elegance, his fashion characterizing him as timid and distinguished. There are some who suppose that Silva suffered from psychological or sexual problems. It was said at times, in Bogotá, that he was crazy.

Upon Silva's return from Europe, the literary gatherings were resumed. Guests gathered in the Silvas' comfortable and luxuriously decorated library, drinking and talking while smoking Turkish cigarettes and discussing popular authors, all in an atmosphere of great refinement. Silva's dandyism continued throughout his life. Later, when he lived in Caracas, even in the midst of economic difficulty he would write, "You know that I am repulsed by cheap pleasures. So, not being able to live in *grand seigneur*, I live without pleasures" (Eduardo Camacho Guizado, *La poesía de José Asunción Silva*, pp. 16–17). In his last days he placed this order: "I ask you to buy the following and send it to me—in postal packages and wooden boxes or metal containers—twelve pounds of black tea, of the finest quality sold by the *United Kingdom Tea Co.*" (pp. 16–17).

His aestheticism is evident in his poetry and in his novel *De sobremesa* (Dinner Conversation, 1925), which display both extravagance and luxury. His works present domestic interiors covered with fine rugs ("Crepúsculo" [Twilight]), walls covered with tapestries ("Nocturno" that begins "Poeta, di paso . . ." ["Poet, in flight . . ."]), a candle placed in a crafted goblet ("El alma de la rosa" [The Soul of the Rose]). His poems, such as "Taller moderno" (A Modern Workshop), contain an abundance of artistic and exotic objects: "un busto del Dante . . . Del arabesco azul de un jarrón chino . . . una armadura . . . un viejo retablo" (a bust of Dante . . . a blue arabesque on a Chinese jar . . . a suit of armor . . . an old altar piece). Silva did not employ an abundance of metaphors and comparisons, but of those that he did use, the great majority derive from luxury, wealth, refinement, gold, opal, satin, silk, lace, and the like.

His contemptuous attitude concerning the bourgeoisie can be seen in a series of satiric poems in which he attacks with cynicism the middle-class ethic and, in some compositions, religion. He rejects materialism, which, according to him, opposes idealism. In some poems he expresses social protest. With contempt for things "vulgar," he shows the contrast between the world of the "dreamer" or poet, which is delicate, sensible, elegant, and beautiful, and the world of the bourgeoisie, which is vulgar and senseless.

Another important aspect of Silva's personality was his rejection of religion. Many critics believe that his lack of religious beliefs was a decisive factor in his premature demise. His lack of faith did not, however, preclude a preoccupation with the other world. In his eagerness to obtain absolutes, Silva tried to resolve his inner conflicts through studies in the occult and esoteric beliefs, clearly manifested in his poetry, above all in the "Nocturno" that begins "Una noche. . ."

In 1887, after his father died, Silva made an effort to manage the family business. It was useless, as he was not temperamentally suited to such work and as his father had left overwhelming debts; soon the situation became unbearable. In 1891 his sister Elvira died suddenly from angina pectoris. Her death was the heaviest blow the poet had ever experienced, and he became even more melancholy and withdrawn from life. In the painful solitude to which he banished himself, Silva found the genesis for his poem "Nocturno" which immortalized him and his sister.

In 1894 Silva was named secretary of the Colombian legation to Caracas. In the Venezuelan capital, he became an important and influential figure for the young editors of Cosmópolis magazine, the initiator of modernism. Between 1885 and 1894 he wrote his finest poetry. Juan Ramón Jiménez, when referring to the poem "Nocturno," affirms that "this nocturne, the seed of so many others, is without a doubt the most representative of the latest romanticism, and of the first modernism that was written, that lived, and that died in Spanish America" (Sur 10/79:14 [1941]). Silva was not, as so many claim, a precursor of modernism, but a real, conscious modernist, not only in his art but also in his life.

Silva returned to his homeland in 1895 on a French vessel, L'Amérique, which was shipwrecked on the Caribbean coast of Colombia, losing with it the best part of the poet's work. Back in Bogotá, he tried unsuccessfully to obtain a high-ranking diplomatic post. Suffering from an incurable melancholy, Silva attempted to establish a business in polychromatic cement tiles. The venture was a failure, and the poet sank into a decline. Bothered by insomnia, he consulted a doctor on 23 May 1896, and on some pretext requested that he indicate the exact location of the human heart. The doctor obliged, mapping out the pectoral region on Silva's chest and marking the location of the heart with a cross. That same day Silva's friends met in his house and spent the usual three or four hours in discussions. Rueda Vargas, one of those in attendance, relates: "It was close to midnight when, one by one, the ten who had gathered began to leave, while José lighted the path with a lamp in his hand" (Betty T. Osiek, José Asunción Silva, Twayne ed., pp. 46–47). The following day the poet was discovered dead in his room. He had put a bullet straight through his heart. No one heard the revolver discharge, since he had carefully closed the doors and windows. He left not even a note to explain the reasons for his suicide. The laws of Colombia did not allow the burial of Silva's body in the Catholic cemetery.

Silva's literary opus is of a reduced size since, like the protagonist of his novel De sobremesa, he preferred to read his compositions to friends rather than publish them, and only a small portion of his work was published. "Los cuentos negros" (Black Stories) was lost in the shipwreck of *L'Amérique.* "Los poemas de la carne" (Poems of Flesh) and the sonnets that he considered naming "Las almas muertas" (Dead Souls) suffered the same fate. Of those works that have been published, only a fraction appeared in newspapers and magazines during the author's lifetime. The majority of his work was published posthumously. His work consists of a book organized by the author, another containing poems that were partially reconstructed by his friends, a series of loose poems, a novel, and some prose essays that deal primarily with literary issues. There are several poems whose authorship is doubtful.

The first book, *El libro de versos* (The Book of Verses, 1928), according to the author was written between 1891 and 1896, although it did contain some poetry written as early as 1883. The book consists of some thirty compositions and constitutes a biographical unity, from the evocation of Silva's childhood to the anticipated confrontation with the funereal world beyond. Silva never intended to publish the second group of poems, entitled "Gotas amargas" (Bitter Drops). Some of the compositions appeared in newspapers and magazines in reconstructed form, published by the poet's friends several years after his death. The third group consists of poems published, usually singly in magazines and newspapers, during the author's lifetime; in collections of Silva's work, they carry the title "Versos varios" (Various Verses). *De sobremesa*, Silva's last work, is a novel written over a span of years, some portions dating from 1892 and others from 1895. A group of nonpoetic items published in newspapers and magazines is entitled "Prosas breves" (Short Prose).

In his first stage of writing, Silva adopted the rounded, sonorous verses of the Spanish romantic style and toiled to clarify the ideas, to make them transparent. Later he developed a liking for French poetry with light, flexible, suggestive verses and musically orchestrated words.

The fundamental theme of Silva's work is the turmoil caused by his present reality. Life and the place where he lives it are repugnant; conversely, the past and the world beyond this life are mysterious and attractive. The desire to transcend this existence carries him to the gates of a world beyond the immediate and the real. He is a poet whose vision is directed toward the past, yet who is condemned to a coarse,

rough, mediocre present, an existence that leaves him with a pessimistic, negative view of the future. He sees a past that is historic, sentimental, and, above all, aesthetic, a past that permits childhood mentalities and fantasies. The novel *De sobremesa,* which documents that flight from contemporary reality, is permeated with strangeness; the protagonist lives in an aesthetic world completely divorced from the American reality that surrounds him.

Another essential theme in Silva's work is death, the primary character in his poetic universe, the decomposing factor of all that might be perfect. The "Nocturno" that begins "Poet, in flight . . .," one of the most beautiful poems, consists of three strophes, each based on the memory of the woman loved; the poem ends with her death in the final strophe. In the work of Silva, death becomes an obsession, sometimes revealed in its most fleshless and naked form ("El recluta" [The Recruit], and "Psicopatía" [Mental Disorder]). At other times it is adorned with morose beauty ("Notas perdidas" [Lost Notes]). Death prevents the enjoyment of life and love, and its wounding proximity causes anguish ("Sonetos negros" [Black Sonnets]). A corollary of this theme is a contempt for life. In the poem "Lázaro" (Lazarus), the resurrected begins to curse his new life after only a short while. At times, the weariness that Silva feels for life precipitates his willing approach to the gates of death ("Día de difuntos" [All Souls' Day]).

Like other modernists, Silva decorates reality with luxury. This decoration occurs on one level through the metaphors derived from precious and magnificent materials, such as gold, silver, jewels, and fine cloths: "El contacto furtivo de tus labios de seda" (The furtive touch of your silken lips) in the "Nocturno" that begins "Poet, in flight . . ."; "mis sueños color de armiño" (my ermine-colored dreams) in "A tí" (To You). The author also achieves these effects through the exaltation of sensory refinement:

> *Vemos tras de la neblina,*
> *Como al través de un encaje*
> ("Poesía viva")

> We gaze beyond the mist
> as if through lace
> (Live Poetry)

Sobre las teclas vuela tu mano blanca,
Como una mariposa sobre una lila
("Nocturno" that begins "A
veces cuando en alta
noche . . .")

over the keys your white hand flies
like the butterfly over the lilac
("Nocturno" that begins
"At times when at the
height of night . . .")

. . . rara historia
que tiene oscuridad de telerañas
Són de laúd y suavidad de raso.
("Vejeces")

. . . a strange history
with the opacity of a spider web,
a tune of lute and silk.

Silva's poetic style can be characterized by his un-realistic attitude. In his world, reality appears illuminated by a dim light through which only a faint, distant glimpse may be obtained. It is shadowy poetry, as Unamuno aptly stated. "Silva sings like a bird, but a sad bird, one that feels death approaching with the setting of the sun." In "La voz de las cosas" he presents the elements of his poetic world—"frágiles cosas" (frail things), "pálido lirio que te deshojas" (you, a pallid lily shedding its petals), "rayo de luna" (a moon-ray), "pálidas cosas" (pallid things), "fantasmas grises" (gray ghosts), "sueños confusos" (confusing dreams), "ósculo triste" (sad kiss)—that is, things that are fragile, evanescent, thin, vague, subtle, and opposed to the immutable, permanent, solid, and strong.

With this heightened poetic sensibility, Silva strives to apprehend an exterior, physical world characterized by vagueness and imprecision. The passages are delineated in dim shadows, in the twilight, beneath the moon's rays (the "Nocturno" that begins "At times when at the height of night . . .," "Paisaje tropical" [Tropical Landscape], "Al pie de la estatua" [At the Foot of the Statue], "Muertos" [The Dead], and "Poesía viva"). One poem in particular, "Día de difuntos," reveals this obsession with darkness and shadows. The shadow that invades the physical world has symbolic connotations, alluding to the past and to death ("Los maderos de San Juan," "Vejeces") and

establishing a clear relationship between the physical, exterior world, and the interior world of the poet.

Silva's poetic vision is also rendered through the other senses. Whispers occupy a position of primary importance: statements are made in hushed voices and sighs, through vague sobs; the poetic universe is "llenos de murmullos" (full of whispers), mysterious and vague. The sense of smell is perceived with delicacy and imprecision, associated in the poem "Vejeces" with a revival of the past. A similar imprecision is used to express feelings: love and nostalgia are softly and vaguely felt ("Crepúsculo," "Luz de la luna" [Moonlight]).

In order to create the sensation of imprecision and vagueness, Silva employs several lexical and syntactic methods. One is the use of the adjective *medio* ("half") with an adjective or another verb.

Del arabesco azul de un jarrón chino,
Medio oculta el dibujo complicado.
("Taller moderno")

A blue arabesque on a Chinese jar
half-hides the intricate drawing

mirar allí, sombría,
medio perdida en la rizada gola
("La ventana")

to see there, somber
half-lost in the wavy molding
(The Window)

La divisa latina, presuntuosa,
Medio borrada por el líquen verde
("Vejeces")

The presumptuous Latin emblem
half-erased by the green lichen.

Another technique is the use of adverbial phrases, in which objects, events, and sensations are compared and related by means of the word *como* ("as" or "like").

Mi oído fatigado por vigilias y excesos
Sintió como a distancia los monótonos rezos!
("Nocturno" that begins "Poeta,
dipaso . . .")

excess and vigilant, my fatigued hearing
sensed, *as* at a distance, monotonous prayers.

He makes comparisons, but without precision, and with the intention of being more precise, leaves one of the terms in vagueness in order to make a more attenuated comparison: ". . . cruza por su espíritu *como* un temor extraño" (. . . crossing through his spirit *like* a strange fear), for example, in "Los maderos de San Juan."

Another theme in Silva's poetry is that of unreality, of fantasy and mystery. Not only is reality unraveled; it becomes totally denied. The poet abandons mundane life to enter a fantastic world. At times, a single word proves sufficient to transfer the verse from normality to unreality:

> *Por el aire tenebroso ignorada mano arroja*
> *Un oscuro velo opaco de letal melancolía.*
> ("Día de difuntos")

Through the gloomy air, an unknown hand throws an obscure, opaque veil of lethal melancholy.

It is the word *ignotas* ("unknown") that places the verse in the realm of unusual suggestion.

> *En unas distancias enormes e ignotas*
> *Que por los rincones oscuros suscita . . .*
> ("Crepúsculo")

In unknown, enormous distances
Which rise up in dark corners . . .

Extraños ("unusual"), *ignotas* ("unknown"), *oscuros* ("dark")—such words force us to depart from our daily sphere of reality.

In order to achieve this transposition, a necessary secret communication is established between the poet and things, through which the poet is able to discover the world that lies beyond appearances. Things speak to the poet with strange voices ("Vejeces"). The new, unreal world opens great panoramas normally only permitted in the realm of fantasy and the unconscious.

In his excellent essay on Silva, Andrés Holguín offers the following explanation:

Perhaps the feeling of mystery in Silva is the result of some frustrated, transcendent desire. It is the sensation of the skeptic who, unable to resolve his religious feelings, falls into the abyss of nothingness. I said before that anguish is the final result of logical failure. This is especially evident in Silva. Silva is profoundly learned, intellectually curious in terms of philosophy, religion, science, and art. But nothing offers him an explanation of the world. In that is his agony born. And there, where his speculative search ends, where his reason is broken, there the night is opened into the unknown and mysterious.

(*Revista de las Indias* 28/90:354 [1946])

Of the seventy-five poems that Silva wrote, not counting those of questionable origin, twenty-nine are based on a single metrical form: six in verses of eleven syllables, six in verses of eight syllables, five in *alejandrinos* (alexandrines), five in verses of nine syllables, four in verses of twelve syllables, two in verses of eight syllables, and one in verses of ten syllables. In other words, he used the traditional Spanish metrical forms. Thirty-two poems are composed using two or three metrical forms, based entirely on verses of eight and nine syllables.

In only three poems —"Luz de luna," "Dia de difuntos" and the "Nocturno" that begins "Una noche"—does the poet experiment with metrical novelties. In each one there is an internal rhythm that provides a constant base, yet each is composed using different meters of verse. In these works the author employs changes in meter and accent that break with the traditional rigid metrical forms, using combinations of eight, sixteen, fourteen, eleven, nine, twelve, six, and seven syllables. In these compositions Silva's stylistic restlessness may be detected; at times, the poet seems to be approaching free verse. The use of a single metrical form proved much too rigid in Silva's search for something more vague and undetermined.

Silva's vocabulary contains an abundance of verbs, most often used in the present tense to express palpitant emotion and action in progress. He also uses gerunds and participles to denote action in progress:

> *Va tornando en pavesas*
> *Tronos, imperios, pueblos y ciudades*
> ("Al pie de la estatua")

Burning into cinders
Thrones, empires, towns and cities

Likewise: "*Dándole* al aire aromado aliento" (*Giving* to the air aromatic breath) in the poem "Psicopatía," and "Y *mirando* dos rayos de la luna" (And *looking* at the moonlight) in "Luz de la luna." He frequently employs the preterit to denote a completed action.

The poet often uses adjectives in groups of two, one before and one after the noun: "la divisa latina presuntuosa" (the presumptuous Latin inscription), "viejas cartas de amor, ya desteñidas" (old love letters faded), "un oscuro velo opaco" (a dark opaque veil). The three words are read as an isolated unit, without a respiratory pause, forming an intense image.

Multiple adjectives are sometimes linked by the conjunction *y* ("and"): "sugestiones místicas *y* raras" (mystical *and* strange suggestions) in "Vejeces," "ramilletes negros *y* marchitos" (black *and* withered bouquets) in "Muertos," and "fragua negra *y* encendida" (black *and* red forge) in "Psicopatía." These condensed images eliminate the need for lengthy descriptions. Silva's adjectives often serve to displace the natural, syntactic progression of an idea, as in "y la *luz* de la luna limpia *brilla*" (and the *light* of the moon *shines* pure) and "de *barrotes* de hierro *colosales*" (of *colossal* iron *bars*) from "La ventana" or "*colores* de anticuada *miniatura*" (*colors* of antiquated *miniature*) from "Vejeces." In this way the author creates an original and surprising expression of his idea.

Silva's poetry is also characterized by the repetition of sounds, words, verses, and even strophes, reinforcing through this technique the impressions that he wishes to provoke. In "Los maderos de San Juan," for example, repetition is used in two ways: at the beginning of the poem in the children's poetry, with its play of repeated sounds, and later in the verses distributed among the three strophes. The accumulation of repetitions and alliterations of sounds causes the poem to move slowly, to unfold with a sad, melancholy moroseness.

Silva frequently overlaps verses. The pauses that normally would fall at the end of a verse are eliminated by the syntax of the phrase. As a result, the syntactic pause is not enforced by the rhythm, as in ". . . adivina / El porvenir de luchas y horrores" (. . . guess / the future of fights and horrors) in "Al

pie de la estatua" or ". . . iluminaba / El paso de la audaz locomotora" (. . . illuminating / the passage of the daring locomotive) in "Obra humana" (Human Work).

Possibly Silva's most significant work is his poem "Nocturno." The crowning jewel of this opus, it is a poem constructed as a concert in vowels, with accents that enhance the words and sounds they touch, as in the line "Por los cielos azulosos, infinitos y profundos esparcía su luz blanca" (Through the infinite, and profound azure skies, its white light spreading). The line begins with the predominance of the *o* sound, followed by a section in *i* that alternates with *u*, and finishes with the final double *a*.

Alliterations abound: "Una noche toda llena de perfumes de murmullos y de músicas de alas" (A night wholly filled with sounds, perfumes, and music of wings). Most important is the placement of accents, which often produces special effects, as in the following verse, in which three grouped words are accented on the antepenult: "en que ardían en la sombra nupcial y húmeda, las luciérnagas fantásticas" (in which fantastic fireflies burn in the nuptial and humid shadow). The effect of the accents is a seeming desire to be identified with the flashing of the insects.

A particular effect is achieved by those verses that are linked by a peculiar rhythmic phenomenon. At the end of each verse, points of suspense are placed to maintain a vagueness that prevents rapid reading. One critic has called it an ideal overlapping reached through diverse techniques. Some of these are syntactic; the verses are full of parenthesis, making them appear static. The words of the first verse, "una noche . . ." (one night . . .) are repeated at the beginning of the second and the third. In the second a verse is begun that does not continue; its progress is halted by means of parenthetical phrases and appositions.

The punctuation of the poem consists entirely of commas; there are no periods. At the end of each verse, one expects the continuation of the idea. The effect is that no single verse ends in itself but continues on into the next. Also contributing to this effect is the tetrasyllabic accentual base of the poem, in spite of the fact that the meter is arbitrary. The accenting produces for the ear an ideal regularity, one that foreshadows rhythmic development. The arbitrary variation of the verse's length clashes with this ideal rhythm, creating tension. Phonetic elements contribute to the development of sensations. The assonance of *a* sounds echoes in the even verses, as the sound is repeated.

Exceptional poetic possibilities are achieved through images of mysterious sounds, perfumes, and the music of wings, illuminated by intermittent fireflies and the moon's pallid light. In this unreal situation, the central action of the poem takes place: two shadows projected by the moon unite in a nuptial embrace. It is not a closeness of actual bodies, but rather of shadows, thin and evanescent, that in their embrace open this world to the world beyond.

The novel *De sobremesa* has been, until now, unjustly ignored by the critics. A characteristic modernist novel, it almost completely lacks a plot and centers exclusively on the thoughts of the protagonist, an anguished aesthete and a model of the modernist hero. José Fernández is neurotic, languid, superrefined, the classic decadent of the turn of the century.

The subject of the novel is simple. A wealthy Latin American writer gathers together in his luxurious and exotic home a group of his friends, requesting that they review the manuscript of his new work, one in which he has solved the mysteries of life. There exist in *De sobremesa* several incidents: the death of the writer's grandmother, a scene in which he stabs his lover, and his encounter with a mysterious young woman with a pre-Raphaelite face, with whom he falls passionately in love. The desperate search for this ideal lover completes the thematic development.

What stands out in the novel is the intensity of emotion provoked by the external events. One sees in these pages the typical modernist use of unusual adjectives, the association of discontinuous sensations, and the perception of what is hidden and how the hidden is linked with the visible. In this novel there are images, scenes, pictures, indicators of stationary and temporal suspense. To these impressions, the protagonist operates as actor, introspective and excessively sensitive.

De sobremesa is a lyric novel that subordinates action to the intensity of an instant's emotion. There is evident in this work the disintegration of the realistic protagonist. The protagonist of these pages loses his corporal nature, but not his humanity. Silva explores the intimate reactions of the hero in minute detail, paying greater attention to the effected impression than to the affecting action. The style is analytical in its observation of various states of being and in its description of objects, placing things observed on the same level as the contemplator.

Silva is essentially a poet of modern times. Principally with the "Nocturno" he delves into irrationalism and the mystery of the world beyond. He restored the use of the eleven-syllable verse favored by later modernist poets and gave it new cadences. He introduced a flexibility in the alexandrine line and created combinations of meters and verses of different measurements. He liberated traditional verse, redefining it as a musical totality with its own laws of rhythm and its own images. Silva, more than any other modernist poet, forged the Spanish language into a tool of powerful suggestiveness and delicate sounds, without falling, as even Rubén Darío did, into excessive adornment and color, never exploiting what would later become the tinsel of modernism.

Translated from the Spanish by Robert Reynolds

SELECTED BIBLIOGRAPHY

Editions

Individual Works

De sobremesa. Bogotá, 1925.
Intimidades. With an introduction by Germán Arciniegas. Edited and with a preliminary study and notes by Hector H. Orjuela. Bogotá, 1977.
El libro de versos, 1883–1896. Bogotá, 1928.
El libro de versos. Fascimile edition. Bogotá, 1945.
_____. Bogotá, 1946.

Collected Works

Los mejores poemas de José Asunción Silva. With a commentary by Manuel Toussaint. Mexico City, 1917.
Obra completa. Bogotá, 1955.
_____. With a prologue by Eduardo Camacho Guizado. Edited and with notes and chronology by Eduardo Camacho Guizado and Gustavo Mejia. Sucre, Venezuela, 1977.

Obras completas. With a prologue by Héctor H. Orjuela. 2 vols. Buenos Aires, 1968.

Poesías. With a prologue by Miguel de Unamuno. Barcelona, 1908.

Poesías. Edicion definitiva. With a prologue by Miguel de Unamuno and notes by Baldomero Sanín Cano. Paris, 1923.

_____. With a study by Baldomero Sanín Cano. Santiago, Chile, 1923.

Poesías. Edited by Franco Meregalli. Milan, 1950.

_____. Edited and with notes and an introduction by Héctor H. Orjuela. Bogotá, 1973.

_____. Critical edition by Héctor H. Orjuela. Bogotá, 1979.

Poesías completas. Buenos Aires, 1941.

Poesías completas, seguidas de prosas selectas. Madrid, 1951.

Prosas y versos. With an introduction, selection, and notes by Carlos García Prada. Mexico City, 1942.

Sus mejores poesías. Edited by Fermín Gutiérrez. Barcelona, 1955.

Biographical and Critical Studies

Argüello, Santiago. "El anunciador José Asunción Silva." In *Modernismo y modernistas* 1. Guatemala City, 1934. Pp. 137–183.

Botero, Ebel. *Cinco poetas colombianos.* Manizales, Colombia, 1964. Pp. 15–40.

Camacho Guizado, Eduardo. *La poesía de José Asunción Silva.* Bogotá, 1968.

Capdevila, Arturo. "José Asunción Silva, el arístocrata." Prologue in *Poesias completas y sus mejores páginas en prosa,* by José Asunción Silva. Buenos Aires, 1944. Pp. 9–22.

Carrier, Warren. "Baudelaire y Silva." *Revista iberoamericana* 7/13:39–48 (1943).

Cuervo Márquez, Emilio. *José Asunción Silva: Su vida y su obra.* Amsterdam, 1935.

Fogelquist, Donald F. "José Asunción Silva y Heinrich Heine." *Revista hispanica moderna* 20/4:282–294 (1954).

Gicovate, Bernardo. "Estructura y significado en la poesía de José Asunción Silva." *Revista iberoamericana* 24/48:327–331 (1959).

Holguín, Andrés. "El sentido del misterio en Silva." *Revista de las Indias* 28/90:351–365 (1946).

Ingwersen, Sonya A. *Light and Longing: Silva and Darío. Modernism and Religious Heterody.* New York, 1986.

Jiménez, Juan Ramón. "José Asunción Silva" in "Españoles de tres mundos." *Sur* 10/79:12–14 (1941).

Lievano, Roberto. *En torno a Silva: Selección de estudios e investigaciones sobre la obra y la vida íntima del poeta.* Bogotá, 1946.

Loveluck, Juan. "*De sobremesa:* Novela desconocida del modernismo." *Revista iberoamericana* 31/59:17–32 (1965).

Miramón, Alberto. *José Asunción Silva: Ensayo biográfico con documentos inéditos.* Bogotá, 1937. 2nd ed. 1957.

Osiek, Betty T. *José Asunción Silva: Estudio estilístico de su poesia.* Mexico City, 1968.

_____. *José Asunción Silva.* Twayne's World Authors Series no. 505. Boston, 1978.

Rico, Edmundo. *La depresión melancólica en la vida, en la obra y en la muerte de José Asunción Silva.* Tunja, Colombia, 1964.

Euclides da Cunha

(1866–1909)

Leopoldo M. Bernucci

The renowned contemporary Peruvian novelist Mario Vargas Llosa once remarked that Euclides da Cunha's life is perhaps just as fascinating as his major literary achievement, *Os Sertões* (*Rebellion in the Backlands*, 1902). There is a mythic and legendary aura surrounding the character and work of this Brazilian writer, and both his life and his book evoke intense and disturbing emotions.

Euclides was born at Santa Rita do Rio Negro on 20 January 1866, in the old province of Rio de Janeiro. When he was three years old his mother died and his father left him to the care of relatives until he began to attend boarding schools in Bahia and Rio. His father, an avid reader and writer of poetry, influenced his son's intellectual orientation. In the Colégio Aquino in Rio (1883–1884), young Euclides studied under the great Republican leader Benjamin Constant. In this school, Euclides and seven of his other schoolmates, founded *O Democrata* (The Democrat), the journal in which Euclides published his first works of poetry and prose.

These were turbulent political years in Brazil, culminating with the abolition of slavery in 1888 and the downfall of Emperor Pedro II and the collapse of the Brazilian Empire in 1889. As an adolescent, Euclides witnessed this political and social turmoil and grew to become a fervent participant in the republican movement, fighting against the monarchy. In 1885, the young man entered the Polytechnic School, but left a year later to enroll in the military school of Praia Vermelha in Rio de Janeiro. Just as he was about to complete his third academic year, in 1888, the passionate youth led a political protest that interrupted his military studies. During a special ceremony paying homage to the minister of defense, Euclides abandoned his line position in the honor guard and, in an act of contempt for the minister, stepped on his sword attempting to break it. When he did not succeed, young Euclides, who was a cadet at the time, violently cast his sword to the ground.

What was seemingly a lone act of defiance by a rebellious young soldier was in reality nothing of the kind. This demonstration of protest had been planned and previously agreed upon with a group of other cadets in the hope of obtaining more adherents to the republican cause. However, at the moment of truth, Euclides was the only one who had the courage to act. When the revolt was initially conceived, Euclides, with the aid of his comrades, plotted to arrest the minister and subsequently the emperor, ultimately proclaiming the republic. As a punishment for this rebellious act, Euclides was immediately expelled from the military school, sent to the military hospital, and then imprisoned in the Fortress of

Santa Cruz. Fortunately, with the aid of his father, he was pardoned by the emperor and the imprisonment lasted only a few days.

Little did Euclides suspect the enormous social and political repercussions of his protest. Shock waves were felt in parliament, in the press, and among military authorities and leading republicans. Even though the impetuous act initially brought about negative consequences for the future writer, it later produced many positive effects. Seen as an ardent supporter of the republican ideology, Euclides established himself as a revolutionary in liberal Brazilian political circles even though he had no direct participation in the birth of the republic in 1889.

After being released from prison, Euclides not only gained widespread recognition from the republicans for his gesture of political discontent but, because he was now free from the military school, could start his brilliant, though struggling, journalistic career. Since his early years as a student he had desired to become a journalist. In late 1888 he left Rio and traveled to São Paulo, where he spent a little more than a month writing for the prestigious newspaper A *Província de São Paulo*. This short period in São Paulo could not have been more fruitful or successful. He published his first articles in A *Província* on 22 December, and on 29 December began a permanent collaboration with the newspaper, writing under the pseudonym Proudhon in the section "Questões Sociais" (Social Questions).

Once back in Rio, Euclides resumed his military education after the republic was created on 15 November 1889. The author's former teacher, Benjamin Constant, became the first minister of defense under the republic and he gave Euclides permission to attend the military academy, from which he graduated in 1892, receiving a military engineering degree. In 1896, Euclides left the military life to take up civil engineering.

Married in 1890 and working as an engineer for the government from 1892 until his death, Euclides traveled constantly on government commissions and quickly became profoundly dissatisfied with his professional instability. In order to maintain his job, he was always dependent on political favoritism. These difficult years were characterized by strained relationships with his colleagues, due mostly to his complex and peculiar personality. Euclides was known as a moody man, quick to anger and given to impulsive rages. For this reason he suffered one setback after another in his professional life as an engineer, but he met his defeats with impressive perseverance and dignity.

Euclides became well known for his first two decisive articles, both written on the War of Canudos and both entitled "A Nossa Vendéia" (Our Vendée; the title refers to the French peasant insurrections of 1793–1796, comparable to the Brazilian rural conflict that lasted twelve months in its worst phase, from October 1886 to October 1887). In them, Euclides described the inhabitants of Canudos as barbarians, who, like those French who fought against the French Revolution, wanted to destroy the new democratic regime of the republic in order to reestablish the ancien régime. However, the War of Canudos was not an isolated case in the history of confrontations between government officials and the group of the messianic leader of Canudos, Antônio Conselheiro (Antônio the Counselor). In fact, since 1874 he had become more and more popular as a missionary, and in 1893 and 1894 other minor clashes with Brazilian authorities had occurred in the state of Bahia. By that time, the Counselor was well known throughout the North of Brazil, where he preached the salvation of the soul to his destitute flock, who had long been suffering the effects of the drought and poverty. Thus, for the followers of his ministry, there was no hope for a better life on earth other than to prepare oneself for the afterlife.

The articles appeared in the newspaper O *Estado de São Paulo*, the first on 14 March 1897 and the second on 17 July the same year. In the beginning, Euclides firmly believed that the leader of Canudos, Antônio Conselheiro, was the epitome of barbarism and a loyal defender of the emperor and monarchy. But Euclides soon discovered that his own view, shaped by the press of the day, was in fact distorted and subjective. His new awareness began in August 1897, when he was sent by O *Estado de São Paulo* to Salvador (Bahia) and the battlefield of Canudos. In the backlands, Euclides spent approximately thirty days, and witnessed scenes of war so horrifying that the experience marked a turning point in his life: a reevaluation of the War of Canudos and of himself.

This change in critical and personal opinion was derived in part from a more extensive change in his ideological perspective—from a basically idealistic ultra-republican view to a more realistic consciousness of Brazil's identity.

The proclamation of the republic had been a victory for the idealistic young republicans representing the progressive forces in Brazil. The Canudos Rebellion appeared to them as an antirepublican movement aimed at restoring the empire and the ancient colonial power. These idealists, including Euclides, believed that Antônio Conselheiro's group was a monarchic residue obstructing the democratic process. For progress to take hold in Brazil the old, traditionalist regime of large landholders had to be completely eliminated.

As a result of the booty left behind by the military armies, the Counselor had strengthened his forces with an impressive arsenal, which made many republicans and official representatives of Brazil believe, as Euclides initially did, that Antônio Conselheiro was allied to the defunct monarchy and was sponsored by the British crown. Likewise, the poverty-stricken peasants who constituted most of the Counselor's group fought the republican armies believing they were fighting the devil and forces of evil, Freemasonry, and heresy. Misperceptions and a general lack of communication between these two groups was responsible for creating a misunderstanding so serious that it ultimately led to the massacre at Canudos.

No other important Brazilian journalist before or since has acquired such a deep understanding of his country's tremendous social problems. What engaged him most in the coverage of the War of Canudos were the tragic ends of the three military expeditions that succumbed to the Counselor's disciples, the *jagunços* (which, in general, might be translated as "backlands ruffians," but in Euclides could be synonymous with *sertanejo*, or inhabitant of the backlands). The first two articles Euclides wrote on Canudos were seminal for the birth of his *Rebellion in the Backlands*. In them, Euclides' analytical exposé clearly outlines the principal cause for the failure of the first three expeditions, which attempted to eradicate the messianic Counselor and his followers. The tactics used by the Brazilian army, based on European war strategy, proved failures. While European tactics were suitable to Europe's topography, they were disastrous in the unique terrain of Brazil's Northeast. Furthermore, Euclides repeatedly observes the sheer negligence of those commanders-in-chief who, in view of the intricate topography, inhospitable vegetation, and torrid climate, had blatantly ignored the inadequacy of the heavy weapons and uniforms with which their troops were equipped.

After returning to São Paulo, away from the battlefield, Euclides began to compose his powerful account of the war at Canudos. Of the various moves made while supervising governmental construction projects, his stay in the rural town of São José do Rio Pardo was by far the most significant to the development of his literary work. Here he spent three years (1898–1901) shuffling the notes he brought back from Canudos while reading extensively in related areas in order to write *Rebellion in the Backlands*. While he supervised the reconstruction of a bridge, his book began to take shape in a nearby shanty that served as the engineer's shelter. Above the door, he inscribed a line from *Hamlet:* "What should a man do, but be merry?"—a statement perhaps too ironic for his personality. In these humble surroundings the most beautiful pages of *Rebellion in the Backlands* were written.

The first edition of the book was financed by Euclides himself because of his publisher's skepticism about its success. But immediately after its publication in 1902, *Rebellion in the Backlands* was critically acclaimed and became a best seller in Brazil. Only three years after its release, two more editions were printed, each meticulously corrected by the author, who always sought perfection in the art of writing. The success of his book guaranteed him membership in the prestigious Brazilian Academy of Letters, which he joined in 1903. Having set this as a goal for himself earlier in life, this long-desired membership represented the peak of his literary career. The success of *Rebellion in the Backlands* was not limited to Brazil. In 1944, when its English translation was published in the United States, reviewers from the nation's major newspapers and magazines responded enthusiastically, acclaiming it a splendid depiction of a nation and its people.

The demanding and isolated existence of an itinerant engineer provided Euclides with the peace and concentration necessary to writing. But his long, repeated absences from his family—which his biographers usually justify on the grounds of his position as a famous public figure—led his wife into an adulterous relationship with a young army officer. Frequently tormented by rumors, Euclides, poisoned with thoughts of his wife's betrayal, took it upon himself in a moment of passion to resolve the situation. On the morning of 15 August 1909, the writer, carrying a pistol, went to the house of his wife's lover and, in an exchange of gunfire, was mortally wounded by his rival. At the time of his death Euclides was writing a book on the Amazon, "Paraíso Perdido" (Paradise Lost), which was to be an expansion of the ideas found in his previous essays, which were posthumously included in À Margem da História (On the Margin of History, 1909). Unfortunately, this new book was not completed.

Euclides da Cunha's "literary" repertoire (as opposed to his essayistic and journalistic work) is surprisingly small. Indeed, Rebellion in the Backlands is the only work of his that experts have labeled as "literary." Aside from this book, he dedicated most of his time to the writing of articles, many of which were ultimately used in the composition of his masterpiece. The majority of these published articles, dispersed among several Brazilian newspapers, were gathered in 1907 to form a single volume entitled Contrastes e Confrontos (Contrasts and Comparisons). In these essays, the thematic interest of Euclides ranges from Brazilian history, geography, nationality, and diplomatic relationships with other countries, to world history and imperialism in Europe and Latin America. They also complement the writer's brilliant reflections in Rebellion in the Backlands. Many other articles and his war correspondence would be published later in his oeuvre and in Canudos e Inéditos (Canudos and Other Unpublished Works, 1967). In 1909, shortly after the author's death, À Margem da História was published. Despite its pronounced scientific orientation, this book comes close in style and tone to Rebellion in the Backlands, and from a literary point of view it is undoubtedly his second most important work. In 1975, another important posthumous publication appeared: Caderneta de Campo (Notebook), Euclides' private notes taken during the fourth military expedition against Canudos.

Hailed at the age of thirty-six as one of the most prominent Brazilian writers of his time, Euclides' reputation has continued to grow with the publication of an impressive number of articles and monographs by distinguished scholars. It has been estimated that the bibliography on Euclides da Cunha is one of the largest in Brazilian literary history, second only to Joaquim Maria Machado de Assis, the great nineteenth-century fiction writer.

Rebellion in the Backlands

Euclides da Cunha's famous Rebellion in the Backlands overshadows his other work. His undeniable journalistic talent alone makes him an extraordinary author, and his masterpiece elevates the author to the pantheon of great Latin American writers, for Rebellion in the Backlands remains unsurpassed among volumes of its kind in world literature.

The central topic of the book lies in the narration of the episodes of the War of Canudos. According to Euclides, since 1874 the messianic leader Antônio the Counselor had been preaching, repairing cemetery walls, and building churches in the local villages in the deserted area of northeastern Brazil. He soon became a legend and countless disciples helped maintain the myth of this messiahlike figure. By 1897, the charismatic religious chief had gathered approximately 25,000 fanatic devotees, who lived in Canudos under their own laws. The Counselor's followers, called the jagunços, were seen by the government as a menace to the fragile republic and, consequently, to the national security.

Three related phenomena triggered the War of Canudos: (1) the great popularity the Counselor enjoyed and the inevitable defection of believers from the Catholic church to his following (reasons which led the church to intervene); (2) the downfall of the monarchy and the practical implications of the creation of the republic (such as the introduction of the decimal system, the civil marriage, the new currency, and the census—innovations that were repudiated by the Counselor and his followers as being the work of the devil); and, perhaps the most critical, (3) the episode of Uauá, described by Euclides in the passage quoted below, in which the local army and the jagunços clashed for the first time in what, apparently, was a commercial dispute. In this conflict the soldiers were defeated by the Counselor's group, and the nightmarish episode gave rise to national military support in the form of two army troops, which in subsequent military expeditions were also massively defeated:

> The conflict in this case arose out of a trifling incident. Antônio Conselheiro had acquired in Joazeiro a certain quantity of lumber which the extremely impoverished caatingas of Canudos were unable to furnish him. He had contracted for it with one of the authorized representatives of that city, but, when the time agreed upon for the delivery of the material, which was to be used in the completion of a new church, came around, there was no lumber in sight. Everything pointed to a deliberated affront, an open break.
>
> The chief magistrate of Joazeiro, the truth is, had an old account to settle with the backlands agitator, one that dated from the period when he was a judge at Bom Conselho and had been compelled to leave town hastily as the result of an attack by the Counselor's followers; and he was simply taking advantage of the present situation, which afforded him the chance he wanted for evening the score. He knew that his enemy would strike back at the slightest provocation. The latter, indeed, even before the contract was broken, had threatened to descend on the attractive little town in the São Francisco Valley and take by force the timber that he needed.
>
> (Putnam trans., 1944, pp. 178–179)

Rebellion in the Backlands is the product of nineteenth-century philosophical ideas that strongly influenced the worldview of Brazilian scholars and politicians contemporary with Euclides. Herbert Spencer's theory of evolution, Charles Darwin's theory of creation, and especially Auguste Comte's and Hippolyte Adolphe Taine's positivism were immediately embraced by the country's most illustrious intellectuals. In Brazil, unlike in the United States, there was no positivist group that could define itself as cohesive or particularly restricted to Comte's philosophical thought. The history of ideas in Brazil shows us that, above all, Taine's postulates were the most enduring and influential. The impact that his theory produced on literature was powerful—so powerful, in fact, that not only did Euclides model his most important book on the Tainian triad of race, milieu, and moment, but so did Aluísio Azevedo, a brilliant novelist contemporary with Euclides and the author of the anthological *O Cortiço* (*A Brazilian Tenement*, 1890).

The disposition of the parts and chapters of *Rebellion in the Backlands* notably reflects the premises of Taine's determinism: "Land" (part 1), "Man" (part 2) and "Rebellion" (part 3). These three parts form the structural tripod that sustains Euclides' argument. Just as Henry Thomas Buckle and Taine had traced the deterministic laws of nature, the Brazilian writer, in similar fashion, had first to explain the land (the backlands) in order to study the man (Antônio the Counselor), and the subrace (the *jagunço*) so as, at last, to give plausible answers to the causes of the social and political phenomenon (the War of Canudos).

The prose of *Rebellion in the Backlands* is rich, metaphorical, twisted, yet familiar, and takes liberties with the use of technical terminology for precision and clarity in the description of the geography of Canudos. Euclides' scientific training is noticeably demonstrated in the symmetrical structure of his syntax, but also visible in his wish rhetorically to contrast distinct realities through his unique dialectical style: his use of antithesis and oxymoron is unprecedented in the history of Brazilian literature. For instance, through this rhetorical device the author names the man of the backlands "Hércules-Quasímodo," and describes him as "at once ridiculous and delightful"; the backlands are depicted as "barbarously fertile, marvelously exuberant"; and Antônio Conselheiro is portrayed as a "demoniac saint." Euclides also searched his dictionaries, along with his botany and geology manuals to discover proper Latin names for the plants, although he juxtaposed arcane and technical terms with colloquialisms from the peculiar vocabulary of the Tupi-Guaraní Indians and with the vernacular of the *jagunços*.

In spite of the authoritative voice of the narrator at the beginning of *Rebellion in the Backlands*, when Euclides presents himself as a model historian, the book is not a completely objective historical account of the War of Canudos. The discrepancy between its artistic achievements and its scientific accuracy is frequently felt, although astute critics have often noted that Euclides sought to pursue truth in a perfectly objective way. In this pursuit, however, he employed metaphor and analogy, and he had to do some daring guessing and arguing, especially since he knew little of geology and botany and had never set sight on the backlands of Brazil before the last thirty-five days of the war. One of the ironies in his quest for scientific precision is that his language was full of creative richness and plurivocality, which poets recklessly exploit and scientists usually avoid. For this reason, he can be considered an original historian who enjoyed narrating for its own sake in order to achieve aesthetic goals. Nonetheless, the man of science predominates throughout the book. Like many nineteenth-century naturalists, Euclides saw the elements of nature and man, set one against the other in an admirable struggle for life:

> The caatinga, on the one hand, stifles him; it cuts short his view, strikes him in the face, so to speak, and stuns him, enmeshes him in its spiny woof, and holds out no compensating attractions. It repulses him with its thorns and prickly leaves, its twigs sharp as lances; and it stretches out in front of him, for mile on mile, unchanging in its desolate aspect of leafless trees, or dried and twisted boughs, a turbulent maze of vegetation standing rigidly in space or spreading out sinuously along the ground, representing, as it would seem, the agonized struggles of a tortured, writhing flora.
>
> (p. 30)

In Rebellion in the Backlands, Euclides' statements, even his choice of words, reveal a tantalizing desire to make use of historiographical and fictional sources. While the Brazilian writer relies heavily on certain sources, at the same time he keeps others partially hidden in the text without referring to their respective authors. It is not clear whether this literary strategy is the result of the writer's desire to be original, or whether it represents an exaggerated precaution for having abusively used his written sources. This question has no easy answer, especially since Euclides left very few clues as to how his book was written. Even today, after many important aspects of this work have been carefully scrutinized, what is known about the original sources of Rebellion in the Backlands is limited to what can be learned from the author's own footnotes.

Although Euclides quotes several authors in Rebellion in the Backlands, many of its written sources (such as newspapers, government documents, and scientific journals) are not explicitly cited. Hence, from a literary and historical perspective, Euclides has rewritten the episodes of Canudos in an aesthetic manner, transforming his nonfictional, nonliterary sources in the process. Moreover, his political awareness and his literary talent led him to believe that utilizing this type of discursive strategy was the most effective way to draw attention to his social theories on Brazilian nationality. It was also his aim to provide the reader with an objective understanding of the true causes underlying the atrocities committed by the military during the campaigns. He wrote with a consciousness that went beyond that of a chronicler outlining a chapter of Brazilian history. Rather, he created an enduring work of art, embellished with aesthetic value.

Perhaps the most important intertextual aspect of Rebellion in the Backlands is not the extent of its borrowings from various academic fields, but rather the influence that it has exerted upon some of the best Latin American writers. The Brazilians, Graciliano Ramos' Vidas Sêcas (Barren Lives, 1938) and João Guimarães Rosa's Grande Sertão: Veredas (The Devil to Pay in the Backlands, 1956), and the Peruvian Mario Vargas Llosa's La guerra del fin del mundo (The War of the End of the World, 1981), to mention only a few, represent, with all their own literary idiosyncrasies, the importance Euclides da Cunha has had on modern narrative in Latin America. Crossing continental boundaries, the Hungarian Sándor Márai's Ítélet Canudosban (Verdict in Canudos, 1970), the Frenchman Lucien Marchal's Le Mage du Sertão (The Sage of Canudos, 1952), and Robert B. Cunningham Graham's pastiche, A Brazilian Mystic (1920), in the United States, all have incisively depended upon Rebellion in the Backlands.

Much of the excellence of Euclides' masterpiece resides in its multifacetedness. Rebellion in the Backlands owes much of its stature as a Brazilian classic to its literary discourse. Scholars have not yet been able to agree fully on how this important book should be generically classified. It has been studied as an epic novel, a sociological treatise, and as a historical account. To many readers, it oscillates between a fictional representation (of imagination) and a purely scientific description of nature and events (of empirical observation). This ontological duality is not gratuitous and plays an important rhetorical role. While in the book these two distinct spheres of representation do not invalidate each other, the book also provides the reader with an aesthetic experience and a journey through the more real and objective world of sciences. But the dynamics of the text are paradoxical and complex: designed to give an objective view of reality, as Euclides states in the "preliminary note," at times the book leaves the reader contemplating the subversion of the author's own desire. Euclides' oral and written sources are not always reliable, and his historical account is contradictory as well.

Most remarkable of all is the way the author of Rebellion in the Backlands succeeds in captivating our sympathies for the authentic heroes of the war who are by no means limited to soldiers of the republican army. The description of the jagunço Pajeú in action, for example, depicts with great precision the qualities of the typical war hero; the same qualities can also be found in the characterization of the army officer Siqueira de Menezes. In rapid succession, Euclides shows sinister scenes of the war, marching armies, hungry, wounded, and agonizing soldiers. His account evokes an acute emotional response in the reader, created by the naturalistic technique that Euclides contrasted with the grandiose epic tone of the description of battles.

À Margem da História

Seldom does a single work by a writer illuminate a process of intellectual maturity. However, À Margem da História, a collection of essays by Euclides, offers an excellent example of the development of his thought over the last eight years of his life. This period begins in 1900, two years before the publication of Rebellion in the Backlands, and ends in 1908. The maturity here cannot be measured in terms of linguistic qualities, in which the author always excelled. Rather, it must be gauged in terms of his intellectual stability. As a writer, he was enjoying fame and living in intellectual serenity. Unfortunately, his private life lacked the tranquillity a man of his caliber and profession should have had.

The essays contained in À Margem da História are not arranged chronologically, since the book is divided in four parts according to theme. The seven essays in part 1, "Terra sem História (Amazônia)" (Land Without History [The Amazon Region]), set the stage for this collection as a whole since the author draws attention to the rigorous social critique that lies beneath the surface of his work. "Impressões Gerais" (General Impressions), "Um Clima Caluniado" (A Slandered Climate), "Os Caucheros" (The Caucheros, or gatherers of India rubber; the word also means an exploiter or owner of a rubber tree plantation) and "Judas-Asvero" (The Wandering Jew) are the highlights of this section and, in fact, of the entire collection. They are reminiscent not only of the best moments of Rebellion in the Backlands, but they also show a more balanced and less passionate writer. Yet, in these pages, the vigor of Euclides' writing has been maintained and he does not hesitate to make use of the linguistic devices of his earlier prose. In a passage from "Os Caucheros," which can serve as a suitable illustration of Euclides' genuine style, he asserts:

> In his oscillating life he [the cauchero] gives to everything he practices, in the land that he devastates and disdains, a temporary character—from the cabin he builds in ten days to last five years, to the most affectionate links which sometimes last years and he destroys in just one day.
>
> (Obra Completa 1, p. 261)

In part 2, the writer discusses with great scientific accuracy the issues related to the geography of Brazil, the Río de la Plata region, and the efforts of the United States to create adequate means of transportation in order to accelerate progress in Latin America. Part 3 includes the longest and earliest essay of this collection: "Da Independência à República" (From Independence to Republic), originally published as "O Brasil no Século XIX" (Brazil in the Nineteenth Century) in 1901. Here Euclides is at his best, writing about the history of his country and, once again, in full command of his exhilarating, passionate style. Finally, part 4 consists of a single essay, "Estrelas Indecifráveis" (Indecipherable Stars), in which the author demonstrates great knowledge of astronomy.

If to the modern reader Euclides da Cunha's ideas seem a bit awkward, this is probably not so much due to his quasi-impenetrable style or to the difficulty posed by his archaic vocabulary. While many feel inclined to ascribe the difficulty found in his writings to his idiosyncratic language, there is no question that some of his theories, for example, on "ecological determinism" (the influence of the backlands upon the individual) or physical anthropology (the degeneration of the white race through miscegenation), though expressed with vitality and intelligence by the author, are arcane and have become obsolete. More fortunate was the future of his sociological theory on cultural "isolation," which is still valid. He not only attributed the isolation of the man of the backlands to geographical phenomena, but went further to study its political and economic causes: the nonsensical distribution of land in colonial Brazil had much in common with land division in the Middle Ages; on 7 February 1701, an absurd royal charter prohibited, with severe penalties for infraction, this part of the north to communicate with the south, with the mines of São Paulo.

Indeed, one cannot help but draw the conclusion that the perennial appeal of Euclides' work lies in the aesthetic power of his discourse. Even though capable of writing in the style of a chronicler, delivering a straightforward message to the reader, Euclides da Cunha preferred to take upon himself the arduous task of artistic writing typical of only the most accomplished authors.

SELECTED BIBLIOGRAPHY

Editions

Individual Works

Os Sertões. Rio de Janeiro, 1902. 2nd. ed., rev. 1903. 3rd. ed., rev. 1905.
Os Sertões. São Paulo, 1985. Critical edition by Walnice Nogueira Galvão.
Relatório da Comissão Mixta Brasileiro-Peruana de Reconhecimento do Alto Purus. Rio de Janeiro, 1906.
Castro Alves e Seu Tempo. Rio de Janeiro, 1907.

Collected Works

Contrastes e Confrontos. Porto, Portugal, 1907.
Peru Versus Bolívia. Rio de Janeiro, 1907.
Obra Completa. Edited by Afrânio Coutinho. 2 vols. Rio de Janeiro, 1966.
À Margem da História. Porto, Portugal, 1909.
Canudos e Inéditos. Edited by Olímpio de Souza Andrade. São Paulo, 1967.

Correspondence, Notebooks

Cartas de Machado de Assis e Euclides da Cunha. Edited by Renato Travassos. Rio de Janeiro, 1931.
Euclides da Cunha e Seus Amigos. Edited by Francisco Venâncio Filho. São Paulo, 1938.
Skidmore, Thomas E., and Thomas H. Holloway. "New Light on Euclides da Cunha: Letters to Oliveira Lima, 1903–1909." Luso-Brazilian Review 8/1:30–55 (1971).
Caderneta de Campo. Edited by Olímpio de Souza Andrade. São Paulo, 1975.

Translations

Putnam, Samuel. Rebellion in the Backlands. Chicago, 1944.
_____. Revolt in the Backlands. London, 1947.

Biographical and Critical Studies

Books

Abreu, Modesto de. Estilo e Personalidade de Euclides da Cunha. Rio de Janeiro, 1963.
Andrade, Olímpio de Souza. História e Interpretação de "Os Sertões." São Paulo, 1960.
Freyre, Gilberto. Atualidade de Euclydes da Cunha. 2nd ed. Rio de Janeiro, 1943.
_____. Perfil de Euclydes e Outros Perfis. Rio de Janeiro, 1944.
Moura, Clóvis. Introdução ao Pensamento de Euclides da Cunha. Rio de Janeiro, 1964.
Oliveira, Franklin de. Euclydes: A Espada e a Letra. Rio de Janeiro, 1983.
Rabello, Sýlvio. Euclides da Cunha. Rio de Janeiro, 1948. 3rd ed. Rio de Janeiro, 1983.
Tocantins, Leandro. Euclides da Cunha e o paraíso perdido. Rio de Janeiro, 1966. 3rd ed. Rio de Janeiro, 1978.

Periodicals, Articles and Prefaces

Amory, Frederic. "Euclides da Cunha as Poet." Luso-Brazilian Review 12/175–185 (1975).
Araripe Júnior, Tristão de Alencar. "Dois Grandes Estilos."

Preface to *Contrastes e Confrontos*. 2nd ed. Porto, Portugal, 1907. Pp. 23–66.

———. "*Os Sertões* (Campanha de Canudos)." In *Obra Crítica de Araripe Júnior* 4. Rio de Janeiro, 1966.

Calasans, José. "Algumas Fontes de *Os Sertões*." *Revista do Instituto de Estudos Brasileiros* 14/91–125 (1973).

Cândido, Antônio. "Euclides da Cunha, Sociólogo." *O Estado de São Paulo*. 13 December 1952. P. 5.

Conrad, Robert. "A Footnote to *Os Sertões*." *Luso-Brazilian Review* 9/2:102–103 (1972).

Galvão, Walnice Nogueira. "O Correspondente de Guerra Euclides da Cunha." In her *Saco de Gatos*. São Paulo, 1976. Pp. 55–63.

———. "De Sertões e Jagunços." In her *Saco de Gatos*. São Paulo, 1976. Pp. 65–85.

———. "Notas." In *Los sertones* (Spanish translation by Estela dos Santos). Caracas, 1980. Pp. 384–409.

———. "Ciclo de *Os Sertões*." In her *Gatos de Outro Saco*. São Paulo, 1981. Pp. 62–110.

———. "Euclides, Elite Modernizadora e Enquadramento." In her *Euclides da Cunha*. São Paulo, 1984. Pp. 7–37.

Lima, Luiz Costa. "Nos Sertões da Oculta Mimesis." In his *O controle do imaginário*. São Paulo, 1984. Pp. 201–241.

Oliveira, Franklin. "*Os Sertões*, Obra de Arte da Linguagem. Espírito e Forma de Euclydes. Euclydes Socialista." In his *A Fantasia Exata*. Rio de Janeiro, 1959. Pp. 248–268.

Proença, Cavalcanti. "O Monstruoso Anfiteatro. Sobre *Os Sertões* de Euclides da Cunha." In his *Estudos literários*. Rio de Janeiro, 1971.

Putnam, Samuel. " 'Brazil's Greatest Book': A Translator's Introduction." In *Rebellion in the Backlands*. Chicago, 1944. Pp. iii–xviii.

Bibliographies

Reis, Irene Monteiro. *Bibliografia de Euclides da Cunha*. Rio de Janeiro, 1971.

Sousa, J. Galante de. "Algumas Fontes para o Estudo de Euclides da Cunha." *Revista do Livro* (Rio de Janeiro) 15/4:183–219 (1959). Also published as an offprint.

Venâncio Filho, Francisco. *Euclides da Cunha: Ensaio Bio-bibliográphico*. Rio de Janeiro. 1931.

Rubén Darío

(1867–1916)

Enrique Anderson Imbert

Rubén Darío's work divides Latin American literary history into a "before" and an "after." In terms of this dividing line, he is the modernist poet par excellence.

Modernism in Latin America was a synthesis of three European movements: romanticism, Parnassianism, and symbolism. In Europe, the romantics had emphasized the spontaneous expression of passions; later, the Parnassians had introduced to literature forms that imitated those of the visual arts; finally, the symbolists had begun to refine a language whose rhythms and harmonies were as suggestive as music. In Latin America, the process was shorter: Poets who began as romantics quickly learned the richly visual Parnassian ways, and with Darío leading the way, they quickly rose to the cadence of symbolism. Latin American modernists coincided in their art not so much for having come to a previous agreement, but, rather, for their common tendency of fixing their gaze upon Europe. Just as money changers know the value of each foreign coin, young people after 1885 could say which were the most prestigious artistic mintages in the international banks. They were convinced that the combining of styles was in itself a new expression; and they prided themselves on being part of a minority that, for the first time in the disorderly social life of Latin America, could specialize in art. They adored literary forms as supreme values and believed that while any topic could be handled within these forms, the old as well as the new (they were antiroutine, not antitraditional), the forms themselves had to be beautiful. The formalist passion of the modernists brought them to aestheticism, the aspect critics have studied the most; but with this same inclination toward form, the modernists celebrated the originality of Latin American society, with its colorful wildlife and its inexplicable history. They were enthusiastic about any creative endeavor as long as it had some distinction, as long as the artist was successful in the expression of elitist tastes.

"Moderns," an old word, used again and again to name new generations who parade through the centuries, thereby partakes of transitoriness; but nevertheless, in literary histories, it serves to refer to two Latin American literary generations active between 1885 and 1910. José Martí, Manuel Gutiérrez Nájera, José Asunción Silva, and Julián del Casal, who all died by 1896, form a "first modernist generation." Darío, because of his age and precocity, had already emerged, but after 1896 he led a "second modernist generation," composed of Leopoldo Lugones, Ricardo Jaimes Freyre, Guillermo Valencia, Amado Nervo, Enrique González Martínez, Manuel Díaz Rodríguez,

Enrique Gómez Carrillo, José Enrique Rodó, Julio Herrera y Reissig, and many more. In the year 1896, with the publication of Darío's *Prosas profanas* (Lay Hymns), aestheticism reached its peak. In addition, with *Prosas profanas*, Latin American writing for the first time would influence the literature of Spain.

Darío was born on 18 January 1867 in Nicaragua. From 1879 to 1892 he wrote *Poesías y artículos en prosa* (Poems and Prose Articles), which remained forgotten in original manuscript until 1967, when the University of Nicaragua reproduced them in a facsimile edition. His first printed book was *Epístolas y poemas* (Epistles and Poems, 1885). By 1880, and still a young boy, he had changed his real name—Félix Rubén García Sarmiento—to the pseudonym Rubén Darío. The "boy poet," as he was called, was an immediate success.

In the first period of his life, Darío was a connoisseur of Spanish literary history, from the *Poema del Cid* to the poetry of Gustavo Adolfo Bécquer, and of French literature, from the romantic Victor Hugo to the Parnassians Charles Leconte de Lisle, François Coppée, and Catulle Mendès. His precocious talent matured in Chile, where he arrived in June 1886. He was dazzled by Valparaíso and Santiago, the first major cities that he had seen, prosperous and with pretentions to the sophistication of Europe. His friends were up to date on the intellectual fads, and thanks to them Darío continued to teach himself about the French poetic inventions. His first innovations did not appear in verse but in prose. The verses in *Abrojos* (Thistles, 1887) and *Rimas* (Rhymes, 1887) were traditional. Nor did he dare to experiment in the verses of the first edition of *Azul . . .* (Azure . . . , 1888). Of course, when one searches in the verses of *Azul* for the first vibrations of modernism, the innovation may be seen developing. Tremors in the four seasons of "El año lírico" (The Lyric Year) indicate, in effect, that Darío was already equipped to take on his big adventure. But he did not take it on. Only in the second edition of *Azul* (1890) do we find fully "modern" poems.

Why did Darío open his prose to change before his verse? Because he had seen the artistic prose of Théophile Gautier, Gustave Flaubert, Edmond and Jules Goncourt, Paul de Saint-Victor, Mendès, and Pierre Loti triumph. Since in Latin America the

beginnings of the change in style had appeared in prose, it seemed safe to him to make his debut with prose. *Azul* owes its historical importance more to its short stories and poetic prose than to its verses; it was such an important book that historians often cite it as the beginning point of modernism. The story "El pájaro azul" (The Blue Bird) masterfully inaugurated the series of those stories. The setting is the artistic bohemia of Paris. Garcin, a poet, punished with poverty by his bourgeois father, opens his own skull with a bullet in order to let the "poor blue bird" escape from its cage. The suffering of the artist in an antiartistic society was more than a theme for Darío; it became a leitmotif repeated in other stories. In the middle of this aestheticist propaganda is "El fardo" (The Bundle), which describes proletarian misery in realistic style. Darío considered Émile Zola's naturalism worthy of including in the collection of novelties he offered the Latin American public.

In 1889, Darío returned to Central America and in the following year, from Guatemala, he launched the second edition of *Azul*, much enlarged. Comparing the edition of 1888 with that of 1890, one appreciates Darío's rapid progress toward modernity. In his verse there is now an audacity that before had shown itself only in prose. Such is the case of the sonnet "Venus." The planet Venus, shining in the black night, "as a divine, golden jasmine encrusted in ebony," suggests myths and stories to the poet, who is nostalgic with love. Moreover, Venus becomes an erotic symbol. To the poet's enamored soul, the planet appears to be an oriental queen waiting for her lover. The poet desires her.

> "¡Oh reina rubia!"—díjele—"mi alma quiere dejar su crisálida
> y volar hacia tí, y tus labios de fuego besar; . . . "

> "Oh blonde queen," I said to her, "my soul wants to leave its chrysalis
> and fly to you, and kiss your lips of fire;. . ."

The metaphor of the body-soul as chrysalis-butterfly initiates a language that takes on more and more esoteric symbols. Listen to the final verse: "Venus, from the abyss, watched me with sad eyes." Abysmal sadness will be the tone of Darío's last years.

The second edition of *Azul* is enriched by additional short stories. Two are memorable. "El sátiro sordo" (The Deaf Satyr) continues the theme of the artist disdained by those who are inept when it comes to beauty: in a forest of Greek mythology, the king, a deaf satyr, follows the advice of the ass, not that of the lark, and banishes Orpheus. The other story is a narrative gem: "La muerte de la emperatriz de la China" (Death of the Empress of China). The lovers Recaredo and Suzette, in Paris, quarrel because she is jealous of the affection that he shows for the porcelain bust of an empress of China. Although in this woman's jealousy of a work of art one recognizes very real and human sentiments, Darío replaces reality with fantastical figures. The story begins with a metaphor that strips Suzette of her womanhood and converts her into a woman-jewel-bird that lives in a house-case-cage. It ends with another metaphor, this time of a blackbird, caged like Suzette, except that it is not a real bird but a confidant of the young lovers; the blackbird, upon seeing them making up with kisses, "was dying of laughter." Among the denaturalized sounds and lights of this poetic prose, we recognize the leitmotif: the conflict between life and art. By jealously breaking the porcelain bust of an empress of China, Suzette gives credence to the philosophy of aestheticism; this humiliating act is, in effect, an admission that art is superior to life. As *Azul* was the only collection of short stories that Darío published, the image of a Frenchified story writer, elegant and artistic, was imprinted on the minds of his readers; only when, long after his death, his complete stories were collected did readers realize that he had been a narrator of various themes and tones.

In the summer of 1892, Darío left for Spain as the secretary of the Nicaraguan delegation to the festivities of the quadracentennial of the discovery of America. (En route through Havana, he met Julián del Casal.) In two months he took a quick look at the literary beehive. The Spain that Darío saw, as a young man of twenty-five, was an old Spain: José Zorrilla, Juan Valera, Emilia Pardo Bazán, Marcelino Menéndez Pelayo, Ramón de Campoamor. In reading them, Darío became convinced more than ever that it was time to reform that old-fashioned style of writing.

In April 1893, he was named consul for Colombia to Buenos Aires. In May, when passing through New York, he met José Martí, and in June he was in Paris: "My dream, to see Paris, to feel Paris," he would record in *Opiniones* (Opinions, 1906), "was fulfilled, and my aesthetic initiation in the womb of symbolism made me proud and enthusiastic. . . . I was sworn in by the gods of the new Parnassus; I had seen the old faun Verlaine; I knew the mystery of Mallarmé and was a friend of Moréas." In August 1893 he arrived in Buenos Aires, then the most prosperous city in Latin America, with more than half a million inhabitants and a very Europeanized elite. More talented than the young poets of Buenos Aires who were already familiar with the French Parnassus, Darío let himself be surrounded and was quickly acclaimed their leader. When the Colombian consulate was abolished in 1894, Darío earned a living as a journalist. He published almost thirty short stories. They were no better than those in *Azul*, but they contained a novelty: horror in the style of Edgar Allan Poe.

The literary atmosphere of Buenos Aires stimulated Darío to labor over fantastical stories. Making use of his recent initiation into theosophy, the occult, and parapsychology, Darío began a series of stories with themes of spiritualism, reincarnation, magic, and miracles. "Thanathopia" was a macabre story. The son of a practitioner of the occult sciences, who until then has boarded at Oxford, goes to London to meet his stepmother and, upon seeing her, understands that his father has married a dead woman, a vampire. "La pesadilla de Honorio" (Honorio's Nightmare) is the story of a dream: The sleeper dreams images of the end of the world that resemble others of Thomas De Quincey, William Beckford, Poe and Stéphane Mallarmé. The best story is metaphysical: "El caso de la señorita Amelia" (Miss Amelia's Case). All the characters grow old except for one, who remains forever a girl of twelve. Darío, through the mouth of the narrator, Dr. Z—cabalist, occultist, orientalist, demonist—propounds a puzzle that, according to him, will someday be explained by theosophy. Before recounting the case, the gnostic Dr. Z vacillates: he fears that he will not be believed. Then Darío has him speak these words: "'I believe,' I answered with a firm and severe voice, 'in God and his church. I believe in miracles. I believe in the supernatural.'" With this, Darío reconciles—because in his own mind they are reconciled—Catholic theology and occult theosophy.

On leaving Buenos Aires, his streak of fantastic narration ended. From then on, he would write short stories only in his spare time. He spent entire years without writing a single one and wrote hardly fifteen between 1899 and 1915. Perhaps he subdued his vocation as a story writer in order to devote himself to his essays and poetry. He did not, unfortunately, collect his stories in a volume; he did collect his essays and poetry in *Los raros* (The Exceptional Ones) and *Prosas profanas*, two important books published in Buenos Aires in 1896.

In *Los raros*, Darío raised a relief map of the culture as he had explored it between 1893 and 1896. Or, rather, he shows us what rarities he honored in those "exceptional ones," the measures he took with each of them, the library and periodicals room that he consulted, the critical authorities that he recognized, anecdotes of his personal relationships with men of letters—in essence, an autobiography in the form of biographies. In these intelligent essays, the sentences frequently shine with poetic dexterity; he has already developed an agile and graceful style. In some passages, we can locate precise sources for his poems. And, as Darío praised in exceptional writers what he felt in himself or desired for himself, he revealed, without intending to, his own aesthetic program.

This program is a challenging one in the "Palabras liminares" (Opening Words) of *Prosas profanas*. It incites the "young of America" to be conscious of the principles of their art. It proclaims "an anarchistic aesthetic," individual and inimitable. Darío declares himself an aristocrat and tells his readers: "You will see in my verses princes, kings, imperial things, visions of faraway or impossible countries, and why not? I detest the life and the time in which birth befell me. . . . My wife is from my land; my darling, from Paris."

Even the title *Prosas profanas* was a provocation. His critics did not understand that the term *prosa* (literally "prose") signified a musical sequence, as in the ecclesiastical poetry of Gonzalo de Berceo. Or, if one prefers a French example, it was an echo of the "Prose (pour des Esseintes)" of Mallarmé. And after the provocation of the title word "prose," there was the provocation of the first poem: "Era un aire suave . . ." (It was a gentle air . . .). From this "gentle air of slow movements" came dreamlike figures. It was an atmosphere of a courtly party—paintings by Antoine Watteau plus poems of Paul Verlaine—that produced hallucinations and altered time. "The divine Eulalia laughs, laughs, laughs." It is the laugh of a goddess who is the beginning and support of the world.

> ¿Fué acaso en el Norte o en el Mediodía?
> Yo el tiempo y el día y el país ignoro;
> pero sé que Eulalia ríe todavía,
> ¡y es crüel y eterna su risa de oro!

Was it in the north or was it in the south? Of the age, the day and the country, I know not; but I know that Eulalia is still laughing, and her laughter of gold is cruel and eternal!

With perfect musical sense, Darío tried all kinds of rhythms. In his experiments, regular versification predominated; it was after 1920 that the torrent of nonmetrical verses broke loose in America. His inventions and restorations modulated the prosody of the Spanish language deliciously. A great part of so much technical ostentation was inspired by the French tendencies toward free verse. And the tendencies were not only French. Darío himself has confessed other debts in the development of his versification. But in reading the sources indicated by him or by his critics, one admires his independence. It is difficult to recognize the model; and when the model appears, Darío is not its inferior. As much as the new sounds—for example, those that produced the scandal of his "Responso a Verlaine" (Anthem for the Death of Verlaine)—the vague melody of musical súggestions was disconcerting. Without such a melody, Darío's landscapes and settings would have been conventional. The gold, the lily, the swan, and the woman; the lake in the garden and the palace in the city; the objects of art, the jewels, and the sumptuous clothing; the parade of mythical figures—all had something of the photographer's backdrop or the theater's props. They would have harmed his work irreparably had it not been for the music of ideas that wrapped everything in waves of emotion. Even in the visual, sculpturelike verses, things were not seen with well-defined outlines, but rather as hazy images in the depths of a dreaming consciousness.

In Darío, aristocratic feeling, disdainful of the reality of the time, showed itself in four thematic types of poetry: exotic ("Sinfonía en gris mayor" [Symphony in Gray Major]), cosmopolitan ("Divagación" [Digression]), reminiscent of art ("Pórtico" [Portico]), and nostalgic of historical eras ("Blasón" [Blazon]). Some compositions partake more of the exotic, others the cosmopolitan, others of values realized in the visual or musical arts, and others the prestige of Greece, Rome, the Middle Ages, eighteenth-century France; but in each composition, we perceive the themes of all the other compositions. And the lyrical unity of *Prosas profanas* shows itself in those compositions with distinct sentimental tones. (1) *The frivolous tone.* Frivolity tends to change into austere poetic ideal. For example, "Sonatina" is a small rococo painting, a small box of music. But it is also an allegory about the act of composing poetry. Upon first reading, it seems a frivolous transposition of a fairy tale: the princess who, in a palace guarded by a dragon, dreams about a prince who comes to love her and a fairy who tells her the prince is on his way. But after a more attentive reading, that princess who "is sad" and "pursues through the eastern sky the vague dragonfly of a vague illusion" is not so frivolous. The poem reveals its serious intention in the last stanza:

> —¡Calla, calla, princesa—dice el hada madrina—
> en caballo con alas, hacia acá se encamina,
> en el cinto la espada y en la mano el azor,
> el feliz caballero que te adora sin verte,
> y que llega de lejos, vencedor de la Muerte,
> a encenderte los labios con su beso de amor!

Oh hush, my princess, hush—says her fairy godmother—the happy knight who adores you without having seen you is riding this way on his winged horse, a sword at his belt and a hawk in his hand, and comes from far off, having conquered Death, to kindle your lips with the kiss of his love.

The princess is the beauty that the poet looks for; but it is a mutual search: the beauty is also looking for the poet. And so they find each other, the dream and its poet, the poet and his dream.

(2) *The hedonistic tone.* Parties, liquor, walks, kisses, flirtation, contemplation of beautiful forms and graceful movements—these subjects indicate that Darío has deliberately instituted pleasure as the goal in life. An excellent example is the poem "Alma mía" (My soul). (3) *The erotic tone.* The erotic experience was the most powerful and permanent for Darío, as seen in "Ite, missa est" (Go, it is the dismissal). (4) *The reflexive tone.* Although the poems slip upon the surface of an aesthetic literature, the poet tends to be absorbed in his inner life, thinking about the meaning of human existence. This meditative tone will sharpen itself over the years. For Darío, the world is enigmatic but harmonious; he feels himself a participant in the mysterious universal harmony, as seen, for example, in "Coloquio de los centauros" (Colloquy of the Centaurs).

José Enrique Rodó, in the study he dedicated to *Prosas profanas*, saw in Darío an exquisite poet who, because of his aristocratic emphasis on form, diminished human content and universality in his poetry. That study reappeared as the prologue to the second edition of *Prosas profanas*, in 1901, but by then Darío had already moved a few steps ahead, and Rodó's judgment was dated and out of focus. In the meantime, in the second edition, Darío had accumulated some poems that announced a more concerned art. They exhibited a philosophical attitude that would become more visible in his next book of verse. These poems, from the series "Las ánforas de Epicuro" (The Amphoras of Epicurus), are noteworthy for their symbolistic art of suggesting, with flowing, barely insinuated images, a conception of the world formulated in Catholicism, theosophy, and the occult sciences. One of the best poems added to the second edition was "Yo persigo una forma . . ." (I Seek a Form . . .). This sonnet, like the mythological Janus who faced both the old and the new year, is at the same time retrospective and prospective: it repeats the exact forms and artistic transpositions that prevailed in Darío's Parnassian period and suggests mysteries and ineffable correspondences that will prevail in his symbolist period. The poem "Yo persigo una forma" belongs to what has been called poetry of poetry, or metapoetry, an ancient genre that, thanks to Poe and Charles Baudelaire, sharpened in the modernist poets an awareness of what poetry is and how it comes to be. At the triumphal moment of his career, when his verbal mastery was being celebrated everywhere, Darío wrote a poem describing how difficult, almost impossible, it is to be a poet.

> Yo persigo una forma que no encuentra mi estilo,
> botón de pensamiento que busca ser la rosa.

I seek a form that my style does not find, a bud of thought that strives to be a rose.

But the form he seeks is precisely that which he has found. He pretends not to be able to communicate what he communicates well. He complains, in an extraordinarily accomplished way, that his poetic capabilities lie unrealized. There is an overlapping of forms: the definite, objective form of the sonnet that the reader has before his eyes, and the vague form that Darío says he tries in vain to find in his mind.

In 1898, La Nación of Buenos Aires gave Darío the task of taking Spain's pulse after its recent defeat by the United States. He arrived in Madrid with the year 1899. The chronicles that he wrote are collected in España contemporánea (Contemporary Spain, 1901). This prose is journalistic, much less elegant and imaginative than that of Los raros. Darío limits himself to describing what he sees, a spectacle of decadence. He is severe but without the accusatory tone of the moralist. Art and literature interest him most. He salutes the new talents: Jacinto Benavente, Antonio and Manuel Machado, Miguel de Unamuno, Azorín, Pío Baroja, Ramiro de Maeztu; the aestheticians Ramón María del Valle-Inclán and Juan Ramón Jiménez. He salutes them but continues to estimate that the American generation is superior to the Spanish generation, at least in reformist restlessness.

In April 1900, Darío began travels in France and Italy. He comments on these in Peregrinaciones (Pilgrimages, 1901), which again offers journalistic prose with occasional bright spots. There was less "artistic writing" in La caravana pasa (The Caravan Passes On, 1902), Darío's chronicles of London, Brussels, Dunkirk, and Paris. In March 1903, the government of Nicaragua named him consul in Paris: he retained this position until 1907. From the journeys that he then undertook came another book of chronicles, superior to his earlier ones: Tierras solares (Sunny Lands or The Lands of Our Ancestral Home, 1904),

in which the most interesting elements are his observations and reflections concerning literature. Now Darío admits that the writers who have emerged in Spain are in tune with the stylistic renovation he promoted. They are the writers of the so-called Generation of '98, and Darío knows that they all admire him. Sure of his importance in America and Spain, Darío focuses his eyes inward and buries himself in his poetry.

He then produced his best book, Cantos de vida y esperanza (Songs of Life and Hope, 1905). In the "Preface," he boasts:

I could repeat here more of the concept of the Opening Words of Prosas profanas. My respect for the aristocracy of thought, for the nobility of art, is always the same. My long-standing hatred of mediocrity, the intellectual jackass, aesthetic smallness, hardly diminishes today with a reasoned indifference. The movement of liberty that it befell me to initiate in America propagated to Spain, and as much here as there the triumph is attained.

In these songs of an emotional timbre, we sense the crisis of aestheticism of Prosas profanas. The precious lamps lit in France are lowered, and the flames of an internal fire grow brighter. Now Darío sings from his abyss, playing the mysterious depths of life. We will hear, in Cantos de vida y esperanza his profound depression. Before, in Prosas profanas, he had spoken of himself but had hid himself behind allegories or masked his states of being in poetic figures. In Cantos de vida y esperanza, the personal presence of Darío imposes itself upon the reader, directly, strongly, convincingly. It is not that there has been a break with the past; rather, a change has taken place in his scale of values. These changes are analyzed in the following paragraphs.

Aristocratic evasion of reality. The exoticism, the cosmopolitanism, the reminiscences of art, and the nostalgia for other eras that we see in Prosas profanas continued in the songs, but they began to form a more complicated structure. Art took root in life. Within the crisis of aestheticism, the aristocratic evasion of reality is still evident, even in a topic as immediate and brutal as war. The "Marcha triunfal" (Triumphal March) is an apotheosis of victory in war but without patriotic goals, without military glorification: "It is a triumph of decoration and of music," said Darío. In effect, the poem is an ode rich in art, not in belligerent emotion; the theme of war is dressed up in civility by reminiscences of mythology and literature.

Return to social concern. Darío's attitudes from before *Azul* reappear, but with an arrogant style: the politics, the morality, the love of Spain, the consciousness of what Spanish America is, the suspicion of the United States. A group of poems attempts a revalidation of the Hispanic culture: "Un soneto a Cervantes" (A Sonnet to Cervantes), "A Goya" (To Goya), "Letanía de nuestro señor Don Quijote" (Litany for Our Lord Don Quixote). Darío takes pride in the historic past of the mother country. He renews his ties with his caste and so shares in his glorious heritage. He usurps the role of defender of hispanism. In "Salutación del optimista" (The Optimist's Salutation) he sings the raison d'être of the Spanish-speaking peoples; of course, after the defeat that Spain suffered, in the war that the United States declared, that optimism sounded forced. The United States, during the era of Theodore Roosevelt's "big stick" policy, committed aggressions against Latin America; Roosevelt had declared, "I took Panama." Darío reacted angrily with his ode "A Roosevelt" (To Roosevelt). All the assaulted people say "no!" to the "future invader of ingenuous America who has indigenous blood" and "still speaks Spanish." The "men of Saxon eyes and barbarous souls" of the United States have it all: strength, money, power, skill, and democracy. But to subjugate the "thousand nimble cubs of the Spanish Lion," the support of God would be necessary, and they cannot count on God. Darío was not indifferent to the evil in the world: he deplored it as ugliness. When he took part, he chose the good causes, but taking part, he would say, was not the job of the poet. He was attentive to the good because he believed that good is also beauty: "Let's do the good because it is beautiful," he says in "Programa matinal" (Morning Program).

Toward a knowledge of life. The poet tends to reflect upon his own existence and what art is, what love is, what religion is, what life is.

The introductory poem in *Cantos de vida y esperanza* is an introspective examination and a program of expression. It begins as follows:

> *Yo soy aquel que ayer no más decía*
> *el verso azul y la canción profana,*
> *en cuya noche un ruiseñor había*
> *que era alondra de luz por la mañana.*

I am the man who just yesterday uttered the azure verse and the lay hymn; in my night there was a nightingale that in the morning turned into a luminous skylark.

He is the poet of *Azul* and *Prosas profanas*, owner of a dream garden, with roses and swans.

> *y muy siglo diez y ocho y muy antiguo*
> *y muy moderno; audaz, cosmopolita;*
> *con Hugo fuerte y con Verlaine ambiguo,*
> *y una sed de ilusiones infinita.*

and I was very eighteenth century, and very ancient, and very modern; bold, cosmopolite; strong like Hugo and ambiguous like Verlaine, and with an infinite thirst for illusions.

He is the poet who in his garden believed himself to be a beautiful statue, but one of living flesh, not of marble, and with a shy soul that would come out to sing in the spring. His song is sincere: "Si hay una alma sincera, ésa es la mía" (Mine was a sincere soul, if any was). But this sincerity is not that of the shout nor of eloquence nor of ideas, but of vague shades, weightless, imprecise, faded, of his intimate impressions.

The erotic impetus is completely aroused throughout his work, at times simple and naked, in a joyous unconsciousness, at times anguished at the premonition of death. In Darío, there is an almost theoretical vision of the value of womankind as summoned by the profound forces of life. It is a sort of paneroticism that exalts the flesh and makes it an agent of history. In the verses "¡Carne, celeste carne de la mujer!" (Flesh, celestial flesh of womankind!), there appears, more ardent, this erotic experience in which the flesh (not of this or that specific woman, but the celestial flesh, the flesh in which mankind buries himself and enjoys the absolute) ends up becoming spiritual: It is clay, ambrosia, eucharist.

The terror before mystery pushes Darío toward religion, not as a solution to problems nor an artistic spectacle, but out of fear, doubt, anguish. Before *Prosas profanas*, Darío's religious topics were insincere: they were given with anticlerical and even antireligious jokes; in *Prosas profanas*, the sacred became iridescent in a beautiful pagan or erotic atmosphere. But now Darío is sincere. Unfortunately, religion does not offer him peace. It is hardly a light to which he aspires in order to save himself. This "hope" in the salvation of the soul is what he put in the title of his book: he called the poems songs "of hope." Nevertheless, from the psychological point of view, they are more like songs of despair. The poet was thinking about the theological virtue of hope that a supernatural bliss promises, in the name of God. All the poems that speak of hope are religious, as in "Canto de esperanza" (Song of Hope) and "Spes" (Hope).

The insistence with which Darío compares his life with autumn is not a reference merely to his age, but also to a philosophy of time: Nature changes, but we feel it change only in the temporality of our own existence. In the "Canción de otoño en primavera" (An Autumn Song in Spring), he gives us the situation, the circumstance, almost the explanation of the bitterness with which he now esteems life.

> Juventud, divino tesoro,
> ¡ya te vas para no volver!

Youth, divine treasure, so soon you are going, not to return!

That good-bye to Youth, that confession that his heart is already autumnal, carries an explicit philosophy:

> La vida es dura. Amarga y pesa.
> ¡Ya no hay princesa que cantar!

Life is hard. It embitters and depresses. There is no princess to be sung.

The first word of the song, *Juventud* (Youth), points out the theme of the poet's meditation: the fleetingness of life in the current of an irreversible time. Darío apostrophizes Youth by using the present tense—"ya te vas para no volver" (so soon you are going, never to return)—as well as the past tense—"te fuiste para no volver" (you left, never to return). Such vacillation results from the fact that Darío does not resign himself to seeing his own youth as completely removed. This following of Youth's path—

still near yet already removed—ends with a verse of several possible interpretations: "¡Mas es mía el Alba de oro!" (But the golden dawn is still mine!). Perhaps the poet consoles himself here, remembering that, when young, he knew how to live intensely; he will become old, naturally, but nothing will be able to take away from him what he has lived or the joy that once, as an adolescent, he experienced when he saw a "golden dawn" in the future.

Cantos de vida y esperanza reveals Darío's existential anguish. The two "Nocturnos" (Nocturnes), "Melancolía" (Melancholy), "No obstante" (Nevertheless), "Filosofía" (Philosophy), and "A Phocás el campesino" (To Phocas the Rustic) are a few of the many poems that we could examine. We will comment on only one.

> Dichoso el árbol que es apenas sensitivo,
> y más la piedra dura, porque ésa ya no siente,
> pues no hay dolor más grande que el dolor de ser vivo,
> ni mayor pesadumbre que la vida consciente.
>
> Ser, y no saber nada, y ser sin rumbo cierto,
> y el temor de haber sido y un futuro terror . . .
> Y el espanto seguro de estar mañana muerto,
> y sufrir por la vida y por la sombra y por
>
> lo que no conocemos y apenas sospechamos,
> y la carne que tienta con sus frescos racimos,
> y la tumba que aguarda con sus fúnebres ramos,
> ¡y no saber adónde vamos,
> ni de dónde venimos . . . !
>
> "Lo fatal"

Happy the tree because it is barely sensitive, and happier the hard rock because it does not feel at all, for there is no pain as great as the pain of a living being nor greater heaviness than conscious life. To be, and to know nothing, and to be without direction, and the fear of having been, and a future terror . . . and the sure dread of being dead tomorrow, and suffering because of life and darkness and because of what we do not know and barely suspect, and the flesh that tempts us with its fresh grapes and the tomb that awaits us with its funeral wreaths, and we know not whither we go nor whence we came . . . !

Fatality

The theme of man's fate—to be conscious and wretched—was not, in Darío, a rhetorical exercise.

Consequently, he exteriorizes it with simplicity and directness. There is nothing of luxurious objects, mythologies, rococo palaces, artistic transpositions, verbal feats, and exquisite harmonies. Those elements belonged to the aestheticism that, years before, had earned him a reputation as a "decadent." Now, with a lump in his throat, Darío is not going in for games. His theme is the deadliness of having to think and tear apart his soul.

There was a neighboring theme, of related content: the religious theme. Darío had already poeticized—and he will do so increasingly—the contrasts between paganism and Christianity, hedonism and asceticism, skepticism and faith, the joy of living and the fear of death, flesh-pleasure and spirit-truth. But not even in "Lo fatal" will he yield to the religious theme. He touches upon it only barely and more on the side of theosophy than on that of the Catholic church. The verse "y el temor de haber sido y un futuro terror" (and the fear of having been, and a future terror) reflects Darío's obsession with reincarnation: If someone else had reincarnated when he was born, in whom would he reincarnate when he dies? This is the obsession of a theosophist, not of a Catholic. Fatality is not a doctrine of Catholicism. Darío himself said it: "In "Lo fatal", contrary to my deep-seated religiosity, and to my regret, rises a ghost of desolation and doubt, like a dark shadow" (*Historia de mis libros* [History of My Books]).

Darío's religiosity was not as deep-seated as he would have us believe, and therefore he adds, a few lines later: "In my desolation I have launched myself at God as a refuge, I have seized prayer as one would seize a parachute." It is not that he is flying toward God in a high heaven, but rather that he is falling upon God, in a deep abyss of doubts. Full of grief, and leaving aside the aesthetic and even the religious theme, Darío chose, in "Lo fatal," the autobiographical theme of why, for him, thinking was a fatal urge.

In many other poems, and also in pages of prose, Darío complained "of the terrible evil of thinking." As Darío was not a thinker—the truth is that he never forced himself to think logically—it is evident that he did not complain about rational thought but rather about the scruples of the conscience. Grim, tasteless, accusing conscience is life's killjoy, gaiety's wet blanket; it sours the wine and embitters the kiss.

Animal, vegetable, and mineral are guilty of nothing because they are what they are. Man, on the other hand, feels guilt because he is one way and wishes he were another. He is always keeping tabs. Darío sought simple pleasures (women, banquets, drunken revelry, social flattery), but later he would be mortified with remorse. The conscience produces thoughts, and the thoughts overwhelm us.

Consequently, in the poem "Lo fatal,"there is the feeling of sorrow. Many regrets weighed heavily upon him: the waste of his life, the ruin of his health, being a "drunkard until death" (as he said), the weakness of his character, the sordidness of his sex life, not writing the poetry of which he felt capable, having been born doomed, seeing a menacing hell on the other side of death. And when in the solitude of interminable insomnia the shouts of a remorseful conscience jolt him, Darío stiffens—solemn and agonizing—and renounces man's unique gift of reason (oh, if only he were stone, tree or beast!), and sobs.

In 1906 Darío published the book of essays entitled *Opiniones*, in which he rectified, explained, and cooled some of his juvenile enthusiasm. He is disconcerted upon seeing that writers who were once "strange" are now popular. In contrast, he declares admirations that would not have fit with the aestheticism of *Los raros*: for example, admirations for Émile Zola, for Arshile Gorky. In praising them, he admits the limitations of a pure, ivory-towerish, aristocratic literature. In general, he views the literary movement of the decadent and symbolistic Parnassians with the distant perspective of a historian. It is not that Darío has changed. He knows that he played a principal role in the renovation of literature. He salutes "Spain's new poets" (offering proof, naturally, that the Latin Americans helped them along), and insists, in the prologue, that he does not want to be imitated: "I'm not looking for anyone who thinks like me, nor for anyone who manifests himself as I do. Freedom! Freedom, my friends!" He is conscious of the fact that times have changed: "Now we all want to be simple."

In July and August 1906, as secretary of the Nicaraguan delegation at the Pan-American Conference in Rio de Janeiro, Darío wrote his "Salutación al águila" (Salutation to the Eagle). In it, the eagle symbolizes the United States and is the brother of the condor, Latin America's symbol.

*Águila, existe el Cóndor. Es tu hermano en las grandes
    alturas.*
Los Andes le conocen y saben que, cual tú, mira al Sol.

O Eagle, the Condor does exist. He is your brother, on
the mighty peaks. The Andes know him and realize that
he, like you, is gazing at the Sun.

Darío's intention was to contribute to an understanding between two cultures; but the foreign policy
of the United States had, at various times, aggravated
the Latin American nations, and there were those
who, invoking the fight against "Yankee imperialism," reproached Darío, for he appeared to them to
be backing down. It was not so. On the contrary,
Darío had the integrity to rise above his antipathy.
The increasing influence of the United States displeased him: its materialism, its excessive economic
power, its vulgarity, its lack of respect toward poor
countries. But he also recognized in the "Yankee
Cyclops" qualities worthy of imitation. Actually,
Darío did not care much about politics. In their
maneuvering and intrigue, politicians lack scruples,
so Darío was unscrupulous with them. This is hardly
an admirable attitude, but it is understandable. All
he wanted to do was to survive, and, although he
scorned politics, he played by the rules of the game.
He applauded this and that obscure Latin American
dictator and kept quiet about this or that oppression.
He temporized with political evils because he never
believed in politics; in contrast, he was proud when it
came to literature, and in his cult of beauty he never
ceded. Darío did not play politics with literature.

Toward the end of 1907, *Parisiana* (From Paris)
appeared, soon followed by *El canto errante* (The
Wandering Song), both published in Madrid. In
Parisiana, Darío moves with grace from journalistic
irony to poetic intuition. Darío always yielded to
contradictory impulses. He liked to enter palaces,
strut his diplomatic finery, live well, and rise socially.
His benevolent attention toward kings and aristocrats
was the version, on this side of the world, of the
mythologies that he cultivated on the other side, in
his literary work. But he knew that the elements of
this bohemian life of false grandeur—precarious
kings, dethroned kings, kings of comic-opera countries, kings from a deck of cards—were of little value.

Not without fear, he saw coming the great democratic and socialist revolution, and on one occasion,
before a certain injustice, notes this spirit in himself:
"The anarchist part inside my being is rising up." He
was not an anarchist, nor was he a socialist, nor even
a convinced democrat. Instead, he tried to make
himself comfortable in a badly made society. He was
kind, no doubt, as many testimonies of those close to
him indicate. But his kindness did not help him to
make common cause with the oppressed masses.

In Paris, in 1906, he had published a small volume:
Oda a Mitre (Ode to Mitre). Now he included it in his
next collection, *El canto errante*. The title indicates
that Darío, the traveler, was conscious of his extreme
mobility and that he, as a poet, was nothing less than
the personification of a song that wanted to become
eternal. He prefaced the book with some "elucidations" dedicated "to the new poets of the Spains." In
this most profound, coherent, and useful of his prologues, he continues the argument against the rhetoricians. An elite, he says, gathers talents, but each
one of these should express not the group's but, rather,
one's own personal originality. He insists on the sincerity of his poetry: "Never have I proposed to amaze
the bourgeois nor martyr my thought on a torture rack
of words. I do not take pleasure in old or new *moldes*
(forms) . . . . My verse has always been born with its
body and soul, and I have never applied to it any sort
of orthopedics." In these "elucidations" of *El canto
errante*, Darío is more explicit than in the Opening
Words of *Prosas profanas* and in the preface to *Cantos
de vida y esperanza*. Now he completes his thought.
Language, he tells us, is physical in its sonority, psy-
chic in its intentions, and social in its communication, all in a structure as indivisible as the body and
soul of a person who is talking with his family. There
is, in language, an external form, perceptible by the
senses (the verbal sound), and an internal form, interpreted by the mind (the ideal meaning). Both forms
merge in the creative energy of the poet, who, in turn,
manifests the infinite unity of the supreme Creator.
No one will resolve the conflicts between the lyric
style of the poet and the codified language of society.
It is best, then, that the poet abide by his own style,
which is creative freedom.

This prologue was better than the previous ones;
but *El canto errante*, as a book, is much less homo-

genous than *Prosas profanas* and *Cantos de vida y esperanza*, and is, on the whole, inferior. Darío must have had difficulty in putting it together. There are signs of all his types of singing, even the most juvenile, for he is still harvesting songs published after 1886. The themes are varied: passionate commentaries and literary medallions; exaltation of art; erotic relief, the philosophy of life and religious and esoteric unrest; intellectual games; moral, political, and civil attitudes; the urge to travel and the landscapes of the journey; descriptions of American wildlife; the myths of indigenous America ("Tutecotzimí"); and the inevitable influence of the United States ("Salutación al águila").

Although these themes exist in his previous work, the poet amazes us with new expressions, like very familiar faces that suddenly smile at us with a movement of the lips we had not seen. At times, Darío shows a grimace, not a smile. More than in other books, we hear irregularities. As usual, Darío is a musician, especially in the old poems, but in the recent ones he tends to allow prosaic rhythms and even the living voice of conversation. One example is the "Epístola (a la señora de Leopoldo Lugones)" (Epistle to the Wife of Leopoldo Lugones), in which he confesses his moral weaknesses, his neurosis, and his incapability of defending himself from human rapacity. These verses seemed out of tune to the ears of those readers educated by modernist music. Today, in contrast, accustomed as we are to the prosaism of communicative literature at the level of the masses, the ironic and conservative autobiography of the "Epístola" seems more modern to us than modernism. At times one hears the babble of a thought broken by perplexity, as in "¡Eheu!" (Ah!).

> Unas vagas confidencias
> del ser y el no ser
> y fragmentos de conciencias
> de ahora y ayer.

> Some vague confidences
> of being and not being,
> and fragments of consciences
> of now and yesterday.

In *Poema del otoño y otros poemas* (Poem of Autumn and Other Poems, 1910), the ensemble is fee-

ble, but here we find one of his best lyric moments: the exultant "Poema del otoño." The poem, itself, as a tree in autumn, has let fall, in magnificent cadences, its ample ornamental foliage; and it shows, if not the dryness, the bareness of the trunk and the branches of Darío's philosophy of time. Time corrodes all and hurries, he says; we grow old, we become bitter, and fatigue makes us pensive. But in view of this certainty of death, why do we not turn around and approach what life we still have left with eagerness? Even if by doing it we sin, life is worth the risk. Let's live. "Cojamos la flor del instante" (Let us pluck the flower of the moment). One must know how to pluck it in adolescence; but even in the autumn, let's live, let's enjoy. Everything passes, and the moment is what offers itself to man, "espuma de un mar eterno" (spindrift of an eternal sea). After all—and here Darío's hedonism becomes pantheism—the pleasure of love makes us participate in the driving force of creation. The universe is a mysterious fecundating force: "la paloma de Venus vuela / sobre la Esfinge" (the dove of Venus is flying over the Sphinx). We are something more than men.

> Pues aunque hay pena y nos agravia
> el sino adverso,
> en nosotros corre la savia
> del universo.

> Nuestro cráneo guarda el vibrar
> de tierra y sol,
> como el rüido de la mar
> el caracol.

> La sal del mar en nuestras venas
> va a borbotones;
> tenemos sangre de sirenas
> y de tritones.

> A nosotros encinas, lauros,
> frondas espesas;
> tenemos carne de centauros
> y satiresas.

> En nosotros la vida vierte
> fuerza y calor.
> ¡Vamos al reino de la Muerte
> por el camino de Amor!

Although there is such a thing as pain, and adversity grieves us, the very sap of the universe flows within us. Our skull keeps the vibration of earth and sun as the shell keeps the beat of the sea. The salt of the sea goes bubbling in our veins; our blood is the blood of mermaids and tritons. Oaks, laurels, thick foliage are for us; we have the flesh of centaurs and satyresses. Life pours into us force and warmth. We go to the kingdom of Death by the path of Love!

These verses prove that it is not true that the erotic theme dominates Darío's poems in the manner of a sun that, from each height, governs the shadows of things. Granted, Darío the man yielded to sexual impulses and Darío the artist let these impulses touch his art. But once in contact with art, the impulses were no longer sexual. In any case, they did not constitute a primordial theme; other themes presided over the erotic. One example is the theme of art itself. From the romantics to the symbolists, it was fashionable to allude to artistic power in terms of sexuality. The poet was a satyr who wanted to possess nature. Mystery took the form of women, such as Isis. Meditation was voluptuous. One impregnated a Muse. The work of art was more desirable than a woman of flesh and blood. Furthermore, in Darío's case, and in that of other occultists, the origin of the world was sexual, and the poet, one of its priests. Many myths were of use to him in these effusions, not because they were erotic, but because they were beautiful: the swan and Leda, Apollo and Daphne, Aphrodite, this nymph, that satyr or centaur. Thanks to his artistic impulse, the erotic myths ended up as the bearers of an illuminating beauty, not of an underhanded sensuality.

In 1911 and 1912, respectively, Darío published his two books of essays: *Letras* (Literature) and *Todo al vuelo* (Just in Passing). In *Letras* Darío again shows us a double attitude: on one hand he reclaims his role as restorer of a new literary regime in the Spanish language; on the other hand, he rejects the idea of fashions, schools, manifestos, and literary chieftains. It is as if he wanted to tell us that he was indeed worthy of joining the vanguard of Parnassians, symbolists, and decadents, but that these aesthetic currents were already a part of the past and that only the imitators have remained in the modernist school.

Todo al vuelo ends the series of books of essays that

he himself authorized. In its pages, Darío remembers his literary career from the easy chair of the historian, beginning with the pleasure of recounting his first steps and first meetings with other writers. He knows that he put himself at the head of a Latin American, and even Spanish, movement; but he also knows that in this movement there were passing fads, desertions, the advent of new values and the constant company of mediocre imitators.

From 1911 to 1914, Darío wrote articles for *La Nación* of Buenos Aires. These were collected, posthumously, under the title *El mundo de los sueños* (The World of Dreams, 1973). They are not worth much as literature but are fundamental to an understanding of Darío's personality. Darío cared more about oneiromancy than about the psychology of dreams. Through his dreams, he looked for the occult, for revelation of the absolute. A large part of his literature was nourished on the mix that he made of dreams with irrational beliefs and nervous disorders.

In these years, Darío tried three different forms of autobiography: anecdotal memoirs, a history of his books, and a novel about his life. While in Buenos Aires, he had scribbled a few pages and dictated others for the weekly *Caras y Caretas* (Faces and Masks), which were published from 21 September to 30 November 1912. A publishing house in Barcelona collected them under the title *La vida de Rubén Darío* (The Life of Rubén Darío, 1915). It is not a good book of memoirs, and Darío does not recount with pleasure. One notices the rush to fulfill a journalistic commitment. He forgets or hardly mentions facts of some consequence; instead, he amplifies, disproportionately, dispensable anecdotes. Nevertheless, in these unorganized pages, the reader sympathizes with Darío the man: meek, sincere, generous, impractical, even-tempered, understanding, capable of good humor, without more vanity than necessary to dedicate himself to poetry.

In his next autobiographical attempt, Darío concerned himself more with his books. In July 1913, he published three articles in *La Nación*—on *Azul, Prosas profanas, Cantos de vida y esperanza* that would be edited posthumously under the title *Historia de mis libros*. These articles, written with more care than those of *La vida de Rubén Darío*, are indispensable for the studious. The poet traces the origins of the three collections that he liked the most; he points out the effects they had on the renovation of poetry; he distinguishes the successive waves of this renovation; he comments on his leadership in the midst of those who resisted, accompanied, followed, or imitated him; he tells about some of his most audacious experiments. He explains that his mastery consisted of a domination of the literary traditions of the Spanish language—from "the primitive and classical"—and also of learning French and European techniques, all in an artistic, aristocratic tension that gave way to the expression of an "internal melody." He enumerates his sources and offers the key to his personal originality with its conflict between sensuality and religious faith, between the exigencies of culture and the desire to be natural, between art and life. He insists that each poet should become independent of scholastic formulas and examine the genesis of his poems.

Darío's third autobiographical attempt, in novel form, was published in *La Nación* between December 1913 and March 1914: *El oro de Mallorca* (Majorcan Gold). The plot is minimal. The musician Benjamín Itaspes, Darío's self-portrait, goes from Marseilles to Majorca to spend a period of rest at a friend's house and begins a relationship with a sculptress. Darío confesses that what he recounts here is the failure of his marriage to Rosario Murillo. In this "species of novel" are Darío's most intimate and indiscreet pages.

Halfway through 1914, Darío published *Canto a la Argentina y otros poemas* (Song to the Argentine and Other Poems), which had appeared in a newspaper in Buenos Aires in 1910 in celebration of that country's centennial. It was the most extensive of his poems, not the best. More significant is "La Cartuja" (The Carthusian Monastery), in which the Catholic concepts of a transcendent God and contempt of the flesh seem to cause Darío to doubt his earlier exalted hedonism and pantheism.

In "Poema del otoño," Darío had expressed his desire to enjoy life until the hour of his death. On the contrary, he now seems to express his contempt for enjoyment before the possible existence of a heaven that prizes asceticism. Darío, man of poetic vocation, admired, from the other side of the fence, religious vocation; and what more impressive religious voca-

tion than that of the Carthusian monks whom he saw in their monastery of Valldemosa, on Majorca. Without a doubt, they were men like himself and, like him, must feel the sexual urge. But those Carthusians saved themselves from the temptations of the devil, thanks to prayer, discipline, and solitude. Alas! he, Darío, had not been elected by God to save himself in this way. Then the poet laments all the sensual powers that, in "Poema del otoño," he had believed to be the force and heat of a universal fecundity. There is a tremendous fight between the faun and the angel who inhabit him, dramatized in quartets in which some verses express what the poet is, others what he would like to be. Oh! If he could only give himself saintliness!

> *Darme otros ojos, no éstos ojos vivos*
> *que gozan en mirar, como los ojos*
> *de los sátiros locos medio-chivos,*
> *redondeces de nieve y labios rojos.*
>
> *Darme otra boca en que queden impresos*
> *los ardientes carbones de asceta,*
> *y no ésta boca en que vinos y besos*
> *aumentan gulas de hombre y de poeta.*
>
> *Darme unas manos de disciplinante*
> *que me dejen el lomo ensangrentado,*
> *y no éstas manos lúbricas de amante*
> *que acarician las pomas del pecado.*
>
> *Darme una sangre que me deje llenas*
> *las venas de quietud y en paz los sesos,*
> *y no ésta sangre que hace arder las venas,*
> *vibrar los nervios y crujir los huesos.*

To give myself other eyes, not these vivacious eyes that take joy in looking at snowy roundnesses and red lips like eyes of mad goat-footed satyrs. To give myself another mouth, burnt by the ardent coals of the ascetic, not this mouth in which wine and kisses augment the gluttony of man and poet. To give myself hands of a flagellant to whip and to bloody my back, not these lascivious lover's hands that caress the apple of sin. To give myself blood that might fill my veins with quietness and my brains with peace, not this blood that burns my veins, vibrates my nerves, and crackles my bones.

The sincerity of this poem lies precisely in that it shows us an incorrigible Darío, habitual sinner until the day he dies. The rest of the book does not have the same depth. It is interesting to see how, since 1914, Darío, overcome with religiosity, took a few steps toward the church, seemed to enter and then did not, wanted to believe but could not, started to cross himself but let his hand fall. He was discouraged by "horrible doubt." His was a religious soul, if by this we mean he felt his own insignificance before a dreadful absolute Being that has created us; but he had never enrolled in any church. We have already seen that when he professed to be Catholic it was with shadings and reservations that a priest would not have approved. He was somewhat superstitious and something of an occultist, a theosophist, a metaphysicist, and a collector of myths, with a preference for Christian terminology, given that his civilization was Christian; but he had no faith in any dogma.

In October 1914, shortly after the outbreak of World War I, Darío distanced himself from Europe to make a "pacifist outing in America." He passed through New York, in whose Hispanic Society he read his poem "Pax" (Peace), continued on to Guatemala, to whose dictator he dedicated the poem "Palas Athenea" (Pallas Athena) and from there returned to his native Nicaragua. In spite of his long absences from his homeland, the Nicaraguans continued to consider him their national poet.

Actually, the homeland, for Darío, was all of Central America. He had dedicated various poems to the cause of the Unión Centroamericana (Central American Union) and, in his essays, tended to speak of "the five countries of my land." We could go further than he and believe that his homeland was Latin America, from Mexico to Chile and Argentina. He always spoke of that "magna patria" (great homeland), as Simon Bolívar called it. He spoke of the towns and their customs, the heroes and their feats, the creators and their creations. He included the indigenous pre-Columbian past in the living history of Latin America ("My poet's pickax . . . works in the terrain of the unknown America," he said in "Tutecotzimí"). He preached that the independent republics should not forget their common Spanish heritage nor become anarchical in civil wars ("I am a son of America, I am a grandson of Spain," he said in "Los cisnes" [The Swans]). He dreamed of the utopia of a vast land of promise ("To your health, homeland, for yours is also mine, / since you are part of humanity!" he said in "Canto a la Argentina").

Darío saw Latin America integrated into Western culture, but he also felt it was distinct because of its racial mixture. "Is there in my blood some drop of blood of Africa or of Chorotega or Nagrandano Indian? It could be, in spite of these hands of a marquis," he said in the opening words of Prosas profanas. On one occasion, Miguel de Unamuno joked that one could see Indian feathers under Darío's sombrero. The intention was not offensive, and Darío answered him with much grace: "It is with a feather that I take from under my hat that I write." Years after Darío's death, Unamuno explained how he was first attracted to Darío's goodness and only later discovered the great poet: "To the Indian—I say this without a hint of irony, rather with a flat tone of reverence—to the Indian who trembled with all his being, like the foliage of a tree whipped by the north wind, before the mystery."

Indian or no, Darío was Latin America's poet. Rodó denied that he was, but that was immediately after reading the Frenchified Prosas profanas. Today, in view of his complete work, no one would dare deny it. The truth is that, even in the "precious" years of Prosas profanas, a perspicacious reader could have glimpsed the Latin American who was hiding in that style. Darío's taste for the aristocracy had its antecedents in viceregal America. After all, Spain had transplanted to its colonies a society with a hierarchy of classes. First the Spaniard, then the creole were individualists, arrogant and ungovernable. They wanted to live like gentlemen, although their surroundings did not always permit it, and as much as they could, they escaped reality with impossible dreams of greatness. Darío went into libraries, museums, and palaces and came out disguised as a marquis; but under his disguise, there was an authentic spiritual aristocrat. Many years have passed and upon passing have taken away that which was artificial in Darío the artist. On the collective artifice of the generations of 1885–1910 was stamped the seal of Rubén Darío: his vitality, his intelligence, his good taste, his wisdom. He filled the whole modernist period. He was modernism.

Rubén Darío left poetry different from what he had found: in this, he was like Garcilaso de la Vega, Fray

Luis de León, San Juan de la Cruz, Lope de Vega, Luis de Góngora, and Gustavo Adolfo Bécquer. But he was not simply a master of rhythm. With incomparable elegance he poeticized the joy of living and the terror of death.

Death, ugly death, overcame him on 6 February 1916, in his beloved Nicaragua.

Translated from the Spanish by Peter Latson

SELECTED BIBLIOGRAPHY

Editions

Epístolas y poemas. Managua, 1885.

Abrojos. Santiago, Chile, 1887.

Rimas. Santiago, Chile, 1887.

Azul . . . . Valparaíso, Chile 1888.

A. de Gilbert. San Salvador, 1889.

Los raros. Buenos Aires, 1896.

Prosas profanas y otros poemas. Buenos Aires, 1896.

España contemporánea. Paris, 1901.

Peregrinaciones. Paris, 1901.

La caravana pasa. Paris, 1902.

Tierras solares. Madrid, 1904.

Cantos de vida y esperanza. Los cisnes y otros poemas. Madrid, 1905.

Opiniones. Madrid, 1906.

El canto errante. Madrid, 1907.

Parisiana. Madrid, 1907.

El viaje a Nicaragua e Intermezzo tropical. Madrid, 1909.

Poema del otoño y otros poemas. Madrid, 1910.

Letras. Paris, 1911.

Todo al vuelo. Madrid, 1912.

Canto a la Argentina y otros poemas. Madrid, 1914.

La vida de Rubén Darío escrita por él mismo. Barcelona, 1915.

Obras desconocidas de Rubén Darío, escritas en Chile y no recogidas en ninguno de sus libros. Edited by Raúl Silva Castro. Santiago, Chile, 1934. Posthumous.

Escritos inéditos. Edited by E. K. Mapes. New York, 1938. Posthumous.

Páginas desconocidas de Rubén Darío. Edited by Roberto Ibáñez. Montevideo, 1970. Posthumous.

El mundo de los sueños. Edited by Ángel Rama. Rio Piedras, Puerto Rico, 1973. Posthumous.

Collected Works

Autobiografías. Prologue by Enrique Anderson Imbert. Buenos Aires, 1976. Includes *Autobiografía, Historia de mis libros,* and *El oro de Mallorca.*

Cuentos completos. Edited by Ernesto Mejía Sánchez. Introductory essay by Raimundo Lida. Mexico City, 1950.

Escritos dispersos de Rubén Darío. Edited by Pedro Luis Barcia. La Plata, Argentina, 1968.

Obras completas. Edited by Sanmiguel Raimúndez and Emilio Gascó Contell. 5 vols. Madrid, 1950–1955.

Poesía. Prologue by Ángel Rama. Edited by Ernesto Mejía Sánchez. Chronology by Julio Valle-Castillo. Caracas, 1977.

Poesías completas. Edited by Alfonso Méndez Plancarte. Corrected and enlarged by Antonio Oliver Belmás. 10th edition. Madrid, 1967.

Rubén Darío, crítico literario; temas americanos. Edited by Ermilo Abreu Gómez. Washington, D.C., 1951.

Translations

Eleven Poems of Rubén Darío. Translated by Thomas Walsh and Salomón de la Selva. New York, 1916.

Prosas Profanas and Other Poems. Translated by Charles B. McMichael. New York, 1922.

Selected Poems of Rubén Darío. Translated by Lysander Kemp. Austin, Tex., 1965.

Swan, Cygnets, and Owl. An Anthology of Modernist Poetry in Spanish America. Translated by Mildred E. Johnson. With an introductory essay by J. S. Brushwood. Columbia, Mo., 1956.

Biographical and Critical Studies

Anderson Imbert, Enrique. *La originalidad de Rubén Darío.* Buenos Aires, 1967.

Bowra, C. M. *Inspiration and Poetry.* New York, 1955. Pp. 242–264.

Capdevila, Arturo. *Rubén Darío, "un bardo rei."* Buenos Aires, 1946.

Carilla, Emilio. *Una etapa decisiva de Darío: Rubén Daíro en la Argentina.* Madrid, 1967.

Contreras, Francisco. *Rubén Darío: Su vida y su obra.* Barcelona, 1930.

Cuadernos hispanoamericanos. 212–213 (1967).

Darío. Universidad de Chile, 1968.

Ellis, Keith. *Critical Approaches to Rubén Darío.* Toronto, 1974.

Giordano, Jaime. *La edad del ensueño: Sobre la imaginación poética de Rubén Darío.* Santiago, Chile, 1971.

Goldberg, Isaac. *Studies in Spanish-American Literature.* New York, 1920. Pp. 101–183.

Homenaje a Rubén Darío. Universidad Nacional Mayor de San Marcos, Lima, Perú, 1967.

Homenjae a Rubén Darío. Revista iberoamericana 33/64 (1967).

Le Fort, E. C. "Rubén Darío and the 'Modernista' Movement." *University of Miami Hispanic-American Studies* 2:220–237 (1941).

Lida, Raimundo. "Los cuentos de Rubén Darío." In *Diez estudios sobre Rubén Darío,* edited by Juan Loveluck. Santiago, Chile, 1967. Pp. 155–207.

Mapes, E. K. "Innovation and French Influence in the Metrics of Rubén Darío." *Publications of the Modern Language Association of America* 49/1:310–326 (1934).

Marasso, Arturo. *Rubén Darío y su creación poética.* Definitive edition. Buenos Aires, 1954.

Mejía Sánchez, Ernesto, ed. *Estudios sobre Rubén Darío.* Mexico City, 1968.

Oliver Belmás, Antonio. *Este otro Rubén Darío.* Barcelona, 1960.

Paz, Octavio. "El caracol y la sirena." In *Cuadrivio.* Mexico City, 1965. Pp. 9–65.

Rubén Darío. Universidad de Concepción, Chile, 1967.

Rubén Darío Estudios reunidos en conmemoración del centenario. La Plata, Argentina, 1968.

Salinas, Pedro. *La poesía de Rubén Darío.* Buenos Aires, 1948.

Sequeira, Diego Manuel. *Rubén Darío, criollo.* Buenos Aires, 1945.

———. *Rubén Darío, criollo en El Salvador.* León, Nicaragua, 1965.

Torres, Edelberto. *La dramática vida de Rubén Darío.* 3rd ed. Mexico City, 1958.

Torres Bodet, Jaime. *Rubén Darío: Abismo y cima.* Mexico City, 1966.

Torres-Ríoseco, Arturo. *Vida y poesía de Rubén Darío.* Buenos Aires, 1944.

Trend, J. B. *Rubén Darío.* Cambridge, England, 1952.

Watland, Charles D. *Poet-errant: A biography of Rubén Darío.* New York, 1965.

Bibliographies

Del Greco, Arnold Armand. *Repertorio bibliográfico del mundo de Rubén Darío,* New York, 1969.

Hebblethwaite, Frank P. "Una bibliografía de Rubén Darío (1945–1966)." *Revista interamericana de bibliografía* 17/2:202–221 (1967).

Jirón Terán, José. *Bibliografía general de Rubén Darío.* Managua, 1967.

Saavedra Molina, Julio. *Bibliografía de Rubén Darío.* Santiago, Chile, 1946.

Woodbridge, Hensley C. *Rubén Darío: A Selective Classified and Annotated Bibliography.* Metuchen, N.J., 1975.

Roberto Jorge Payró

(1867–1928)

John F. Garganigo

Roberto Jorge Payró, Argentinean novelist, short story writer, dramatist, political man of action, and dedicated journalist, was born in Mercedes (Buenos Aires) on 19 April 1867. The Payró family had settled in Buenos Aires in 1828 during the regime of Juan Manuel de Rosas. Although Roberto's father, originally from Catalonia, Spain, had married into an aristocratic Uruguayan family, thus attaining a measure of respectability, it was very difficult during this period of strict social stratification for any immigrant to be fully accepted into society. The Payró family remained on the periphery, a fact that would condition the writer's view of society.

From an early age, Payró demonstrated a keen interest in literature. In 1882, together with a number of young friends, he was instrumental in founding Los Pickwickianos (The Pickwickians), a literary circle inspired by the popularity of Charles Dickens. It was also during this time that Payró was attracted to politics, aligning himself with the liberal ideology of Bartolomé Mitre, a statesman who served as Argentina's president from 1862 to 1868. Mitre's presidency saw the emergence of Buenos Aires as the center of government. He encouraged foreign immigration and investments, and curbed the power of local, provincial *caudillos* (political bosses), who were supporters of the land-owning oligarchy. By 1891,

Payró had become firmly entrenched within the ranks of a newly founded, middle-class political party, the Unión Cívica Radical, embracing at the same time a social-democratic ideology based on the works of Eduard Bernstein and Karl Kautsky. In 1894, he began his association with the recently established Socialist party.

Payró's literary career began with the publication in 1883 of the poem *Un hombre feliz* (A Happy Man), a youthful book that he later destroyed as an act of self-criticism. This work displayed a nonconformist attitude that was to become one of his trademarks. Soon after his marriage to María Ana Bettini in 1888, Payró launched *La Tribuna* of Bahía Blanca, a newspaper that became the organ of the Unión Cívica Radical. Its initial success was short-lived, and in 1890, after declaring bankruptcy, he moved to Buenos Aires, where, after a series of positions with a number of newspapers, he became affiliated with *La Nación*, Argentina's most prestigious publication.

As a roving reporter, he traveled to Chile in 1895 and wrote "Cartas chilenas escritas por un argentino" (Chilean Letters Written by an Argentine), a series of impressions based on a close scrutiny of Chilean customs and culture. His vivid portrayal of the Chilean *roto*, or peasant, was a penetrating psychological study with realistic overtones. It showed

413

Payró's ability to capture the main characteristics of certain types of individuals against a sociopolitical backdrop. It is precisely this ability that constitutes Payró's greatest contribution to Argentinean letters.

Firsthand accounts of travelers made up a large body of literature in nineteenth-century Latin America. When Payró began commenting on his own country after visits to Patagonia in 1898 and a journey to the northern provinces of Argentina in 1899, he was continuing a tradition that was well established. His *La Australia argentina* (Argentinean Australia, 1898) and *En las tierras del Inti* (In the Lands of the Inti, 1909) had as a model *Una excursión a los indios ranqueles* (An Excursion to the Land of the Ranquel Indians, 1870), by another great Argentinean writer, Lucio Victorio Mansilla.

Payró was at his best when he analyzed the causes and effects of political turmoil, as in his accounts of the uprising of Aparicio Saravia, the Uruguayan *caudillo* who in 1903 sought to overthrow the legitimate government of president-elect José Batlle y Ordóñez. Payró's interest in history inspired him to contemplate a grandiose project along the lines of the *Episodios nacionales* (National Episodes), by Spain's leading nineteenth-century writer, Benito Pérez Galdós. Their main purpose was to trace the development of a nation throughout history by capturing the lives of key figures at crucial moments in time. Although Payró never completed this project, he returned to it at various times in his life. Two works that stand out are *El falso Inca* (The False Inca) of 1905 and *El mar dulce* (The Calm Sea) of 1927. The latter is of particular interest because it traced the discovery of the river Plate region, underlining the cultural ties with conquering Spain.

At the turn of the century, Payró gravitated toward theater, producing *Un drama vulgar* (A Vulgar Drama) and *Canción trágica* (Tragic Song), both of 1900. These were followed by *Sobre las ruinas* (Upon the Ruins), of 1904, and *Marco Severi*, of 1905. *Canción trágica* and *Marco Severi*, conceived within the prevailing dramatic current of theater of ideas, or "thesis theater," are fraught with social implications. They deal respectively with the conflict between progress and tradition, and the implementation of the newly formulated law of extradition with an emphasis on its human repercussions. Marco Severi, for example, is

forced to return to Italy to pay for an earlier crime, after having lived an exemplary life in Argentina for ten years. Payró was a faithful chronicler of this delicate period of transition, during which Argentina changed from a rural to an urban nation.

By 1907, Payró was recognized as one of the leading writers of his generation. In the theater he was as influential as Florencio Sánchez, the noted Uruguayan dramatist, while in the narrative his closest competitors were the Uruguayans Javier de Viana and Carlos Reyles, and his compatriots José Sixto Álvarez (Fray Mocho) and Francisco A. Sicardi. For the most part, these writers and journalists had been able to raise writing to the level of a profession and to dedicate their lives to the production of literature. As evidence that writers considered themselves members of a profession, they founded La Sociedad Argentina de Escritores (The Society of Argentinean Writers) and elected Payró as its president in 1906. The influence of this society is still felt today.

An unexpected inheritance from a long-lost relative took Payró to Barcelona in 1907. He was joined there by his family two years later, and they remained in Europe until after the end of World War I. The family lived in Belgium from 1909 to 1919, actively supporting the Allied effort. While Payró wrote newspaper articles denouncing German actions, his wife and his youngest son, Roberto, joined the Belgian army as volunteer hospital workers. The German military command ransacked Payró's Brussels apartment and confiscated all of his papers. After a period in jail, Payró was released, and his papers were returned to him shortly before he embarked for his native country.

Payró's fame as a writer is based mainly on three major works: *El casamiento de Laucha* (*Laucha's Marriage*, 1906), the country tales of *Pago Chico* (1908), and *Divertidas aventuras del nieto de Juan Moreira* (Entertaining Adventures of the Grandson of Juan Moreira, 1910).

Laucha's Marriage is a short novel written in the picaresque mode. Laucha, the protagonist, is a typical rogue, or *pícaro*, who embodies many of the ills that afflicted Argentina at the turn of the century. Although depicted as having a certain amount of charm, not unusual in a picaresque character, Laucha is a despicable human being who is lazy, cruel, amoral, self-centered, and unscrupulous in his dealings. While he laments that he is a victim of bad fortune, or fate, he remains blind to his many shortcomings. According to Enrique Anderson Imbert, Laucha is a character who derives an almost perverse delight in blaming fate for his condition. Through Laucha, Payró is presenting a totally chaotic and uncontrollable world. Laucha accepts this world because he knows he cannot change it. Unlike other picaresque novels, the protagonist's voice is never overtly moralizing, although by implication this presentation of reality suggests the conquering effects of barbarism over civilization. Noé Jitrik, a respected Argentinean critic, sees this aspect as the novel's main intent, as Payró's predominant theme. The presentation of the development of Argentinean society as a struggle between the forces of civilization and those of barbarism, first voiced by Domingo Faustino Sarmiento in his monumental *Civilización y barbarie: Vida de Juan Facundo Quiroga* (Civilization and Barbarism: Life of Juan Facundo Quiroga, 1845), underscored this social phenomenon. If the city of Buenos Aires was the center of civilization, then the countryside, and by extension the inhabitants of the pampa, became synonymous with barbarism. In order for the country to progress, barbarism had to be eradicated.

In the novel, Laucha takes advantage of Carolina, a recently widowed, matronly Italian immigrant who is the owner of a small but successful business. By playing on her emotions, Laucha convinces her to make him a full partner in the enterprise. His machinations eventually lead to a proposal of marriage, a union that will allow Laucha complete freedom to squander Carolina's hard-earned fortune. One of the most vivid scenes occurs when Laucha arranges the wedding with the equally corrupt Father Papagna, a Neapolitan priest whose greed characterizes that of some immigrants who settled in Argentina with no intention of becoming an integral part of the society. While many immigrants worked diligently to become assimilated, others came to Argentina hoping to "fare l'America," to get rich quickly and to return home. Payró's indictment of Father Papagna is scathing.

This loathsome individual offers Laucha a special type of marriage. For a hefty fee, he will deliver the wedding license to Laucha but fail to record it in the local registry. In effect, this allows the rogue to dissolve the marriage at any time. When Laucha eventually leaves Carolina, after informing her that the wedding had been a sham, we witness the disintegration of a society in which nothing is held sacred. The only decent and moral person in the novel, Carolina, is left in abject poverty, her life shattered. Papagna returns to Naples, and Laucha tries to rationalize his behavior by suggesting that the breakup of the marriage was the best thing for both parties. While Laucha continues to roam from place to place, showing a total disregard for society, Carolina is able to pick up the pieces. She starts life anew as a nurse in a local hospital. Implicit in the novel's ending is Payró's belief that progress and hard work eventually will triumph. Unlike others, who considered the immigrant to be an outcast, Payró was able to see that human beings like Carolina could be incorporated into the nation.

If *Laucha's Marriage* was the story of one *pícaro*, the tales of *Pago Chico* present a collection of rogues, set against a rural background. The twenty-two stories are based on common characters, some ot whom, like Laucha and Papagna, had appeared in the previous novel. The rural setting of Pago Chico symbolizes a closely knit society governed by political corruption and chicanery. It is a mirror of Payró's days in the provincial town of Bahía Blanca during the years 1880 to 1890. With humorous undertones, Payró unmasks the intricate machinery of the oligarchy by presenting the various types who inhabit the town. With an objective eye, he narrates the events of the daily lives of the local political bosses, electoral *caudillos*, police commissioners, judges, lawyers, doctors, shopkeepers, immigrants, and enlightened do-gooders. A third-person narrator allows the characters to comment on different situations. The resulting observations of the world are presented in a humorous way, yet they underscore serious social problems. Payró's biting remarks are directed toward those who are members of the establishment as well as those who are working in the name of progress. Payró was not blind to the faults of those who professed a progressive ideology.

A memorable character who comments on one of

the pertinent issues of the day is Silvestre, the local chemist and self-proclaimed town crier. His views closely reflect Payró's own. Silvestre's straightforward account of events in the local elections reveals corruption and abuse of political power, as dishonest electoral officials, controlled by minor *caudillos*, undermine the democratic process at will. His account is humorous yet shocking:

> Yesterday's election was so peaceful that no one bothered to set up the polls. . . . Can you believe that! Those who were to count the ballots completely forgot about the election until Bustos, the local secretary, brought the tally sheets to Ferreiro's house, so that they could sign them and send them to the Capital. I heard someone say to him: "What's the rush! The elections aren't until next Sunday!" . . . When all is said and done, without anyone leaving his house, without paying one single cent, two thousand votes were delivered to the party: this gives Pago Chico enormous political clout. It shows how well we all pull together for the good of the fatherland!
>
> (*Pago Chico*, p. 167)

This type of attitude shows that the system contains residues of barbarism that impede progress. This issue was one of many debated in public forums as Argentina was celebrating its first century of independence from Spain.

Critics are unanimous in their praise of *Divertidas aventuras del nieto de Juan Moreira*, considered to be Payró's unquestioned masterpiece. Anderson Imbert, who has written a penetrating study of the *pícaro* in the three works discussed above, emphasizes Payró's serious intent in this last novel. According to this critic, although the Argentinean reality and the characters remain the same as those in his earlier novels, Payró has injected into this work a definite, theoretical social plan along progressive lines. The life of Mauricio Gómez Herrera, descendant of the legendary outlaw Juan Moreira, is offered as an example of the negative forces that impede progress. Gómez Herrera narrates his life through a series of memoirs delivered to a scribe. His life parallels the course of Argentinean history in the transitional period from the late nineteenth century to the beginning of the twentieth century.

Gómez Herrera's life is as complex as the historical period reflected. At a time in Argentinean history

when the country was trying to gain a foothold in the modern era, many forces were diametrically opposed to the progressive ideals formulated by Sarmiento and Mitre. There were no facile solutions to the perplexing questions raised by opposing sides. For this reason, Payró's portrayal of Gómez Herrera is not one-sided. If, on the one hand, Gómez Herrera embodies certain characteristics worthy of emulation, among them a strong individualism, a charismatic personality, and a dynamism that all great men possess, these qualities must be tempered and used for the achievement of common goals. On the other hand, Gómez Herrera, as the last remnant of the amoral, selfish, unscrupulous *caudillo*, represents the negative forces that kept Argentina tied to outdated, reactionary values.

In a progressive society, there was no room to place the *caudillo* on a pedestal, as so many writers had done, pretending to espouse the ideals of a national literature. Those who romanticized the *gaucho*, and all *caudillos* were *gauchos*, were inventing a human being who bore little resemblance to reality. Others, like Payró, were more realistic in their appraisal. The *gaucho* stood in the way of real democratic progress. Payró's message implied that there was no turning back. The essence of the *gaucho* that lived on in Gómez Herrera's personality had to be eradicated. Payró's views were expressed in no uncertain terms in one of the *Charlas de un optimista* (An Optimist's Musings), published in 1931. He said:

> Society's onward march has certain requirements that appear to be cruel ones but that are at the same time beneficial to the majority. . . . Today's *gaucho* is a static element, a useless and embarrassing one. He has to disappear, and he will disappear, through degeneration that is tantamount to death and through absorption that is transformation.
>
> (Ghiano, p. 25)

Payró was a great observer who turned to history in order to find answers to the present. He traced the evolution of his characters within a historical context, at the same time assessing the social evolution of an entire nation. It should not surprise us that his assessment of Gómez Herrera as an opportunistic individual who was continuing in the footsteps of his infamous predecessor, Juan Moreira, suggested a deterministic view of society. This pessimistic view, a product of the prevailing current of naturalism in vogue at the time, was tempered, however, when Payró allowed Mauricio Rivas, the illegitimate son of Gómez Herrera, to be the most outspoken critic of the system. When Mauricio attacks Gómez Herrera, not knowing his true identity, he is attacking the very foundations of a corrupt political system. At the same time, he offers a glimmer of hope for the future by suggesting a total reconstruction of Argentina, based on new ideals of progress.

Roberto Payró died on 5 April 1928. Although not all of his work merits critical acclaim, he was a faithful observer of Argentinean reality in troubled times. He felt the pulse of an age as few before or after him have done.

SELECTED BIBLIOGRAPHY

First Editions

Poetry

Un hombre feliz. Buenos Aires, 1883.

Plays

Canción trágica. Buenos Aires, 1902.
Sobre las ruinas. Buenos Aires, 1902.
Marco Severi. Buenos Aires, 1907.

Prose

La Australia argentina. 2 vols. Buenos Aires, 1898.
El falso Inca. Buenos Aires, 1905.
El casamiento de Laucha. Buenos Aires, 1906.
Pago Chico. Barcelona and Buenos Aires, 1908.
En las tierras del Inti. Buenos Aires, 1909.

Divertidas aventuras del nieto de Juan Moreira. Barcelona, 1910.
El mar dulce. Buenos Aires, 1927.
Charlas de un optimista. Buenos Aires, 1931.

Modern Editions

El casamiento de Laucha. Buenos Aires, 1940. Includes *El falso Inca.*
Pago Chico y nuevos cuentos de Pago Chico. Buenos Aires, 1939.
Cuentos de Pago Chico. Havana, 1965.
Divertidas aventuras del nieto de Juan Moreira. Buenos Aires, 1939, 1957.
El mar dulce. Buenos Aires, 1940.
Teatro completo. Introduction by Roberto F. Giusti. Buenos Aires, 1956.

Translations

"The Devil in Pago Chico." Translated by Anita Brenner. In *Tales from the Argentine.* Edited by Waldo Frank. New York, 1930. Pp. 153–178.
Laucha's Marriage. Translated by Anita Brenner. In *Tales from the Argentine.* Edited by Waldo Frank. New York, 1930. Pp. 1–76.

Biographical and Critical Studies

Anderson Imbert, Enrique. *Tres novelas de Payró con pícaros en tres miras.* Tucumán, Argentina, 1942.
Ghiano, Juan Carlos. "Roberto J. Payró: Un testigo de excepción." In *Al azar de las lecturas.* La Plata, Argentina, 1968. Pp. 19–31.
González Lanuza, Eduardo. *Genio y figura de Roberto J. Payró.* Buenos Aires, 1965.
Jitrik, Noé, and Estela dos Santos. "Realismo y picaresca: Roberto J. Payró." In *Capítulo: La historia de la literatura argentina 28.* Buenos Aires, 1968.
Larra, Raúl. *Payró: El hombre—la obra.* Buenos Aires, 1938.
Vergara de Bietti, Noemí. *Payró, humorista de la tristeza.* Buenos Aires, 1980.

Ricardo Jaimes Freyre

(1868–1933)

Darío A. Cortés

Ricardo Jaimes Freyre, considered by many to be one of the major figures of Latin American modernist literature, is perhaps the most widely celebrated of all Bolivian writers. Born on 12 May 1868 to one of the most prominent intellectual families of Bolivian society, Jaimes Freyre inherited his writing talents from both parents, who were noted authors in their own right. During his early years the family lived in Peru, Bolivia, and Argentina as a result of his father's many diplomatic assignments. At age twenty-four Jaimes Freyre served as executive secretary to Argentine president Mariano Batista, and about 1889 he decided to stay permanently in Buenos Aires to pursue his literary and journalistic career. Ten years later he published his most important collection of poems, *Castalia bárbara* (1899), a work that is considered—along with Rubén Darío's *Prosas profanas* (Profane Prose, 1896) and Leopoldo Lugones' *Las montañas de oro* (Mountains of Gold, 1897)—part of the classic trilogy of Latin American modernist literature. During the next two decades he lived in the northern Argentine province of Tucumán and devoted most of his efforts to researching the history of that region. He dedicated the latter part of his life to public office, representing Bolivia's political interests in diplomatic posts in a number of Latin American countries. His final days were spent in Buenos Aires, where he died on 24 April 1933.

Jaimes Freyre's main literary production consists of two exceptional collections of modernist poems, *Castalia bárbara* and *Los sueños son vida* (Dreams Are Life, 1917), and a fundamental manual on poetic theory, style, and art entitled *Leyes de la versificación castellana* (Laws on Spanish Versification, 1912). He also published two dramatic pieces, *La hija de Jefte* (The Daughter of Jefte, 1899), a biblical work of two acts in prose, and *Los conquistadores* (The Conquerors, 1928), a short drama in verse; and four chapters of an incomplete novel, *Los jardines de Academo* (The Gardens of Academo). Jaimes Freyre also launched two important journals in Argentina: *Revista de América*, coedited with Rubén Darío from 1894 to 1900, which attracted articles of a modernist orientation; and *Revista de letras y ciencias sociales*, established in 1905 to promote topics of historical, literary, and national interest.

In a letter to his brother Raul, Jaimes Freyre recalls the process of his poetic inspiration:

My *Castalia* was born during those gloomy days of my life in Peropolis. My other books were written during my busy and continuous work in Tucumán. Yesterday I wrote four notes and a poem. I never worry about publicity; my works sleep until there is moment of goodwill that all of a sudden is born in me, and then I send them to the world. Afterwards, I let them make their way, without pushing them.

Most critics divide Jaimes Freyre's life and literary production into three major periods: his induction into the literary, political, and diplomatic circles of Buenos Aires (1868–1901); his historical studies and university experience in Tucumán (1901–1921); and his political and diplomatic involvement in Bolivia (1921–1933). Following approximately these same subdivisions, this study will examine his literary production in relation to the modernist movement and will identify his role and place in Latin American contemporary literature.

Ricardo Jaimes Freyre belongs to the generation of Latin American modernist authors who were writing approximately from the 1880's through the first decades of the twentieth century. Among the most representative of this group are Rubén Darío, the spiritual and political leader, Leopoldo Lugones, José Martí, Julián del Casal, Manuel Gutiérrez Nájera, José Asunción Silva, and Santos Chocano. Like many of his contemporaries, the Bolivian poet was influenced by French symbolist and Parnassian writers, such as Charles Baudelaire, Paul Verlaine, Stéphane Mallarmé, C.-M. Leconte de Lisle, and Théodore Banville, who often introduced exotic elements, evoked and re-created archaeological histories, and followed the pessimistic and escapist tendencies of the fin de siècle. The early modernist generation in Latin America adopted an ivory tower attitude toward the rest of society. They cultivated a literature based on "art for the sake of art," explored irresolvable existential dilemmas (death, resurrection, and the like), and experimented with the musical possibilities and complexities of poetic prose.

The many parallels between Jaimes Freyre and the Nicaraguan poet Rubén Darío deserve mention, since they shed additional light on the literary formation and experience of the Bolivian writer. Both poets made Buenos Aires their second home and spent some of their most important developmental years in Argentina. When Darío arrived in the Argentine capital he was already an internationally celebrated poet, while Jaimes Freyre was just beginning to explore his poetic talent. Nevertheless, there was a very tangible link between these men, beginning with their strong mutual affection and extending throughout their life and work experiences. They were both diplomats, journalists for the same newspapers, and coeditors of a magazine; they honored each other's works, traveled widely through Latin America and Europe, and spearheaded the modernist movement from the River Plate region. In addition, several of their most important works are very similar—not only in form and style but also in theme and message. For example, many critics have recognized the affinities between Darío's *Prosas profanas* and Jaimes Freyre's *Castalia bárbara*, and between *Cantos de vida y esperanza* (Songs of Life and Hope, 1905) and *Los sueños son vida*. Even after Darío's death in 1916 the linkage continued, when Jaimes Freyre pronounced the most passionate and widely publicized elegy for his friend.

Castalia bárbara—the untranslatable title refers to the Castalian Spring on Mount Parnassus, source of poetic inspiration—contains thirteen poems and a prologue written by Lugones. For the first time Jaimes Freyre introduces into Latin American literature the exotic world of Nordic and Scandinavian mythology as a contrast to the Christian and mystical traditions. The titles alone of some of these poems—"Los héroes" (The Heroes), "La muerte del héroe" (The Death of the Hero), "Las hadas" (The Fairies), "El himno" (The Hymn), and "Los cuervos" (The Crows)—suggest a turbulent medieval setting, where warfare, fantasy, and worship join together to create a magical and poetic world. In "Aeternum vale," the best-known poem of this collection, the poet interposes the image of Christ among a number of Scandinavian mythological figures, such as Thor, in order to underline the confusion, fear, and sense of despair of contemporary man:

Un Dios misterioso y extraño visita la selva
Es un Dios silencioso que tiene los brazos abiertos
Cuando la hija de Nhor espoleaba su negro caballo,
le vio erguirse, de pronto, a la sombra de un anoso fresno.
Y sintio que se helaba su sangre
ante el Dios silencioso que tiene los abrazos abiertos.

A mysterious and foreign God visits the jungle.
He is a silent God with arms wide open
When Thor's daughter spurs her black horse

she sees him, all of a sudden, standing in the shadows
    of an old ash tree.
And feels her blood freeze
in front of the silent God with arms wide open.

The passage of time, death, and immortality are
among the recurrent themes of *Castalia bárbara*,
which presents the symbolic burials of Nordic heroes,
the vivid image of an agonizing crucified Christ,
and—in a four-line poem entitled "La espada" (The
Sword)—the description of the death of a warrior
after a battle:

   La roja, sangrienta espada del soldado,
   cuando el Corcel luminoso con su roja crin la bana,
   cubierta de polvo yace, como un ídolo humillado,
   como un viejo Dios, hundido en la montaña.

The red, bleeding sword of the soldier,
when the luminous horse bathes it with his red mane,
remains covered in dust, like a humiliated idol,
like an old God, caved in the mountain.

In *Los sueños son vida*, published eighteen years
later, the theme of death remains important, but now
as a manifestation of the philosophical dilemma of
the passage of time—"Los fugaz" (Fleeting),
"Tiempos idos" (Time That Has Gone)—or as part
of an elegy on the death of a popular figure—"Al
borde de la tumba de Tolstoi" (At Tolstoy's Tomb)—
or simply as a means to make a social or political
commentary on the human condition—"La verdad
eterna" (The Eternal Truth). In the third section of
this book, "Víctimas," Jaimes Freyre includes a poem
written in 1906 entitled "Rusia," in which he re-
examines the abortive revolution of 1905 and antic-
ipates the events of the Russian Revolution. In this
short poem he strongly criticizes the injustice and
despotism of the ruling class and describes the deplor-
able condition of the exploited working classes:

   Enorme y santa Rusia, la tempestad te llama!
   Ya agita tus nevados cabellos, y en tus venas
   la sangre de Rurico, vieja y heroica inflama. . . .

Large and saintly Russia, the storm is calling you!
It has already agitated your snow-colored hair, and in
   your veins
Rurico's blood, ancient and heroic ignites. . . .

With *Leyes de la versificación castellano* Jaimes
Freyre became one of the very few Latin American
authors to make a major contribution to poetic
theory. In ten short chapters he proudly announces a
new theory on rhythmical creation and explains the
laws of melody, harmony, and metrical pattern in
Spanish verse. Although the theories expressed in
this book are not totally new, he develops a clear set
of justifications, using examples from Spanish and
world literature to make convincing arguments that
have become widely accepted in Spanish-American
letters.

As is the case with most Latin American modernist
writers, Jaimes Freyre is recognized more for his
poetic talents than for his prose contributions. Although his narrative fiction consists of only five short
stories and an incomplete novel, these works offer
clear examples of the author's changing and contradictory aesthetic and thematic tendencies and are
also typical of the dual tendencies of his entire
generation. For, while modernism initially strove to
re-create the splendor of exotic lands and mysterious
peoples as a means of escaping society's bourgeois
values, at a later period, it focused on genuine Latin
American characters and settings in order to defend
native rights and traditions.

In his first three stories—"Zoe" (1894), "Los
viajeros" (The Travelers, 1900), and "Zaghi, mendigo" (Zaghi the Tramp, 1905)—Jaimes Freyre captures the spirit and essence of old and remote civili-
zations, using the established poetic language and
refined prose of modernism. In "Zoe," subtitled
"Mosaicos bizantinos" (Byzantine Mosaics), the author places a beautiful Greek woman in the city of
Byzantium, a world of riches, grandeur, and religious
conflict. As in "Aeternum vale," the contrasts between the pagan and Christian worlds are apparent.
Among provocative paintings, incense, and Arabian
perfumes, the beautiful and idolatrous Zoe questions
her own vague religious beliefs: "Do you think that
the Father originates from the Son?"

On the other hand, in his last two stories—"En las
montañas" (In the Mountains, 1906), subtitled
"Justicia india" (Indian Justice), and "En un hermoso
día de verano" (On a Beautiful Summer Day,
1907)—Jaimes Freyre rediscovers the American continent and introduces social and political themes. In

"En las montañas" the characters form two antagonistic groups. On one side are the white exploiters, and on the other, the abused Indians. In hate and vengeance, the Indians rebel against those who have profited from their work and dispossessed them of their land. In a scene of intense realism, filled with pagan and Christian symbolism, the Indians crucify their white oppressors: "Pedro Quispe pulled out Cordobas' tongue and burned his eyes. With a small knife Tomas carved small wounds in Alvarez' body." These stories are early examples of the Indian social protest literature that originated in Peru, Bolivia, and Ecuador at the beginning of the century. From the first novel on this topic, Clorindo Matto de Turner's *Aves sin nido* (Birds Without Nests, 1889), to the Bolivian Alcide Arguedas' *Wuata wuara* (1904) and *Raza de bronce* (Race of Bronze, 1919), Latin American writers, including Jaimes Freyre, have denounced the exploitation, injustice, and expropriation suffered by the Andean Indians through most of their history.

Jaimes Freyre's work in historiography is important for the unsurpassed value of the previously unknown material he collected and the size and comprehensiveness of his work. He spent twenty years studying and describing the history of the Argentine province of Tucumán. This vast and detailed project traces all aspects of the early stages of colonization and independence, ranging from social and political structures to geographical boundaries to the makeup of the indigenous population. These pioneering efforts are contained in the volumes *Tucumán en 1810* (1909), *Historia de la República de Tucumán* (1911), *El Tucumán del siglo XVI* (1914), *El Tucumán colonial* (1915), and *Historia del descubrimiento de Tucumán* (1916). In *El Tucumán colonial*, to take one example, Jaimes Freyre presents the history of this province, using documents and maps found in the Archivo de Indias during a research trip in Spain. He also identifies the original name of the province, describes the difficulties experienced by the first explorers, and includes official documents, such as nine letters sent by the king of Spain to the governor of Tucumán.

Ricardo Jaimes Freyre's literary career, which covers almost thirty years, includes work in poetry, prose fiction, drama, and the essay. Although he will be remembered as a Bolivian modernist writer and the author of *Castalia bárbara*, his impact on Latin American letters and history has been much greater than that. His accomplished diplomatic and public service career in Argentina and Bolivia, and his political and social involvement on behalf of the disadvantaged have had a lasting effect. Jaimes Freyre's rich and comprehensive description of Tucumán represents a valuable historical document and personal testament regarding that region. His pioneering efforts in the study of Spanish versification have not been surpassed. In sum, Jaimes Freyre merits a place of distinction in modern Latin American literature.

SELECTED BIBLIOGRAPHY

Editions

Poetry

Castalia bárbara. Buenos Aires, 1899.
Los sueños son vida. Buenos Aires, 1917.

Prose Narratives

"Zoe." Buenos Aires, 1894.
"Los viajeros." Buenos Aires, 1900.
"Zaghi, mendigo." Buenos Aires, 1905.
"En las montañas." Caracas, 1906.
"En un hermoso día de verano." Buenos Aires, 1907.
Los jardines de Academo. Incomplete novel.

Plays

La hija de Jefte. Buenos Aires, 1899.
Los conquistadores. Buenos Aires, 1928.

Nonfiction

Historia de la edad media y de los tiempos modernos. Buenos Aires, 1895.
Tucumán en 1810. Buenos Aires, 1909.
Historia de la República de Tucumán. Buenos Aires, 1911.
Leyes de la versificación castellana. Buenos Aires, 1912.
El Tucumán del siglo XVI. Buenos Aires, 1914.
El Tucumán colonial. Buenos Aires, 1915.
Historia del descubrimiento de Tucumán. Buenos Aires, 1916.

Collected Works

Poesías completas. Edited by Eduardo Joabin Colombres. Buenos Aires, 1944.

Poesías completas. Edited by F. Díez de Medina. La Paz, Bolivia, 1957.

Biographical and Critical Studies

Baptista Gumucio, Mariano. *Narradores bolivianos*. Caracas, 1969.

Carrilla, Emilio. "Jaimes Freyre, cuentista y novelista." *Thesaurus* 16:664–698 (1961).

_____. *Ricardo Jaimes Freyre*. Buenos Aires, 1962.

Castañon Barrientos, Carlos. *Cuentos de Ricardo Jaimes Freyre*. La Paz, Bolivia, 1975.

Cortés, Darío Alvaro. "Los cuentos de Ricardo Jaimes Freyre." *Cuadernos americanos* 256:197–214 (1984).

Echevarría, Evelio. *La novela social de Bolivia*. La Paz, Bolivia, 1973.

Francovich, Guillermo. *Tres poetas modernistas de Bolivia*. La Paz, Bolivia, 1971.

Gisbert, Teresa. "Aproximación a Ricardo Jaimes Freyre." *Cuadernos hispanoamericanos* 237:752–769 (1969).

Gosalvez, Bothelo Raul. "Ricardo Jaimes Freyre en el modernismo americano." *Cuadernos americanos* 156–157:238–250 (1968).

Guzman, Augusto, et al. *Ricardo Jaimes Freyre: Estudios*. La Paz, Bolivia, 1978.

Jaimes-Freyre, Mireya. *Modernismo y 98 a través de Ricardo Jaimes Freyre*. Madrid, 1969.

Ocampo Moscoso, Eduardo. *Personalidad y obra poética de don Ricardo Jaimes Freyre*. Cochabamba, Bolivia, 1968.

Otero, Gustavo Adolfo. *Figuras de la cultura boliviana*. Potosi, Bolivia, 1953.

Torres-Rioseco, Arturo. "Ricardo Jaimes Freyre (1870–1933)." *Hispania* 16:389–398 (1933).

Amado Nervo

(1870–1919)

Frank Dauster

A mado Nervo was born on 27 August 1870, in the small city of Tepic, in the rather remote Mexican province of Nayarit, the first child of a modest family of Spanish roots. Nayarit was still heavily Indian, and indigenous myths formed a background for Nervo's youth, along with his mother's devout Catholicism. These may have influenced in part his later fascination with various kinds of spiritualism. When his father's death in 1883 left the family in reduced circumstances, they moved to Zamora, in the state of Michoacán, where Nervo studied in the seminary, which was also a secondary school not exclusively devoted to theological studies. After beginning the study of law, he abandoned plans for a legal career, and in 1891 began studies for the priesthood. A year later he abandoned these in turn, probably because of the need to find employment to help alleviate the family's economic difficulties, and quite possibly owing to doubts about his religious vocation, raised by a stormy first love. The increasing financial problems of his family led him to journalism, a difficult career but widely regarded as an alternative to poverty for talented and impecunious young men. He worked first in Tepic, but in 1892 moved to Mazatlán, where he worked in a law office and on newspapers, primarily writing social notes. In 1894 Nervo moved to the capital, Mexico City.

Initially, he seems to have supported himself and helped his family through humble employment, but soon he had his first short stories published, and began to work intensively as drama critic, author of articles and essays, and chronicler of social news.

In 1895 Nervo attracted a good deal of attention with his novel *El bachiller* (The Student), which he claimed to have written in a deliberate search for fame. It deals in relatively graphic seminaturalistic fashion with the sexual problems of a seminary student. Soon he was widely known. With Jesús Valenzuela, he coedited the *Revista moderna* (Modern Review), spokespiece of the modernist movement and one of the most important literary reviews in Mexico and all Spanish America. At the same time he published his first important books of poetry, *Perlas negras* (Black Pearls, 1898) and *Místicas* (Mystical Poems, 1898). In 1900 the newspaper *El Imparcial* (Impartial) sent him as special correspondent to Paris, where he participated in the end-of-century bohemian life and became a friend of the great Nicaraguan poet Rubén Darío, leader of the modernist movement, and of many of the French poets of the period. Although the paper soon ended its payments and he was forced to work as a translator, Nervo chose to remain in Paris and traveled widely in Europe. In 1903 he returned to Mexico, where his increasing reputation as a poet and the protection of influential friends enabled him to support himself through teaching. In 1905 he entered the diplomatic service; from that year until 1918 he resided in Madrid, where the bulk of his poetry was written. Appointed minister plenipotentiary to Argentina and Uruguay, he died in Montevideo on 24 May 1919, shortly after taking up his duties there. Meanwhile, he had achieved an extraordinary renown; both intellectual elites and the mass of popular readers acclaimed him, and his body was returned to Mexico in a naval cruiser escorted by ships of Argentina, Mexico, Cuba, and the United States.

Nervo was one of the first international literary celebrities, and his death and interment in Mexico some months later received enormous response. An incident in 1914 reveals the growth of his reputation and the esteem in which he was held in Spain: the chaos of the Mexican Revolution led to the virtual cessation of Mexican diplomatic services, and a group of Spanish writers proposed successfully that Nervo receive a pension from the government of Spain. The poet refused the gesture, and supported his household through writing and editorial work until 1916, when he resumed work as a member of the foreign service.

One of the critical dates in Nervo's life was 1901, when he met Ana Cecilia Luisa Dailliez, the Ana who was his great love and of whom so little is known. For unknown reasons they never married, although they lived together until her death in 1912, an event that left Nervo stricken and that had a profound impact on his work. Given Nervo's increasing reputation as a poet and the official nature of his employment, the relationship forced him into a curious double life. Officially unmarried and forced to attend unending social, diplomatic, and literary functions, he kept Ana's existence hidden from all but friends.

Nervo's youth and his earliest poetry were under the influence of the prevailing school of romanticism. Although the major part of his work corresponds to modernism, the cosmopolitan new movement that rejected outworn romanticism, many of the emotional attitudes reflected in his verse are still predominantly romantic. Influenced by the new French currents, symbolism and Parnassianism, and by the outstanding genius of the movement, Darío, the

modernists experimented with colors and images, renewed verse forms long forgotten or brought others from exotic corners of the world, and enriched the poetic vocabulary and syntax through adaptations from French and even classical Greek. Perhaps their greatest innovation was the reform of rhythm, in search of a greater subtlety, a poetry more suggestive and less obvious. As one of their models, Paul Verlaine, had said, poetry was, above all, music, and after music, shading.

This was, of course, a sophisticated urban movement that had its roots in the relatively prosperous metropolis. Under the rule of the dictator Porfirio Díaz, Mexico had seen considerable progress and modernization, but the benefits of these were restricted to a small group of wealthy absentee landholders and industrial entrepreneurs. The majority of the country's population, the laboring classes and especially the rural Indians and mestizos, those of mixed ancestry, lived untouched by either the economic benefits or the literary excitement. This situation led to the revolution of 1910, a cataclysm that drastically altered Mexican society and literature. Although Nervo was a member of his nation's diplomatic corps, his writing was virtually untouched by the revolution, and he seems to have been affected primarily through the temporary loss of his position because of the social chaos provoked by the revolution. In the same way, the war of 1898 between Spain and the United States appears to have aroused little, if any, echo in his work. Darío and many of the other leading modernists evolved toward a poetry that, if not always entirely committed in a contemporary sense, expressed the author's social and political concerns, but if Nervo's newspaper articles and chronicles record his awareness of the world around him and the crisis of bourgeois faith in progress, in his poetry the world about him finds expression only in occasional political or folkloric verses. Nervo never really ceased to be a modernist of strong romantic leanings, with his ear and his eye turned inward toward the mysterious connections between his psyche and another kind of reality.

Nervo's complete works number thirty titles, and the superior part is poetry. Fundamentally, Nervo is a religious poet, although in a broad and nearly metaphorical sense. His work reflects his constant religious concerns, from the doubts of the youth tormented by the desire for perfection, to the struggle with the demands of the flesh. The themes that were to dominate all his poetry are already visible in the earliest books. His first poems show the influence of Verlaine and vacillate between these two sentiments of carnality and religiosity. Thus, in "Delicta carnis" (Sin of the Flesh) from Místicas, while he pleads for divine aid to help him resist the call of the flesh, he lovingly describes the sinfully attractive marble tones of a woman's shoulders. In "A Kempis" (To Kempis), from the same book, Nervo balances his love for life against the awareness of inevitable death.

Nervo's earliest work corresponds to Mañana del poeta (Morning of the Poet), a collection of poems and prose written between 1886 and 1891 and posthumously assembled for the complete works. In Perlas negras, the first volume of poetry published during his lifetime, there is a typically modernist mixture of musicality and sensuality under the influences of Verlaine and the Mexican Manuel Gutiérrez Nájera. Along with the romantic posturing characteristic of a good deal of modernist poetry, there was a mixture of religious and sensual themes, including liturgical imagery. This note was heightened in Místicas, which includes an emphasis on poetic parallels with the litany, but with the exception of a very few poems, Nervo did not reach the extremes of erotic content and sacrilegious imagery that so fascinated some of his fellow modernists. Curiously, but not unusually in Latin America, where the literary currents of the period did not always proceed in orderly fashion, after the symbolism of the earlier books, Nervo turned to the Parnassian search for purity of form in Poemas (Poems, 1901) and El éxodo y las flores del camino (The Exodus and the Flowers of the Road, 1902). From this period are the delightful variations on Darío's experimentation with unusual meters in poems like "Doña Guiomar" or "El metro de doce" (The Meter of Twelve), the latter not published until Los jardines interiores (The Inner Gardens) in 1905. Also from Poemas is Nervo's most famous and probably his best poem, "La hermana agua" (Sister Water), although it was later reworked. It combines the Parnassian emphasis on purity of form in its austerity and emphasis on the color white, with a Franciscan religious attitude that prefigures

some of the later developments of Nervo's work. It is perhaps Nervo's most ambitious and complicated effort in its examination of the multiple forms that water can take, and there is a suggestion of the metaphysical speculation on the nature of reality that hints at an influence on José Gorostiza's brilliant development of the same theme, Muerte sin fin (Death Without End, 1939). By the publication of En voz baja (In a Low Voice, 1909), Nervo's long pilgrimage toward a different kind of poetry was well under way, a process still more visible in Serenidad (Serenity, 1914), where Nervo sought consolation for the death in 1912 of Ana, the great love of his life. This disaster also inspired La amada inmóvil (The Unmoving Beloved), never published in complete form until the complete works. The book is a confession of the poet's anguish at her death and the recognition of his own inexorable fate.

After his first books, Nervo's interests turned toward spiritual matters, as he became increasingly absorbed by his essential theme, the mystery of being and the limitations of life, a process exacerbated by the death of Ana. Slowly his work began to be purified of modernism's ornate garb. He was increasingly less interested in form, his rhymes and rhythms became progressively simpler, and the poems were less clearly autobiographical. In the later works very often what remains is only a somewhat formless whisper composed of ordinary words and—the only formal concern—popular sayings that helped to create a secretive atmosphere. In the succeeding books Nervo repeatedly trod this same path of resignation, until his poetry took on a spiritual nudity somewhat remote from art. Unfortunately, the lack of care led him at times to stumble; such poems as "Los muertos" (The Dead), from La amada inmóvil, may reveal to us the most intimate sentiments of the speaker, but they are questionable as poetry. By Elevación (Elevation, 1917), technique had been reduced to a minimum, and there were few images.

During Nervo's last years, spiritualism played a major role in his life. Although he had received a profoundly Catholic formation and he continued to read widely in Christian authors, he immersed himself in readings about theosophy, the transmigration of souls, reincarnation, and other Oriental doctrines. His favorite author was the German romantic poet and seer Novalis, so influential on the symbolist movement. On another level, Nervo was influenced by the contradictory philosophical currents of irrationalism and nineteenth-century positivism with its emphasis on progress through science; despite the pronounced emphasis of the former in his poetry, Nervo was fascinated by science and the idea of progress. He was not a systematic thinker; rather, his work reflects the syncretic use of themes that on the surface are mutually contradictory. These interests are visible in the Orientalism of his last poems, such as *El estanque de los lotos* (The Lotus Pool, 1919), the last volume published during the poet's life. Throughout Nervo's life and work, these two tendencies, pessimistic resignation and hopeful faith, fought for control, uniting occasionally to struggle against the call of the flesh. Rather than a mystic, as he was often called during the period of his greatest fame, he seems today a man who had an immense desire to believe; as Rufino Blanco-Fombona said of him, "He lacks faith and does everything he can to find it." His vision of the world was pantheistic, which sometimes achieved profundity of thought and depth of expression, as in "La hermana agua."

Nervo exercised an extremely important influence on Spanish-American poetry, and he was long considered one of its giants. Since his death, his reputation has suffered drastically. Because the succeeding generation in Mexican letters was highly critical of the anti-intellectual nature of his poetry, today he is much less highly regarded and is nearly forgotten by academic critics, although many readers still consider him to be one of the greatest poets in the language.

It is difficult to come to an aesthetic evaluation of Nervo; critics are far from agreement. If he was often elegantly perceptive, he was also often cloyingly sentimental and distressingly vague. For some, he is a great poet, for others his work is blemished by the air of secretive intimacy. Certainly, poems such "La hermana agua" and some others from the earliest period are worthy of their great reputation, but his last books represent a retreat. The closer he approached the intimate confessional whisper, the farther behind he left poetry. He is often compared to Baudelaire or to a fellow Mexican, Ramón López Velarde, because of the struggle between the spirit and the flesh—Ana's death, however deeply it af-

fected Nervo, did not prevent him from a further series of passionate relationships, including a frustrated love for Ana's daughter—but where Baudelaire and López Velarde wrote poetry that was an anguished record of this struggle, Nervo chose to eliminate the erotic aspect and progress toward silence. Rather than a battle between eroticism and the spirit, Nervo's poetry is a record of the struggle for suppression of the former. Just as Occidental poetry was moving, in the postwar ferment, toward a greater complexity of form and content, Nervo's long process of simplification from initial modernist melancholy complexity toward mystical pantheistic simplicity led him toward poetic silence.

Although less important, Nervo's prose is far more abundant than his poetry. His prose work includes newspaper articles, essays, novels, short stories, including even some fantasy, drama reviews, and poetic prose. His *Juana de Asbaje* offers a subjective and sympathetic appreciation of the magnificent nun poetess of the seventeenth century. *El bachiller* was so successful that it went through a second edition after its introduction and was even published in a French version in Paris in 1901. *Pascual Aguilera* provides a description of life on the rural ranch; written before *El bachiller*, it was published a good deal later. Although all but forgotten because of the enormous success of the poetry, Nervo's articles were also widely read. One example is the series "Semblanzas íntimas" (Intimate Sketches), a group of brief verbal portraits of writers published in *El Nacional* in 1895. Nervo's prose, however, is not always what one would expect based on his poetry. His articles and essays show a greater awareness of the world about him; they are also much more ironic and less intimate, which is understandable since they were, in the majority, written as commercial articles for the purpose of earning money. Since Nervo tended to move in elegant society his finances usually were in need of the additional income provided by his articles and essays. The themes of Nervo's prose also tend to be rather different from his poetry; he displays a greater interest in science, in social affairs, and the world of books. The prose works reveal an Amado Nervo of broader and more varied interests and intellectual capacities than the poet of the whispers and sighs.

SELECTED BIBLIOGRAPHY

First Editions

Poetry

Místicas. Mexico City, 1898.
Perlas negras. Mexico City, 1898.
Poemas. Paris, 1901.
El éxodo y las flores del camino. Mexico City, 1902.
Lira heroica. Mexico City, 1902.
Cantos escolares. Mexico City, 1903.
Las Voces. Paris, 1904.
Los járdines interiores. Mexico City, 1905.
En voz baja. Paris, 1909.
Serenidad. Madrid, 1914.
Elevación. Madrid, 1917.
El estanque de los lotos. Buenos Aires, 1919.

Collected Works

Obras completas. Edited by Alfonso Reyes. Vols. 1–29, Madrid, 1920–1928; vol. 30, Mexico City, 1938.
Obras completas. 2 vols. Edited by Francisco González Guerrero and Alfonso Méndez Plancarte. Madrid, 1962.
Poesías completas. Madrid, 1935.

Biographical and Critical Studies

Castagnino, Raúl. *Imágenes modernistas.* Buenos Aires, 1967.
Durán, Manuel. *Genio y figura de Amado Nervo.* Buenos Aires, 1968.
Feustle, Joseph. "La metafísica de Amado Nervo." *Hispanófila* 40:45–65 (1970).
García Prada, Carlos. "Amado Nervo." *Américas* 22/10: 9–14 (1970).
Hernández de López, Ana María. "Amor, dolor y muerte en cuatro poemas de Amado Nervo." *Cuadernos americanos* 237/4:135–148 (1981).
Jensen, Theodore. "Christian-Pythagorean Dualism in Nervo's 'El Donador de Almas.'" *Kentucky Romance Quarterly* 28/4:391–401 (1981).
Kress, Dorothy. *Confessions of a Modern Poet: Amado Nervo.* Boston, 1935.
Leal, Luis. "La poesía de Amado Nervo: A cuarenta años de distancia." *Hispania* 43:43–47 (1960).
_____. "Situación de Amado Nervo." *Revista iberoamericana* 36/72:485–494 (1960).
Mejía Sánchez, Ernesto. "Darío, Nervo y el modernismo en el siglo XIX." In *Literatura iberoamericana del siglo XIX,* edited by Robert Anderson and Renato Rosaldo. Tucson, Ariz., 1974.
Meléndez, Concha. *Amado Nervo.* New York, 1926.
_____. "Poesía y sinceridad en Amado Nervo." *Cuadernos americanos* 173/6:206–221 (1970).
Molina, Rodrigo. "Amado Nervo: His Mysticism and Franciscan Influence." *The Americas* 6/2:173–196 (1949).
Ortiz de Montellano, Bernardo. *Figura, amor y muerte de Amado Nervo.* Mexico City, 1943.
Porrata, Francisco, and Jorge Santana, eds. *Antología comentada del modernismo.* Sacramento, Calif., 1974.
Reyes, Alfonso. *Tránsito de Amado Nervo.* Santiago, Chile, 1937.
Umphrey, George. "Amado Nervo and Hinduism." *Hispanic Review* 17:133–145 (1949).
_____. "Amado Nervo and Maeterlinck: On Death and Immortality." *The Romantic Review* 40:35–47 (1949).
Wellman, Esther. *Amado Nervo, Mexico's Religious Poet.* New York, 1936.

Manuel Díaz Rodríguez

(1871–1927)

Hugo Achugar

The most important novelist of Spanish-American modernism became a writer in order to win a bet. Manuel Díaz Rodríguez himself relates the paradoxical story in *Sermones líricos* (Lyric Sermons, 1918):

> We were chatting one day after a generous meal when my friend broke out in praise of a little travel book by a Venezuelan author that we had been reading at the time. Animated by a contradictory spirit that wasn't really mine, but rather belonged to the wine's soft, subtle, treacherous soul, I objected that the book was rather mediocre and somewhat common. Further, any good reader of moderate education could, with sufficient travel and desire, write a book of his personal impressions, a book which, if not of great style, would be a worthy and pleasurable work. I added, over dessert, that given the opportunity, I could do it with more skill and better results than the author we were discussing. My friend responded maliciously: "Prove it. Go ahead and try." "Why not?" I answered. *

Manuel Díaz Rodríguez was born on 28 February 1871 on his family's estate, Los Dolores, located at

the foot of Mt. Avila in what is now midtown Caracas. His parents had become farmers after emigrating to Venezuela from the Canary Islands. In 1878, Díaz Rodríguez went to the nearby capital to study, staying there until he received his medical degree in 1891. By 1892, when he went to Paris to pursue postgraduate medical studies, there still was nothing to hint at his future literary career.

Venezuela's literary Generation of 1895, which included Díaz Rodríguez, is noted for the aesthetic renovation it brought to Venezuelan letters. This renovation consisted of literary cosmopolitanism but also creolism and Spanish-American *modernismo* (different from Anglo-Saxon or Brazilian modernism, which is closer to the Spanish-American avant-garde). Venezuelan *modernismo* had special characteristics that differentiated it from the rest of Spanish America. Mariano Picón Salas has remarked that this aesthetic change came to Venezuela not only through poetry (especially the work of Rubén Darío) but also, fundamentally, through prose. At the beginning of the 1880's José Martí was in Caracas, contributing crackling articles to local newspapers; his presence was especially important in the years before the appearance of *El cojo ilustrado* (1892–1915) and *Cosmópolis* (1895–1900), the two great journals of Venezuelan *modernismo* in which Díaz Rodríguez was

---

*Manuel Díaz Rodríguez, *Obras Selectas*. Madrid, Caracas, 1968. P. 796. All subsequent quotations are from this edition, hereafter referred to as OS. Translations are the work of this essay's translator.

431

to collaborate. The modernist generation of 1895 had another peculiar characteristic: its special alliance with positivism set it still further apart from other Spanish-American countries. Spanish-American *modernismo* as a whole rejected the scientific security of positivism. In Venezuela, though, the antimetaphysical "rigor" of the Spenserian doctrine was considered compatible with the spiritualistic aestheticism of the artistic style of *modernista* writers. Positivists and modernists shared rostrums and journals, differing only—and not always visibly—in that the former had, as Picón Salas said, "more social emotion than aesthetic emotion." Hence aestheticist cosmopolitanism mixed with an interest in the native land, and the protagonist of Díaz Rodríguez' *Idolos rotos* (Broken Idols, 1901) could thus create his "Creole Venus."

Díaz Rodríguez' student years in Paris and Vienna provided him not only with deeper medical knowledge but also brought him into his first direct contact with European culture. Domingo Miliani and Oscar Sambrano Urdaneta suggest that Díaz Rodríguez could have learned of Freudian theory during his stay in Vienna, since Sigmund Freud was developing his methods of psychoanalytic therapy there at that time. These critics point out that the novelist "describes the symptoms of his afflicted characters with professional exactitude."

This idea seems to be accepted as a possibility by most of the critics who have read Díaz Rodríguez, as all of them note his rich, diverse education. Orlando Araujo describes him as one of the most cultivated writers of his period. He read and spoke French, Italian, and German. To many of his critics his profound knowledge of Gabriele D'Annunzio is visible in his novels; he read Charles Baudelaire, Stéphane Mallarmé, Arthur Rimbaud, Paul Verlaine, Walter Pater, Henri Conti, Ernest Renan, Oscar Wilde, and Thomas Carlyle. He studied Friedrich Nietzsche in detail. Among authors who wrote in Spanish, he was interested in Gabriel Alomar, Ramón del Valle Inclán, and José Enrique Rodó.

Before going to Europe in 1892, Díaz Rodríguez was already well educated and familiar with Venezuela's diverse and conflicting cultural panorama. As a student of Dr. Adolf Ernst at the medical school of Caracas, he had come in contact with the positivistic scienticism of his country's university environment and with the philosophical arguments of the time. But it was in Paris, in Vienna, and in his travels through Italy where the young doctor completed his education. His first book, *Sensaciones de viaje* (Travel Impressions, 1896), expresses this educational process as well as the novice writer's talent. The book contains six descriptions of Italy and one of Constantinople, alternating orientalism, aestheticism, and sentimentalism with moral reflections and autobiographical elements. The chapter describing the Naples area was Díaz Rodríguez' first publication; it appeared in *El cojo ilustrado* on 15 August 1895.

In *Sensaciones de viaje,* so surprising to his compatriots, the young physician employed a prose that, like Martí's, broke with the prevailing style, seen as overly academic and careless of its aesthetic effects. Díaz Rodríguez described the panorama of Lake Maggiore and the Swiss Alps as "a colossal turquoise of soft hues, set among gigantic emeralds; and in the background Cyclopean cones whose intense, radiant whiteness pales the blueness of the skies" (OS, p. 1042).

But there is more besides chromatism and mere aestheticism. The youthful doctor also states: "We, the refined sons of the nineteenth century, go rash and wild from one perversion to the next, following the phantasm of true happiness, which in reality we have very near ourselves, inside ourselves" (OS, p. 1069). As with other Spanish-American *modernistas,* ethical judgment is aesthetic judgment and vice versa. Beginning with *Sensaciones de viaje,* Díaz Rodríguez applied himself to the study and description of "beautiful souls" and, at the same time, to mastering the *écriture artistique,* which prevailed in the antimaterialistic spiritualism of his generation. The same ambiance and nearly the same chords comprise *De mis romerías* (From My Pilgrimages, 1898), his second travel book, which appeared in 1898. The difference between *Sensaciones de viaje* and this second travel book lies in an increase in narrative and novelistic elements and also in a greater expressiveness and the presence of the fantastic.

Díaz Rodríguez' first book was published in Paris during his second trip to Europe; after staying little more than a year (1895–1896) he returned to Caracas. By then his compatriots recognized him as a master, and upon his arrival he received the award for best literary work of the year from the Academia de la Lengua (Academy of Language). The award caused controversy as some academy members with ties to the church opposed honoring a work they considered "saturated with pagan ideas." In his acceptance speech Díaz Rodríguez synthesized his thinking on aesthetics and ethics:

> [T]he artist's greatest compensation is perhaps in the torturous delight of creation, in that state of the soul which is composed of deep sadnesses and divine exaltations and which governs the birth of art, especially the flowering of the fluid, harmonious phrase, perfumed with the balsam of exquisite sentiment, containing the idea like a perfectly adjusted mold.
>
> (OS, p. 875)

In June 1896 Díaz Rodríguez became a regular contributor to *El cojo ilustrado,* and under its editorial seal he published his first book of short stories, *Confidencias de psiquis* (Secrets of the Psyche, 1896). The volume contains six stories—four narrated in the first person—centered on the psychological analysis of extremely sensitive individuals. Set in Paris, these stories are about dilettantes, men and women who succumb to sensuality or to unhealthy passions. Action is practically absent from the narrative, appearing only in support of the psychological study. Instead, the stories are charged with moral and aesthetic reflection, often displaying a paternalistic attitude toward the common people and "ignorant souls." The world of this first book of stories reached its peak in *Cuentos de color* (Color Tales, 1899). Composed of nine chromatic narrations, the book is very much in the canonical modernist style, postulating an aesthetic universe in which the aesthetification of reality is a dominant value. Many critics have seen it only as useless prose or sterile beauty. Some of the stories resemble the Darío of *Azul,* especially in the theme of the artist's plight in the face of a "deaf," uncomprehending bourgeois plutocracy.

Díaz Rodríguez' third trip to Europe was his honeymoon and marked the beginning of his literary maturity. He married Graziela Calcaño on 7 July 1899, and shortly thereafter they traveled to Paris. At

this time, General Cipriano Castro carried out his revolution; his corrupt and violent government was later opposed by Díaz Rodríguez and other Venezuelan intellectuals. Between 1899 and 1902 Díaz Rodríguez reached his novelistic prime: he wrote or outlined the three novels he was to publish during his lifetime: *Idolos rotos,* 1901; *Sangre patricia* (Patrician Blood, 1902); and *Peregrina, o El pozo encantado* (Peregrina, or The Enchanted Well, 1922), then titled "Barroco criollo" (Creole Baroque).

The first two novels represent the author's maturity. The critics have recognized his stylistic mastery, but until recently have been chiefly concerned with the "escapist" and "uprooted" nature of his narrative. The evaluation of the literary production of Díaz Rodríguez and other Spanish-American *modernistas* of this period has been marked by "pseudo ethical" accusations concerning the authors' alienation from their environment and by appraisals that value only their verbal fancywork. Raúl Agudo Freites has spoken of Díaz Rodríguez' "literary anachronism"; Mariano Picón Salas maintains that his "art (was) excessively refined, aristocratic and solitary" and mentions the author's "escapist tendencies"; Max Henríquez Ureña notes the "sometimes excessive elegance" of his prose. Nevertheless, in recent years a partial revision of this evaluation has begun. Orlando Araujo, for example, in 1982 modified his 1966 judgment: "I once wrote a book about Díaz Rodríguez that had a beautiful but unfair title (*La palabra estéril,* The Sterile Word), although the content was not unjust. . . . New writers, less prejudiced than we, will return to the work of this great Venezuelan author and in it they will find things unseen by us" (Díaz Rodríguez, *Narrativa y ensayo,* p. xxvi).

The Venezuelan assessment of Díaz Rodríguez' work may have been influenced by his political activity during the Juan Vicente Gómez dictatorship and by his privileged status as owner of a large estate. But a review of international criticism shows much the same process at work; here the 1933 judgment of Dillwyn F. Ratcliff is of interest. In his *Venezuela in Prose Fiction* Ratcliff asserts that "Díaz Rodríguez' aesthetic sensibility leaned toward an appreciation of sound, form, and color. He was by nature indifferent toward reality and toward the ideas and principles behind appearances. As a writer, he delighted in hollow flourishes." More recent studies, however, are beginning to value not only the author's stylistic merits but also his expression of a mentality and a cultural discourse characteristic of his period.

Miliani and Sambrano Urdaneta consider *Idolos rotos* "the most representative novel of Spanish-American modernism." The story concerns a young doctor, Alberto Soria, who, having gone to Paris for postgraduate study, returns home as a promising sculptor. Alluding in part to Díaz Rodríguez' own change in career, the novel centers on the shock that the artist experiences on returning, and allows the author to sketch an acid portrait of Venezuela at century's end. The novel also contains the predictable emotional conflict and, even more characteristic of modernist narrative, the theme of the clash between the artistic soul of the protagonist and the bourgeois flatness of his familial and social milieu. Ideological and social conflicts constitute the greater part of the novel and give the narrator an opportunity to expand his criticism of Venezuelan society.

The description of the country that Soria finds upon returning is one of the novelist's ways of showing that the reality of Venezuela had little in common with the "azure" ideal that Spanish-American *modernista* writers so eagerly sought. But it is in Soria's statues, the "broken idols" of the novel's title, that symbolism is most clearly present; indeed, Picón Salas calls it a "symbolic novel." Soria returns from Paris with a replica of his prize-winning sculpture, composed of a faun and a nymph. The statue represents not only art but also the aesthetic ideal alluded to by Darío when he spoke of "French Greece." Back in his own country the protagonist creates a "Creole Venus," in an attempt to become "creolized" but also to transcend his country's spiritual poverty and enlighten his homeland through art. In addition to grappling with his own emotional, ethical, and aesthetic conflicts, Soria witnesses a revolution. At one point the triumphant soldiers wantonly destroy his statue, which leads Soria to condemn the failure of his country and his society:

Alfonzo was right: nobody has the right to sacrifice his own ideal. The artist's supreme duty is to preserve his ideal of beauty. And I never, never will realize my own ideal in my country. I will never, never be able to live my ideal in my country. My homeland! My country! Is this my homeland? Is this my country? And before the words are written in the barbarian language by the iron boot of the new conquerors, the conquerors of today, also coming from the north like the conquerors before them, written for the vile masses, blind to the truth, deaf to warning, the artist, slandered, insulted, humiliated, wrote them with the blood of his wounded ideals, within his heart and on the ruins of his home and the tombs of his dead loves, wrote those irrevocable and fateful words: FINIS PATRIAE.

(OS, p. 240)

Alberto Soria is the misunderstood artist facing the unrefined barbarism of bourgeois society and, in this sense, is a typical modernist hero. But he is more: Soria is the artist who attempts to settle the conflict between cosmopolitanism and creolism, so debated in the Spanish-American art of the period. Díaz Rodríguez' solution to the conflict is intimately related to that offered by Venezuelan modernism as a whole. Still, they differ in that his narrative belongs to an aesthetic that pretends to evoke and suggest rather than to name direct, immediate reality. *Idolos rotos* did not include the note of realism or commitment that Díaz Rodríguez' contemporaries expected. Rufino Blanco Fombona, who had so appreciated the irrealistic aesthetic twists of Julio Herrera y Reissig and other canonical modernists, commented in 1902 that his compatriot's novels, although "national . . . are a hundred leagues from 'creolism' . . . and paint . . . [only] souls of the *élite*."

The alienation and escapism for which the majority of Díaz Rodríguez' critics reproach him, however, were no more than an aesthetic device for reflecting a reality seen as lacking and empty. The elitist attitude of his work was not so much a result of a non-nationalist theme or landscape as one of a position within Venezuelan society that did not allow the author to exceed the limits of his own ideology. The lack of authenticity that Araujo attributed to the characters may show a lack of folklorism, but even so, Alberto Soria's socioethical messianism is not very different from that felt by many intellectuals of Díaz Rodríguez' generation.

Sangre patricia, or "Uvas del trópico" (Grapes of

the Tropic), as Díaz Rodríguez planned to call it, appeared in 1902. This novel is one of the most representative examples of modernist narrative. It presents all the typical characteristics: predominance of description over action, symbolism, aestheticism and verbal richness, spiritual aristocraticism, and the necessary antagonism between bourgeois spirit and artistic sensibility. Most characters in the novel are sickly and hyperaesthetic. And of course, there is a high regard for the spiritual and the accompanying disdain for plutocratic materialism. Although critics have not esteemed this novel as highly as *Idolos rotos* or *Peregrina*, Miliani points out that studies note its importance and suggests that some of its "poetic visions . . . clear the way for the psychological novel and bring surrealism forward."

The predominance of description over narration makes *Sangre patricia* a lyric novel. According to José Antonio Castro, the novelistic structure itself dissolves—a trait common to Spanish-American modernist writing and, to a certain extent, to French and Italian symbolist and decadent prose. In any case, the dominance of description is not simply a formal device without relation to the story narrated. Indeed, the protagonist's neurosis consists mainly of his incapacity for action and his tendency to daydream. It is this characteristic that makes him so similar to other neurasthenic protagonists of Spanish-American *modernismo*.

The plot is minimal: a young woman named Belen sets sail from Venezuela to join Tulio Arcos, whom she has married by proxy. During the voyage she falls ill and dies, and her body is thrown to the sea. The groom remains in Paris, obsessed by the memory of his beloved. He tries to overcome his pain in the company of artist friends and by traveling about the Mediterranean; unable to alleviate his depression, he finally decides to return to his own country. During the trip he commits suicide, casting himself into the sea to be reunited with his siren-lover. If the story is slight, the psychological analysis of the protagonist is not; the discourse is wrought with great care. Aesthetic commentary, description of the protagonist's daydreams, and analysis of exquisite sensations occupy most of the novel.

The protagonist, Tulio Arcos, belongs to a patrician family that views with displeasure the encroach-ment of the bourgeoisie, whose unwelcome advances are described through the transformations visited on the ancestral homes of Caracas' patricians: "Many facades now had replaced the thick angular windows of old with thin, fragile windows and ridiculous little balconies. Little by little, like an indecent mask, an effeminate smile was disguising the august relics of the old fortress" (OS, p. 255). But Tulio Arcos is a refined soul who can appreciate and enjoy the spiritual values of the world and of society without being restricted by the norms that a degraded society attempts to impose. The narrator says of the protagonist: "He fled from idle silliness, from common talk, from the common man, and everywhere sought beautiful souls and enlightened attitudes" (OS, p. 254). He does not reject the plebian rabble only because of aristocratic elitism; in addition to the despiritualized masses, he rejects the wealthy bourgoisie who, represented in the novel by Señor Perales, also lack "beautiful souls and attitudes." In this line of thinking, Díaz Rodríguez coincides with other modernists and intellectuals of his period. Something of this disdain for the spirit of the masses can be seen in Rodó's *Ariel*.

The young bride's death and Tulio Arcos' daydreams of the sea form the novel's symbolic nucleus. The sea obsesses the protagonist and becomes a leitmotif in the novel. Near the end, before Arcos' suicide, the sea symbolizes the supernatural forces that rule the universe and that so strongly attract the protagonist.

> Along the steamship's sides, the *grapes of the tropic* mimicked islands, garlands, crowns, mysterious epitaphs and indecipherable hieroglyphs. The sea, under the shadow of a night attired in stars and adorned with the discrete jewel of a golden sickle moon, sang and laughed placidly, filling the steamer's belly with the murmuring echo of the laughter and song.
>
> (OS, p. 343)

The "grapes of the tropic" (an aquatic plant that usually grows near the seashore but is sometimes found far away from the shore, in deep water) earlier considered as a possible title for the novel reappear here as signs of transcendence. The aestheticism of the description and the substitution of common reality by a spiritualized reality express Díaz Rodríguez' universe. *Sangre patricia* thus marks a culmination in Venezuelan modernist narrative and opens the doors to another reality.

The writer who criticized Venezuela from a platform of tradition and aesthetics left fiction, temporarily, and entered the realm of action. Díaz Rodríguez faced the same conflict as his characters Alberto Soria and Tulio Arcos and seems to have resolved it through his engagement in agriculture and politics.

In 1902, at his father's death, his mother asked him to take over the family estate, Los Dolores. The writer became farmer and left literary life for several years. His daughter Yolanda was born in 1905. In 1908 he completed his book of essays, *Camino de perfección* (Road of Perfection, published in Paris in 1910). The same year marked the beginning of his public life as journalist, university administrator, and politician. In 1909, along with intellectuals like Blanco Fombona, Cesar Zumeta, Pedro Manuel Arcaya, and Simon Barceló, he took charge of the newspaper *El progresista*; he was also named vice-president of the Central University of Venezuela. These were years of intense political activity, during which his name became associated with the regime of the dictator Juan Vicente Gómez. However, as Araujo clarifies, there is no evidence that Díaz Rodríguez' participation in Venezuela's public life was tainted by the rampant corruption of the time nor that his pen was employed in praise of the tyrant.

Still, the years he dedicated to working the family farm were not ones of complete silence, for a writer like Díaz Rodríguez could not help but to exercise his craft. The 1908 publication of *Camino de perfección* presupposes arduous labor in itself, but the author also occasionally published short stories in this period. Among them is "Música bárbara" (Barbaric Music), according to Miliani a creolist story, published in 1922 with his last novel, *Peregrina.*

But Díaz Rodríguez' most interesting work during these years is not that of the fiction writer, but rather that of the essayist and speaker. *Camino de perfección*, for some his most memorable work, and *Sermones líricos* are both products of these years. By 1908 Díaz Rodríguez was considered an undeniable master by the literary youth of the period.

The 1908 collection of essays, which Araujo calls "a minor masterpiece," centers on the analysis of literary creation and criticism. Max Henríquez Ureña maintained that "these admirable essays give Díaz Rodríguez a reputation as a thinker who, within modernism, is rivaled only by Rodó." In the brief "Advertencia al lector" (Note to the Reader) that introduces the essays, the author requests that the hypothetical reader retain his "faith in art." Especially, he asks that the reader remember the admonition that "arises from time to time" in his pages, inveighing against society's increasing materialism. The central passage runs,

> Amid the progressive and universal yankeefication of the earth, when men and societies have made gold life's only goal; when more and more often literature is reduced to bare travel notes . . . everything a trinket for sale in the market . . . it is well to remember that only selflessness, divine selflessness, can make the act of heroism, or science, or art, incorruptible and eternal. And these pages recall it. They venerate altruism as the best armor of the ideal, as the arch-saint of the spirit
>
> (OS, pp. 633–634)

It is not superfluous to recall that the author of this celebration of selflessness is a landowner who in the coming years would increase his fortune with the acquisition of the San José estate, now Caracas' East Park, which he inherited from his mother upon her death in 1911. The highly praised *Sermones líricos* unites a series of academic and politico-cultural lectures that Díaz Rodríguez presented during those years. Although the prose and ideas of *Sermones* offer nothing new, they do demonstrate their author's stylistic mastery and allow an appreciation of the value system and worldview proposed in his narrative universe.

Díaz Rodríguez held several political posts in these years: he was minister of foreign relations in 1914, senator in 1915 and 1918, and ambassador to Italy between 1919 and 1923. In 1910 he traveled to Buenos Aires for the Fourth Pan American Conference; in 1916 he became minister of economic development. The roles of politician and farmer partially supplanted that of novelist, but the creative silence of this period was only of the creator of fiction, not the intellectual, and much less the man of letters. In any case, Díaz Rodríguez' path during these years was little different from that of many Latin American artists, and in fact closely resembled the life of many of his modernist colleagues.

Díaz Rodríguez returned to Europe in 1919 as an ambassador, and his four-year stay in Italy allowed him to finish an old project: *Peregrina, o El pozo encantado*, his third and last novel, was published in Madrid in 1922.

It was creolism's moment, a time to reevaluate modernism. Three short stories, "Música bárbara," "Las ovejas y las rosas del padre Serafín" (The Sheep and the Roses of Father Serafín), and "Égloga del verano" (Summer's Eclogue), were published along with the novel. To Henríquez Ureña, the stories are "noteworthy"; Miliani and Sambrano Urdaneta refer to them as "creolist stories." Juan Liscano has spoken of a sort of "magical realism" *avant la lettre* in Díaz Rodríguez' work of this period, especially in "Las ovejas y las rosas." Here the style is purified and the use of adjectives is not that of *Cuentos de color*. The narrator treats nearly the same themes, but now with increased "local color." In this case, his maturity is visible in his restraint from past "youthful excess," but the writer's evolution fails to result in a really important work. Hence it is Díaz Rodríguez the modernist who will be remembered in literary history.

Peregrina has been called by one critic a "creolist novel of rural setting," while others have said that "rather than a novel it is a book of illustrations . . . excessively artistic." While some criticize the novel's verbosity, none fail to point out the change in Díaz Rodríguez' fictional universe. The step from aestheticist modernism to creolism, as mentioned, was made not only by Díaz Rodríguez but was characteristic of Venezuelan modernists in general. The novel takes the tone of a "rural idyll" as it narrates the adventures of the young Peregrina. She is seduced by Bruno, a sort of country rogue, at the foot of Mt. Avila, amid a richly described landscape; later, Bruno abandons her. The novel allows the narrator to evoke traditions, superstitions, and customs of rural Venezuela. This Venezuela is unlike that of his previous novels, much more rosy and playful, containing the

magical realm of the "enchanted well." Yet, in *Peregrina* the presence of local tradition overshadows the question of "magical realism." The enchanted well that gives the novel its subtitle, although magical, is the natural space where the protagonist's destiny is decided. Similarly, Love and Death, who govern Peregrina's luck, are siblings who rule all of nature.

The critics unanimously note that the countryside, not the characters nor the customs depicted, is the essence of the novel. The landscape is aestheticized, as it must be with Díaz Rodríguez, but it is landscape nonetheless. The "beautiful souls" are still present, and the degraded bourgeoisie still pass through the background, in automobiles now, but Nature is the central character. Unavoidably, the landowner novelist sings the praises of the region of his own estates; this is self-acceptance and reconciliation of his narrative world with his homeland. The *locus amenus* is extolled now and there is no room for neurotic spaces nor for the controversy of *Idoles rotos* and *Sangre patricia*.

Returning to Venezuela in 1923, Díaz Rodríguez entered the Academy of History (1924) and was named governor of Nueva Esparta (1925) and then of Sucre (1926). His literary activity became markedly reduced. His family collected his last writings posthumously and published them in *Entre las colinas en flor* (Among the Flowering Hills, 1935), a volume that adds nothing to Díaz Rodríguez's work.

Díaz Rodríguez died of an "affection of the throat," certainly cancer, on 24 August 1927 in New York, after being treated in a medical facility there. His remains were moved to Caracas a few months later. His end was consistent with his work: the narrator of journeys and absences, emulating some of his own characters, died far from home. When he died, little remained of the Venezuela of his novels. The agricultural world lauded in *Peregrina* was beginning to give way to the fierce oil industry. Díaz Rodríguez' worst fears for the traditional life of Venezuela, which he had mythified and of which Tulio Arcos was the best representative, were becoming reality. His world of translucent beauty was disappearing and the violence of the 1926 revolt against the dictator Gómez was fast approaching.

Translated from the Spanish by Jane A. Johnson

SELECTED BIBLIOGRAPHY

First Editions

Fiction

Confidencias de psiquis. Caracas, 1896.
Cuentos de color. Caracas, 1899.
Idolos rotos. Paris, 1901.
Sangre patricia. Caracas, 1902.
Peregrina, o El pozo encantado. Madrid, 1922. This edition also includes three short stories: "Las ovejas y las rosas del Padre Serafín," "Égloga del verano," and "Música bárbara."

Essays

Sensaciones de viaje. Paris, 1896.
De mis romerías. Caracas, 1898.
Camino de perfección y otros ensayos. Paris, 1910.
Motivos de meditación ante la guerra y por Hispanoamérica. Caracas, 1918.
Sermones líricos. Caracas, 1918.
Entre las colinas en flor. Barcelona, 1935.

Collected Works

Manuel Díaz Rodríguez 1: With a preface by Rafael Angarita Arvelo. 2: With a preface by Lowel Dunham. Caracas, 1964.
Narrativa y ensayo. With a preface by Orlando Araujo. Caracas, 1982.
Obras selectas. With a preface by José Antonio Calcano. Caracas and Madrid, 1968.
Páginas de la patria. With a preface by Luis Correa. Caracas, 1971.

Biographical and Critical Studies

Alegría, Fernando. In *La novela hispanoamericana del siglo XX.* Buenos Aires, 1967. Pp. 62.
Anderson, Robert Roland. In *Spanish American Modernism: A Selected Bibliography.* Tucson, Ariz., 1970. Pp. 66–67.
Anderson Imbert, Enrique. In *Historia de la literatura hispanoamericana* 1. Mexico City and Buenos Aires, 1962. Pp. 405–407.
Angarita Arvelo, Rafael. In *Historia y crítica de la novela en Venezuela.* Berlin, 1938. Pp. 59–67.
Araujo, Orlando. *La palabra estéril.* Maracaibo, Venezuela, 1966.
Arráiz, Rafael Clemente. "*Cuentos de color; Sangre patricia.*" *Revista nacional de cultura* 13/90–93:390–392 (1952).

Blanco Fombona, Rufino. In *Letras y letrados en Hispano América.* Paris, 1908. Pp. 65–66, 233–235, 251–255.
Carrera, Gustavo Luis. In *Bibliografía de la novela venezolana.* Caracas, 1963. Pp. 69.
Castro, José Antonio. In *Narrativa modernista y concepción del mundo.* Maracaibo, Venezuela, 1973. Pp. 183.
Crema, Edoardo. "Armonía de tendencias en *Peregrina.*" *Revista nacional de cultura* 21/136:59–106 (1959).
Debicki, Andrew P. "Díaz Rodríguez' *Sangre patricia*: A Point of View Novel. *Hispania* 53:59–66 (1970).
Dunham, Lowell. *Manuel Díaz Rodríguez, vida y obra.* Mexico City, 1959.
Earle, Peter G., and Robert G. Mead. In *Historia del ensayo hispanoamericano.* Mexico City, 1973. Pp. 64–65.
Flores, Angel. In *The Literature of Spanish America* 3. New York, 1968. Part 1: pp. 401–410.
Fraser, Howard M. "El universo psicodélico en *Sangre patricia.*" *Hispanofila* 50:9–18 (1974).
Guerrero, Luis Beltrán. *Manuel Díaz Rodríguez o el estilista.* Caracas, 1971.
Henríquez Ureña, Max. *Breve historia del modernismo.* Mexico City, 1962.
Hernández, Hugolino. *Manuel Díaz Rodríguez, un mirandino.* Caracas, 1980.
Holland, Henry. "Manuel Díaz Rodríguez, estilista del modernismo." *Hispania* 39:281–286 (1956).
Liscano, Juan. In *Panorama de la literatura venezolana actual.* Caracas, 1973.
Matteson, Marianna. "Imagery in Díaz Rodriguez' *Sangre patricia.*" *Hispania* 56:1014–1020 (1973).
Miliani, Domingo, and Oscar Sambrano Urdaneta. In *Literatura hispanoamericana. Manual-Antología.* Caracas, 1986. Pp. 172.
Monguió, Luis. "Manuel Díaz Rodríguez y el conflicto entre lo práctico y lo ideal." *Revista iberoamericana* 11/21:49–54 (1946).
———. In *Estudios sobre literatura hispanoamericana y española.* Mexico City, 1958. Pp. 71–77.
Moreno García, Alberto. *Manuel Díaz Rodríguez o la belleza como imperativo.* Bogotá, 1957.
Nervo, Amado. "Díaz Rodríguez." *El Heraldo* (Caracas), 2 September 1927. P. 1.
Núñez, Enrique Bernardo. In *Ensayos biográficos.* Caracas, 1931. Pp. 112.
Pascual Buxó, José. *La perfección del amor en los cuentos de Manuel Díaz Rodríguez.* Maracaibo, Venezuela, 1966.
Paz Castillo, Fernando, ed. *Manuel Díaz Rodríguez entre contemporáneos.* Caracas, 1973.
Picón Febres, Gonzalo. *La literatura venezolana en el siglo diez y nueve.* With a preface by Domingo Miliani. Caracas, 1972. Originally published in 1906.

Picón Salas, Mariano. In *Formación y proceso de la literatura venezolana.* Caracas, 1984.

Ratcliff, Dillwyn F. In his *Venezuela in Prose Fiction.* New York, 1933. Pp. 173–189. Translated into Spanish by Rafael di Prisco as *La prosa de ficción en Venezuela.* Caracas, 1966.

Salvi, Adolfo. *Apuntes para una biografía (a Manuel Díaz Rodríguez).* Madrid, 1954.

Sánchez, Luis Alberto. In *Proceso y contenido de la novela hispanoamericana.* 2nd ed. Madrid, 1968. Pp. 664.

Semprun, Jesús. In *Estudios críticos.* Caracas, 1938. Pp. 83–102.

Torres Rioseco, Arturo. In *Grandes novelistas de la América hispánica.* Berkeley, Calif., 1949. Pp. 61–88.

Unamuno, Miguel de. "*Sangre patricia* por Manuel Díaz Rodríguez." *El cojo ilustrado,* 15 June 1903. P. 371.

Uslar Pietri, Arturo. In *Letras y hombres de Venezuela.* Caracas, 1948. Pp. 139–141.

Veiravé, Alfredo. In *Literatura hispanoamericana. Escrituras, autores, contextos.* Buenos Aires, 1976. Pp. 331.

Vidal, Hernán. "*Sangre patricia* y la conjunción naturalista simbolista." *Hispania* 52:183–192 (1969).

Woods, Richard D. "*Sangre patricia* and the Doors of Perception." *Romance Notes* 12/302–306 (1971).

José Juan Tablada

(1871–1945)

Adriana García de Aldridge

One of the most cosmopolitan of all Latin American poets, the Mexican José Juan Tablada derived aesthetic inspiration from Japan, China, and France, as well as from other European nations. Paradoxically his connections with the literature and the literati of the United States, where he lived at various periods, appear to be relatively minor. An exponent of the international symbolist movement, he is known in his native Mexico as a creator of *calligrammes* (picture-poems), originally made famous in France by Guillaume Apollinaire, and for introducing a new type of verse form based on the Japanese haiku. He is widely considered the father of modern Mexican poetry.

During his life Tablada published nine books of poetry, including a drama in verse, as well as a number of prose volumes on travel, on politics, and of personal recollections. In addition to ventures in journalism and periodical essays, he experimented with the novel and short fiction. But his chief contribution to letters was the introduction of the techniques and tones of oriental verse to the Latin American world.

Tablada was born in Mexico City on 3 April 1871 and died in New York City on 2 August 1945. He probably received in childhood the original impulse toward orientalism that characterized his poetic ma-

turity. The reminiscences of a friend of his mother's about exotic places inspired his novel "La nao de China" (The Ship from China). In his memoirs, he describes the source of these reminiscences as the widow of the Comandante General de las Naos de China (Admiral of the Chinese Fleet), but the defunct may have been merely a Mexican sailor in the China trade. Tablada's novel was never published because the manuscript disappeared during the Mexican Revolution. Tablada studied French during his childhood and became familiar with the works of Charles Baudelaire, Edmond and Jules Goncourt, Paul Verlaine, Arthur Rimbaud, and Stéphane Mallarmé. Later, in the United States, he earned his living as a private tutor of French.

In his youth, Tablada developed an interest in the plastic arts and aspired to study painting in Europe, but his father's sudden death put an end to his dream. Because his mother and sisters could not control his exuberant pranks, he was enrolled in a military school. Although he was not cut out for military service, the congeniality of his classmates compensated for the barrenness of the curriculum in regard to the humanities. He later revealed his fond memories of these classmates in various autobiographical passages of his published work. During this period, Tablada developed an interest in nature that later became evident in his pictorial verse inspired by Japanese writers.

In 1889, Tablada published his first poem, entitled "A . . ." (To . . .), in the periodical *La patria ilustrada* (The Enlightened Country). In 1891, while working as a clerk at the Central Railroad, he wrote verses on the margins of invoices, including the poem "Fecundación" (Fecundity), published a decade later. Tablada's poems were brought to the attention of Rafael Reyes Spíndola, who offered him a job as a reporter for his newspaper *El Universal.* He thus began his literary career writing a column entitled "Rostros y máscaras" (Faces and Masks) in a newspaper that was noted for following the American rather than the European model. In September 1893, Tablada published "Ónix" (Onyx) in *El siglo XIX* (The Nineteenth Century). It was reprinted in June 1894 in *Revista azul* (The Blue Review), the journal that sponsored the French symbolist movement in Mexico. For Amado Nervo, it was this poem that brought *modernismo* to Mexico. Others viewed the poem as the incorporation of the aesthetic spirit of Charles Baudelaire in Mexican letters.

Another poem inspired by the alleged satanism of Baudelaire was "Misa Negra" ("Black Mass"). Erotic for the nineteenth century, it enjoyed a *succès de scandale.* In his memoirs, entitled *La feria de la vida* (The Fair of Life, 1937), Tablada asserted that the poem appeared in 1898, but later scholars have ascertained that the poem had seen the light five years earlier, in the newspaper *El País* (The Country). The poet further stated in his memoirs that he had resigned from his employment as a journalist because of the threat of censorship, but no supporting evidence has been found concerning this alleged interference with his aesthetic ideals. According to Tablada, his employers told him to write for Mexico and not for Montmartre, and in disgust he wrote an open letter to the people of Mexico, condemning them for hypocrisy in allowing brothels and gambling houses to exist openly at the same time that they opposed erotic overtones on the printed page. He came to the conclusion that it was impossible to introduce promising works of art in newspapers that depended on the financial support of their subscribers. He proposed, therefore, the creation of a new literary-artistic journal that would adhere to aestheti-

cism as its main premise. In this spirit of innovation, he recommended that it be named *La revista moderna* (The Modern Review). This relationship between his poem "Black Mass" and the creation of this journal has generally been accepted. Although "Black Mass" appeared in 1893, *La revista moderna* was not established until 1898.

Tablada's career developed concomitantly with the literary movement *modernismo,* originally a Latin American version of French Parnassianism and symbolism. As the movement grew, American writers in Spanish, while not rejecting French influences, began to widen their horizons by reading works from other countries. In 1899 Tablada published his first collected book of poems, *Florilegio* (Floral Wreath), and it was followed by a second edition in 1904, which included new works. Although elements of nineteenth-century romanticism may be seen in these poems, most critics agree that they, like Tablada's entire production at this period, fit within the modernist tradition. Some poems, particularly those published after 1900, clearly show the influence of French symbolism, a major element of modernism. Indeed, because of *El florilegio,* Tablada has been labeled, with his contemporaries Rubén Darío and Manuel Gutiérrez Nájera, a propagator of French aesthetics as well as poetic innovation. The most important evidence of the new spirit in Tablada's verse is his devotion to the Orient, apparent for the first time in poems inspired by Japanese culture and topography, added to the 1904 edition of *El florilegio.*

Tablada's youthful fascination with the Orient led him to visit Japan in 1900 for a period of several months. He was indebted for the financial support of this trip to one of his patrons, Jesús Luján, the same Maecenas who had previously provided the funding for the review *La revista moderna.* Even before his journey to the land of the rising sun, Tablada was already interested in its culture. He enjoyed dressing in kimonos, receiving his guests in oriental costumes, and reading French writers who treated oriental themes. As a result of his trip to Japan, Tablada published vignettes on different aspects of Japanese culture and life, which he entitled *En el país del sol* (In the Land of the Sun). The articles were written in 1900, although the collection was not published until 1919. *En el país del sol* includes some very negative opinions about the way of life and culture of the Chinese living in Japan, an adverse attitude toward China that appears to have changed by 1920, when Tablada published *Li-Po y otros poemas* (Li-Po and Other Poems), a poetic glorification of China's great poet of the sixth century.

After returning to Mexico, Tablada led a bohemian existence, publishing only sporadically in literary journals and newspapers and not bringing out another complete book of lyrical poetry until 1918. During this bohemian period, Tablada married Evangelina, the niece of Justo Sierra, the teacher of many poets in Mexico. The marriage ended in divorce, apparently as a result of Tablada's dissipated way of life. After serving briefly in the Department of Education, he established himself as a wine merchant, a position lucrative enough to enable him to build a house in Coyoacán, where he employed servants and lived in opulence laced with orientalism.

Tablada turned away temporarily from aesthetic concerns in his next extensive work, the verse satire *La epopeya nacional: Porfirio Díaz* (The National Epic Poem: Porfirio Díaz, 1909), which defends the regime of the unpopular dictator. The poet's material prosperity may have caused him to cater to the party in power. In 1911, in the early stages of the Mexican Revolution, the Díaz regime fell. As a result of his political writing, Tablada's house was pillaged and his library destroyed. His *Tiros al blanco* (Shots at the Target, 1909) is a collection of articles that had appeared in the newspaper *El Imparcial*; they had been written to discredit Bernardo Reyes, who was running for the vice-presidency of Mexico. Tablada favored the official candidate of the regime, Ramón Corral. During this time, Tablada wrote a libelous closet drama, *Madero-Chantecler,* (Madero-Chantecler), a zoological allegory in verse that attacked powerful governmental figures. Although the play was published anonymously in 1910, its authorship was immediately attributed to Tablada, and he was later forced to write an apology to Victoriano Huerta, later president of the nation. It has been said that in *Tiros al blanco* and in *Madero-Chantecler*, Tablada does not present any political doctrine but only intends to combat the opposition press through irony and sarcasm. Tablada was anticlerical, praised Benito Juárez, and shared democratic convictions with a generally respected literary figure, Salvador Díaz Mirón, but conspired for personal reasons against the incumbent president of Mexico, Francisco I. Madero.

While living in Paris from 1911 to 1912, Tablada wrote chronicles of Gallic life for the *Revista de revistas* (Review of Reviews), which he later collected in *Los días y las noches de París* (Parisian Days and Nights, 1918). From 1912 to 1913 he became the chief editor of *El Imparcial.* By 1914 he was forced to leave the country because of *La defensa social: Historia de la campaña de la división del norte* (The Social Defense: A History of the Campaign of the Northern Division, 1913), a political prose narrative praising Huerta, which he had been paid to write. Obviously his loyalties were subject to change. Today very few speak about his prose, and he wished to have his writings from this period forgotten. During his exile, Tablada went first to Galveston, Texas, and then to New York, where in 1918 he married Nina Cabrera. During that year, another president of Mexico, Venustiano Carranza, pardoned him, and he returned briefly to Mexico before his October wedding. In November he departed for South America, where he had been given a diplomatic appointment by the Mexican government. Before reaching Colombia, his first post, the newly wedded couple made a brief stop in Cuba to meet Nina's father. They were well-received there by many writers, and similar warm receptions were awarded him in Colombia and Venezuela.

In the midst of his diplomatic career, Tablada published a collection of miscellaneous poems, *Al sol y bajo la luna* (In the Sun and Under the Moon, 1918). The title suggests the ephemeral landscapes portrayed in Chinese and Japanese verse. Significant in the collection is "El poema de Okusai" (The Poem of Hokusai), which lavishly praises the genius and universal scope of the Japanese painter's depiction of nature. The volume carried an introductory poem by Leopoldo Lugones, one of the most admired of the modernist coterie. This book of poems marks the transition from modernism to the *vanguardia* style, which is characterized by the incorporation of the latest experiments in Dadaism and surrealism. The collection also includes some of Tablada's earlier poems that contain romantic elements. Other poems that have received particular attention are "Lawn-tennis" and ". . . ?" The latter poem presents a different type of woman from the model admiringly envisioned by the modernists, not a hysterical female, but one who is "diabolic." A friend revised the poem and recommended that Tablada rename it "Quinta Avenida" (Fifth Avenue).

Tablada's next book of poetry, *Un día . . . Poemas sintéticos* (One Day . . . Synthetic Poems, 1919), introduced to Latin America the Japanese haiku, a verse form composed of a mere seventeen syllables in three lines, with five syllables in the first line, seven in the second, and five in the third. Tablada's experimentation represented a revolutionary departure in Spanish poetry, and it exercised a continuing influence on later generations, including the group named the Contemporáneos and a subsequent one called the Taller, the Spanish word for workshop. *Un día*, consists entirely of haikus, and others appear in Tablada's *El jarro de flores* (The Flower Vase, 1922). When Tablada published his first haikus in *Un día*, he did not know how to describe them in Spanish; for this reason he labeled them "synthetic poems." He uses the word *hokkú* and the plural form *hai-kais*, however, in *El jarro de flores*. Tablada dedicated *Un día* to two of the classic poets of Japan of the seventeenth century and eighteenth century, respectively: Matsuo Basho and Shiyo.

In 1920, Tablada demonstrated his versatility with *Li-Po y otros poemas*, a work that brought together his interests in oriental poetry and the fine arts; through it he acquired his greatest fame. As a direct result of his Japanese sojourn, he had earlier published an illustrated book on the Japanese painter Hiroshige entitled *Hiroshigué: El pintor de la nieve y de la lluvia, de la noche y de la luna* (Hiroshige: Painter of the Snow and the Rain, of the Night and the Moonlight, 1914). His knowledge of the plastic arts was not limited to the Far East, for he also treated both the ancient and the contemporary art of his own country in essays and lectures written in English, and edited an English-language journal in the same field, *Mexican Art and Life* (1938–1939), printed in Mexico City.

The outstanding feature of *Li-Po y otros poemas* is a group of verses shaped to resemble objects in nature. Critics and the public in general immediately saw in these poems the influence of Apollinaire's *Calligrammes* (Picture-Poems, 1918), despite Ta-

blada's insistence that his inspiration derived from other sources. The publication of his complete poetical works in 1971 vindicated his claim: hitherto unpublished verses proved that Tablada had admired the work of the French poet Judith Gautier to such a degree that he had translated three of her Chinese-inspired poems into Spanish (they appeared in the posthumous publication not as translations, but as original creations of Tablada). They are important because they reveal that in *Li-Po y otros poemas*, as in his other writings, Tablada was an inventor. His major source of inspiration, however, was Gautier, not Apollinaire. Indeed the second part of *Li-Po*, entitled "Otros poemas ideográficos" (Other Ideographic Poems), with individual poems dated 1915, 1917, and 1918, made some critics wonder whether Tablada had preceded Apollinaire in the use of shaped verse; it is appropriate to note, however, that Apollinaire circulated two hundred copies of his *Idéogrammes lyriques* (Lyrical Ideograms) as early as 1914, and it is possible that Tablada had seen one of these copies.

Tablada's diplomatic career took him to Ecuador, but since his health did not permit him to live in the high altitude of Quito, he had to resign his post in 1920. After a few days in Mexico, he returned with his wife to New York, where he opened a bookstore, at 28 East 118 Street, called Librería de los Latinos (Bookstore of the Latins). The following year he gave up the business and built a house in the Catskill Mountains.

In 1922, Tablada received recognition for his stylistic innovations by being included in the *Antología de jóvenes poetas mexicanos* (Anthology of Young Mexican Poets). In the following year, in a ceremony at the National Museum of Mexico, he was proclaimed by students and young writers "the representative poet of youth."

In the 1920's, Tablada dedicated himself to propagating the culture and art of Mexico in the United States, a task he considered difficult because of the unfavorable image of Mexico in the United States at that time. As editor in New York of the journal *Mexican Art and Life*, he attempted to educate the American public about the history and general culture of his native land. In the few issues that appeared, he treated the painters Rufino Tamayo,

Diego Rivera, and José Clemente Orozco. His most ambitious undertaking in the art world, *Historia del arte en México* (History of Art in Mexico), was published in Mexico City in 1927. It had been preceded by the printing of the text of a lecture given in Venezuela, *Cultura mexicana: Artes plásticas—Periodos precortesiano, colonial, y moderno* (Mexican Culture: Plastic Arts—Pre-Cortez, Colonial, and Modern Periods, 1920).

In a novel with autobiographical elements, *La resurrección de los ídolos* (The Resurrection of the Idols, 1924), Tablada revealed his attraction to theosophy and occult religions and attempted to explain his somewhat mystical views about life and the universe. In his book of poems *Al sol y bajo la luna*, he had included references to these beliefs but had not elaborated them in a systematic manner. In 1926, he published *El arca de Noé* (Noah's Ark), a collection of readings on animals for primary-school children. The subtitle suggests that he had collaborated with other writers, but most of the stories are his own translations of French authors like Pierre Loti and J. H. Favre. The book also contains selections by his countryman Manuel José Othón, the Spaniard Jacinto Benavente, and the Frenchman Francis Jammes.

Tablada returned to Mexico in 1936 and the following year published the first volume of his memoirs, *La feria de la vida*. He settled in Cuernavaca, but a heart ailment made him return to New York for treatment. In 1944 he brought out a book of jokes, satirical vignettes, and anecdotes, *Del humorismo a la carcajada* (From Humor to a Peal of Laughter). That year he was given a pension for life by the Mexican government, which shortly afterward he gave up for an appointment as vice-consul in the Mexican consulate in New York. He never occupied this last post, for he died of a heart attack in a New York hospital in 1945.

On 3 September 1945, one month after Tablada's death, Octavio Paz delivered his eulogy in New York. For Paz, Tablada's introduction of the haiku into Spanish letters in *Un día* and *El florilegio* was more than a metrical innovation. "The form gave liberty to the image and rescued it from the poem that had plot, in which it was drowning" (*Las peras del olmo* [translated literally as "The Pears of the Elm Tree,"

but idiomatically as "To Look for the Impossible"], p. 80). Tablada's haiku had many imitators. Indeed, until 1945, a whole school of Mexican poets wrote in that fashion. Tablada's real importance, however, as Paz indicated, lies in his giving poets "an awareness of the value of the image and the power of the concentrated word" (p. 81). Tablada was the only Mexican poet, Paz added, who transmitted the essence of nature "without converting it into a symbol or decoration" (p. 84).

SELECTED BIBLIOGRAPHY

First Editions

Poetry

El florilegio. Mexico City, 1899; 2nd ed. Paris and Mexico City, 1904.
La epopeya nacional: Porfirio Díaz. Mexico City, 1909.
Al sol y bajo la luna. Mexico City and Paris, 1918.
Un día . . . : Poemas sintéticos. Caracas, 1919.
Li-Po y otros poemas. Caracas, 1920.
El jarro de flores: Disociaciones líricas. New York, 1922.
Intersecciones. Mexico City, 1924.
La feria (Poemas mexicanos). New York, 1928.
Los mejores poemas de José Juan Tablada. Mexico City, 1943.

Plays

Madero-Chantecler. Mexico City, 1910.

Translations by Tablada

El rey Galaor. [Dramatic poem by Eugenio de Castro. Translated from the Portuguese.] *Revista moderna* (April–July 1902).
El arca de Noé. Mexico City, 1926. Contains several original pieces by Tablada.

Prose

Tiros al blanco (Actualidades políticas). Mexico City, 1909.
La defensa social: Historia de la campaña de la división del norte. Mexico City, 1913.
Hiroshigué: El pintor de la nieve y de la lluvia, de la noche y de la luna. Mexico City, 1914.
Los días y las noches de París. Paris and Mexico City, 1918.
En el país del sol. New York, 1919.
Cultura mexicana: Artes plásticas—Períodos precortesiano, colonial, y moderno. Caracas, 1920.

La resurrección de los ídolos. Mexico City, 1924.
Historia del arte en México. Mexico City, 1927.
La feria de la vida. Mexico City, 1937.
Del humorismo a la carcajada. Mexico City, 1944.

Journal Articles

SPANISH
"Calles." *Del México actual* 6:17–46 (1933).

ENGLISH
"Mexican Pride and Commissioner Cabrera." *Latin American News Association* (1916). Pp. 3–7.
"Mexican Painting of Today." *International Studio*, January 1923. Pp. 267–276.
"Art in Mexican Education." *Survey Graphic*, January 1923.
"Mexican Cartoonists." *Shadowland*, April 1923.
"Old Mexican Art and Elie Faure." *The Arts*, August 1923.
Mexican Art and Life. Edited by José Juan Tablada. Nos. 1–7 (January 1938–July 1939).

Collected Works

Antología general de José Juan Tablada. Edited by Enrique González Martínez. Mexico City, 1920.
Obras 1: Poesía. Edited by Hector Valdés. [Contains extensive bibliography.] *2: Sátira política.* Edited by Jorge Ruedas de la Serna and Esperanza Lara Velázquez. Mexico City, 1971–1981.

Translations

Anthology of Mexican Poetry. Edited by Octavio Paz. Translated by Samuel Beckett. Bloomington, Ind., 1958.
New Poetry of Mexico. Edited with notes by Octavio Paz, Alí Chumacero, José Emilio Pacheco, and Homero Aridjis. New York, 1970. Bilingual edition.

Biographical and Critical Studies

Cabrera de Tablada, Nina. *José Juan Tablada en la intimidad.* Mexico City, 1954.
Ceide-Echevarría, Gloria. *El haikái en la lírica mexicana.* Mexico City, 1967.
Cramer, Mark. "José Juan Tablada and the Haiku Tradition." *Romance Notes* 16/2:530–535 (1975).
Dauster, Frank. *Breve historia de la poesía mexicana.* Mexico City, 1956.
——. *Ensayos sobre poesía méxicana: Asedio a los "Contemporáneos."* Mexico City, 1963.

Faurie, Marie-Josephe. *Le modernisme hispano-américain et ses sources françaises.* Paris, 1966.
Forster, Merlin. "The Contemporáneos: A Major Group in Mexican Vanguardismo." *University of Texas Studies in Literature and Language* 3/4:425–438 (1962).
Galván, Delia V. "José Juan Tablada y su haiku: Aventura hacia la unidad." *Cincinnati Romance Review* 2: 110–120 (1983).
García de Aldridge, Adriana. "Las fuentes chinas de José Juan Tablada." *Bulletin of Hispanic Studies* 60/ 2:109–119 (1983).
González de Mendoza, José María. In *Ensayos selectos.* Mexico City, 1970.
Holdsworth, Carole A. "José Juan Tablada: Crítico modernista." *Inter-American Review of Bibliography* 29/ 1:65–69 (1979).
Lemay, Albert H., and Thomas W. Renaldi. "The Friendship Between Ramón del Valle Inclán and José Juan Tablada." *The American Hispanist* 3/21:12–14 (1977).
List Arzubide, Germán. *El movimiento estridentista.* Jalapa, Mexico, 1927.
Mariscal Acosta, Amanda. *La poesía de José Juan Tablada.* Mexico City, 1949.
Mendieta Alatorre, Ángeles. *Tablada y la gran época de la transformación cultural.* Mexico City, 1966.
Mitre, Eduardo. "Los Ideogramas de José Juan Tablada." *Revista iberoamericana* 40/89:675–679 (1974).
Nieves Alonso, María. "'Nocturno Alterno' de José Juan Tablada." *Acta literaria* 9:109–119 (1984).
Núñez y Domínguez, José de J. "José Juan Tablada." Mexico City, 1951. Speech read before the Mexican Academy of Letters on 28 January 1946.
Paz, Octavio. "Estela de José Juan Tablada." In *Las peras del olmo.* Mexico City, 1957. Pp. 76–85.
——. "A Tradicao do Hai-Kai." *Minas Gerais: Suplemento literário* 14/788:6–8 (1981).
Phillips, Allen W. "El primer José Juan Tablada: Modernismo y decadentismo." In *Homage to Irving A. Leonard: Essays on Hispanic Art, History and Literature.* East Lansing, Mich., 1976. Pp. 181–196.
Renaldi, Thomas W. "José Juan Tablada: Imágenes vanguardistas entre formas modernistas." *Texto crítico* 12:253–260 (1979).
Roggiano, Alfredo A. "José Juan Tablada: Espacialismo y vanguardia." *Hispanic Journal* 1/2:47–55 (1980).
Schneider, Luis Mario. *El estridentismo: Una literatura de la estrategia de México.* Mexico City, 1970.
Young, Howard Thomas. "José Juan Tablada: Mexican Poet (1871–1945)." Ph.D. diss., Columbia University, 1956.